PUBLIC LAW
and
PUBLIC ADMINISTRATION

PUBLIC LAW
and
PUBLIC ADMINISTRATION

Phillip J. Cooper
Georgia State University

 MAYFIELD PUBLISHING COMPANY

Library of Congress Catalog Card Number: 82-062054

International Standard Book Number: 0-87484-525-2

Manufactured in the United States of America
Mayfield Publishing Company
285 Hamilton Avenue
Palo Alto, California 94301

Sponsoring editor: Chuck Murphy
Manuscript editor: Linda Rageh
Managing editor: Pat Herbst
Art director: Nancy Sears
Cover designer: William Nagel
Production manager: Cathy Willkie
Compositor: Columbia Phototype
Printer and binder: George Banta Company

To my wife Lynn

The author gratefully acknowledges permission to use the following copyrighted material:

Quotation on p. 122, from Harold H. Bruff and Ernest Gellhorn, "Congressional Control of Administrative Regulation: A Case Study of Legislative Vetoes," 90 *Harvard L. Rev.* 1376–77 (1977). Copyright © 1977 by The Harvard Law Review Association. Used by permission of *Harvard Law Review* and the authors.

Quotations on pp. 185, 188, from Carl McGowan, "Reflections on Rulemaking Review," 53 *Tulane L. Rev.* 686, 690–91, 693 (1979). Used by permission of *Tulane Law Review*.

Quotations on pp. 213, 214, 215, from William Lockhart, "Discretionary Clemency: Mercy at the Prosecutor's Option," 1976 *Utah L. Rev.* 57, 59, 60, 64 (1976). Used by permission of *Utah Law Review*.

Quotations on pp. 216, 218–19, 224–25, from Abraham D. Sofaer, "Judicial Control of Informal Discretionary Adjudication and Enforcement," 72 *Columbia L. Rev.* 1296–97, 1300–01, 1301–02, 1313, 1374 (1972). Used by permission of *Columbia Law Review*.

Quotations on pp. 220–21, 233, from Richard B. Stewart, "The Reformation of American Administrative Law," 88 *Harvard L. Rev.* 1976, n. 25, 1965 (1975). Copyright © 1975 by The Harvard Law Review Association. Used by permission of *Harvard Law Review* and the author.

Quotations on pp. 245–46, 252, 253, from James Q. Wilson, "The Politics of Regulation," in Wilson, ed., *The Politics of Regulation* (New York: Basic Books, 1980), pp. 362–63, 366, 368, 369. Copyright © 1980 by Basic Books, Inc. Used by permission of Basic Books, Inc., Publishers, New York.

Quotation on p. 264, from Abraham Ribicoff, "Congressional Oversight and Regulatory Reform," 28 *Ad. L. Rev.* 418 (1976). Used by permission of *Administrative Law Review*.

Quotation on p. 297, from Aubrey Milunsky and Philip Reilly, "The New Genetics: Emerging Medicolegal Issues in the Prenatal Diagnosis of Hereditary Disorders," 1 *American J. of Law & Medicine* 78 (1975). Used by permission of *American Journal of Law & Medicine* and Aubrey Milunsky.

Quotations on pp. 297, 298, 313, from Leonard I. Riskin and Philip P. Reilly, "Remedies for Improper Disclosure of Genetic Data," 8 *Rutgers Camden L. J.* 480, 483, 489 (1977). Used by permission of *Rutgers Camden Law Journal*.

Quotations on pp. 365, 366, 367, from James H. Haviland and Michael B. Glomb, "The Disability Insurance Benefits Program and Low Income Claimants in Appalachia," 73 *West Virginia L. Rev.* 113–14, 115–16, 128 (1971). Used by permission of *West Virginia Law Review*.

Chapter 11, "Acquisition, Use, and Dissemination of Information: A System of Information Policy," appeared in different form in 33 *Ad. L. Rev.* 81 (1981).

Contents

Part One
Foundations of Administrative Justice

v

Part Two
The Formal Administrative Process

Part Three
Law, Politics, and Administration

Appendixes

Preface

Many books on law and courts begin with Alexis de Tocqueville's familiar observation that almost all important political problems in America sooner or later are recast as legal problems. But if Tocqueville had visited this country in the second half of the twentieth century rather than early in the nineteenth, he might have changed the observation to something like: "Sooner or later most important political problems in America are transformed into administrative problems which, in turn, find their way into the courts." In our country, there is a complex, ongoing interaction between matters legal and administrative. This book is about that interaction. It is a book about administrative law, but it is administrative law broadly defined. Its premise is that administrative law problems are not merely legal but are also administrative and political.

Public Law and Public Administration is not intended as a law school primary text, though it might be used in that manner with appropriate cases or case book supplements. I wrote this book with the following readers in mind. First, it is specifically aimed at those who plan to enter government service and those engaged in mid-career education for public administration. Second, it is written for those who must deal with administrative agencies as consumers of administrative decisions. It is partly intended for law students or lawyers who wish to place their formal study of administrative procedure in administrative and political context. Finally, it is written for scholars of law and administration with the hope that this volume will raise new issues, frame some important existing debates in a new way, and suggest alternative conceptualizations of long-standing problems.

Two primary factors motivated me to prepare this volume. The first was that I could not find a book for my public law and public administration classes that students could understand and would read with interest. Also, the book is a product of ongoing studies of the relationships among law, politics, and administration, relationships that have not been adequately described or understood. If students and teachers find it useful and others are prompted to further explore the themes that this work only introduces, it will have served its purposes.

As with any book of this type, the most difficult decisions were what to omit.

xiii

However, I have made an effort to supply thorough and extensive footnotes, bibliographies, and case references to help readers better understand the interpretations I have made here and to take the issues beyond the point where I have necessarily left them in this work. One of the basic decisions on content was that a full-length case study from the initial dispute to the Supreme Court would be more useful than several reproduced judicial opinions. The *Mathews v. Eldridge* case study is the result.

A point or two on organization is in order. The material in the appendixes was designed to be used and not merely to serve as a general reference collection. For that reason, I developed selected references in law and administration at state and local as well as national levels. The case study was made an appendix because it can be used in a variety of ways—as introductory reading, as a second reading assignment following something like Fritschler's *Smoking and Politics*, in connection with the adjudications chapter, or as a capstone case study. Finally, Chapter 2, "The Law in Books," may seem a break in flow to teachers or others with an extensive legal process or research background, but I have found that, for students new to judicial process and research, it works well in its present position. Those using the book may of course elect to alter that position through their assignment schedules.

Many people have provided invaluable assistance in the development of this book. Some years ago, Professors Michael O. Sawyer, Dwight Waldo, John Clarke Adams, and Spencer Parratt encouraged my work in the area of law and administration and suggested the need for books like the present project. I would like to acknowledge a number of colleagues who have graciously read and commented on portions of the manuscript: F. Glenn Abney of Georgia State University; Howard Ball of the University of Utah; Richard Campbell of the University of Georgia; Stephen R. Chitwood of George Washington University; Donald Fairchild of Georgia State University; A. Lee Fritschler of the Brookings Institution; Ron Hoskins of Institute of Government of the University of Georgia; Thomas Lauth, University of Georgia; Lloyd Nigro of Georgia State University; Christopher Pollitt of England's Open University; William Richardson of Georgia State University; and John A. Rohr of Virginia Polytechnic Institute and State University. Their help and encouragement are sincerely appreciated. Of course, I alone am responsible for any errors of fact or interpretation.

My appreciation goes as well to the editorial and production staff at Mayfield Publishing Company. As managing editor, Pat Herbst has been cordial and helpful as well as efficient. Linda Rageh gave outstanding service as copy editor. Her precision as well as her sensitivity and understanding contributed a great deal to the project.

Finally, the contributions of Ms. Lucy Cheely in typing the manuscript can really be appreciated only by those who have had the pleasure of working with a truly professional typist. Her assistance is gratefully acknowledged.

P.J.C.

PUBLIC LAW
and
PUBLIC ADMINISTRATION

PART ONE

FOUNDATIONS
OF
ADMINISTRATIVE
JUSTICE

Introduction:
Defining the Field

Think of yourself as a member of the Federal Communications Commission, the independent regulatory commission charged with regulating broadasting on the airwaves in the public interest. Ask yourself what you would do in the following situation.

A man is driving into New York City with his eight-year-old son at two o'clock in the afternoon. The radio is tuned to a public broadcasting station. For various reasons, the driver doesn't take note of the program currently being aired. Suddenly, to the surprise of the boy and the consternation of the father, a long string of profanity issues from the radio.

The program on the air was playing a monologue recorded by a nightclub comedian concerning "seven dirty words." The monologue focused on words that, according to the comedian in question, "you couldn't say on the public airwaves, the ones you definitely wouldn't say ever." The recording was played as a part of program on the use and abuse of language in American culture.

When the man arrived home, he promptly phoned the field office of the Federal Communications Commission to complain. Such language, he said, should not be broadcast over the public airwaves and, in any case, it certainly should not be aired during the middle of the day when the audience was likely to contain large numbers of children.

The radio station's response was that the monologue was broadcast as part of a legitimate inquiry into the uses of language, including verbal taboos. Moreover, the broadcasters argued, the monologue had been preceded by a warning that the presentation would include language that might offend some listeners. The warning further noted that concerned listeners could tune back in for the rest of the discussion following the monologue, which would last approximately fifteen minutes. Besides, they said, radios are equipped with channel selector switches and on/off knobs for the purpose of permitting nonconsenting listeners to exercise discretion in selecting what material they will or will not listen to.

3

As a member of the commission, what would you do? What means would you employ in investigating the complaint? Would you sanction the station or would you merely warn its management? Would you ban the broadcast altogether or would you direct the managers of the station to move the program to an hour when children were not likely to be in the audience? How would you decide?[1]

Consider also the following example. In this situation you are a member of the Federal Trade Commission, the regulator charged with preventing fraudulent or deceptive trade practices. From a group representing roughly ten thousand concerned parents, teachers, and dentists you receive a petition that asserts that all advertising directed at children under the age of eight is inherently deceptive because minors of that age are unable to discriminate between the content of programming and advertising. The children are, it is argued, unable to make rational choices and decisions in consumer matters and therefore can be easily manipulated. The group is joined by another group known as the Center for Science in the Public Interest, which claims to represent four thousand members who are interested in improving nutrition and health. The two groups show that more than $400 million is spent annually in advertising directed at young children, of which more than $80 million is spent by processed cereal firms alone. They also present evidence showing that young children are unable to discern which aspects of programs are entertainment and which are commercial advertisements. They further argue, with supporting evidence, that advertisers know and capitalize on the fact that

> when you sell a woman a product and she goes into the store and finds
> your brand isn't in stock, she'll probably forget about it. But when you sell
> a kid your product, if he can't get it he will throw himself on the floor,
> stamp his feet and cry. You can't get a reaction like that out of an adult.[2]

In addition to their complaints about deceptive efforts to increase sales, the groups argue that there exists a fundamental health problem in the ads targeted at children. Specifically, they sampled Saturday programming on all three television networks and found that foods with high sugar content were advertised "as many as four times per hour on each network, and as many as seven times per half hour if fast-food advertising is taken into account."[3] They contend that this influence on children's eating habits has direct implications for tooth decay and obesity, as well as indirect effects on likely cases of heart disease and diabetes.

The advertisers respond by arguing that it is up to the parents to regulate the television viewing of their children and family nutrition. Parents should have more will power; it is their responsibility to exercise judgment and to teach their children to do the same. The same is true of responsibility for establishing proper nutrition and oral hygiene habits.

What would you do? Would you reject the petitions of the groups? Would you ban all advertising directed at young children? Would you bar ads for high sugar foods directed at young children? If so, how young is young in such circumstances—eight years of age? Would you, as an alternative, require advertisers of such foods to pay a tax to be used to pay for commercials aimed at teaching children good nutrition and the need for dental care?[4]

Finally, think of yourself as a veteran tenured employee of an agency of the federal government. In the course of your work you conclude that your supervisor is engaged in illegal practices. In fact, you charge him with extortion on grounds that you think he threatened a group with denial of a federal grant unless they assisted him politically and financially. You make your charges known to agency officials.

Your supervisor sends you a letter informing you that you are to be dismissed for the "efficiency of the service." You are told that you have thirty days to respond in writing to the dismissal and that you may speak with your supervisor concerning the termination. You write a letter objecting to being fired, but your supervisor indicates that, as much as he hates to say so, you'll just have to go. He indicates that you may, after termination, pursue an administrative appeal that may eventually culminate in a hearing before an administrative law judge or a panel.

After some checking, you file for the appeal and begin cleaning out your desk. Colleagues inform you that it takes an average of eleven months to get a hearing in such a case. You're now making a good salary and have a family, car payments, and a mortgage to think about. Your friends know this and inquire about how you will get by without the money and the fringe benefits such as health insurance that you'll be missing while you fight your dismissal.

What would you do? How would you go about it? What would your prospects for alternative employment be?[5]

These are only three of the important problems of public law and public administration that will be addressed in this book. The situations that will be dealt with are problems of public law as opposed to private civil conflicts. Private law conflicts are the types of disputes that arise following the Saturday morning "fender bender" in the local shopping center parking lot or when a neighbor chops down the half of your cherry tree that happens to hang over his property line. Public law conflicts, on the other hand, usually involve the government more directly. The term "public administration" is a part of the book's title because governmental actions are defined and controlled by special provisions of the Constitution and laws. As such, government actions must be accomplished in particular ways. The need for responsiveness and responsibility in government agencies requires that legal guidelines be carefully drawn in cases where government acts.

DEFINITION OF ADMINISTRATIVE LAW

The body of law that is concerned with actions by administrative agencies is known as administrative law. To ensure that this term, which in this book serves as shorthand for public law and public administration, is properly understood, it is necessary to spend some time on the problem of definition. There is no single commonly accepted definition of "administrative law." Indeed, as Frank E. Cooper has said, "There is not even to be found any generally accepted definition of the term 'administrative law.' Defining the term thus becomes the first element of any discussion of the subject."[6]

Nevertheless, the legal literature does provide evidence of some similarity in the approaches to defining the term. In surveying a number of these works,[7] one finds that "administrative law" is to be defined in two senses. On the one hand, the concept has a broad sense that includes "not only administrative powers, their exercise, and remedies but also such subjects as the various forms of administrative agencies; the exercise of and limitations upon regulatory power; the law of the civil service; the acquisition and management of governmental property; public works; and administrative obligations."[8] Having recognized this broad sense, however, most legal practitioners dismiss that perspective in favor of a narrower conception.

There are at least two reasons why most of the literature tends toward the narrow view. First, much of what has been written in this area is intended to provide guidance primarily to attorneys, and they are generally in need of clearly defined and narrowly drawn categories. Second, some authors, like Bernard Schwartz, indicate that the broad definition exceeds the range of questions appropriately addressed by lawyers:

> To the American lawyer, these are matters for public administration, not administrative law; they are primarily the concern of the political scientist. In this country, administrative law is not regarded as the law relating to public administration, the way commercial law is the law relating to commerce, or land law the law relating to land. It is limited to powers and remedies and answers the questions: (1) What powers may be vested in administrative agencies? (2) What are the limits of those powers? (3) What are the ways in which agencies are kept within these limits?[9]

Since the purpose of this book is to understand a number of perspectives of the administrative justice systems, including those of lawyers, public administrators, benefit claimants, regulated groups, courts, legislators, and political scientists, we will proceed by using a broad definition of "administrative law."

The authors who work from a narrow view of administrative law base their definition on a number of specific decisions that should not be quickly or uncritically made. First, there is the oft-repeated assumption that administrative law is procedural and not substantive. According to this view, neither the substantive decisions made by the agencies involved nor the substantive mandate directed to the agencies by the legislature are administrative law.[10] Martin Shapiro, a political scientist, has correctly observed that "such a procedural focus tended to leave in some sort of nonlegal limbo the substantive policies and decisions of administrative agencies."[11] Administrative law questions do not arise without reference to substantive administrative decisions, to the legislation that controls the administrative action, and to the complex fact pattern that gave rise to the governmental decision.[12]

A second distinction on which the narrow definition rests concerns what is sometimes called the internal versus external dichotomy. This view asserts that the proper scope of administrative law is limited to agency actions that affect the rights of private parties.[13] The legal relationships among governmental officers, government departments, or different levels of government are excluded. The view is that the "administrative lawyer is not concerned with administrative powers as such; only when administrative power is turned outward against the person or property of private citizens does he deem it a proper subject of administrative law."[14] Given the complex set of intergovernmental relations that influences public policy,[15] this view is myopic.

More attention will be given to the concept of intergovernmental relations and administrative law in later chapters.[16] For the present, consider the controversy over the effort by the British and French to gain landing rights in the United States for their cooperative venture in aviation, the supersonic Concorde. Concorde was a controversial airplane from its inception. Designed to fly at more than twice the speed of sound, Concorde began its record-breaking flights in 1969 and 1970. The British and French felt that the craft would be economical only if it could ply the transatlantic air routes from London and Paris to New York, Washington, and other American cities. Air France and British Airways applied to the United States for landing rights.

Two and a half years after Concorde made its first friendship flight to this country, Secretary of Transportation William Coleman authorized a test period of sixteen months, which permitted one flight daily into Dulles Airport in Washington and Kennedy Airport in New York.[17] That decision, announced on February 4, 1976, intensified the existing conflict among federal authorities, British Airways, Air France, the state of New York, the state of New Jersey, residents in the area of Kennedy Airport, and the Port Authority of New York, which operates the airport. The controversy centered on anticipated noise, not from supersonic flight, but from takeoff and landing of the craft. The foreign governments were pressuring the United States to permit landings on pain of losing some of this country's routes abroad. The federal government was pressuring the Port Authority to cooperate in the experimental landing period, but the residents were protesting. Their protests took the forms of political pressure on state lawmakers and demonstrations, the most significant of which were long, slow automobile caravans that blocked entrances and exits to and from the airport.

On February 28, 1976, the New York legislature voted to bar landings of the Concorde.[18] The Port Authority issued a ban, beginning March 11, against landings at the airport pending the outcome of a study of approximately six months' duration of the probable impact of Concorde traffic into Kennedy. During the following year, Secretary Coleman's original order permitting the Concorde landings was challenged and upheld in the Supreme Court, test flights into Dulles began, and the Port Authority ban was also challenged.

In March 1977, a federal district court found that the Port Authority order was discriminatory and vacated it. The Port Authority appealed but was unsuccessful in the Second Circuit Court of Appeals. The case went to the United States Supreme Court, which in October 1977 formally refused to review the findings of the lower court.

This case clearly shows how major public policy questions that are "internal" are classic administrative law questions. In fact, many administrative law questions cannot be fully understood without a proper respect for the significance of intergovernmental relations.

A third distinction that has been employed as the basis for narrow definition of "administrative law" is the dichotomy between so-called quasi-legislative action and quasi-judicial action. Louis L. Jaffe and Nathaniel L. Nathanson suggested that "it will serve our purposes to identify the administrative process as rule making when not done by the legislature and adjudication when not done by the courts."[19] As will be indicated in Chapters 4 through 7, it is often difficult in specific cases to determine whether an agency action is legislative or adjudicatory[20] in nature. This is an important classificatory device. It was at the heart of the enactment of the Administrative Procedure Act, with which the reader will become familiar in later chapters.[21] But it does not easily explain or accommodate some agency activities or processes. It should not and will not limit our inquiry into administrative law.

For purposes of this study, administrative law is the branch of law that deals with public administration, providing the authority on which administrative agencies operate as well as the limits necessary to control them. The term is broadly defined to include both substantive and procedural concerns, internal as well as external issues, and aspects of the legal environment of administration that exceed simple quasi-legislative and quasi-judicial categories.

ORIENTATION TO THE ADMINISTRATIVE JUSTICE SYSTEM

The institutions, actors (referred to here as repeat players and single shot players), and processes that together produce administrative law decisions may be thought of as the administrative justice system. Before one can begin to deal in depth with the details of law, politics, and administration, it is necessary to acquire a rudimentary understanding of the parts of the system and interrelationships among them.

Institutions

Administrative agencies differ greatly in form and responsibility. Since each agency is created by statute or executive order to respond to unique needs at different periods in history, it is natural that they vary considerably. For present purposes there are two ways to conceptualize the nature and function of administrative agencies. From the perspective of traditional government institutions, one can think of agencies as either executive branch agencies or independent commissions that report primarily to Congress and yet retain a great deal of independence. Using a functional classification, there are regulatory bodies, social service agencies, and what will be referred to here as second-generation regulatory agencies.

The functional classifications are significant and will be discussed in greater detail in Chapters 5, 6, and 10. For quite some time, at least since World War II, legal literature about the administrative justice system has tended to emphasize the major independent regulatory commissions, while scholars of public administration have paid particular attention to social service agencies. Both are important.

Regulatory Commissions   The Interstate Commerce Commission,[22] created in 1887, is generally referred to as the prototype for the medium-size independent regulatory commissions. These commissions are often referred to in the literature on regulation as the "Big Seven" or "Big Ten" (depending on who is counting) federal commissions. These agencies were created by Congress as collegial bodies with a great deal of independence from the executive branch and Congress to protect the agencies from political interference. Some of the most important of the commissions are:

- Nuclear Regulatory Commission (NRC): nuclear safety enforcement
- Civil Aeronautics Board (CAB)[23]: regulation of airline routes and rates
- Federal Communications Commission (FCC): regulation of broadcasting
- Economic Regulatory Administration, which is a part of the Department of Energy[24]: pricing and allocation of oil and gas

- Federal Trade Commission: elimination of unfair or deceptive trade practices and antitrust enforcement
- Securities and Exchange Commission: regulation of stock and bond markets
- National Labor Relations Board: regulation of labor-management relations
- Federal Maritime Commission: regulation of shipping
- Federal Reserve Board: regulation of the money market

These commissions are usually headed by from three to five commissioners appointed for fixed terms by the President with the advice and consent of the Senate. They are protected against arbitrary removal by the President except for just cause.

Regulatory agencies perform a number of functions. They occasionally control access to a particular industry or profession, usually by some form of licensing. For example, for obvious technical reasons there is a limit to the number of radio or television stations that can broadcast in a particular geographic area without causing interference. Since the airwaves are a national resource, an agency was created to grant licenses in the public interest to broadcast various kinds of programming. The Federal Communications Commission grants the licenses and conducts renewal proceedings on a regular basis to determine whether the broadcaster deserves to retain the license.

Watchdog agencies, as they are sometimes called, also establish and enforce standards of fair market or professional practice. Federal Trade Commission actions against deceptive or false advertising are obvious examples. Medical and bar association enforcement of professional codes of ethics are further examples.[25] The power to regulate in this fashion has been called by Ernst Freund, a leading scholar on the subject, the power of corrective intervention.[26]

Regulatory bodies are frequently called on to set routes and rates where market forces do not appear to operate effectively, as in the case of local utility companies, which are by definition monopolies within their service areas. The problem in such cases is to determine what is a fair rate where "fair" is defined as an amount that covers costs plus a reasonable return on investment for investors in order to ensure the continued availability of capital needed by the utility.

Social Service Agencies Despite the high visibility of the major regulatory agencies, in terms of personnel and dollars they are small by comparison with social service agencies such as the Social Security Administration and the Veterans' Administration. In recent years the Social Security Administration has processed several times the combined number of cases listed on the dockets of all the federal courts in the nation.[27] According to one recent analysis, the VA employed "fifteen times as many [personnel] as the seven [major regulatory] agencies in combination."[28]

Social service agencies generally respond to requests for benefits or services. The claims are generally made by individuals who know little about government. The problem of the government is to give aid provided for by law with a sensitivity to individual problems while simultaneously guarding the public treasury against fraud and maintaining sufficient professional distance and rules of general applicability so that arbitrariness is avoided.

The social service agencies have a heavy intergovernmental component.[29]

Programs such as Social Security disability and community development were designed to involve several levels of government. Not surprisingly, that interconnection between governmental units involves complex communication and coordination problems.

Second-Generation Regulators Some agencies, especially a number of those created within the last decade or so, perform both regulatory and social service functions. The Occupational Safety and Health Administration (OSHA), the Environmental Protection Agency (EPA), the Consumer Product Safety Commission (CPSC), and the Equal Employment Opportunity Commission (EEOC) are examples. These agencies have varying degrees of regulatory power. In addition to their watchdog roles, they provide direct services to individuals or communities. The EPA provides aid to water purification and waste disposal efforts in local communities. The EEOC clears civil suits by individuals who feel that they have been discriminated against in hiring and promotions in violation of Title VII of the Civil Rights Act of 1964. On occasion these agencies may be negotiators, and at other times they may act as the enforcement arm of government.

In recent years the general tendency has been to place these agencies within the executive branch, as contrasted with the New Deal focus on extremely independent regulatory commissions. This change and the significance of organizational form will be discussed in Chapter 10.

Repeat Players and Single Shot Players

Just as the types of administrative organizations differ, so too do the kinds of individuals and groups that deal with the agencies. In particular, it is useful to distinguish two significantly different categories of parties who place demands on the administrative justice system—single shot players and repeat players. The terms are borrowed from analyses of the criminal justice process.[30] Single shot players are generally individuals who rarely deal with government agencies. Examples include those who apply for benefits from the Veterans' Administration or the Social Security Administration. They are not usually represented by legal counsel; they are generally under pressure to get a response quickly; and they know very little about the agencies and programs with which they are dealing.

Repeat players, on the other hand, are often organizations with more or less continuous, long-term relationships with particular agencies. They generally have in-house or outside counsel to represent them. These firms or groups frequently have substantial financial and technical resources at their command and consequently operate with comparatively greater flexibility in their dealings with the agencies. Repeat players are perhaps best typified by regulated businesses as drug companies or manufacturing firms.

It is important to note very clearly in an analysis of a problem in law and administration what sort of parties are involved in both sides of the debate. The assumption that most agencies or most parties before the agencies are alike will distort a consideration of the operation of the administrative justice system.

It is useful to bring the definitions and categories together into a simple descriptive model of administrative processes. Figure 1-1 outlines the relationships among the various actors and institutions in the administrative justice system. Each agency differs somewhat in its method of dealing with administrative law problems, but this general description provides a kind of road map.

Single shot and repeat players place demands on the system. The demands of the former may be nothing more than a telephone call to the Veterans' Administration requesting information on the procedure to apply for educational benefits, or something much more complex. Repeat players frequently seek different kinds of information. Whatever the demand, it is usually passed through an informal process filter, in which an attempt is made to resolve problems short of formal or legalistic actions. Chapter 8 explains how and why most administrative law questions are resolved informally rather than in the more formal stages of the administrative justice system.

A common first step in cases requiring more formal process is consideration of the matter by a hearing examiner, generally known as an administrative law judge (ALJ).[31] The ALJ develops a record containing pertinent documents, written evidence, and in some cases transcripts of oral testimony, decides questions of fact, and makes preliminary conclusions as to the disposition of the matter under consideration. If an appeal is needed, it will usually be an administrative appeal in which the record will be examined by other officers within the agency. In rulemaking procedures, the record developed by the ALJ moves up to agency heads for a final decision on whether and in what form to issue a regulation. Given the number and complexity of the decisions that department heads or commissions are called on to make, the work of agency staff members in aiding the decisionmakers is important. They frequently prepare digests of hearing records and highlight important questions and problems in the records that allow the decisionmakers to focus quickly on the most pertinent considerations. Because the decisions that issue from agencies involve so many individuals and because they are, unlike judicial opinions, rarely signed by the author of the opinion, the term "institutional decision" is often used to describe them.

Some form of review of agency decisions can be sought in the courts, although there are significant limits on the scope and nature of judicial review. If a case presents important legal questions, there may be appeals within the judicial system leading to a possible—though rare—hearing in the U.S. Supreme Court.

There are also institutional inputs to the administrative justice system. Congress creates, and conducts oversight of the agencies. The statutes are vital because they define and limit the authority of an agency. Any action taken that exceeds the statutory authority is by definition unlawful and is referred to as *ultra vires* action.[32] After all, nothing in the Constitution requires administrative agencies or grants them any authority. Most are created by statutes under the Article I, section 8, powers of the Congress. Budget authority is, of course, also critical since an agency without the funds necessary to use its statutory authority is a paper tiger.

The executive branch, aside from its general policymaking and management functions, provides specific inputs. Specific policy directives to agencies are of

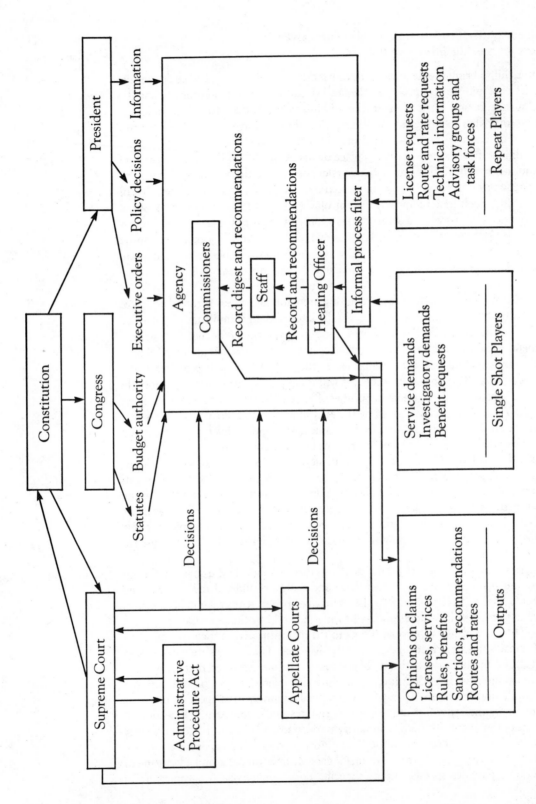

Figure 1-1 *A Simple Model of the Administrative Justice System*

obvious importance. Executive orders are also significant. Two examples of specific orders will provide an indication of their importance. The rules governing classification of government documents stem from an executive order issued by President Eisenhower.[33] A more recent example is the so-called Philadelphia Plan established by President Johnson under an executive order requiring affirmative action in hiring of employees by firms doing business with the government.[34] Another major input, discussed in detail in Chapter 11, is information that is supplied to the agency by other agencies.

The judiciary supplies inputs and also what might more appropriately be called feedback. The agency receives as inputs the decisions of courts interpreting the Constitution, statutes related to its operations, and the agency's enabling act, which is the statute that establishes the agency and defines its authority. The courts also provide feedback by responding in cases brought for review to questions about the accuracy of agency interpretations of statutes and also to the adequacy of the agency's procedures. The key source of law on fair and adequate administrative procedure is the Administrative Procedure Act (APA).[35]

PRODUCER AND CONSUMER PERSPECTIVES ON ADMINISTRATIVE DECISIONS

How one evaluates the success or failure of one agency or the entire administrative justice system, as in most other fields, depends on one's perspective of the system. Consumers of administrative decisions, whether they are single shot or repeat players, necessarily perceive the system differently from producers of administrative decisions. The case of *Mathews v. Eldridge*, presented in Appendix A, describes the plight of a man who had a series of misfortunes in his personal life and faced a long, difficult legal battle with the Social Security Administration over his claim for disability benefits. It is easy to be sympathetic to one who appears to have suffered grievously at the hands of the bureaucracy. From the producer's side in that case, administrators must try to clear more than a million and a quarter disability claims in a year as rapidly, fairly, and cost effectively as possible and still meet demands from the general public to cut costs, reduce the size of social service payment roles, and implement enough checks in the system to guard the public treasury against unwarranted claims.

A complicating factor in the attempt to develop a balanced perspective on questions of law and administration is that, at various times, the producer becomes a consumer, and vice versa. For example, the state disability agency that renders the decision on whether to grant or deny a benefit claim receives directives (in the Disability Insurance State Manual) from the federal agency headquartered in Baltimore. The policies that guide the state agencies change from time to time and, in this context, local administrators may find themselves feeling much the same as the claimant. That is a specific example, but the concept of shifting producer and consumer roles is significant in a more general sense.

Our form of government presupposes that all citizens are both producers and consumers of government decisions. Clearly, government officials are often more directly involved in the production process, but citizen participation in political and administrative matters, to the degree that the two differ, also affects decisionmaking.

Additionally, a Department of Energy official may be simultaneously a decision-maker on solar power technology development programs and a consumer of decisions before the Veterans' Administration in search of educational benefits to support college courses in public administration.

Careful analysis and decision in any problem of law and administration requires the attempt to deal with both the producer and the consumer perspectives on the matter. That is not to say that everything is relative or that there is no such thing as an erroneous or unfair output from the administrative justice system. These comments merely advise caution when intuition pushes one to choose sides quickly and uncritically.

FOUR-PART APPROACH TO PROBLEMS IN PUBLIC LAW AND PUBLIC ADMINISTRATION

The development of a useful conceptual framework with which to approach problems raised in the administrative justice system is a continuing challenge. A useful rule of thumb, however, is that one should always test a problem at the outset for the presence of each of the following types of issues: (1) constitutional, (2) statutory, (3) procedural, and (4) factual. Most administrative law problems contain more than one of these elements.

Constitutional questions concern such matters as whether the due process clause of the Fifth or Fourteenth amendments requires that an individual be afforded the opportunity to appear in person to argue his or her case before benefit payments are terminated. Statutory questions ask for explanations of legislation as applied to particular problems and often, either explicitly or implicitly, present inquiries as to the scope of administrative discretion in a particular policy area.

Procedural questions focus not on what the agency has done or proposes to do, but highlight the manner in which the agency goes about its actions. A challenge to a regulation issued by an agency may rest on the assertion that the agency did not provide adequate opportunity for interested parties to make their criticisms known before the rule was published in its final form. Factual matters are of major significance because problems of law and administration are frequently highly technical and complex. For example, the attempt to determine questions regarding regulations on air quality involves scientific, economic, and medical considerations. Though actors in the administrative justice system prefer to leave such matters to the experts, some understanding is needed to deal with air quality questions at any level. This four-part approach departs significantly from the traditionally narrow procedural method discussed earlier and presents a more accurate picture of administrative law problems.

SUMMARY

The resolution of problems of public law and public administration involves the attempt to deal with difficult questions under conditions of pressure. In general, the field of law that deals with these problems is called administrative law. For purposes of this study, administrative law is defined broadly. It includes substantive as well as procedural problems. It is concerned with the intergovernmental problems of law and administration and applies to other kinds of matters in addition to the traditional quasi-legislative and quasi-judicial types of decisions.

Agencies exist within a loosely defined system often called the administrative justice system. Different types of individuals and groups, referred to here as single shot players and repeat players, make demands on the system for several different kinds of decisions. The demands are resolved through a number of processes and institutions.

In approaching problems of administrative law, one must be alert to both consumer and producer perspectives. A careful consideration of the elements of decisions in each case begins with a search for constitutional questions, factual issues, statutory problems, and procedural matters.

NOTES

[1]For the story of what actually happened in this case, see *Federal Communications Comm'n v. Pacifica,* 438 U.S. 726 (1978). Chapter 2 will explain how to read this citation and find the report in the library.

[2]An advertising executive quoted in Federal Trade Commission, *FTC Staff Report on Television Advertising to Children* (Washington, D.C.: Government Printing Office, 1978), p. 17.

[3]Id., at p. 22.

[4]This case has been a lengthy battle not altogether different from the cigarette controversy of the sixties. See A. Lee Fritschler, *Smoking and Politics,* 2d ed. (Englewood Cliffs, N.J.: Prentice-Hall, 1975).

For the background of the children's advertising case, see *FTC Staff Report on Television Advertising to Children,* supra.

[5]To learn what happened to someone in this situation, see *Arnett v. Kennedy,* 416 U.S. 134 (1974). In particular examine the dissenting opinion by Justice Marshall for comments on the impact of the termination on the employee.

[6]Frank E. Cooper, *Administrative Agencies and the Courts* (Ann Arbor: University of Michigan Law School, 1951), p. 3. The same is true today more than a quarter century after Cooper's admonition.

[7]The following works were surveyed for a definition of administrative law: Frank Goodnow, *The Principles of the Administrative Law of the United States* (New York: Putnam, 1905); James M. Landis, *The Administrative Process* (New Haven: Yale University Press, 1938); James Hart, *An Introduction to Administrative Law with Selected Cases* (New York:

Crofts, 1940); Roscoe Pound, *Administrative Law: Its Growth, Procedure and Significance* (Pittsburgh: University of Pittsburgh Press, 1942); Frank E. Cooper, supra note 6; J. Forrester Davison and Nathan D. Grundstein, *Administrative Law: Cases and Readings* (Indianapolis: Bobbs-Merrill, 1952); Morris D. Forkosch, *A Treatise on Administrative Law* (Indianapolis: Bobbs-Merrill, 1956); E. Blythe Stason and Frank E. Cooper, *The Law of Administration Tribunals: A Collection of Judicial Decisions, Statutes, Administrative Rules and Orders and Other Materials,* 3d ed. (Chicago: Callaghan, 1957); Kenneth Culp Davis, *Administrative Law Treatise* (St. Paul: West, 1958); David L. Sills, ed., *International Encyclopedia of the Social Sciences* (New York: Macmillan, 1968); Robert S. Lorch, *Democratic Process and Administrative Law* (Detroit, Mich.: Wayne State University Press, 1969); Ernest Gellhorn, *Administrative Law and Process in a Nutshell* (St. Paul: West, 1972); Walter Gellhorn and Clark Byse, *Administrative Law: Cases and Comments* (Mineola, N.Y.: Foundation Press, 1974); Edwin W. Tucker, *Text–Cases–Problems on Administrative Law, Regulation of Enterprise and Individual Liberties* (St. Paul: West, 1975); Louis L. Jaffee and Nathaniel L. Nathanson, *Administrative Law: Cases and Materials* (Boston: Little, Brown, 1976); and Bernard Schwartz, *Administrative Law* (Boston: Little, Brown, 1976).

[8]Schwartz, supra note 7, at p. 2.

[9]Id.

[10] "Administrative law is not, by this definition, the substantive rules made by administrators, nor is it the adjudicative decisions they make." Robert S. Lorch, *Democratic Process and Administrative Law* (Detroit, Mich.: Wayne State Uni-

versity Press, 1969), p. 59. See also Kenneth Culp Davis, *Administrative Law Treatise* (St. Paul: West, 1958), §1.01, and Schwartz, supra note 7, at p. 3.

[11]Martin Shapiro, *The Supreme Court and Administrative Agencies* (New York: Free Press, 1968), p. 106.

[12]For an example of how the nature, form, and purpose of legislation and agency action blend with complex facts and policy issues, see *Volkswagen Aktiengesellschaft v. Federal Maritime Comm'n*, 390 U.S. 261, 309–10 (1968), Justice Douglas dissenting.

[13]Davis, supra note 10, at §1.01.

[14]Bernard Schwartz in David L. Sills, ed., *International Encyclopedia of the Social Sciences* (New York: Macmillan, 1968), p. 68.

[15]See generally Deil S. Wright, *Understanding Intergovernmental Relations: Public Policy and Participants' Perspectives in Local, State, and National Governments* (North Scituate, Mass.: Duxbury Press, 1978); James D. Carroll and Richard W. Campbell, eds., *Intergovernmental Administration: 1976—Eleven Academic and Practitioner Perspectives* (Syracuse, N.Y.: Syracuse University, 1976); and Michael D. Reagan, *The New Federalism* (New York: Oxford University Press, 1972).

[16]See Chapters 4, 7, and the *Eldridge* case in Appendix A.

[17]See *New York Times*, Tuesday, October 18, 1977, p. 1, and Thursday, October 13, 1977.

[18]Id., October 18, p. 28.

[19]Louis L. Jaffee and Nathaniel L. Nathanson, *Administrative Law: Cases and Materials* (Boston: Little, Brown, 1976), p. 2.

[20]For some indication of the difficulties encountered, see *United States v. Florida East Coast Railroad*, 410 U.S. 224 (1973), and *United States v. Allegheny–Ludlum Steel Corp.*, 406 U.S. 742 (1972).

[21]"The basic scheme underlying the legislation is to classify all proceedings into two categories, namely, 'rulemaking' and 'adjudication.' " Attorney General Tom C. Clark to Bureau of the Budget Director Harold D. Smith, June 3, 1946, Truman Papers, Truman Library.

[22]See generally Isaiah Sharfman, *The Interstate Commerce Commission* (New York: The Commonwealth Fund, 1937), and Robert Fellmeth, *The Interstate Commerce Commission* (New York: Grossman, 1970).

[23]The CAB is scheduled to meet its demise in 1985 under the provisions of the Airline Deregulation Act of 1978.

[24]See Administrative Conference of the United States, *U.S.*

Government Manual (Washington, D.C.: Government Printing Office, 1981–82), p. 250.

[25]See, e.g., *Withrow v. Larkin*, 421 U.S. 35 (1975), and *Bates v. State Bar*, 433 U.S. 350 (1977).

[26]Ernest Freund, *Administrative Powers over Persons and Property* (Chicago: University of Chicago Press, 1928), chap. 1.

[27]As the *Eldridge* case study indicates, even in 1974 the disability program had 1,250,400 filings. U.S. House of Representatives, Subcommittee on Social Security of the Committee on Ways and Means, *Delays in Social Security Appeals*, 94th Cong., 1st Sess. (1975), p. 34. In that year the combined total of major federal court filings was less than 200,000. See *Management Statistics for United States Courts* (Washington, D.C.: Administrative Office of U.S. Courts, 1975).

[28]Kenneth Culp Davis, *Administrative Law: Cases–Text–Problems*, 6th ed. (St. Paul: West, 1977), p. 2.

[29]"The service polity is a formidable political-administrative entity, characterized by pressures upon public budgets by clients and public employees; demands for humane, equitable, and responsive service by clients; demands for evidence of productivity by politicians and the public; a challenge to the nature of professionalism and administrative expertise in face-to-face relations; and related factors. Questions of collective bargaining by public employees, of productivity and equity in the provision of services, and of the political rights and responsibilities of public employees as a large segment of the public are the heart of the service polity." James D. Carroll, "Service, Knowledge, and Choice: The Future as Post-Industrial Administration," 35 *Public Admin. Rev.* 578 (1975).

[30]See, e.g., Marc Galanter, "Why the Haves Come Out Ahead: Speculations on the Limits of Legal Change," 9 *Law & Society Rev.* 95 (1974).

[31]37 *Fed. Reg.* 16787 (1972)

[32]The term *ultra vires* comes from corporate law. It derives from the idea that corporate ownership and control rest not with managment but with the owners. Some of that control is delegated to management, but actions beyond those delegated are not binding on the corporation as a body or on the owners of the corporation. The relationship of citizens, legislators, and administrators is analogous to the corporate example.

[33]Executive Order No. 10501 (1953). Eisenhower's order superseded related programs ordered by Franklin Roosevelt in 1940 and Truman in 1950 and 1951. See Arthur M. Schlesinger, *The Imperial Presidency* (Boston: Houghton Mifflin, 1973), pp. 339–40.

[34]Executive Order No. 11246 (1967).

[35]5 U.S.C. §551 et seq.

The Law in Books:
An Orientation to Legal Research

"That's the law!" When people make such a claim they mean at least two things. First, they are asserting that the law as it is written requires or prohibits some action. This is a reference to the law in books or, as it is frequently referred to, the "black letter law." Second, the claim of legality suggests implicitly or explicitly that the courts will interpret and apply the written law in a predictable manner. This is a reference to the law in action.

Chapter 3 will deal with those aspects of legal theory and judicial policymaking that comprise the law in action. Chapter 2 will address the problem of locating and using the law in books.

Legal research is not simple, but neither is it magical or exotic. Techniques of legal research are based on the need to find the most authoritative statements, rulings, and commentaries on specific problems in the shortest possible time. Like most other skills, for example, using a computer, the only way to learn legal research is through practice. To set the stage for working with the law in books, we must first consider the sources of the law and the process through which the law is developed.

SOURCES OF LAW

When the television or newspaper reports major legal decisions affecting public policy, the cases discussed are frequently disputes that have been decided by the United States Supreme Court. However, since the Supreme Court deals with relatively few cases, some comment on the manner in which legal disputes work their way through the legal system and which sources of law are used to resolve them is necessary.

17

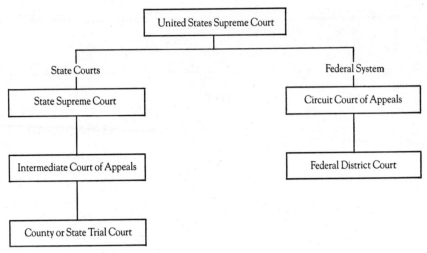

Figure 2-1. *The Dual Court System*

The Dual Court System

Most potential legal disputes never go to court. They are resolved through discussion and compromise. Of the controversies that do develop into formal legal cases, most are dealt with in the state courts. Most criminal and domestic relations problems, for example, are judged in state courts according to state rules. With this caveat in mind, let us turn briefly to a description of the American dual system of courts. See Figure 2-1.

Cases that come from state courts usually begin in a county court with a trial before a judge and, in some cases, a jury. The jury is the trier of fact whose duty it is to determine whether, for example, Mary Smith really punched Harry Jones in the nose. The judge must interpret the law to determine how the law should be applied in the particular case before the court.

If the case is lost at the trial court level, an appeal to an intermediate appellate court may be made on questions of law. Normally, the appeals court will not review questions of fact decided by the jury. The facts on appeal are taken directly from the trial court record.

Should the decision at the appellate level be found unsatisfactory, one may have recourse to the state supreme court,[1] which is the highest authority on the law of that state. In many cases, that court also has administrative responsibility for the operation of the entire state court system. If one asserts a question of federal law, there may be an opportunity to have the case reviewed in the United States Supreme Court.[2]

Cases that come up through the federal court system begin in the federal district courts.[3] There are some ninety-seven federal district courts staffed by approximately four hundred judges.[4] Each district court interprets the federal law within its district; and most states have several such districts within their borders.[5]

Appeals from decisions made in the federal district courts are taken to the United States Circuit Courts of Appeals. There are twelve judicial circuits in this country. See Figure 2-2.

Figure 2-2. *The Twelve Federal Judicial Circuits*

SOURCE: *Federal Reporter*, 2d series (St. Paul: West, 1982). Used by permission of West Publishing Company.

The circuit courts rule over activities within their respective circuits. Judges in the circuit courts sit in three-judge panels; a majority vote is needed to decide a case. Obviously, given the number of different panels within the circuits and the number of circuits within the United States, there are bound to be conflicting interpretations of law. Within a circuit, such conflicts are resolved by having all of the judges sit together to review a case "en banc." Conflicts among the circuits must be resolved by the Supreme Court.

Cases come to the Supreme Court in one of three forms. Disputes may be taken on appeal from state supreme courts,[6] circuit courts of appeals,[7] or other special courts.[8] Appeals are cases that may be taken to the Supreme Court as a matter of right.[9] Second, cases are taken to the Court on certification.[10] In this situation, a lower court certifies a particular question of law to the Supreme Court in an effort to get a clear interpretation of an ambiguous area of the law. Finally, most cases come to the Court on a writ of *certiorari*.[11] The decision to grant a writ of *certiorari* is purely discretionary and is reached through what has come to be known as "the rule of four." If four of the nine justices vote to hear the case, the writ is issued to the lower court directing that the record in the case be sent up for review. Less than ten percent of the requests for *certiorari* are granted in a given year.

Repositories of the Black Letter Law

The decisions of appellate courts are, under the Anglo-American system of precedent, the law within their respective jurisdictions. But precedent is only one of a number of sources of black letter law. There are several:

- Constitutions
- Statutes
- Administrative regulations
- Executive orders
- Treaties
- Appellate court decisions

Constitutions are by definition fundamental laws and are superior to any other legal enactment whether in the form of a bill or a joint resolution. Treaties are negotiated by the President and ratified by the Senate. There are also other forms of international agreements that, though they are not ratified by the Senate, have the force of law. Executive agreements or diplomatic protocols are examples.[12] In case of a conflict, the provisions of a treaty are superior to state law.[13] Executive orders are proclamations issued by the President[14] or, in the states, by the governor.[15] They have legal authority but are generally limited in scope. Administrative regulations are promulgated by an administrative agency within the area of authority delegated to the agency by the legislature. They will be the subject of extensive consideration in Chapter 5.

BEGINNING LEGAL RESEARCH

Anyone who will have occasion to do research in the law should consider purchasing a basic legal reference book such as Morris Cohen's *How to Find the Law,*[16] or one of several similar works. A number of aids to legal research are available free from law book publishers.[17]

Legal materials are published by official sources at various levels of government and by private commercial houses. The two largest private legal book firms presently in the market are West Publishing Company and the Lawyers Cooperative Publishing Company. In doing legal research work, the researcher must frequently move from materials prepared by one publisher to those of the government or another publisher. Unfortunately, the three reference systems do not cross-refer well in all cases. In our discussion, therefore, we shall be somewhat redundant so that users will be able to understand the resources and problems of each system of books.

After one has developed a familiarity with the tools of legal research, it is normal to select favorite research strategies for different types of research problems. At present we shall take a general approach. Most students of the craft agree that there are three parts to legal research : (1) finding the law; (2) reading the law; and (3) supplementing the law.

FINDING THE LAW

Every year Congress enacts many new laws; the Supreme Court hands down more than 150 full opinions in major cases; U.S. Circuit Courts of Appeals dispose of nearly 18,000 cases;[18] the district courts add another 155,000 cases;[19] administrative agencies produce hundreds of regulations, and legislatures, courts, and agencies in all fifty states add their share to the law already "on the books." The problem then is to locate the law on the specific topic that one wishes to learn about.

First, one must be aware that words are important. The researcher must get into the habit of searching for key words. Therefore, learning the language of the area of law that one is investigating is one of the first steps. Do not be put off by legalisms or exotic words. No one can know all areas of the law, or even the language or jargon currently in vogue in a particular specialty. Attempt to discover clear descriptive terms in the study of a subject to aid in the law finding process.

Suppose, for example, that one wanted information on the topic of discrimination in employment. "Discrimination" and "employment" are two obvious words that one would use to find material on the topic, but there are any number of other possible terms. One might check various indexes under "sex discrimination," "age discrimination," "race discrimination," "aliens," "equal protection," "labor," "equal opportunity," "affirmative action," or "employment tests."

Make a list of the terms that come to mind or words that are mentioned in titles or early reading in the research area. It will not be long before one finds certain terms repeated in research sources. Using these words, the researcher will be able to focus on his or her specific interest and save time.

Indexes, Dictionaries, and Encyclopedias

Finding the law begins much like any other kind of research. The beginning researcher will need to refer to dictionaries for definitions of new terms. Two of the most commonly available legal dictionaries are *Black's Law Dictionary*[20] and *Ballentine's Law Dictionary*.[21] In law, unlike some other fields, words usually have an authoritative definition derived directly from the definition given to the words by courts that have considered them. Legal dictionaries provide the reader with the definitions and references to cases in which those definitions were developed.

Some research problems may seem to demand more detailed explanations or alternative definitions. A multivolume work called *Words and Phrases*[22] provides this additional information.

If one knew nothing about a topic of general interest in any field, an encyclopedia would be a likely first stop. In the social sciences, for example, one might refer to the *International Encyclopedia of the Social Sciences*.[23] In legal research, the researcher would go to West's *Corpus Juris Secundum*[24] ("second body of law") or to the Lawyers Cooperative's *American Jurisprudence*, second series (frequently referred to as Am. Jur. 2d).[25] Despite their somewhat forbidding titles, both sets are encyclopedias in that they do two things: (1) they present the beginning researcher with an encyclopedic article on major topics like any other encyclopedia; and (2) they footnote almost every statement of any consequence in the article to legal cases that discuss the point.

Most law reference books are much too expensive to republish each year as new developments occur in the law. To accommodate changes, many research volumes contain a "pocket part," so named because it is a paperback part added by means of a pocket in the binding on the inside back cover. Whenever using a legal volume, be certain to check for a pocket part updating the material from the main body of the book.

Legal encyclopedias are organized by topic and alphabetically arrayed in several volumes. If key words do not yield a complete entry, refer to listings for those terms in the volumes of the set called the "Descriptive Word Index." Entries in that index send the researcher to a specific section of an encylopedic entry. Check as many key words as possible because there may be several different entries that discuss a topic in different ways.

One of the most important legal research tools, especially for a public administration student or practitioner, is the index. The *Index to Legal Periodicals*[26] provides access to law review articles referenced by subject, author, case title, and book review title. If one's research begins with the name and citation to a case, he or she may turn to the *Index to Legal Periodicals* case table and find commentaries written specifically about that case. The most recent editions of the *index* are published in paperback pamphlet form. They are combined each year into a single volume and combined again every three years in a hardback volume. Because of the format, it is relatively easy to search several bound volumes, single year issues, and the last few months for a rapid survey of all articles published on one's topic in the last decade. Like most index volumes, the legal periodicals index has an abbreviations list and entry description at the beginning of each volume.

One of the most common mistakes made by beginning legal researchers is to overlook the obvious. The card catalog may well contain a reference to a legal treatise or summary monograph of the topic under consideration. For the appropriate key words, one should examine the *Library of Congress Subject Headings List. Law Books in Print* is indexed by author, subject, and title and may provide useful references to legal works that are available but not presently in a card catalog if the book is not in the library's current collection. Particularly where law and public policy questions are at issue, do not forget the various dissertation indexes. In addition to the fact that someone may have done recent research on the topic under consideration, most dissertations contain fairly complete literature reviews and bibliographies that help, especially where a long-term broad-based research program is the task at hand. Finally, various newspaper indexes, such as the *New York Times Index,* may be available to lead the reader to research resources stored as microfilm or microfiche.

Digests and A.L.R.s

Another important law-finding tool is the set of indexes prepared by the Lawyers Cooperative to accompany its *American Law Reports* (A.L.R.) series. The A.L.R. editors prepare and publish selected court opinions and accompany these with detailed annotations, which are small essays or treatises on very specific legal topics. Each entry in the A.L.R. or other Lawyers Coop publications begins with a mini-index, which the publisher calls the "Total Client Service Library." See Figure 2-3.

West relies heavily on its digest system for cross-referring, using the West key number system to index court decisions. The system sounds complex but is very logical and relatively simple to use. West publishes court reports from all fifty states and all the federal courts. As court opinions are prepared for publication, editors develop short paragraphs that highlight the points of law discussed in the opinion,[27]

TOTAL CLIENT-SERVICE LIBRARY® REFERENCES

25 Am Jur 2d, Elections § 11.

USCS, Constitution, 14th and 15th Amendments

US L Ed Digest, Appeal and Error §§ 1641, 1677; Civil Rights § 5; Constitutional Law § 334

L Ed Index to Annos, Elections; Equal Protection of the Laws

ALR Quick Index, Discrimination; Elections

Federal Quick Index, Equal Protection of the Laws; Fifteenth Amendment

ANNOTATION REFERENCES

Racial discrimination in voting, and validity and construction of remedial legislation. 27 L Ed 2d 885.

Diluting effect of minorities' votes by adoption of particular election plan, or gerrymandering of election district, as violation of equal protection clause of Federal Constitution. 27 ALR Fed 29.

Binding effect upon state courts of opinion of United States Supreme Court supported by less than a majority of all its members. 65 ALR3d 504.

Figure 2-3 *Mini-Index to A.L.R.*

SOURCE: *Mobile v. Bolton,* 64 L. Ed. 2d 47, 49 (1980). *U.S. Supreme Court Reports, Lawyers Edition,* 2d series, vol. 64 (Rochester, N.Y.: Lawyers Cooperative, 1980), p. 49. Used by permission of the publisher.

for example: "Presidential communications are presumptively privileged, and such privilege is fundamental to operation of government and inextricably rooted in separation of powers under the Constitution" *United States v. Nixon,* 94 S. Ct. 3090, 3091 (1974). The notes are placed at the beginning of the case report as headnotes. Each headnote is then classified by subject and assigned a key number. "The West Key Number classification system divides the entire body of case law into Seven Main Divisions, thirty-two Subheadings and over four hundred Digest Topics.[28]

All notes with similar subjects and key numbers are collected and organized alphabetically by subject in the same fashion as in the encyclopedias. Each state has a digest. A series of digest volumes, West's *Federal Practice Digest 2d,* contains only points of law from federal cases. There are also *Decennial Digests,* published every ten years, which compile points of law from decisions across the nation rendered during that period.[29]

There are several ways to use digests as law finders. The researcher may begin by using the "Descriptive Word Index" volume (usually the last volume in the set), to find specific subject headings and key numbers of cases on the topic under study. If the researcher begins with the name of a case, he or she may go to the case table to find the complete citation to the case, the history of that case, and the subjects and key numbers in the main digest volumes that deal with the case and mention other decisions related to it. See Figure 2-4. The digest may be used as an encyclopedia by

84 F P D 2d—515

References are to Digest Topics and Key Numbers

U S v. NORMAN

U S v. Nine Parcels of Land in City of Grand Forks, Grand Forks County, State of N D, DCND, 215 FSupp 771 —Em Dom 152(1); Fed Civ Proc 2656; Mun Corp 519(5), 529.

U S v. 19.897 Acres of Land, More or Less, in Town of Islip, Suffolk County, State of N Y, DCNY, 27 FRD 420—Fed Civ Proc 1508, 1509.

U S v. 1964 Ford Thunderbird, Motor and Serial No 4Y85Z156657, CANJ, 445 F2d 1064, cert den Bivens v. U S, 92 SCt 1181, 405 US 964, 31 LEd2d 239—Arrest 63.4(2, 13), 71.1(2); Autos 349; Drugs & N 183, 192, 195, 196; Fed Cts 706, 841; Forfeit 5.

U S v. 1967 Cadillac Fleetwood El Dorado Auto, DCTex, 296 FSupp 991—Drugs & N 190; Forfeit 3, 9.

U S v. 9,947.71 Acres of Land, More or Less, in Clark County, State of Nev, DCNev, 220 FSupp 328—Em Dom 83, 195, 257, 319; Evid 21; High 9; Mines 14(1), 23(2); Pub Lands 45.

U S v. 9,101.24 Acres of Land, More or Less, In Sierra and Otero Counties, State of N M, CANM, 521 F2d 13. See U S v. 46,672.96 Acres of Land, More or Less, In Dona Ana, Et Al Counties, State of N M.

U S v. 9,345.53 Acres of Land, More or Less, in Cattaraugus County, N Y, DCNY, 256 FSupp 603—Indians 5, 16, 16(1, 2).

U S v. 90.39 Acres of Land, More or Less, in Polk County, State of Iowa, DCIowa, 413 FSupp 91—Em Dom 138, 234(1), 237(1, 5).

U S v. 94 Acres of Land, More or Less, in Town of Hyde Park, Dutchess County, State of N Y, DCNY, 299 FSupp 668—Em Dom 76, 130, 131, 223; Tax 537.

U S v. 91.69 Acres of Land, More or Less, in Oconee County, State of S C, CASC, 334 F2d 229—Em Dom 58, 198(1), 240, 262(1); Fed Cts 527, 554; Mand 4(1).

U S v. 96 Cases, More or Less, of Fireworks, DCOhio, 244 FSupp 272 —Fed Civ Proc 2445.

U S v. 93 Court Corp, CANY, 350 F2d 386, cert den 86 SCt 560, 382 US 984, 15 LEd2d 473—Fed Cts 770; Lim of Act 4(1), 11(1, 4); U S 53(13), 133.

U S v. Niro, CANY, 338 F2d 439—Crim Law 643, 1167(1), 1169.1(1); Fraud 68.10(4); Jury 31(11).

U S v. Nitti, CAIll, 444 F2d 1056—Rec 8 Goods 3, 8(3, 4).

U S v. Nitti, CAIll, 374 F2d 750, cert den 87 SCt 2141, 388 US 920, 18 LEd2d 1366—Consp 47(3); Counterfeit 18; Crim Law 627.9(5), 742(1), 1144.13(3), 1177.

U S v. Nix, CAAla, 548 F2d 1159—Crim Law 369.2(6), 406(1); P O 49(6, 12).

U S v. Nix, CAIll, 501 F2d 516—Crim Law 774; Escape 1, 6.

U S v. Nix, CALa, 465 F2d 90, cert den 93 SCt 455, 409 US 1013, 34 LEd2d 307, reh den 93 SCt 918, 409 US 1119, 34 LEd2d 704—Crim Law 121, 126(1), 393(1), 591; Jury 131(2); Searches 7(25, 26); Weap 17(4).

U S v. Nix, CACal, 437 F2d 746, cert den 91 SCt 2173, 402 US 999, 29 LEd2d 166—Armed S 20.8(4).

U S v. Nixon, DistCol, 94 SCt 3090, 418 US 683, 41 LEd2d 1039—Const Law 50, 67, 72, 76, 266(1), 268(1, 5); Crim Law 412(1), 423(1, 4), 427(2, 5), 627.5(1, 2, 3, 4, 6), 627.6(2), 627.7(4), 627.8(1, 3, 4, 6), 639(2), 662(1), 736(1), 1023(2), 1131(2), 1134(1), 1158(2), 1192; Fed Cts 12, 13, 491, 571; U S 26; Witn 2(2), 331½.

U S v. Nixon, CAAriz, 571 F2d 1121 —Crim Law 412.2(5), 414.

U S v. Nixon, CACal, 545 F2d 1190, cert den 97 SCt 1148, 429 US 1110, 51 LEd2d 565—Crim Law 273(1); Stip 5.

U S v. Nixon, DCMich, 395 FSupp 395—Hus & W 147, 158.

U S v. Nixon, NCMR, 2 MJ 609—Mil Jus 265.

U S v. N L Industries, Inc, CAMo, 479 F2d 354—Civil R 9.10, 9.12, 9.13, 38, 39, 44(1, 4), 46.

U S v. NL Industries, Inc, DCMo, 338 FSupp 1167, rev 479 F2d 354 —Civil R 9.10, 43, 44(1, 2).

U S v. Noa, CAHawaii, 443 F2d 144 —Crim Law 412.2(3); Searches 7 (27).

U S v. Noah, CAWash, 475 F2d 688, cert den Ross v. U S, 94 SCt 119, 414 US 821, 38 LEd2d 54, cert den 94 SCt 728, 414 US 1095, 38 LEd2d 553—Consp 28(1), 40, 47(12), 48.2 (2); Crim Law 37(2), 317, 622(2), 730(8), 770(2), 772(6), 788, 855(5), 984, 1035(6), 1165(1), 1173.1, 1177, 1184(4); Drugs & N 123; Hab Corp 85.5(12); Ind & Inf 56, 124(1); Jury 33(1).

U S v. Nobile, CACal, 451 F2d 1121—Armed S 20.8(1); Crim Law 1186.1.

U S v. Noble, DCNY, 269 FSupp 814—Infants 78(1), 81.

U S v. Noble, AFCMR, 2 MJ 672—Mil Jus 51, 113, 332.

U S v. Nobles, Cal, 95 SCt 2160, 422 US 225, 45 LEd2d 141, on remand 522 F2d 1274—Crim Law 393(1), 683, 627.5(3, 6), 627.6(5), 627.7(1, 3), 641.12(1), 655(1), 661, 699, 1028, 1153(1), 1154; Witn 2(1), 266, 271 (1), 297(1), 306, 390, 391.

U S v. Nobles, Cal, 95 SCt 801, 419 US 1120, 42 LEd2d 819. See U S v. Brown, 501 F2d 146.

U S v. Nobles, CACal, 501 F2d 146. See U S v. Brown.

U S v. Nocar, CAIll, 497 F2d 719, cert den 95 SCt 526, 419 US 1038, 42 LEd2d 315—Const Law 258(3); Drugs & N 42, 78, 123, 183.

U S v. Nocerino, CANY, 474 F2d 903 Cert den 93 SCt 2785, 412 US 942, 37 LEd2d 402—Drugs & N 31.

U S v. Noel, CATenn, 490 F2d 89—Crim Law 778(11).

U S v. Noel, CMA, 3 MJ 328—Mil Jus 193, 332.

U S v. Noftall, CAMass, 553 F2d 731. See U S v. Bailleul.

U S v. Nogueira, CACal, 403 F2d 816 —Fed Civ Proc 2504; Fed Cts 41, 47; Mines 14(1), 38(1, 6, 7), 51(1); Pub Lands 103(4).

U S v. Nolan, CAOkl, 571 F2d 528—Atty & C 92; Courts 100(1); Crim Law 997.5, 997.7.

U S v. Nolan, CAKan, 564 F2d 376—Bail 75, 79(1, 2).

U S v. Nolan, CAKan, 551 F2d 266, cert den 98 SCt 302—Crim Law 304 (2), 338(1), 342, 369.1, 369.2(1, 3), 369.15, 370, 371(1, 12), 372(1, 13), 517(2), 517.2(3), 552(3), 720(6), 768 (1), 827.4(6), 834(2), 899, 1037.1 (2), 1144.13(3), 1153(1), 1159.3(1), 1159.4(1), 1169.1(7); Drugs & N 124.

U S v. Nolan, CAKan, 450 F2d 934 —Crim Law 778(11), 1172.2.

U S v. Nolan, CALa, 420 F2d 552, cert den 91 SCt 36, 400 US 819, 27 LEd2d 47—Crim Law 394.5(1, 4), 394.6(4), 627.8(2), 1038.2, 1038.3.

U S v. Nolan, CAIll, 416 F2d 588, appeal after remand 450 F2d 934— Arrest 71.1(1); Autos 357; Crim Law 394.4(2), 404(4), 438(8), 656 (7), 721(1), 1037.1(2), 1166.22(4), 1171.5; Searches 3.8(2).

U S v. Nolan, CAOhio, 413 F2d 850—Crim Law 394.4(6), 1186.1; Searches 3.6(2, 5).

U S v. Noland, CAVa, 510 F2d 1093 —Infants 69.

U S v. Noland, CATex, 495 F2d 529 Cert den 95 SCt 228, 419 US 966,

42 LEd2d 181—Const Law 259; Crim Law 113, 121, 1171.1(1), 1202 (1).

U S v. Noland, DCTex, 367 FSupp 571 aff 495 F2d 529, cert den 95 SCt 228, 419 US 966, 42 LEd2d 181—Crim Law 1202(7); Ind & Inf 114.

U S v. Noles, CAFla, 524 F2d 1262—Crim Law 762(1), 1172.3.

U S v. Noll, DCPa, 377 FSupp 203—U S 75(4).

U S v. Nolte, CATex, 440 F2d 1124, cert den 92 SCt 49, 404 US 862, 30 LEd2d 106—Crim Law 507(1), 780(1), 942(2), 1020(1), 1037.1(2).

U S v. Nolte, DCCal, 39 FRD 359—Fed Civ Proc 627.6(2).

U S v. Nomura Trading Co, DCNY, 213 FSupp 704—Consp 28(1), 40.1; Crim Law 394.6(1), 618, 622(1, 3), 627.9(5), 649(2); Ind & Inf 10.1(1), 10.2(1, 6), 71.2(1), 87(2), 121.2(3), 121.3, 125(3, 5½), 144.1(2).

U S v. Nooks, CAGa, 446 F2d 1283, cert den Hughes v. U S, 92 SCt 299, 404 US 945, 30 LEd2d 261—Arrest 63.4(16); Courts 100(1); Crim Law 394.4(12), 881(3), 893, 1169.1(5); Searches 7(10).

U S v. Noonan, CAPa, 434 F2d 582, cert den 91 SCt 1190, 401 US 981, 28 LEd2d 333—Armed S 20.8(4, 7, 10), 20.9(3), 40.1(7, 11).

U S v. Nooner, CAOkl, 565 F2d 633 —Crim Law 1026.

U S v. Nooney, CAMo, 487 F2d 355. See Diversified Brokers Co, Inc, In re.

U S v. Norber, CAMich, 492 F2d 1367. See U S v. Stephens.

U S v. Norcome, DCDC, 375 FSupp 270, aff U S v. Cook, 162 USApp DC 98, 497 F2d 686, 162 USAppDC 99, 497 F2d 686, U S v. Silvers, 162 USAppDC 99, 497 F2d 686, U S v. Staton, 162 USAppDC 99, 497 F2d 686—Infants 69.

U S v. Nordic Baking & Importing Co 47 CCPA 78—Cust Dut 12, 38(9), 85(3).

U S v. Nordlof, CAIll, 440 F2d 840, cert den 92 SCt 936, 405 US 935, vac 454 F2d 739—Armed S 20.8(4, 7, 10), 40.1(5, 7).

U S v. Noreikis, CAIll, 481 F2d 1177 cert den in part, gr in part 94 SCt 1398, 415 US 904, 39 LEd2d 461—Drugs & N 123, 188, 189; Searches 3.8(1).

U S v. Norfolk & W Ry Co, Ohio, 87 SCt 255, 385 US 57, 17 LEd2d 162. See Illinois Cent R Co v. Norfolk & W Ry Co.

U S v. Norfolk, Baltimore & Carolina Line, Inc, CAVa, 382 F2d 208—Adm 118.7(5); Crim Law 4; Ship 16; Statut 174.

U S v. Norfolk Dredging Co, DCMd, 242 FSupp 175. See Maloof v. U S.

U S v. Norgi, CMA, 2 MJ 96—Mil Jus 170, 171, 318, 333.

U S v. Nori, CAIll, 352 F2d 910—Arrest 63.4(18); Crim Law 394.6(5); Searches 3.3(9).

U S v. Norman, CANC, 518 F2d 1176 —Crim Law 394.1(3), 556.

U S v. Norman, CATenn, 413 F2d 789, cert den 90 SCt 585, 396 US 1018, 24 LEd2d 510, reh den 90 SCt 962, 397 US 958, 25 LEd2d 145—Armed S 40.1(10); Crim Law 322.

U S v. Norman, CACal, 412 F2d 629—Armed S 20.8(4); Crim Law 274(7), 997.4.

U S v. Norman, CACal, 402 F2d 73, cert den 90 SCt 949, 397 US 938, 25 LEd2d 119—Const Law 268(8); Crim Law 662(1), 940, 1044.1(5), 1170½(5); Drugs & N 124; Poisons 9; Witn 18, 267, 344(2).

U S v. Norman, CAOhio, 391 F2d 212, cert den 88 SCt 1265, 390 US 1014, 20 LEd2d 163—Comp Off 5; Crim Law 997.1; Ind & Inf 201.

U S v. Norman, DCTenn, 301 FSupp 53, aff 413 F2d 789, cert den 90

Figure 2-4 *A Typical Page from Digest Case Table*

SOURCE: *Federal Practice Digest*, 2d series, vol. 84 (St. Paul: West, 1978), p. 515. Used by permission of West Publishing Company.

turning to the general topic under study and examining the expanded table of contents under that subject to find the key numbers that appear likely to further research.

Once the researcher finds the subject and the appropriate key number, he or she will find a collection of those short paragraphs from case headnotes discussed earlier, arranged by date and by the court that rendered the ruling. See Figure 2-5. If, on examining the notes from cases related to the subject under study, there are case references that appear to be useful or obviously important, one may take the citation from the digest and go directly to the full report of the opinion.

A digest, a dictionary, or any encyclopedia is never cited as a primary legal source. They are secondary sources—the cases are the primary references. A second caveat is that one should not simply adopt the point of law noted in a secondary source without carefully examining the primary source. These research tools are intended to assist the researcher in finding the law, not to present the law itself.

Law Review Articles as Law Finders

From a social scientist's or administrator's point of view law review articles are some of the best law finders. They accomplish a number of goals. Survey articles on the topic under study frequently provide the neophyte in a particular area of law with:

- An introduction to the field of interest[30]
- Basic familiarization with the jargon in use in a specialty
- A survey of the major statutes and leading cases in the field
- References to leading treatises, government reports, and other journal articles on the topic
- A conceptualization of the major issues and conflicts surrounding a particular policy area
- A brief who's who in the field and how the major actors are arrayed on the policy under consideration

When using the law reviews as law finders, try scanning the introduction, the first footnote, which identifies the credentials of the author, the conclusion, which is usually a survey paragraph, the section headings in the body of the article, and the footnotes. After reading the body of the article, read the footnotes separately.

Before proceeding to the discussion of reading the law, go to the library and use the law finders described above to obtain reference and citations to the law in an area of interest.

READING THE LAW

We turn now to an examination of the manner of presentation of the law by the government and private publishers. However, to get from the law finder to the black letter law, one must understand the use of legal citations.

The citation consists for present purposes, of two parts: the case or article title and the reference. The following example uses *San Antonio Independent School District v. Rodriguez*, 411 U.S. 1 (1973). A title is italicized as a proper title. The reference indicates where the cited case or article may be found. It begins with the volume

11A F P D 2d—555   **CONSTITUTIONAL LAW**   ⚫⇒76

For references to other topics, see Descriptive-Word Index

(C) EXECUTIVE POWERS AND
FUNCTIONS.

⚫⇒76. **Nature and scope in general.**

Library references

C.J.S. Constitutional Law § 167.

U.S.Dist.Col. 1974. Executive Branch has exclusive authority and absolute discretion to decide whether to prosecute case.

U. S. v. Nixon, 94 S.Ct. 3090, 418 U.S. 683, 41 L.Ed.2d 1039.

Presidential communications are presumptively privileged, and such privilege is fundamental to operation of government and inextricably rooted in separation of powers under Constitution.

U. S. v. Nixon, 94 S.Ct. 3090, 418 U.S. 683, 41 L.Ed.2d 1039.

To extent that President's interest in confidentiality of communications with aides and advisors relates to effective discharge of President's powers, it is constitutionally based.

U. S. v. Nixon, 94 S.Ct. 3090, 418 U.S. 683, 41 L.Ed.2d 1039.

C.A.D.C. 1973. The Executive's prosecutorial discretion does not imply an unreviewable power to withhold evidence relevant to a grand jury's criminal investigation.

Nixon v. Sirica, 487 F.2d 700, 159 U.S. App.D.C. 58.

C.A.D.C. 1971. Doctrine of executive privilege is inherent in constitutional requirement of separation of powers.

Soucie v. David, 448 F.2d 1067, 145 U.S. App.D.C. 144.

C.A.D.C. 1966. Specific congressional action to remedy an evil does not by itself indicate that executive branch lacks authority to act under other statutory provisions.

Udall v. Littell, 366 F.2d 668, 125 U.S.App. D.C. 89, certiorari denied 87 S.Ct. 713, 385 U.S. 1007, 17 L.Ed.2d 545, rehearing denied 87 S.Ct. 952, 386 U.S. 939, 17 L.Ed.2d 812.

C.A.2 1975. While Federal Communications Commission acted properly in adopting amendments to prime time access rule which allowed network broadcasting in access time for public affairs, documentary and children's programs, it was improper delegation of Commission's duty of policing rule when it admonished licensees not to use exemption for network programs during access time on Saturday except for "compelling public interest reasons." Communications Act of 1934, § 307(d), 47 U.S.C.A. § 307(d).

National Ass'n of Independent Television Producers and Distributors v. F. C. C., 516 F.2d 526.

see United States Code Annotated

C.A.Ala. 1966. When Congress declares national policy, duty that other coordinate branches owe to nation requires that, within the law, the judiciary and executive respect and carry out such policy.

U. S. v. Jefferson County Bd. of Ed., 372 F.2d 836, corrected 380 F.2d 385, certiorari denied Caddo Parish School Bd. v. U. S., 88 S.Ct. 67, 389 U.S. 840, 19 L.Ed.2d 103, and Board of Ed. of City of Bessemer v. U. S., 88 S.Ct. 77, 389 U.S. 840, 19 L.Ed.2d 104.

C.A.Ill. 1965. Powers of law enforcement are not wholly assigned to executive department under United States Constitution. U.S. C.A.Const. art. 2, §§ 1, 3.

I. C. C. v. Chatsworth Co-op. Marketing Ass'n, 347 F.2d 821, certiorari denied 86 S.Ct. 390, 382 U.S. 938, 15 L.Ed.2d 349, rehearing denied 86 S.Ct. 535, 382 U.S. 1000, 15 L.Ed.2d 490.

The enforcement of any judgment resulting from the initiating of a judicial proceeding for enforcement of legislative act remains with the judicial or executive departments.

I. C. C. v. Chatsworth Co-op. Marketing Ass'n, 347 F.2d 821, certiorari denied 86 S.Ct. 390, 382 U.S. 938, 15 L.Ed.2d 349, rehearing denied 86 S.Ct. 535, 382 U.S. 1000, 15 L.Ed.2d 490.

C.A.La. 1966. When Congress declares national policy, duty that other coordinate branches owe to nation requires that, within the law, the judiciary and executive respect and carry out such policy.

U. S. v. Jefferson County Bd. of Ed., 372 F.2d 836, corrected 380 F.2d 385, certiorari denied Caddo Parish School Bd. v. U. S., 88 S.Ct. 67, 389 U.S. 840, 19 L.Ed.2d 103 and Board of Ed. of City of Bessemer v. U. S., 88 S.Ct. 77, 389 U.S. 840, 19 L.Ed.2d 104.

C.A.Mich. 1971. Constitutional design was to require sharing of "sovereign power" by three coordinate branches of government.

U. S. v. U. S. Dist. Court for Eastern Dist. of Mich., Southern Division, 444 F.2d 651, certiorari granted 91 S.Ct. 2255, 403 U.S. 930, 29 L.Ed.2d 708, affirmed 92 S.Ct. 2125, 407 U.S. 297, 32 L.Ed.2d 752.

C.A.Neb. 1975. The President may not act as a lawmaker in the absence of a delegation of authority or mandate from Congress. U.S.C.A.Const. art. 2, § 3.

Independent Meat Packers Ass'n v. Butz, 526 F.2d 228, certiorari denied 96 S.Ct. 1461, 424 U.S. 966, 47 L.Ed.2d 733, Consumer Federation of America v. Butz, 96 S.Ct. 1461, 424 U.S. 966, 47 L.Ed.2d 733 and National Ass'n of Meat Purveyors v. Butz, 96 S.Ct. 1461, 424 U.S. 966, 47 L.Ed.2d 733.

Figure 2-5   *A Page from a West System Digest*

SOURCE: *Federal Practice Digest*, 2d series, vol. 11A (St. Paul: West, 1978), p. 555. Used by permission of West Publishing Company.

number in which the item is found. The initials abbreviate the name of the publication in which the item is printed. The second number indicates the page on which the case or article begins. Finally, the date in parentheses tells the reader the year in which the case or article was published. *San Antonio*, then, may be found in volume 411 of the *United States Reports* (the official reporter for the U.S. Supreme Court), beginning on page 1, decided in 1973.[31]

Legislative Enactments

During a given year, Congress may enact several hundred statutes. There are also fifty state legislators more or less continuously engaged in enacting laws. Using statutes is not particularly difficult once the researcher understands the various forms in which a piece of legislation appears as it moves from introduction through passage and into use in legal disputes.

When a congressman or senator introduces a legislative proposal, it is assigned a bill number.[32] Once the bill has been enacted into law, it is assigned a public law number. For example, the Education for All Handicapped Children Act is Public Law 94-142, meaning that the statute was the 142d law enacted by the 94th Congress. Each year the statutes are compiled chronologically by public law number into the *Statutes at Large*.

As the new laws emerge, the West series *U.S. Code Congressional and Administrative News* reports the text of the statute and the legislative history of the new law, including the background of the law, changes made during the legislative process, and interpretations suggested during the enactment process.

Volumes of chronologically arranged laws would be very difficult to use by themselves. For this reason, statutes are codified or arranged by subject. The official government version of this compilation is the *United States Code*, abbreviated U.S.C.[33] Private publishers have developed annotated codes, e.g., the *United States Code Annotated* (West) and the *United States Code Service* (Lawyers Cooperative). The annotated codes contain the same verbatim statement of the legislation, but they also give additional references to the background of the legislation and to the interpretations of the various sections of the statute made over the years by courts. Remember when reading statutes always to check for recent changes in the pocket part of the volume!

State legislative enactments are reported in a similar fashion. Compilations of statutes enacted annually are often referred to as "session laws." Frequently, the states do not publish an official code, but instead recognize a commercial code as having official status.

To locate a particular statute, one may use the index volume of the code annotated or *Shepard's Acts and Cases by Popular Name*. However, statutes may be difficult to interpret in specific cases. The words of a statute may necessarily be vague because the legislature, among other reasons, must enact laws that are general enough to cover a range of problems to cover future circumstances. In consequence, courts and administrators must frequently attempt to find evidence of exactly what the legislators had in mind at the time the bill was enacted. The search for this legislative intent is known as legislative history, which includes a consideration of the reasons that prompted the legislation, the form of the measure as it is initially introduced and its sponsors, amendments made during the process as well as the reasons advanced to support them, conference committee changes during efforts to resolve differences between the houses of the legislature on different versions of the bill, debates on the floor, and statements made at the executive bill signing ceremony.[34]

The U.S. Code Congressional and Administrative News has attempted to aid the researcher in finding recent legislative histories. For some major pieces of legislation, Congress will carefully compile and publish a one-volume sourcebook on a bill. An example is the U.S. Senate Committee on Government Operations and House Committee on Government Operations, Sourcebook on Privacy, *Legislative History of the Privacy Act of 1974*, S. 3413 (Public Law 93-579), 94th Cong., 2d Sess. (1976). Some histories are catalogued as separate volumes within the card catalog general collection.

Finally, another finding tool for legislative histories is the *Union List of Legislative Histories.*[35] Unfortunately, many state governments have such complex processes or poor reporting systems that legislative history research becomes extraordinarily difficult.[36]

Executive Lawmaking

In most cases, statutes are implemented through the use of administrative regulations that have the force of law. Until 1935, there was no uniform system for reporting regulations and other official executive branch rulings. After a major New Deal decision in the Supreme Court illustrated the fact that only a handful of people may have had access to regulatory guidelines affecting the entire nation,[37] Congress enacted the Federal Register Act of 1935.[38]

The federal government is required by the Register Act to publish in the *Federal Register* administrative orders and regulations, executive department announcements, presidential proclamations and executive orders, and any other announcements or material that Congress may require be publicized in the *Register*. The *Federal Register* is published daily and distributed throughout the country to U.S. depository libraries (e.g., most universities), and other subscribers. The daily editions, which come in a stapled newsprint format, are periodically bound with indexes.

The *Register* is like the *Statutes at Large* in that it is chronologically arranged. As with legislative enactments, the regulations are later arranged by subject, or codified, and appear as the *Code of Federal Regulations*, abbreviated C.F.R. The C.F.R. is updated completely once each year. In the interim, of course, new regulations are constantly in publication. These interim changes are reported in the "C.F.R. Parts Affected" pamphlet located with the "Index" at the end of the C.F.R. volumes. These parts-affected tables send the researcher to the *Federal Register* pages published since the last C.F.R. revision that contain additions or deletions.

Like most legal reference tools, the C.F.R. Index is very detailed. Along with the regular title and subject portion, the index contains tables by *United States Code* section number which tell the reader where to find regulations interpreting specific statutes.

Because the C.F.R. prints only the language of the regulation, the researcher must return to the *Federal Register* for background material published at the time the

regulation was announced. This shuffling among regulations, when coupled with
the myths and fears that abound concerning regulations, can trigger mild panic in
someone who is told to find the regulations on a particular subject. Believe it or not,
regulations really are written by human beings who speak and write English. On the
other hand, one should not expect regulations governing, for example, the licensing
of nuclear power plants to read like a newspaper article. The attempt by those who
draft regulations to walk the fine line between loose overgeneralized prose and
bureaucratic legalese is a constant battle.

One who must deal with administrative agencies on a regular basis should also
be aware of two general sources. The first is the *U.S. Government Manual*, which is
extremely easy to use. See Figure 2-6. The entries are organized by agency. The
section on each agency begins with a list of officers. Then follows a background
statement on the mission of the agency and the legislation that brought it into
existence, as well as other statutes the agency is assigned to administer. Most entries
include an organization chart. Finally, the entries comment on specific departments
or task groups and frequently list telephone numbers and addresses to contact for
further information.

Second, most agencies publish annual reports. The reports contain the same
type of information as the *U.S. Government Manual*, but in much greater detail.
Additionally, the reports generally contain budgetary information, personnel data,
workload analysis in terms of type and quantity, and current problems and issues.
These reports can be found through the card catalog or by the use of indexes of
government publications, which will be described shortly.

Judicial Decisions

Since our courts work on a system of precedent, it is extremely important that case
reports be widely available. That is easier said than done in a nation with so many
legal disputes resolved in diverse forums. To meet the challenge, case reports are
organized by type of tribunal and by type of controversy.

The decisions of the United States Supreme Court apply nationally. They are
reported officially in the *United States Reports*, published by the federal government.
The two major private publishers also print Supreme Court decisions. West Publishing Company prepares the *Supreme Court Reporter*, abbreviated S.Ct. The S.Ct. is
designed to cross-refer to the West research tools, like the digests, through the key
number system explained earlier. The Lawyers Cooperative Publishing Company
distributes the *U.S. Supreme Court Reports, Lawyers Edition* (second series), abbreviated L. Ed. 2d. Like West, L. Ed. 2d cross-refers to other Lawyers Cooperative
works, most notably the *American Law Reports* (A.L.R.) series, which will be
described below.

The text of the opinion reported in all three reporters is exactly the same. In
fact, the two private reporters even show the *United States Reports* page numbers at
corresponding points in the text of the decision. When taking notes on Supreme
Court cases, always use the *U.S. Reports* pagination to avoid confusion.

There are really three reasons why researchers select the private reporters. First,
they are generally available sooner in both the advance sheets, which present very
recent opinions, and in the full bound volumes. Second, they are slightly less

Figure 2-6 is a reproduction of pages 528 and 529 of the U.S. Government Manual:

---

528   U.S. GOVERNMENT MANUAL

Reserve System—Purposes and Functions, pamphlets entitled *What Truth in Lending Means to You* (English and Spanish), *U.S. Currency*, *If You Borrow To Buy Stock*, *Fair Credit Billing*, *Truth in Leasing*, *Equal Credit in Housing*, and several pamphlets describing the Equal Credit Opportunity Act. Copies of these pamphlets are available free of charge. Information regarding publications may be obtained in Room MP-510 (Martin Bldg.) of the Board's headquarters. Phone, 202-452-3244.

Employment Inquiries regarding employment should be addressed to

Director, Division of Personnel, Board of Governors of the Federal Reserve System, Washington, D.C. 20551.

Procurement Firms desiring to do business with the Board should address their inquiries to Director, Division of Support Services, at the above address.

For further information, contact the Office of Public Affairs, Board of Governors, Federal Reserve System, Washington, D.C. 20551. Phone, 202-452-3204.

Approved.

James McAfee,
Assistant Secretary of the Board.

FEDERAL TRADE COMMISSION

Pennsylvania Avenue at Sixth Street NW., Washington, D.C. 20580
Phone, 202-523-3598

DAVID A. CLANTON   *Acting Chairman*

Commissioners

Paul Rand Dixon
Michael Pertschuk
Robert Pitofsky
Patricia P. Bailey

Carol M. Thomas   *Secretary*
James Sneed   *Acting General Counsel*
Howard E. Shapiro   *Deputy General Counsel*
Barry R. Rubin   *Assistant General Counsel, Legal Counsel*
William D. Cross   *Assistant General Counsel, Litigation & Environmental Policy*

Kathleen D. Sheekey   *Director, Office of Congressional Relations*
Deborah Leff   *Director, Office of Public Information*
Christian S. White   *Executive Director*
Barry J. Kefauver   *Deputy Executive Director*
Robert B. Reich   *Director, Office of Policy Planning*
Ernest G. Barnes   *Chief Administrative Law Judge*
E. Perry Johnson   *Director, Bureau of Competition*
Benjamin Sharp   *Deputy Director, Bureau of Competition*
Alan Palmer   *Deputy Director, Bureau of Competition*
Albert H. Kramer   *Director, Bureau of Consumer Protection*
Tracy A. Westen   *Deputy Director, Bureau of Consumer Protection*
Richard C. Foster   *Deputy Director, Bureau of Consumer Protection*
Michael Lynch   *Acting Director, Bureau of Economics*
Ronald S. Bond   *Deputy Director, Bureau of Economics*
John L. Peterman   *Deputy Director, Bureau of Economics*

FEDERAL TRADE COMMISSION   529

[For the Federal Trade Commission statement of organization, see Code of Federal Regulations, Title 16, Part 0]

The basic objective of the Federal Trade Commission is the maintenance of strongly competitive enterprise as the keystone of the American economic system. Although the duties of the Commission are many and varied under law, the foundation of public policy underlying all these duties is essentially the same: to prevent the free enterprise system from being stifled, substantially lessened or fettered by monopoly or restraints on trade, or corrupted by unfair or deceptive trade practices.

In brief, the Commission is charged with keeping competition both free and fair.

This basic purpose finds its primary expression in the Federal Trade Commission Act, cited below, and the Clayton Act (38 Stat. 730; 15 U.S.C. 12), both passed in 914 and both successively amended in the years that have followed. The Federal Trade Commission Act lays down a general prohibition against the use in commerce of "unfair methods of competition" and "unfair or deceptive acts or pactices." The Clayton Act outlaws specific practices recognized as instruments of monopoly. As an administrative agency, acting quasi-judicially and quasi-legislatively, the Commission was established to deal with trade practices on a continuing and corrective basis. It has no authority to punish; its function is to "prevent," through cease-and-desist orders and other means, those practices condemned by the law of Federal trade regulation; however, court ordered civil penalties up to $10,000 may be obtained for each violation of a Commission order.

Regional Offices—Federal Trade Commission

Region	Regional Director	Address
ATLANTA Alabama, Florida, Georgia, Mississippi, North Carolina, South Carolina, Tennessee, Virginia.	Harold E. Kirtz	1718 Peachtree St. NW., Atlanta, Ga. 30309
BOSTON Connecticut, Maine, Massachusetts, New Hampshire, Rhode Island, Vermont.	Lois G. Pines	150 Causeway St., Boston, Mass. 02114.
CHICAGO Illinois, Indiana, Iowa, Kentucky, Minnesota, Missouri, Wisconsin.	Paul W. Turley	55 E. Monroe St., Chicago, Ill. 60603.
CLEVELAND Michigan, Western New York, Ohio, Pennsylvania, West Virginia, Delaware, Maryland.	Paul E. Eyre	118 St. Clair Ave., Cleveland, Ohio 44144.
DALLAS Arkansas, Louisiana, New Mexico, Oklahoma, Texas.	Juereta P. Smith	2001 Bryan St., Dallas, Tex. 75201.
DENVER Colorado, Kansas, Montana, Nebraska, North Dakota, South Dakota, Utah, Wyoming.	Paul C. Daw	1405 Curtis St., Denver, Colo. 80202.
LOS ANGELES Arizona, Southern California.	Robert J. Enders	11000 Wilshire Blvd., Los Angeles, Calif. 90024.
NEW YORK New Jersey, eastern New York.	LeRoy C. Richie	26 Federal Plaza, New York, N.Y. 10007.
SAN FRANCISCO Northern California, Hawaii, Nevada.	Judith Ford	450 Golden Gate Ave., San Francisco, Calif. 94102.
SEATTLE Alaska, Idaho, Oregon, Washington.	Randall Brook, Acting	915 2d Ave., Seattle, Wash. 98174.

The Federal Trade Commission was organized as an independent administrative agency in 1914, pursuant to the Federal Trade Commission Act of

---

Figure 2-6   A Typical Page from the U.S. Government Manual

SOURCE: Administrative Conference of the United States, *U.S. Government Manual* (Washington, D.C.: U.S. Government Printing Office, 1981–82), pp. 528, 529.

cumbersome because they generally print two of three *U.S. Reports* pages per page of L. Ed. 2d or S. Ct. Finally, the private reporters provide more introductory material and headnotes as well as the cross referencing capability.

Official reporters are also available for many other courts, but the private reporters are more widely used. As a matter of form, however, where there is an official reporter, that publication is cited alone, or is cited first if it is cited with a private reporter.[39]

Most of the major opinions of the U.S. Circuit Courts of Appeals are reported in West's *Federal Reporter,* now in its second series and cited F. 2d. The courts do not consider all decisions significant enough to warrant adding more volumes of reports to already large and expensive libraries. When reading the decisions of circuit courts (or any court, for that matter), take care to record which court rendered the ruling. For example, a district court ruling for the Southern District of New York might read 457 F. Supp. 1284 (SDNY 1978). A circuit court decision in the same geographic area would read 589 F. 2d 1116 (2d Cir. 1979).

There are two major reasons for keeping track of which court one is dealing with. For example, the binding authority of the Federal District Court for the Northern District of Georgia is limited to that geographic area. The same is true of the courts of appeals. Second, as the law develops, disagreements are bound to occur among some of the courts. The researcher will soon spot trends by noting which courts are going in specific doctrinal directions. Plotting the trends and comparing conflicting opinions helps to focus controversies.

Federal district court opinions are reported in the *Federal Supplement,* cited as F. Supp. District court opinions are usually rendered by only one judge, but in a few instances the researcher will encounter decisions prepared by a three-judge district court.

West's National Reporter System also publishes opinions by state supreme courts and, on occasion, state appeals courts. For purposes of the system, the country is divided into seven reporting regions. See Figure 2-7. These regions were established in the late nineteenth century based on economic rather than political similarity. Hence, some of the states seem intuitively out of line with the name of the volume that reports their opinions. However, the states reported are listed on the title page of each volume.

Annotated Reports

The Lawyers Cooperative *American Law Reports* series (the A.L.R. and the A.L.R. Fed.) is an annotated reports system. It is in many ways like the West digest system, but to avoid confusion the two sets are discussed separately here.

The A.L.R. is, of course, keyed to the *Lawyers Edition* of the Supreme Court cases. It does not attempt to publish verbatim many opinions. Instead, the editors select particularly important opinions of specific points of law and prepare annotations on the subject. The annotations are exhaustively documented essays on the point of law under consideration along with references to practical problems encountered in dealing with that body of law. The annotations, the *Lawyers Edition,* and other Lawyers Coop tools are linked by two devices. First, the L. Ed. 2d reports and other materials that provide references to other volumes have cross references

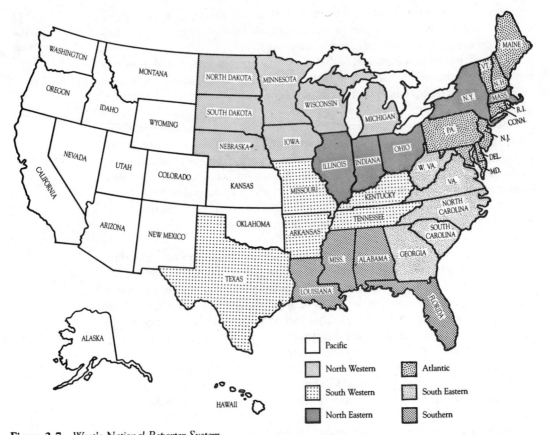

Figure 2-7 *West's National Reporter System*

SOURCE: *The West Law Finder* (St. Paul: West, 1978), p. 2. Used by permission of West Publishing Company.

noted. Second, the materials are arranged by subject in what is known as the A.L.R. Quick Index. The A.L.R. Fed. and its Quick Index are, not surprisingly, limited to federal questions. Like all such tools, the A.L.R. indexes take a bit of familiarization. Again, remember the pocket part!

Other Case Reporters

Occasionally one encounters a reference to the F.R.D., which refers to a West series called the *Federal Rules Decisions*. The F.R.D. series contains opinions interpreting federal rules of civil and criminal procedure issued by any of the federal courts. An administrator might, for example, encounter a case concerning consumer or environmental class action suits in this reporter.

Many administrative agencies also publish opinions to support their findings in adjudicatory proceedings. Like court cases, the agencies often publish an official reporter. The *National Labor Relations Board Decisions* and the *Interstate Commerce Commission Reports* are examples. The Commerce Clearing House (CCH) and the Bureau of National Affairs (BNA) are two of the major private publishers that print administrative reporters.

Supplementing legal research involves at least two distinct kinds of work. First, one must ensure that materials are current. Second, the researcher must round out the research or place it in proper context. Failure to follow through in legal research by supplementing materials, as in most other things, can nullify the hard work expended in finding and reading the law.

Updating Knowledge

This chapter began by defining legal research in terms of access to the most authoritative and most recent statement of law by the highest possible decision-maker. Given the great number of courts that deliver opinions every day, this seems an almost impossible task. Fortunately, there are a number of tools specifically designed to help the researcher ensure that currency is maintained.

Shepard's Citations is the primary tool to use in updating case materials. The citator is organized by the citation of the case under consideration. It indicates where the researcher can go to find other cases in any major court in the country that has rendered a decision that mentions the researcher's case. Shepard's also notes whether the more recent decisions explained the earlier opinion, overruled it, or followed the earlier holding as a statement of controlling law. Shepard's seems a bit intimidating on first glance, but it is easy to use.[40] Consider the following example.

San Antonio Independent School District v. Rodriguez, 441 U.S. 1 (1973), mentioned earlier in this chapter, was a major case on the responsibilities of states and local school districts versus individual rights in the area of public school financing. Suppose an administrator desired to know whether the holding in *San Antonio* was still current and what more recent case materials might be available that show how that case has been applied and interpreted.

Turn first to the *Shepard's U.S. Citations,* which is the citator for decisions of the United States Supreme Court. (All the citators indicate on the binding the type of material cited.) Turn to the part of the book with the *United States Reports* designation at the top of the page. The volume numbers are noted in the upper right-hand corner of the page. Where volume 411 is indicated, look down the page until you find a boldface number 1 with a line under it. This volume, page, and title format is used in all the case citators.

The initial entry is the history of the case, followed by a long list of citations to the *U.S. Reports,* the *Federal Reporter,* the *Federal Supplement,* and other case reporters in the states. These are pages in various cases in which the *San Antonio* decision has been mentioned. The context in which the case was mentioned is indicated by the small letters to the left of the case citations. The abbreviations are explained fully at the beginning of each volume. An "o," for example, indicates that the case being researched was overruled. An "f," on the other hand, shows that the ruling was cited as the controlling law in a more recent case. In addition to indicating whether a case is still "good" law, the citator can be used as a law finder to locate more recent cases that cited the basic case as controlling (f), explained it (e), or harmonized that case with what appeared to be conflicting rulings (h).

With practice, one can learn to use the Shepard's volumes quickly and for even more intricate research techniques than those outlined above Of course, the use of a citator requires specific knowledge about a particular case or statute. There are volumes that aid the researcher in remaining current in a general sense in a given area of law.

Loose-Leaf Services

Commercial publishers have made quite a business out of carving out specific areas of the law and public policy that are of interest to professionals who want rapid updating on that law in the shortest possible time. These tools are referred to as loose-leaf services; the name is derived from the loose-leaf format in which the reporters are distributed.

General updating materials on the U.S. Supreme Court and other federal courts may be found in Commerce Clearing House and Bureau of National Affairs volumes. The CCH distributes the *CCH Supreme Court,* which contains docket information on pending cases and on cases recently appealed to the Court as well as hearing schedules and actual reports of the decisions of the Court filed only days after the decision has been delivered. BNA's *United States Law Week: Supreme Court* is published weekly. *Law Week* contains material similar to that of the CCH but in a slightly different format. *Law Week* also attempts to include review essays through the year on the kinds of cases pending before the Court and summary reports on portions of the oral argument before the Court in particularly important or interesting cases.

BNA also publishes a more general loose-leaf service, *United States Law Week General. Law Week General* surveys all federal courts and many major administrative agency cases pending before the courts. The journalistic format is usually a two- or three-paragraph description of a case and its implications with citations to the actual opinion.

A number of more specialized loose-leafs exist for particular subject areas, e.g., the *Media Law Reporter,* the *Criminal Law Reporter,* and the *Environmental Law Reporter.* An administrator in broadcasting, for example, can keep abreast of recent developments and be alerted to major developments in the offing for which more research ought to be done.

Finally there are specialized law journals or annual surveys in standard law reviews for those who have little time to keep up with the major developments across the nation over the year. In the general area of administrative law, for example, the Section on Administrative Law of the American Bar Association publishes the *Administrative Law Review.* For a general review of the U.S. Supreme Court's most recent term, the *Harvard Law Review* November survey issue is first-rate. The *Duke Law Journal* produces an annual administrative law survey. The key to using loose-leafs and summary reviews or specialized journals is to select a few of them and develop a routine for reviewing those chosen.

Rounding Out Research

For law and public administration practitioners or scholars, the great strength of legal research is paradoxically also its great weakness. Legal research tools and techniques are designed to methodically narrow the study to a very small part of a massive body of law. Tunnel vision is always dangerous, and particularly so in public law and public administration problems.

Administrative law problems arise from and are affected by a wide range of factors. There are statutory problems, which are continually dealt with in one way or another by Congress or the state legislature. Financial matters affect an agency's ability to investigate, to litigate, and to counsel. Appropriations hearings in the legislature often deal with more substantive policy questions than the protection of the public fisc. Interest groups lobby in all branches of government, including the judiciary. New scientific, economic, and administrative developments are always in progress. For all these reasons, it is wise for anyone who is doing research in law and administration to step back after completing the problem-oriented research in case law and take notice of the larger environment in which the problem exists.

The easiest tools for this purpose are periodicals aimed at the informed public. The two most popular are the *Congressional Quarterly* and the *National Journal*. Both can be found in most major libraries and are very well indexed. A relatively brief look at these publications will tell the researcher whether the topic under study is currently a matter of significant debate in government. Some states, like California and Illinois, have similar publications.

The primary index for quick public affairs updating is the *Public Affairs Information Service* (PAIS). Similar in format to the *Index to Legal Periodicals* and the *Reader's Guide*, PAIS references popular news magazines, some law review articles, and many government publications. In addition, PAIS frequently notes recent statutes enacted in particular subject areas and sources of statistics in those areas.

Finally, government publications can be useful, offering valuable information that is both timely and carefully prepared. More important, the person who does not round out research with government documents may fail to accurately perceive a law and policy conflict. The *Eldridge* case study in Appendix A provides a case in point. A check of congressional documents in the months leading up to the argument before the U.S. Supreme Court would have shown that the government had no intention of arguing the case on grounds of precedent, but focused instead on financial and policy problems.

A specific example of a generally useful and widely respected set of materials is the General Accounting Office Reports. These reports are the result of analyses conducted by GAO teams at the request of congressmen or congressional committees. GAO reports provide current useful data on a wide range of subjects. One free copy of any GAO report is available to anyone who requests it.

Generally, two major indexes will lead the researcher to government documents. The *Monthly Catalog of United States Government Publications* is the official index and is referenced by title, subject, or by the institution that issued the document. Since 1970 a private index known as the *Congressional Information Service* (CIS) has been available. The CIS references only Congress-related publications, and uses an index and abstract system to save the researcher from expending time obtaining a document only to learn that it does not contain useful information. The CIS index is arranged by subject, name, committee, bill title, and public law number. To use it, find a reference number for the subject under study, for example, H171-2. Then turn to the abstract under the same number H171 and look for item H171-2. The abstract will provide size, cost, date, issuing agency, availability, and other data along with detailed information on contents.

USING LEGAL RESEARCH TOOLS

Most books on legal research contain discussions of the best research routines, but the following simplified technique will do for most research in law and administration.

Use a law-finding tool.

1. If a case citation is already available, one has a starting point.
2. From a subject, go to an encyclopedia for introduction.
3. Using any available case names and all subject headings or key words that come to mind, go to the Index to Legal Periodicals in search of law review articles.
4. Check the A.L.R. quick index to see if an annotation has been written on the subject under consideration.
5. Use the law review articles as law finders, noting major cases cited, and references to other articles, treatises, statutes, or regulations. Keep a running list of citations.

Read the law.

1. Examine the statutes involved using an annotated code to get both the letter of the law and court interpretations.
2. Check applicable regulations in the C.F.R. using the C.F.R. index. Remember to check the "C.F.R. Parts Affected" pamphlet for material recently published in the *Federal Register.*
3. Read the cases, noting which court ruled, precedents cited, law reviews noted and statutes interpreted.
4. If using West publications, be alert for the key numbers for use in cross-referencing to digests or other books in their series.

Supplement the authorities.

1. Check pocket parts in all reference volumes used.
2. Refer to Shepard's citations for later cases.
3. Use key numbers to find related cases in digests.

Round out the research.

1. Check *National Journal* or *Congressional Quarterly* indexes for recent debate on the topic.
2. Refer to PAIS for recent articles, government publications, and statistics.
3. Check CIS for recent government documents or studies, especially major hearings with expert testimony, Congressional Research Service studies, and other reprinted articles or analyses.

SUMMARY

The law in books, or black letter law, is important and available to most students and practitioners of public law and public administration. Hands-on experience is necessary to learn this skill well, but time, practice, and persistence will demonstrate that legal research is not particularly difficult. The goal is to find current, high-level authority on the specific points of law under study. The process begins with the use of law finders to locate statutes, regulations, and cases. One then reads the law itself and supplements the law through any of a number of devices. Finally, the researcher places the research in a larger context through consulting public documents and public affairs journals, which note whether and to what extent the law and policy problem under study is currently on the public agenda.

NOTES

[1]On state court systems generally, see Fannie J. Klein, *Federal and State Court Systems—A Guide* (Cambridge, Mass.: Ballinger, 1977), chaps. 2–5.

[2]The types of cases and methods for getting them to the Supreme Court are nicely set forth in Henry Abraham, *The Judicial Process, 3d ed.* (New York: Oxford University Press, 1975), Chart B, pp. 180–81.

[3]For an in-depth discussion of the nature of the federal judicial system, see Howard Ball, *Courts and Politics: The Federal Judicial System* (Englewood Cliffs, N.J.: Prentice-Hall, 1979).

[4]*Annual Report of the Director—1979* (Washington, D.C.: Administrative Office of U.S. Courts, 1979), pp. 20–22.

[5]The numbers of courts, their staffing, jurisdiction, and caseloads are presented in *Management Statistics of U.S. Courts* (Washington, D.C.: Administrative Office of U.S. Courts, 1979), published annually.

[6]28 U.S.C. §1257.

[7]28 U.S.C. §1254 or §1252.

[8]These include the Court of Claims, 28 U.S. C.2 §1252; Court of Customs and Patent Appeals, 28 U.S.C. §1251; Customs Court, §1251; or in some circumstances three-judge federal district courts, 28 U.S.C. §§1253, 1284.

[9]The Court may still avoid most of these cases if it wishes by refusing to note probable jurisdiction.

[10]U.S. Circuit Courts of Appeals, 28 U.S.C. §1254, or Court of Claims, 28 U.S.C. §1255.

[11]State supreme courts, 28 U.S.C. §1257, courts of appeals, 28 U.S.C. §1254, and Court of Claims, 28 U.S.C. §1255.

[12]See generally *United States v. Pink*, 315 U.S. 203 (1942); *United States v. Belmont*, 301 U.S. 324 (1937); *United States v. Curtiss-Wright*, 299 U.S. 309 (1936); *B. Altman & Co. v. United States*, 224 U.S. 583 (1912).

[13]Laurence Tribe, *American Constitutional Law* (Mineola, N.Y.: Foundation Press, 1978), pp. 167–72.

[14]Louis Fisher, *The Constitution Between Friends: Congress, the President and the Law* (New York: St. Martin's Press, 1978), pp. 128–32.

[15]See, e.g., "Note: Gubernatorial Executive Orders as Devices for Administrative Direction and Control," 50 *Iowa L. Rev.* 78 (1964).

[16]Morris Cohen, *How to Find the Law*, 7th ed. (St. Paul: West, 1976).

[17]Examples are *The West Law Finder* (St. Paul: West, 1978) and *The Living Law: A Guide to Modern Legal Research* (Rochester, N.Y.: Lawyers Cooperative, 1979).

[18]*Management Statistics for United States Courts—1978* (Washington, D.C.: Administrative Office of U.S. Courts, 1978), p. 13. These are total case terminations from whatever form of disposition comes to the case.

[19]Id., p. 129.

[20]*Black's Law Dictionary*, 5th ed. (St. Paul: West, 1979).

[21]William S. Anderson, ed., *Ballentine's Law Dictionary*, 3d ed. (Rochester, N.Y.: Lawyers Cooperative, 1969).

[22]*Words and Phrases* (St. Paul: West, 1964).

[23]David L. Sills, ed., *International Encyclopedia of the Social Sciences* (New York: Macmillan, 1968).

[24]*Corpus Juris Secundum* (St. Paul: West, 1952).

[25]*American Jurisprudence*, 2d series (Rochester, N.Y.: Lawyers Cooperative, 1970).

[26]*Index to Legal Periodicals* (Bronx, N.Y.: Wilson, 1980).

[27]On the digests generally, see *The West Law Finder*, supra note 17, chap. 2

[28]Id., at p. 16.

[29]See Cohen, supra note 16, chap. 2. The ten-year compilations are updated annually in the *General Digest*.

[30]For example, a first-time investigator in Social Security Disability programs might find the following articles useful: Fred Davis and James Reynolds, "Profile of a Social Security Disability Case," 42 *Missouri L. Rev.* 541 (1977); Gerald Hayes, "Social Security Disability and the Administrative Law Judge," 1975 *Air Force L. Rev.* 73 (1975); and James Smith, "Social Security Appeals in Disability Cases," 28 *Admin. L. Rev.* 13 (1976).

[31]For a complete list of legal citation forms and their uses, see *A Uniform System of Citations*, 13th ed. (Cambridge, Mass.: Harvard Law Review Association, 1981).

[32]On the specifics of the legislative process, see Charles J. Zinn, *How Our Laws Are Made* (Washington, D.C.: Government Printing Office, 1971).

[33]References to parts of a code are made by title and section number. Note, for example, that the Civil Rights Act provision presented is Title 42 of the U.S. Code at Section (§) 1983.

[34]See generally Gwedolyn B. Folsum, *Legislative History: Research for the Interpretation of Laws* (Charlottesville: University of Virginia Press, 1972), and Robert Goehlert, *Congress and Law-Making: Researching the Legislative Process* (Santa Barbara, Calif.: CLIO Books, 1979).

[35]Law Librarians' Society of Washington, D.C., *Union List of Legislative Histories*, 3d ed. (Vienna, Va.: Coiner, 1967).

[36]Folsum, supra note 34, at p. 36.

[37]*Panama Refining Co. v. Ryan*, 293 U.S. 388 (1935).

[38]49 Stat. 500 (1935).

[39]For example, the following opinion was published in both the official reporter of New York and the commercial West edition. In either case, it should be cited as *Fresh Meadows Medical Associates v. Liberty Mutual Insurance Co.*, 49 N.Y. 2d 98, 400 N.E. 2d 3030 (1979).

[40]On Shepard's generally, see *How to Use Shepard's Citations* (Colorado Springs: Shepard's Citations, 1971).

The Law in Action: Judicial Policymaking

C hapters 1 and 2 defined the field of public law and public administration and demonstrated the role of the administrative justice system as a subset of the larger American legal system. The essential institutions and black letter law provisions of the government have been discussed. However, anyone who reads newspaper accounts of important legal controversies quickly learns that law is not simply a mechanical process into which one feeds elements of a legal conflict and from which one draws an automatic response. This chapter addresses those elements of jurisprudence, legal reasoning, and judicial policymaking that, together with the law in books, make up the law in action.

PROBLEMS OF JUDICIAL DECISIONMAKING: "THE CASE OF THE SPELUNCEAN EXPLORERS"

In 1949 Professor Lon Fuller developed a hypothetical case that affords students of law an opportunity to deal with some of the complexities involved in deciding hard cases. The case, entitled "The Case of the Speluncean Explorers,"[1] is outlined below. Come to a decision in the matter and consider arguments on both sides of that conclusion.

As developed at trial, the facts that gave rise to the case occurred in the spring of the year 4299 in the nation of Newgarth. Five members of a cave exploring club, the Speluncean Society, set out to explore a cavern recently discovered by one of the club's members. The five were all in good physical condition and properly outfitted for their foray into the cave. In accordance with society rules, the group left an outline of their planned exploration with the society's secretary and each member left information with his family.

Not long after entering the cave, the spelunkers felt a severe earth tremor. They retraced their steps to the cave entrance, but found that it had been blocked by a massive rock slide. The five sat down near the cave entrance to assess their supplies and await rescue. They hoped for a quick rescue since, although all were in good physical condition and unharmed by the slide, they had little food and only a moderate amount of water.

When the group did not return home at the appointed time, the society officers initiated a rescue effort. It did not take long for the experts called to the scene to determine that extricating the trapped explorers would be a major undertaking. Engineers, medical personnel, troops, police officials, and others were summoned to the site. During the second week of excavation, ten rescuers were killed when a new rock slide caught them by surprise. Along with the death toll, the costs of the effort rose alarmingly.

Twenty days after the spelunkers had entered the cave, it was learned that the group had a small radio transceiver in the cave. Radio contact was established and, to the delight of the rescuers, it was learned that the men in the cave, though weak, were all alive. The initial elation soon gave way to fear and frustration. The engineers in charge of the rescue informed the men in the cave that an additional twelve days would be the minimum time required to break through based on the view from outside and the description from within the cave. After a brief consultation with a team of doctors concerning their conditions and supplies, it was determined that the men could not survive for the required twelve days. The doctors conveyed the information to the spokesman for the trapped men, a fellow named Roger Whetmore. Whetmore asked for any suggestions or instructions from the rescuers. There were none.

Communication ceased for several hours. Then Whetmore made contact with the rescue team, and asked whether it would be possible for four members to survive if they drew sustenance from the flesh of one of their own number. The doctors answered reluctantly that it would be possible. Whetmore and his colleagues inquired whether anyone on the outside would advise them how the victim should be selected. The doctors refused to respond. The men asked for a legal opinion. No legal officials would answer. They asked for moral guidance. None of the ministers on hand would reply. Radio contact was terminated.

The rescuers broke through to the men in the cave after the predicted total of thirty-two days. They found four men suffering from exposure and shock, but alive. Roger Whetmore had provided the necessary nourishment for his colleagues.

The Newgarth criminal law clearly states that "whoever shall willfully take the life of another shall be punished by death." It has no other provisions regarding homicide. After they recovered in a hospital from their ordeal, the four survivors were tried for the murder of Roger Whetmore.

At trial, it was determined that it had been Whetmore's suggestion that the men should survive at the expense of one of their number. After much discussion, his fellow prisoners agreed to the plan. When authorities on the outside refused to provide guidance as to the manner of selection, it had been Whetmore who advanced the idea of rolling dice. And it had been Whetmore who produced the dice, which he always carried as good luck pieces. But when it had come time to roll the dice and carry out the plan, Whetmore changed his mind, arguing that it was too drastic a solution. The others refused his desire to withdraw since it was he who had developed the plan and convinced the others of its necessity. They rolled the dice for him, but permitted him an opportunity to object if he thought the manner of rolling the dice was unfair. He raised no objection. He lost and the others carried out the plan.

The jury asked to be allowed to issue a finding of facts, but wished the judge to apply the law to those facts and render the final verdict. All parties agreed to this arrangement. The jury found the facts as described above and the judge concluded on those facts that the four were guilty of a violation of the statute. He added that the death sentence was, of course, the only possible sentence under the statute. As soon as the trial ended, the judge and the members of the jury jointly prepared a letter requesting executive clemency for the four condemned men.

When the decision and the sentence were reported in the press, there was a massive public outcry against what was perceived to be a gross miscarriage of justice. Speculation ran rampant concerning the possibility of a reversal of the ruling in the Supreme Court. Some reporters concentrated on information which seemed to indicate that the President would not grant clemency.

If the case came to the Supreme Court and the reader were a member of it, how should it deal with the case? Would one say that the words of the statute of murder are clear and must be applied exactly as they are written? Should the Court decide the case by a verbatim application of the law, but unofficially join the petition for executive clemency?

Or would one reverse, arguing that, under the conditions in the cave, the men were in a state of nature in which the ordinary laws of Newgarth were inapplicable? If so, would the social contract entered into willingly by all the members of the group be binding? Could they demand specific performance from Whetmore as the contract law might provide?

What of the argument that the seemingly clear and absolute law of murder was not all that clear? If self-defense is not a willful taking of life, were these men guilty given the inevitable death they faced in the cave? Would enforcement of the death penalty in this case fit the spirit of the law as well as the letter?

If the Court overturned the ruling, would it appear that the law of contract was more important than laws regarding murder? If the view that a social contract had been made in the cave was accepted, how remote from ordinary circumstances must one be to declare the accepted laws of the community inapplicable? Could a plan as carefully developed as this one was, and which had been discussed over a lengthy period of time, realistically not be understood to be a willful taking of life?

Should the court be permitted to make one official ruling and join in an unofficial communication to another branch of government? Is this a responsible position? Assuming that the judge is aware that the law will cause an obvious injustice if applied as written, should he or she ignore the harm to be done and apply the law strictly? Is it the business of the judge to make decisions on the rightness or wrongness of the law?

Is the problem here less a question of dogmatic applications of strongly held judicial philosophies on either side and more a matter of how to handle these particular defendants, since the uniqueness of the facts in this case make it unlikely that any precedent that emerges from the decision will ever be applied in the future? Should the judges give any consideration to the clear statements of public opinion on the matter?

To be sure, decision on a case like this requires an explicit understanding of the law involved and of the facts; but it also demands at least an implicit set of beliefs about the nature and purpose of law.[2] Decisions in cases that have considerable legal and political significance also require that the judge understand his or her own role in the judicial process. Jurisprudence is the study of the philosophy that provides these underpinnings for legal decisionmaking.

PURPOSES OF LAW AND APPROACHES TO LEGAL THEORY

A decision in the case of the Speluncean explorers could depend on the view one has of the purpose of the law. If the purpose is to have justice done between parties involved in litigation, the decision might hold for the defendants. On the other hand, if the purpose of law is primarily to preserve civil society by maintaining order, one may wish to treat these four men more harshly. One who reads in the Anglo-American legal tradition can readily identify a number of purposes of law that appear to coexist, although different authors have emphasized different goals at various times in history.

Purposes of Law

For many, the law exists to provide justice in the society as a whole and for the specific participants in the case at issue. The problem is to define justice as a concept and then to apply it in a particular case.

Another commonly accepted purpose is the management of change. For example, laws that govern credit cards and computer credit records help to facilitate economic change, and ensure that the change is orderly and under some measure of control. The flexibility of the legal process permits marginal change through judicial interpretation of existing law. During the debate over ratification of the United States Constitution critics argued that the new charter of government was too vague. To be useful, they asserted, the fundamental law should be specific and clearly applicable to particular situations. James Madison, generally regarded as the father of the Constitution, rejected that notion. Writing in *Federalist Paper* No. 44, Madison argued that a set of laws, especially a constitution, that attempted to completely codify every aspect of the legal system would be both under- and overinclusive.[3] It would be underinclusive because no lawmaker, however prescient, could draft laws that would cover every possible contingency that might arise in the future. Yet the body of law would also be overinclusive because it would be rigid, and would freeze the norms and problems of one period into the law that would be imposed in the future when circumstances had changed.

A third purpose of law is to maintain stability. One of the benefits of the legal system that permits us to live and work together in civil society is a certain predictability. While the law does allow for change, it is also, especially in the Anglo-American tradition, inherently conservative. *Stare decisis*, the rule that precedent should govern new cases, is strong. One learns, for example, that a driver of an automobile that strikes another vehicle from the rear will generally be held responsible for the accident. One can guide his or her actions in the future based on the knowledge that the same rule of liability will likely be applied if he or she is involved in a similar accident.

A fourth purpose of the law is to provide for orderly and peaceful resolution of disputes. If there is an accident, one need not jump from the car to have it out with the other party in the middle of the street. Instead, we generally retain an attorney to resolve the dispute in the accepted forum, a court. The society provides the courts and sets rules for their operation to provide a fair forum in which grave controversies may be resolved on the basis of reason. It is clear that this system is not perfectly fair or absolutely unbiased. Even so, we know that there is a systematic civilized means to settle disputes.

Law is also a means of facilitating private arrangements. Adoption is an example. Through legal process we make someone, to all intents and purposes, a child of a mother and father when they are not biologically related. The law allows the creation of unique legal entities to help those who wish to accomplish personal goals. For example, through incorporation, several people can join together for business purposes in a way that protects their personal property and limits their individual liability to the amount invested in the corporation. There are many similar examples of situations in which the law provides support for private endeavors.

Finally, the law is a mechanism that maintains a sense of historical continuity in the society. For example, the American way of life as it has developed in this century is reflected in our laws. One can trace changes in social and legal norms and relate them to the circumstances that brought them about. These long-term trends and historical connections in the law help the society develop for the future.

These are just some of the many purposes of law.[4] Over the centuries, various legal scholars have developed substantial theories of law based on one or more of these purposes. Such bodies of theory and the writings of those associated with each are often referred to as "schools of jurisprudence."

SCHOOLS OF JURISPRUDENCE: THEORETICAL APPROACHES TO LEGAL DECISIONMAKING

In addition to offering theories about the purpose of law, schools of jurisprudence differ as to the role of the legal process in the state, the role of the judge, and the relationship between the law and the society it serves. A judge's jurisprudence provides a general approach to legal decisionmaking. Scholars who have studied approaches to legal theory generally have classified them into a number of philosophical schools.[5] Among the most commonly acknowledged schools are natural law, analytic jurisprudence, historical, sociological, realist-behavioralist, political jurisprudence, and deterministic jurisprudence.

Natural Law Jurisprudence

One of the oldest of the approaches to the law, the natural law school of jurisprudence is represented in its various manifestations by such people as Aristotle, Cicero, Hugo Grotius, Saint Thomas Aquinas, John Locke, and a more contemporary legal scholar, Lon Fuller. Natural law jurisprudence has been of major importance to western law in general and to American law in particular.[6] At its heart, this body of theory rests heavily on the proposition that man is part of a natural order of things and he should act in harmony with that order. Particularly in its more modern manifestations, the theory suggests that while man's relationship to the world is a matter of natural order, his relationship with his fellows is in large part a matter of social contract.

Our ability to live together under such a social compact stems from the fact that man is both a rational and a social being who, under the right conditions, can govern himself. But the social contracts under which the society operates, such as the U.S. Constitution, must be in harmony with the law of nature and the natural rights of all citizens. At the time of the American Revolution, these natural rights were known as the rights of Englishmen. As developed in our Constitution, they were in general terms those rights to life, liberty, and property referred to by Locke and discussed by Jefferson in the Declaration of Independence.[7]

Judges who operate within a natural law context share one or more of the following decision principles in resolving cases. There does exist a natural law that is prior to man-made law. There is some conception from natural law of truth and justice. The true and just decision can be found by reasonable men if they have access to information and search for the right decision. There should be some relationship between the law that is and what ought to be. Judges, rather than making law, should discover the law from principles of natural law and reason.

Like most such philosophies, natural law has adherents who range from ardent apostles, such as Saint Thomas Aquinas,[8] who developed a complete typology of law based on the relationship between man and his creator and man and his fellows, to Lon Fuller,[9] who merely suggested that there are some moral principles that come before man-made laws and must be considered in any legal system. In part, Fuller was reacting to the analytical school of jurisprudence.

Analytical Jurisprudence

The scholars of analytical jurisprudence include such writers as Thomas Hobbes, John Austin, and Hans Kelsen, who reject the idea that anything apart from man-made law is of concern to the jurisprudential scholar.[10] Law is positive or man-made. Natural order is not expected. The analytical approach has a more pessimistic view of the nature of man. Hobbes assumed that life outside a powerful government, in a state of nature, would be the "war of all against all," in which life would be "solitary, poor, nasty, brutish and short."

Under the analytical approach, people are not presumed to be especially rational. They are not basically very good in any moral sense, but obey laws because the laws are backed by sanctions. For whatever reason, the analytical scholars insist that it is the *logic* of man-made laws that is important.

From these premises John Austin launched his attempt to develop a fully articulated logical system of law. He began with the idea that law is the command of the sovereign backed by a sanction. The task is to develop from that premise a system that is logically coherent and consistent. Hans Kelsen began from what he called a "grund norm", a basic principle, to do the same.

Under this approach to jurisprudence the task of the lawyer and the judge is not to find the law in a natural law sense, but to maintain the logical integrity of the legal fabric. This process of rationalizing rules is a continuous one. The concern is not for historical continuity, but rather for consistency among the pronouncements of the lawgiver.

Historical Jurisprudence

Historical jurisprudential scholars reject the idea that the law can be understood either as an analytical system or as an enduring reflection of the natural order. They insist that law is the product of the custom and history of a people. The two leading scholars of this persuasion are Sir Henry Maine and Friedrich Karl von Savigny.[11] Maine demonstrated that existing English law was in fact primarily a product of the historical development of legal principles from the Roman period to the British nation state era. Savigny, studying German law, made the point that the law consists of the "volksgeist," the spirit of the people, and the "zeitgeist," spirit of the times. The changing patterns of societies are the underpinnings of the law as it exists in any single time and place. Hence, it should not be surprising that nineteenth-century German law and twentieth-century American law differ in major ways. Although Maine and Savigny developed their theories from quite different directions, both concluded that history is the primary factor in the development of law. It is the task of the judge to apply the law in light of this historical dynamic.

Sociological Jurisprudence The sociological approach to jurisprudence is concerned with the spirit of the people, but in a different sense. Probably the most influential of the modern writers in this area was Roscoe Pound.[12] Pound summarized the approach as follows:

Comparing sociological jurists with jurists of other schools, we may say:
1. They look more to the working of the law than to its abstract content.
2. They regard law as a social institution which may be improved by intelligent human effort, and hold it their duty to discover the best means of furthering and directing such effort.
3. They lay stress upon the social purposes which law subserves rather than upon sanction.
4. They urge that legal precepts are to be regarded more as guides to results which are socially just and less as inflexible molds.
5. Their philosophical views are diverse.[13]

In other words, the law is, and ought to be, concerned with the maximization of social wants and needs and the minimization of social tensions and costs.

That courts are engaged in balancing important interests is basic to this approach. It is eclectic in origin and method, but clearly normative in its actual operation.[14]

Realist-Behavioralist Tradition of Law

The legal realists also reject the mechanical notion of clear response from clearly analyzed principles of law. Three major groups writing at different periods during the last century have developed a body of writings that are best understood as the realist-behaviorialist tradition.

The first group wrote at about the turn of the century. Justice Oliver Wendell Holmes is the leading figure.[15] Holmes rejected the idea that the law was some "brooding omnipresence in the sky" that can be discovered through pure reason. The life of the law, he said, is experience. Holmes asserted that scholars of analytical jurisprudence were guilty of the "fallacy of logical form," those of the historical approach faced the "pitfall of antiquarianism," and the natural law philosophers were operating "in that naive state of mind that accepts what has been familiar and accepted by them and their neighbors as something that must be accepted by all men everywhere."[16] However, unlike the scholars of sociological jurisprudence, Holmes was less concerned with the relationship between the moral or social "ought" and the legal "is." "The prophecies of what the courts will do in fact, and nothing more pretentious, are what I mean by the law."[17]

Holmes, along with such other writers as John Chipman Gray,[18] acknowledged that judges make law. For various reasons, the judges, at least in a "nation [with a] common law heritage like America's," cannot avoid issuing decisions that are the law. The important thing, according to these writers, is to understand how judges make law so that we may understand the law better and improve it in the future.

A second group of legal realists came along during the 1930s and includes such writers as Jerome Frank and Karl Llewellyn.[19] They add at least two dimensions to their predecessors' work. First, they suggest that the process of legal decisionmaking is important for understanding what the law is and why judges are important. A fact skeptic, Jerome Frank argued that a legal decision is more than a product of a legal rule applied to a specific set of facts. The processes through which we determine facts, most notably the "fight theory of law" and the jury system as presently used, add several variables that affect the final determination of the facts in a case. Frank acknowledged others who, like Llewellyn, suggested that the interpretation of rules was far more complicated than a simple clean analytical process. Second, they argued that judges make decisions on a wide range of bases, only some of which are conscious, rational, and analytic. Other elements of decisionmaking are more complex and less obvious.

Glendon Schubert and other behaviorialists took the importance of the judge and the significance of nonrational aspects of decisionmaking and legal process as the starting point for their work. They went further, to suggest that the study of law, at least from a political science perspective, should emphasize process rather than product. "The orientation is Bentleyan, behavioristic, actional and nonmotivational."[20] What matters is the law in action, and that should be studied scientifically to understand the nonrational aspects of legal decisions.

In a very general sense the basic assumptions of the realist-behavioralist scholars are as follows. Law consists of a set of decisions made by persons in power. These decisions are not necessarily rational. Judges have preferences and values, and their decisions, for good or ill, are affected by the inherited and acquired traits that they bring to the bench. The behavior of judges is also affected, especially in appellate courts, by the fact that such courts are collegial bodies that operate with all the strengths and weaknesses imposed by small group dynamics.

Political Jurisprudence

Another group of scholars is closely related to the judicial realists in the Jerome Frank tradition. These people may be referred to as students of political jurisprudence. Martin Shapiro, Walter Murphy, and J. Woodford Howard are contemporary authors in this tradition.[21] In many respects, they are like the behavioralists, but they tend to emphasize the study of political relationships that affect the law. Judges are important as individual actors, as are legal institutions and interest groups that affect the court, internally and from the outside. These authors' works evidence a concern for policy-oriented judges.[22] They assume that judges are policymakers and they ask questions about how the judges actually make the policy and the implications of that policy for other parts of government.

Deterministic Jurisprudence

Over the years, a number of writers have suggested that law is deterministic. Some, like Michael Parenti,[23] assert that since all law is designed to preserve the status quo, judicial decisions are not especially important. The Marxist view is the clearest example. In that perspective the law exists to keep those in power in place and those out of power subservient. This view has had relatively few adherents in American legal literature.

Justice Cardozo's Eclecticism

Several authors have been cited whose work can be classifid loosely into various schools of jurisprudential thought. But many of us approach legal problems from a more eclectic perspective. Justice Cardozo explained this process well in a lecture that was later published as *The Nature of the Judicial Process.*[24] Asked to give an address on the subject of how he decided cases, Cardozo found it to be a very difficult task. Up to a point, it was easy enough to comment on statutory interpretation and common law development but he had to acknowledge that the judge must also play a significant role in the development of the law.

> Where does the judge find the law which he embodies in his judgment? There are times when the source is obvious . . . [but] codes and statutes do not render the judge superfluous, nor his work perfunctory and mechanical. There are gaps to be filled.[25]

He recognized "judge-made laws as one of the existing realities of life."[26] The problem is to understand the direction that a judge takes in deciding a case that will doubtless make new law. Cardozo gave the following summary:

> The directive force of a principle may be exerted along the line of logical progression, this I will call the rule of analogy or the method of philosophy; along the line of historical development, this I will call the method of evolution; along the line of customs of the community, this I will call the method of tradition; along the line of Justice, Morals and Social Welfare, the mores of the day, and this I will call the method of sociology.[27]

Cardozo concluded that he and other judges use most of these methods depending on the kind of case and the nature of the facts.

Whether one has developed an eclectic view of law, as did Justice Cardozo, or one that is more exclusive, such as one of those advanced in one of the schools of thought discussed above, it is important to understand the philosophical base from which one approaches a legal controversy. Assumptions about the purposes of law and approaches to legal decisions set limits on decisionmaking. Failure to deal with the theoretical underpinnings of legal disputes can, as Justice Holmes suggested, be deadly to one who must deal with the law.

> Theory is the most important part of the dogma of the law, as the architect is the most important man who takes part in the building of the house. . . . It is not to be feared as impractical, for, to the competent, it simply means going to the bottom of the subject. For the incompetent, it sometimes is true, as has been said, that an interest in general ideas means an absence of particular knowledge.[28]

With this survey of legal thought as a basis, let us turn to a consideration of the specific skills used in making legal decisions. The collection of analytical techniques employed to resolve legal controversies is known as "legal reasoning."

LEGAL REASONING

Recognizing the need to protect the integrity of the judicial process as much as possible from the possible arbitrariness of judges and others, members of the legal community have developed a body of procedures and rules to govern legal decision-making. These constraints on the decisionmaking process seek to regularize the process of legal problem solving to permit orderly development of the law and at the same time maintain stability in the legal system. Most of these decision rules and rules of self-restraint are imposed by courts on themselves and are policed by the judges. The legal community has a number of methods for reminding the judges of their limitations and criticizing decisionmakers who breach those professional norms. One of the most effective of these is criticism and praise in law reviews. What are some of the professional guidelines for judges?

Institutional Influences on Decisionmaking

One of the more significant characteristics of the courts as decisionmakers is that they are not self starters. They must wait for cases to be properly brought before them for resolution. And, when a case is brought to a court, it must be dealt with as it stands, not as the judge would like it to be presented. For example, it was clear to the legal community that the U.S. Supreme Court would be called on in the mid-1970s to decide whether affirmative action programs for admission to graduate and professional schools violated either the equal protection clause of the Constitution or the Civil Rights Act of 1964. The case that finally reached the Court, *Regents v. Bakke,*[29] was a complicated one involving a challenge by a California man to the affirmative action program of the University of California Medical School at Davis. The facts of this particular suit were even more complex than the usually complicated fact patterns of affirmative action cases. In part because of the difficult issues in the case, but also partly because of the facts that caused this particular man to sue, the Supreme Court was badly split in its decision.[30] The Court rendered six opinions in the case with no more than five judges joining in any one part of Court's opinion, and then only with respect to those two parts of the opinion prepared by Justice Powell.

Another example of the problems of reactive decisionmaking is the body of case law in which courts have ordered school desegregation or intervened in the operation of prisons and mental health facilities.[31] Many judges attempted to dodge decisions in these cases, but found themselves faced with cases properly before their courts that required decisions. They faced the dilemma of telling a deserving litigant that he or she, though advancing a just claim, was not entitled to a legal remedy, or else producing a remedy that was certain to bring down an avalanche of political criticism and social outrage.

Another factor that influences judicial decisonmaking is "equity," which has a rich heritage extending back at least as far as Aristotle. There are difficulties involved in writing law that make it highly likely that some laws will fall with undue and unintended harshness on citizens. The Speluncean Explorers situation is an example. Most people react with horror at the idea of sacrificing a life only to execute the men who were saved from the cave. On the other hand, it seems undesirable to appear to give official approval to the actions taken by the men in the cave. One option for the judge is to argue that equity dictates that, while the men must receive some punishment since society cannot condone the taking of life, the statute was never intended to cover a situation like the one at bar and the full weight of its sanction should not fall on these defendants.

Equity is, in a sense, the deliberately unequal treatment of some people before the law for some very limited purposes where equal application would be unjust. As a formal institutionalized practice, equity reaches back to the time when it was believed that the sovereign was possessed of a sense of perfect justice. When the king no longer dispensed justice but delegated that task to judges there were bound to be difficulties. Some cases were brought on appeal to the king acting in equity to ameliorate the harsh judgments of the courts. Eventually, even this task overwhelmed the Crown and the task of decisionmaking concerning equity was delegated to the Lord High Chancellor, who came to be known as "my Lord Keeper" for his role as the keeper of the king's conscience. Since then, equity law has become much more formal and limited, but the idea of equity remains a major factor in judicial decisions.

Another longstanding concept of major importance is the "legal fiction." It permits one to make assumptions about the world that are not real in an empirical sense for legal purposes. The practice of permitting a corporation to sue or be sued in its own name is one such fiction. The personality of a ship is another example. Douglas cited this practice in a discussion about who should represent some environmental interests.

> Our case law has personified vessels: "A ship is born when she is launched, and lives so long as her identity is preserved. Prior to her launching she is a mere congeries of wood and iron. . . . In the baptism of launching she receives her name, and from the moment her keel touches water she is transformed. She acquires a personality of her own."[32]

When such fictions are involved in litigation, they may cause the decision-maker difficulties in matching the fictional concepts to real outcomes in the law. For example, a bank recently brought a case to the Supreme Court in which it claimed that the First Amendment of the Constitution, which protects freedom of speech, barred the state of Massachusetts from restricting its expenditure of corporate funds to defeat a tax measure then pending on the ballot.[33] If a corporation can sue and be sued, can it claim protection under the First Amendment?

In general, Anglo-American legal decisionmaking is guided by the doctrine of *stare decisis,* or the rule of precedent. More will be said about this approach to legal decisionmaking. For the present, it is important to understand that the idea that previous rulings should govern new cases makes the law inherently conservative. A judge attempts to decide whether actions taken at some point in the past by a person or persons now involved in a legal dispute violated the law. The decision is predicated on the existing rules of law at or before the time the actions were taken.

As each new decision of a court of record is rendered in the form of a judicial opinion, new law is, in a very real sense, made by the judge. Consider again the cave explorers. A judge could decide the case any number of ways. Two possible approaches are:

(1) The agreement to take one life to save the lives of the rest when all were under clear threat of death, if entered into voluntarily by all parties, is lawful, and enforcement of that agreement is not a willful taking of life within the meaning of the statute.

(2) Even if the taking of one life will save the lives of a substantial number of others who face imminent death, a homicide is a willful taking of life under the law.

Whichever decision is adopted, there is an official interpretation that will be presumed to be the law. In the first approach, the judge is interpreting the actions in the cave as a form of self-defense that has not traditionally been considered a "willful" action as required by the murder statutes. In the second, the interpretation may mean that the law makes no allowance for life-threatening situations except for traditional notions of self-defense. Hence, when a judge renders an opinion, no matter how much he or she may attempt to circumscribe the ruling of law, it will be treated as the new interpretation of law to guide the actions of those who may in the future face a similar or even a related legal situation.

Since all such opinions are new law, courts generally seek to resolve legal problems on the narrowest principle available. This self-imposed rule, sometimes honored as much in the breach as in the observance, is important to the maintenance of that critical balance between change and stability in the law.

Rules of Self-restraint in Federal Courts

Over the years the United States Supreme Court has developed a set of rules governing legal decisionmaking in federal courts. These rules, sometimes referred to in general terms as the *Ashwander* rules (from a case that attempted to synthesize and describe rules of self-restraint),[34] describe the kinds of controversies that the courts will resolve and caveats to be observed by judges in dealing with them. We shall come to these rules again in our discussion of judicial review of administrative actions in Chapter 7, but it is necessary to touch on them briefly here since they so heavily condition the law in action.

Though there are a number of specific rules of self-restraint, most fall into two categories. The first concerns the Article III authorization for federal courts to decide actual "cases and controversies" that arise under the Constitution or federal law. That is, does the court have jurisdiction to hear the case? Second, is it the kind of case that the courts can hear and do something about? This category is covered by the concept of justiciability. Writing for the Supreme Court in *Baker v. Carr*, Justice Brennan described the concept as follows:

> The distinction between the two grounds is significant. In the instance of nonjusticiability, consideration of the cause is not wholly and immediately foreclosed; rather, the Court's inquiry necessarily proceeds to the point of deciding whether the duty asserted can be judicially identified and its breach judicially determined, and whether protection for the right asserted can be judicially molded. In the instance of a lack of jurisdiction the cause either does not "arise under" the Federal Constitution, laws or treaties (or fall within one of the other enumerated categories of Art. III, §2), or is not a "case or controversy" within the meaning of that section; or the cause is not one described by any jurisdictional statute.[35]

Whether a particular case presents legal questions that are within the jurisdiction of the court and justiciable must be decided before the court reaches any decision on the substance of the claims made by those involved in the case.

Among the rules by which the courts make such determinations is the rule that the person who brings a lawsuit must have legal standing to do so. He or she must have been injured or stand in imminent danger of being injured by the party being sued.[36] The idea is that the people who bring suits should be the right parties to get the case before the court. Under an adversary system such as ours, the appropriate person is one who stands to win or lose something significant in the resolution of the case. Our "fight theory" of law operates on the premise that those who stand to be seriously affected will put forward the best case for their respective positions.[37] With both sides advancing the best arguments, the judge sees the case with the legal issues carefully defined and the various alternatives properly arrayed. The judge is then able to focus the decision process on the narrow aspects that must be decided to resolve the problem at hand. Standing, then, has to do with the persons or groups bringing a suit and not with the nature of the questions of law those people would like the court to resolve.

Related, in some respects, to the problem of standing is the rule that federal courts will not decide collusive suits or provide advisory opinions.[38] Agencies and private individuals would like to avoid taking actions that might later open them to a lawsuit. Similarly, legislatures would sometimes like to get some reaction on the constitutionality of a new measure before time and money are wasted on implementing a law that will fall before a court order. These concerns have given rise to what are known as "collusive suits" in which the parties at interest agree to a legal action in an attempt to get a legal opinion clarifying their respective positions under the law. In general terms, collusive suits are not considered actual "cases or controversies."[39] There is no "concrete adversity" as required under our judicial rules. Although some state courts do provide advisory opinions,[40] most state courts and all federal courts refuse to produce such decisions. If, for example, one wishes an opinion on the legality of an agency action before an actual suit is instituted in court, the standard procedure is to ask the U.S. Attorney General for an advisory opinion on the matter.

Courts generally refuse to hear cases that do not present live issues. Such cases are rejected as moot. *De Funis v. Odegaard* provides an example. Marco De Funis sought admission to the University of Washington School of Law. He was unsuccessful on his initial application to the school, but other students with lower test scores and grade-point averages were admitted through a special admissions program. De Funis sued, claiming discrimination in violation of the equal protection clause. But by the time his suit reached the United States Supreme Court, his situation had changed. He had been admitted to the school the next year and was in his final term of law school when the case came before the Court. The school indicated that De Funis would not be dismissed from the school even if he lost his appeal. The Court held that De Funis no longer had a live controversy or case against the school.[41]

Before one's case is heard in appellate courts, all remedies in lower courts and agencies must have been exhausted. This doctrine serves a number of purposes. First, it helps to clear the docket of higher courts. Second, it discourages needless opinion production in higher courts that would add to the already massive body of law. Third, it protects the integrity of the decision processes in lower courts and agencies. These tribunals are afforded the opportunity to shape litigation as needed and to correct their own errors before matters are taken up on review. Finally, where there is federal court review of state action, exhaustion permits state officials to resolve problems short of federal court action that might raise important questions of federalism.

Appellate courts generally limit their review to questions of law and accept lower court findings on questions of fact. There are some exceptions, but in most cases a reviewing court limits its inquiry to whether the law was properly interpreted and applied in lower courts or agencies. This rule of restraint is based in part on the idea that the "cold record" that comes up to a reviewing court of appeal is not sufficiently complete to determine the facts of a case. Appellate judges cannot see or hear the responses of witnesses. The transcripts contain their words but not their inflections or facial expressions, which may be quite helpful to the decisionmaker.

Judges will refuse to decide some legal issues because they are "political questions" and therefore nonjusticiable. There are at least two important aspects to the political question doctrine. First, the courts use the doctrine to restrain themselves in cases where an issue should not be resolved by the judiciary. Second, from a practical standpoint, the political question is a device by which courts can escape making decisions they would rather avoid for the present. From a doctrinal perspective, the Supreme Court has held that there are some cases in which the decisions involved were constitutionally committed to someone other than the judiciary. This is a matter of respect for the separation of powers. On the other hand, there are some cases that the courts have found intrinsically unfit for judicial resolution. Justice Brennan has written one of the most succinct descriptions of the doctrine.

> Prominent on the surface of any case held to involve a political question is found a textually demonstrable constitutional commitment of the issue to a coordinate political department; or a lack of judicially discoverable and manageable standards for resolving it; or the impossibility of deciding without an initial policy determination of a kind clearly for nonjudicial discretion; or the impossibility of a court's undertaking independent

resolution without expressing lack of respect due coordinate branches of government; or an unusual need for unquestioning adherence to a political decision already made; or the potentiality of embarrassment from multifarious pronouncements by various departments on one question.[42]

The Court has always had some practical concern for its position in the polity. Since the Court has neither the "power of the purse not the sword,"[43] it depends on support from the other branches of government and a strong sense of legitimacy of judicial actions from the general public to gain compliance with its judgments. For this and other reasons, the Court occasionally uses rules of self-restraint, especially the political question doctrine, to avoid cases it feels should be avoided. On this use of the doctrine, John P. Frank has written:

> The term "political question" is a magical formula which has the practical result of relieving a court of the necessity of thinking further about a particular problem. It is a device for transferring the responsibility for decision of questions to another branch of the government; and it may sometimes operate to leave a problem in mid-air so that no branch decides it.[44]

Examples of problems considered political questions include decisions to call out the militia, determinations regarding general foreign policy, and internal disciplinary rules in Congress. In the final analysis, a political question is anything the Court says it is.

Another rule of self-restraint relating to the concern for respect among the branches and the effective operation of the government is the presumption in favor of government action. Normally, a court will presume that a statute passed by a legislature, a regulation issued by an agency, or a decision of a government official is lawful and any challenger carries the burden to prove the contrary. That presumption does not depend on an assumption about the wisdom or fairness of government officials.

The narrowest principle approach to legal decisionmaking applies with even greater force to decisions that may involve interpretation of the Constitution. Since the Constitution is the basic charter of government, decisions about its meaning are not to be taken lightly or unnecessarily. The Court will attempt to avoid deciding a case on constitutional grounds. If it is necessary to reach a constitutional question, the Court will generally attempt to limit the breadth of the decision.[45]

The Process of Hearing a Case

At this point we have a court made up of judges each of whom approaches legal decisionmaking with some sort of jurisprudential view of his or her role, and each of whom has an understanding of institutional factors that influence the resolution of cases and an explicit commitment to a flexible but significant set of rules of self-restraint. Chapter 2 detailed the procedure through which a case winds its way up on appeal. What happens when the case comes before a major appeals court, e.g., the United States Supreme Court? There are a number of procedures involved in getting a case from the docket to a decision published as an opinion in the Court's reports.

The first problem is getting a case onto the docket. If the Court finally accepts a case for review on the merits, there has already been extensive development of the suit in the lower courts and agencies. That material is made available to the Court. Given the nature of the crowded docket that the Court faces, acceptance of the case generally means that the questions raised in the case are important. Even so, the Court has a relatively small amount of time to deal with each dispute. Consequently, the process of argument is fairly standardized.

The parties in the case file written briefs that identify the issues, develop the law on the subject as it presently exists, apply that law to the facts established in the lower court or agency, and recommend a specific disposition of the case by the Court. The briefs ask for an interpretation of the Constitution, a statute, or one of the Court's prior opinions. In addition to case law, historical evidence, legislative histories, and sociological or other forms of data, the advocates may offer commentaries published in law reviews or treatises as support for their views. These briefs are considered along with the record and whatever *amicus curiae* (friends of the court) briefs are accepted in the case.

Some, but not all, cases brought before the Supreme Court are then set down for oral argument before the Court. Unless the case is of major importance, the Court rarely gives the advocates in a case more than an hour to present arguments. Unlike the trial before a jury, an appellate argument is more of an interchange between advocates and judges than a lecture by a lawyer.[46] The advocates begin with a brief restatement of the facts and issues and move on to emphasize or clarify important points raised in the briefs submitted to the Court.

The justices have had an opportunity to read the briefs and to do some research into the case prior to the argument. They come to the argument with different perspectives. Some will feel strongly about a case based on their reading of it, consideration of previous decisions, or for jurisprudential reasons. Others may be concerned about the public policy implications involved in attempting to resolve the case. Still others will be uncommitted and may be swayed by the oral presentation.

At argument the justices question the advocates about their briefs, the public policy implications of their positions, and the applicability of the Court's prior decisions. Often the questions come in the form of hypothetical situations in which the advocates are asked to project the results of their reading of the law into possible future circumstances. A judge who has grave doubts, to put it mildly, about a position may ask what is known as the "jugular question," which seeks to go to heart of the argument with a strong challenge to the position presented by an attorney.[47] Some of the questions are raised with an eye toward the need felt by one judge to persuade other members of the Court to his (or her) point of view. Another motivation for questioning is an attempt by some judges to probe the arguments in search of promising directions for an opinion they may have to write in the case. In any event, when the Chief Justice indicates that "the case is submitted," the arguments by attorneys end and consideration by the judges begins.

Appellate courts hold conferences at which the cases are discussed and votes taken on the disposition of the dispute. In the Supreme Court, the standard practice is for the Chief Justice to assign the task of drafting an opinion to a member of the majority in the case. If the Chief Justice is not with the majority, that task falls to the senior member of the majority.

After the case is assigned, the judge prepares a draft of an opinion and circulates it for consideration by his colleagues. The idea is to attract as many members of the court to one's position as possible. A unanimous opinion is the most powerful statement a court can make. The members of the court can make changes in their voting posture at any time before the decision is rendered. Thus, there is always a chance that one can win over votes cast on the other side of the case at conference. Of course, there is also the possibility of losing votes. Hence, one must be concerned about drafting an opinion that will gain the support of the court, receive the support or at least the acquiescence of the public, and be accepted by the legal community as providing a well-crafted and cogent statement of the law.

In addition to changing votes, members of a court have other options in responding to the draft opinion. If a judge wishes to agree with the actual outcome of a case but for different reasons from those advanced in the majority opinion, he or she may enter a concurring opinion or join in a concurring opinion written by another member of the court. Those who disagree with the majority may enter dissenting opinions individually or as a group. Judges who write separate opinions enjoy greater latitude in what they write and in the manner in which their argument is presented, since they speak only for themselves and not for the court as a whole. These opinions provide a certain dynamic in the law. They may be drawn upon by future jurists and commentators in drafting new opinions.

However, if several opinions are issued in a case, although they may be interesting and helpful in understanding the views of particular members of the Court, it is difficult to know which direction the Court will take in the future.

Logic in the Law

The techniques of decisionmaking that judges employ to arrive at a determination of the meaning of the law in a particular case are known collectively as "legal reasoning."[48] As the leading author on the subject, Edward Levi, notes, there are really three different sets of techniques within the general rubric of legal reasoning. They are application of constitutional principles, statutory interpretation, and common law development.[49]

In the early years of national development, Chief Justice John Marshall explained the Court's view on the nature of constitutional decisionmaking. In *Marbury v. Madison*, the Court declared an act of Congress, section 13 of the Judiciary Act of 1789, unconstitutional.[50] In the opinion, Justice Marshall indicated that the Constitution is a "superior paramount law, unchangeable by ordinary means." It is, he wrote, "emphatically the province and duty of the judicial department" to say what that fundamental law means. The primary difficulty in understanding the meaning of the Constitution is that a fundamental law designed to remain useful over a long period must be rather general in its terms. One of the criticisms leveled by those who opposed ratification was that the document was vague. Writing in *The Federalist*, James Madison noted that an attempt to write a basic charter of government would become impossible if narrow specificity and precision were to be the benchmarks of draftsmanship. It would, he said, be necessary to develop a fully detailed code of all rights, duties, and privileges for all time to come. Such an undertaking would destroy the purpose of a Constitution and would, in any case, be impossible since no set of framers could have such prescience as to predict all possible developments that would call for special interpretations by the Congress.

Interpretation of the Constitution involves, at the least, a consideration of the language of the document, an understanding of the intent of the framers, the circumstances that have given rise to the problem under consideration, and the possible need for change in the law of the Constitution to keep the document current.

An interpretation of the language of the Constitution begins with a reading of the document, but it continues through a reading of the gloss the courts have placed on those words during the history of American constitutional development. For example, the Constitution gives the president the power to make treaties by and with the advice and consent of the Senate.[51] But does the word "treaties" mean executive agreements and diplomatic protocols? Does the language mean that, if any agreement is made by the executive branch, it must be ratified by the Senate? The Supreme Court has held that, although executive orders are for some purposes like treaties and may therefore be made by the president under article II, they are not exactly the same and do not require Senate approval in all cases.[52]

Even if the language of a constitutional provision appears to provide a simple answer, one must look further to the spirit or intent of the provision in question. The First Amendment is one of the best examples of this problem. The language is seemingly clear and absolute: "Congress shall make no law" abridging freedoms of religion, speech, press, and peaceful assembly. As Justice Black was so fond of pointing out, it doesn't say "may make no bad laws" or "unfair laws," but *no law*. However, Justice Black was alone in reading the language literally, since it is clear that the framers of the Constitution were well aware of existing law, which proscribed some kinds of expression. The Court has summarized these restrictions as matters of defamation, obscenity, or fighting words.[53] There are a number of sources to which one may refer on the intent of the framers, including Madison's *Notes on Debates in the Federal Convention of 1787*,[54] Max Farrand's *The Framing of the Constitution . . .* ,[55] Robert Rutland's *The Birth of the Bill of Rights, 1776–1791*,[56] Jonathan Elliott's *Debates . . . on the Adoption of the Federal Constitution . . .* ,[57] and *The Federalist Papers*.[58] There is also a substantial body of historical material on the Constitution and early national period that is helpful.[59]

Often, although the language does not speak directly to a particular problem and there is no specific mention of the purpose of a particular provision so clear as to resolve a dispute, the circumstances in which a case arises are helpful to an understanding of a case. This was the situation facing the Supreme Court in one of its early cases. *McCulloch v. Maryland.*[60] The Congress had chartered the Bank of the United States as its central financial institution based on its understanding of the powers granted under article I of the Constitution. But article I says nothing of the power of the legislature to charter a bank, or anything else. We know from the history of the framing of the Constitution that Congress was given a number of specifically enumerated powers—including especially financial authority—in section 8 of article I to remedy some of the problems that had caused the downfall of the Articles of Confederation. This did not settle the question whether the so-called "necessary and proper" clause gave Congress power to incorporate a bank. Marshall wrote for the Court, reminding critics that "it is a constitution we are expounding." Such a frame of government must be flexible. In this case, Marshall went into a lengthy consideration of the circumstances in which the bank had been created and the logical connections between the creation of the bank and the accomplishment of some of the matters specifically delegated to Congress by the Constitution to demonstrate that the chartering of the bank was constitutional.

Finally, courts do consider the need for change in interpretation. The framers of the Constitution made no mention of privacy either in the document itself or in the amendments later enacted. Does that mean there is no right to privacy under the Constitution? The Ninth Amendment states: "The enumeration in the Constitution, of certain rights, shall not be construed to deny or disparage others retained by the people." There is little else one can point to as a direct source. The Supreme Court held in 1965 that there was indeed a constitutionally protected right to privacy, which was a "penumbral" right flowing from the First, Third, Fourth, Fifth, and Ninth amendments.[61] The decision in *Griswold* and others delivered since make clear the view of the justices that it is necessary for a document that protects liberty in modern America to include that protection.

Statutes are different: they may be altered whenever the legislature—state or federal—wishes to change them. In part for this reason, the courts have generally held that one should read them and apply them more literally than is possible or desirable with constitutional provisions.[62] Like constitutional interpretation, statutory language must be read with an eye toward the judicial gloss that language has received since its enactment. Additionally, it is a convention that one should also look to contemporaneous administrative interpretation of the language of a statute.[63] This deference comes from the view that administrators charged with implementing pieces of legislation are usually given the authority to administer the laws because they are considered experts in the general field dealt with by the legislation. For this and other reasons, the courts often defer to interpretations made by those administrators.

The spirit of the law or the intent of the writers of the statute is an important issue in statutory interpretation. The Supreme Court ruling in *United Steelworkers v. Weber*[64] is a case in point. This case arose when a white employee of the Kaiser Aluminum Gramercy Works sued claiming that an affirmative action plan developed voluntarily as a part of a contract between the company and the union was discriminatory on the basis of race and therefore unlawful under Title VII of the Civil Rights Act of 1964. The program established a craft training plan in the plant that would accept applicants who wished to participate, with selections based on seniority. Within the overall plan was the requirement that 50 percent of those selected were to be minority group members until the level of participants met some approximation of the local population. The language of Title VII makes clear that, absent a finding of past discrimination, hiring quotas cannot be imposed on a business but there is some question whether voluntary programs are also prohibited. The case turned on the intent of the statute. The law had undergone a lengthy debate and a number of compromises during its development. Was the statute meant to bring an end to discrimination on the basis of race against minority groups and to permit voluntary efforts to eliminate the effects of past discrimination? Or was the statute meant to cut off any consideration of race in the future unless there was a specifically proven violation, in which case a race-conscious equitable remedy could be imposed by a court? Justice Brennan, writing for the Court, argued the former. Justice Rehnquist wrote for himself and Chief Justice Burger, arguing the latter view of the purpose of the statute.

Even though statutes may be more easily changed than constitutional provisions, it is still impossible for those who draft legislation to foresee all the problems that might arise under the administration of a statute in the future. Neither is it possible to get a change in a statute every time a new situation develops during the implementation of a legislative enactment. For this reason, changing circumstances must also be considered in matters of statutory interpretation. The recent developments of cable and community antenna television service provides an example. The law that established the jurisdiction of the Federal Communications Commission was enacted long before commercial television in any form was developed. The question arose whether the FCC could regulate cable under the law. The commission concluded that the regulation of the new technology was reasonably ancillary to its other specifically defined duties and fell within its jurisdiction. The courts have agreed.[65]

Case law or common law development is a somewhat different problem. The techniques of common law analysis are used in all judicial decisionmaking, but primarily these methods developed when there were no statutes or legislative enactments to apply to new cases. Common law decisionmaking involves the classification of facts and the application of rules found in existing law and applied through a process of analogy either directly or with some changes to fit the different circumstances of a particular set of facts.

As a judge prepares to hear a case, he or she looks to the briefs to determine whether there is a specifically applicable statute or court precedent that might be applied to the present case. In some instances, referred to as "cases of first impression," there is no precedent that is sufficiently helpful in resolving the case before the court. In such cases, the judge must develop a rule based on the law as it is applied in other jurisdictions or other related but different areas of the law. At argument the advocates attempt to convince the judge that a favorable case is the appropriate precedent.

From an analytic perspective, the judge undertakes a process of discovery, synthesis, and analogy. The facts of various precedents advanced by the parties in the case are studied to determine whether they are sufficiently like the pending case to be appropriate precedents. The motivating theory is that the law should treat like parties similarly in like situations. If a judge determines that a particular case is applicable, he or she must analyze that case to synthesize from the opinion what is known as the rule of the case. That is, he or she must determine a specific rule or test that was the basis of the decision in the precedent case. Such analysis can be quite difficult, for a number of reasons. Among them, one must recall that judges frequently compromise or add explanatory materials in their opinions to get approval of colleagues and the acquiescence of the parties to the case. Thus, some of the material in the opinion is ncessary to the holding in the case while the remainder of the opinion is extra information. The former is known in the law as the *ratio decidendi* and the latter as *obiter dicta*. Much of the discussion in legal cases and law review literature concerns differences of opinion about just what parts of the opinion are essential and therefore applicable as precedent and which are mere dicta.

Having developed the rule of the precedent case, the judge must apply that rule by analogy to the case at hand. Sometimes the fit is a good one and the answer to the problem before the court is easily resolved. However, it is rare that there is an exact fit. In the first place, if there is a clear precedent, a competent attorney would advise a client of that fact and advise against litigation. Second, no two cases are ever exactly alike. Hence, one frequently finds legal decisions resting on the ability of one side to differentiate existing precedents from the case at hand. If the rule of the earlier case does not easily fit, the judge must decide whether the earlier rule can be modified to apply to the new case. If not, the judge must craft a new rule and justify it. If a modification is necessary, it is encumbent on the judge to justify that change in approach.

Consider the following simple example. Assume that one is a judge when the first automobile rear-end collision occurred. There is no statutory guidance with which to determine which party in the accident will be held responsible for any damages in the collision. From an examination of other areas of law, one concludes that a driver should be in control of his or her vehicle and that a vehicle that approaches from the rear is required to avoid the accident or face a presumption of liability for failure to control the car. Assume that a similar case arises later. Unlike the first incident, this does not involve a stopped vehicle being struck from the rear by an approaching car. Instead, a driver backs out of a driveway that is partially obstructed by shrubbery in the early evening. The car has defective backup lights, and is struck from behind by another car. The differences between the two situations are important. In the second abstract case, there are several possible options. One might still apply the rule that driver approaching from the rear should have had the last clear chance to avoid the accident and is therefore liable. The judge might hold that the rule of the first case does not apply because there both vehicles were clearly in the mainstream of traffic while here one vehicle failed to exercise due care in entering the roadway. Another option would be to find the driver approaching from the rear responsible, but hold that that driver's responsibility should be mitigated by the contributory negligence of the driver whose defective vehicle improperly blocked the roadway.

Reading Cases

The institutional, legal reasoning, opinion crafting, and jurisprudential factors come together in the judicial opinion. For the beginner, there are several points to consider in approaching opinions.

First, attempt to understand the precise facts that gave rise to the suit and the stages of legal action the case has moved through on its way to its present position. Second, consider the issues in the case. More precisely, what questions has the court been asked to address in the case and which questions has it dealt with? What was the court's response to each of those questions? When considering the rationale advanced by the court in support of its decisions, attempt to understand what is essential to the holding in the case and what may be classified as dicta. Look for doctrinal development, that is, are there tests or rules used or developed that seem relatively detailed and fit into a pattern of cited precedents? Finally, consider the judge's view of the policy implications in a particular opinion.

Thus far we have approached the law in action from the perspective of a particular judge on a specific court attempting to resolve a case. It is also important to consider courts from a more general perspective as parts of the judiciary and the judiciary as part of the government. That is, it is important to understand some of the relationships among courts as well as between courts and other branches of government at the federal, state, and local levels.

Intercourt Relations

Judges are important political actors in government. The decisions rendered by courts are exercises in policymaking.[66] But the judiciary is not a monolith, nor is it a neatly defined hierarchy in which the lines of authority are clearly defined and well separated.[67] Different courts have different procedures for the appointment of judges,[68] serve widely diverse communities,[69] and approach decisionmaking from different practical if not jurisprudential perspectives. The case load and case mix faced by various courts influence the conditions in which the judges in that court work. Some judges are secure in what amounts to life tenure, legally enforced institutional independence, and stable, if sometimes inadequate, support budgets. Other judges must stand for reelection, are staffed by patronage appointees who may or may not be professionally competent and who are not necessarily stable occupants of an office, and face budgets that are affected by county governments, disputes in the state legislature, and the vagaries of property tax policy. These political and administrative factors shape the politically complex relations among judges and courts. For the present, consider the following two aspects of judicial politics.

Which judge or court one will file suit with is not necessarily a neutral or narrow legal question. Two important major determinants of forum selection are political in nature. First, interest groups have learned that litigation can be an effective tactic to achieve their ends where appeal to a legislative body or an administrative agency appears unlikely to be successful.[70] To improve the chances of a favorable outcome, an interest group, e.g., an environmental group or a civil rights organization, may select a particular jurisdiction because of certain political conditions in the area or special legal factors that operate there.[71] If a case can be shaped in a favorable manner, the likelihood of a particular outcome may be considerably enhanced. Second, there is outright forum shopping by many groups, businesses, and institutions. Forum shopping—the selection of a forum in which to raise a suit—is based on analyses of the personal or jurisprudential proclivities of the judges sitting in a particular court and the political forces in the environment that operate to dispose judges favorably toward the party bringing the suit.[72] It is not easy, for example, for a local judge of a federal district court to decide against a tobacco company in the Carolinas or Virginia. There is no allegation of bias, but there is an awareness of the political environment. Another example is the selection of some Bible Belt locations for major prosecutions of obscenity charges.[73]

In addition to the problems of forum selection, important questions arise in the area of what is called "impact analysis."[74] As one scholar of the judiciary has said, "The Constitution may mean what the Supreme Court says it does, but Supreme

Court opinions mean what the district court judges say they mean."[75] When the Supreme Court renders a decision, the case is not at an end. Appellate courts do not speak to the individuals in the case as much as they do to the lower courts. The decision directs a lower court to correct an error or to take some further action. Not all Supreme Court decisions have the impact they were expected to produce. Lower courts can use a number of tactics to evade higher court rulings.[76] One of the best-known problems of impact has been evasion of school desegregation rulings.[77]

The Judiciary and Other Parts of Government

Judicial policymaking is also very much affected by the relationships among courts and other branches and levels of government. Federal courts, for example, are part of the political process.[78] Recent cases on school busing to remedy racial segregation and intervention in unequal provision of government services at the state and local levels indicate just how political an environment these judges face. Circuit Courts of Appeals must attempt to resolve some of the differences among district courts and deal with other problems, such as appeals from rulings made by the President or by administrative agencies.[79] State supreme courts are the ultimate arbiters of the law of their respective states, but they must also deal with various branches of the federal government when there is alleged to be a conflict between federal law and state law.[80] Finally, the local courts often face the most direct effect of the political environment since they are not afforded the isolation and academic calm of the appellate courts.[81] Judges at the local level must face highly charged issues of fact and law in an emotion-laden and politically volatile atmosphere. Whether the political relationships between these judicial tribunals and other actors on the political scene are major open conflicts or subtle pressures, they are factors that mold the cases and the decision environment within which the law develops.

SUMMARY

When legal challenges are launched, the law in books is debated. But the debate becomes a product of other factors in addition to the letter of the law. These influences on the law shape the law in books into the law in action. Among the influences one must consider is the jurisprudential perspective of the judges who decide the cases. There are many views on the nature and purpose of the law and each jurist is influenced, often unconsciously, by his or her own approach to these conceptions of law. The analytical tools and rules used by judges to resolve cases also shape the law in action. Some of the constraints on decisionmaking are institutional, such as rules of self-restraint. Other tools are conventions on the manner in which judges are to interpret constitutions, statutes, and cases. In addition to the techniques of legal reasoning, there are other factors to be considered, such as the need to develop consensus in support of a decision among a judge's colleagues.

Finally, decisionmaking in courts does not take place in a political vacuum. Complex and delicate political factors are part of the decision environment. Some of these result from the problem of maintaining cooperation among courts at various levels of government and in different parts of the nation. Still other political variables result from the important and sometimes fragile relationships between courts and other actors in the political environment at all levels of government. An understanding of public law and public administration requires a sensitivity for both the law in books and the law in action.

NOTES

[1]Lon Fuller, "The Case of the Speluncean Explorers," 62 *Harvard L. Rev.* 616 (1949).

[2]Another case raises a number of these questions and adds a variety of others. See Lon Fuller, "The Case of the Grudge Informer," *The Morality of the Law*, (New Haven, Conn.: Yale University Press, 1969), pp. 245–53.

[3]Alexander Hamilton, James Madison, and John Jay, *The Federalist Papers* (New York: Mentor, 1961), pp. 284–88.

[4]For a further discussion of the purposes of law, see Harold Berman and William Greiner, *The Nature and Functions of Law* (Mineola, N.Y.: Foundation Press, 1972).

[5]These schools are described differently by various scholars of jurisprudence. Anyone wishing to pursue this line of inquiry would do well to survey some of the leading texts on jurisprudence, including George W. Paton and David P. Derham, *A Textbook of Jurisprudence*, 4th ed. (London: Oxford University Press, 1972); Julius Stone, *The Province and Function of Law* (Cambridge, Mass.: Harvard University Press, 1950); Carl J. Friedrich, *The Philosophy of Law in Historical Perspective*, 2d ed. (Chicago: University of Chicago Press, 1963); George C. Christie, *Text and Readings on Jurisprudence—The Philosophy of Law* (St. Paul: West, 1973); and Roscoe Pound, *An Introduction to the Philosophy of Law* (New Haven, Conn.: Yale University Press, 1954), particularly the bibliography, pp. 169–87.

[6]An edited collection of the most apropos writings by these authors is Clarence Morris, ed., *The Great Legal Philosophers: Selected Readings in Jurisprudence* (Philadelphia: University of Pennsylvania Press, 1971).

[7]See, e.g., E. S. Corwin, "The 'Higher Law' Background of American Constitutional Law," 42 *Harvard L. Rev.* 149 (1928–29), and Carl L. Becker, *The Declaration of Independence: A Study in the History of Political Ideas* (New York: Vintage, 1958).

[8]Morris, supra note 6, at pp. 56–79.

[9]Fuller, supra note 2.

[10]Morris, supra note 6, at pp. 335–63.

[11]Id., at pp. 289–300. Maine's major contribution was *Ancient Law* (London: Dent, 1972). Savigny's works were *Law of a People as an Emanation of Its Common Consciousness* (1814), *History of the Roman Law in the Middle Ages* (1815–31), and *System of the Roman Law* (1840–48).

[12]Morris, supra note 6, at pp. 532–37. See also Pound, supra note 5.

[13]Roscoe Pound, "The Scope and Purpose of Sociological Jurisprudence," 25 *Harvard L. Rev.* 487, 516 (1912).

[14]Like any aspect of a philosophical school, the quasi-economic rationality operating in the Pound's sociological school can be taken to extremes. See, e.g., Gordon Tullock, *The Logic of the Law* (New York: Basic Books, 1971).

[15]Oliver Wendell Holmes, Jr., "The Path of the Law," 10 *Harvard L. Rev.* 61 (1897).

[16]Oliver Wendell Holmes, Jr., "Natural Law," 32 *Harvard L. Rev.* 40, 41 (1918).

[17]Holmes, supra note 15, at pp. 460–61.

[18]John Chipman Gray, *The Nature and Sources of Law* (New York: Macmillan, 1927), chap. 4.

[19]Jerome Frank's leading jurisprudential works include *Law and the Modern Mind* (New York: Coward-McCann Brentanos, 1930) and *Courts on Trial* (New York: Atheneum, 1971). Karl Llewellyn's most widely known work is *The Bramble Bush* (New York: Oceana, 1951).

On the neorealists generally, see Julius Paul, *The Judicial Realism of Jerome Frank* (The Hague: Mertinus Nijhoff, 1959), and Wilfred E. Rumble, Jr., *American Legal Realism* (Ithaca, N.Y.: Cornell University Press, 1968).

[20]Jack W. Peltason, *Federal Courts in the Political Process* (Garden City, N.Y.: Doubleday, 1955), p. 1.

[21]See, e.g., Walter F. Murphy, *Elements of Judicial Strategy* (Chicago: University of Chicago Press, 1964); J. Woodford Howard, *Mr. Justice Murphy: A Political Biography* (Princeton, N.J.: Princeton University Press, 1968); and Martin Shapiro, "Political Jurisprudence," 52 *Kentucky L. J.* 294 (1964).

[22]Walter Murphy defined a policy-oriented judge or justice as follows: "By this term I mean a Justice who is aware of the impact which judicial decisions can have on public policy, realizes the leeway for discretion which his office permits, and is willing to take advantage of this power and leeway to further particular policy aims." Murphy, supra note 21, at p. 4.

[23]Michael Parenti, *Democracy for the Few* (New York: St. Martin's Press, 1977). On class theory relating to law, see generally Renzo Sereno, *The Rulers* (New York: Harper & Row, 1968).

[24]Benjamin N. Cardozo, *The Nature of the Judicial Process* (New Haven, Conn.: Yale University Press, 1921).

[25]Id., at p. 14.

[26]Id., at p. 10.

[27]Id., at p. 30.

[28]Holmes, supra note 15, at p. 477.

[29]*Regents v. Bakke*, 438 U.S. 265 (1978).

[30]There were two special problems in Bakke's situation. First, while his grades and test scores were higher than some students admitted through the affirmative action program, it is not clear that he would have been admitted on the scholastic basis even if there had been no such program. Second, many medical schools might have considered his age a problem.

[31]On desegregation, see *Green v. County School Board*, 391 U.S. 430 (1968), and *Swann v. Charlotte Mechlenburg*, 402 U.S. 1 (1971). On the mental health facility, see *Wyatt v. Stickney*, 325 F. Supp. 781 (M.D. Ala. 1971). See also Frank M. Johnson, Jr., "The Role of the Judiciary with Respect to the Other Branches of Government," in Walter F. Murphy and C. Herman Pritchett, eds., *Courts, Judges and Politics: An Introduction to the Judicial Process*, 3d ed. (New York: Random House, 1979), pp. 66–71.

[33]*Sierra Club v. Morton*, 405 U.S. 727, 742, n. 2 (1972), Justice Douglas dissenting.

[33]*First National Bank v. Bellotti*, 435 U.S. 765 (1978).

[34]*Ashwander v. Tennessee Valley Authority*, 297 U.S. 288 (1936), Justice Brandeis concurring.

[35]*Baker v. Carr*, 369 U.S. 186, 198 (1962). See also Laurence H. Tribe, *American Constitutional Law* (Mineola, N.Y.: Foundation Press, 1978), §§3-7-3-27.

[36]"The fundamental aspect of standing is that it focuses on the party seeking to get his complaint before a federal court and not on the issues he wishes to have adjudicated. The 'gist of the question of standing' is whether the party seeking relief has 'alleged such a personal stake in the outcome of the controversy as to assure that concrete adverseness which sharpens the presentation of issues upon which the court so largely depends for illumination of difficult constitutional questions.' . . . In other words, when standing is placed in issue in a case, the question is whether the person whose standing is challenged is a proper party to request an adjudication of a particular issue and not whether the issue itself is justiciable." *Flast v. Cohen*, 392 U.S. 83, 99 (1968).

[37]Frank, *Courts on Trial*, supra note 19, chap. 6.

[38]*Muskrat v. United States*, 219 U.S. 346 (1911). See also Tribe, supra note 35, at §3-10.

[39]An exception to this rule in the judicial proceeding is a declaratory judgment, under which it is sometimes possible to obtain from a judge a declaration of the rights and obligations of people before the court. 28 U.S.C. §2201. This is true even though as of the time of the suit there has been no direct legal injury. But declaratory judgments are exceptions to the general rule and usually require a showing that there will be irreparable harm to the person before the court if declaratory relief is not granted.

[40]Examples include Colorado and Massachusetts. See Tribe, supra note 35, at p. 57 n. 4.

[41]*DeFunis v. Odegaard*, 416 U.S. 312 (1974).

[42]*Baker v. Carr*, 369 U.S. 186, 217 (1962).

[43]Hamilton, Madison, and Jay, *Federalist* 78, supra note 3, at p. 465. See also Alexander M. Bickel, *The Least Dangerous Branch* (Indianapolis: Bobbs-Merrill, 1975), chap. 1.

[44]John P. Frank, "Political Questions," in Edmund Cahn, ed., *Supreme Court and Supreme Law* (New York: Simon & Schuster, 1971), p. 37. See also Charles G. Post, *The Supreme Court and Political Questions* (New York: Da Capo Press, 1969).

[45]See, e.g., *Rescue Army v. Municipal Court*, 331 U.S. 549 (1947).

[46]For in-depth consideration of this process prepared for a wide audience, see Anthony Lewis, *Gideon's Trumpet* (New York: Random House, 1964), and Alan F. Westin, *The Anatomy of a Constitutional Law Case* (New York: Macmillan, 1958). To see the process more from the vantage point of the judge, see Leon Friedman, ed., *United States v. Nixon: The President Before the Supreme Court* (New York: Chelsea House, 1974).

[47]Excerpts from recent arguments before the Supreme Court may be found in *United States Law Week—Supreme Court* (Washington, D.C.: Bureau of National Affairs, 1933–date).

[48]For a comprehensive treatment of legal reasoning, see Lief Carter, *Reason in Law* (Boston: Little, Brown, 1979).

[49]Edward Levi, *An Introduction to Legal Reasoning* (Chicago: University of Chicago Press, 1949).

[50]*Marbury v. Madison*, 5 U.S. (1 Cranch) 137 (1803).

[51]U.S. Constitution, article II, §2.

[52]See, e.g., *Dames & Moore v. Regan*, 69 L. Ed. 2d 918 (1981); *United States v. Pink*, 315 U.S. 203 (1942); *United States v. Belmont*, 301 U.S. 324 (1937); and B. *Altman & Co. v. United States*, 224 U.S. 583 (1912).

[53]*Chaplinsky v. New Hampshire*, 315 U.S. 568 (1942).

[54]James Madison, *Notes on Debates in the Federal Convention of 1787* (Athens: Ohio University Press, 1966).

[55]Max Farrand, *The Framing of the Constitution of the United States* (New Haven, Conn.: Yale University Press, 1913); and Max Farrand, ed., *Records of the Federal Convention of 1787*, rev. ed., 4 vols. (New Haven, Conn.: Yale University Press, 1966).

[56]Robert A. Rutland, *The Birth of the Bill of Rights, 1776–1791* (Chapel Hill: University of North Carolina Press, 1955).

[57]Jonathan Elliott, *Debates in the Several States on the Adoption of the Federal Constitution as Recommended by the General Convention at Philadelphia in 1787*, 2d ed. (New York: Burt Franklin, 1888).

[58]Hamilton, Madison, and Jay, supra note 3.

[59]See, e.g., Robert Wood, *The Creation of the American Republic, 1776–1787* (Chapel Hill: University of North Carolina Press, 1969).

[60]*McCulloch v. Maryland*, 17 U.S. (4 Wheat.) 316 (1819).

[61]*Griswold v. Connecticut*, 381 U.S. 479 (1965).

[62]See Levi, supra note 49, and Carter, supra note 48. See also

William O. Douglas, "Judges and Legislators," in Alan F. Westin, ed., *The Supreme Courts: Views from Inside* (New York: Norton, 1961).

[63]*United States v. Rutherford*, 442 U.S. 544, 553–54 (1979).

[64]*United Steelworkers v. Weber*, 443 U.S. 193 (1979).

[65]*United States v. Southwestern Cable Co.*, 392 U.S. 157 (1968) and a later related case, *United States v. Midwest Video*, 406 U.S. 649 (1972).

[66]See generally Glendon Schubert, *Judicial Policy Making* rev. ed. (Glenview, Ill.: Scott, Foresman, 1974).

[67]Sheldon Goldman and Thomas P. Jahnige, *The Federal Courts as a Political System*, 2d ed. (New York: Harper & Row, 1976), chap. 2.

[68]See Burt Neuborne, "The Myth of Parity," 90 *Harvard L. Rev.* 1105 (1977); Kenneth Dolbeare, *Trial Courts in Urban Politics* (New York: Wiley, 1967); Richard J. Richardson and Kenneth L. Vines, *The Politics of Federal Courts* (Boston: Little, Brown, 1970); and John R. Schmidhauser, *Judges and Justices* (Boston: Little, Brown, 1979).

[69]See, e.g., S. Sidney Ulmer, *Courts, Law and Judicial Processes* (New York: Free Press, 1981); James Eisenstein and Herbert Jacob, *Felony Justice* (Boston: Little, Brown, 1977); and James R. Klonoski and Robert I. Mendelsohn, *The Politics of Local Justice* (Boston: Little, Brown, 1970).

[70]See, e.g., Clement E. Vose, *Caucasians Only: The Supreme Court, the NAACP, and the Restrictive Covenant Cases* (Berkeley: University of California Press, 1959). See also Jack W. Peltason, *Fifty-eight Lonely Men* (Urbana: University of Illinois Press, 1971).

[71]A recent example is the challenge to petrochemical industry regulation brought in the Fifth Circuit Court of Appeals, headquartered in New Orleans, Louisiana.

[72]See Robert Ash, "Forum Shopping Has Distinct Advantages in Seeking Declaratory Judgments on Exemptions," 51 *Journal of Taxation* 112 (1979), and Comment, "Forum-Shopping in the Review of NLRB Orders," 28 *U. Chicago L. Rev.* 552 (1961).

[73]See Ted Morgan, 'United States versus the Princes of Porn," *New York Times Magazine*, March 6, 1977, p. 16.

[74]See Stephen L. Wasby, *The Impact of the United States Supreme Court* (Homewood, Ill.: Dorsey Press, 1970) and Theodore L. Becker and Malcolm M. Feeley, *The Impact of Supreme Court Decisions*, 2d ed. (New York: Oxford University Press, 1973).

[75]Jack W. Peltason, *Federal Courts in the Political Process* (Garden City, N.Y.: Doubleday, 1955), p. 14.

[76]See Walter F. Murphy, "Lower Court Checks on Supreme Court Power," 53 *American Political Science Rev.* 1017 (1959); Jerry K. Beatty, "State Court Evasion of United States Supreme Court Mandates During the Last Decade of the Warren Court," 6 *Valparaiso U. L. Rev.* 260 (1970); Bradley C. Cannon, "Reactions of State Supreme Courts to U.S. Supreme Court Civil Liberties Decisions," 8 *Law and Society Rev.* 109 (1973); and Donald E. Wilkes, Jr., "The New Federalism in Criminal Procedure: State Court Evasion of the Burger Court," 62 *Kentucky L. J.* 421 (1973).

[77]See Wasby, supra note 74, at pp. 169–85.

[78]See Richardson and Vines, supra note 68.

[79]Many administrative agency statutes permit appeals from agency rulings to circuit courts of appeals in Washington, D.C., or in the circuit in which one's business is headquartered.

[80]See, eg., *Hodel v. Virginia Surface Mining and Reclamation Ass'n*, 101 S. Ct. 2352 (1981).

[81]See Dolbeare, supra note 68.

A History of
Law and Administration

Mr. Withers was a commissioner of sewers. During a routine inspection, Withers discovered a small defect in a flood control wall that protected a small farm next to a river. The commissioner had considerable discretion in assessing a repair fee. Withers chose to assess the fee against the farm, but the resident of that property sued claiming that the fee should have been assessed against all property owners who benefited from the flood control wall. The court held that, although Withers had a great deal of latitude in performing his duties, this levy against the single property owner was an abuse of administrative discretion. The river was the Thames, the tribunal was the Court of Common Pleas, and the date was 1599.[1]

The point of the reference to *Rooke's Case,* of course, is that problems of law and administration did not begin with the creation of the Occupational Safety and Health Administration, President Johnson's Great Society programs, the expansion of social services during the fifties, the enactment of the Administrative Procedure Act in 1947, the rise of the New Deal, the Progressive Era's reform movements, or even with the creation of the Interstate Commerce Commission in 1887. Similarly, concern over abuses of administrative discretion, efficiency and effectiveness in administration, and fear of judicialization of the administrative processes of government are not new phenomena. There are at least two reasons for devoting attention to the historical foundations of public law and public administration. First, students and practitioners of administration ignore the historical underpinnings of their field at the risk of Santayana's dictum that those who ignore history are doomed to repeat it. Second, and of much more immediate concern for this study, is the fact that administrative law has evolved in an ad hoc fashion over the years without a clear understanding of its theoretical underpinnings. The developing concepts and approaches to administrative law have not been synthesized and integrated with the larger legal and governmental literature. In part, the ad hoc development of the field is a function of important historical events that have changed both theories and practices in administration. Writing in 1941, Walter Gellhorn described the pragmatic origins of administrative law: "The striking fact is that new agencies have been created or old ones expanded not to satisfy an abstract governmental theory, but to cope with problems of recognized public concern."[2] An understanding of the concepts and practices that together comprise administrative law requires a study of the historical roots of the subject.

The history of administrative law will be divided into four periods during which practical and theoretical problems influenced the growth and development of this field of law. The first period extends from the founding of the republic to 1928. The second period is the so-called "Golden Age of Administrative Tribunals"[3]—the New Deal, World War II with its monumental administrative operations, and the postwar period, including the enactment of the Administrative Procedure Act, which remains the basic statute governing the operation of the administrative law process. The third period extends from 1950 to 1969. The final period begins at the end of the Johnson administration. At that time the literature on administrative law and court rulings experienced a marked change. The change was also reflected in popular responses to the energy crisis and other events of the 1970s.

A number of significant themes and conceptual conflicts flow through these periods of development. In broad compass, one might map them as follows. During the first hundred years of the republic, we came to the realization that powerful administrative agencies were essential and turned our attention to the important problems of ensuring that administrative activities took place within an administrative justice system governed by the rule of law. During the New Deal years, theoretical discussions gave way to the practical problems of the moment. Concern for the rule of law was disposed of as procedural protections against arbitrary administrative activities were developed and buttressed by increased judicial review of agency activity. In the third period, we realized that procedural regularity, general requirements for some kind of due process, and the availability of judicial review had not resolved some very basic problems of law and administration. The final period has been marked by attempts to respond to some of the problems of the administrative justice system, with varying degrees of success.

LAW AND ADMINISTRATION IN AMERICA TO 1928

A history of administrative law is a story both of the unfolding of events and of the development of ideas. Many of the important ideas and events that would shape the rise of administrative law in the years following the industrial revolution were products of forces that guided the early years of our nation. It is to those early foundation years that we now turn.

The Early Years

Public administration in America can be traced back to the first colonial settlements. Indeed, John Winthrop, governor of the Massachusetts Bay Colony, had been a justice of the peace in England before his departure for the New World.[4] At that time, justices of the peace in England were as much administrative officers as judicial officials.[5] The problems of administering the colonies involved both public and private matters: public insofar as the colonies were, by and large, societies of free people who entered into social compacts and private inasmuch as they were communities founded on the authority and financing of joint stock companies or proprietors. As the colonies grew in numbers and population, it became necessary to develop structures and processes for their governance.

About 1763, following the French and Indian War, the British began to strengthen their administrative system in the colonies. Indeed, some of the reaction against British rule had to do with the scope and methods of administration by British governors and administrators, rather than their form of government.[6]

The years during which America functioned under the Articles of Confederation were administrative disasters in part because of a lack of power on which to construct an effective administrative operation.

> The government of the Confederation had run steadily down until its movements almost ceased. . . . When [Washington] entered New York late in April 1789, to become the first President under the new Constitution, he took over almost nothing from the dying confederation. There was, indeed, a foreign office with John Jay and a couple of clerks to deal with correspondence from John Adams in London and Thomas Jefferson in Paris; there was a Treasury Board with an empty treasury; there was a "Secretary at War" with an authorized army of 840 men; there were a dozen clerks whose pay was in arrears, and an unknown but fearful burden of debt, almost no revenue, and a prostrate credit.[7]

Alexander Hamilton and John Marshall experienced this dearth of administration during the Revolutionary War and under the Articles of Confederation.[8] Both became strong advocates of an effective structure for public administration during the debates over the ratification of the Constitution and in the years that followed. In fact, Hamilton, with James Madison and John Jay, wrote the leading campaign document for the Constitution, *The Federalist Papers*.[9] The argument advanced in the *Papers*, reduced to its most basic form, was that the people needed a strong, effective government and the proposed Constitution promised to provide such a government while establishing sufficient safeguards to ensure against abuses of power by those in positions of authority.

When the officials of the new government took office, they lost no time in constructing the various governmental units necessary to remedy the defects of the Articles of Confederation.

> In 1789, the first Congress esablished a complete administrative machinery for the collection of customs and duties, necessitating administrative adjudication of disputes; it provided for the payment of pensions to disabled soldiers "under such regulations as the President of the United States may direct"; granted power to the Secretary of State, the Secretary for the Department of War, and the Attorney General or any two of them to grant patents "if they shall deem the invention or discovery sufficiently useful and important"; and provided that persons trading with Indians must procure a license, and that such license shall be governed in all things touching upon said trade and intercourse by such rules and regulations as the President shall prescribe.[10]

By 1790 there was a federal regulatory statute "for protecting seamen against unseaworthy ships," with judicial action being the primary means of enforcement until a substantial administrative structure was established to deal with the problem in the mid-nineteenth century.[11] In 1797 and 1798 New York established a pair of statutes for New York City to regulate "noxious trades" that were believed to be dangerous to health, with enforcement responsibility vested in the commissioner of health, the mayor, and a judicial tribunal.[12] In sum: "Of the fifty-one major federal agencies which the Attorney General's Committee on Administrative Procedure selected for its study of the administrative process in 1941, eleven traced their beginnings to statutes enacted prior to the close of the Civil War."[13]

Chief Justice John Marshall led the Supreme Court into the nineteenth century with opinions in important cases that established the judiciary as a co-equal third branch of government.[14] Two Marshall Court decisions are particularly important in the development of administrative law. *McCulloch v. Maryland,* which gave a broad interpretation to the "necessary and proper clause" of the legislative article of the Constitution, provided clear constitutional authority for Congress to create a wide variety of administrative institutions.[15] *Gibbons v. Ogden* and later cases maintained that the article I, §8, power to regulate interstate commerce was also to be read broadly.[16] Taken together, these two constitutional provisions provide the authority for most of the federal agencies in existence.

The Industrial Revolution and the Progressive Era

Presidential leadership in public administration floundered during the term of President Andrew Jackson, whose philosophy was that no task of government was so complex that it could not be performed by the average citizen.[17] Expertise was of no value. He also held that the best administration of the people's business resulted from frequent rotation in office. These simplistic notions fell before the demands of national development and events brought about by the Civil War.

The mobilization of the nation for war and the accompanying administrative nightmares transformed the public administration. Difficulties of communication, transportation, and management of resources afflicted both North and South. One of the major results of the Civil War was increased industrialization, particularly the dramatic growth of the railroads.

The importance of public administration underwent a quantum leap in the closing decades of the nineteenth and early decades of the twentieth century. The industrial revolution brought not only new technology, but also the destruction of the insular agricultural community, the burgeoning growth of urban areas, and an increasingly complex, interrelated, and machine-oriented economy.

The Populist and Progressive reform movements were in part reactions to the social, economic, and political upheavals of the postwar period; it was the beginning of the end of what Richard Hofstadter has termed "the Agrarian Myth."[18] The Granger movement's battle with the railroads gave rise to state regulation of some aspects of the grain trade and was a major factor in the creation of the Interstate Commerce Commission in 1887.[19] The ICC is generally acknowledged to be the prototype for the several major independent regulatory commissions established in the twentieth century.

Even though the first three decades of the twentieth century were the time of laissez faire economics, public administration assumed proportions and objectives never before attempted. Market manipulations by large corporations, monopolies, and holding companies brought about a number of investigations and were instrumental in the creation of the Federal Trade Commission in 1914.[20] World War I brought a blurring of the lines between the public and private sectors of the economy. The 1920s were prosperous years for some Americans, but they were also years of turmoil[21] and unstable economic development. The 1920s witnessed the onset of severe agricultural depression.[22] Progressive reformers worked at all levels to rectify political corruption and to deal with the social spillovers of the new industrial age. Their efforts were based on two fundamental principles that are of continuing importance to administrative law. The first was an emerging social conscience, which required that the society through government had an obligation to deal with social problems that developed as the nation grew and industrialization increased.[23] Not content with Herbert Spencer's social Darwinism, the Progressives argued that someone must deal with the problems that the marketplace did not resolve. The second important idea that emerged from this movement was a new faith in professionalism and expertise. The growth of the professions was seen as a promising means of applying newly discovered scientific and technological knowledge to social and economic problems.

During the years before the crash of 1929, many of the problems of law and administration that were to be of importance in the next decade were recognized. Investigations of market manipulations and other financial chicanery were undertaken.[24] Utilities began to develop, and with them came problems of regulating the companies, necessarily monopolies, formed to deliver utility services.[25] Power generation policies became increasingly important with a new statute, the Federal Water Power Act,[26] created to be administered by the Federal Power Commission.

The law in general was not well structured to meet new controversies brought to court over administrative decisions. That fact was recognized as early as 1915 by Elihu Root:

> There is one special field of law development which has manifestly become inevitable. We are entering upon the creation of a body of administrative law quite different in its machinery, its remedies, and its necessary safeguards from the old methods of regulation by specific statutes enforced by the courts. As any community passes from simple to complex conditions the only way in which government can deal with the increased burdens thrown upon it is by the delegation of power to be exercised in detail by subordinate agents, subject to the control of general directions prescribed by superior authority. The necessities of our situation have already led to an extensive employment of that method. The Interstate Commerce Commission, the state public service commissions, the Federal Trade Commission, the powers of the Federal Reserve Board, the health departments of the states, and many other supervisory offices and agencies are familiar illustrations. . . . There will be no withdrawal from these experiments. We shall go on; we shall expand them, whether we approve theoretically or not, because such agencies furnish protection to rights and obstacles to wrongdoing which under our new social and industrial conditions cannot be practically accomplished by the old and simple

procedure of legislatures and courts in the last generation. Yet the powers that are committed to these regulating agencies, and which they must have to do their work, carry with them great and dangerous opportunities of oppression and wrong. If we are to continue a government of limited powers these agencies must themselves be regulated. The limits of their powers must be fixed and determined. The rights of the citizen against them must be made plain. A system of administrative law must be developed, and that with us is still in its infancy, crude and imperfect.[27]

Some efforts were already under way to establish those principles and to deal with the problems Root noted. Indeed, the year 1928 was chosen as the end point for this period in part because it saw the publication of Freund's *Administrative Powers over Persons and Property*,[28] which was the last major work in the first phase of literature development in the area of public administration and law.

The Literature of Public Law and Public Administration Emerges

The important authors of this period presented an agenda of problems and set the terms of political and legal discourse for years to come. They were concerned with three major questions. First, could there legitimately be such a thing as administrative law in the United States, given our Anglo-American jurisprudential heritage? Second, are these administrative bodies legitimate or are they products of constitutionally illegitimate delegations of power? Third, assuming they are constitutional, how does one go about setting limits on them such that they can be said to comport with the rule of law? The authors of particular importance who addressed these questions were A. V. Dicey, Frank Goodnow, John Dickinson, and Ernst Freund.

The British scholar A. V. Dicey examined the British legal and constitutional tradition and concluded that: "There can be with us nothing really corresponding to administrative law."[29] By this injunction Dicey meant that the rule of law requires that any action which results in injury to the liberty or property interests of a citizen or any challenge to actions of government officials is subject to final determination in the ordinary courts according to common law.[30] Clearly, the purposes of administration and administrative law, among which were interests in the establishment of tribunals better suited than ordinary courts for resolving special administrative problems, required a different form of operation than the strict regime demanded by Dicey. He eventually abandoned that "extravagant version of the rule of law," but it was an important interpretation and had significant consequences for administrative law in the years to come.[31]

Frank Goodnow is often referred to as the father of American administrative law. Writing at the turn of the century, Goodnow dismissed Dicey's extreme argument and asserted that administrative law and major administrative agencies are not only possible but necessary.[32] The problem, according to Goodnow, is how to limit appropriately some of the discretionary authority necessarily exercised by administrators.

Any attempt to deal with possible abuses of authority by administrators must be dealt with, in Goodnow's view, with a sensitivity for the complex environment within which administration takes place. Administrators execute the will of the state. When the will of the state is expressed as "unconditional commands" specifically stated and narrowly defined by the legislature, the administrator need do no more than seek out violators of the law and enforce the statute.[33] The room for administrative arbitrariness in such circumstances is small. Goodnow then attempted to come to grips with a problem not recognized by Dicey.

> There are many duties which the government is called upon to perform in a complex civilization which cannot be performed under a system of unconditional commands. No legislature has such insight or extended vision as to be able to regulate all the details in the administrative law, or to put in the form of unconditional commands rules which will in all cases completely and adequately express the will of the state. It must abandon the system of unconditional commands and resort to conditional commands which vest in the administrative officer large powers of a discretionary character. The legislature, therefore, enacts a series of general rules of administrative law which in distinction from those we have just considered may be called relative or conditional statutes.[34]

Under conditional statutes, administrators are called on to interpret the "will of the state. "In the case of conditional statutes, the administration has not merely to execute the state's will, but has as well to participate in its expression as to the details which have not been regulated by the legislature."[35]

Goodnow feared that abuses of discretion might be a problem even with efforts to control them, but he was willing to concede that at some point the requirements of administration are sufficiently important to justify some inconvenience to individuals in their dealings with administrators. Government, after all, involves the balancing of priorities. For Goodnow, the priorities were: (1) efficient operation of the people's business; (2) the protection of individual rights and interests; and (3) efforts to achieve the general goals of social welfare.

John Dickinson, writing some years later, arrayed the priorities somewhat differently than Goodnow.[36] He suggested that the law is an instrument designed to protect the individual from government.[37] Hence, individual rights and liberties are prior to administrative convenience or efficiency. Dickinson understood that there must be a significant number of administrative bodies and that these agencies will make determinations that affect the liberty and property interests of individuals. Nevertheless, he found several major aspects of the developing administrative law in need of reform.

First, he found that the existing administrative structure lacked a clear set of regular procedures sufficient to satisfy even the most charitable view of the requirements of the rule of law. "Summarizing, we can say that a regime of law requires a logically coherent system of general rules based on precedent and accepted principles of justice."[38] He saw no such logically coherent system in administrative law. Second, where he found something that approximated due process protections, Dickinson viewed the protections for the citizen to be less acceptable than those available in law courts. Common law rules of evidence and authority did not apply in a formal sense.[39] Jury trials weren't available. The rules by which disputes were to be governed were often developed in the course of the resolution of the matter rather than before the fact. Third, unlike judges, administrators who drafted rules and decided cases enjoyed little independence from government or politics. Finally, the very expertise that made administrators effective rendered them myopic when it came time to draft rules of general applicability.[40]

After a long and careful analysis, Dickinson recognized the legitimacy of agencies and the administrative justice system subject to certain conditions. Administrative procedure must be regularized. Minimum due process protections must be available. A full judicial review of agency decisions must always be available as a check. "Administrative justice exists in defiance of the supremacy of law only in so far as administrative adjudications are final or conclusive and not subject to corrections by a law court."[41]

Writing in 1928, Ernst Freund suggested that administrative law was necessary, but that the problem of its inclusion in the American system of justice was the need to find and maintain appropriate grants of and limitations on administrative power.[42] In his works, Freund was interested in setting limits on discretion while allowing sufficient latitude to ensure the effective operation of government. He was primarily concerned that the legislature should be the body to limit power by ensuring the preparation of statutes that would structure and limit discretion.

In a major study published in 1917, *Standards of American Legislation*, Freund discussed some of the events and problems that required Congress to become more active in drafting new measures for regulatory purposes and to meet demands for social welfare programs.[43] In the early days it was possible for neighbors or businessmen to obtain relief in court through common law suits for fraud or nuisance.[44] But as the society changed and grew individual remedies became less feasible and legislatures were called on for regulatory legislation that required administrators for enforcement. Freund argued that the courts' inability or unwillingness to come to grips with changing social, political and economic reality added to the pressure on the legislatures.[45] But Freund was also aware that the legislatures faced the problem of drafting major legislation in a period of laissez faire economics, when many judges would carefully scrutinize regulatory or social welfare statutes for weaknesses that would lead to their demise.

In his *Administrative Powers over Persons and Property*, Freund went further to suggest that legislatures had to construct statutes carefully to ensure that the necessary power granted to administrators would not be abused. He recognized two types of administrative power—control and service—and two means of exercising those powers—with and without discretion. Control powers could be subdivided into enabling powers and directing powers. Enabling powers are exemplified by licensing and the like. Directing powers, or "powers of corrective intervention," are those normally ascribed to regulatory administration. Freund touched only lightly on service powers, but at that time government services and problems associated with providing them were limited compared to contemporary administrative functions.

Freund used this typology of administrative powers as a framework to deal with uses and abuses of administrative discretion. He understood that administrative discretion must be viewed as a continuum with one end marked by a rigid impersonal system of rules bound to work hardship on those who are affected by them.[46] At the other end, one finds complete administrative arbitrariness; what Freund refers to as the "principle of unfreedom."[47] Some discretion is necessary.

The plausible argument in favor of administrative discretion is that it individualizes the exercise of public power over private interests, permitting the adjustment of varying circumstances and avoiding undesirable standardization of restraints, disqualifications, and particularly of government.[48]

By understanding the types of power and the methods of their use and abuse, legislators can draft laws that will meet the needs for which they are created and will be administered with the appropriate degree of properly exercised discretion.

In summary, the early period of administrative law and administration presented the problems and the terms of political, social, and economic discourse for the years to come. Dicey's denial of the possibility of administrative law gave way to Dickinson's demand for justice with law through procedural reform and judicial review in administration. Goodnow and Freund made clear the reasons for the new body of law, but also raised some of the important theoretical problems that must be dealt with in constructing an acceptable administrative justice system. All recognized the need to deal with administrative discretion. However, just as the theoretical development of the field began to gain momentum, the Great Depression diverted attention to day-to-day problems in administration.

THE GOLDEN AGE OF ADMINISTRATIVE TRIBUNALS: 1928–1950

The years from the onset of the Great Depression through the early post-World War II years were marked by a veritable explosion of administrative activity. This dramatic increase, coupled with problems noted by the authors of the earlier period, brought attempts at reform and development in administrative law. Those efforts gave rise to sharp disagreements in the literature over the new, decidedly pragmatic, approach to administrative law.

The New Deal and Administrative Law Problems

The stock market crash of 1929 was of seminal importance for law and administration for a variety of reasons. It demonstrated the complexity and interrelatedness of the society which, until then, had prided itself on rugged individualism. Hard-working, conscientious men and women lost everything just as quickly and painfully as did the market manipulators and others who had engaged in what has been termed "predatory finance."[49] The crash also showed that while the market system did many things very well, it required some policing to ensure that the competition was indeed fair and open.[50] By the time Franklin Roosevelt took office, President Hoover's assurances that this was merely a temporary downturn in the economy, a time of market correction, was unacceptable. The government was expected to do something about the state of the economy and the social consequences of the depression.[51] President Roosevelt felt an obligation to try new techniques to meet these demands: "The country needs, and unless I mistake its temper, the country demands bold, persistent experimentation. It is common sense to take a method and try it: If it fails, admit it frankly and try another. But above all, try something."[52]

The Roosevelt administration moved on two fronts. It sought to stabilize the marketplace through several types of legislative programs including bank regulation, market regulation, agricultural incentives and controls, codes of competition developed by members of the business community under provisions of the National Industrial Recovery Act, and related policies. FDR and his colleagues also moved on the social welfare front with jobs programs and other techniques designed to realize more personal security for individuals than could be provided within the twentieth-century American market economy.[53]

Many of the statutes enacted by the Congress during the New Deal, such as the Securities and Exchange Act, the Public Utility Holding Company Act, the Federal Power Commission legislation, and agricultural market legislation, were products of the investigations conducted and policies advocated during the twenties. But there is no doubt that the broad jurisdiction administrative agencies of the New Deal marked a new era in public administration by virtue of the size and scope of operations.

The New Deal is often thought of as two related though distinct periods, the first and second New Deals. The dividing point is roughly set at the 1936 presidential campaign. During the first part of the New Deal there was a relatively high degree of cooperation between the federal government and the business community. After the markets stabilized and economic recovery was under way, more private sector groups became disenchanted with programs and agencies established after the crash. They were no happier about other regulatory programs that had their beginnings in earlier years but were implemented during the New Deal, such as the Securities and Exchange Commission. The decline of cooperative spirit turned into outright conflict by 1936, with Roosevelt building his campaign around opposition to those he referred to as "economic royalists."[54]

The breakpoint is also important because it marked a turning point in the relationship between the Supreme Court and the New Deal administration and Congress. Before the so-called "switch in time that saved nine," the Court had been dominated by a group of justices trained and appointed at the high point of laissez faire economic and political fervor. Citing abuses of the commerce power, the taxing and spending powers, and other provisions of the Constitution, the Court struck down several major New Deal programs.[55] However, two members of the Court switched their position on some of the powers of the Congress and FDR was able during the latter years of the New Deal to appoint a majority of the members of the Court, making the second New Deal a much more philosophically favorable forum for New Deal programs.[56]

The onset of World War II meant mobilization of the entire nation. Such a task required administration on an unprecedented scale. Mobilization further blurred the lines between the public and private sectors of the economy. Government contracting and government-supported scientific research and development became major areas of growth.

The end of the war, however, did not mean the end of the administrative programs created to deal with the conflagration. Education, housing, and employment were needed for thousands of returning veterans. The arrival of the United States on the scene of international politics brought with it requirements for American aid in restoring the nations ravaged by war. The birth of the nuclear age created an awesome responsibility to administer peacetime uses of fissionable materials. As the nation entered the 1950s, the questions presented for discussion were whether the administrative branches of government were equal to the tasks before them and whether the law provided sufficient safeguards to ensure that a government powerful enough to meet modern needs could be controlled.

In May 1933, the Executive Committee of the American Bar Association created the Special Committee on Administrative Law to come to grips with the administration explosion. Louis G. Caldwell, chairman of the committee, opened his remarks to the first session of the Special Committee by obeserving:

> The first Session of the 73rd Congress . . . left more than the usual quota of footprints in the field assigned to our committee. If fact, last spring witnessed a more formidable legislative output than has ever before found its way into the statutes at large in time of peace.[57]

As Caldwell and his colleagues went to work, it became clear that the overriding theme of the gathering was the fear of burgeoning administrative power without clear constraints on that power sufficient to ensure responsiveness and responsibility of those in administrative positions. It was recognized that one reason for the increase in administrative tribunals was dissatisfaction with orthodox judicial proceedings and legislative actions and the need for continuity and expertness in administration.[58] Caldwell announced his intention that the committee should place the bridle of the rule of law on government agencies.[59] The conference began a study of the administrative process to be used as a basis for regularizing administrative procedure and clarifying standards for judicial review of agency decisions.

Progress in reforming the administrative justice system was slow for the next several years. Pressure for change increased with the change in the political and economic climate of the second New Deal. The Brownlow Commission criticized the agencies as a "headless fourth branch of government."[60] Roosevelt rejected that assessment and directed the Attorney General to appoint a study commission to perform a complete analysis on the state of the administrative justice system and provide recommendations. The Attorney General's Committee on Administrative Procedure was created in February 1939.[61] The committee, like other groups studying the topic, approached the subject with the assumption that the most effective way to deal with public law and public administration problems was by examining and modifying administrative procedures used in adjudications done by agencies, the procedural aspects of administrative rulemaking, and problems of judicial review of agency actions.[62]

The report of the Attorney General's Committee was published in 1941.[63] The most extensive and authoritative study produced during this period, the report had three major consequences. First, it suggested that the administrative system could be usefully and adequately dealt with by a statutory formulation of administrative procedure, which would (1) address rulemaking, adjudications, the nature and scope of judicial review, and matters related to the form and content of administrative rulings, and (2) establish the role and responsibility of the hearing examiners who conducted many administrative proceedings. Those suggestions were enacted into law as the McCarren-Summers Bill, now more commonly known as the Administrative Procedure Act.[64]

Although the commitee never claimed that its recommendations would solve all the problems of law and administration, the statute that resulted was the only source of law that specifically applied to most areas of administrative decisionmaking by most agencies of the federal government. The APA has, unfortunately, come to be thought of as a kind of constitution of administrative law and the report itself as an administrative treatise analogous to Farrand's *Records of the Federal Convention of 1787.*[65] In any event, the report was a superior piece of work on law and administration and as such deserves consideration as one of the most important pieces of literature in law and administration of that period.

Literary Conflict over Administrative Law Development

The efforts to develop an adequate system of administrative justice were carried out amidst a hard-fought conflict, much of it conducted in the legal literature and court opinions. The disagreement reflected the political and economic tensions of the New Deal years. Surprisingly, the discussion tended to ignore much of the literature published earlier and the history of administration before the creation of the Interstate Commerce Commission in 1887.[66] Also rather surprising was the fact that on both sides most of the arguments were fairly narrowly drawn with a certain pragmatism, explicit in some works and implicit but still present in others. Perhaps these characteristics can be explained by the fact that the debate over the legitimacy of administrative agencies and the proposed methods to control their activities was literally a battle of professional advocates.

In general terms, the critics of administrative law as it existed during this period made two major arguments.[67] The first was that administrative agencies with the power to make rules that carried the force of law were unconstitutional because they operated on the basis of unconstitutional delegations of legislative power. The intensity of this argument varied from those who said that any authorization of rulemaking power to nonelected civil servants and political appointees exceeded the legislative power of Congress, to those who grudgingly accepted the need to delegate some authority to fill in the ambiguous terms of statutes enacted by Congress, but refused to accept broad standardless delegations of authority to administer a particular policy area in "the public interest."

The argument ran along the following lines. An administrative agency exists by virtue of the statute that created it. The powers delegated to the agency by the legislature define the boundaries of agency activity. Similarly, the legislature has only the powers delegated to it by the people through the Constitution. A long standing legal maxim holds that a person who possesses a delegated power may not delegate away the power given to him. The people delegated the power to make laws to the legislature and that power may not be delegated away to an administrative agency. In addition to being an abuse of the legislative power, such a grant of authority to the agency would violate the separation of powers since the agency would have the power to make and enforce the law.[68] The less strident nondelegation partisans admitted some delegation was necessary because the legislature could not make sufficiently detailed statutes for all future circumstances, but they could and should do more than give administrators a blank check.

The second major attack on the rise of administrative law focused on a perceived violation of the rule of law arising from a lack of court-like protections in administrative adjudications and the so-called "combination-of-functions" problem.[69] Combination of functions referred to the fact that many of the agencies made rules, enforced the rules, and then adjudicated disputes arising from enforcement of the rules.

Criticism hit a high point with the "headless fourth branch" condemnation by the Brownlow Commission. James M. Landis, a leading New Dealer and member of the Securities and Exchange Commission, entered the lists in defense of administrative processes.[70] Landis began with the premise that administrative powers grew in part because of the deficiencies of the judiciary and the legislature. "Without much political theory but with a keen sense of the practicalities of the situation, agencies were created whose functions embraced the three aspects of government."[71] Specifically, Landis argued that efficient and effective responses to problems of administering the people's business could only be achieved by experts with an ongoing interest in particular policy areas. These expert administrators must have some discretion to accomplish their tasks.[72] Responding to the argument against delegation of authority, he asserted that there are tasks which government must perform. As the society becomes more complex, those tasks multiply. When legislators identify a matter that requires government action, one of two factors may result in a rather broad grant of discretion to administrators to deal with the problem. First, the issue (e.g., health code administration) may be so complex that legislators cannot possibly understand at the outset the many specific problems involved in administering a policy. Or, competing interests within the legislature may agree that some kind of policy and administrative mechanism is necessary, but they may not be able to achieve consensus on details. Rather than do nothing, the legislature settles on a general statute and vests the agency involved with considerable discretion to fill in the details.

In the end, Landis seemed satisfied that the existing checks were sufficient to prevent administrative arbitrariness. He argued that because agencies specialize in rather narrow fields, they can be checked fairly quickly. Their discretion within that narrow range of activity is limited by statutes and subject to judicial review. Because judicial review is available, he asserted, administrators will take care to provide reasoned opinions in support of their decisions.

The next major defense of administrative justice came with the publication of the report of the Attorney General's Committee in 1941. On the way to its conclusions about regularization of procedures, the report noted several important aspects of law and administration worthy of further consideration. First, the committee recognized a central dilemma of administrative law. There is a basic conflict between those who demand complete standardization of procedures like that expected in the judicial system and those who argue for more flexibility so that administrators may use their expertise in the changing administrative environment to accomplish the purposes for which their agencies were created. The committee recognized that neither extreme was acceptable.

Second, the committee emphasized a generally unstated fact. Most cases that arise in administrative law are disposed informally rather than by formal procedures. The committee went so far as to label informal procedures the "lifeblood of the administrative process."[73] Third, and somewhat related to the prevalence of informal proceedings, administrative disputes involve more than two parties. It is one thing for an administrator to produce a decision satisfactory to the person or group before an agency as well as the administrator, but quite another if the finding comes at the expense of the public interest. Since most such decisions are not made in public proceedings, it is difficult to ensure that all interests are adequately protected.

Procedural regularity should help check abuses, as should judicial review, but both are better devices to ensure protection for individual participants in a dispute than they are controls to ensure that agencies are sufficiently vigorous in administering policy.[74] Ultimately, the committee sought refuge from administrative arbitrariness in the time-honored legal commandments of procedural regularity, due process, and judicial review.

Probably the strongest defense of the contemporary administrative system was written by the director of the study for the Attorney General's Committee, Walter Gellhorn.[75] Gellhorn, like Landis, began with the premise that the large-scale administrative state exists because circumstances and existing weaknesses in traditional government structures require it.[76] The developing approach to administration and law offered expertise, continuity (which he preferred to call "specialization"), and understanding or sympathetic administration.[77] It also made possible the processing of the huge volume of disputes before the government. Gellhorn saw contemporary administrative law in the third phase of its development. The first stage was a struggle over the legitimacy of administrative law as a field of law. The second was an inevitable growth of administration, accompanied by a call for strict judicial review. The third phase was the development of administrative procedure. He thought that development had gone well and he defended it with vigor. Gellhorn felt that the greatest danger was that critics of administration would succeed in overjudicializing the administrative process. He argued that courts and agencies perform different government roles and should have different procedures tailored to their respective functions. Specifically, he argued in favor of informal proceedings and for flexible elements in formal proceedings. He asserted that most of the combination-of-functions arguments concerning rulemaking, enforcement, and adjudication are based on gross generalization. In the first place, Gellhorn wrote, most agencies have no prosecutorial powers, and those that do rarely use them. Even where such cases arise, he contended that there was no more reason to suspect administrators of bias or arbitrariness than judges. Beyond that, the combination-of-functions argument assumes that agencies are monoliths when in fact they are highly complex structures with many parts and some structural and operational separations among their various divisions.[78] Gellhorn summarized his view nicely as follows:

> I have attempted to show that neither the existence nor the form of the Federal administrative machinery is in itself an alarming phenomenon. To be sure, there is a danger that any power, once granted, may be abused by its possessor. Having recognized that fact, however, we need not conclude that power must be wholly withheld. In each instance we must decide whether the intended objective of Federal control is important enough to warrant assuming the inherent risks of mis-government. . . . What is needed today is alert determination that the agencies shall in purpose and in method prove themselves to be efficient instruments of democratic government.[79]

Like Gellhorn, Jerome Frank was fearful of overjudicialization of the administrative process. The government and the critics of administration might "substitute a 'lawyercracy' for democracy, to turn our entire government into a government of lawyers, or a government solely by the judiciary."[80] He took issue with the idea that rigid procedural guidelines would be helpful. Those who demanded rigorous checks and denied the validity of the role performed by agencies on grounds that they threatened the rule of law were, in Frank's view, infatuated with the words "a nation of laws and not of men." What is needed, he wrote was "a government of laws administered by the right kind of men."[81]

> Curiously, it often happens that the very men who one day stress that truth [that public officers are human], the next day help to obscure it, by distorting the real truth contained in the phrase "a government of laws, and not of men." . . . Hypnotized by those words, we picture as an existing reality—or at least as a completely achievable ideal—a government so contrived that it matters not at all what men, at any given moment, constitute government. Such an idea is a narcotic. It is bad medicine. It does not protect us from bad government. On the contrary, it invites bad government.[82]

He argued that when one examines specific operations of particular agencies, it becomes clear that administrators are no more or no less trustworthy than judges. To the degree that the discussion focuses on the discretion used by administrators, Frank argued that it was often not the administrator who sought to exercise his (or her) own discretion, but rather the agency's clientele, who wanted individual, differential treatment for each case. In his view, the federal government was in fact fairly meeting the requirements of basic democratic values, maintaining a balance between government power sufficient to accomplish its tasks and limits on government adequate to the maintenance of individual liberty.[83]

> It is imperative that in a democracy it should never be forgotten that public office is, of necessity, held by mere men who have human frailties. . . . To pretend, then, that government, in any of its phases, is a machine—that it is not a human affair; that the language of statutes—if only they are adequately worded—plus appeals to the upper courts, will alone do away with the effect of human weaknesses in government officials is to worship illusion. And it is a dangerous illusion.[84]

The eminent jurisprudential scholar Roscoe Pound responded to such arguments in his *Administrative Law: Its Growth, Procedure and Significance*.[85] Dean Pound set out to bury the debate over whether there can be such a thing as a powerful administrative system within a democracy. He was willing to dispose of the separation-of-powers arguments about delegation of power. Administrative agencies had "very real grievances against the common law and judicial review as developed under the common law in the United States." The imposition of overly strict rules of evidence in some areas and complete retrials on judicial review had placed intolerable burdens on administrative actions. Pound agreed that there was a need for flexibility and expertise, but he was not prepared to allow the relative youth of the field and the need for flexibility to excuse the denial of basic justice. "I am not here to preach a going back to eighteenth-century doctrines of natural rights and natural law as such. But I do insist upon the role of ideals."[86] Any body of law must be based on "a set of received ideals." The primary problem lay not in the argument over details on how to provide instrumental checks on administrators, but rather in that there was no consensus on the ideals for administrative law. In Pound's view, the nation was experiencing a "time of transition when men are struggling to adapt the machinery of justice to new conditions imperfectly grasped . . . seek[ing] short cuts through a reversion to justice without law—not without a judicial or administrative process, of course, but without authoritative precepts or an authoritative technique of applying them."[87] Until such a theoretical foundation could be established, Pound argued that judicial review would have to be used carefully and effectively to guard against abuses in the name of efficiency or expertise.

> I am not attacking administration as a means of government in the society of today nor deploring the rise of administrative justice and delegation to standards, or determinations of fact necessary to the exercise of their functions. But administration is not all of the ordering of human relations. We may pay too high a price for efficiency. We must pay a certain price for freedom; and a reasonable balance between efficiency and individual rights is that price. If the balance does not leave absolute power to administrative agencies, it does not follow that it may not leave them enough power to function intelligently and efficiently under a government of laws and not men. I grant that a government of law must yet be a government of men. Laws govern as they are applied by men. But they may and should be applied by men according to law.[88]

The years from 1928 to 1950 may have been golden years for administrative tribunals, but a great deal of heat was engendered by the process by which the gilt was polished. The views of the efficacy of administrative law and means necessary to accomplish public purposes within the bounds of law ranged from those who rejected outright the legitimacy of the administrative justice system, notwithstanding the significant body of literature developed in the earlier years, to those who were afraid that needed discretion and flexibility would be strangled by rigid procedural requirements and exhaustive judicial review.

The ardent foes of administration were doomed from the outset. The delegation-of-powers argument had been settled years before. The first Congress gave the president authority to administer benefits to veterans of the Revolutionary War under such regulations as he saw fit to issue. In 1813, in the case of *The Brig Aurora*, the Supreme Court sanctioned the principle of delegation by the Congress.[89] Since the early years, the delegation doctrine had been tested repeatedly.[90] Administrative actions were sustained in all but three major cases, two involving the National Industrial Recovery Act; *Panama Refining Co. v. Ryan*[91] and *Schechter Poultry Corp. v. United States*.[92] The other case was in the area of coal mining.[93] The combination-of-functions argument was met in the Administrative Procedure Act by including protection for the independence of hearing examiners. Procedural regularity, due process provisions, and some availability of judicial review, although not as much as such critics as Pound would have liked, was also provided by the APA.

But the Administrative Procedure Act was a limited starting point for administrative law development. Narrow and procedural, it lacked the kind of consensus on larger ideals sought by Pound. With its enactment a new concern arose: whether the APA would be interpreted in such a manner as to render administrative agencies impotent.[94] Would the APA be sufficient to protect against abuses of power or would it prevent agencies from accomplishing the tasks for which they were designed?

FROM THE NEW DEAL TO THE NEW FEDERALISM: LAW AND ADMINISTRATION, 1950–1969

The years from early post-World War II demobilization through the decades of the 1950s and the turbulent '60s were years of important development in law and administration. They were years of testing the Administrative Procedure Act approach to problems facing administrators in a complex administrative environment and those facing individuals and groups attempting to deal with those administrators. By 1969, the APA approach would be found wanting and the search would be under way for new answers. The evaluation of the operation of the administrative justice system during this period was affected by a reordering of academic priorities and methodologies. In government and in the larger legal community, authors who were once ardent defenders of existing administrative law became its strongest critics.

Toward a New Administrative Environment

In his history of the years 1945 to 1960, Eric Goldman wrote:

> Beneath everything, two critically important questions were pressing to be answered. One of the questions concerned affairs inside the United States: would America continue through extensions of the welfare state and welfare capitalism and through a variety of other techniques, the economic and social revolution which had marked the previous decades? The other question concerned foreign affairs: would the United States keep moving along the path marked out in the early Truman Years, a path suggested by the words "containment" and "coexistence" and one which represented a sharp departure from deep-seated American traditions?[95]

The attempt to answer these two questions shaped the environment of administration.

The war ended, but international concerns still demanded the nation's attention. The Cold War was beginning. A somewhat warmer conflict was brewing in Washington, where President Truman found himself battling congressional opponents.[96] For Truman, it was one crisis after another; Alger Hiss, Israel, China, the Berlin blockade, Joe McCarthy, and Korea. When these issues captured the national limelight, administrative problems declined in importance on the policy agenda.

Truman attempted to make some headway on the administrative front by calling on Herbert Hoover. The President, who had great respect for Mr. Hoover, called for a commission to study the federal administrative establishment. Congress, with a unanimous vote for the Lodge–Brown Act[97] in July 1947, created the President's Commission on Organization of the Executive Branch of Government, more popularly known as the Hoover Commission.[98] The commission's report, delivered in February 1949, called for a more streamlined administration organized to be more responsive to presidential direction.[99] Although it deferred to the 1941 Report of the Attorney General's Committee on most matters of administrative law, the report concluded: "Administrative justice today unfortunately is not characterized by economy, simplicity, and dispatch. It remains, however, a necessity in our complex economic system."[100] The commission recommended an administrative conference for further study.

By 1953 when President Eisenhower took office, there had been a number of calls for a conference on administrative law problems. As a result, questions of law and administration were included in the second Hoover Commission report, the result of the commission's work from 1953–1955.[101] The commission established the Task Force on Legal Services and Procedures staffed by leading legal scholars, several of whom had served on the Attorney General's Committee and had been instrumental in enactment of the APA.[102] The second report, which will be treated in more detail later, was highly critical of the administrative justice system and issued seventy-four separate recommendations for change. Among these was a call for a major administrative conference. Congress was not generally receptive to the recommendations of the second Hoover Commission, and those advanced by the Task Force on Legal Services and Procedures fared no better than the rest.[103] The American Bar Association seemed content with the status quo; reports of meetings during this period suggest that the bar was more interested in settling into practice under the APA than in major change.[104]

The 1950s were marked by a plethora of important political, economic, and social developments. Major Supreme Court desegregation rulings were as controversial as they were necessary.[105] Joe McCarthy did not last long as a Senate power, but others on the House Un-American Activities Committee carried on the campaign of fear and intimidation with loyalty programs and strained security investigations threatening government workers.[106] In addition to foreign policy crises in Europe and the Middle East, Eisenhower was faced with a vexing administrative problem in this country: control over the growth of technology. When he left office, the President warned of the problems of administering a burgeoning military-industrial complex.

In the late 1950s there was a dramatic shift in importance in administration from regulatory administration to social service delivery. Development of health, safety, and other social services had begun earlier at the local level with the Progressive era providing a particular impetus for urban reform. But social service problems during the Depression and the two wars that followed were national in scope and required national assistance. Suburban housing development became important. New parts of the country felt growing pains as servicemen relocated families to the West Coast and other places they had seen during their service days.[107] Veterans' housing, health, and educational benefits created administrative problems that were complex and numerous. By the late 1950s the baby boom came to school, and the need for capital expenditures for schools, costs of training teachers, and attempts to ensure some uniformity in education practices added to the strain on public administration. During this period the Social Security Administration also began to experience an increase in its workload with the enactment of the Social Security Disability Program and increases in other programs.[108]

John F. Kennedy assumed office with the best intentions of examining and responding to problems of law and administration, as indicated first by his call for a major study with specific recommendations and later by his appointment of an administrative conference. Unfortunately, attention was again diverted by events abroad. It was post time for the space race. Kennedy's international relations skills were tested by the Soviet Union. The world went to the brink of nuclear war in the Cuban missile crisis. Other important issues during Kennedy's administration included the intensification of civil rights efforts, the Bay of Pigs fiasco, and growing involvement in the conflict in Southeast Asia.

The Johnson years saw dramatic increases in administrative activity. In particular, the "War on Poverty," which Johnson pursued as one of several routes to the Great Society, was waged in part by the use of grants and contracts which increased the complexity of intergovernmental relations.[109] The war in Vietnam, enactment and implementation of the Civil Rights Act, domestic unrest, and continued strain on human services in all areas added task after task to an already strained administrative state. Again, many of these tasks were as controversial and as difficult as they were necessary. The burgeoning growth in science and technology, spurred by the goal of placing a man on the moon before the decade ended, and war mobilization had positive and negative consequences. Among the positive results was development of electronic technology, which advanced the state of the art in a variety of areas, but none so dramatically as the field of automated data processing. But that progress had disadvantages as well. The increased use of computers meant the development of massive data banks with information about all aspects of one's life.[110] The decade came to an end with growing political and social turmoil. The future was very much in doubt.

Intellectual Fragmentation on Administrative Law Development

Writing in 1950, James Hart asserted:

> The relationship of administrative justice to the supremacy of law is, however, but the lawyer's way of expressing the central problem not only of administrative law, but of political science as a whole. In abstract terms, that problem is the adjustment of authority and liberty. At the relatively concrete level of administrative law, it may be called the adjustment of the public and the private interest. The student who fails to approach administrative law in terms of this problem will fail to see the subject as part of political science and hence will be unable to make intelligent administrative law judgments."[111]

The relationship between practice and theory, problems of making day-to-day adjustments of the public and private interests in administration, and the interconnections among law, public administration, and political science are all important ingredients of a balanced and comprehensive perspective on the problems of public law and public administration. Unfortunately, for a variety of reasons, that synthesis of views and concepts broke down, with important consequences for the manner in which the administrative justice system operated, was evaluated, and ultimately modified.

The attempts to meld theory and practice of administrative law development had already begun to break down during the 1930s, as Gellhorn, Landis, and others insisted that practice, not theory, should shape and must control the administrative process. Despite the criticisms of writers like Dean Pound, many observers felt that the practical or instrumental view of administrative law prevailed and was enacted into law as the Administrative Procedure Act. Problems of adjustment of authority and liberty, or of adjustment between public and private interests, had been remedied as much as they were going to be by regularizing procedures, specifying rules of due process, and making judicial review available in some areas of administrative activity. The task for someone proceeding from an analytical jurisprudence base was to carefully develop a logically coherent system of rules and categories for problem solving from the initial set of statutory requirements. That task, and establishing its own role in the administrative justice system, is precisely what the legal community turned to during the 1950s and '60s.

Political science had no such unity of purpose or perspective in the postwar years. The two subfields of that discipline most concerned with administrative law were experiencing major changes which took both in directions that meant a break with the lawyers and an abandonment of important administrative law questions.

Public administration was undergoing an "identity crisis."[112] For a number of reasons, public administrators wanted to establish the field as a unique area of practice and study. In the preface to his now famous work, *Introduction to the Study of Public Administration*, Leonard D. White asserted that "the study of administration should start from the base of management rather than the foundation of law."[113] His attitude was at least in part a response to the existing overemphasis on law by those interested in the study and practice of public administration. It was also a reaction to the domination of the public service by those with legal training.[114] After all, efficiency was the new end of administration since the scientific management movement had appeared on the scene.[115] The need for change became apparent following postwar publication of the seminal works by Dwight Waldo[116] and Herbert Simon,[117] which sought to bring public administration to a more mature level. Based on the work of Simon and others, administration grew as a generic area of study that sought to avoid exclusive identification with either public administration or business administration. The result was that public administrators had little time or page space for administrative law matters during the 1950s and '60s. An additional influence was the fact that schools that continued to teach administrative law (and over the years the number dwindled at which the subject was required) tended to use law school materials or to favor books on the regulatory environment of business. By 1968, Waldo concluded that the antilaw bias had gone too far:

> Perhaps I have been subverted by two years of association with the Continental administration, but I am of the opinion that we now suffer from lack of attention to constitutional-legal matters. Our early antilegal and antilawyer bias is understandable and forgivable, but it is dangerously obsolete and self-defeating.[118]

Political science, as a discipline, was also undergoing a postwar change. The new direction was oriented toward process and based on a behavioral methodology and conceptual framework that avoided normative concerns. More predictive research was favored, focused on political activity by groups rather than substantive policy decisions made by specific individuals or issued by particular institutions. In the subfield known as public law there were two important developments. First, public law declined in popularity, compared with other subfields.[119] Second, it followed the track of the larger discipline by becoming "Bentleyan, behavioristic and process oriented."[120] As a result, questions on the substantive development of law and administration attracted little scholarly attention.[121]

In summary, much of the literature on law and administration during these years was written by legal practitioners and some government investigators. It tended to take an analytical approach that stressed the need to clarify categories, concepts, and procedures in the APA.

The Administrative Procedure Act Under Pressure: Commentary and Criticism of the APA

The report of the Task Force on Legal Services and Procedure is important in part because of the substantive findings it presents and also because the task force was staffed by men who had been instrumental in administrative law during the 1950s and '60s. After examining nearly a decade of operation under the Administrative Procedure Act, the task force concluded that the administrative justice system was not operating satisfactorily.

> The task force examined the effectiveness of legal procedures under the Administrative Procedure Act enacted by Congress in 1946. It found that the statute had not always been implemented and followed by agencies in the executive branch to the extent intended by Congress and concluded that substantial amendments should be made to the act to strengthen it as the charter of due process of law in administration. [122]

The task force began with the premise that efficiency in administration requires efficient and effective legal practices with regard to relationships between one agency and another and between the agency and the citizen served by that agency. But at each stage of the report where the need for efficiency and effectiveness is stressed, an admonition is added: "Economy in Federal Government operations through improvements in legal procedures is an end earnestly sought by this task force. Procedural safeguards cannot be sacrificed to economy or efficiency."[123] The goal was efficiency, effectiveness, *and* fundamental fairness in administrative justice.

The report specifically rejected the conventional wisdom among administrators that wide discretion permits flexibility in administration, which in turn yields efficiency. On the contrary, discretionary authority may in fact result in inefficiency:

> Positive limitations should be imposed by statute upon the exercise of administrative powers, authority, or discretion, to the end that statutes are faithfully executed, the rights of the parties are fully protected, and the administration of matters committed to agency action is prompt, fair and efficient. [124]

The task force lamented the ad hoc manner in which agencies were established. Lack of planning and coordination had led to conflicts among federal agencies and between federal and state agencies. Even where no jurisdictional controversies arose, agency authority was vague because of the lack of standards in many of the statutes that created the agencies. [125]

The group saw the need for long-range congressional action to correct deficiencies in the administrative justice system, but urged self-help by administrators as the first step in the needed reform. Most urgent was the need for administrators to define the means by which their agencies planned to exercise their authority. The Administrative Procedure Act was constructed on the theory that agencies promulgate future policies through rulemaking or quasi-legislative procedures, and apply existing policies to current problems using quasi-judicial adjudicatory procedures. In practice, the task force found, agencies were not carefully articulating policy through rulemaking, but were loosely using adjudications to make policy and to resolve contemporary disputes. This common-law-development approach to administration might be less of a problem if the rule of *stare decisis,* or the binding effect of precedent, was followed as rigorously in administration as it was in the judiciary, but the task force found that agencies often took advantage of the less strenuous concept of precedent often applied to agencies:

> It is a manifest hardship to subject an individual to a penalty, or other sanction, for continuing to do that which for long was considered by him, and others, to be permissible under the law. Unfortunately, situations have arisen where, as a result of an adjudicatory proceeding initiated by an agency, a sanction has been imposed upon an individual for engaging in such conduct, even though no statute or rule had been enacted or promulgated specifically condemning it. . . . A clear inequity arises when persons rely in good faith upon authoritative agency opinions, only to be informed in subsequent proceedings that the opinion is not binding upon the agency.[126]

In sum, agencies should use rulemaking as much as possible to guide the public and should avoid policymaking through adjudication.[127]

Where agencies *do* adjudicate, they have a burden to ensure prompt action primarily because the expense of protracted administrative proceedings may effectively deny due process and fundamental fairness to the person before the agency. The task force urged that more be done to ensure that persons appearing before agencies be made more aware of their options and the nature of the process they are confronting.[128]

The task force also took note of some of the special problems of law and administration in the areas of social services and benefits. In 1941, Gellhorn had written that this might be a problem in administrative law, but that benefit claims only required a claimant to carry the burden of proving that he or she was eligible for the benefit claimed.[129] The task force, with the benefit of a study of several years of practice and a clearer perspective on postwar social programs, concluded that there was more at stake than proof by a claimant. There was more involved, they wrote, than the question of whether the claimant had a legal right to a benefit or was merely granted the benefit as a matter of privilege by the government. The report argued that the fairness and effectiveness of benefit claims case processing was a concern of citizens generally and not merely of those with claims. Benefit programs are based on legislative determinations of the public interest, and are funded from tax revenues. Therefore the people have a right to ensure that administrators execute the programs for the purpose and in the manner prescribed by the legislature.[130]

Given their observations of existing practices, the members of the task force concluded that, at least in the short term, judicial review would have to be relied on to ensure proper operation of the administrative justice system. "A plain, simple and prompt judicial remedy should be available for every legal wrong because of agency action or failure to act. Judicial controls over administrative action should be expanded and strengthened."[131]

James M. Landis was a member of the task force of the second Hoover

Commission. In fact, Landis had been the leading defender of the faith, administrator and a member of most of the major study groups that had examined administrative law since the 1930s. So it came as no surprise when President-elect Kennedy asked Landis to prepare a report on the state of administrative justice and make recommendations for upgrading existing practices. The Landis report was an indictment of the administrative justice system: "Effective procedural solutions, so necessary to the proper functioning of the administrative agencies, have admittedly not been achieved despite the sweeping studies which culminated in the Administrative Procedure Act of 1946 and the many studies which have followed."[132]

The *Report on Regulatory Agencies to the President-Elect* did not mince words.[133] Landis recognized the need for the agencies, the complexity of their work environment, and the stakes involved in the cases and policies with which they dealt. Even so, he was angry at the conduct, bordering on influence peddling, practiced by attorneys.[134] He was dissatisfied with the manner in which agencies had implemented procedural requirements. He felt that administrative law problems had effectively halted administrative planning and policy formulation. "Inordinate delay characterizes the disposition of adjudicatory proceedings before substantially all of our regulatory agencies."[135] If administrative law procedures had been developed to save time and money, they had failed.[136] Even with all of the complex procedures, Landis was not satisfied that agency decisions were characterized by fundamental fairness. In addition to political interference or unethical *ex parte* contacts with agency decisionmakers, he saw an increasing tendency toward institutional decisionmaking.

> Generalizations as to the organization of administrative agencies are not only difficult but dangerous to make. Unlike the judges of the federal judiciary, members of administrative commissions do not do their work.
> . . . But worse than this, it is a general belief founded on considerable evidence, that briefs of counsel, findings of hearing examiners, relevant portions of the basic records, are rarely read by the individuals theoretically responsible for the ultimate decisions.[137]

Landis made a number of suggestions to the President on ways to deal with some of the problems noted in his survey. But the more important result of this report was the complete reversal of one of the major proponents of the administrative procedure solution as to the problems of administrative justice. He had come full circle to the conclusion that much remained to be done before we could rest satisfied with the state of administrative law.[138]

Peter Woll was one of the few political scientists writing on law and administration during this period.[139] In his *Administrative Law: The Informal Process*,[140] Woll concentrated on the point made by the Attorney General's Committee in 1941, largely ignored since then, that informal procedures are "the lifeblood" of the administrative process. With some of the earlier writers, Woll acknowledged the key words of administrative law from the administrators' perspective: speed, flexibility, cost effectiveness, continuity expertise, and sympathetic administration.[141] "Congress and the judiciary have voluntarily relinquished power and permitted the broad exercise of discretion on the part of administrators."[142]

Woll asserted that "requirements of public policy, expertise, and speed have rendered administrative adjudication today primarily informal in nature."[143] Even in cases where agencies are involved in adversary processes or adjudications, Woll argues, "full-fledged legal procedure is rarely employed."[144] His survey of agency workloads suggested that informal conferences and other devices had become alternatives to formal procedures. Even where formal procedures were used, informal agreements developed in prehearing conferences were used to limit the scope of the formal proceedings. He concluded that the gradual increase in the use of informal processes had been accepted because it was assumed that a person dissatisfied with agency actions would have recourse to all the protections of the formal process. But Woll found that for reasons of cost and time there was some doubt about the availability of alternatives; indeed, informal process had "replaced" formal procedures.[145]

> Because of the widespread use of informal procedures in the administrative process, it is no longer possible to say that private parties subject to the jurisdiction of administrative agencies have recourse to traditional adjudicative procedure to settle their cases.[146]

He was critical of those who had spent so much time on problems of administrative law without understanding that the majority of administrative justice activity is informal and has little to do with narrow debates over close interpretation of the Administrative Procedure Act. To those who would propose reforms for administrative law, Woll advised a balanced perspective that recognized the complaints of those before agencies, but also included concern for the problems faced by administrators.[147]

Dissatisfaction of many with implementation of the APA, the apparent unwillingness of Congress to develop innovative reforms for administrative law, and the ambiguity of the contemporary administrative environment, led many writers in the 1950s and 1960s to focus on judicial review as the centerpiece of administrative justice.[148] Judges continued to defer to the expertise of administrators, imposing relatively mild forms of review on agency decisions.[149] The debate over whether that situation should change was the focus of much of the literature in law reviews during this period.

One of the most prominent authors writing on administrative law was Kenneth Culp Davis. Davis's first major work was his 1951 treatise.[150] In that pathbreaking work, Davis set out to develop a body of administrative law based on the Administrative Procedure Act with elaborations that sought to give guidance to judges and attorneys in this developing area of the law. By the late 1950s Davis's categories of administrative process, based on the APA, court decisions, and his own thinking, had grown into the multivolume *Administrative Law Treatise*, later updated by regular supplements.[151]

Davis was relatively satisfied with the APA approach to operation of the administrative justice system and was engaged in the task of refining that body of law. Among other things, this work led Davis to conclude that there were areas of administrative law activity that were not subject to judicial review "even for arbitrariness or abuse of discretion."[152] Davis's assertions touched off a decade of debate with writers like Louis Jaffe,[153] who argued that public administration depended for its legitimacy on judicial review as well as regular procedures and minimal due process protections. Davis's leading adversary was Raoul Berger. Davis based his argument primarily on statutory grounds, but it was precisely that narrowness that drew Berger's fire.[154] Berger argued that no statute could justify arbitrary government action, prohibited in his view by the Constitution and principles of justice.

The debate reflects some of the larger problems of this period. Davis made a great many contributions to the day-to-day development of the guidelines needed to deal with ongoing problems that could not await the promulgation of a new administrative law. Berger and others, dissatisfied by what they saw as the narrow APA approach to administrative justice, recognized that a broader approach was necessary if administrative law was to succeed in the long run in integrating emerging law into the larger legal and governmental system. For both practical and theoretical reasons, the administrative justice system had been found wanting. But all agreed that administrative law had to grow. Since 1969 there has been a search for incremental reforms and attempts at experimentation with those reforms.

ADMINISTRATIVE JUSTICE IN THE CONTEMPORARY CONTEXT: SINCE 1969

The decade of the 1970s was a period of rapid change in law and administration. In part the changes resulted from a number of historic events that followed in quick succession. Other developments arose from deliberate attempts to deal with problems vividly demonstrated during the 1960s. Like most changes in law and politics, these changes will affect "who gets what, where, when, and how," as Lasswell put it in his definition of politics. It is too early to tell what the results of the wave of renewed attention to problems of law and administration will be, but one can at least note the trends and the criticisms.

Administrative Environment Shaped by Conflict

Richard Nixon came to the White House at a turbulent time. The mood of the population alternated between fear and anger, aroused by both foreign and domestic concerns. There was an unpopular war in Vietnam and social activism in the streets at home. United States prestige declined abroad. In this country, citizens locked and bolted doors, installed burglar alarms, and armed themselves in an unprecedented manner. The fear of violent crime brought cries for tougher law enforcement, which resulted in more policy for government to implement, such as the Omnibus Crime Control and Safe Streets Act and the creation of the Law Enforcement Assistance Administration.[155]

In addition, a number of political movements were growing. Environmental interests, women's groups, Chicanos, Blacks, and poverty organizations came to the seat of government on some occasions, took to the streets on others, and became increasingly sophisticated in the use of litigation as another forum for interest group conflict. Soon it could be said that legal challenge and response was a predictable part of any major policy activity.

The Nixon administration pronounced the Great Society a failure and substituted for it the New Federalism, which purported to return decisionmaking in social programs and other policy areas to states and local governments.[156] The dismantling of the Great Society meant transfer of essential services to other levels of government, and with this came revenue sharing and other complex grant programs.

While the President's men were engaged in eliminating some agencies, Congress and the administration itself were responding to new demands for regulation in consumer product safety, occupational health and safety, and environmental quality with the establishment of new agencies.

The problems of administration had changed. The government faced an increasingly complicated intergovernmental environment and heavy social service demands. Administrative programs, services, regulatory devices, and benefit claims processes had all become politicized. Even so, it might have been possible to employ new techniques of administration to reduce governmental confusion—but for Watergate and the energy crisis.

The nation was badly shaken by the events that led to the downfall of the Nixon administration. Aftershocks continued to rock Washington, including revelations on domestic and foreign misdeeds of the CIA and on improper use of income tax records by the White House, attempts to influence regulatory decisions affecting those perceived to be enemies of the administration, and FBI violations of civil liberties. These tremors seriously damaged an image that is important to the functioning of modern administration.

The picture that has emerged, correct or not, is that of government against the people. Those who remembered the days when the "best and the brightest" went to Washington to fight the Depression were shaken. Cynics, on the other hand, felt vindicated. It must be recalled that administration had grown up largely based on faith: first, the faith born in the Progressive era that professionals in different disciplines could solve national problems and, second, that these people were committed to the common good. There had never been any particular love of bureaucracy, but after Watergate the level of distrust increased dramatically. For the administrator in the 1970s, the problem became—and remains—how to carry out difficult and necessary administrative tasks in a hostile environment.

The energy crisis that had its first effects in 1973 continues to influence policy in ways few would previously have imagined. Among other things, the energy crisis clearly demonstrated that the idea that experts can solve society's problems without drastic alterations in standards and modes of living is a myth. The day of the administration quick fix is at an end. However, the first thought that occurred to many to deal with the energy crisis was to create new administrative agencies to meet regulatory needs and to develop innovative policies. At the same time that national demands to decrease the size and role of government generally were heard, equally strident demands were made for the government to solve the energy problem, with each interest group claiming first priority in whatever policy would be developed in Washington.

The judiciary also felt major change during this period. By 1975, the Supreme Court had changed its identity from the Warren Court to the Nixon-appointed Burger Court.[157] The views of the Warren Court majority, coupled with the new militancy, knowledge, and skills of minorities, the poor, and other groups called "public interest" lobbies, had resulted in an expanding sphere of activity for the federal courts. The Burger Court was appointed with the definite purpose of reducing that involvement and the new majority has, in several areas, done just that.[158]

In the academic community, problems of law and administration have again been recognized as significant by public administrationists and some political scientists. Among the reasons for this resurgence of interest, though it may be a bit premature to use such a term, are the increased number of law and policy conflicts, the high visibility of some law and administration problems, such as detailed orders to administrators on operation of prisons and mental health facilities following suits by inmates and patients,[159] and the increasing importance of policy studies as a popular part of these disciplines. Policy studies attempts to apply some of the methods and concepts of the 1950s and '60s to the substance of government policy as well to as the processes of government. This shift to policy studies involves both methodological changes in approach and, more important, attention to what is studied. Attention to the substance of policy as well as to the processes that produced it means attention to public law questions.

Reform Efforts in Action and in Literature

On the positive side, the 1970s witnessed attempts to ameliorate the problems noted in earlier years. Attempts at reform have been relatively limited and largely incremental, but they have been significant. Each year Congress has considered a variety of bills, at least one of which is entitled something like "the Administrative Procedure Reform Act of _____." Most are efforts to patch up deficiencies in the APA. There have been few attempts to go beyond this to a more comprehensive attempt to construct a coherent administrative law theory on which to build specific procedures and institutions, but that may not yet be possible. In fact, one may view some of the failures of the APA in light of Sir Henry Maine's warning that premature codification of developing areas of law may be dangerous.[160]

Some experimental reform has been attempted. Many such efforts are intended by the interest groups who support them to advance their own goals, but that is no reason to reject suggestions or experiments out of hand. Executive experiments have included reorganization of agencies, attempts to reduce interagency conflicts through the use of interagency working groups, limited deregulation initiatives, civil service reform, and proposals to deal with privacy and freedom-of-information problems. The jury is still out on all these efforts and much more will be said about them in future chapters. It is clear that, at least in the near term, no President with a sense for recent history will attempt to ignore the bureaucracy or make the mistake of assuming that simplistic methods can be used to manage important agencies.

Congress was extremely active during the 1970s in efforts to come to grips with administrative problems. Ironically, one of the methods used by Congress is its own counterbureaucracy—administrative offices designed to prepare research and monitor activities of other administrative agencies on behalf of Congress. Some of the statutes enacted in the 1970s reacted to earlier criticisms about vague and open-ended wording that leaves administrators free to roam in a given policy area. An example is the Education for All Handicapped Children Act,[161] which some observers feel may even have gone too far in the direction of specificity.[162] Congress appointed a number of study groups that have, unlike some of their predecessors, seemingly had a very real policy impact. For example, the Commission on Procurement's efforts led to substantial changes in the system of grants and contracts administration. The Ribicoff Committee *Study on Federal Regulation* has figured prominently in recent regulatory reform efforts. Congress has also had the benefit of recommendations from the Administrative Conference of the United States, a prestigious body of experts from several areas of scholarship and practical experience in administration. Although the statute creating the conference was enacted at the request of President Kennedy and signed into law by President Johnson, it did not become effective until after staffing began in 1968.[163]

One of the most controversial of the experiments used in recent years has been the legislative veto concept. Legislative veto provisions have been attached to a number of bills, permitting Congress by various means to veto a rule promulgated by an administrative agency.[164] Congress has enacted a series of information laws that provide for protection of privacy and for access to government documents. A related package of statutes includes the Government in the Sunshine Act,[165] which responds to some of the complaints on the difficulty many individuals and groups encounter in participating in rulemaking processes, and the Federal Advisory Committee Act,[166] which attempts to meet criticisms made since the Landis Report about the dangers of off-the-record contacts by regulated groups and special access by interest groups to administrators.

The courts have been part of this period of experimentation, although different courts have approached the subject differently. On the basis of the criticisms of the earlier period and the experiences of the courts with agencies, some judges were less willing to grant wide deference with only cursory review of administrative decisions. Judge Bazelon summarized the concern of these judges.

> We stand on the threshold of a new era in the history of the long and fruitful collaboration of administrative agencies and reviewing courts. For many years, courts have treated administrative policy decisions with great deference, confining judicial attention primarily to matters of procedure. On matters of substance, the courts regularly upheld agency action, with a nod in the direction of the "substantial evidence" test, and a bow to the mysteries of administrative expertise. Courts occasionally asserted, but less often exercise, the power to set aside agency action on the ground that an impermissible factor had entered into the decision, or a crucial factor had not been considered. Gradually, however, that power has come into more frequent use, and with it, the requirements that administrators articulate factors on which they base their decisions.[167]

Judges at all levels have been more willing than before to send opinions or rules back to agencies for clarification and for a demonstration that the procedures of the APA had been followed in letter and in spirit. One device is the demand for hybrid rulemaking.[168] Developed in response to calls by scholars on judges to press administrators for guidelines and assurances of fairness to those before agencies, hybrid rulemaking requires a minimum level of material in records supporting agency rules to show that administrators made decisions based on some kind of evidence and did not arbitrarily reject evidence offered by citizens or groups to the agency. While the Supreme Court has been less willing than before to grant automatic deference, it has also not been well disposed toward some of the new techniques, such as hybrid rulemaking, if imposed by courts.[169] However, although the Court has limited the authority of federal courts to interfere with administrative action in progress, it has expanded opportunities to sue administrators and units of government after the fact to recover damages.[170]

As these experiments get under way, a number of authors continue to probe for new directions in the reform of law and administration. One reason for selecting 1969 as the break point between the contemporary period and preceding decades was the change in presidential administrations, but a major intellectual rationale is that 1969 is the year in which Kenneth Culp Davis published his *Discretionary Justice: A Preliminary Inquiry*[171] and a related article, "A New Approach to Delegation."[172] A longstanding supporter of conventionally defined administrative law had arrived at the conclusion that much remained to be done before it could be said that the administrative justice system was functioning properly. Davis made a strong case that discretion is widespread and open to abuse. The dangers of abuse are exacerbated, in his view, by the lack of public proceedings and by the burdens placed on those who attempt to get judicial review of agency actions.[173] Davis, confident that the discretion could be controlled, structured, and limited with relative ease,[174] would rely primarily on self-help by administrators. He asked only that they expand the use of rulemaking to announce their own view of agency discretion and means for its use,[175] and that agencies avoid interposing technical defenses in cases where a citizen decided to seek judicial review.[176] If agencies would not take these steps, Davis suggested that courts should encourage them to do so.[177] Davis recognized that "our system is the result of long-term, rudderless drift,"[178] but he felt that by avoiding massive efforts at reform—given the major conflicts implied in such reform campaigns—important and effective incremental changes could be achieved.[179]

Louis Jaffe and Judge J. Skelly Wright, two of Davis's reviewers, agreed with his assessment of the problems of the administrative justice system, but disagreed with his call for voluntary change by administrators.[180] Both concluded that careful judicial review would likely be necessary until congressional action was taken.[181]

Abraham Sofaer is another critic of the position that administrators will make rules to control their own discretion.[182] In his study of the Immigration and Naturalization Service, an agency with perhaps the widest range of discretionary authority of any federal administrative body, Sofaer agreed with the dangers of discretion noted by Davis and others. Based on his study, Sofaer concluded that not only was such broad discretionary authority dangerous to those who might suffer from arbitrary agency action, but it also led to major inefficiencies and high reversal rates on appeal.[183] He did not believe that administrators were likely to divest themselves of discretion, and reported an attempt by the Administrative Conference to convince INS officials to promulgate rules defining their own discretion. The INS responded by memorandum, indicating that they were not going to limit their own flexibility by issuing standards.[184] Sofaer suggested that courts should prod legislatures and executives to mandate agency rulemaking and other reforms.[185] Ernest Gellhorn and Glen O. Robinson were in general agreement,[186] as was Richard B. Stewart.[187] Stewart summarized the several suggestions with the most support during this period, including "deregulation and abolition of agencies; enforcement of the doctrine against delegation of legislative power; a requirement that agencies crystallize their exercise of discretion through standards and adoption of allocational efficiency as a substitute yardstick for agency decisions."[188] He concluded that no one of these would solve the problems, and that experimentation ought to continue. These authors had concluded that it was time to stop asking whether the APA was in good health and begin treatment for the difficult, but probably curable, ailments that all could readily diagnose.

SUMMARY

One of the weaknesses of much of the literature and law in public law and public administration is the lack of consideration of the historical underpinnings of the present administrative justice system. That system can be traced back to the very beginning of our country. Certainly, it is inaccurate to assume that our problems in law and administration have sprung full blown from the New Deal, the Great Society, or the New Federalism.

An examination of the history of law and administration in the United States may conveniently be divided into four major periods defined by important political and economic events, problems of governmental administration and attempts to remedy them, and the literature which has provided a continuous record of ongoing problems and possible solutions. From the founding of the republic to about 1928 we experienced the development of public administration, the contest over the legitimacy of broad administrative authority in light of the requirements of the rule of law, and thoughtful theoretical consideration of bases from which to develop a coherent body of administrative law.

Attempts at theory building gave way to the practical needs that arose during the Great Depression, requiring for immediate solutions to pressing problems. A compromise solution was adopted with the agreement in government and the legal community that basic due process protections, regular procedure, and the availability of judicial review would provide sufficient protection from administrative arbitrariness. That compromise was enacted into law as the Administrative Procedure Act.

The third period of administrative law development indicated that the APA was no substitute for a coherent theory of administrative law or for more comprehensive techniques of ensuring necessary flexibility for administrators while simultaneously providing safeguards against arbitrariness. The 1970s marked the beginning of specific attempts at significant change. Although highly controversial and admittedly politicized, a number of incremental changes in the operation of the administrative justice system are being attempted in several areas of government.

NOTES

[1]*Rooke's Case*, 5 Co. Rep. 996, 77 Eng. Rep. 209 (1599).

[2]Walter Gellhorn, *Federal Administrative Proceedings* (Baltimore: Johns Hopkins, 1941), p. 5.

[3]Louis G. Caldwell, "Remarks to the ABA Convention," 58 *Rep. ABA* 197, 201 (1933).

[4]Edmund S. Morgan, *The Puritan Dilemma: The Story of John Winthrop* (Boston: Little, Brown, 1958).

[5]Frank Goodnow, *Comparative Administrative Law* (New York: Putnam, 1893), vol. 2, book 5, chap. 3.

[6]See generally Bernard Bailyn, *The Ideological Origins of the American Revolution* (Cambridge, Mass.: Harvard University Press, 1967).

[7]Leonard D. White, *The Federalists: A Study in Administrative History* (New York: Macmillan, 1959), p. 1. See also Leonard D. White, *The Jeffersonians: A Study in Administrative History, 1801–1829* (New York: Macmillan, 1959).

[8]John C. Miller, *Alexander Hamilton and the Growth of the New Nation* (New York: Harper & Row, 1959), and Albert Beveridge, *The Life of John Marshall* (Boston: Houghton Mifflin, 1916–1919).

[9]Alexander Hamilton, James Madison, and John Jay, *The Federalist Papers* (New York: Mentor, 1961).

[10]Milton M. Carrow, *The Background of Administrative Law* (Newark, N.J.: Associated Lawyers, 1948), p. 6.

[11]Ernst Freund, *Administrative Powers over Persons and Property: A Comparative Survey* (Chicago: University of Chicago Press, 1928), p. 145.

[12]Id., at pp. 143–44.

[13]Carrow, supra note 10, at p. 6.

[14]*Marbury v. Madison*, 5 U.S. (1 Cranch) 137 (1803); *Cohens v. Virginia*, 19 U.S. (6 Wheat.) 264 (1821); *Fletcher v. Peck*, 10 U.S. 87 (1810); and *United States v. Judge Peters* 5 Cranch 115 (1809).

[15]*McCulloch v. Maryland*, 17 U.S. (4 Wheat.) 316 (1819). The necessary and proper clause is found in article I, §8, clause 18, of the U.S. Constitution.

[16]*Gibbons v. Ogden*, 22 U.S. (9 Wheat.) 1 (1824) and the *Daniel Ball*, 77 U.S. (10 Wall.) 557 (1871).

[17]See Robert Remini, *Andrew Jackson* (New York: Harper & Row, 1966), and G. Van Deusen, *The Jacksonian Era* (New York: Harper & Row, 1959).

[18]Richard Hofstadter, *The Age of Reform* (New York: Random House, 1955), chap. 1.

[19]Carrow, supra note 10, at pp. 7–9. See also Isaiah Sharfman, *The Interstate Commerce Commission* (New York: Commonwealth Fund, 1937).

[20]Gerald C. Henderson, *The Federal Trade Commission: A Study in Administrative Law and Procedure* (New Haven, Conn.: Yale University Press, 1924).

[21]William Leuchtenburg, *The Perils of Prosperity* (Chicago: University of Chicago Press, 1958).

[22]See generally John Kenneth Galbraith, *The Great Crash of 1929* (Boston: Houghton Mifflin, 1961).

[23]Hofstadter, supra note 18, chap. 5.

[24]Galbraith, supra note 22.

[25]See, e.g., U.S. Senate, *Report of the Federal Trade Commission on Utility Corporations*, Sen. Doc. no. 92, 70th Cong., 1st Sess., 1935, pt. 73A.

[26]41 Stat. 1063 (1920).

[27]Elihu Root, "Public Service by the Bar," in Robert Bacon and James B. Scott, eds., *Elihu Root: Addresses on Government and Citizenship* (Cambridge, Mass.: Harvard University Press, 1916), pp. 534–35.

[28]Freund, supra note 11.

[29]A. V. Dicey, *Introduction to the Study of the Law of the Constitution* (London: Macmillan, 1965), p. 203.

[30]"When we say that the supremacy or the rule of law is characteristic of the English constitution, we generally include at least three distinct though kindred conceptions. . . . We mean, in the first place, that no man is punishable or can be lawfully made to suffer in body or goods except for a distinct breach of law established in the ordinary legal manner before the ordinary courts of the land. In this sense the rule of law is contrasted with every system of government based on the exercise by persons in authority of wide or arbitrary discretionary powers of constraint. We mean in the second place, when we speak of the 'rule of law' as a characteristic of our country, not only that with us no man is above the law, but (what is a different thing) that here every man, whatever be his rank or condition, is subject to the ordinary law of the realm and amenable to the jurisdiction of the ordinary tribunals. . . . There remains yet a third and a different sense in which the "rule of law" or the predominance of the legal spirit may be described as a special attribute of English institutions. We may say that the constitution is pervaded by the rule of law on the ground that the general principles of the constitution are with us the result of judicial decisions determining the right of private persons in particular cases brought before the courts." Id., at pp. 188–196.

[31]Dicey, in 1915, responded with regret but understanding when the King's Bench Division and the House of Lords handed down their opinions in *Board of Education v. Rice*, A.C. 179, 80 L.J.K.B. 796 (1911), and *Local Government Board v. Arlidge*, A.C. 120, 84 L.J.K.B. 72 (1915). He stated (p. 497):

"There remain two checks upon the abuse of judicial or quasijudicial powers by a government department. In the first place, every department in the exercise of any power possessed by it must conform precisely to the language of any statute by which the power is given to the department, and if any department fails to observe this rule the courts of justice may treat its action as a nullity. . . . In the second place, a Government department must exercise any power in the spirit of judicial fairness."

Thus, Dicey still defended the English system based on his belief that administrative discretion would be carefully limited and that agencies would be required to act like courts in the disposition of cases.

For a discussion of the "extravagant version of the rule of law," see Jerome Frank, *If Men Were Angels: Some Aspects of Government in a Democracy* (New York: Harper & Brothers, 1942), and Kenneth Culp Davis, *Discretionary Justice: A Preliminary Inquiry* (Baton Rouge: Louisiana State University Press, 1969).

[32]See Goodnow, supra note 5, and his *The Principles of Administrative Law in the United States* (New York: Putnam, 1905).

[33]Id., at pp. 323–24.

[34]Id.

[35]Id., at p. 325.

[36]John Dickinson, *Administrative Justice and the Supremacy of Law in the United States* (New York: Russell & Russell, 1927).

[37]"In Anglo-American jurisprudence, government and law have always in a sense stood opposed to one another; the law has been rather something to give the citizen a check on government than an instrument to give the government control over the citizen. There is a famous passage, which was long attributed to Bracton, to the effect that the king has a superior, to wit, the law; and if he be without a bridle, a bridle ought to be put on him, namely, the law." Id., at p. 32.

[38]Id., at p. 113.

[39]"The crucial qualities of a common-law court which are absent from administrative tribunals are at least three, two of them being procedural and one substantive. Administrative tribunals are not bound by procedural safeguards which would mould the outcome of an action at law; more specifically they are, in the first place, not bound by the common law rules of evidence and in the second place, parties to proceedings before them do not have the benefit of jury trial. The substantive differences between the administrative procedure and the procedure at law is that the administrative tribunal decides controversies coming before them, not by fixed rules of law, but by the application of governmental discretion or policy." Id. at pp. 35–36.

[40]Id., at p. 234.

[41]Id., at pp. 37–38.

[42]Freund, supra note 11.

[43]Ernst Freund, *Standards of American Legislation* (Chicago: University of Chicago Press, 1917).

[44]Id., chap. 3.

[45]"First, its standards had failed to keep pace with advancing or changing ideals; it was most emphatic in maintaining order and authority, least emphatic in relieving social weakness and inferiority; it developed no principles of reasonableness regarding economic stands or equivalents . . . ; its ideal of public policy was too exclusively the advantage of the many and not sufficiently the regard for claims of individual personality; equity was absorbed with property interest to the neglect of nonmaterial human rights." Id. at p. 70.

[46]Freund, supra note 11, at p. 72.

[47]Id., at p. 74.

[48]Id., at p. 97.

[49]William O. Douglas, "Address to the International Management Congress" in James Allen, ed., *Democracy and Finance: The Addresses and Public Statements of William O. Douglas as a Member and Chairman of the Securities and Exchange Commission* (New Haven, Conn.: Yale University Press, 1940), p. 56.

[50]The confession of a former president of the stock exchange to misappropriation of clients' securities was one of the most devastating examples. Memorandum, William O. Douglas to Stephen A. Early, October 27, 1938, OF 1060 Whitney Folder, Franklin Delano Roosevelt Papers, Franklin Delano Roosevelt Library. See also Louis D. Brandeis, *Other People's Money* (New York: Harper & Row, 1967).

[51]See generally James MacGregor Burns, *Roosevelt: The Lion and the Fox* (New York: Harcourt, Brace & World, 1956); William E. Leuchtenburg, *Franklin D. Roosevelt and the New Deal, 1932–1940* (New York: Harper & Row, 1963); and Arthur M. Schlesinger, *The Coming of the New Deal* (Boston: Houghton Mifflin, 1958).

[52]Franklin D. Roosevelt, speaking at Oglethorpe University, in Howard Zinn, ed., *New Deal Thought* (Indianapolis: Bobbs-Merrill, 1966), p. 83. See also Jerome Frank, "Experimental Jurisprudence," 78 *Congressional Record* 12412 (1934).

[53]Franklin D. Roosevelt, addressing the Commonwealth Club in San Francisco, in Zinn, supra note 52. See also Leuchtenburg, supra note 51, p. 165.

[54]Burns, supra note 51, chap. 14.

[55]*Panama Refining Co. v. Ryan*, 293 U.S. 388 (1935); Schechter *Poultry v. United States*, 295 U.S. 995 (1935); *Carter v. Carter Coal Co.*, 298 U.S. 238 (1936); and *United States v. Butler* 297 U.S. 1 (1936).

[56]See generally Fred Rodell, *Nine Men: A Political History of the Supreme Court of the United States from 1790 to 1955* (New York: Random House, 1955).

[57]Louis G. Caldwell, "Remarks to ABA Convention," 58 *Reports of the ABA* 197, 197 (1933).

[58]Id.

[59]"A little later I may attempt partially to define an administrative tribunal; for the present let us assume that it is something that looks like a court and acts like a court, but some how escapes being classified as a court whenever you attempt to impose any limitation on its powers." Id.

[60]Brownlow Commission, *Report of the President's Committee on Administrative Management* (Washington, D.C.: Government Printing Office, 1937).

[61]The committee was a distinguished body chaired by Dean Acheson with Walter Gellhorn as executive director. Other members were Francis Biddle, Ralph F. Fuchs, Lloyd K. Garrison, Lawrence Groner, Harry M. Hart, Jr., Carl Mc-

Farland, James W. Morris, Harry Schulman, E. Blythe Stason, and Arthur T. Vanderbilt.

[62]The committee specifically rejected any suggestion that it should consider the wisdom, propriety, or correctness of legislation or administration. See the report cited in note 63, pp. 1–2.

[63]U.S. Senate, Report of the Attorney General's Committee on Administrative Procedure, *Administrative Procedure in Government Agencies*, Sen. Doc. no. 8, 77th Cong., 1st Sess. (1941).

[64]5 U.S.C. §551 et seq.

[65]Max Farrand, ed., *Records of the Federal Convention of 1787*, rev. ed., 4 vols. (New Haven, Conn.: Yale University Press, 1911).

[66]Even the Attorney General's Committee Report focused on relatively recent problems and did not reflect a particularly strong concern for historical continuity.

[67]In later years Kenneth Culp Davis would argue that these debates of the thirties over narrow, albeit significant, topics sapped much of the creative energy available to build a new and better administrative jurisprudence. Davis, supra note 31, pp. 50–51.

[68]Carrow, supra note 10, chap. 7, "The So-Called Rule Against Delegation."

[69]Frank, supra note 31, chap. 12, and later Davis, supra note 31, pp. 28–42, argued that these concerns stemmed from a belief in an "extravagant version of the rule of law."

[70]James M. Landis, *The Administrative Process* (New Haven, Conn.: Yale University Press, 1938).

[71]Id., at p. 2.

[72]Id., at p. 24.

[73]"Enough [examples] have been given, however, to make clear that even where formal proceedings are fully available, informal procedures constitute the vast bulk of administrative adjudication and are truly the lifeblood of the administrative process. No study of administrative procedure can be adequate if it fails to recognize this fact and focus attention upon improvement at these stages." Attorney General's Committee Report, supra note 63, at p. 35.

[74]On judicial review, the committee observed: "In the whole field of administrative law the functions that can be performed by judicial review are fairly limited. Its objective, broadly speaking, is to serve as a check on the administrative branch of government—a check against excess of power and abusive exercise of power in derogation of private right. But that relates only to one or two more or less equally important aspects of administration. From the point of view of public policy and public interest, it is important not only that the administrator should not encroach on private rights but also that he should effectively discharge his statutory obligations. Excessive favor of private interest may be as prejudicial as excessive encroachment." Id., at p. 76.

[75]Gellhorn, supra note 2; this work is taken from his James Schouler Lectures at Johns Hopkins, delivered in May 1941, just after publication of the report of the Attorney General's Committee.

[76]Id., at p. 5.

[77]By "sympathetic administration" Gellhorn meant effective administration carried out by people who know enough

about the special problems of the regulated industry or the group seeking services to be sensitive to practical problems.

[78]Gellhorn, supra note 2, at p. 25.

[79]Id., at pp. 39–40.

[80]Frank, supra note 60, at p. 181.

[81]Id., at p. 9.

[82]Id., at p. 3.

[83]"It has been widely said that the first problem of today is to reconcile the Expert State and the Free State. Our American democracy, while accommodating itself to new factors heretofore unknown, will have to achieve a balance—which wise political thinkers have always regarded as the chief task of sound government—between two opposed tendencies: enough power to make the government effective but enough liberty to leave the citizens a free agent; it must mediate between absolute dependence and absolute independence for its citizens. In new and difficult circumstances, we must solve the age-old fundamental problem of government, that of reconciling liberty and authority." Id., at p. 18.

[84]Id., at pp. 3–7.

[85]Roscoe Pound, *Administrative Law: Its Growth, Procedure and Significance* (Pittsburgh, Pa.: University of Pittsburgh Press, 1942).

[86]Id., at p. 113.

[87]Id., at pp. 19–20.

[88]Id., at p. 55.

[89]*The Brig Aurora*, 11 U.S. (7 Cranch) 382 (1813).

[90]See, e.g., *Field v. Clark*, 143 U.S. 649 (1892); *United States v. Grimaud*, 220 U.S. 506 (1911); *Butterfield v. Stranahan*, 192 U.S. 470 (1904); and *J. W. Hampton, Jr., & Co. v. United States*, 276 U.S. 394 (1928).

[91]*Panama Refining Co. v. Ryan*, 293 U.S. 388 (1935).

[92]*Schecter Poultry Corp. v. United States*, 295 U.S. 495 (1935).

[93]*Carter v. Carter Coal Co.*, 298 U.S. 238 (1936).

[94]See, e.g., F. Blachly, "Critique of the Federal Administrative Procedure Act," in G. Warren, ed., *The Federal Administrative Act and the Administrative Agencies: Proceedings of an Institute Conducted by the New York University School of Law on February 1–8, 1947* (New York: New York University School of Law, 1947).

[95]Eric Goldman, *The Crucial Decade—And After: America, 1945–1960* (New York: Vintage, Books, 1960), p. vi.

[96]Id. See also Robert Griffin, *The Politics of Fear: Joseph B. McCarthy and the Senate* (New York: Hayden, 1970), and Merle Miller, *Plain Speaking: An Oral Biography of Harry S Truman* (New York: Putnam, 1973).

[97]97 Stat. 246 (1947).

[98]Commission members included Herbert Hoover (chairman), Dean Acheson (vice chairman), Arthur S. Flemming, James Forrestal, George H. Mead, George D. Aiken, Joseph P. Kennedy, James K. Pollock, Clarence J. Brown, Carter Monasco, and James H. Rowe, Jr.

[99]Commission on Organization of the Executive Branch of

Government, *The Hoover Commission Report on the Organization of the Executive Branch of Government* (New York: McGraw-Hill, Inc., 1949).

¹⁰⁰Id., at p. 436.

¹⁰¹For an excellent commentary on the work of the Hoover Commission and its reports, see Neil MacNeil and Harold W. Metz, *The Hoover Commission Report, 1953–1955: What It Means to You as Citizens and Taxpayers* (New York: Macmillan, 1956). Mr. MacNeil served as editor-in-chief for the commission's report.

¹⁰²Task Force members included James March Douglas (chairman), Herbert W. Clark, Cody Fowler, Albert J. Harne, James M. Landis, Carl McFarland, Ross L. Malone, Jr., David F. Maxwell, Harold R. Medina, David W. Peck, Reginald H. Smith, E. Blythe Stason, Elbert Par Tuttle, and Edward L. Wright. Consultants were former Justice Robert H. Jackson, George Roberts, and Arthur T. Vanderbilt.

¹⁰³There is speculation that the reason that the second Hoover Commission report recommendations were not followed relates to perceptions in Congress that the second round of Commission efforts went beyond efficiency oriented reorganization proposals to more substantive policy criticisms.

¹⁰⁴See the reports of the ABA Administrative Law Section in 80–84 *Reports of the ABA* (1955–1959).

¹⁰⁵Jack W. Peltason, *Fifty-eight Lonely Men* (Urbana: University of Illinois Press, 1971). See also Richard Kluger, *Simple Justice* (New York: Knopf, 1976).

¹⁰⁶See generally Griffin, supra note 96.

¹⁰⁷See, e.g., John R. Owens, Edmond Costantini, and Louis F. Weschler, *California Politics and Parties* (London: Macmillan, 1970), chap. 1.

¹⁰⁸Robert G. Dixon, *Social Security Disability and Mass Justice: A Problem in Welfare Adjudication* (New York: Praeger, 1973).

¹⁰⁹Michael D. Reagan, *The New Federalism* (New York: Oxford University Press, 1972).

¹¹⁰Alan F. Westin, *Privacy and Freedom* (New York: Atheneum, 1967).

¹¹¹James Hart, *Introduction to Administrative Law With Selected Cases*, 2d ed. (New York: Appleton-Century-Crofts), 1950), p. 23.

¹¹²Dwight Waldo, *The Enterprise of Public Administration: A Summary View* (Novato, Calif.: Chandler & Sharp, 1980), p. 69.

¹¹³Leonard D. White, *Introduction to the Study of Public Administration*, 4th ed. (New York, Macmillan, 1955), p. xvi.

¹¹⁴Frederick C. Mosher, *Democracy and the Public Service* (New York: Oxford University Press, 1968), chaps. 2–4, and Dwight Waldo, *The Administrative State* (New York: Ronald Press, 1948), pp. 79–80.

¹¹⁵Waldo, supra note 114, chap. 10. See also Henri Fayol and Frederick W. Taylor, in D. S. Pugh, ed., *Organization Theory* (Baltimore: Penguin, 1971).

¹¹⁶Waldo, supra note 114.

¹¹⁷Herbert Simon, *Administrative Behavior*, 3d ed. (New York: Free Press, 1976).

¹¹⁸Dwight Waldo, "Scope of the Theory of Public Administration" in James C. Charlesworth, ed., *Theory and Practice of Public Administration: Scope, Objectives, and Methods*, monograph no. 8, *Annals of the American Academy of Political and Social Science* (1968), pp. 14–15.

¹¹⁹See C. Herman Pritchett, "Public Law and Judicial Behavior," 30 *Journal of Politics* 480 (1968).

¹²⁰See the discussion of this trend in Chapter 3.

¹²¹That is, they attracted little attention from the leading public law scholars.

¹²²U.S. House of Representatives, Task Force on Legal Services and Procedure, *Report on Legal Services and Procedure Prepared for the Commission on Organization of the Executive Branch*, House Doc. no. 128, 84th Cong., 1st Sess. (1955), p. 2.

¹²³Id., at p. 19.

¹²⁴Id., at p. 30.

¹²⁵"Administrative agencies exercise powers delegated to them by Congressional enactment. The scope and meaning of these powers are sometimes inadequately formulated in the legislation. Vague and general statutory terms confer an unnecessarily broad range of discretionary authority upon the administrative officials entrusted to carry out legislative objectives. Such grants of authority, inadequately limited by statutory safeguards and standards are encountered throughout the administrative process." Id., at p. 22.

¹²⁶Id., at p. 31.

¹²⁷"The primary method which agencies should use to effectuate legislative provisions is the adoption of implementing rules which will give information and guidance to the public. In principle, agencies should not proceed by adjudication where the subject matter permits the determination and statement of a policy by a rule of general applicability." Id., at p. 24.

¹²⁸"All persons should be able to understand administrative processes and to protect their just rights before administrative agencies. They should have reasonable notice of regulations, information concerning the manner in which they defend their position, and knowledge of the means and extent of judicial relief from administrative error." Id., at p. 19.

¹²⁹Gellhorn, supra note 2, at p. 104.

¹³⁰Task Force report, supra note 122, at p. 209.

¹³¹Id., at p. 28.

¹³²U.S. Senate, *Report on Regulatory Agencies to the President-Elect*, 86th Cong., 2d Sess. (1960). (Hereafter referred to as Landis Report.)

¹³³Landis's description of the situation at the Federal Power Commission is an excellent example of the tenor of the Landis Report: "The Federal Power Commission without question represents the outstanding example in the federal government of the breakdown of the administrative process. The complexity of its problems is no answer to its more patent failures." Id., at p. 54.

¹³⁴"One of the worst phases of this situation is the existence of groups of lawyers in Washington itself, who implicitly

hold out to clients that they have means of access to various agencies off the record that are more important than those that can be made on the record." Id., at p. 14.

[135]Id., at p. 5.

[136]Id., at p. 9.

[137]Id., at pp. 19–20.

[138]For an interesting commentary on the Landis Report, see Carl McFarland, "Landis' Report: The Voice of One Crying in the Wilderness," 47 *Virginia L. Rev.* 373 (1961).

[139]Another notable political scientist at work in this area was Martin Shapiro, *The Supreme Court and Administrative Agencies* (New York: Free Press, 1968).

[140]Peter Woll, *Administrative Law: The Informal Process* (Berkeley: University of California Press, 1963).

[141]"The raison d'etre of the administrative process is the increasing need for more flexibility than is provided by either Congress or the courts. Modern regulation requires specialization, expertise, continuity of service, and flexibility for utilization of a variety of skills which would not be possible operating within a strict common-law framework. Even the formal administrative process was intended to be more flexible than a court of law, and the courts have permitted this utilization of more flexible procedure; however, it is actually the informal administrative process that epitomizes those characteristics for which there was a felt need at the time of the creation of the administrative agency as a regulatory device." Id., at p. 188.

[142]Id., at p. 5.

[143]Id., at p. 2.

[144]Id., at pp. 29–30.

[145]Id., at p. 34.

[146]Id., at p. 61.

[147]"Present day criticisms of the independent regulatory agencies by the American Bar Association and some of its representatives concentrates upon administrative proceeding though proper use of formal judicial techniques. Criticism from the administrative standpoint, on the other hand, focuses upon the importance of proper policy formulation and coordination, and upon the need for greater efficiency in handling the adjudicative and legislative tasks of the agencies. The orientation of each group is reflected in their respective proposals for administrative law reform." Id., at p. 177.

[148]See, e.g., Louis L. Jaffe, *Judicial Control of Administrative Action* (Boston: Little, Brown, 1965).

[149]Chapter 7 describes this tradition of deference.

[150]Kenneth Culp Davis, *Administrative Law* (St. Paul: West, 1951).

[151]Kenneth Culp Davis, *Administrative Law Treatise* (St. Paul: West, 1958).

[152]Id., §28.16.

[153]Jaffe, supra note 148.

[154]Raoul Berger, "Administrative Arbitrariness and Judicial Review," 65 *Columbia L. Rev.* 55 (1965); Davis, *Administrative Law Treatise*, 1965 Supplement, §28.16; Berger, "Administrative Arbitrariness—A Reply to Professor Davis," 114 *U. Pennsylvania L. Rev.* 783 (1966); Davis, "A Final Word," 14 *U. Pennsylvania L. Rev.* 814 (1966); Berger,

"Rejoinder," 114 *U. Pennsylvania L. Rev.* 816 (1966); Davis, "Postscript," 114 *U. Pennsylvania L. Rev.* 823 (1966); Berger, "Sequel," 51 *Minnesota L. Rev.* 601 (1967); Davis, "Not Always," 51 *Minnesota L. Rev.* 643 (1967); Berger, "Synthesis," 78 *Yale L. J.* 965 (1969).

[155]See generally Report of the Twentieth Century Fund Task Force on the Law Enforcement Assistance Administration, *Law Enforcement: The Federal Role* (New York: McGraw-Hill, 1976).

[156]Reagan, supra note 109.

[157]See James F. Simon, *In His Own Image: The Supreme Court in Richard Nixon's America* (New York: McKay, 1973).

[158]See U.S. House of Representatives, Hearings before the Subcommittee on Courts, Civil Liberties, and the Administration of Justice of the Committee on the Judiciary, *The State of the Judiciary and Access to Justice*, 95th Cong., 1st. Sess. (1977). See also R. A. Sedler and A. W. Houseman, eds., "Symposium: Access to Federal Courts: Rights Without Remedies," 30 *Rutgers L. Rev.* 841 (1977).

[159]See *Rhodes v. Chapman*, 69 L. Ed. 2d 59 (1981).

[160]Sir Henry Maine, *Ancient Law* (New York: Everyman, 1972), chap. 1.

[161]Public Law 94-142, 89 Stat. 773, 20 U.S.C. §§1232, 1401, 1405, 1406, 1411–1420, 1453 (1976). See Erwin L. Levine and Elizabeth M. Wexler, *PL94-142: An Act of Congress* (New York: Macmillan, 1981).

[162]Stephen R. Chitwood, "Legalizing American Public Administration—Practical and Theoretical Implications for the Field," unpublished paper presented at 1978 annual meeting of the American Society for Public Administration.

[163]Since that time the ACUS has published annual recommendations with supporting scholarly studies.

[164]See the legislative veto provision of the Federal Trade Commission Improvement Act of 1980, reproduced in Chapter 5.

[165]Public Law 94-409, 90 Stat. 1241, 5 U.S.C. §5526, (1976).

[166]5 U.S.C. app. I. See generally Jerry W. Markham, "The Federal Advisory Committee Act," 35 *Pittsburgh L. Rev.* 557 (1974).

[167]*Environmental Defense Fund, Inc. v. Ruckelshaus*, 439 F. 2d. 584, 597 (D.C. Cir. 1971).

[168]See, e.g., Ralph F. Fuchs, "Development and Diversification In Administrative Rule Making," 72 *Northwestern L. Rev.* 83 (1977), and Stephen Williams, " 'Hybrid Rulemaking' under the Administrative Procedure Act: A Legal and Empirical Analysis," 42 *U. Chicago L. Rev.* 401 (1975).

[169]*Vermont Yankee Nuclear Power Corp. v. Natural Resources Defense Council*, 435 U.S. 519 (1978). See Antonin Scalia, "Vermont Yankee: The APA, the D.C. Circuit, and the Supreme Court," 1979 *Supreme Court Rev.* 345 (1979), and "Vermont Yankee Nuclear Power Corp. v. Natural Resources Defense Council, Inc.: Three Perspectives," 91 *Harvard L. Rev.* 1805 (1978).

[170]*Maine V. Thiboutot*, 448 U.S. 1 (1980); *Owen v. City of Independence*, 445 U.S. 622 (1980); *Butz v. Economou*, 438

U.S. 478 (1978); *Monell v. New York City Dep't of Social Service,* 436 U.S. 658 (1978); and *Wood v. Strickland,* 420 U.S. 308 (1975).

[171]Davis, supra note 67.

[172]Kenneth Culp Davis, "A New Approach to Delegation," 36 *U. Chicago L. Rev.* 713 (1969).

[173]Davis, supra note 67, at p. 113. Several statutes have been enacted in this area since Davis wrote his criticism, but the critique remains valid a decade after it was originally published.

[174]Id., chaps. 3–5.

[175]Id., chap. 3.

[176]Id., at pp. 159–61.

[177]Id., at pp. 57–59.

[178]Id., at p. 159.

[179]"My opinion is, paradoxically, today's excessive discretionary power is largely attributable to the zeal of those who a generation ago were especially striving to protect against discretionary power. If they had been less zealous they would have attempted less, and if they had attempted less they might have succeeded. They attempted too much—so much that they could not possibly succeed—and they were decisively defeated. They tended to oppose all discretionary power; they should have opposed only unnecessary discretionary power." Id., at pp. 27–28.

[180]Louis L. Jaffe, "Book Review," 14 *Villanova L. Rev.* 773 (1969), and J. Skelly Wright, "Beyond Discretionary Justice," 81 *Yale L. J.* 575 (1972).

[181]See, e.g., Wright, supra note 180, at p. 595.

[182]Abraham Sofaer, "Judicial Control of Informal Discretionary Adjudication and Enforcement," 72 *Columbia L. Rev.* 1293 (1972).

[183]"The call for greater control of informal discretionary action deserves sympathetic attention. Ample evidence has accumulated of the need for legislative, judicial, and administrative reform to narrow discretionary power in numerous areas. Broad discretion in adjudication and enforcement at INS causes inconsistency, arbitrariness, and inefficiency." Id. at p. 1374.

[184]Id., at p. 1313.

[185]Id., at p. 1358.

[186]Ernest Gellhorn and Glen O. Robinson, "Perspectives on Administrative Law," 75 *Columbia L. Rev.* 771 (1975).

[187]Richard B. Stewart, "The Reformation of American Administrative Law," 88 *Harvard L. Rev.* 1667 (1975).

[188]Id., at p. 1688.

PART TWO

THE FORMAL ADMINISTRATIVE PROCESS

Chapter 5

Agency Rulemaking

The chapters in Part One have considered the operation of the administrative justice system as a whole. Particular attention has been given to the need for a broad understanding of administrative law, a concern for producer and consumer perspectives on administrative decisionmaking, a multifaceted approach to administrative law problems, and the need for sensitivity to the relationship between the law in books and the law in action. The next several chapters will be more particular in orientation, focusing on specific elements of administrative justice. There are problems of informal process, discretion, and power law to be considered. But first we turn to the formal processes of administrative law that have developed, as Chapter 4 indicated, out of several decades of administrative practice and legal challenge.

These formal procedures are agency rulemaking, administrative adjudication, and judicial review of administrative activity. This chapter focuses on the methods by which rules and regulations are adopted.

Before considering the formal aspects of administrative law, it is necessary to gain at least a general understanding of the Administrative Procedure Act, which governs administrative practice in federal agencies. Most states have a similar statute intended to ensure a degree of uniformity in agency operations.[1]

THE ADMINISTRATIVE PROCEDURE ACT

The Administrative Procedure Act (APA) can be understood by observing in some detail its basic components, which include: (1) an introduction; (2) fair information practices rules; (3) rulemaking; (4) adjudications; (5) qualifications and conduct of the presiding officer in administrative proceedings; and (6) judicial review of administrative decisions. It is important to bear in mind that these six parts evolved historically, as was sketched in Chapter 4, and not from some coherent theory of administrative law. They correspond to concerns about the need to establish general guidelines for federal agencies with due process protections, procedural regularity, and judicial review as the cornerstones of administrative law.

For example, one point of particular interest in the years just before the act was adopted in 1946 was the combination-of-functions problem. The Attorney General's Committee gave considerable attention to methods for dealing with this problem by ensuring the independence of hearing examiners from those outside the agency and also from pressures within the agency. Civil Service protections and procedural guidelines were given to the hearing officers for their work. Another set of provisions in the act arose when Congress determined that the basic statute governing administrative activity ought to include sections that ensured open administrative practices and access to information held by government. Over the course of several years these provisions were enacted as amendments to the APA. Other matters are dealt with in the statute, but the six main sections provide its core.

In the search for a conceptual framework to use as an organizing tool for the statute, the framers of the APA emphasized the idea that most matters of administrative law, as the term was understood at the time, could be classifid as quasi-legislative, which resulted in the making of rules, or quasi-judicial, which, like court decisions, produced orders governing particular cases.[2] It was around this dichotomy that the act was structured.[3]

With these organizing principles in mind, let us turn to a brief introduction to the APA provisions. Follow the discussion using the copy of the APA reprinted in Appendix B.

The Introduction Section

Title 5 of the United States Code contains statutes that control the internal operations of government in general and administrative concerns, e.g., government personnel laws, in particular. The APA begins with §551 of that title.[4] Statutes generally begin with a presentation of authoritative definitions of terms important to the new law. The APA has a substantial introduction that contains a lengthy list of definitions. This lexicon represents an effort by the legislature to work out a common language for administrative law from the many conflicting interpretations that had grown up around court decisions and agency practices.

One of the first problems was to define the actors and institutions in the administrative process. Just what is an administrative agency? Are all government organizations "agencies" within the meaning of the APA? From a brief look at the statute, one can see that the Congress exempted its own internal operations, those of the judiciary, some aspects of military activity, and a few other organizations from the coverage of the APA.[5] Section 551 defines "agency" as "each authority of the Government of the United States whether or not it is within or subject to review by another agency." But is a government corporation to be governed by the strictures of the APA? What of the Executive Office of the President? These important ambiguities led to amendment of the act in 1974. The new section [§552(3)] indicates that, at least for the information practices portion, the definition of agency "includes any executive department or military department, Government corporation, Government controlled corporation, or other establishment in the executive branch of the Government (including the Executive Office of the President), or any other regulatory agency."[6]

Another major point of confusion defined in the introduction concerns the processes or types of actions taken by agencies that are to be covered. Categories of agency action are not easily divided up, since they overlap. Therefore, some convention on the meaning of terms is necessary. In particular, the framers of the APA wanted to clarify, to a limited extent at least, the difference between quasi-legislative activities or rulemaking, which produce rules, and quasi-judicial activities or adjudications, which yield orders. This process of definition began with the nature of a rule [§551(4)]. In general terms, the act defines as orders any final agency decisions that are not rules [§551(6)]. The definitions of rulemaking and adjudication were then simply stated in terms of the processes for making rules and orders [§551(5) and (7)]. There are, however, a variety of administrative activities that are neither simply rulemaking nor adjudication. Two examples are ratemaking and licensing, discussed later in this chapter. When a television station requests a license to operate from the Federal Communications Commission, is it seeking an adjudication of a dispute in the hope of receiving an order or is it asking the agency to engage in rulemaking? When a public utility requests that electrical user rates be increased, is it asking the Public Service Commission to engage in rulemaking or is it requesting an adjudication of its claim to increased revenues? The convention that resulted defined ratemaking within the rule definition and set special descriptive terms for licensing [§551(9)], but treated it as a species of adjudication.

The definitions or introduction section of the Administrative Procedure Act, then, is an important section. Its provisions are more than cold definitions. This section represents a continuing attempt to work out a common language for the administrative justice system.

Fair Information Practices

The longest of the provisions of the APA is the set of rules governing fair information practices. These amendments were developed as separate pieces of legislation and enacted over a ten-year period from the mid-1960s to the mid-1970s. Section 552 is the Freedom of Information Act[7] (FOIA), which establishes the policy that government documents and materials should be available to the public, prescribes the means by which requests for information are to be processed, and fixes methods of redress for those who are, for one reason or another, denied access to requested information. Section 552(b) sets out a number of types of materials that are exempt from these open access rules.

APA §552a is the Privacy Act of 1974,[8] which seeks to protect against the unwarranted or inaccurate reporting of information about individuals which the government may have collected for any of several purposes. The Privacy Act makes a significant number of exceptions to the general rule against disclosure of information about an individual, which allows for criminal investigations and other particularly sensitive types of proceedings. Like the FOIA, the Privacy Act sections of the APA establish procedures and remedies for abuses by administrators.

There are two other parts to the fair information practices part of the APA. These two provisions focus on the need to encourage openness in proceedings undertaken by agencies as well as to provide for a better opportunity for interested groups or individuals to participate in agency activities. Related provisions attempt to ensure that participation is equally available to all significant groups and not merely to a limited set of special interest organizations. The Government in the Sunshine Act[9] (§552b) performs the first task. The Federal Advisory Committee Act[10] (5 U.S.C. app. I,) accomplishes the second goal. In both cases, the sections of the APA provide a set of procedures for monitoring compliance and remedial steps that may be taken to redress violations.

Rulemaking

Section 553 of the APA describes the processes an agency must perform to make a rule. Discussion of these requirements will occupy much of the remainder of this chapter. For the present, it is important to note again that the statute exempts some activities from its provisions. In particular, the rulemaking section exempts military or foreign affairs [§553(a)(1)]; "a matter relating to agency management or personnel or to public property, loans, grants benefits, or contracts" [§553(a)(2)]; activities such as internal agency reorganizations and the like [§553(b)(A)]; or cases where there are emergency circumstances of a special nature that require some deviation from the normal requirements for rulemaking [§553(b)(B)].

Section 553 goes on to describe procedures to ensure that rulemaking will be based on proper legal authority; is within the power granted by the legislature; that there is some opportunity in one form or another for public participation in the process; that the rule is properly and clearly stated by the agency, and is promulgated in a manner that will afford interested people a fair opportunity to know what the rule will require and to have some advance warning when the new rule will be implemented.

Adjudication

Section 554 describes the nature of administrative adjudication. Specifically, §554 requires the minimum procedures necessary to guarantee that those who have a case adjudicated by the government are afforded the basic due process requirements of notice, an opportunity to be heard in some form, and a decision by an impartial decisionmaker.

Qualifications and Conduct of the Presiding Officer in Administrative Proceedings

The APA speaks to two problems regarding the administrative law judge (who was until recently referred to in the statute as the hearing officer) or others who might conduct hearings for an administrative agency. First, it states the authority and responsibility of the ALJ for the manner in which the hearing is conducted and the form in which the initial findings are rendered. Sections 556 and 557 provide relatively detailed procedures for formal hearings; these rules are applicable when the statute that guides the agency's work requires that a rule or decision be made "on the record after an opportunity for an agency hearing," as required by §§553(c) and

554(c) and (d).[11] Sections 556 and 557 prescribe the methods of proceeding and the means for taking evidence during the hearing.

Second, the statute provides, in §§554(d), 557(d)(1), 3105, 7521, 5362, 3344, and 1305, for means of ensuring the independence of hearing examiners from inappropriate influences from outside the agency and from pressure from within the agency, whether directly applied in a particular case or even indirectly exercised by pay judgments, threats to job security, or possible job assignments.

Judicial Review of Agency Decisions

Sections 701 through 706 prescribe the scope and method of judicial review of agency proceedings. They attempt to provide a structure for judicial review of agency actions that preserves an opportunity for a judicial check on possible arbitrary actions or abuses of discretion, and at the same time maintains some warnings against premature or excessive intervention by courts into areas properly the business of the agency.

Each of the parts of the Administrative Procedure Act noted above will be discussed in detail in future chapters. Two caveats should be observed to understand administrative law and the operation of the APA. First, its provisions should not be read in splendid isolation. The Administrative Procedure Act is always applied in conjunction with a particular statute or set of statutes; it arises with respect to a particular problem or set of facts and may be involved in a controversy that also raises constitutional questions. Second, the Administrative Procedure Act (commentary in the legal literature notwithstanding), is not a constitution of administrative law. It is merely one statute with a variety of sections and particular provisions. The provisions are quite likely to change. Therefore, it is useful to think of the statute in terms of its major sections rather than particular provisions.

The remainder of this chapter will focus on the rulemaking segment of the act.

RULEMAKING IN CONTEXT

Because rulemaking occurs in connection with particular problems confronted by one or more agencies acting under some statutory authority, it is useful to come to the black letter law of rulemaking with a sense of the context in which this sort of administrative action takes place.

Assume, for example, that Congress responds to the controversy over the continued use and possible expansion of nuclear power plants by completely reconsidering all the statutes that govern the licensing of nuclear power facilities. In the new statute, the Congress states that it will be the policy of the United States to make prudent use of nuclear power at least through the next several decades, recognizing that this course poses a number of major problems. It proposes that the Nuclear Regulatory Commission completely rewrite all its regulations on nuclear-powered electrical generating facilities within the next 180 days. The statute contains a provision that will force complete review of the nuclear use policy and all agency regulations made to implement it in ten years.[12] The NRC is told that it is to establish separate systems of regulation for (1) medical or scientific uses of nuclear energy and (2) commercial purposes. Decisions on licensing of commercial nuclear power plants will be made in two parts, with the first clearance to be made for construction and the final permit decision to be rendered prior to operation of the facility.[13] The commission's statute directs it to produce a uniform system of licensing rules.

Now, how should the commission proceed? What information do the commissioners need to know? Should they develop a list of descriptive factors that applicants for licenses will be asked to provide? If not, where should they begin?

If the commissioners chose first to array the important questions about proposed plants, they might proceed as follows. They might say that what is involved, in reality, is the design of the application forms that will bring information to the commission from would-be plant developers. Perhaps it would help to conceptualize a fictional plant and ask questions about it. In that way, the commissioners may be able to focus on just what information they need to make future licensing decisions. Where should the description of the plant begin? A physical description of the facility might be a useful starting point. How should the location and structure be discussed? If the commissioners want to begin with the location of the plant, what is meant by location: the address, the geographical coordinates, or the location on a local road map? Or perhaps it is more important to describe the location in terms of its proximity to a population center. In that case, do the commissioners wish to know the distance from the plant to the center of the nearest city or the distance to the nearest residential area, whether it is the center of the nearest city or not? Are these descriptive materials sufficient to describe the location and physical nature of the facility? If not, what other information is needed?

Another important factor in licensing decisions might be the security of the facility, in terms of both its physical integrity and its plans for defense against internal and external threats to the safety of the plant and its environs. The commissioners would perhaps like to have materials that describe the reputation and capabilities of the applicant who will build and operate the plant. But how much do they wish to know? In addition, in security questions, what information should be demanded? The commissioners could request data on the size and training of the security force, alarm systems, and other physical security devices to be employed. Some of those involved in the construction and operation of the plant might be required to have security clearances. If so, what level of clearance would be required and for which employees? After all, security clearances are expensive to perform. Would the contractors be required to obtain clearances? If so, would subcontractors be included? After all, there might be real dangers in having subassemblies made by uncleared workers in plants away from the construction site itself that would later lead to catastrophic failure of the entire facility. As the list lengthens, the costs in time and money increase dramatically.

The applications might contain a separate section for technical assessments. A major area of interest here could be the fuel cycle and its possible impact on the safety of the plant and the environment. As laymen, are the commissioners capable of assessing the data they might receive from the applicants? Unsuccessful applicants might very well argue that the commission lacks sufficient expertise to make technical assessments. If there is a problem, can the members of the commission adequately evaluate claims made by the applicants and operators of the facility? The commission will doubtless call on its staff for help here.

Thus far, the discussion has been limited to substantive questions about proposed plants for which licenses may be sought. But what of the procedures by which the applications will be processed and their contents evaluated? If a construction permit is issued, does it follow that an operating permit will more or less automatically issue in due course unless specific and serious problems arise during construction?[14] If not, and the operations certification can be kept completely separate from the construction permit process, what appeal will the would-be operator have from an initial adverse finding? After all, by the time the operations certification process arises, millions will have been spent on the project with no hope of recovery.[15] If, on the other hand, the second part of the licensing process is more or less automatic, barring some major problem, what procedure will be available for groups claiming to represent the public interest to intervene if they assert that a major problem does indeed exist that justifies terminating the project?[16]

Finally, will any means be provided by which those planning future projects can obtain interpretive guidelines to clarify agency rules after they are issued? If so, how will the guidelines be formulated and promulgated? To what degree will the commission be bound to the guidelines in its future decisionmaking?

This example suggests some of the concerns with which an administrator must deal in developing rules within the modern governmental context. Such problems as developing sufficiently precise language, adherence to a systematic method in considering a large variety of detailed issues, a practical yet sensitive feel for the scope and impact of the proposed rules, an understanding of the political forces that operate with respect to a particular policy problem, and the ever-present issue of costs of the new rules, are all significant.

From the perspective of the formal administrative law, rulemaking is a process that is governed by the Administrative Procedure Act and the statutes that establish the agency involved and grant it authority. This process may be understood through responses to the following questions: (1) What is a rule? (2) What are the specific types of rules? (3) By what procedure are rules promulgated? (4) Are rulemaking processes changing and, if so, in what ways?

WHAT IS A RULE?

To understand what the Administrative Procedure Act requires in any particular agency action, it is necessary first to determine whether the action is a rulemaking activity or an adjudication. When an administrator makes rules, he or she is acting as a policymaker, not unlike a legislator albeit with a limited range of authority. When one contemplates an adjudication, however, the appropriate image is of a courtlike proceeding. There are no particular due process rights involved in a quasi-legislative procedure. After all, one has no rights of any significance to get a policy enacted by a legislature or to play an active role in that process. Rights are associated with courtlike proceedings, which have an adversarial cast to them. In the latter situation, one takes a very active personal or group role in the decision process. The Administrative Procedure Act incorporates that difference in perspective and process. Unfortunately, as noted in Chapter 1, many administrative activities do not fit neatly into either of the two categories. Two of the most obvious examples of ambiguous proceedings are rate-setting problems and licensing processes. Rate requests by utility companies appear to be requests for some decisionmaker to sit in judgment on the merits of the company's immediate case, but policy decisions for the future are also involved. The former is a courtlike activity, but the latter more closely resembles the work of a legislature. In the case of broadcasting, licensing looks to the future public interest of the community served by the station, but it also settles a claim—often disputed—over control of a valuable business enterprise for particular companies or individuals, often on the basis of past events. The former resembles a policymaking decision and the latter has the characteristics of a court proceeding. For these and other reasons, classification of administration activity within the APA categories is important.

Administrative Procedure Act Definitions

Section 553(4) of the APA states that

> "rule" means the whole or part of agency statement of general or particular applicability and future effect designed to implement, interpret, or prescribe law or policy or describing the organization, procedure, or practice requirements of an agency and includes the approval or prescription for the future of rates, wages, corporate or financial structures or reorganization thereof, prices, facilities, appliances, services or allowances therefor or of valuations, costs, or accounting, or practices bearing on any of the foregoing.

This definition describes what a rule is, the types of rules noted in the APA, and resolves the question about rate-setting decisions: prescriptions for rates are developed as rules. Rulemaking is described as the "agency process for formulating, amending, or repealing a rule."[17] The act continues to employ the rule definition as the base for other terms by defining an "order" as the final disposition "of an agency in a matter other than rule making but including licensing."[18] The licensing problem is settled in general terms. "Adjudication" is then, not surprisingly, an "agency process for the formulation of an order."[19]

General Characteristics of Rules and Rulemaking

When one refers to rules and rulemaking, one usually means that the action being taken by the administrator is quasi-legislative—the agency is acting more like a legislature than a court. Rules are usually general in scope. They are made to govern all those under the authority of an agency rather than one particular individual or business firm. Like legislation, rules are made to cover a class of people and a class of actions. Rules, again like legislation, are intended to guide future actions rather than to evaluate actions that have already taken place. Conversely, adjudications are quasi-judicial. They are most often specific, applying to particular named parties involved in a case. Finally, the purpose of adjudication is to resolve a dispute over matters that have already occurred.

The Constitution does not grant power to any administrative agency. Agencies are created by the Congress and, in the states, by the state legislatures. The authority the agency possesses is defined and limited by the provisions of the legislation creating it, generally referred to as the enabling act or the organic act. Whatever actions the agency takes in excess of the authority delegated to it by the legislature are by definition unlawful. If a court finds that an agency has adopted a regulation that exceeds statutory authority, the regulation is held to be *ultra vires* and therefore unlawful.[20] That is to say, the authority of the government will not be available to enforce the rule. The concept of *ultra vires* action comes from corporation law, which noted that the owners of a firm cannot be called to answer for actions taken by the officers of the firm who acted beyond their proper range of authority. Similarly, since administrators function on the basis of authority delegated to them by the legislature, the government should not be held responsible and cannot be made to support actions taken by officials who exceed their proper authority. As the APA defines it, rules should not be "in excess of statutory jurisdiction, authority, or limitations, or short of statutory rights."[21]

The APA also requires judges to strike down agency rules that are "arbitrary, capricious, an abuse of discretion, or otherwise not in accordance with law,"[22] or if they were made "without observance of procedure required by law."[23] In simple terms, these provisions require that administrative actions generally should have some reasonable basis, they should be related to the purposes the administrator is intended to accomplish, and they should be made according to the procedures for rulemaking prescribed by the APA and the enabling statute of the agency.[24]

TYPES OF RULES

Agencies make different kinds of regulations, each of which carries different requirements for making the rule and varying degrees of legal force. The three types come from the APA and are referred to as substantive or legislative rules, procedural rules, and interpretive rules.

Substantive Rules

Substantive or legislative rules are those rules, described in the definition of a rule in §551(4), that "implement, . . . or prescribe law or policy." Legislative rules, to return to nuclear power plant example, cover such matters as the safety requirements for construction of the generating facility or the regulations governing transportation of the fuel to and from the plant. Another example is the attempt by the Federal Trade Commission to issue rules limiting advertising directed at children, discussed in Chapter 1.[25]

Legislative or substantive regulations are legally binding and can be enforced in court.[26] As long as the rules are properly enacted and published in the *Federal Register*, organizations and individuals must obey substantive rules as they would a statute enacted by Congress and published in the *Statutes at Large.*

The amount of authority given different agencies to promulgate substantive rules varies with the statute that guides the agency's actions. Some organizations are given a virtual carte blanche to issue such regulations as are needed to accomplish the purposes assigned by Congress. If those purposes include, for example, the obligation to ensure that broadcasting is conducted in accordance with the public interest, the rulemaking authority is broad indeed. Other statutes are somewhat more specific and yet quite generous in their grants of authority. For example, the following rulemaking authority is granted to the administrator of the National Oceanic and Atmospheric Administration (NOAA), under provisions of the Deep Seabed Hard Mineral Resources Act:

> Application for issuance or transfer of licenses for exploration and permits for commercial recovery [from the ocean floor] shall be made in such form and manner as the Administrator shall prescribe in general and uniform regulations and shall contain such relevant financial, technical and environmental information as the Administrator may by regulations require as being necessary and appropriate for carrying out the provision of this title. In accordance with such regulations, each applicant for the issuance of a license [to mine or explore on the ocean floor] shall submit an exploration plan.[27]

Of course, the courts are the final arbiters of the meaning of a statute and the limits of agency statutory authority.[28]

Procedural Rules

Procedural rules "describe the organization, procedure, or practice requirements of an agency."[29] The APA and the agency enabling act may establish procedures for an agency, but the organization may go beyond such recommendations to add additional guidelines. In general, agencies have inherent powers to promulgate procedural rules.[30] Indeed, they are encouraged to establish such rules. Good management requires some flexibility in agency procedures, but standardization and publication of procedures lend an air of fairness and impartiality to agency interactions with individuals, groups, and other agencies. Although agencies may not be required to issue procedural rules, and need not follow APA rulemaking requirements if they do make procedural rules, the rules of procedure the agency *does* choose to issue must be published in the *Federal Register*.[31] Once procedural rules are promulgated, agencies are required to honor them.[32]

Interpretive Rules

The third variety of administrative rule is the interpretative (or interpretive) rule. Interpretive rules are statements issued by agencies that present the agency's understanding of the meaning of the language in its regulations or the statutes it administers. These rules are not legislative or substantive rules. They are specifically exempted from the normal rulemaking processes required by the APA,[33] although they must be published in the *Federal Register* if they are enacted.[34] Three important questions remain. First, what is the difference between an interpretive rule and a substantive or legislative rule? Second, if interpretive rules do not carry complete binding legal force, why have them at all? Third, since by claiming that a regulation it issues is interpretive rather than substantive an agency can avoid costly and time-consuming rulemaking procedures, who is to determine the appropriate category for any particular rule?

Interpretive rules are not intended to add to or subtract from the existing body of statutory law or regulations in any particular field. They are merely explanatory statements that provide guidance on the understanding that an administrator has of existing law. It is helpful to think of an interpretive rule as a quasi-legislative analog of the advisory opinion.[35]

Suppose one wished to know whether it would be lawful to deduct from one's income tax the price of a new automobile as a business expense. The Internal Revenue Service provides answers to some tax questions by telephone or on a walk-in basis at IRS offices. If an IRS adviser indicated that one was correct in interpreting the code to allow the price of the car to be written off as a business expense, should one accept the advice? If called in for an audit at a future date, should one be able to hold the auditor to the advice given by the agency employee?

Consider another example. Suppose a struggling farm community receives word from the Department of Agriculture that the federal government will underwrite loans for financially pressed farmers suffering the combined effect of high interest rates and drought. The loan programs begin and the farmers are assured that they will continue. They plan their finances and plant accordingly. A new administration is elected and determines that the loan program must be substantially cut back to eliminate abuses in the program. If a farmer who had previously been assured of help at the local office is told that he will not receive the promised loan, does he have any way to hold the government to the earlier promise? Should he have?

In such cases one is tempted to demand enforcement of advisory opinions or interpretative rules on the ground that citizens acted in good faith on the basis of what they believed to be an authoritative statement of government policy. On the other hand, these are useful examples of why one who would understand the administrative justice system must deal with the perspective of the producers of administrative decisions as well as the consumers of those rulings. Can agencies be held to every comment or promise allegedly made by any employee at any level of an organization? It is in everyone's best interest to have agency employees give accurate information on particular problems and interpretations of more general policies. Such information or advice will likely save the agency lengthy disputes later. The same may be said of interpretive rules. A published interpretation guides all who deal with an agency, but should interpretations be treated like substantive rules, as binding on agency officials? If so, the administrator faces a system that would discourage any rulemaking beyond that which is absolutely necessary, since any additional interpretations would be treated to all intents and purposes as substantive binding rules. They would presumably be binding on the agency, but only guidelines to anyone else. Why then should an administrator issue guidelines or provide advice? Why limit one's own flexibility with nothing in return? And if, from an administrator's viewpoint at least, interpretive rules are going to be treated like substantive rules, why not call as much of the necessary rulemaking interpretive rather than substantive, thereby avoiding the work and cost of APA-mandated substantive rulemaking processes?

For these and other reasons, opinions are divided on the binding force of interpretive as opposed to substantive rules.[36] In the near term, consumers of administrative decisions in or out of government would probably be wise to assume that interpretive rules do not bind the agency. In drafting interpretive rules, producers of such decisions should consider at least the possibility that a court will give the rule binding force against the agency.

Interpretive rules are useful devices even if their binding force is questionable. In the years since enactment of the APA several reports and studies have urged agencies to use rulemaking as much as possible and avoid adjudication as a mode of policymaking.[37] In this way, consumers of agency decisions can get information ahead of time on what agency policy is and the probable direction of future agency decisions. Interpretive rules offer administrators a simple method of conveying information on current agency thinking without complex procedures. The idea is to give guidance and to avoid, as much as possible, future conflict. From the standpoint of consumers, interpretive rules provide information from an authoritative source to guide their actions.

Finally, either because an administrator perceives the effect of an interpretive rule as indistinguishable or because he or she sees a possibility of saving time and effort, a substantive rule may be treated as an interpretive rule. Consider the following example.

The Occupational Safety and Health Act provides for inspections of workplaces in search of safety hazards, and also prohibits employers from discriminating against employees who exercise their rights under the act. The agency issued a rule saying that employers who refused to pay a worker representative who accompanied the OSHA inspector during the time required to complete the walkaround inspection would be in violation of the antidiscrimination provisions of the statute. The National Chamber of Commerce contested the rule on the ground that OSHA had not followed the requirements of the APA and its enabling act in promulgating the walkaround rule. The agency countered that the rule was merely an interpretive rule defining employer discrimination as the concept was used in the statute. Since the rule was interpretive, OSHA argued, it was exempt from standard procedures. The D.C. Circuit Court of Appeals disagreed. The court held that: "A rule is interpretive, rather than legislative, if it is not issued under statutory authority to make rules having the force of law or if the agency intends the rule to be no more than an expression of its construction of a statute."[38] The walkaround rule was, in the court's view, clearly intended to be a rule promulgated under the OSHA authority to make rules having the force of law that did more than merely clarify an agency understanding of statutory language. Therefore, the agency was required to follow normal rulemaking procedures.

The courts will decide on judicial review whether a rule is interpretive or substantive regardless of the label the administrator prefers to apply.[39]

HOW ARE RULES MADE?

The manner in which rules are made by administrative agencies is important for many of the same reasons that the processes by which a bill is enacted into law by the Congress are significant. Both are lawmaking activities. But the activities of the legislature are somewhat more visible than those of administrative agencies and are subject to the judgment of the ballot box. The authority to issue rules with relatively limited checks on that power was one of the reasons why those worried about possible administrative arbitrariness referred to administrative agencies as a "headless fourth branch of government." Among the cures for this potentially dangerous situation was the establishment of regular procedures for rulemaking, included in the Administrative Procedure Act.

The APA, enabling legislation enacted since the APA, executive branch policies, and various court decisions have given us essentially three types of processes through which substantive administrative regulations are made: (1) informal rulemaking; (2) formal processes; and (3) hybrid rulemaking procedures. Informal rulemaking is referred to as a "notice and comment" procedure and is governed by §553 of the Administrative Procedure Act. Formal rulemaking is so named because it involves a formal hearing that looks very much like a court proceeding. It is governed by §§556 and 557 of the APA. A hybrid procedure, as the term implies, is a compromise between the formal and informal processes and is governed by the requirements of the agency's enabling act and judicial interpretations of agency processes.

Before discussing the types of rulemaking, it is necessary to clarify the potentially confusing use of the terms "formal" and "informal." Chapter 1 discussed the very important fact that much of what is done by administrative agencies is done through informal discussions and exchanges of information and is guided by no particular set of processes except habit, individual and group interaction, and circumstance. But the term "informal" as it is used in rulemaking does not mean without standards or procedures. One might be well served to think of informal rulemaking as simplified rulemaking. Both formal and informal rulemaking are standardized processes.

Notice and Comment Rulemaking

Informal or simplified rulemaking is generally governed by APA §553. This section identifies those few sorts of rulemaking that are exempted from the act and describes the steps that most administrative agencies must accomplish in order to promulgate a rule.

The rulemaking section exempts military and foreign affairs functions of the federal government, for rather obvious reasons.[40] It also exempts matters "relating to agency management or personnel or to public property, loans, grants, benefits or contracts."[41] At about the same time that the APA was enacted, another set of statutory provisions—the Federal Property and Administrative Services Act, among others—were enacted to deal with some of these problems.[42] Over the years, there has been some question about whether it would be advisable to include rulemaking in formerly exempted areas in the APA requirements and eliminate overlap and confusion. Procedural and interpretive rules are not required to be made in accordance with the APA procedures. Finally, emergency rulemaking may sometimes be required. For example, dangers to health and safety may require immediate promulgation of a rule without the usual opportunities for comment and calm deliberation. The APA exempts emergency rulemaking "when the agency for good cause finds (and incorporates the finding and a brief statement of reasons therefor in the rules issued) that notice and public procedure thereon are impracticable, unnecessary, or contrary to the public interest."[43]

For all other substantive rules made under §553, the administrative agency should proceed as follows. First a notice of proposed rulemaking is published in the *Federal Register.* (See Figure 5-1.) The notice must contain: "(1) a statement of the

FOR FURTHER INFORMATION CONTACT:

Bernard J. Phillips, Attorney, Federal Trade Commission, Washington, D.C. 20580, telephone 202-523-1642.

SUPPLEMENTARY INFORMATION: Comments at this stage of the proceeding are received pursuant to § 1.13(h) of the Commission's Rules of Practice. Accordingly, comments must be confined to information already in the record, new evidence will not be accepted.

Comments should be submitted, when feasible in four copies.

These articles have not been reviewed or adopted by the Commission, and their availability should not be interpreted as reflecting the views of the Commission or any individual member thereof.

CAROL M. THOMAS,
Secretary.

[FR Doc. 79-2250 Filed 1-19-79; 8:45 am]

[6450-01-M]

DEPARTMENT OF ENERGY

Federal Energy Regulatory Commission

[18 CFR Part 285]

[Docket No. RM79-10]

POWERPLANT AND INDUSTRIAL FUEL USE ACT OF 1978

Proposed Criteria for Powerplant's Design Capacity

AGENCY: Federal Energy Regulatory Commission, DOE.

ACTION: Proposed Rule.

SUMMARY: The Powerplant and Industrial Fuel Use Act of 1978 requires the Commission to promulgate rules under which a powerplant's design capacity may be determined. Determination of a powerplant's capacity is necessary because it is an element of various statutory definitions in the Act. By this notice, the Commission has established certain criteria for the design rating and requests comments on how well the proposed rules support the criteria established by the Commission.

DATES: Comments due on or before January 30, 1979.

ADDRESS: Comments referencing Docket No. RM79-10 should be sent to: Kenneth F. Plum, Secretary, Federal Energy Regulatory Commission, 825 North Capitol Street, NE., Washington, D.C. 20426.

FOR FURTHER INFORMATION CONTACT:

Kenneth F. Plum, Secretary, Federal Energy Regulatory Commission, 825 North Capitol Street, NE., Washington, D.C. 20426, 202-275-

4166.

SUPPLEMENTARY INFORMATION: Section 103(a)(18)(D) of the Powerplant and Industrial Fuel Use Act of 1978 (Act) Pub. L. 95-1749, requires the Federal Energy Regulatory Commission (Commission) to promulgate rules under which a powerplant's design capacity may be determined. The determination of a powerplant's design capacity is necessary because it is an element of each of the statutory definitions of the terms"peakload powerplant", "intermediate load powerplant", and "base load powerplant" as provided in section 103(a)(18) of the Act. The definitions of those terms will be used to determine the applicability of certain temporary and permanent exemptions from sections 201 and 202 of the Act, which proscribe the use of natural gas or petroleum as a primary energy source in new electric powerplants, under sections 212(g) and 212(h). The definitions are also to be used to determine the applicability of certain temporary and permanent exemptions from sections 301 and 302 of the Act, relating to existing electric powerplants, under sections 311(f), 312(f), and 312(g) of the Act. Finally, determinations regarding design capacity are necessary under section 501 of the Act, Electric Utility System Compliance Option, in order to determine if existing electric utilities are in compliance with Title III of the Act.

DISCUSSION

The Commission proposes that the rules contained herein be used to determine a powerplant's design capacity. There are a number of powerplant capacity ratings used by the electric power industry. However, these are used principally for operational purposes, reflecting seasonal weather conditions, degradation of a powerplant, or other factors, and may be substantially different from a powerplant's design capacity. The Commission has established criteria that the design rating should be (1) determinable unequivocably from the manufacturer's data and ordinarily not change during a powerplant's physical life, unless there is substantial modification of the unit; (2) a familiar and recognizable quantity throughout the electric power industry; and (3) a published value readily available to any party interested in obtaining it. These criteria and the proposed rules evolving therefrom were developed in consultation with the Staff of the Secretary of Energy. The proposed rules are summarized below:

(1) The design capacity of a steam-electric generating unit shall be its maximum generator nameplate rating which has been reported to the Energy Information Administration

on EIA Form——(formerly FPC Form 12).

(2) The design capacity of a combustion turbine shall be its peak load rating as defined by both the American National Standards Institute (ANSI) and by the International Standards Organization (ISO). This peak load rating, which applies to units operating for peaking service with a maximum of 2,000 hours per year operation, is based on an ambient temperature of 59 degrees Fahrenheit (15 degrees Celcius) and a pressure of 14.696 psia (sea level). This should be the capacity rating reported to the Energy Information Administration on EIA Form——(formerly FPC Form 12). If those reported ratings are based on different conditions, they will be adjusted to ISO standard conditions for the purposes of the Powerplant and Industrial Fuel Use Act.

(3) The design capacity of a combined cycle unit shall be the sum of its combustion turbine peak load rating, based on ANSI/ISO standard conditions, and the maximum generator nameplate rating of the steam turbine portion of the unit.

(4) The design capacity of an internal combustion engine shall be the capacity rating which has been reported to the Energy Information Administration on EIA Form——(formerly FPC Form 12).

The Commission solicits comments from interested parties concerning how well the proposed rules support the criteria established by the Commission. Also, the Commission is interested in any problems or concerns regarding the applicability of the proposed rules in meeting the requirements of the Act.

PUBLIC COMMENT PROCEDURES

Interested persons may participate in this proposed rulemaking by submitting written data, views or arguments to the Office of the Secretary, Federal Energy Regulatory Commission, 825 North Capitol Street, N.E., Washington, D.C. 20426, on or before January 30, 1979. Each person submitting a comment should include his name and address, identify the notice (Docket No. RM79-10), and give reasons for any recommendations. An original and 14 conformed copies should be filed with the Secretary of the Commission.

Comments should indicate the name, title, mailing address, and telephone number of one person to whom communications concerning the proposal may be addressed. Written comments will be placed in the Commission's public files and will be available for public inspection at the Commission's Office of Public Information, Room 1000, 825 North Capitol Street, N.E., Washington, D.C. 20426, during regular business hours.

Figure 5-1 A Notice of Proposed Rulemaking

SOURCE: U.S. Federal Register, vol. 44 (Washington, D.C.: U.S. Government Printing Office, 1979), pp. 4500, 4501.

(Department of Energy Organization Act, Pub. L. 95–91, E.O. 12009, 42 F.R. 46267, Powerplant and Industrial Fuel Use Act of 1978, Pub. L. 95–1749)

In consideration of the foregoing, the Commission proposes to amend Chapter I of Title 18, Code of Federal Regulations, as set forth below.

By the Commission.

LOIS D. CASHELL,
Acting Secretary.

Chapter I of Title 18 is amended by adding a new Subchapter J, Part 285 Consisting of § 285.101 to read as follows:

SUBCHAPTER J—REGULATIONS UNDER THE POWERPLANT AND INDUSTRIAL FUEL USE ACT OF 1978

PART 285—RULES GENERALLY APPLICABLE TO POWERPLANT AND INDUSTRIAL FUEL USE

§ 285.101 Determination of powerplant design capacity.

For purposes of this subchapter, a powerplant's design capacity shall be determined as follows:

(a) *Steam-electric generating unit.* The design capacity of a steam-electric generating unit shall be taken as the maximum generator nameplate rating which has been reported to the Energy Information Administration on EIA Form——(formerly FPC Form 12).

(b) *Combustion turbine.* The design capacity of a combustion turbine shall be taken as its peak load rating as defined by both the American National Standards Institute (ANSI) and by the International Standards Organization (ISO). This peak load rating, which applies to units operating for peaking service with a maximum of 2,000 hours per year operation, is based on an ambient temperature of 59 degrees Fahrenheit (15 degrees Celsius) and a pressure of 14.696 psia (sea level). If capacity ratings as reported to Energy Information Administration on EIA Form——(formerly FPC Form 12) are based on different conditions, these reported ratings will be adjusted to ISO standard conditions.

(c) *Combined cycle unit.* The design capacity of a combined cycle unit shall be taken as the sum of its combustion turbine peak load rating, based on ANSI/ISO standard conditions, and the maximum generator nameplate rating of the steam turbine portion of the unit.

(d) *Internal combustion engine.* The design capacity of an internal combustion engine shall be taken as the capacity rating which has been reported to the Energy Information Administration on EIA Form——(formerly FPC Form 12)

(FR Doc. 79-2312 Filed 1-19-79; 8:45 am)

[4310–84–M]

DEPARTMENT OF THE INTERIOR

Bureau of Land Management

[43 CFR Part 8370]

USE AUTHORIZATIONS

Special Recreation Permits—Allocations and Transfers; Extension of Comment Period

AGENCY: Bureau of Land Management, Interior.

ACTION: Extension of Comment period.

SUMMARY: The Bureau of Land Management extends the time for filing comments on its notice of intent regarding use authorizations for river areas requiring limited use or river areas of scarce recreation resources.

DATE: The comment period is extended to February 23, 1979.

ADDRESS: Send comments to: Mr. William Brown, Bureau of Land Management (D–370), Denver Federal Center, Building 50, Denver, Colorado 80225.

FOR FURTHER INFORMATION CONTACT:

Mr. William Brown, Bureau of Land Management, 303-234-5094 or Mr. Larry R. Young, Bureau of Land Management, 202-343-9353.

SUPPLEMENTARY INFORMATION:

In a notice of intent to develop proposed rulemaking published in the FEDERAL REGISTER on December 6, 1978 (43 CFR 57167), the Bureau of Land Management gave notice of its intention concerning special recreation permit allocations and transfers in river areas of the public lands administered by the Bureau of Land Management.

In the notice comments were requested by February 8, 1979. It has now been determined to extend the comment period by 15 days. Comments received on or before February 23, 1979, will be considered before action is taken to develop the proposed rulemaking.

ARNOLD E. PETTY,
Acting Associate Director.

JANUARY 15, 1979.

[FR Doc. 79-2156 Filed 1-19-79; 8:45 am]

[6712–01–M]

FEDERAL COMMUNICATIONS COMMISSION

[47 CFR Part 73]

[BC Docket No. 78–313; RM-3052]

TELEVISION BROADCAST STATION IN SAN DIEGO, CALIFORNIA

Order Extending Time for Filing Reply Comments

AGENCY: Federal Communications Commission.

ACTION: Order.

SUMMARY: Action taken herein extends the time for filing reply comments in a proceeding involving the proposed assignment of a television channel to San Diego, California. Petitioner, Center City Complex, Inc., states that the additional time is needed for review of comments filed in the proceeding.

DATE: Reply comments must be filed on or before February 16, 1979.

ADDRESSES: Federal Communications Commission, Washington, D.C. 20554.

FOR FURTHER INFORMATION CONTACT:

Mildred B. Nesterak, Broadcast Bureau (202-632-7792).

SUPPLEMENTARY INFORMATION:

In the matter of amendment of § 73.606(b), Table of Assignments, Television Broadcast Stations. (San Diego, California); Order extending time for filing reply comments. See 43 FR 59404, December 20, 1978.

Adopted: January 12, 1979.

Released: January 15, 1979.

By the Chief, Broadcast Bureau:

1. On September 22, 1978, the Commission adopted a *Notice of Proposed Rule Making,* 43 FR 46049, concerning the above-entitled proceeding. The date for filing comments has expired and the date for filing reply comments is presently January 12, 1979.

2. On January 5, 1979, counsel for Center City Complex, Inc., filed a timely request seeking an extension of time for filing reply comments to and including February 16, 1979. Counsel states that the additional time is needed to analyze the whole allocation situation in the San Diego-Mexico border area, taking into account such matters as existing U.S. and Mexican assignments. Counsel adds that the Land Mobile and Translator objections also require legal review and analysis in close conjunction with the engineering facets developed by the consulting engineers.

time, place, and nature of public rulemaking proceedings; (2) reference to the legal authority under which the rule is proposed; and (3) either the terms or substance of the proposed rule or a description of the subjects and issues involved."[44] The agency must give individuals and groups "an opportunity to participate in the rule making."[45] Participation can be made available in any of several forms, but the most common is simply the presentation of a name and address of someone in the agency designated to receive public comment on the proposed rule. As in Figure 5-1, there is usually a name, address, and telephone number for the contact person and a date by which all comments are to be in the hands of agency decisionmakers.[46]

After giving notice of the proposed rulemaking and a general opportunity for comment, the agency is free to produce its final version of the new regulation. The final rule must be published in the *Federal Register* thirty days before its effective date. Presumably, those concerned will have an opportunity within that time to learn of the issuance of the regulation and bring themselves into conformity with it. The final rule must contain, in addition to the actual text of the rule, a "concise general statement" setting forth the purpose of the rule and the legal basis on which it was issued.[47]

The notice and comment procedure is very simple. No more is required of an agency issuing a rule, unless the specific statutes that govern its operation require more or if the enabling act requires that rules be "made on the record after an agency hearing."[48] If the language "on the record after . . . hearing" is used, the agency involved must use formal rulemaking procedures rather than the notice and comment technique just described.

Formal Rulemaking Under the APA

There are only a dozen or so statutes in federal administrative law that require formal rulemaking processes. Food and drug regulatory matters are major examples of the formal approach. The arguments in favor of formalized procedures are: (1) they ensure that all aspects of the development of a new regulation are spelled out in detail on the record; (2) full opportunity is given to all interested groups to participate at length in the deliberations over the proposed new rule; (3) they provide careful limits on the information used in the decisionmaking process to ensure that every bit of evidence can be tested in a hearing; (4) all objections to findings of law or fact in the development of the rule can be decided and reasoned opinions provided; and (5) the burden-of-proof requirement ensures that those likely to be adversely affected by the new rule can be assured that it is necessary and justified by clear evidence on the record developed at hearing. The arguments against formalized rulemaking, which resembles a full dress trial-type hearing, are not difficult to guess. Such procedures are tremendously costly and involve extensive delay. The great dispute over 3 percent limits on non-peanut product in peanut butter stretched on for appoximately twelve years.[49] Formalized procedures leave little administrative flexibility within which expert administrators can perform the functions for which their agencies were created. There is a great danger that the administrative process will be replaced by a heavily judicialized decision process not well suited to policymaking.[50] But there are still some areas of administration where the consequences of the risks of poor quality or arbitrary rulemaking by administrative agencies are so great that legislatures have been unwilling to dispense with the admittedly burdensome formal process.

In a formal §§556 and 557 rulemaking proceeding, the administrative law judge (ALJ) or members of the regulatory commission involved hold a formal trial-type hearing. It is an adversary proceeding with many, although not all, of the requirements of a formal civil trial. On completion of the proceeding, the ALJ makes findings of fact, decides questions of law raised during the hearing, and issues a preliminary opinion. All the material developed at hearing is sent to the members of the commission or to the secretary, if it is a single head cabinet department, for a final decision. That decisionmaker examines the record, or a digest of the record prepared by agency staff personnel, and considers the recommendations of the ALJ. The decision of the ALJ is not binding on the policymaker, but it must be considered. Any final rule must be based on substantial evidence on the record before the agency at the time of the decision.[51]

Table 5-1, based on a discussion in Kenneth Culp Davis's *Administrative Law*

Table 5-1 Formal versus informal rulemaking requirements

Informal Requirements (§553)	Formal Requirements (§§556 and 557)
Few oral proceedings No specific presiding officer	Agency, member of agency, or a hearing examiner (ALJ) must preside
No burden of proof problem	Proponent of the rule or order has the burden of proof
No major ruling on the record insured	§556(d): Decision must be based on the whole record and supported by substantial evidence
No cross-examination	§556(d): Such cross-examination is available as may be required for full and true disclosure of the facts
Agency must maintain a record	§556(e): Agency must maintain a transcript, exhibits, and papers that make up the exclusive record
No initial opinion required	§557(b): The presiding officer must issue an initial decision
No specific input or petitions required	§557(c): Parties may present proposed findings, conclusions, and exemptions and the record must include a rule on each of these
Requires a concise general statement of basis and purpose	§557(c): Must include findings of fact, conclusions of law, and reasons for all materials issues of fact, law, or discretion presented on the record
No limit on the types of permissible communications	§557(d)(1): Limits *ex parte* communications

SOURCE: Based on Kenneth Culp Davis, *Administrative Law Treatise*, 2d ed. (San Diego, Calif.: Kenneth Culp Davis, 1979), p. 460. Used with the permission of Kenneth Culp Davis.

Treatise,[52] provides a view of the differences between informal notice and comment rulemaking and the formal process. The informal process offers maximum administrative flexibility, permits the use of a wide variety of information drawn from diverse sources, and involves no presumed rights on the part of individuals or groups who would like to influence the rulemaking process. On the other hand, notice and comment rulemaking does not, at least on the face of the statute, guarantee that comments offered by the public will be considered, that information used will not be biased, or that evidence and method of evaluating data used by the agency will be open to challenge. The formal process does safeguard the integrity of the evidence by permitting some degree of testing through the use of cross-examination or the submission of contradictory evidence. The formal process insulates the fact-finding process from unseen or unchallenged influence and establishes a strong record that can be used to determine whether the administrator was acting arbitrarily or not. It does presume a need for fairness to contending parties in a policy dispute. However, the formal process is unmercifully burdensome, expensive, and constraining to an administrator.

Hybrid Rulemaking

Given the existing choices between an excessively formal procedure and a weak informal process, it was natural that a compromise third alternative would be developed. Hybrid rulemaking has been favored by Congress, the president, and the courts, but the prime mover behind the development of the hybrid process from the late 1960s through the mid-1970s has been the judiciary. The principal catalyst was the growing number of disputes over regulations issued by various agencies that involved a significant and complex scientific or technological debate. One who would understand recent trends in the administrative process must understand the reasons for the process of hybrid rulemaking development.

Two of the criticisms of the administrative process heard most often, especially following the report of the Task Force on Legal Services and Procedures of the second Hoover Commission from the mid-1950s trhough the 1960s were: (1) administrative agencies ought to make policy decisions through rulemaking proceedings rather than in case-by-case adjudications;[53] and (2) for a variety of reasons, effective judicial review would be necessary to ensure the responsiveness and responsibility of administrators.[54] Rulemaking did increase during the '60s, perhaps in part because of the demands for it, but certainly also because the number of agencies and the scope of administration also increased. In particular, regulation of the environment, implementation of the civil rights laws, and changes in the marketplace brought rapid administrative policy generation and saw legal challenges and responses increase. Many of these policies involved complex technical issues. In such an environment the problem for judges is how to respond to the call for effective judicial review while at the same time respecting the well-understood doctrine of deference to administrative expertise. One must keep administrators within the law without second-guessing their policy judgments.

In a series of cases, several courts worked out solutions.[55] The general line of reasoning ran somewhat as follows. The APA and other statutes and common-law doctrines required courts, on judicial review of agency action, to ensure that the agency was not acting in violation of constitutional provisions, was acting within the authority granted to the agency by statute, and was not acting in a way that was "arbitrary, capricious, an abuse of discretion or otherwise not in accordance with law."[56] In terms of a policy promulgated in the form of a rule, what does it mean to ask whether the rulemaking was arbitrary, capricious, or an abuse of discretion? There are several possibilities. First, an administrator might have included some factors in the decisionmaking process that were impermissible, e.g., whether a certain racial or religious group would be advantaged or disadvantaged. Second, since the APA requires an opportunity for some form of public participation, an administrator might be acting arbitrarily if he or she refused to consider obviously relevant and important information offered in response to notice and comment announcements. Finally, and in the most general sense, arbitrary action is commonly thought of as action without a basis in reason. But how is a reviewing court to determine whether the rule was issued as a matter of fiat or as a reasoned determination? Probably the best way is to examine the record, or more generally the set of information in whatever form, that was before the administrator when he or she made the decision to issue the rule, and inquire as to how the decision was arrived at.[57]

The processes required came to be known as hybrid rulemaking.[58] From the judges' point of view, it was a workable way of meeting their responsibilities without interference with the operation of government. If, after all, presumptions are made in judicial review of the rulemaking record in favor of the validity of agency action and the review is indeed limited to that record, one can perhaps ensure against administrative arbitrariness and at the same time avoid judicial usurpation of administrative authority.

The cornerstone of hybrid rulemaking is the rulemaking record. One of those involved in the development of the hybrid process, Judge David L. Bazelon, commenting on the *Vermont Yankee* ruling,[59] summarized his views on the usefulness and appropriateness of this form of rulemaking:

> Courts do not have resources to get deeply into the area of agency expertise. The court can make sure the agency did its task by ensuring that a good rule-making record is established. Such a record provides for:
>
> (1) Judicial review—because the judge understands what was considered and how it was considered;
>
> (2) Peer review—because it gets all the material out where the professional scientific community can see the record and respond to it;
>
> (3) Legislative oversight—so that we can learn from [agency performance];
>
> (4) An adhesive force in public opinion in that there is no sense of secrecy or cover up;
>
> (5) Reconsideration of policy—because as values change we can reconsider policy. We can look back five months, five years, fifty years, or two hundred years to judge the bases for decisions to know how to evaluate them in light of changing values.[60]

Gellhorn and Bruff summarized the nature and purposes of this new form of rulemaking as follows:

Several purposes are discernible in these new statutory and judicial requirements. One is to assure fair treatment of persons submitting comments by requiring actual agency consideration and response. A second is to foster reasoned agency decisionmaking by exposing thinking within the agency to public criticism and by requiring reasoned resolution of the issues. A third is to facilitate judicial review by providing a record to justify a final rule. Obviously, these purposes are closely intertwined.[61]

In general terms, hybrid rulemaking involves the §553 process plus such specific procedures as are needed to establish that when a rule is promulgated it will be supported by a rulemaking record, which:

1. Gives a statement of the basis and purpose of the rule and cites supporting documentation;
2. Sets forth the data on which the agency relied in developing the rule;
3. Describes the methodology the agency employed in analyzing its data and developing the final policy;
4. Provides evidence that there was adequate notice to those who might be interested in commenting on the proposed rule;
5. Shows that a sufficient amount of time was provided so that comment could be prepared and submitted to the agency;
6. Indicates that comments could challenge the data admittedly relied on by the agency, either on paper or by some form of oral argument;
7. Gives evidence that the agency did examine relevant significant public comments and responded, albeit perhaps in a limited way, to those criticisms and suggestions.[62]

But these judicially imposed reforms quickly became controversial.[63] Were the judges really simply demanding substantial compliance with the provisions of the APA and agency-enabling acts as opposed to rubber-stamping agency decisions, or were they second-guessing the legislature and substituting judicial policy views for the discretion that was properly the province of the expert administrator? Although it is an interesting topic for debate some of the significance of the controversy has been rendered moot by the fact that Congress and the president have imposed a hybrid rulemaking process on a variety of agencies since the technique was first launched in judicial opinions. Congress has included some additional requirements above the basic §553 notice and comment process in most of the major pieces of legislation enacted during the 1970s that contained significant rulemaking authority.[64]

The provisions of the Toxic Substances Control Act[65] include hybrid or §553-plus requirements for rulemaking by the Environmental Protection Agency in the area of hazardous substances regulation.

SEC. 4. TESTING OF CHEMICAL SUBSTANCES AND MIXTURES.

(a) Testing Requirements.—If the Administrator finds that—
(1)(A)(i) the manufacture, distribution in commerce, processing, use, or disposal of a chemical substance or mixture, or that any combination of such activities, may present an unreasonable risk of injury to health or the environment,

(ii) there are insufficient data and experience upon which the effects of such manufacture, distribution in commerce, processing, use, or disposal of such activities on health or the environment can reasonably be determined or predicted, and

(iii) testing of such substance or mixture with respect to such effects is necessary to develop such data. . . .

the administrator shall by rule require that testing be conducted on such substance or mixture to develop data with respect to the health and environmental effects for which there is an insufficiency of data and experience and which are relevant to a determination that the manufacture, distribution in commerce, processing, use, or disposal of such substance or mixture, or that any combination of such activities, does or does not present an unreasonable risk of injury to health or the environment.

(b) (1) TESTING REQUIREMENT RULE.—A rule under subsection (a) shall include—

(A) identification of the chemical substance or mixture for which testing is required under the rule,

(B) standards for the development of test data for such substance or mixture, and

(C) with respect to chemical substances which are not new chemical substances and to mixtures, a specification of the period (which period may not be of unreasonable duration) within which the persons required to conduct the testing shall submit to the Administrator data developed in accordance with the standards referred to in subparagraph (B). . . .

(5) Rules issued under subsection (a) (and any substantive amendment thereto or repeal thereof) shall be promulgated pursuant to section 553 of title 5, United States Code, except that (A) the Administrator shall give interested persons an opportunity for the oral presentation of data, views, or arguments, in addition to an opportunity to make written submissions; (B) a transcript shall be made of any oral presentation; and (C) the Administrator shall make and publish with the rule the findings described in paragraph (1)(A) or (1)(B) of subsection (a) and, in the case of a rule respecting a mixture, the finding described in paragraph (2) of such subsection.

(d) NOTICE.—Upon the receipt of any test data pursuant to a rule under subsection (a), the Administrator shall publish a notice of the receipt of such data in the Federal Register within 15 days of its receipt. Subject to section 14, each such notice shall (1) identify the chemical substance or mixture for which data have been received; (2) list the uses or intended uses of such substance or mixture and the information required by the applicable standards for the development of test data; and (3) describe the nature of the test data developed, except as otherwise provided in section 14, such data shall be made available by the Administrator for examination by any person.

•   •   •

SEC. 6. REGULATION OF HAZARDOUS CHEMICAL SUBSTANCES AND MIXTURES.

(a) SCOPE OF REGULATION.—If the Administrator finds that there is a reasonable basis to conclude that the manufacture, processing, distribution in commerce, use, or disposal of a chemical substance or mixture, or that any combination of such activities, presents or will present an unreasonable risk of injury to health or the environment, the Administrator shall by rule apply one or more of the following requirements to such substance or mixture to the extent necessary to protect adequately against such risk using the least burdensome requirements:

(1) A requirement (A) prohibiting the manufacturing, processing, or distribution in commerce of such substance or mixture or (B) limiting the amount of such substance or mixture which may be manufactured, processed, or distributed in commerce.

(2) A requirement—

(A) prohibiting the manufacture, processing, or distribution in commerce of such substance or mixture for (i) a particular use or (ii) a particular use in a concentration in excess of a level specified by the Administrator in the rule imposing the requirement, or

(B) limiting the amount of such substance or mixture which may be manufactured, processed, or distributed in commerce for (i) a particular use or (ii) a particular use in a concentration in excess of a level specified by the Administrator in the rule imposing the requirement.

(3) A requirement that such substance or mixture or any article containing such substance or mixture be marked with or accompanied by clear and adequate warnings and instructions. . . .

(4) A requirement that manufacturers and processors of such substance or mixture make and retain records of the processes used to manufacture or process such substance or mixture and monitor or conduct tests which are reasonable and necessary to assure compliance with the requirements of any rule applicable under this subsection.

(5) A requirement prohibiting or otherwise regulating any manner or method of commercial use of such substance or mixture.

(6)(A) A requirement prohibiting or otherwise regulating any manner or method of disposal of such substance or mixture, or of any article containing such substance or mixture, by its manufacturer or processor or by any other person who uses, or disposes of, it for commercial purposes. . . .

(7) A requirement directing manufacturers or processors of such substance or mixture

(A) to give notice of such unreasonable risk of injury to distributors in commerce of such substance or mixture and, to the extent reasonably ascertainable, to other persons in possession of such substance or mixture or exposed to such substance or mixture,

(B) to give public notice of such risk of injury, and

(C) to replace or repurchase such substance or mixture as elected by the person to which the requirement is directed. . . .

(c) PROMULGATION OF SUBSECTION (a) RULES.—

(1) In promulgating any rule under subsection (a) with respect to a chemical substance or mixture, the Administrator shall consider and publish a statement with respect to—

(A) the effects of such substance or mixture on health and the magnitude of the exposure of human beings to such substance or mixture,

(B) the effects of such substance or mixture on the environment and the magnitude of the exposure of the environment to such substance or mixture,

(C) the benefits of such substance or mixture for various uses and the availability of substitutes for such uses, and

(D) the reasonably ascertainable economic consequences of the rule, after consideration of the effect on the national economy, small business, technological innovation, the environment, and public health.

If the Administrator determines that a risk of injury to health or the environment could be eliminated or reduced to a sufficient extent by actions taken under another Federal law (or laws) administered in whole or in part by the Administrator, the Administrator may not promulgate a rule under subsection (a) to protect against such risk of injury unless the Administrator finds, in the Administrator's discretion, that it is in the public interest to protect against such risk under this Act. In making such a finding the Administrator shall consider (i) all relevant aspects of the risk, as determined by the Administrator in the Administrator's discretion, (ii) a comparison of the estimated costs of complying with actions taken under this Act and under such law (or laws) and (iii) the relative efficiency of actions under this Act and under such law (or laws), and (iv) the relative efficiency of actions under this Act and under such law (or laws) to protect against such risk of injury.

(2) When prescribing a rule under subsection (a) the Administrator shall proceed in accordance with section 553 of title 5, United States Code (without regard to any reference in such section to sections 556 and 557 of such title), and shall also

(A) publish a notice of proposed rulemaking stating with particularity the reason for the proposed rule;

(B) allow interested persons to submit written data, views, and arguments, and make all such submissions publicly available;

(C) provide an opportunity for an informal hearing in accordance with paragraph (3);

(D) promulgate, if appropriate, a final rule based on the matter in the rulemaking record (as defined in section 19(a)), and

(E) make and publish with the rule the finding described in subsection (a).

(3) Informal hearings required by paragraph (2)(C) shall be conducted by the Administrator in accordance with the following requirements:

(A) Subject to subparagraph (B), an interested person is entitled—

(i) to present such person's position orally or by documentary submissions (or both), and

(ii) if the Administrator determines that there are disputed issues of material fact it is necessary to resolve, to present such rebuttal submissions and to conduct (or have conducted under subparagraph (B)(ii) such cross-examination of persons as the Administrator determines (I) to be appropriate, and (II) to be required for a full and true disclosure with respect to such issues.

(B) The Administrator may prescribe such rules and make such rulings concerning procedures in such hearings to avoid unnecessary costs or delay. Such rules or rulings may include (i) the imposition of reasonable time limits on each interested person's oral presentations, and (ii) requirements that any cross-examination to which a person may be entitled under subparagraph (A) be conducted by the Administrator on behalf of that person in such manner as the Administrator determines (I) to be appropriate, and (II) to be required for a full and true disclosure with respect to disputed issues of material fact.

(C) (i) Except as provided in clause (ii), if a group of persons each of whom under subparagraphs (A) and (B) would be entitled to conduct (or have conducted) cross-examination and who are determined by the Administrator to have the same or similar interests in the proceeding cannot agree upon a single representative of such interests for purposes of cross-examination the Administrator may make rules and rulings (I) limiting the representation of such interest for such purposes, and (II) governing the manner in which such cross-examination shall be limited.

(ii) When any person who is a member of a group with respect to which the Administrator has made a determination under clause (i) is unable to agree upon group representation with the other members of the group, then such person shall not be denied under the authority of clause (i) the opportunity to conduct (or have conducted) cross-examination as to issues affecting the person's particular interests if (I) the person satisfies the Administrator that the person has made a reasonable and good faith effort to reach agreement upon group representation with the other members of the group and (II) the Administrator determines that there are substantial and relevant issues which are not adequately presented by the group representative.

(D) A verbatim transcript shall be taken of any oral presentation made, and cross-examination conducted in any informal hearing under this subsection. Such transcript shall be available to the public.

(4)(A) The Administrator may, pursuant to rules prescribed by the Administrator, provide compensation for reasonable attorneys' fees, expert witness fees, and other costs of participating in a rulemaking proceeding for the promulgation of a rule under subsection (a) to any person—

(i) who represents an interest which would substantially contribute to a fair determination of the issues to be resolved in the proceeding, and

(ii) if—

> (I) the economic interest of such person is small in comparison to the costs of effective participation in the proceeding by such person, or
>
> (II) such person demonstrates to the satisfaction of the Administrator that such person does not have sufficient resources adequately to participate in the proceeding without compensation under this subparagraph.[66]

The act requires the kinds of items generally included in demands for hybrid rulemaking in situations in which the Environmental Protection Agency (EPA) either promulgates a rule for the testing of a substance or in which the agency decides actually to regulate the manufacture or distribution of particular substances found through the testing process to be toxic.

The trend toward hybrid procedures has not been limited to the courts and the legislature. President Carter issued Executive Order 12044 on March 23, 1978.[67] Among other things, this announcement required some executive branch agencies not otherwise required to do so to employ the additional requirements of adequate notice, openness, participation, and development of a rulemaking record usually included in hybrid rulemaking.

NEW DIRECTIONS IN AGENCY RULEMAKING

As well as the steps to be followed in rulemaking described above, agencies have been increasingly required to add two further elements to rulemaking requirements. Both Congress and the president have compelled administrators to perform regulatory analyses on proposed rules. The legitimacy of the second requirement is hotly disputed by the executive branch, but, through provisions in agency-enabling legislation—and other vehicles—Congress appears to be, temporarily at least, able to force procedures that permit legislative review and veto of proposed regulations.

Regulatory Analyses

Several recent presidents have been concerned that some agencies were not taking sufficient care in rulemaking to ensure that a new regulation was necessary and that its probable economic impact had been considered. President Ford issued Executive Order 11821 in 1974, authorizing the Office of Management and Budget to require inflation-impact assessments by agencies that wished to promulgate new rules.[68] President Carter expanded on the theme dramatically in his regulatory improvement policy order of 1978:

TEXT OF EXECUTIVE ORDER 12044: IMPROVING GOVERNMENT REGULATIONS

As President of the United States of America, I direct each Executive Agency to adopt procedures to improve existing and future regulations.

Section 1. Policy. Regulations shall be as simple and clear as possible.

They shall achieve legislative goals effectively and efficiently. They shall not impose unnecessary burdens on the economy, on individuals, on public or private organizations, or on State and local governments.

To achieve these objectives, regulations shall be developed through a process which ensures that:

(a) the need for and purposes of the regulation are clearly established;

(b) heads of agencies and policy officials exercise effective oversight;

(c) opportunity exists for early participation and comment by other Federal agencies, State and local governments, businesses, organizations and individual members of the public;

(d) meaningful alternatives are considered and analyzed before the regulation is issued; and

(e) compliance costs, paperwork and other burdens on the public are minimized.

Sec. 2. Reform of the Process for Developing Significant Regulations. Agencies shall review and revise their procedures for developing regulations to be consistent with the policies of this Order and in a manner that minimizes paperwork.

Agencies' procedures should fit their own needs but, at a minimum, these procedures shall include the following:

(a) Semiannual Agenda of Regulations. To give the public adequate notice, agencies shall publish at least semiannually an agenda of significant regulations under development or review. On the first Monday in October, each agency shall publish in the FEDERAL REGISTER a schedule showing the times during the coming fiscal year when the agency's semiannual agenda will be published. Supplements to the agenda may be published at other times during the year if necessary, but the semiannual agendas shall be as complete as possible. The head of each agency shall approve the agenda before it is published. At a minimum, each published agenda shall describe the regulations being considered by the agency, the need for and the legal basis for the action being taken, and the status of regulations previously listed on the agenda.

(b) Agency Head Oversight. Before an agency proceeds to develop significant new regulations, the agency head shall have reviewed the issues to be considered, the alternative approaches to be explored, a tentative plan for obtaining public comment, and target dates for completion of steps in the development of the regulation.

(c) Opportunity for Public Participation. Agencies shall give the public an early and meaningful opportunity to participate in the development of agency regulations. They shall consider a variety of ways to provide this opportunity, including (1) publishing an advance notice of proposed rulemaking; (2) holding open conferences or public hearings; (3) sending notices of proposed regulations to publications likely to be read by those affected; and (4) notifying interested parties directly. Agencies shall give the public at least 60 days to comment on proposed significant regulations. In the few instances where agencies determine this is not possible the regulation shall be accompanied by a brief statement of the reasons for a shorter time period.

(d) Approval of Significant Regulations. The head of each agency, or the designated official with statutory responsibility, shall approve significant regulations before they are published for public comment in the FEDERAL REGISTER. At a minimum, this official should determine that:

(1) the proposed regulation is needed;

(2) the direct and indirect effects of the regulation have been adequately considered;

(3) alternative approaches have been considered and the least burdensome of the acceptable alternatives has been chosen;

(4) public comments have been considered and an adequate response has been prepared;

(5) the regulation is written in plain English and is understandable to those who must comply with it;

(6) an estimate has been made of the new reporting burdens or recordkeeping requirements necessary for compliance with the regulation;

(7) the name, address and telephone number of a knowledgeable agency official is included in the publication; and

(8) a plan for evaluating the regulation after its issuance has been developed.

(e) Criteria for Determining Significant Regulations. Agencies shall establish criteria for identifying which regulations are significant. Agencies shall consider among other things: (1) the type and number of individuals, businesses, organizations, State and local governments affected; (2) the compliance and reporting requirements likely to be involved; (3) direct and indirect effects of the regulation including the effect on competition; and (4) the relationship of the regulations to those of other programs and agencies. Regulations that do not meet an agency's criteria for determining significance shall be accompanied by a statement to that effect at the time the regulation is proposed.

Sec. 3. Regulatory Analysis. Some of the regulations identified as significant may have major economic consequences for the general economy, for individual industries, geographical regions or levels of government. For these regulations, agencies shall prepare a regulatory analysis. Such an analysis shall involve a careful examination of alternative approaches early in the decision-making process.

The following requirements shall govern the preparation of regulatory analyses:

(a) Criteria. Agency heads shall establish criteria for determining which regulations require regulatory analyses. The criteria establish shall:

(1) ensure that regulatory analyses are performed for all regulations which will result in (a) an annual effect on the economy of $100 million or more; or (b) a major increase in costs or prices for individual industries, levels of government or geographic regions; and

(2) provide that in the agency head's discretion, regulatory analysis may be completed on any proposed regulation.

(b) Procedures. Agency heads shall establish procedures for developing the regulatory analysis and obtaining public comment.

(1) Each regulatory analysis shall contain a succinct statement of the problem; a description of the major alternative ways of dealing with the problems that were considered by the agency; an analysis of the economic consequences of each of these alternatives and a detailed explanation of the reasons for choosing one alternative over the others.

(2) Agencies shall include in their public notice of proposed rules an explanation of the regulatory approach that has been selected or is favored and a short description of the other alternatives considered. A statement of how the public may obtain a copy of the draft regulatory analysis shall also be included.

(3) Agencies shall prepare a final regulatory analysis to be made available when the final regulations are published.

Regulatory analyses shall not be required in rulemaking proceedings pending at the time this Order is issued if an Economic Impact Statement has already been prepared in accordance with Executive Orders 11821 and 11949.

Congress has required some of the same kinds of analyses in particular agency-enabling acts, although attempts to required governmentwide regulatory analyses have not been enacted.[69]

The requirement that agencies perform a regulatory analysis prior to issuance of a new rule requires essentially three types of information: (1) the agency is expected to show that the new regulation is really necessary; (2) the administrator is to indicate what other alternative policy instruments were available and why they were rejected in favor of the regulation. Finally, (3) the agency is generally expected to show that it has considered the likely costs of the proposed regulation.

Legislative Veto Provisions

Both the regulatory analysis requirements and the legislative veto device have been and are likely to remain extremely controversial, with the latter causing particularly lively debate.[70] The reasons for the controversy will be discussed in the consideration of regulation in Chapter 10. For the present, it is important to note what the legislative veto is and how it works.

The legislative veto requires that agencies submit proposed rules to the legislature before they are issued. The legislature may then vote to prevent the publication of the rule or allow some predetermined time period, usually sixty to ninety days, to pass without action, in which case the regulation is presumed to be cleared. The agency enabling act indicates whether a legislative veto process is required. Attempts to require a governmentwide (or generic) veto as an amendment to the APA has not succeeded as yet.

Three basic types of vetoes are in use. The first is a veto by concurrent resolution, in which a resolution must pass both houses of the legislature to veto the rule. In a concurrent resolution the president is not permitted a veto. The second type of legislative veto is the one-house veto in which either house of the legislature may reject a rule by simple resolution. Finally, there is what is known as the committee veto, which by various means permits a legislative committee to kill the proposed rule.

A sample of the legislative veto requirements is provided in the provisions that follow, taken from the Federal Trade Commission Improvement Act of 1980:

FEDERAL TRADE COMMISSION IMPROVEMENT ACT, 1980
THE LEGISLATIVE VETO PROVISION

Congressional Review of Rules

SEC. 21 (a)(1) The Federal Trade Commission, after promulgating a final rule, shall submit such final rule to the Congress for review in accordance with this section. Such final rule shall be delivered to each House of the Congress on the same date and to Each House of the Congress while it is in session. Such final rule shall be referred to the Committee on Commerce, Science, and Transportation of the Senate and to the Committee on Interstate and Foreign Commerce of the House, respectively.

(2) Any such final rule shall become effective in accordance with its terms unless, before the end of the period of 90 calendar days of continuous session after the date such final rule is submitted to the Congress, both Houses of the Congress adopt a concurrent resolution disapproving such final rule.

(b)(1) The provisions of this subsection are enacted by the Congress—

(A) as an exercise of the rulemaking power of the Senate and the House of Representatives, respectively, and as such they are deemed a part of the rules of each House, respectively, but applicable only with respect to the procedure to be followed in that House in the case of concurrent resolutions which are subject to this section, and such provisions supersede other rules only to the extent that they are inconsistent with such other rules; and

(B) with full recognition of the constitutional right of either House to change the rules (so far as relating to the procedure of that House) at any time, in the same manner and to the same extent as in the case of any other rule of that House.

(2)(A) Any concurrent resolution disapproving a final rule of the Commission shall, upon introduction or receipt from the other House of the Congress, be referred immediately by the presiding officer of such House to the Committee on Commerce, Science, and Transportation of the Senate or to the Committee on Interstate and Foreign Commerce of the House, as the case may be.

(B) If a committee to which a concurrent resolution is referred does not report such concurrent resolution before the end of the period of 75 calendar days of continuous session of the Congress after the referral of such resolution to the Committee on Commerce, Science and Transportation of the Senate or to the Committee on Interstate and Foreign Commerce of the House, as the case may be, under subsection (a)(1), it shall be in order to move to discharge any such committee from further consideration of such concurrent resolution.

(C)(i) A motion to discharge in the Senate may be made only by a Member favoring the concurrent resolution, shall be privileged (except that it may not be made after the committee has reported a concurrent resolution with respect to the same final rule of the Commission), and debate on such motion shall be limited to not more than 1 hour, to be divided equally between those favoring and those opposing the motion. An amendment to the motion shall not be in order, and it shall not be in order to move to reconsider the vote by which the motion was agreed to or disagreed to. If the motion to discharge is agreed to or disagreed to, the motion may not be renewed, nor may another motion to discharge the committee be made with respect to any other concurrent resolution with respect to the same final rule of the Commission.

(ii) A motion to discharge in the House may be made by presentation in writing to the Clerk. The motion may be called up only if the motion has been signed by one-fifth of the Members of the House. The motion is highly privileged (except that it may not be made after the committee has reported a concurrent resolution of disapproval with respect to the same rule). Debate on such motion shall be limited to not more than 1 hour, the time to be divided equally between those favoring and those opposing the motion. An amendment to the motion is not in order, and it is not in order to move to reconsider the vote by which the motion is agreed to or disagreed to.

(3)(A) When a committee has reported, or has been discharged from further consideration of, a concurrent resolution, it shall be at any time thereafter in order (even though a previous motion to the same effect has been disagreed to) to move to proceed to the consideration of the concurrent resolution. The motion shall be privileged in the Senate and highly privileged in the House of Representatives, and shall not be debatable. An amendment to the motion shall not be in order, and it shall not be in order to move to reconsider the vote by which the motion was agreed to or disagreed to.

(B) Debate on the concurrent resolution shall be limited to not more than 10 hours, which shall be divided equally between those favoring and those opposing such concurrent resolution. A motion further to limit debate shall not be debatable. An amendment to, or motion to recommit, the concurrent resolution shall not be in order, and it shall not be in order to move to reconsider the vote by which such concurrent resolution was agreed to or disagreed to.

(4) Appeals from the decision of the Chair relating to the application of the rules of the Senate or the House of Representatives, as the case may be, to the procedure relating to a concurrent resolution shall be decided without debate.

(5) Notwithstanding any other provision of this subsection, if a House has approved a concurrent resolution with respect to any final rule of the Commission, then it shall not be in order to consider in such House any other concurrent resolution with respect to the same final rule.

(c)(1) If a final rule of the Commission is disapproved by the Congress under subsection (a)(2), then the Commission may promulgate a final rule which relates to the same acts or practices as the final rule disapproved by the Congress in accordance with this subsection. Such final rule—

(A) shall be based upon—
(i) the rulemaking record of the final rule disapproved by the Congress; or
(ii) such rulemaking record and the record established in supplemental rulemaking proceedings conducted by the Commission in accordance with section 553 of title 5, United States Code, in any case in which the Commission determines that it is necessary to supplement the existing rulemaking records; and

(B) may contain such changes as the Commission considers necessary or appropriate.

(2) The Commission, after promulgating a final rule under this subsection, shall submit the final rule to the Congress in accordance with subsection (a)(1).

SUMMARY

Rulemaking is one of the primary devices through which administrative agencies make authoritative policy statements. There is some regularity to the rulemaking process, although the starting point for an understanding of any particular agency's work is the agency-enabling act. The Administrative Procedure Act sets forth the standard procedures, based on understandings of the nature of a rule, the type of rule involved in specific situation, and the manner in which that type of rule must be promulgated. The determination of the rule type, whether substantive, procedural, or interpretative, determines the formality involved in rulemaking and the degree of legal force involved in any rulemaking procedure. Those procedures may be formal, informal (simplified), or hybrid processes. The hybrid procedure is a compromise form developed from a variety of sources, most notably the courts. For several reasons there appear to be new procedures on the horizon designed to ensure that agencies remain responsible and responsive to the legislature and the electorate.

The standardization of rulemaking as a process was one of the cornerstones of formal judicial process developed in earlier years and codified in the Administrative Procedure Act. Judicial review is a second fundamental concept. The regularization of adjudications to provide for fundamental fairness in decisionmaking by agencies is the third basic element, and it is to this subject that we turn in Chapter 6.

NOTES

[1]For material on specific areas of state administrative law, see Appendix D.

[2]"The basic scheme underlying the legislation is to classify all proceedings into two categories, namely, 'rulemaking' and 'adjudication.' " U.S. Attorney General Tom C. Clark to Director Harold D. Smith, Bureau of the Budget, June 3, 1946, Truman Papers, Truman Library.

[3]But see the discussion of this dichotomy in Chapter 1.

[4]5 U.S.C. §551 et seq. Because there have been a number of amendments to the act over the three decades since its passage, and because some of the APA provisions, such as those governing hearing examiners, have several overlapping areas of importance, the sections of the APA are not all numbered in sequence.

[5]5 U.S.C. §551 (a)(A)–(E).

[6]The debate came to the boiling point during the Nixon administration when the Executive Office of the President was expanded into a counterbureaucracy. Congress may have granted some deference to internal executive branch operations, but the claims by the White House against requests for information by Watergate investigators and the liberal use of security classification stamps prompted Congress to add the clarification during their strengthening amendments to the Freedom of Information Act (see note 7).

[7]Public Law 89-554, 80 Stat. 383 (1966); Public Law 90-23, 81 Stat. 54 (1967); Public Law 93-502, 88 Stat. 1561–1564 (1974); Public Law 94-409, 90 Stat. 1247 (1976).

[8]Public Law 93-579, 88 Stat. 1896 (1974).

[9]Public Law 94-409, 90 Stat. 1241 (1976).

[10]Public Law 92-463, 86 Stat. 770 (1972); Public Law 94-409, 90 Stat. 1241 (1976).

[11]The Supreme Court has held that for a statute to be interpreted to require the formal process it must contain precisely the correct language. It must require that rules be made "on the record after an agency hearing." Merely stating that rules be made "after a hearing" is not sufficient to trigger the form §§556–557 process. *United States v. Florida East Coast Ry. Co.*, 410 U.S. 224, 234–38 (1973).

[12]This type of statutory provision is referred to as a "sunset" clause, so named because it will set on the policy unless specific action is taken to reenact it within a specified period. See, e.g., "Zero Base Sunset Review," 14 *Harvard J. on Legislation*, 505 (1977).

[13]This format approximates existing requirements. See Donald W. Sever, Jr., *Seabrook and the Nuclear Regulatory Commission: The Licensing of a Nuclear Power Plant* (Hanover, N.H.: University Press of New England, 1980).

[14]See generally *Power Reactor Dev. Co. v. International Union of Electrical Radio and Machine Workers*, 367 U.S. 396 (1961).

[15]Id., Justice Douglas dissenting. This problem is discussed in detail in Chapter 10.

[16]See supra note 14 and *Northern Public Service Co. v. Porter County Chapter of the Izaak Walton League of America*, 423 U.S. 12 (1975), particularly Justice Douglas, concurring.

[17]5 U.S.C. §551(5).

[18]Id., at §551(6).

[19]Id., at §551(7).

[20]On the delegation of power doctrine and its limits, see Bernard Schwartz, *Administrative Law* (Boston: Little, Brown, 1976), pp. 151–52. See also Walter Gellhorn, Clark Byse, and Peter Strauss, *Administrative Law: Cases and Comments*, 7th ed. (Mineola, N.Y.: Foundation Press, 1979), pp. 52–77.

[21]5 U.S.C. §706(2)(C).

[22]Id., at §706(2)(A).

[23]Id., at §706(2)(D).

[24]Schwartz, supra note 20, at pp. 152–53.

[25]For an interesting example of a similar problem, see A. Lee Fritschler *Smoking and Politics: Policymaking and the Federal Bureaucracy*, 2d ed. (Englewood Cliffs, N.J.: Prentice-Hall, 1975).

[26]*Chrysler Corp. v. Brown*, 441 U.S. 281, 301–302 (1979); *United States v. Nixon*, 418 U.S. 683, 695–96 (1974). See Kenneth Culp Davis, *Administrative Law Treatise*, 2d ed. vol. 2 (San Diego, Calif.: Kenneth Culp Davis, 1979), §7:21.

[27]Deep Seabed Hard Minerals Act, Public Law 69-283, 94 Stat. 553 (1980), §103.

[28]*International Brotherhood of Teamsters v. Daniel*, 439 U.S. 551, 566–67 (1979); *Securities and Exchange Comm'n v. Sloan*, 436 U.S. 103, 117–19 (1978); *United States v. Nixon*, 418 U.S. 683, 704–706 (1974); *Halperin v. Kissinger*, 606 F. 2d 1192, 1211 (D.C. Cir. 1979); *National Treasury Employees Union v. Nixon*, 492 F. 2d 587 604, 612–16 (D.C. Cir. 1974); *National Automatic Laundry and Cleaning Council v. Schultz*, 443 F. 2d 687, 695 (D.C. Cir. 1971).

[29]5 U.S.C. §551(4).

[30]Schwartz, supra note 20, at p. 153.

[31]5 U.S.C. §553(b)(A) exempts procedural and interpretive rules from standard rulemaking proceedings, but §552(a)(1)(C) requires that such procedural rules as an agency does promulgate must be published.

[32]*United States v. Caceres*, 440 U.S. 741, 751 n. 14 (1979); *Morton v. Ruiz*, 415 U.S. 199, 235 (1974); *Vitarelli v. Seaton* 359 U.S. 539 (1959); and *Service v. Dulles*, 354 U.S. 363, 388 (1957).

[33]5 U.S.C. §§553(b)(A), 553(d)(2).

[34]Id., at §552(a)(1)(D).

[35]It is helpful, but it is no substitute for further development of the law. See *Chrylser Corp. v. Brown*, supra note 26, at 301–302.

[36]Compare Davis, supra note 26, vol. 2 §§7:13 and 7:21, with Schwartz, supra note 20, at pp. 160–61.

[37]See generally Henry J. Friendly, *The Federal Administrative Agencies: The Need for Better Definition of Standards* (Cambridge, Mass.: Harvard University Press, 1962), and Kenneth Culp Davis, *Discretionary Justice: A Preliminary Inquiry* (Baton Rouge, La.: Louisiana State University Press, 1969). See also the discussion of the findings of the Task Force on Legal Services and Procedure of the second Hoover Commission in Chapter 4.

[38]*Chamber of Commerce v. Occupational Safety and Health Agency*, 636 F. 2d 464, 488 (D.C. Cir. 1980).

[39]"The administrative agency's own label is indicative but not dispositive; we do not classify a rule as interpretive just because the agency says it is." See *Citizens to Save Spencer County v. United States Environmental Protection Agency*, 600 F. 2d 844, 879 n. 171 (D.C. Cir. 1979); *Citizens Communication v. FCC*, 447 F. 2d 1201, 1204 n. 5 (D.C. Cir. 1971.)" Id., at 468.

[40]5 U.S.C. §553(a)(1).

[41]Id., at §553(a)(2).

[42]These laws are discussed in Phillip J. Cooper, "Government Contracts in Public Administration: The Role and Environment of The Contracting Officer," 40 *Public Admin. Rev.* 459 (1980).

[43]5 U.S.C. §553(b)(B).

[44]Id., at §553(b)(1), (2), (3).

[45]Id., at §553(c).

[46]The APA does not establish any minimum required time between publication of the notice of proposed rulemaking and the date of the publication of the final rule. In a number of instances serious questions have been raised regarding the adequacy of the notice.

[47]5 U.S.C. §553(c).

[48]Id. See note 11 supra.

[49]Mark J. Green, *The Other Government*, rev. ed. (New York: Norton, 1978), pp. 137–45.

[50]. . See, e.g., Jerome Frank, *If Men Were Angels: Some Aspects of Government in a Democracy* (New York: Harper & Brothers, 1942), p. 181, and Walter Gellhorn, *Federal Administrative Proceedings* (Westport, Conn.: Greenwood Press, 1941), chap. 2.

[51]See, e.g., *American Textile Manufacturers Inst. v. Donovan*, 69 L. Ed. 2d 185 (1981). The need for substantial evidence to support a rule is rather confusing. The letter of the APA, 5 U.S.C §706(2)(E), requires only substantial evidence justification in formal rulemaking, but for several reasons, discussed in detail in chapter 7, the substantial evidence concept in rulemaking is more broadly applied than a narrow reading of the APA would suggest.

[53]Davis, supra note 26.

[53]U.S. House of Representatives, Task Force on Legal Services and Procedure, *Report on Legal Services and Procedure Prepared for the Commission on Organization of the Executive Branch*, House Doc. no. 128, 84th Cong., 1st Sess. (1955), p. 24.

[54]See, e.g., J. Skelly Wright, "Beyond Discretionary Justice," 81 *Yale L. J.* 575 (1972), and Louis Jaffe, "Book Review," 14 *Villanova L. Rev.* 773 (1969).

[55]Some of the most widely discussed of these cases were *Mobil Oil v. Federal Power Comm'n*, 483 F. 2d 1238 (D.C. Cir. 1973); *International Harvester Co. v. Ruckelshaus*, 478 F. 2d 615 (D.C. Cir. 1973); *Appalachian Power Co. v. Environmental Protection Agency*, 477 F. 2d 495 (4th Cir. 1973); *Walter Holm & Co. V. Hardin*, 449 F. 2d 1009 (D.C. Cir. 1971); *American Airlines v. Civil Aeronautics Board*, 359 F. 2d 624 (D.C. Cir. 1966).

[56]5 U.S.C. §706(2)(A).

[57]*Citizens to Preserve Overton Park v. Volpe*, 410 U.S. 402 (1971).

[58]See, e.g., Stephen Williams, "Hybrid Rulemaking Under the Administrative Procedure Act: A Legal and Empirical Analysis," 42 *U. Chicago L. Rev.* 401 (1975).

[59]*Natural Resources Defense Council v. Nuclear Regulatory Comm'n*, 547 F. 2d 633 (D.C. Cir. 1976), reversed in *Vermont Yankee Nuclear Power Corp. v. NRDC*, 435 U.S. 519 (1978).

[60]This particular quotation comes from an interview of Judge Bazelon by the author. The *NRDC* opinion contains his views on this subject, supra note 59, 547 F. 2d, at 644–46.

[61]Harold H. Bruff and Ernest Gellhorn, "Congressional Control of Administrative Regulation: A Study of Legislative Vetoes," 90 *Harvard L. Rev.* 1369, 1376–77 (1977).

[62]This summary is taken from the cases cited at note 55 supra; Richard B. Stewart, "Vermont Yankee and the Evolution of Administrative Procedure," 91 *Harvard L. Rev.* 1805 (1978); Bruff and Gellhorn, supra note 61; and William Pederson, "Formal Records and Informal Rulemaking," 85 *Yale L.J.* 38 (1975).

[63]See generally Stewart, supra note 62; Charles Byse, "Vermont Yankee and the Evolution of Administrative Procedure: A Somewhat Different View," 91 *Harvard L. Rev.* 1823 (1978); Stephen Breyer, "Vermont Yankee and the Courts' Rule in the Nuclear Energy Controversy," 91 *Harvard L. Rev.* 1833 (1978); and Antonin Scalia, "Vermont Yankee: The APA, the D.C. Circuit and the Supreme Court," 1978 *Supreme Court Rev.* 345.

[64]See, e.g., Occupational Safety and Health Act, 29 U.S.C. §651 et seq. (1976), and the Consumer Product Safety Act, 15 U.S.C. §2051 et seq. (1976). See also Consumer Product Safety Commission Improvement Act of 1974, 15 U.S.C. §1193 et seq.

[65]Toxic Substances Control Act, 15 U.S.C. §2601 (1976).

[66]15 U.S.C. §§2603, 2605.

[67]Executive Order No. 12044, 43 Fed. Reg. 12661 (1978).

[68]Executive Order No. 11821, 39 Fed. Reg. 41502 (1974).

[69]Chapter 10 discusses the regulatory analysis movement in general and the Regulatory Flexibility Act of 1980 in particular. This act mandates analyses for virtually all agencies when the rules involved will have a significant impact on small businesses or small units of government.

[70]See, e.g., Robert G. Dixon, "The Congressional Veto and Separation of Powers: The Executive on a Leash," 56 *North Carolina L. Rev.* 423 (1978).

Chapter 6

Administrative Adjudications

otwithstanding popular concern about administrative power, which focuses on the profusion of government regulations, administrators make many times more quasi-judicial decisions than they do rulemaking judgments. Is a particular firm in violation of air quality standards? Should a specific coal miner's widow be entitled to benefits under the black lung compensation program?[1] In some situations, the administrator is attempting to resolve a particular case according to existing rules or standards, while in others the agency is engaged in policymaking through adjudication following an administrative analog of the common law process of legal development. In any event, the administrator is making decisions that matter, judgments that determine one's rights or status under the law. The consequences of administrative decisions can be of major importance, and therefore the means by which they are made are also significant. Consider the following examples.

THE RANGE OF ADJUDICATORY PROBLEMS

Mr. Greene was general manager of the Engineering and Research Corporation (ERCO), a company that developed and produced electronic devices under contract to the federal government and the U.S. Navy in particular. Greene had been with the firm from 1937 to 1951, when ERCO received a communication from the Army–Navy–Air Force Personnel Security Board. Greene had been cleared for security three times by the services during World War II and thereafter. But on November 21, 1951, his firm was informed that the company would lose its access to classified materials because Greene was considered a security risk. In December, Greene was formally notified that his clearance had been revoked because his associations and activities from 1942 to 1947 suggested that he was a Communist or a Communist sympathizer.

In January 1952, Greene was granted a hearing before the Industrial Employment Review Board at which he presented a substantial amount of evidence and testimony himself and through former associates at ERCO and in the military, which indicated that Greene's contacts with Soviet embassy personnel during the war and immediately after were official visits on behalf of ERCO as a representative to sell materials to an ally. Greene's witnesses testified that they knew Greene to be a trustworthy citizen with an impeccable record of contribution to American military efforts in both World War II and the Korean War. No testimony was offered by the government. Evidence was taken from reports compiled by various investigators, none of whom were members of the deciding body. None of the sources of the information testified before the board. Greene requested an opportunity to know and face his accusers, which request was denied on security grounds. The board reinstated Greene's clearance.

Just over a year later, ERCO was again contacted about Greene's security clearance—this time by the secretary of the Navy. The loyalty–security program for defense industries had been reorganized. The secretary had reviewed the earlier decision of the Industrial Employment Review Board on his own motion without further hearings or other notice to Greene and had determined that he would recommend that the Secretary of Defense reverse the board's decision. In the interim, ERCO was advised to remove Greene from any area of the plant's activities in which he might come in contact with Navy projects. Since their operation was based on defense department contracts, ERCO had no choice but to terminate Greene's employment, although both the president of the firm and the chairman of the board wrote the Secretary of the Navy protesting the Navy's actions and lauding Greene's sixteen-plus years of service to the company and the Navy. The company asked for some process through which the decision might be discussed or reconsidered, to which the Navy replied that as "far as the Navy Department is concerned, any further discussion on this problem at this time will serve no useful purpose."[2]

It was not until fall 1953 that Greene's attorney was able to get the Navy to produce a statement of the charges against Greene from the Eastern Industrial Personnel Board, which had been given jurisdiction in the case. The allegations were of the same general nature as the charges first leveled in 1951, with no additional material. In April 1954, Greene was given another hearing at which he again presented a great deal of personal testimony and supporting material from others. Greene also testified that since he had been terminated by ERCO, he had been unable to obtain employment as an engineer in the aircraft industry and had finally landed a job as an architectural draftsman, at a much lower pay scale. The board, offering no reasons for its decision and again without permitting Greene to examine the evidence against him, or to face the investigators who had gathered the evidence or the witnesses who had given the evidence, upheld the determination by the Secretary of the Navy. Greene protested the decision and asked for a review. The Industrial Personnel Security Review Board reviewed the record in the case, but gave Greene no opportunity to present arguments. It affirmed the earlier decision, again without reasons, only restating the generalized assertions about his associations and his questionable veracity. The ruling came in 1954.

Greene sought judicial review in the District Court for the District of Columbia, which dismissed his petition without a hearing. That lower court decision was upheld by the Circuit Court of Appeals. The case was finally decided in Greene's favor by the United States Supreme Court in 1959.

What had Greene done to deserve all this? What was the evidence introduced against him? Given the testimony of his supervisors at ERCO and military officials, why did the process ever go as far as it did? What was the nature of the evidence that was so sensitive that the names of the informants could not be made available to Greene and his attorney?

The following excerpts are taken from the Supreme Court's opinion in *Greene v. McElroy*.[3] The bracketed language is that of the Supreme Court.

The specifications were contained in a letter to petitioner's council dated April 9, 1954, which was sent nineteen days before the hearing. That letter provided in part:

"Security considerations permit disclosure of the following information that has thus far resulted in the denial of clearance to Mr. Greene:

"1. During 1942 subject was a member of the Washington Book Shop Association, an organization that has been cited by the Attorney General of the United States as Communist and subversive.*

"2. Subject's first wife, Jean Hinton Greene, to whom he was married from approximately December 1942 to approximately December 1947, was an ardent Communist during the greater part of the period of the marriage.

"3. During the period of Subject's first marriage he and his wife had many Communist publications in their home including . . . Karl Marx's 'Das Kapital.'

"4. Many apparently reliable witnesses have testified that during the period of Subject's first marriage his personal sympathies were in general accord with those of his wife, in that he was sympathetic towards Russia; followed the Communist Party 'line'; presented 'fellow traveller arguments'; was apparently influenced by 'Jean's wild theories'; etc." [Nothing in the record established that any witnesses "testified" at any hearing on these subjects and everything in the record indicates that they could have done no more than make such statements to investigative officers.]

"5. In about 1946 Subject invested approximately $1000 in the Metropolitan Broadcasting Corporation and later became a director of its Radio Station WQQW. It has been reliably reported that many of the stockholders of the Corporation were Communists or pro-Communists and that the news coverage and radio programs of Station WQQW frequently paralleled the Communist Party 'line'." [This station is now Station WGMS, Washington's "Good Music Station." Petitioner stated that he invested money in the station because he liked classical music and he considered it a good investment.]

"6. On 7 April 1947 Subject and his wife Jean attended the Third Annual Dinner of the Southern Conference for Human Welfare, an organization that has been officially cited as a

*In 1942 no justification was required to place an organization on that list. This process was later overturned in *Joint Anti-Fascist Refugee Committee v. McGrath*, 341 U.S. 123 (1951).

Communist front." [This dinner was also attended by many Washington notables, including several members of this Court.]

7. Beginning about 1942 and continuing for several years thereafter Subject maintained sympathetic associations with various officials of the Soviet Embassy." [High-level executives of ERCO, as above noted, testified that these associations were carried on to secure business for the corporation.][4]

As the Court indicated, none of this "evidence" was submitted by witnesses under oath subject to cross-examination. Greene, of course, provided several notable witnesses who did testify under oath and were therefore subject to cross-examination by the government. The opinion of the Court describes their experience.

And the following questions were asked of various witnesses presented by petitioner evidently because the Board had confidential information that petitioner's ex-wife was "eccentric."

"Q. Now you were in Bill's home, that red brick house that you're talking about. . . .

"Q. Was there anything unusual about the house itself, the interior of it, was it dirty? . . .

"Q. Were there any beds in their house which had no mattresses on them? . . .

"Q. Did you ever hear it said that Jean slept on a board in order to keep the common touch? . . .

"Q. When you were in Jean's home did she dress conventionally when she received her guests? . . .

"Q. Let me ask you this, conventionally when somebody would invite you for dinner at their home, would you expect them, if they were a woman, to wear a dress and shoes and stockings and the usual clothing of the evening or would you expect them to appear in overalls?"[5]

The Court later describes the cross-examination to which Greene was subjected in the government's attempt to show that the evidence introduced against his ex-wife was applicable to him.

"Q. I'd like to read to you a quotation from the testimony of a person who had identified himself as having been a very close friend of yours over a long period of years. He states that you, as saying to him one day that you were reading a great deal of pro-Communist books and other literature. Do you wish to comment on that? . . .

"Q. Incidentally this man's testimony was entirely favorable in one respect. He stated that he didn't think you were a Communist but he did state that he thought that you had been influenced by Jean's viewpoints and that he had received impressions definite that it was your wife who was parlor pink and that you were going along with her. . . .

"Q. This same friend testified that he believed that you were influenced by Jean's wild theories and he decided at that time to have no further association with you and your wife."[6]

The Court struck down this process, developed by administrators, which permitted citizens to be deprived of the opportunity to pursue a lawful occupation without the opportunity to confront witnesses against them and to cross-examine those witnesses.

The second situation was quite different from that faced by Mr. Greene. A suit on behalf of two boys, aged twelve and thirteen, was brought against the commissioner of the Georgia Department of Human Services, officials of the department responsible for mental health treatment, and the office in charge of Family and Children's Services. Attorneys for the boys argued that the state law that gave minors who were committed to mental health facilities, by their parents or by the state, no right to a hearing to determine whether they should be confined was an unconstitutional denial of due process in violation of the Fourteenth Amendment. The facts that gave rise to the case as it reached the United States Supreme Court are as follows:

> J.R. was born on August 14, 1962. Approximately three months after birth a juvenile court, because of severe parental neglect, removed him from his parents' home and placed him in a foster home under the supervision of the Georgia Department of Family and Children Services. After having lived in a total of seven different foster homes, when he was almost eight years of age he was admitted by the defendant on June 25, 1970, to Georgia's oldest and largest mental hospital, called Central State Hospital at Milledgeville, Georgia. In each foster home it seemed that he had lost his place to a more favored child. On October 27, 1966, a juvenile court order had given "permanent custody for the purpose of placing said child for adoption" to the Georgia Department of Family and Children Services. Adoption did not materialize, and without further court hearing or order J.R. remained in the custody of the Department of Family and Children Services in said foster homes until that department applied directly to said mental hospital for his admission to said mental hospital pursuant to §88-503.1. Upon admission he was found by hospital personnel to be mentally ill, and his mental illness was described as "1. Borderline mental retardation 310.90-2. Unsocialized aggressive reaction of childhood. 308.40" Exhibit 7. In early 1973, hospital personnel began requesting the Department of Family and Children Services to remove J.R. from hospital confinement and place him in a long-term foster or adoptive home because of the feeling that he "will only regress if he does not get a suitable home placement, and as soon as possible." Exhibit 9-A-2. On August 9, 1973, hospital personnel "felt that efforts to obtain a foster placement should be primary at this time, lest [J.R.] become a permanently institutionalized child." Exhibit 10-A-2. A foster home was not obtained for J.R., and he remained in confinement. On October 24, 1975, when this lawsuit was filed, he had been confined for five years and four months of his thirteen years, two months of life.[7]

> J.L. at birth on October 1, 1963, was adopted. His parents divorced when he was three, and he went to live with his mother. She remarried and soon gave birth to a child. On May 15, 1970, his mother and step-father, pursuant to the previously quoted state law §88-503.1, applied for his admission to what is now Central State Hospital; he was admitted. Hospital personnel found that J.L. was mentally ill and diagnosed his illness as "Hyperkinetic Reaction of Childhood 308.00." On September 8,

1972, he was discharged to his mother, but she brought him back to the hospital and readmitted him ten days later. He then remained in the hospital in confinement, and at the time this lawsuit commenced had been in confinement for five years and five months of his twelve years, one month of life. In 1973 hospital personnel indicated to the Department of Family and Children Services that J.L. needed to be removed from hospital confinement and placed in specialized foster care. His records show that the Department of Family and Children Services indicated that the department could not pay for institutionalized (private) foster care unless J.L. was eligible for such care to be paid for by A.F.D.C. [Aid to Families With Dependent Children] or Social Security funds. He was not an A.F.D.C. eligible child. See Exhibit 1. Specialized foster care was not obtained for J.L. by the defendants.[8]

Under the state's voluntary commitment law, the child generally remains confined without a hearing unless the parents, or the state in the case of a ward of the state, ask for the release. It is then up to the adult or the state to find appropriate care outside the institution. The district court found that although many parents commit their children with all the right intentions and motives, there are problems.

> While parents generally make such applications with the best of intentions and with the sincere desire to seek help for their child, the defendants nevertheless recognize what society knows but had rather not admit—"there are a lot of people who still treat [mental hospitals] as dumping grounds." [Dr. John P. Filley, Director, Child and Adolescent Mental Health Services, deposition at 48.][9]

The court also found that once children are sent to a facility, it is likely that a reason can be found for confining them.

> Then the statutory concept is that "if found to show evidence of mental illness and to be suitable for treatment, such person may be given care and treatment . . . and . . . may be detained by such facility for such period and under such conditions as may be authorized by law." . . . In practice the language "evidence of mental illness and to be suitable for treatment" is as indefinite and elusive to the psychiatrists employed by the state as it is to a layman. Note the . . . following deposition of Dr. John Filley, Director, Child and Mental Health Services: . . . In sum and substance Dr. Filley testified that the decision to hospitalize for care and treatment comes about in the following manner: "The parent may come in saying, 'I can't handle it any more; do something.' And, they say at the hospital or it might be the psychiatrist who says, 'I think hospitalization is indicated.' The parent would agree and that would decide it."[10]

The state often commits a juvenile for whom adoptive parents cannot be found or adequate foster placement secured.

The district court received testimony from employees and supervisors of Georgia's mental hospitals that a substantial portion of the nonpsychotic older juveniles being held in confinement were there solely because funds had not been made available for suitable placement or because the families would not take the children for whom discharge had been recommended.

The three-judge district court concluded that the Georgia voluntary commitment statute was unconstitutional insofar as it permitted children to be held without an opportunity for a hearing at which the state would show cause why the children should be confined.

> By this statute the state gives to parents the power to arbitrarily admit their children to a mental hospital for an indefinite period of time. "Where the state undertakes to act in parens patriase, it has the inescapable duty to vouchsafe due process," . . . and this necessarily includes procedural safeguards to see that even parents do not use the power to indefinitely hospitalize children in an arbitrary manner. . . .
>
> It is thus apparent that this statute supplies not the flexible due process that the situation of the plaintiff children demands, but, instead, absolutely no due process. It is also apparent that it affords to parents, guardians, the Department of Human Resources as Custodian, and superintendents the "unchecked and unbalanced power over [the] essential liberties" . . . of these children that is universally mistrusted by our "whole scheme of American government." The doublecheck that is needed is that which is guaranteed by the Fourteenth Amendment—due process of law. There being none the statute in question violates the Due Process Clause of the Fourteen Amendment and is unconstitutional.[11]

In 1979, the United States Supreme Court reversed the district court ruling and held that the initial screening process at the hospital and the good intentions of the parents and the state were sufficient protection for the child's rights to due process of law.[12]

The *Greene* case, the juvenile commitment suit, the employee dismissal case described in Chapter 1, and the *Mathews v. Eldridge* Social Security disability benefits conflict, presented in Appendix A, all involved decisions by government officials or agencies of an adjudicatory nature that carried important consequences. These cases are all unusual in that they were addressed by the United States Supreme Court, but they do illustrate several of the major recurring aspects of administrative law that guide administrators in making decisions about individual claims and disputes. *Parham* concerned a demand that children be afforded a hearing on their hospitalization and, in effect, confinement. The case of the government employee discharged for allegedly accusing his superior of improprieties and the *Eldridge* case both involved demands for a hearing before, rather than after, government acted against the individuals concerned. The employee insisted that he be given a hearing before his pay and benefits were terminated, and not months down the road. Eldridge argued that a hearing should be available before the disability benefit checks were cut off. Mr. Greene was able to present his case in a hearing, but he argued that the hearing was not a fair proceeding because he was not accorded certain of the elements of due process, namely, the right to confront his accusers and to test the veracity of their testimony by cross-examination, generally required by the concept that one should have a fair hearing before being injured by a government action.

THE ESSENCE OF THE DUE PROCESS CLAIM

Administrative justice rules governing the conduct of adjudicatory proceedings make up the second major category of formal administrative law. They result from the understanding that, despite a number of ambiguities in definition, in making adjudicatory decisions agencies act rather like courts, and are required to employ the traditional elements of fair decisionmaking that fall under the rubric of due process of law. The guidelines ensure not that one will win a dispute, but that the dispute will be resolved fairly through a regular procedure. The centerpiece of the Anglo-American concept of due process of law is that before suffering injury one is entitled to a fair hearing at which one may present arguments and evidence in one's behalf.[13] Unlike the discussion of rulemaking procedures, which were more legislative, albeit by degrees, adjudicatory procedures that are quasi-judicial involve assertions of rights. Due process rights are protected by the Constitution, statutes, judicial interpretations, and agency regulations. The requirements of administrative adjudication may be understood through consideration of questions that have to do with a fair hearing. One can ask: (1) Is a hearing required in a particular situation? (2) If so, at what point in an administrative action is the hearing required? (3) What kind of hearing is required? (4) What are the essential elements of an administrative hearing?

The responses to these questions will be more understandable if the discussion is informed by an understanding of the procedural due process model of administrative justice.

PROCEDURAL DUE PROCESS MODEL OF ADMINISTRATIVE JUSTICE

The rules that govern administrative adjudications are very much products of the historical developments detailed in Chapter 4. They represent compromises between the recognized need that administrators must function with some flexibility and dispatch and the fear of administrative arbitrariness, which has grown as government has become more involved in day-to-day life. In much the same way that rulemaking requirements developed in an attempt to control nonelected officials who could make rules that had the force of law, so the adjudication requirements developed in an effort to limit judicial-type decisions having the force of law made without some of the formalities normally available in a court of law.

Due Process and the Rule of Law

Notwithstanding the numerous dangers inherent in the "extravagant version of the rule of law," the United States is, and prides itself on being, a nation committed to the rule of law. On the need to control abuses of administrative discretion, J. Skelly Wright observed:

> If that consensus is properly marshalled and the legal tactics carefully planned, King Rex [an administrator who would like unbounded authority] can indeed be turned into a constitutional monarch. Failing that, we may still be able to pull off a bloodless coup d'etat and send the King packing to a land that does not purport to govern its affairs by rules of law.[14]

Reminding administrators that administrative law is but one aspect of the American governmental system and, like the others, functions under the rule of law, Louis L. Jaffe wrote:

An agency is not an island entire of itself. It is one of the many rooms in the mansion of the law. The very subordination of the agency to judicial jurisdiction is intended to proclaim the premise that each agency is to be brought into harmony with the totality of the law; the law as it is found in the statute at hand, the statute book at large, the principles and conceptions of the "common law" and the ultimate guarantees associated with the Constitution.[15]

By almost any standard, the concept that government should not take any action that seriously injures an individual without providing at least some of the elements of due process of law is at the heart of the Anglo-American definition of the rule of law. The idea of due process can be traced at least as far back as the Magna Carta. "King John promised that 'no free man shall be taken or imprisoned or exiled or in any way destroyed, nor will we go upon him nor send upon him, except by the lawful judgment of his peers or by the law of the land.'"[16] The "law of the land," of course, included all the protections afforded by the entire fabric of the law.[17] The term "due process of law" was first used in England in 1354. "No man of what state or condition he be, shall be put out of his lands or tenements nor taken, nor disinherited, nor put to death, without he be brought to answer by due process of law."[18]

During the colonial period and early nationhood, many of the state governments adopted statements in their constitutions or laws requiring due process protections.[19] In part to bolster the principles of fair and independent adjudications, the framers of the U.S. Constitution established a co-equal judiciary as opposed to the subordinate status accorded that branch of government in England. Included in the Fifth Amendment to the new Constitution was the protection against the deprivation of life, liberty, or property without due process of law. But that provision only protected citizens against abuses of authority by the national government and not the governments of the states or localities.[20] Experience before and after the Civil War indicated that the states were just as capable of abusing citizens as were officials in Washington.[21] Hence, when the Fourteenth Amendment was drafted, it included an admonition that no state shall "abridge the privileges or immunities of citizens, . . . nor deprive any person of life, liberty, or property without due process of law, nor deny to any person the equal protection of the laws."

Of course, although "supremacy of law" and "due process of law" are important symbolic terms and concepts praised and ascribed to by all Americans, they are very difficult to define in individual cases. This is true even in the area of criminal law, where one would think the precepts of due process of law would be most clearly understood.

Defined stringently enough, due process would require any government official to proceed with a formal court trial in any situation in which the citizen involved might suffer a loss, for example, of money, in bringing a business into compliance with a regulation. Some authors who were writing about the developing administrative state at the end of the nineteenth and the beginning of the twentieth centuries defined the term exactly that way, with A. V. Dicey leading the attack on any adjudication not conducted in an "ordinary court" under the rules of ordinary common law.[22] The debate over just what due process required was a cornerstone of the entire argument over whether administrative law was or was not legitimate.[23] As

Chapter 4 indicated, some of those anxieties were exacerbated as administrative activities increased during the New Deal. However, courts were not well equipped to deal with administrative adjudications. Indeed, it was the failure of the courts in the regulatory arena that was one of the strongest reasons for the development of administrative law.[24] The courts provided a scrupulously fair forum, but their rules were much better suited to civil cases between individuals, to be argued before juries, than for the complex problems of regulation and social service. There was no way that judges could acquire the kind of expertise that was needed to resolve expeditiously some of the problems agencies faced.

The courts, in a number of decisions, and the Congress, in enacting the APA, reached a compromise on administrative adjudications by ensuring that they would be regular, would be guided by the basic principles of due process, and could be reviewed by a court to ensure that the agency had indeed fulfilled the technical requirements of due process of law and, in a larger way, also fulfilled the fundamental fairness demanded by due process and the concept of supremacy of law.

Procedural Versus Substantive Due Process

It is important to note some of the limits that the concept of due process imposes on administrators. First is a recognition of the difference between substantive and procedural due process.

Procedural due process permits government to take action that may have grave consequences for a person (or a group) as long as it follows fair procedures. Thus, the Fifth Amendment requires that one may not be deprived of life, liberty, or property without due process. But if all the procedures needed to ensure a fair decision process are followed, the government may take property, it may sentence citizens to jail, and it may even mandate execution. Procedural due process does not mean that a person before a government organization is entitled to win a dispute, but only that the government must deal with the case fairly and in accordance with all the requirements of law.

The idea that due process prevents government from taking some actions against an individual regardless of the procedural protections provided is frequently referred to as substantive due process. The classic example of substantive due process in action was a case challenging a New York law that limited the working hours of bakery employees to no more than 60 hours in a week or ten hours per day.[25] The law was a safety statute to protect workers in what the legislature deemed to be an unsafe work environment. The conservative pre-New Deal Supreme Court found that the law interfered with the liberty of bakery workers and owners to enter into contracts to sell or purchase labor on any terms they might set. The opinion for the divided Court, written by Justice Peckham, ruled that the legislature had no authority in that area. "There is no reasonable ground for interfering with the liberty of person of the right of free contract, by determining hours of labor, in the occupation of a baker."[26] That line of decisions was later overturned. Although there remain a few situations in which the Court is willing to take a substantive due process in barring government actions,[27] such cases are very rare and are generally limited to disputes over the constitutionality of a piece of legislation and not the administration of a policy.

As early as the 1930s the Supreme Court spoke to the limits on requirements on administrative adjudications.

> If the statutory benefit is to be allowed only in his [the administrator's] discretion, the courts will not substitute their discretion for his. . . . If he is authorized to determine questions of fact, his decision must be accepted unless he exceeds his authority by making a determination which is arbitrary or capricious or unsupported by evidence . . . , or by failing to follow a procedure which satisfied elementary standards of fairness and reasonableness essential to due conduct of the proceeding which Congress has authorized.[28]

In general, then, when someone refers to due process in connection with an administrative adjudication, procedural due process is what is meant. But even these requirements of minimal courtlike procedures are not required in everything that looks like a quasi-judicial action.

Investigations Versus Adjudications

Agencies may hold hearings on individual problems that appear to be courtlike or adjudicatory procedures, but are in fact merely investigatory activities. In such situations people who may see themselves as being injured by the administrative procedure are nevertheless not entitled to participate in the same manner or with the same procedural protections that one normally thinks of in a courtlike proceeding.

The Supreme Court dealt with the problem not long ago in *Withrow v. Larkin.*[29] Its opinion began with the recognition that

> concededly, a "fair trial in a fair forum is a basic requirement of due process." *In re Murchison,* 349 U.S. 133, 136 . . . (1955). This applies to administrative agencies which adjudicate as well as to courts. *Gibson v. Berryhill,* 411 U.S. 564, 579 . . . (1973).[30]

In the end, however, the Court found that the fact that the administrative body was merely engaged in an investigative process rather than an actual adjudication was enough to justify the decision not to allow the doctor whose activities were at issue in the proceeding to participate as fully as he might in a full-scale adjudication. The Court held that the investigatory hearing was rather like a grand jury proceeding, in that the board was merely determining whether a formal proceeding to discipline the physician should be pursued just as a grand jury would decide whether there was probable cause to believe that a crime had been committed, that the individual accused may have committed it, and that a formal procedure for determining guilt or innocence should be instituted.

This is a somewhat simplified, and indeed clarified, interpretation of the Court's decision. Dr. Larkin was a Michigan physician who was licensed in Wisconsin under a reciprocal licensing agreement. Dr. Larkin allegedly performed abortions in his office in Wisconsin. The Wisconsin licensing authorities informed Larkin that they would hold "uncontested" hearings to determine whether there was probable cause to follow through with a formal administrative procedure looking toward a revocation of his license and possibly a recommendation that the public prosecutor should institute a criminal prosecution. Larkin and his attorney were permitted to attend the hearing, but not to present a case directly or indirectly by cross-examining witnesses against Larkin. At the end of the hearing, Larkin was allowed to "explain" the evidence presented against him.

The board decided to launch a formal hearing to remove his license. Larkin brought suit in a federal district court claiming that the hearing was in violation of due process for several reasons. Most prominent among the abuses, he asserted, was the board's refusal to permit him to participate in the uncontested hearing and the fact that the same body that had heard evidence against him without benefit of cross-examination and had made a preliminary finding that his license should be revoked, would be judging his fitness to practice medicine. It was, in Larkin's view, an unfair procedure conducted by a biased decisionmaking body.

The Court concluded that the hearing was investigative and not adjudicative. It also decided that the board was not inherently biased any more than a judge who found probable cause to issue an arrest warrant or determined as a result of a preliminary hearing that a defendant should be bound over for trial was too biased to preside at a trial of the same individual.

The *Withrow* decision was not a good ruling,[31] but it serves to point up the fact that agencies are not courts and not every administrative procedure that looks like an adjudication will be treated like one. Additionally, the decision supports the proposition that administrative due process is allowed to be considerably less formal than the judicial variety.

Administrative Versus Judicial Due Process

What are some of the differences between due process in court and the limits of due process in agency adjudications? Specific elements of administrative due process will be considered in detail later in this chapter, but consider the problem, for the moment at least, in broad compass.

What is meant by due process in a judicial proceeding? In general, Anglo-American jurisprudence requires that a citizen should not be called upon to appear before a court unless a violation of a properly enacted law is alleged. The person summoned has a right to expect that he or she will be notified of the purpose of the proceeding and the nature of the charges being asserted in order to prepare an adequate defense. He or she is entitled to be represented by an attorney who will present the case. He or she may call witnesses and present evidence in his or her own behalf and challenge the evidence presented on the other side by cross-examination. The judge who presides should be unbiased and independent. In serious matters, a trial by jury is available. The process should result in a reasoned decision supported by the evidence developed at trial in accordance with interpretations of law that are explained by the decisionmaking judge. The citizen should be entitled to at least one appeal on the correctness of the interpretations of law to a higher tribunal.

In administrative adjudications, some of these procedures are slightly different. First, there is no recourse to a trial by jury. Second, the procedures for presentation of evidence are slightly less formal than in a court trial since there is no jury to be deceived by inappropriate offers of proof. Third, the decisionmaker is not totally independent. He or she is employed by the agency involved, although there are provisions to ensure that the administrative law judge has some protection against attempts at pressure. Indeed, the fact that the judge is a part of the agency permits him or her to bring an expertise to the case and to maintain continuity in decisions. One is entitled to an appeal from an administrative decision, but it is necessary to accomplish all stages of administrative appeal before moving to a totally separate tribunal.

ADMINISTRATIVE DUE PROCESS: A DEVELOPING PROCESS

Administrative adjudications became increasingly significant as the nineteenth century ended and the twentieth began. Decisions that affected the railroads and other businesses were appealed to the highest courts which led to a significant body of judicial opinions explaining the minimum requirements of due process. State and local administrative rulings in zoning decisions and a host of other areas of regulation contributed to this growing body of law.[32]

These early cases, while granting considerable deference to the substance of administrative rulings, reminded officials that the Constitution does "not mean to leave room for the play and action of purely personal and arbitrary power."[33] Actions by government that cause serious harm to an individual require an opportunity for a hearing.[34] Due process protections extend to all who live under the jurisdiction of American law, whether they are citizens or aliens.[35] Rejecting the idea that a hearing to satisfy the due process requirements should consist merely of an opportunity to submit written objections to the administrative authority, the Supreme Court held:

> Many requirements essential in strictly judicial proceedings may be dispensed with in proceedings of this nature. But even here a hearing in its very essence demands that he who is entitled to it shall have the right to support his allegations by argument, however brief; and, if need be, by proof, however informal.[36]

The case law required that administrative orders would be voided if no hearing was afforded the individual or firm involved, if the hearing was not fair or adequate, if there was no reasoned decision, or if that decision was not supported by the evidence acquired during the adjudication.[37]

The second period was, as the commentary in Chapter 4 noted, significant for the growth in administrative activity because of New Deal activities and wartime mobilization. It was a period of debate over what to do about administrative law. To one examining the decisions of the Supreme Court, however, there is an apparent agreement that while there may have been arguments concerning what Congress could authorize agencies to do, there was no disputing the fact that when administrators conduct courtlike proceedings, they must obey the general requirements of due process of law.[38] Guidelines were slowly developing, through a common law process, which avoided second-guessing on the substance of decisions but did mandate minimal requirements for a fair hearing in a fair forum decided by a fair decisionmaker. The adjudications sections and the requirements and procedures for hearing examiners section of the APA were drafted in an attempt to codify the requirements laid down in the judicial opinions.[39]

In the third period, also described in Chapter 4, several factors led to increased procedural due process protections for consumers of administrative decisions and concomitant burdens on administrators. The growth in administrative activity was one of the most important influences on the refinement of due process requirements for administrative adjudications. Increases in social services, e.g., education, the administration of New Deal and postwar social welfare programs, and the responsibilities of the major regulatory agencies meant more quasi-judicial activities in more areas raising new problems.

Another aspect of the increasing importance of due process was growing awareness of the fact that in an increasingly interdependent society, with no frontiers to escape to for a new start and diminishing privacy, an adverse governmental decision regarding a job or a benefit claim could have profoundly harmful consequences.

> Employability is the greatest asset most people have. Once there is a discharge from a prestigious federal agency, dismissal may be a badge that bars the employee from other federal employment. The shadow of that discharge is cast over the area where private employment may be available. And the harm is not eliminated by the possibility of reinstatement, for in many cases the ultimate absolution never catches up with the stigma of the accusation. . . . Unlike a layoff or discharge due to fortuitous circumstances such as a so-called energy crisis, a discharge on the basis of the captious or discriminatory attitudes of a superior may be a cross to carry the rest of an employee's life. And we cannot denigrate the importance of one's social standing or the status of social stigma as legally recognized harm. . . .
>
> There is no frontier where the employee may go to get a new start. We live today in a society that is closely monitored. All of our important acts, our setbacks, the accusations made against us go into the data banks, instantly retrieved by the computer.[40]

In a commuter society, the loss of a driver's license may have more severe consequences than a short jail sentence. In an urban society with a highly mobile workforce, in which the extended family has ceased to exist and can no longer care for the aged or the infirm, the responsibility of the state becomes complex. When disability benefits are terminated, residents of a public housing project are evicted, a young person is expelled from school, or subsidies or government-guaranteed loans to a business person are canceled, the administrator involved is making decisions that will have profound effects on the consumer of the decision.

Another point obvious to all, including the judges, was the critical literature, which indicated that administrative adjudications under the early years of implementation of the APA left much to be desired. In particular, the Task Force on Legal Services and Procedures of the second Hoover Commission and the Landis Report expressed concern about arbitrariness and breaches of fundamental due process protections.

Finally, the excesses brought about by the Cold War, particularly those associated with the various loyalty and security programs, made a mockery of the concept of due process. The programs never succeeded in locating subversives in government who were proven to be Communists. They did drive nearly two thousand men and women from government work, and many more from work in private industry. The courts were, or became, concerned about violations of substantive rights such as freedom of speech and association,[41] but they were equally concerned about the arbitrariness and lack of procedural fairness involved in government treatment of those accused of disloyalty, whether in public employment or in the private sector. The case of *Greene v. McElroy* is one example. There were others.

Groups were listed by the Attorney General as subversive or Communist organizations with no evidence or opportunity for their members to respond until the Supreme Court barred the practice.[42] Those who were members of the organizations so listed were treated as outcasts. State governments enacted laws barring the state treasurer from paying employees who did not, within a specified period, sign vague loyalty oaths that required one to assure that one had not been a member of any subversive group. In one such situation, college professors refused to sign for several reasons, among which was the fact that they could not know which groups were acceptable and which were not. In the course of the litigation, the state supreme court ruled that the proscribed organizations were only those named on the Attorney General's list. Given that explanation, the professors requested another opportunity to take the oath. It was denied. The Supreme Court struck down the state law, finding:

> There can be no dispute about the consequences visited upon a person excluded from public employment on disloyalty grounds. In the view of the community, the stain is a deep one; indeed, it has become a badge of infamy. Especially is this so in a time of cold war and hot emotions when "each man begins to eye his neighbor as a possible enemy!" . . .
>
> We need not pause to consider whether an abstract right to public employment exists. It is sufficient to say that constitutional protection does extend to the public servant whose exclusion pursuant to a statute is patently arbitrary or discriminatory.[43]

Some who were harmed by these abuses were later vindicated in the courts, but other stories had no happy ending. Judge Henry Edgerton described one case.

> Without trial by jury, without evidence, and without even being allowed to confront the accusers or to know their identity, a citizen of the United States has been found disloyal to the government of the United States.
>
> For her supposed disloyal thoughts she had been punished by dismissal from a wholly nonsensitive position in which her efficiency rating was high. The case received nationwide publicity. Ostracism inevitably followed.[44]

Dorothy Bailey was terminated from her administrative job and barred from re-applying for three years. The only specific allegation against her was that fifteen years earlier she had attended a Communist Party meeting. She answered that a professor had required her and other undergraduate students in a political science seminar at Bryn Mawr to visit different groups to gather information about party platforms.

The Loyalty Board's decision was affirmed in part by the Circuit Court of Appeals in a split decision. Mrs. Bailey appealed to the Supreme Court, which deadlocked with four votes to affirm and four to reverse.[45] Her dismissal stood.

In his dissent from the Circuit Court decision, Judge Edgerton discussed in detail some of the more gross abuses involved in the loyalty cases. After noting that

Bailey had presented several witnesses and some seventy affidavits from character references, Edgerton turned to the government's case.

> Appellant sought to learn the names of the informants, or if their names were confidential, then at least whether they had been active in appellant's union, in which there were factional quarrels. The Board did not furnish or even have this information. Chairman Richardson said: "I haven't the slightest knowledge as to who they were or how active they might have been in anything. All that the Board knew or we know about the informants is that unidentified members of the Federal Bureau of Investigation, who did not appear before the Board, believed them to be reliable."[46]

Edgerton found evidence to indicate that the evidence in the record had not been taken under oath and that there was no information about the credibility of the reports. Speaking to the kind of evidence often used in such "proceedings," Edgerton wrote:

> In loyalty hearings the following questions have been asked of employees against whom charges have been brought. . . . "Do you read a good many books?" "What books do you read?" "What magazines do you buy or subscribe to?" "Do you think that Russian Communism is likely to succeed?" "How do you explain the fact that you have an album of Paul Robeson records in your home?" "Do you ever entertain Negroes in your home?" . . . "Is it not true . . . that you lived next door to and therefore were closely associated with a member of the I.W.W.?" . . . "A woman employee was accused of disloyalty because, at the time of the seige of Stalingrad, she collected money for Russian war relief (she also collected money for British and French Relief)." A record filed in this court shows that an accused employee was taken to task for membership in Consumers Union and for favoring legislation against racial discrimination.[47]

As the Supreme Court moved into the 1960s the increasing ability of administrators to make important and harmful adjudicative decisions became more apparent. The effects appeared to be wide ranging. There was evidence, from the most flagrant abuses of the loyalty security programs to less widespread but equally dangerous practices, of a tendency toward administrative arbitrariness.[48] The courts, with the Supreme Court leading the way, responded with several types of rulings that afforded more individuals in more situations more procedural protections. Much of the case law on this subject is discussed in the *Eldridge* case study in Appendix A, but it is useful to consider the kinds of administrative problem situations that the Court addressed and its approach to solving these difficulties.

The Right-Privilege Dichotomy

As the *Eldridge* case study notes,[49] one of the developments in the due process area was the Warren Court's elimination of the remnants of the so-called right versus privilege dichotomy.[50] This dichotomy was based on the idea that government has different responsibilities in its quasi-judicial activities depending on whether an agency decision affects a right or a privilege. A right is protected against government intervention by law, for example, one's right to acquire, use, and dispose of property.

This right, or legal claim, is based on the Constitution, which limits the government's ability to interfere with the exercise of one's property interests. In such situations, due process protections clearly apply. But there are other situations in which an individual or group may be seriously affected by an adjudicative decision and yet be unable to identify a basic legal right that is clearly being endangered. For example, it was argued that since there is not right per se to a government job, one who does not agree with limitations that go with the position, e.g., rules that limit political speech, should simply resign. Alternatively, he or she may be terminated without any particular due process limitations.[51] Similarly, it was argued that welfare programs were merely gifts of public largesse which, by definition, could be granted under any conditions or requirements that the society promulgates. Since these are privileges, one can make no legal demand on the state for any particular mode of administration of the program, whether it is arbitrary or not.

But the lessons of the loyalty-security programs and the changing social, economic, and political circumstances were understood. The Supreme Court rejected the right versus privilege dichotomy and held that government may not impose unconstitutional or arbitrary conditions on public employment or the receipt of public benefits.[52] Nor may government deny procedural due process protections to those whose benefits are terminated or denied on the ground that these benefits are mere privileges. The protections apply across a broad range of adjudicatory decisions that cause serious harm to the affected individuals.[53]

The Demise of Irrebuttable Presumptions

For various reasons, generally having to do with administrative convenience, some laws have been written with so-called irrebuttable presumptions. These are assumptions about one's situation that are part of an enacted policy about which one may not argue. Consider the following example.

Reverend Bell was a circuit-riding minister in Georgia. One Sunday following services he joined a parishioner's family for dinner, leaving his automobile parked in front of the house at the curb. While the reverend was enjoying his dinner, a five-year-old girl named Sherry Capes "rode her bicycle into the side of his automobile."[54] The girl's parents filed an accident report alleging injury to Sherry in the amount of $5,000. Reverend Bell was not covered by liability insurance. Under existing Georgia law, he was required to file a bond equal to claimed damage regardless of the possibility of his innocence and also to provide proof of continuing financial resources against future claims or face a suspension of his license. Bell argued that deprivation of his license would mean an extreme hardship and, further, that there was no way that he could be found liable for the girl's injuries. He called for a hearing to contest his possible liability. However, the state code made fault, guilt, or innocence irrelevant to the suspension of the license. In effect, the Georgia law presumed that an uninsured motorist involved in an accident would be held liable for the total amount of damages claimed regardless of the facts in the case. The state supreme court upheld the code, but the United States Supreme Court reversed, holding that

> once licenses are issued, as in petitioner's case, their continued possession may become essential in the pursuit of a livelihood. Suspension of issued

licenses thus involves state action that adjudicates important interests of the licensees. In such cases the licenses are not to be taken away without procedural due process required by the Fourteenth Amendment.[55]

The absolute presumption of liability is unacceptable. Before the state can suspend the minister's license, he must at least be given the opportunity to argue that he could not possibly be found liable. The question was not whether there was any state ban on issuance of licenses without insurance, but rather that, given the fact that the state did not require insurance, it could not deprive the driver of an important interest without an opportunity to be heard.

A second case that reached the Supreme Court was that of a woman who contested a Connecticut statute, alleging due process violations on the ground that the statute contained an irrebuttable presumption.[56] The state law was that a student who began study in the university as an out-of-state resident would be, for tuition purposes, considered an out-of-state student throughout the period of his or her education in the state. A woman who came to the state university as a nonresident later married a lifelong Connecticut resident and became a citizen of the state with respect to taxes, voting registration, driver's license, etc. She argued that due process required that she at least be given an opportunity to argue her bona fides as a Connecticut resident and citizen. The Court agreed. The Court recognized that a state has a legitimate interest in protecting its taxpayers against undue burdens on the educational system, but maintained that such concerns do not justify blanket presumptions about individual situations. Administrative convenience does not justify depriving residents who are apparently citizens in all other respects of the opportunity to argue against administrative classifications that make them academic nonresidents.

The Court has struck down other irrebuttable presumptions that served the general purpose of administrative convenience and efficiency. The Court struck down a state law that held that servicemen stationed or claiming citizenship in the state would be presumed to be nonresidents,[57] a law that required schoolteachers to take maternity leave five months before the projected delivery date, whether it was medically necessary or not,[58] and an Illinois law that presumed that all fathers of illegitimate children even if they had lived with the mother and provided support as did other, married fathers, were unfit parents and hence were unable to receive custody of the children in the event of the death of the mother.[59] The Court's opinion in the Illinois case well summarizes its reasons for rejecting irrebuttable presumptions:

> Illinois has declared that the aim of the Juvenile Court Act is to protect "the moral, emotional, mental, and physical welfare of the minor and the best interests of the community" and to strengthen the minor's family ties whenever possible, removing him from the custody of his parents only when his welfare or safety or the protection of the public cannot be adequately safeguarded without removal. . . . These are legitimate interests, well within the power of the State to implement. We do not question the assertion that neglectful parents may be separated from their children.
>
> But we are not asked to evaluate the legitimacy of the state ends, rather, to determine whether the means used to achieve these ends are

constitutionally defensible. What is the state interest in separating children from fathers without a hearing designed to determine whether the father is unfit in a particular disputed case? . . . Illinois . . . [argues] that Stanley and all other unmarried fathers can reasonably be presumed to be unqualified to raise their children.

It may be, as the State insists, that most unmarried fathers are unsuitable and neglectful parents. It may also be that Stanley is such a parent and that his children should be placed in other hands. But all unmarried fathers are not in this category; some are wholly suited to have custody of their children. This much the state readily concedes, and nothing in this record indicates that Stanley is or has been a neglectful father who has not cared for his children. Given the opportunity to make his case, Stanley may have been seen to be deserving of custody of his offspring. . . .

Despite Bell and Carrington, it may be argued that unmarried fathers are so seldom fit that Illinois need not undergo the administrative inconvenience of inquiry in any case, including Stanley's. The establishment of prompt efficacious procedures to achieve legitimate state ends is a proper state interest worthy of cognizance in constitutional adjudication. But the Constitution recognizes higher values than speed and efficiency. Indeed, one might fairly say of the bill of rights in general, and the Due Process Clause in particular, that they were designed to protect the fragile values of a vulnerable citizenry from the overbearing concern for efficiency and efficacy that may characterize praiseworthy government officials no less, and perhaps more, than mediocre ones.

Procedure by presumption is always cheaper and easier than individualized determination. But where, as here, the procedure forecloses the determinative issues of competence and care, when it explicitly disdains present realities in deference to past formalities, it needlessly risks running roughshod over the important interests of both parent and child. It therefore cannot stand.[60]

Other Areas of Due Process Development

In addition to these two broad doctrinal areas, the Court found in a number of particular policy areas that government must afford some kind of a hearing to those injured by government action. Cases requiring a hearing included termination of benefits to welfare recipients,[61] parole and probation revocation and prison disciplinary actions,[62] school disciplinary actions, e.g., suspensions for more than a limited period,[63] driver's license suspension,[64] the use of government institutions for debt collection through such mechanisms as garnishment of wages and repossession and sequestration of property,[65] protection of reputation from public branding by authorities as an alcoholic,[66] and termination of tenured public employees or termination of nontenured public employees where the manner of termination holds the employee up to public scorn or ridicule and threatens the possibility of future employment.[67]

In sum, due process is seen as requisite to protect individuals from arbitrary governmental action, particularly by nonelected officials; the everchanging environment, which citizens cannot escape and in which they are more vulnerable than ever before to government excesses is acknowledged; and the view that administrative convenience is sufficient ground to override protections is rejected. Finally, the opinions were written from well-documented experience which showed that administrative arbitrariness was a continuing problem and resulted in severe hardships on those who must deal with agencies (particularly single shot players). The opinions maintain that administrative quasi-judicial procedures must be carefully watched to ensure that they are fair in substance as well as in form, that fair process requires a hearing of some kind at which a party may present a case, and that the hearing should be accorded before and not after governmental action which harms the citizen.

Burger Court Reformulations of Administrative Due Process

By 1974 and 1975, however, the environment of administrative law was again changing. The composition and philosophy of the Supreme Court had changed.[68] In serveral cases agencies had adopted fair hearing regulations in one form or another.[69] Questions were now being raised about how far what was being termed as "due process explosion" would go. Critics of more and earlier hearing opportunities for agency clients focused on the fact that more hearings meant increased costs, higher costs from maintaining benefit recipients on programs pending hearings, reduced administrative flexibility in handling agency decision processes, and the potential for agency proceedings to become so formalized that all individual decisions would take on the trappings of a court trial.[70] These and other factors led to two significant developments. First, in recent years there has been a significant shift in the manner in which administrative due process is conceptualized. Second, cases arose in several of the specific areas in which due process requirements had been expanding that either marked an end to expansion or the beginning of actual relaxation of due process requirements.

The Burger Court rulings on administrative adjudications show a significant shift in general approach to the concept of procedural due process. The Court has moved away from a view of due process as protection against government arbitrariness and toward due process as a tool for protecting specifically, and relatively narrowly, defined vested legal rights. This distinction is aptly described in Laurence Tribe's discussion of the intrinsic and instrumental approaches to due process.[71] The intrinsic approach uses relatively specific procedures not merely to protect the interests of a particular individual in a specific case in a correct decision regarding well-established liberty or property rights, but also to provide a sense of legitimacy in the quasi-judicial decisions by permitting those adversely affected by a government decision to participate in the process by which their situation is determined. More generally, the procedures are used to provide a mechanism as a check on government to prevent arbitrariness. The instrumental approach holds that due process is more a set of techniques used to arrive at accurate decisions in a particular type of decision, namely, one in which a citizen can demonstrate particular injury to a well-defined legal right, specifically, a liberty or property right. In fact, these two approaches are different poles on a continuum along which different justices would quite likely space themselves. The movement of the Court from the intrinsic side of the instrumental took some time, but can be considered to have begun with *Board of Regents v. Roth* in 1972 and became firm around 1975, when the Burger Court was fully established.[72]

David Roth was an assistant professor of political science at Wisconsin State

University at Oshkosh. Like most young professors, he was hired on a year-to-year contract until he was able to qualify for tenure. Before the end of his first year, however, Roth was informed that he would not be rehired. Roth claimed that the refusal to grant another contract, which was to all intents and purposes termination of his employment, was based on Roth's criticism of the university and in particular of its summary suspension of a number of minority students. Under university rules, the college was not required to tell Roth why his contract would not be renewed or to give him a hearing at which he could present his arguments. He sued the state authorities, contending that the due process clause of the Fourteenth Amendment gave him a right to a hearing at which he could show that he had been terminated for exercising his First Amendment right to freedom of speech. If he could establish that this was indeed the cause, previous cases barred the university from terminating him. The federal district court agreed with Roth's request for a hearing, and its decision was affirmed by the court of appeals. The Supreme Court was divided but reversed the lower courts. In a five-to-three decision, (Justice Powell did not participate), the Court concluded that Roth had not identified a liberty or property right that entitled him to a hearing.

The Court held that there are two parts to judging a case that involves a procedural due process claim to a hearing. First, it must be determined that the plaintiff has a liberty or property interest sufficient to demonstrate that he or she is entitled to procedural due process. Only if that initial finding is made, does one get to the question of what kind of process is due.

> The requirements of procedural due process apply only to the deprivation of interests encompassed by the Fourteenth Amendment's protection of liberty and property. When protected interests are implicated, the right of some kind of prior hearing is paramount. But the range of interests protected by procedural due process is not infinite.[73]

Recognizing that the definition of the interests that are constitutionally protected is difficult, and given the fact "that the property interests protected by procedural due process extend well beyond actual ownership of real estate, chattels, or money,"[74] the Court tried to set limits on the concepts as they might apply to Roth.

Given past precedents, Roth's liberty interests might have been implicated if, for example, the state made "any charge against him that might seriously damage his standing and associations in the community. It did not base the nonrewal of his contract on a charge, for example, that he had been guilty of dishonesty or immorality. Had it done so this would be a different case."[75] "Similarly, there is no suggestion that the State, in declining to re-employ the respondent, imposed on him a stigma or other disability that foreclosed his freedom to take advantage of other employment opportunities."[76] Since Roth couldn't show such an injury, he was not entitled to due process.

But if he were able to identify a property right, he might qualify:

> Certain attributes of "property" interests protected by procedural due process emerge from these decisions. To have a property interest in a benefit, a person clearly must have more than a unilateral expectation of it. He must, instead, have a legitimate claim of entitlement to it. . . .
>   Property interests, of course, are not created by the Constitution.

Rather, they are created and their dimensions are defined by existing rules or understandings that stem from an independent source such as state law-rules or understandings that secure certain benefits and that support claims of entitlement to those benefits. . . .

Just as the welfare recipients' "property" interest in welfare payments was created and defined by statutory terms, so the respondent's "property" interest in employment at Wisconsin State University-Oshkosh was created and defined by the terms of his appointment. . . . In these circumstances, the respondent surely had an abstract concern in being rehired, but he did not have a *property* interest sufficient to require the university authorities to give him a hearing when they declined to renew his contract of employment.[77]

Thus Roth had no right to a hearing. The narrower instrumental approach to procedural due process has guided most of the Court's decisions since 1974–75, with varying support in particular cases by individual justices.

The dissenters in *Roth*, Justices Brennan, Douglas, and Marshall, argued that the narrow instrumental approach misunderstands the meaning and importance of due process. William Van Alstyne summarized the criticisms of *Roth* and later rulings.

The two-step inquiry of Mr. Justice Stewart in *Roth* may seem to have the advantage of settled authority, but only to those who started reading cases in 1972. The fact is, . . . that *Roth* was itself a wholly unprecedented case—no case prior to that time had even hinted at *Roth*'s wizened view that liberty in a free society can be conceived as something having nothing to do with fundamental fairness of how facts are determined and standards applied in the Administrative State. Indeed, as others have noted, the *Roth* approach is shot through with anomalies. First, the plaintiff must overcome the often insurmountable burden of the *Roth–Arnett–Bishop* challenge to show in what sense he was vested with a substantive property interest greater than that circumscribed by the procedural restrictions laid upon it. He may utterly fail in this endeavor . . . although it may be true, even as the Court will concede, that the administrative decision was mistaken and the loss to the individual is grievous. Yet failing at this stage no amount of grievous loss and no degree of probable mistake entitle him to even trivial adjudicative due process. Anomolously, however, no matter how trivial the loss in fact may be, if the litigant is able to meet the vested property test, he then will be able to have the matter reconsidered according to due process of law, although under the circumstances that due process may be minimal.[*][78]

A Reemerging Right-Privilege Distinction

Parallel and in some respects related to the recent shift in the Supreme Court away from broad readings of the due process hearing requirements is a shift toward reinstituting the right-privilege dichotomy. Two examples illustrate the point. The first concerns a person claiming due process rights against an irrebuttable presumption. Mrs. Salfi was married to her husband for only a month before he suffered a heart attack. He was by all accounts in perfect health before they were married, with no history of heart disease or any other significant malady. He was hospitalized for several months following the attack and died, leaving his wife and her two children by a previous marriage. Mrs. Salfi applied for Social Security survivor's benefits, but her claim was rejected on the basis of an irrebuttable presumption that a spouse married to an insured person less than nine months before the death of the insured married solely to take advantage of the benefits. Salfi demanded a hearing, under the due process clause of the Fifth Amendment, at which she might prove that there is no possible way that she could have known of her new husband's impending demise when they were married. Writing for the Court, Justice Rehnquist upheld the presumption.

"Unlike the claim in Stanley [the claim of deprivation of parental rights without a hearing] . . . , a noncontractual claim to receive funds from the public treasury enjoys no constitutionally protected status."[79] If Salfi has a claim to a hearing it must be because of a deprivation of liberty or property. *Roth* had defined liberty narrowly so as *not* to include the idea that any arbitrary government action that meant grievous harm to a particular citizen required a hearing. Therefore, if Salfi had a claim it must be because of a property interest. But *Roth* had ruled that property interests are created and defined by statute and this statute authorized no hearing. With regard to irrebuttable presumptions, the argument is obviously circular.

Both the affirmation of the presumption and the statement that such benefit claims enjoy "no constitutionally protected status" are significant departures from earlier rulings. The effect is to treat the Salfi claim more in the nature of a request for a privilege rather than as a request by a citizen for rectification of arbitrary government action.

Bishop v. Wood[80] is the second example that suggests the reemergence of the right-privilege dichotomy. The language of the case is quite similar to the old overruled view that employment is a privilege. The case was also important because it further limited the meaning of liberty under the due process clause, holding that harm to one's reputation may not be sufficient to require a hearing.

Carl Bishop, a policeman who was classified as "a permanent employee" (as opposed to a probationary employee), was fired by the city manager of Marion, North Carolina. Though he was later informed that he had been fired for alleged "failure to follow certain orders, poor attendance at police training classes, causing low morale, and conduct unsuited to an officer,"[81] he was not accorded a hearing. Bishop and other policemen filed affidavits denying the allegations. Bishop argued that under *Roth* and other cases he had a property interest and a liberty interest that supported his claim to be heard.

Bishop claimed that his firing for cause would bring him into disrepute and severely injure his chances for future employment as a police officer. Whether the reasons had been made public or not, he would be known as having been fired from the police department. Further, any potential employer would be informed of the reasons for his termination. Since he had had no opportunity to defend himself, the charges would be accepted as true. The Supreme Court ruled against Bishop.

By 1976, the Court had shifted its approach to such issues dramatically since 1971, when it decided *Wisconsin v. Constantineau.*[82] Under a Wisconsin statute a local sheriff had posted a notice at all establishments selling liquor in his county that Norma Grace Constantineau was not to be sold any liquor, under penalty of law. She had been given no hearing at which to learn the basis for this action, which presumably would be taken by all to mean that she abused alcohol, nor had she been given any opportunity to defend herself. The Court wrote:

> Where a person's good name, reputation, honor, or integrity is at stake because of what the government is doing to him notice and an opportunity to be heard are essential. "Posting" under the Wisconsin Act may to some be merely the mark of an illness, to others it is a stigma, an official branding of a person. The label is a degrading one. Under the Wisconsin Act, a resident of Hartford is given no process at all. This appellee was not afforded a chance to defend herself. She may have been the victim of an official's caprice. Only when the whole proceedings leading to the pinning of an unsavory label on a person are aired can oppressive results be prevented.[83]

That broad protection against official labeling changed in 1976 when the Court decided *Paul v. Davis.*[84] A local sheriff circulated flyers to merchants identifying Davis and others of being "active shoplifter[s]." Davis had never been convicted of such a crime. His employer told him to get the problem straightened out or lose his job. Davis sued claiming that he had been deprived of liberty without due process. The Court disagreed:

> While we have in a number of our prior cases pointed out the frequently drastic effect of the "stigma" which may result from defamation by the government, this line of cases does not establish the proposition that reputation alone, apart from some more tangible interests such as employment, is either "liberty" or "property" by itself sufficent to invoke the procedural protection of the Due Process Clause.[85]

Mr. Justice Stevens, writing for a five-to-four majority in *Bishop,* concluded that although the statements made about the policeman were damaging, they were not publicly disclosed. Therefore, no name clearing hearing was required for the protection of liberty interests. The claim to a property interest was rejected because neither Bishop's contract nor state law guaranteed the policeman a right to a hearing.

The four dissenters argued that this decision misinterpreted previous decisions, undermined the protections of liberty by permitting an employer to stigmatize an employee in future job opportunities as long as the reasons for the firing were not made public, and, finally, undermined protected property interests of nonprobationary public employees by dramatically limiting the definition of property interests to the statutory language. As Justice Brennan correctly observed, "the Court's approach is a resurrection of the discredited rights/privileges distinction."[86]

Just how far the Supreme Court will press the new approach to due process rights and how the lower courts will respond remains to be seen. Several specific rulings in doctrinal terms or in effect cut back on previously recognized hearing requirements or stop expansion of such requirements. They include: a decision upholding an Illinois law permitting drivers' licenses to be revoked without a hearing after three suspensions;[87] an opinion that permits removal of a medical student from a state university without a hearing for reasons other than grades;[88] a decision that school disciplinary actions need not allow any particular protections;[89] and opinions rejecting claims to hearings of particular kinds in prison discipline or transfer,[90] claims for pretermination hearings in disability benefits cases,[91] and demands for pretermination hearings by tenured federal employees and others.[92]

These rulings did not purport directly to overturn the earlier decisions. Therefore, statements about the requirements of due process for hearings in administrative adjudications must be approximations, based on understanding of how the concept of due process developed and how it is changing, trends in Supreme Court rulings, recognition that the law in action in the lower courts is in flux, examination of statutory requirements, and a sense of one's position in the administrative justice system. For producers of administrative decisions, the message of the recent decisions is positive to the degree that it means more flexibility and perhaps less judicialized proceedings. They should not signal a retreat from the proposition that administrative adjudicative decisions ought to embody fundamental fairness, which is generally obtained by using at least minimal procedural due process techniques. For consumers of administrative rulings, the decisions suggest somewhat less flexibility and a need for careful and well-documented interactions with administrators, since disputes may have to be resolved on narrower statutory and administrative rule grounds rather than in adjudications where administrative arbitrariness is alleged. Recognizing the caveats discussed above, let us attempt to answer the questions raised at the beginning of the chapter.

IS A HEARING DUE?

In general, a party in an adjudicative or quasi-judicial decision is entitled to a hearing if a statute, regulation, or the Constitution requires it. If the enabling act of the agency or the particular act being enforced and the associated regulations do not specifically require a hearing, if the consumer feels the hearing comes too late in the decision process, or if he or she finds the hearing inadequate, the consumer may argue that the due process clause of the Constitution requires more procedural protections from the agency.

In general, one may claim a due process right to a hearing under the Constitution if one is "condemned to suffer grievous loss" to protected interests.[93] But, as the Court held in *Roth,* "the requirements of procedural due process apply only to the deprivation of interests encompassed by the Fourteenth Amendment's protection of liberty and property."[94] Therefore, the claimed interests must be defined in each case. Property interests are perhaps broader than standard views of real property, and may include such matters as receipt of public benefits once one has qualified or, in some cases, public employment where the statutes or regulations establish tenure rights. In general, however, such property interests are limited and defined by the statute.[95] Liberty interests may be asserted as the basis of a demand for a hearing where one claims protection of specific Bill of Rights guarantees, such as protection against having children removed from one's custody,[96] or where liberty is deprived by holding a person up to public scorn or ridicule[97] or acting in a manner that injures the person's opportunity to find future employment.[98]

The court will also consider the government's interest in avoiding the hearing. The costs of administrative due process will be included in that consideration.

In sum, the Supreme Court has established a general balancing test to be applied in administrative cases to determine whether the situation is one that requires due process, and, if so, when, and what kind of process is due. One must consider

> first, the private interest that will be affected by the official action; second, the risk of an erroneous deprivation of such interest through the procedure used, and the probable value, if any, of additional or substitute safeguards; and, finally, the Government's interest, including the function involved and the fiscal and administrative burdens that the additional or substitute procedural requirements would entail.[99]

In addition to asking whether the liberty or property interest for which protection is claimed is adequate, the court will seek to determine how much and what kind of protections are necessary and how much such procedures will improve decision-making. Finally, it will be concerned about cost and administrative flexibility.

WHEN IS A HEARING REQUIRED?

The American theory of procedural due process requires that one be accorded notice and a hearing before and not after one suffers at the hands of government. But how does one know when that point is reached? Frequently, the right to a hearing is presented in terms of entitlement to hearing before final action by the government. But what is final agency action? There are at least two answers; one practical and one legally defined. In practical terms, the government has acted when the consumer of administrative action is actually affected, e.g., when his paycheck stops or his disability payments cease. In legal terms, the action is final when the decision process in the agency, which may involve a number of steps, is completed. The *Eldridge* case study discussed this problem in detail, but consider one other example.

In Chapter 1, a fact pattern was outlined in which a nonprobationary federal employee accused his superior of illegal activities. The employee was fired for cause, including allegedly false and abusive accusations. No one doubted that as a public employee he was entitled to be heard at some point; the question was whether he had to be accorded a hearing before his pay and benefits were terminated. The government argued that its decision in his case would not come to the hearing stage until a number of other administrative steps had been taken. He had to be informed by his superior in writing of the allegations against him, to which he could respond in writing. Following that, he could be terminated although a review of the decision would continue. At the end of the agency review process, the terminated employee could obtain a full hearing before an independent decisionmaker. If he prevailed, he would be reinstated with back pay. The employee answered that since the government average for reaching the hearing stage was approximately eleven months, he and his family would be deprived of income and health care benefits as well as be saddled with the stigma of being fired without having an opportunity to be heard. A fragmented Court did manage to get five justices to agree that as long as the employee did get a hearing at some point before the final decision to terminate him was made, due process was satisfied, even though that decision came after his paycheck stopped.[100]

This case, the *Eldridge* decision, and others rendered after the shift in the Court's approach to administrative due process suggest that in deciding at what point in the administrative decision process a hearing is required, the Court will weigh the cost and harm to the government against the cost and harm to the consumer of the decision. For example, the Court would not require pretermination hearings for Social Security benefits in *Eldridge* or for the nonprobationary federal employee in *Arnett,* but it still supports a requirement for pretermination hearings for welfare recipients on the ground that their loss outweighs the increased cost in time and money to the government since they may very well have no resources to press their claim through the entire decision process.

WHAT KIND OF HEARING IS NEEDED?

Assuming one is entitled to a hearing at some point in the decision process, what does a hearing look like? The answer is in two parts. First, what are the various forms of hearings? Second, what kind of hearing must be accorded in a particular agency?

The forms in which consumers of administrative decisions may be heard vary from what have been referred to as "full-blown trial-type hearings" to "paper hearings." One might classify administrative hearings into four types, ranging from the least to the most formal. All are directed to the resolution of a dispute over a decision that has government sanction and that decides the legal status or entitlements of a specific citizen or group.

First, there are alternative dispute resolution techniques. Based on the idea that agreements voluntarily arrived at and mutually agreed on are preferable to adversary proceedings, in which there is a winner on whose behalf an edict is imposed on the loser, government officials and those in the private sector have pressed for the increased use of negotiation, conciliation, arbitration, ombudsmen, neighborhood justice centers, and other alternatives to adjudications.[101] Even where there will be a more or less formal adjudication, prehearing conferences are often held to attempt to reach settlement or at least to limit the range of disagreements. The APA encourages such practices: "The agency shall give all interested parties opportunity for . . . the submission and consideration of facts, arguments, offers of settlement, or proposals of adjustment when the time, the nature of the proceedings, and the public interest permit."[102]

Second, in some areas it is acceptable to use a procedure known as a "paper hearing."[103] All the evidence and arguments are submitted in writing, with no oral arguments contemplated. Paper hearings are like the process known as summary judgment in other areas of the law. Where there is no material dispute over the facts or the facts can be adequately determined by an examination of documentary evidence, actual hearings may not be necessary. Arguments on questions of law may be resolved by submission of legal briefs or memoranda. The chief advantage of a paper hearing is the saving of both time and expense for the agency and the consumer.

There are many problems with paper adjudications, a few of which are examined in detail in the *Eldridge* case study in Appendix A. That is particularly true when the consumer of the decision is without legal counsel. It is also true when questions that appear at the outset to be clear and relatively simple turn out to be very complex. For example, in a disability case, like that discussed in *Eldridge,* the claimant's physician is required to submit his or her findings on the claimant's disability. This is often a letter or summary statement stating that, in the doctor's view, the claimant is unable to perform his normal occupation. But the agency requires detailed clinical findings describing the specific problems that render the claimant completely disabled and unfit to perform any gainful employment. A further complicating factor is that a number of foreign-born physicians practice in rural communities in the United States and have difficulty communicating their findings and conclusions. For these and many other reasons, it should not be surprising that each time Mr. Eldridge filed and paper submissions were reviewed, his claim was denied, and each time he was afforded an oral hearing at which he could appear and give testimony he prevailed.

Discussions about the usefulness and difficulties of paper hearings generally take an instrumental approach to due process. That is, given the savings in time and money, is it possible to avoid oral hearings and still make accurate adjudicative decisions? The results of such analyses are mixed, but there is still more to be considered. The intrinsic importance of providing a measure of face-to-face due process exists both because the courts have recognized the changing governmental context and the history of abuses when adequate due process protections were not provided and because the legitimacy of government action is strengthened when a citizen is permitted, even in very informal proceedings, to tell his or her story before the decisionmaker.

The third type of hearing might be referred to as a simple oral hearing, not necessarily in a trial-like setting, perhaps no more than an opportunity to be told by an administrator why some particular action is being taken and given a chance to object. Such a process gives the consumer the opportunity to convince the decision-maker, provides the cathartic effect of telling one's story, and preserves the option for later redress since the exchange can be the basis for a later dispute to recompense the consumer for injury.

A recent example of the need for this type of due process came about when several children were suspended from school for allegedly participating in an illegal assembly at another school. They were not afforded an opportunity to tell their side of the story even though they asserted that they were nowhere near the other school at the time and could prove it. Their loss of education, possible harm to grade averages, public embarrassment, and potential harm based on school records showing a suspension were deemed sufficient harm to require some kind of due process. The Supreme Court held that the Constitution requires some minimal due process protection for children suspended from school for ten days or more, or for other similarly stern disciplinary measures. Fears that the Court would require formal trial-type hearings have been rejected in later decisions.

> In *Goss v. Lopez,* . . . we held that due process requires, in connection with the suspension of a student from public school for disciplinary reasons, "that the student be given oral or written notice of charges against him and, if he denies them, an explanation of the evidence the authorities have and an opportunity to present his side of the story." . . . All that *Goss*

required was an informal give-and-take between the student and the administrative body dismissing him that would, at least, give the student the opportunity to characterize his conduct and put it in what he deems the proper context.[104]

Finally, the Court has concluded that important actions that could inflict grievous loss require trial type hearings, which, although not nearly as formal as court trials, require the standard minimum elements of due process. The chapter has discussed several such situations.[105]

WHAT ARE THE ESSENTIAL ELEMENTS OF AN ADMINISTRATIVE HEARING?

As this chapter has indicated, just what process is due in any particular case, when it is due, and what general form it must take vary considerably. So, too, the elements of a hearing vary from agency to agency, depending on the requirement of the agency's enabling legislation, the particular act being enforced, agency regulations, and judicial interpretations of the Constitution and statutes applicable to the agency. However, under the APA, a number of general characteristics of administrative adjudicatory hearings apply broadly and are required of most federal agencies. These provide the traditional due process requirements of notice, an opportunity to be heard, to submit evidence on one's behalf, and to challenge opposing evidence, and a hearing before an impartial decisionmaker who will render a reasoned decision on the record that may be challenged on appeal.

Notice

The APA describes the basic requirements of a hearing in §§554, 555, 556, and 557. The first requirement of an adjudication is that the person involved should be notified of the nature and progress of the proceeding.

> An elementary and fundamental requirement of due process in any proceeding which is to be accorded finality is notice reasonably calculated, under all the circumstances, to appraise interested parties of the pendency of the action and afford them an opportunity to present their objections.[106]

Of particular importance are the adequacy of the notice, the timeliness of the information, and the proper distribution of the notice. As to adequacy, the APA requires that: "Persons entitled to notice of an agency hearing shall be timely informed of—(1) the time, place, and nature of the hearing; (2) the legal authority and jurisdiction under which the hearing is to be held; and (3) the matters of fact and law asserted."[107] Notice must be "timely," that is, it must afford interested parties sufficient time to prepare. How much time is required may vary considerably. Perhaps the most difficult question is the proper distribution of notice. Who must be notified and in what form? The named parties must be personally informed, usually by mail. Other interested parties may be sufficiently notified by constructive notice, or by notice in newspapers of general circulation.

Others may be involved in an administrative adjudication apart from the two named parties: the agency and the party with a case pending. In licensing pro-

proceedings, e.g., those involving broadcasters[108] or power plant facilities,[109] there may be others who assert a sufficiently strong interest in the outcome of the decision to be included, at least to some degree, in the hearing process. How are all those involved in a proceeding to be notified? It has been argued that notice that is not adequately distributed to ensure that all significantly interested parties are made aware of the hearing can jeopardize its integrity because those with important evidence may not be able to present it.[110]

Interested parties who wish to participate but are not the primary or named parties are referred to as "intervenors." In general, federal agencies have come to deal with the problem of notice to intervenors by maintaining service-of-process lists that contain the names of likely participants. Notice is given to those on the list as a matter of routine.

The Hearing

An oral hearing allows one to present evidence, to challenge adverse evidence, to present an argument as to the proper interpretation of the evidence and the law, and to petition for particular kinds of relief. The Administrative Procedure Act and other sources of administrative law acknowledge and seek to implement these objectives. The APA provides that where parties are unable to reach a conclusion to the proceeding by consent, a hearing is to be held in accordance with §§556 and 557 of the act.[111] Further, "in fixing the time and place for hearings, due regard shall be had for the convenience and necessity of the parties or their representatives."[112] "A party is entitled to present his case or defense by oral or documentary evidence, to submit rebuttal evidence, and to conduct such cross-examination as may be required for a full and true disclosure of the facts."[113] Recognizing the complexity of the adjudicatory process, the APA provides that: "A person compelled to appear in person before an agency or representative therefor is entitled to be accompanied, represented, and advised by or with counsel or other duly qualified representative. A party is entitled to appear in person or by or with counsel or other duly qualified representative in an agency proceeding."[114] The government is not, however, required to provide counsel at the public expense.[115] If the agency has subpoena authority granted by statute, "agency subpoenas authorized by law shall be issued to a party on request and, when required by rules of procedure, on a statement or showing of general relevance and reasonable scope of the evidence sought."[116] That is, one may seek the agency's help under its power to issue subpoenas in order to prepare one's case. However, since agencies do not have the power to hold someone in contempt, which is the normal manner in which subpoenas are enforced, they must go to court to ask the court to enforce a subpoena if cooperation is not immediately forthcoming from a person or organization holding evidence.[117] If it comes to that, the APA provides that: "On contest, the court shall sustain the subpoena or similar process or demand to the extent that it is found to be in accordance with law."[118]

At the heart of the hearing process is the presentation of evidence. There are at least two aspects to discussions of evidence in administrative adjudications.[119] First, what evidence is to be admitted into the record for consideration by the decision-maker? The administrative adjudicatory process was deliberately designed to be more flexible and less formal than a court trial. In particular, because there is no jury, it was intended to allow much less formality in the presentation of evidence. The decision-maker is a properly trained and experienced evaluator of evidence who is less likely than members of a jury to be misled by weak or improperly presented evidence. For these reasons, the APA provides that: "Any oral or documentary evidence may be received, but an agency as a matter of policy shall provide for the exclusion of irrelevant, immaterial, or unduly repetitious evidence."[120] In general, administrative law judges tend to admit most of the evidence that is offered since his or her decision is less likely to be overturned if proffered evidence is accepted than if evidence was offered and rejected.

The second problem, then, is to determine how all the evidence that is collected is to be evaluated. The APA states: "A sanction may not be imposed or rule or order issued except on consideration of the whole record or those parts thereof cited by a party and supported by and in accordance with the reliable, probative, and substantial evidence."[121] The requirement that one consider the whole record is intended to ensure that the decisionmaker consider all the evidence and not merely portions of it that would favor one side. "Substantial evidence" has been interpreted to mean "the kind of evidence on which responsible persons are accustomed to rely in serious affairs."[122] "Probative" evidence is evidence that tends to prove, which is nicely circular.[123] The term "substantial evidence" has been interpreted to require that a decision be supported by a "scintilla" of evidence.[124] In the end, whether the weight of evidence is adequate to support is a matter of judgment. That judgment may be tested on appeal.

Judgment exercised by the administrative law judge in the evaluation of evidence is most severely tested when the decisionmaker must weigh different types of evidence. Probably the best example of this problem arose in *Richardson v. Perales*.[125] To make an extraordinarily long story short, Mr. Perales applied for disability insurance, claiming a back injury. Government physicians examined him and found no disability. Perales sought an agency hearing. Accompanied by his attorney and Dr. Morales, one of his physicians, Perales sought to prove the disability. The government introduced medical reports from the government doctors, who did not appear at the hearing. Instead, a physician who had not examined Perales appeared for the government as a consultant to interpret the reports submitted by the other government doctors. Since the reports of the government physicians who had examined Perales were interpreted by another person who had not examined him, the evidence was hearsay rather than direct evidence. One of the main reasons why hearsay evidence is such a problem is that the sources of evidence are not on hand to be cross-examined. The decisionmaker cannot observe the demeanor of the witness as a key to judging his or her veracity, and no questions can be asked to round out the cold reports. On the other hand, Perales's doctor was present and prepared to face cross-examination. Perales's attorney argued two points. First, the government's medical consultant should not be permitted to testify since he had no direct knowledge of Perales's condition and hence could not corroborate the hearsay evidence offered by the government in the medical reports. Second, he argued that the government's case was strictly hearsay while Perales offered direct evidence. Therefore, Perale's offers of proof should outweigh the government's.

We conclude that a written report by a licensed physician who has examined the claimant and who sets forth in his medical findings in his area of competence may be received as evidence in a disability hearing and, despite its hearsay character and an absence of cross-examination, and despite the presence of opposing direct medical testimony and testimony by the claimant himself, may constitute substantial evidence supportive of a finding by the hearing examiner adverse to the claimant, when the claimant has not exercised his right to subpoena the reporting physician and thereby provide himself with the opportunity for cross-examination of the physician.[126]

The Court simply stated that it is the duty of the trier of fact, the ALJ in this case, to weigh the evidence and his or her actions are to be guided by the general concern for fundamental fairness.[127]

The Presiding Officer

Some formal hearings are conducted by members of regulatory commissions or high-ranking administrators, but most are done by administrative law judges (ALJ), about whom more will be said in later chapters. Whoever conducts the hearing has essentially three responsibilities: management of the hearing, development of an adequate and properly prepared record, and the rendering of a reasoned decision that is based on the record and is responsive to the claims and arguments of the parties involved.[128] A primary obligation that affects all three of these functions of the ALJ is the maintenance of the integrity of the proceeding. To aid the decisionmaker in this effort, he or she is granted certain protections by the Administrative Procedure Act against attempts to influence the development of the record or the decision. The attempt by one party to a case to communicate arguments or information to an ALJ outside the normal hearing process is referred to as an *ex parte* communication. The APA provides procedures for dealing with such attempts at influence and states that the "agency may, to the extent consistent with the interests of justice and the policy of the underlying statutes administered by the agency, consider a violation of section 557 (d) [the *ex parte* communication rules] of this title sufficient grounds for a decision adverse to a party who has knowingly committed such violation or knowingly caused such violation to occur."[129] Agencies may sometimes go outside the evidence produced by the parties at the hearing for information but the parties do have the right to enter rebuttals to this kind of "official notice."[130]

Finally, it is the obligation of the ALJ to prepare a reasoned decision setting forth the findings of fact and conclusions of law according to the requirements of §557 of the APA. If no appeal is taken from the decision of the ALJ, it becomes final.

Administrative Appeal

A hearing will often be conducted by an ALJ on behalf of the commissioners or other high agency officials. In that case there may be either an opportunity for one to appeal the decision of the ALJ or, in other situations, an automatic review of his or her decision. The agency may affirm, modify, or reject the ruling, but it must at least consider the ALJ's findings.[131] The reason for this requirement is that the ALJ actually heard the presentation of the case, and saw the witnesses. The initial decision was based on more than the cold record. Therefore, while the ALJ ruling is not binding, it is a matter to be considered even by agency heads.

SUMMARY

In sum, administrative adjudications are attempts to ensure that the basic American values of fairness and due process of law are maintained in administrative agency operations. The rules governing what process an agency must provide are prescribed by the Constitution, the agency enabling statute, the particular statutes being enforced, agency regulations, and court decisions interpreting all of these. Administrative adjudications are more flexible and informal than court trials. To understand them, one must consider the development of the concept of administrative due process and be mindful of the concepts that together make up procedural due process in administration. With regard to particular kinds of adjudications, one must ask a series of questions to understand what is required. Is a hearing required? At what point in an administrative action is a hearing required? What kind of a hearing is required? What are the essential elements of an administrative hearing? In the end, administrative decision makers are required to exercise a great deal of judgment and discretion because of the nature of the controversies they decide and also because of the flexible and informal nature of the administrative adjudicatory process. The developers of administrative law have been optimistic that this relative flexibility and informality are necessary and workable, given the availability of access to judicial review in courts of law to correct mistakes made in agency activities. We turn to the process of judicial review in the next chapter.

NOTES

[1]See J. Randolph and R. Humphreys, "Black Lung Benefits Reform: Mirage or Reality?" 19 *Labor L. J.* 555 (1977), and Brit Hume, *Death and the Mines* (New York: Grossman, 1971), chaps. 3, 4.

[2]*Greene v. McElroy*, 360 U.S. 474, 483 (1959).

[3]Id.

[4]Id., at 484.

[5]Id., at 487.

[6]Id., at 498.

[7]*J.L. v. Parham*, 412 F. Supp. 112, 116–17 (M.D. Ga. 1976).

[8]Id., at 117.

[9]Id., at 133.

[10]Id., at 134.

[11]Id., at 138–39.

[12]*Parham v. J.R.*, 442 U.S. 584 (1979).

[13]"The fundamental requisite of due process is the opportunity to be heard." *Grannis v. Ordean*, 234 U.S. 385 (1914).

[14]J. Skelly Wright, "Beyond Discretionary Justice," 81 *Yale L. J.* 575, 597 (1972).

[15]Louis L. Jaffe quoted in Wright, id., at p. 596.

[16]U.S. House of Representatives, *Constitution of the United States of America: Analysis and Interpretation*, 92d Cong., 2d Sess. (1973), pp. 1137–38.

[17]The Supreme Court has traced our concept of due process to that British tradition. "As we have said on more than one occasion, it may be difficult, if not impossible, to give the term 'due process of law' a definition which will embrace every permissible exertion of power affecting private rights and exclude such as are forbidden. They come to us from the law of England, from which country our jurisprudence is to a great extent derived, and their requirement was there designed to secure the subject against the arbitrary action of the Crown and place him under the protection of the law. They were deemed to be equivalent to 'the law of the land.' In this country, the requirement is intended to have a similar effect against legislative power, that is, to secure the citizen against any arbitrary deprivation of his rights, whether relating to his life, his liberty, or his property." *Dent v. West Virginia*, 129 U.S. 114, 123–24 (1889).

[18]*Constitution*, supra note 16, at p. 1138.

[19]Robert A. Rutland, *The Birth of the Bill of Rights, 1776–1791* (Chapel Hill: University of North Carolina Press, 1955), chaps. 2, 3.

[20]*Barron v. Mayor and City Council of Baltimore*, 32 U.S. (7 Pet.) 243 (1883).

[21]Rutland, supra note 19, at p. 222.

[22]See Chapter 4, note 29.

[23]See the commentary on Dicey, Goodnow, Freund, Dickinson, Landis, and Gellhorn in Chapter 4, pp. [142]–[147].

[24]See, e.g., Walter Gellhorn, *Federal Administrative Proceedings* (Westport, Conn.: Greenwood Press, 1941), pp. 6–14.

[25]*Lochner v. New York*, 198 U.S. 45 (1905).

[26]Id., at 57.

[27]See, e.g., *Moore v. East Cleveland*, 431 U.S. 494 (1977).

[28]*Dismuke v. United States*, 297 U.S. 167, 1972 (1936).

[29]*Withrow v. Larkin*, 421 U.S. 35 (1975).

[30]Id., at 46–47.

[31]In the first place, a judge is legally trained to understand and differentiate between matters properly considered in a legal decision; administrators may or may not be. Additionally, this hearing cannot be compared with binding a defendant over for trial since a good deal more protection is afforded a defendant in a preliminary hearing than was accorded to Larkin. But see *Hannah v. Larch*, 363 U.S. 420 (1960).

[32]As touched on in Chapter 4, it was during this period that federal suits were being brought against state and local government action under the Fourteenth Amendment. It was the time of the rise of the large corporations able to sustain long-term large-scale litigation against government actions viewed as hostile. Also during this period, the newer statutes tended to provide for enforcement by administrative adjudication rather than through private suits in civil courts. Finally, the courts were growing into the judicial system as we now know it. The bar was developing and providing a group of attorneys who would attempt to answer Elihu Root's call to develop a sophisticated body of administrative law. Frank Goodnow, Ernst Freund, Woodrow Wilson, and John Dickinson were teaching them how this might be accomplished.

[33]*Yick Wo v. Hopkins*, 118 U.S. 356, 369 (1886). *Yick Wo* was decided primarily on equal protection grounds, but the

Court related both equal protection and due process to the central problem of administrative arbitrariness that could render a statutory program unconstitutional. Though the statute was lawful as written, it would be void if administered in an arbitrary manner.

[34]*Grannis v. Ordean*, 234 U.S. 385 (1914) and *Dent v. West Virginia*, 129 U.S. 114 (1889).

[35]*Yamataya v. Fisher*, 189 U.S. 86 (1903).

[36]*Londoner v. Denver*, 210 U.S. 373, 386 (1908).

[37]"A finding without evidence is arbitrary and baseless. And even if the government's contention is correct, it would mean that the Commissioner had a power possessed by no other officer, administrative body, or tribunal under our government. It would mean that, where rights depended upon facts, the Commission could disregard all rules of evidence, and capriciously make findings by administrative fiat. Such authority, however beneficently exerted in one case, could be injuriously exerted in another, is inconsistent with rational justice, and comes under the Constitution's condemnation of all arbitrary exercise of power.

"In the comparatively few cases in which such questions have arisen it has been distinctly recognized that administrative orders, quasi-judicial in character, are void if a hearing was denied; if that granted was inadequate or manifestly unfair; if the finding was contrary to the 'indisputable character of the evidence [cities]; or if the facts found do not as a matter of law, support the order made." *Interstate Commerce Comm'n v. Louisville & Nashville Ry. Co.*, 227 U.S. 88, 91–92 (1913). See also *Crowell v. Benson*, 285 U.S. 22, 50 (1932).

[38]*Morgan v. United States*, 304 U.S. 1 (1938); *St. Joseph Stock Yards v. United States*, 298 U.S. 38 (1936); and *Dismuke v. United States*, 297 U.S. 167 (1936).

[39]See generally the discussion of the act in *Wong Yang Sung v. McGrath*, 339 U.S. 33 (1950).

[40]*Sampson v. Murray*, 415 U.S. 61, 95–97 (1974), Justice Douglas dissenting.

[41]*Keyishian v. Board of Regents*, 385 U.S. 589 (1967), and *United States v. Robel*, 389 U.S. 258 (1967).

[42]*Joint Anti-Fascist Refugee Committee v. McGrath*, 341 U.S. 123 (1951).

[43]*Wieman v. Updegraff*, 344 U.S. 184, 191–92 (1952).

[44]*Bailey v. Richardson*, 182 F. 2d 46, 66 (D.C. Cir. 1950).

[45]*Bailey v. Richardson*, 341 U.S. 918 (1951).

[46]*Bailey v. Richardson*, supra note 44.

[47]Id., at 72–73.

[48]See, e.g., *U.S. ex rel. Accardi v. Shaughnessy*, 347 U.S. 260 (1954).

[49]See Appendix A.

[50]William Van Alstyne, "The Demise of the Right–Privilege Distinction in Constitutional Law," 81 *Harvard L. Rev.* 1439 (1968).

[51]This theory is generally traced to an opinion written by Justice Holmes while he was a member of the Massachusetts Supreme Court. "The petitioner may have a constitutional

right to talk politics, but he has no constitutional right to be a policeman. There are few employments for hire in which the servant does not agree to suspend his constitutional right of free speech, as well as of idleness, by the terms of his contract." *McAuliffe v. Mayor of New Bedford,* 155 Mass. 216, 220, 29 N.E. 517 (1892).

[52] *Slochower v. Board of Higher Education,* 350 U.S. 55 (1956); *Speiser v. Randall,* 357 U.S. 513 (1958); *Sherbert v. Verner,* 347 U.S. 398 (1963); *Keyishian v. Board of Regents,* 385 U.S. 589 (1967); *Pickering v. Board of Education,* 391 U.S. 563 (1968); *Shapiro v. Thompson,* 394 U.S. 618 (1969); *Goldberg v. Kelly,* 397 U.S. 254 (1970); *Perry v. Sinderman,* 408 U.S. 593 (1972); *Mt. Healthy Board of Education v. Doyle,* 429 U.S. 274 (1977); and *Givhan v. Board of Education of Western Line Consolidated School Dist,* 439 U.S. 410 (1979).

[53] *Goldberg v. Kelly,* 397 U.S. 254, 263 (1970).

[54] *Bell v. Burson,* 402 U.S. 535, 537 (1971).

[55] Id., at 539.

[56] *Vlandis v. Kline,* 412 U.S. 441 (1973).

[57] *Carrington v. Rash,* 380 U.S. 89 (1965).

[58] *Cleveland Board of Education v. LaFleur,* 414 U.S. 632 (1974).

[59] *Stanley v. Illinois,* 405 U.S. 645 (1972).

[60] Id., at 652–57.

[61] *Goldberg v. Kelly,* supra note 53.

[62] *Wolff v. McDonnell,* 418 U.S. 539 (1974); *Gagnon v. Scarpelli,* 411 U.S. 778 (1973); and *Morrissey v. Brewer,* 408 U.S. 471 (1972).

[63] *Goss v. Lopez,* 419 U.S. 565 (1975). See also *Wood v. Strickland,* 420 U.S. 308 (1975), and *Carey v. Piphus,* 435 U.S. 247 (1978).

[64] *Bell v. Burson,* supra note 54.

[65] *North Georgia Finishing v. Di-Chem,* 419 U.S. 601 (1975); *Fuentes v. Shevin,* 407 U.S. 67 (1972); and *Sniadach v. Family Finance,* 395 U.S. 337 (1969).

[66] *Wisconsin v. Constantineau,* 400 U.S. 433 (1971).

[67] *Board of Regents v. Roth,* 408 U.S. 564 (1972). See also *Wieman v. Updegraff,* supra note 43 at 191.

[68] See the discussion in the *Eldridge* case study in Appendix A on change in the composition of the Court and the particular positions of various Burger Court justices on administrative due process requirements.

[69] See, e.g., *Smith v. Organization of Foster Families,* 431 U.S. 816 (1977).

[70] One of the leaders in this discussion of administrative due process was Henry J. Friendly, "Some Kind of a Hearing," 123 *U. Pennsylvania L. Rev.* 1267 (1975).

[71] Laurence Tribe, *American Constitutional Law* (Mineola, N.Y.: Foundation Press, 1978), §10-7.

[72] *Board of Regents v. Roth,* supra note 67.

[73] Id., at 569–70.

[74] Id., at 571–72.

[75] Id., at 573.

[76] Id.

[77] Id., at 577–78.

[78] William Van Alstyne, "Cracks in 'The New Property': Adjudicative Due Process in the Administrative State," 62 *Cornell L. Rev.* 445, 489–90 (1977).

[79] *Weinberger v. Salfi,* 422 U.S. 749, 771–72 (1975)

[80] *Bishop v. Wood,* 426 U.S. 341 (1976)

[81] Id., at 689.

[82] *Wisconsin v. Constantineau,* supra note 66.

[83] Id., at 437.

[84] *Paul v. Davis,* 424 U.S. 693 (1976).

[85] Id., at 701.

[86] *Bishop v. Wood,* supra note 80 at 353 n. 4, Justice Brennan dissenting.

[87] *Dixon v. Love,* 431 U.S. 105 (1977).

[88] *Board of Curators v. Horowitz,* 435 U.S. 78 (1978).

[89] *Ingraham v. Wright,* 430 U.S. 651 (1977).

[90] *Meachum v. Fano,* 427 U.S. 215 (1976). See generally *Moody v. Daggett,* 429 U.S. 78 (1976), and *Baxter v. Palmigiano,* 425 U.S. 308 (1976).

[91] *Matthews v. Eldridge,* 424 U.S. 319 (1976).

[92] *Arnett v. Kennedy,* 416 U.S. 134 (1974), and *Bishop v. Wood,* supra note 80.

[93] *Goldberg v. Kelly,* supra note 53 at 262, 263 (1970).

[94] *Board of Regents v. Roth,* supra note 67 at 471, 481 (1972).

[95] See supra note 86.

[96] *Stanley v. Illinois,* 405 U.S. 645 (1972).

[97] See *Board of Regents v. Roth,* supra note 67, and *Wieman v. Updegraff,* supra note 43. But see *Paul v. Davis,* supra note 84.

[98] *Owen v. City of Independence,* 445 U.S. 622, 633 n. 13 (1980). See also *Board of Regents v. Roth,* supra note 67, *Arnett v. Kennedy,* supra note 92, and *Bishop v. Wood,* supra note 86.

[99] *Matthews v. Eldgridge,* supra note 91 at 335.

[100] *Arnett v. Kennedy,* supra note 92, at 157.

[101] See generally American Bar Association, "Report of Pound Conference Follow-Up Task Force," 74 *Federal Rules Decisions* 159 (1976); Judicial Conference of the United States, Conference of Chief Justices, and American Bar Association, *National Conference on the Causes of Popular Dissatisfaction* (St. Paul, Minn.: American Bar Association, 1976), pp. 61–97.

[102] 5 U.S.C. §554(c).

[103] "In rulemaking or determining claims for money or benefits or applications for initial licenses an agency may, when a party will not be prejudiced thereby, adopt procedures for the submission of all or part of the evidence in written form." 5 U.S.C. §556(d).

[104] *Board of Curators v. Horowitz,* supra note 88 at 85–86. See also *Ingraham v. Wright,* supra note 89.

[105] See, e.g., *Goldberg v. Kelly,* supra note 53.

[106] *Mullane v. Central Hanover Trust Co.,* 339 U.S. 306, 314 (1950).

[107] 5 U.S.C §554(b)

[108]*Office of Communications of the United Church of Christ v. Federal Communications Comm'n*, 359 F. 2d 994 (D.C. Cir. 1966).

[109]*Scenic Hudson Preservation Conf. v. Federal Power Comm'n*, 354 F. 2d 608 (2d Cir. 1965)

[110]See generally C. Case and D. Schoenbod, "Electricity on the Environment: A Study of Public Regulation Without Public Control," 61 *California L. Rev.* 961 (1973).

[111]5 U.S.C §554(c)(2).

[112]Id., at §554(b).

[113]Id., at §555.

[114]Id.

[115]*Lassiter v. Department of Social Services*, 68 L. Ed.2d 640 (1981). That does not mean that government units do not in fact help a person—particularly single shot players—obtain counsel. This is occasionally accomplished through legal aid programs. Another mechanism is a set fee to be drawn from benefit claims that are proven meritorious. See the *Eldridge* Case study, pp. [7–8], for a discussion of this practice. Some government organizations, such as the Veterans' Administration, set the maximum permitted fee so low that attorneys are discouraged from practicing before the agency.

[116]5 U.S.C §s55 (d).

[117]The authority that different agencies have to demand evidence or information varies significantly. One of the most dramatic examples of agency subpoena authority backed by statutory authority to impose sanctions is that possessed by the Securities and Exchange Commission. See 15 U.S.C. §77 et seq.

[118]5 U.S.C. §555(d).

[119]Kenneth Culp Davis, *Administrative Law: Cases–Text–Problems*, 6th ed. (St. Paul, Minn.: West, 1977), p. 385.

[120]5 U.S.C. §556(d).

[121]Id.

[122]*National Labor Relations Board v. Remington Rand*, 94 F. 2d 862, 873 (2d Cir. 1938), cert. denied, 304 U.S. 576 (1938), rev'd on other grounds, 110 F. 2d 148 (2d Cir. 1940), cited in Ernest Gellhorn, *Administrative Law and Process in a Nutshell* (St. Paul, Minn.: West, 1972), pp. 183–84.

[123]*Black's Law Dictionary*, 4th ed., (St. Paul: West, 1968), p. 1367.

[124]*Richardson v. Perales*, 402 U.S. 389, 401 (1971), and *Consolidated Edison Co. v. NLRB*, 305 U.S. 197, 229 (1938).

[125]*Richardson v. Perales*, supra note 124.

[126]Id., at 402.

[127]*Richardson* undermined what is generally referred to as the "residuum rule." This rule was developed in an early state case. "The act may be taken to mean that while the Commission's inquiry is not limited by the common law or statutory rules of evidence or by technical or formal rules of procedure, and it may in its discretion, accept any evidence that is offered, still in the end there must be a residuum of legal evidence to support the claim before an award is made." *Carroll v. Knickerbocker Ice Co.*, 218 N.Y. 435, 113 N.E. 507 (1916)

[128]See generally 5 U.S.C. §§556, 557.

[129]5 U.S.C. §556(d).

[130]Id., at §556(e).

[131]See *Universal Camera Corp. v. National Labor Relations Board*, 340 U.S. 474 (1951).

Chapter 7

Judicial Review

In Chapters 5 and 6, we discussed two major areas of formal administrative law. The third is judicial review of agency decisions. The availability of law courts for appeal and review of administrative actions is one of the primary underpinnings of the administrative justice system. (See Chapter 4.) In this chapter we consider the nature of judicial review and some of the problems in its operation.

Earlier chapters have approached problems of administrative law from the perspectives of producers and consumers of administrative decisions. Judicial review can be better understood if the subject is approached from the perspective of the judge. Judges were intentionally made important actors in the administrative justice system. Knowledge of their problems and responsibilities can help both producers and consumers of administrative decisions appreciate the limitations and importance of judicial review and—what might seem at first to be a rather odd idea—suggest ways in which parties can aid the judges in their tasks.

The dilemma judges face in reviewing administrative actions is this: judges ought to presume that government officials act lawfully and should not second-guess the substance of administrative decisions. On the other hand, they perform a vital function in assuring that administrators obey the law. Unfortunately, there is no clear line between excessive judicial deference to arbitrary or unlawful administration and inappropriate interference with decisions that are properly the province of expert administrators. When a judge affirms an administrator's decision the challenger will likely claim abdication of judicial responsibility for failure to hold the administrator accountable. Yet, when the same judge reverses or remands an agency judgment, the agency and its supporters will complain about excessive judicial activism and attempts to substitute judicial preference for properly authorized and executed expert administrative judgment.

What students of judicial review can do is examine the purposes of review, the judges' role, and, in general, the limitations on the review process. Again, it is useful to begin with consideration of a representative example of the problem.

Development of the national system of interstate and defense highways began in the 1950s. In major urban areas federal government assistance was granted to local governments and planning units to construct express highways around the cities as bypasses and through the cities as limited access expressways. Memphis, Tennessee, planned such road construction; among other things, it planned to construct a stretch of I-40 through the city. A group of local residents organized to stop the construction through a central city park.

> Overton Park is a 342-acre, municipally owned park in midtown Memphis used for a zoo, a 9-hole golf course and other recreational purposes. The proposed section of the interstate highway extends in an east-west direction through the Park over the presently existing paved, non-access highway used by diesel buses which is approximately 4800 feet in length. The existing highway is 40 to 50 feet wide. The proposed interstate will consist of six lanes—three running in each direction, separated by a median strip approximately 40 feet wide. The interstate right-of-way will vary from approximately 250 feet in width to approximately 450 feet in width, and will require the use of approximately 26 acres of the Park. The proposed design requires that a large portion of the highway be depressed sufficiently to remove traffic from the sight of users of the Park; however, five or six feet of fill will be required where a creek runs across the right-of-way. A 1200-foot access ramp will be located within the eastern end of the park.[1]

Initial approval was given by the U.S. Bureau of Public Roads (which later became part of the Department of Transportation) in 1956. Following that, hearings and other discussions were conducted on the route of the new highway and various design alternatives.

In the 1960s while final decisions were pending a number of provisions were enacted to protect the environment from burgeoning development. Of particular importance to the citizens of Memphis were identical provisions in the Department of Transportation Act of 1966 and the Federal Aid Highway Act of 1968, which conditioned grants of federal funds for highway construction on the satisfaction of environmental requirements.

> It is hereby declared to be the national policy that special effort should be made to preserve the natural beauty of the countryside and public parks and recreation lands, wildlife and waterfowl refuges, and historic sites. The Secretary of Transportation shall cooperate and consult with the Secretaries of the Interior, Housing and Urban Development, Agriculture, and with the States in developing transportation plans and programs that include measures to maintain or enhance the natural beauty of the lands traversed. After August 23, 1968, the Secretary shall not approve any program or project which requires the use of any publicly owned land from a public park, recreation area, or wildlife or waterfowl refuge of national, State, or local significance as determined by the Federal, State or local officials having jurisdiction thereof, or any land from an historic site of national, State, or local significance as so determined by such officials unless (1) there is no feasible and prudent alternative to the use of such land, and (2) such program includes all possible planning to minimize harm to such park, recreational area, wildlife and waterfowl refuge, or historic site resulting from such use.[2]

In November 1969, the Secretary of Transportation gave final approval to federal funding of 90 percent of the cost of the Memphis project.

A suit was filed by two property owners and taxpayers of Memphis, the Citizens to Preserve Overton Park (a group that had been actively opposing the construction for some time),[3] the Sierra Club, and the National Audubon Society against the Secretary of Transportation and the commissioner of the Tennessee Department of Highways. The plaintiffs asserted that: (1) the Secretary of Transportation had ignored his statutory responsibility since he had issued no findings or statements of reasons or opinions showing, as the statutes require, that there "is no feasible and prudent alternative to the use of such land" and the "program includes all possible planning to minimize harm" to the park; (2) to the degree that these judgments are implicit in approval of the project, the secretary's actions were arbitrary and capricious, not based on fact and reason but on administrative inertia and agreement with local politicians who chose the route through the park as the path of least resistance (so to speak); and (3) the procedures used in the route and design hearings were inadequate and not in compliance with regulations.[4]

The secretary replied that: (1) the suit should be dismissed because those bringing the action did not have standing; (2) if the case were to proceed, it should be decided on summary judgment since the record was adequate for judicial review and there were no material issues of fact; (3) administrative procedures had been observed in substance even if there had been minor technical weaknesses in form; (4) the statute did not require the secretary to make the findings demanded by the plaintiffs; and (5) his actions were not arbitrary and capricious but were exercises of expert discretionary judgment based on a lengthy consideration of the route and design of the highway.

Summary judgment (a decision based on briefs and the record without a trial) was granted to the secretary by the district court. The court found no problem of standing, but neither did it feel it necessary to advance beyond summary judgment since many documents and supporting publications were in the record along with the briefs in the case. The court found no material breaches of procedural requirements. Judge Brown found no requirement in the statute that the secretary enter formal findings concerning the existence of feasible alternatives or adequacy of planning. Finally, the court found no cause for concluding that the secretary had acted in an arbitrary and capricious manner. The primary reason advanced in support of this ruling was that "it was not the intent of Congress to prohibit the building of an expressway through a park if there was any alternative; rather, by providing that such should not be done if there is any feasible and prudent alternative, it was the intent of Congress to avoid the park if, after considering all relevant factors, it is preferable to do so."[5] No systematic investigation was required, but merely a mandate that the secretary consider the relevant factors that together suggest which route and design are feasible and prudent, determined with a sensitivity for environmental values.

By the time the case came to the Sixth Circuit Court of Appeals for review of Judge Brown's summary judgment, ten attorneys from seven different firms were on the briefs. In a split decision, the appellate court upheld the lower court. Judge Weick, writing for himself and Judge Peck, concluded that the documents submitted to the district court provided enough evidence to decide the case and that there were no material issues of fact that would require more than a summary judgment. Specifically, Weick relied on an affidavit prepared for the secretary at the time the suit was decided in the lower court. The affidavit was that of a Mr. Swick, a long-time official in the federal public roads office. Swick's affidavit stated that the route for the highway was selected in 1956 with a concern for avoiding the park, but officials had concluded that too many people would be displaced and the costs would be too high to go around the park. Besides that, by the time Volpe made his final decision, the right of way had been purchased and construction had begun on the part of the road that would run to the park. Any change of plans would have meant great expense and further displacement of people and buildings. Press releases and correspondence were also submitted to suggest the damage that would be caused if an alternative was chosen.

Judge Celebreeze dissented, arguing that Mr. Swick's affidavit was not prepared at the time of the decision, but was developed for his superior at the time of the litigation. He also referred to statements in the record that disputed the affidavit. For example, a former federal highway administrator had testified before a congressional committee "that the decision to build the highway through the park was left 'completely in the hands of the city council' of Memphis." In short, the federal administrators had not taken responsibility for alternative route consideration. Celebreeze further argued that it would have been difficult for the administrator to have considered the statutory environmental protection requirements, as suggested by Swick, when the statute was enacted twelve years later. Finally, the court, according to Celebreeze, was in no position to know what the secretary had decided because no finding by the secretary was on the record, nor was any suggestion as to exactly what the secretary *did* consider when the highway was approved. He would reverse and remand for a full evidentiary hearing.

The Supreme Court agreed with Judge Celebreeze. Justice Marshall wrote for the Court. The Court agreed that the statute did not require formal findings by the secretary; however, the secretary is clearly subject to judicial review under the Administrative Procedure Act.[6] In this case the central problem of review is to determine whether the administrator properly interpreted and applied the statutes that govern his agency's activities. The particular statute under consideration contained "a plain and explicit bar to the use of federal funds for construction of highways through parks—only the most unusual situations are exempted."[7] The only exemption is in cases where there are no feasible alternatives. "For this exemption to apply the Secretary must find that as a matter of sound engineering it would not be feasible to build the highway along any other route."[8] The government argued that the statute implied a general balancing test, but the Court rejected that interpretation.

> They contend that the Secretary should weigh the detriment resulting from the destruction of parkland against the cost of other routes, safety considerations, and other factors, and determine on the basis of the importance that he attaches to these other factors whether, on balance, alternative feasible routes would be "prudent."
> But no such wide-ranging endeavor was intended. It is obvious that in most cases considerations of cost, directness of route, and community disruption will indicate that parkland should be used for highway construction whenever possible. Although it may be necessary to transfer funds from one jurisdiction to another, there will always be a smaller outlay required from the public purse when parkland is used since the public

already owns the land and there will be no need to pay for right-of-way. And since people do not live or work in parks, if a highway is built on parkland no one will have to leave his home or give up his business. Such factors are common to substantially all highway construction. Thus, if Congress intended these factors to be on an equal footing with preservation of parkland there would have been no need for the statute.

Congress clearly did not intend that cost and disruption of the community were to be ignored by the Secretary. But the very existence of the statutes indicates that protection of parkland was to be given paramount importance.[9]

The Court then summarized its responsibility in reviewing the decision of the Secretary to approve the construction.

The Court is first required to decide whether the Secretary acted within the scope of his authority. . . . This determination naturally begins with a delineation of the scope of the Secretary's authority and discretion. . . . As has been shown, Congress has specified only a small range of choices that the Secretary can make. Also involved in this initial inquiry is a determination of whether on the facts the Secretary's decision can reasonably be said to be within that range. The reviewing Court must consider whether the Secretary properly construed his authority to approve the use of parkland as limited to situations where there are no feasible alternative routes or where feasible alternative routes involve uniquely difficult problems. And the reviewing Court must be able to find that the Secretary could have reasonably believed that in this case there are no feasible alternatives or that alternatives do involve unique problems.

Scrutiny of the facts does not end, however, with the determination that the Secretary has acted within the scope of his statutory authority. Section 706 (2)(A) requires a finding that the actual choice made was not "arbitrary, capricious, an abuse of discretion, or not otherwise in accordance with law." . . . To make this finding the Court must consider whether the decision was based on a consideration of the relevant factors and whether there has been a clear error of judgment. . . . Although this inquiry into the facts is to be searching and careful, the ultimate standard of review is a narrow one. The Court is not empowered to substitute its judgment for that of the agency.[10]

The only way to make such a review is to examine the record that was before the administrator at the time the decision was made. But no such record had been submitted in court, merely documentation that tended to support the decision that had already been made and affidavits that were obviously prepared after the fact to support the secretary's decision against the court challenge.

That administrative record is not, however, before us. The lower courts based their review on the litigation affidavits that were presented. These affidavits were merely "post hoc" rationalizations, *Burlington Truck Lines v. United States*, 371 U.S. 156, 168–169 (1962), which have traditionally been found to be an inadequate basis for review. . . . And they clearly do not constitute the "whole record" compiled by the agency; the basis for review required by §706 of the Administrative Procedure Act.[11]

The Court sent the case back to the district court for a full review, as described in the

Court's opinion, of the whole record that was before the secretary when he made his decision in 1969 giving final approval to the Memphis project. The Court did not reverse the secretary's decision; it did require the lower court to take a more careful look.[12]

By the time the case was returned to the district court more parties had become involved in the case. There were fifteen lawyers on record as having worked on the briefs. The National Wildlife Federation has joined the plaintiffs. Several groups intervened on behalf of the secretary and the commissioner, including the Memphis Chamber of Commerce, Future Memphis, Inc., and the Downtown Association.[13] Just after the Supreme Court decision was announced, Judge Brown met with the attorneys to discuss the future litigation of the case. Lawyers for the government informed the judge that it would take several weeks to assemble the whole record that had been before the secretary. The fact that it actually took nearly four and one-half months to do so did not encourage observers to believe that such a record had ever actually existed. The court held twenty-five days of hearings in the fall of 1971, at which some 240 exhibits were taken into evidence. After the hearings, 287 pages of briefs were also submitted.[14] While the government continued to argue that the secretary had made his judgment based on the fact that there were no "feasible and prudent alternatives," the judge disagreed.

> However, we find that, whether or not we consider the affidavit and deposition as a "post hoc rationalization," the evidence is overwhelming that Secretary Volpe did not so consider alternatives.[15]

Even if he had considered some alternatives, his interpretation of the requirement of the statute was in error. These two defects in the secretary's decision required that the case be remanded to the secretary to reconsider the facts and the law in light of the judicial rulings.

However, the case was still not over. After the district court decision, Secretary of Transportation Volped required that the project be restudied in light of the requirements discussed in the judicial opinions. He also noted that he considered the National Environmental Policy Act of 1969 and the noise pollution limitations required by the 1970 Federal Aid Highway Act applicable to the decision. On January 13, 1973, the secretary issued a decision in which he concluded that the project could not be approved. The Memphis I-40 project did not satisfy the requirements of any of the three statutes involved. He ended his opinion as follows:

> Among the possible alternatives which the State of Tennessee may wish to consider are the use of the I-240 circumferencial combined with improvements to arterial streets, alternative routes such as the L & N Railroad corridor and a broadened use of public transportation facilities and services or combinations of the above to meet the transportation needs in and around Memphis. . . . Listing these possible alternatives should not, of course, be construed either as an endorsement of any of them or as an exclusion of any other alternatives that I have not mentioned. Likewise it should not be construed as a finding that the "no build" alternative has been rejected.

At this point the state of Tennessee sued the Secretary of Transportation, arguing that his latest decision was inadequate. In particular, the state asserted that the secretary must find that there were no "feasible and prudent" alternatives, for if there are such alternatives, he must identify them and authorize the state to employ them. The district court agreed and the decision was again remanded to the secretary.

By this time, a new Secretary of Transportation, Claude Brinegar, had been appointed. Represented by a new group of attorneys from the Justice Department, attorneys not involved in earlier stages of the case, and joined by the Citizens Preserve Overton Park, the secretary appealed the district court decision to the Sixth Circuit Court of Appeals. The case was heard by the same three judges who had originally heard the first appeal in 1970. On April 3, 1974, the court of appeals announced an unanimous decision in favor of the secretary, finding that the secretary had no affirmative obligation to provide the state with an alternative. The secretary's sole job under the statute was to approve or disapprove plans submitted by the state or local governments seeking federal assistance.[16]

MYTH AND REALITY IN JUDICIAL REVIEW

Overton Park is an unusual case in terms of the large number of people involved, the length of time of the legal conflict, and the number of judicial opinions formulated to deal with one controversy. It does, however, illustrate a number of characteristics of judicial review of administrative action. In addition to demonstrating the kinds of questions that judges ask administrators, the case gives the lie to several more or less widespread myths about the process.

Judicial review is not a simple one-stop gate at which some gatekeeper is charged with deciding whether to allow the administrative decision to go forward or not. As the simple system model of the administrative justice system discussed in Chapter 1 indicated, decisions can exist at several points without going to courts. In fact, only a small percentage of administrative decisions are ever taken to judicial review.[17] If it were otherwise both the courts and administrative agencies would be in serious trouble. Neither could handle the burden. When cases do go to court, they may be sent back (remanded) for clarification. The decision may not be reversed, but the court may find that the decisionmaker needs to supplement the ruling that was made. In fact, judicial review has been described as more of a dialogue over the requirements of law between courts and officials in the executive and legislative branches than a dictating of terms in one grand, final decision.

As *Overton Park* indicates, cases that come for review often do not fit the neat rulemaking or adjudication categories. As noted in Chapter 1, administrative decisions can take a variety of forms. Judges who review those decisions, in whatever form they are presented, must ensure that they conform to the requirements of law.

In public law cases, unlike private legal disputes where the government is not a party, frequently more than two individuals or organizations are involved. Part of this can be explained, as it will be in Chapter 10, in terms of the practice of litigation as an interest-group tactic.[18] But there is another important reason. As the members of the Attorney General's Committee on Administrative Procedure noted as long ago as 1941, it is one thing to get agreement between an agency and someone with an interest in an agency decision, but quite another to serve the public interest. For example, it is frequently in the political interests of some regulatory officials to avoid confrontation with the groups they regulate, but, at some point, failure to confront an individual or business organization for pollution or safety violations is failure to perform the responsibility assigned to the agency by the legislature. Other parties may become involved in an effort to force administrators to honor the statutory obligations. In *Overton Park,* clearly the local political officials wanted to build through the park and the Secretary of Transportation had an interest in assisting them. Outside parties intervened to challenge the secretary's cooperation on the ground that it was not in the public interest as declared by congressional enactment. The local chamber of commerce entered on the other side of the case. The fact that there may be several parties means that the case requires careful coordination and management by the judge.

As in *Overton Park,* several attorneys may be involved in an administrative case. Some may be from prestigious firms and have a great deal of experience in policy-related adjudications, while others may be from local firms without such experience. On the government side, there may be several government units represented by a number of attorneys. In some cases there can be conflict between government units. There can also be difficulties in litigation if there is a dispute between the Department of Justice, which generally controls federal government litigation, and agency attorneys who may legitimately feel that they have more detailed knowledge in a particular case.

Suits brought for judicial review of administrative actions often arise in a complex political environment. By the time a decision gets to the judicial review stage, various groups and government agencies may have already invested considerable economic and political resources in the controversy. The intensity of interest and conflict varies, but, whatever the level of political debate, the judge must be aware of the nature of the controversy before him or her and sensitive to the environment in which it arose and is played out.

Finally, *Overton Park* demonstrates that judges who review administrative actions have complex tasks to perform. They certainly do not engage in simplistic mechanical jurisprudence in which only narrow clean procedural questions are presented for a plain yes or no judgment. The factors discussed in Chapter 3 that make up the law in action come together to frame the responsibilities and opportunities of the judge in administrative law.

JUDGES AND AGENCIES

The various questions that must be dealt with as administrative decisions come for judicial review are conditioned by the legal bases for review, the particular purposes that such review is designed to serve, and the several tasks that together make up the role of the judge in reviewing agency decisions.

The APA on Judicial Review

There are several bases for judicial review, beginning, of course, with the requirements of the Constitution. Statutes and judicial decisions also describe the need for particular types of review of agency action in specific situations. The general underpinning for judicial review in administrative law is the APA, 5 U.S.C. §701 et seq. Section 702 provides that: "A person suffering legal wrong because of agency action, or adversely affected or aggrieved by agency action within the meaning of a relevant statute, is entitled to judicial review thereof." The type of inquiry to be accomplished by the court is set forth in section 706.

> To the extent necessary to decision and when presented, the reviewing court shall decide all relevant questions of law, interpret constitutional and statutory provisions, and determine the meaning or applicability of the terms of an agency action. The reviewing court shall—
>
> (1) compel agency action unlawfully withheld or unreasonably delayed; and
>
> (2) hold unlawful and set aside agency action, findings, and conclusions found to be—
>
> (A) arbitrary, capricious, an abuse of discretion, or otherwise not in accordance with law;
>
> (B) contrary to constitutional right, power, privilege, or immunity;
>
> (C) in excess of statutory jurisdiction, authority, or limitations, or short of statutory right;
>
> (D) without observance of procedure required by law;
>
> (E) unsupported by substantial evidence in a case subject to section 556 and 557 of this title or otherwise reviewed on the record of an agency hearing provided by statute; or
>
> (F) unwarranted by the facts to the extent that the facts are subject to trial de novo by the reviewing court.
>
> In making the foregoing determinations, the court shall review the whole record or those parts of it cited by a party, and due account shall be taken of the rule of prejudicial error.

Functions of Judicial Review

A review such as that prescribed by the APA serves a number of purposes. (1) It establishes the boundaries of administrative authority through interpretation of the Constitution and statutes. (2) It provides feedback to the legislature, agencies, and the public on the meaning of law and the nature of agency authority. (3) It helps agencies develop orderly and regular processes for change and resolution of disputes. (4) It discourages, to some extent at least, abuses of discretion. (5) It provides some protection from majoritarian pressures on agencies. (6) It forces the development of records for use in later policymaking.

Role of the Public Law Judge

The judge who reviews an administrative action is obligated to accomplish the purposes described above in the manner set forth in the APA, and in accordance with statutory and constitutional law. However, there are also other aspects to the judge's role in such cases.[19]

Judges have an obligation to keep administrators within the law. However, they are able to do so only sporadically, as cases arise; and the way in which cases are structured is largely out of their control. The courts are for the most part passive participants in the administrative process. (There are some exceptions, to which we shall turn in later chapters.) By means of technical points, judges can avoid some decisions, but the ability to duck tough cases is somewhat limited, particularly in the lower courts. Judges are to some degree captives of the manner in which the advocates cast the case. If the advocates are effective and thorough, the judges have a better case to work with than if the opposite were true.

Second, as a court administrator once said, judges are in a business in which at least half the customers leave dissatisfied. In judicial review of administrative decisions, it is not uncommon for both sides to leave grumbling, one because the court did too much, the other because the court didn't do enough. It is important that the judge draft solid, effective opinions. Opinions explain to the winners the judges' reasoning and give guidance for the future. They also explain to the losers why they did not prevail. The judges must—or ought to—craft opinions in such a way that the decision may be understood, reasonably well accepted, and complied with.

Judges in public law cases must be more than umpires. They must play an active part in managing the cases that come to their courts. In cases where there are twenty-five or more briefs and forty or more parties, this may be very difficult.

Part of case management is the task of dealing with conflicting units of government. To do this, judges must interpret and relate statutes that are administered by different agencies. In *Overton Park*, for example, the secretary was obligated by statute to consult with two other cabinet-level departments. The secretary was concerned about three statutes, all of which affected his decision in the case. Sometimes, as in the construction of dams, eight or more statutes may be involved with coordination required among a number of agencies, some primarily interested in environmental protection, and others in construction. The judge may ask the government to consolidate its position in the case where possible, request written arguments on possible areas of conflict in statutes or agency policy, press attorneys at oral argument for clarifications, and draft opinions that attempt to systematically relate the various authorities involved and note points of conflict.

The judge must also guard against preference for what might be termed glamour cases. Illinois Congressman Railsback once observed: "I had the experience of representing a couple of social security disability claimants, and . . . on appeal to the Federal District Court . . . I got the distinct feeling that the district court judge could have cared less that I was representing this woman who happened to suffer from emphysema, I was taking up his valuable time."[20] It can be very difficult for judges who have reviewed major government administrative policy decisions to turn to reviews of individual social security cases, freedom of information disputes, and National Labor Relations Board enforcement cases, which have less interest and prestige. But there are many more of the latter cases and they are of extreme importance to the parties bringing them. Judges must guard against the temptation to underestimate when the consequences of an unlawful decision may be of no major consequence to the nation, yet are of crucial importance to individual citizens.

Finally, the judge must learn to work on the balance point between careful and thorough review of administrative action and judicial usurpation of administrative authority.

These responsibilities and how they are performed can be understood in part through considering the questions that are asked as a case comes on for and proceeds through judicial review. Two general questions, each with a number of subsidiary aspects, should be asked: (1) Should the case be allowed to get through the courthouse door for review? (2) If the case is properly presented for review, what kind of review should be provided?

ENTRANCE THROUGH THE COURTHOUSE DOOR: PROCEDURAL ROADBLOCKS TO JUDICIAL REVIEW

Whether a case for judicial review will be allowed to get through the door of the courthouse involves three considerations. First, the case must be presented to a tribunal that has the authority to decide it. Second, the case must be ready for review and the proper parties must be bringing it. The third question is whether the judges will use the discretion they possess in interpreting procedural rules to block the case.

Jurisdiction

A case can be properly brought only in a court that has jurisdiction, that is, the authority to decide the issues presented. The judicial power is the power to decide cases and controversies;[21] jurisdiction is the authority to apply judicial power in a particular case.[22] That authority is provided by the Constitution and by statute. To obtain judicial review, then, one must show that the court in which the case is brought has jurisdiction to hear it.

The Case and the Parties

The judge may be called on to determine whether the rules of judicial self-restraint, discussed in Chapter 3, have been met.[23] Is the case justiciable? That is, is it the kind of a case the court can hear and do something about? If all lower court or administrative remedies have not been exhausted, the case is not ready for adjudication. Apart from the preparation of the case itself, the parties bringing the case must also be properly before the court. Do they have standing to litigate the case?

To have standing for judicial review one must demonstrate that there has been injury in fact to one's legally protected rights or interests and that the injury was actually the result of the government's action or lack of action.[24] The requirement of an actual substantial injury is intended to ensure that the parties to a suit have the "concrete adverseness" that makes for a serious effort to present sharp and clearly defined legal issues to a court.[25] The term "injury in fact" to one's protected interests implies that one has actually been injured or stands in imminent danger of being harmed, rather than that one is merely concerned about some hypothetical injury that might or might not occur.[26] The frequent reference in commentaries on standing regarding injury to one's legally protected interest is also important.[27] All citizens are affected in one way or another by almost all government policies and any number of them may feel injured by government action. But the courts have held that "generalized undifferentiated injury," which a citizen may feel with regard to, say, the operation of U.S. intelligence agencies' activity, is an insufficient basis for a lawsuit challenging official action.[28] Instead, one must point to more specific injury, such as interference with one's freedom of religion or one's right to see government records.[29]

Courts have held that organizations can sue on behalf of the interests of their members.[30] But, in general, neither an individual nor a group may ask for judicial review to protect the interests of a third party not involved in the litigation.[31] Referred to as the "prudential standing rule," this limitation is intended to ensure that the parties before the court are well suited to argue the case.[32]

Standing can be, and these days often is, a very complex and hotly disputed legal concept. Unless one can meet the requirements for standing to sue one cannot get through the courthouse door, even though all other procedural requirements have been satisfied.

Judicial Gatekeeping

Most of the procedural rules that control access to judicial review are judicially created.[33] The courts may act as gatekeepers and interpret those rules so as to encourage or block litigation. The clear pattern established in Burger Court rulings of the past several years is to restrict access to the courts for judicial review.

The procedural rules allow a great deal of flexibility for a judge in determining whether a particular case is heard. The judge will usually be called on to exercise that discretion, since technical defenses will almost always be raised to block an appeal of an administrative decision.[34] After all, the surest way to prevent a judgment that overturns a favorable ruling is to prevent the case from getting into court in the first place. There are pressures on judges to deal with cases on these narrow procedural grounds, e.g., heavy dockets, or the desire to avoid particularly complex and politically charged issues. Some judges interpret the procedural rules narrowly to discourage certain types of cases and to encourage others.

In acting as gatekeepers to judicial review, judges fall at points along a continuum. At one extreme is the philosophy that all significant disputes ought to have the fullest possible legal consideration without obstruction by procedural technicalities. At the other extreme is the view that the judge's job is to perform a narrow and carefully prescribed function, with respect to cases fully developed according to rigid procedural rules, regardless of any consequences of lack of access to the courts. Fortunately, very few jurists operate at these extremes. Most realize that for the judicial process to operate, cases must be presented in a manageable and appropriate format and that rules of judicial self-restraint are also important, especially among judges who do not stand for election and who are frequently protected by life tenure. Most are also aware that they are often asked to decide issues that cannot be neatly and completely developed within very narrow and rigid guidelines without causing substantial injustices—injustices having the most severe impact on those least able to endure the hardship.[35]

The Burger Court has been moving toward limitation on access to federal courts for resolution of public law disputes.[36]

Although the pattern is not uniform, it is clear enough: The Supreme Court is making it harder and harder to get a federal court to vindicate federal constitutional and other rights. In some cases, prior decisions have been overruled, either explicitly or silently; in other contexts, restrictive implications in prior cases have been taken up and expanded; in still other situations, new approaches developed by lower courts have been repudiated. . . . That there is indeed a pattern, and that it is more than accidental, seems clear from the scope and pervasiveness of the phenomenon.[37]

Apparently motivated by anxiety over increasing dockets and ideological disagreements with earlier decisions, a majority of the Court has made it difficult to obtain standing to challenge government action,[38] substantially reduced the availability of the class action lawsuit,[39] attempted to block the awarding of attorneys' fees to those who prevail in so-called private attorney general suits,[40] interpreted procedural rules and doctrines so as to discourage federal court activity,[41] and limited the authority of federal district courts to impose equitable remedies that require specific changes in proven cases of maladministration.[42]

Congress has enacted some statutes to provide access or assist litigants where the Court was unwilling to recognize or permit suits or reward those who prevailed.[43] The lower courts may or may not cooperate in the Supreme Court's effort to trim federal court activity.[44] A few supreme courts have reacted to the narrowing of some federal doctrines by expanding state rulings, but this creates a very uneven legal fabric and does not apply to federal administrative actions.[45] Judges who oppose limiting access to the courtroom are fond of citing Alexis de Toqueville's observation of almost a century and a half ago.

> The American judge is brought into the political arena independent of his own will. He only judges the law because he is obliged to judge a case. The political question which he is called upon to resolve is connected with the interest of the parties and he cannot refuse to decide it without abdicating the duties of his post.[46]

These critics also observe that the rulings on standing and the like have not reduced the caseload on the federal courts, but have actually increased the burden, because additional space in briefs and hearing time are needed to resolve procedural disputes before the court can proceed to the merits of the case at hand.[47]

WHAT KIND OF REVIEW IS PROVIDED?

If a request for review of an agency decision survives the initial procedural challenges, what kind of review will be made? The type of review afforded is conditioned by the applicable statutes and other variables, but, in most cases, the judge examines the record that was before the administrator at the time of the decision, and asks five questions.

1. Has the administrator acted within his or her proper range of authority?

Deciding this question entails consideration of the enabling act of the agency and any other statutes that the administrator is charged to administer. If the authority the administrator claims is not to be found in the statutes or in an executive order properly issued by the president, the administrative action is *ultra vires,* beyond authority, and is by definition illegitimate. The court will grant the agency considerable deference in interpreting the statute, but the court remains the final arbiter of the meaning of statutes.[48]

2. *Were proper procedures followed?*

The judge will want evidence to show that the proper procedures were followed by the administrator. Procedural requirements are established by statute, by provisions of the APA, and by agency regulations. Procedural rules established by the agency are binding on the agency.[49] If an argument is made on the point, the judge might want some indication that the agency procedures were adequate in substance as well as in form. For example, the FCC at one time dealt with license contests by hearing one applicant, deciding the case, and then hearing the other. The second applicant was given a hearing in any event, but this was meaningless if the agency had already decided to award the license to the first party. The Supreme Court required a consolidated hearing procedure in which both parties could participate.[50]

3. *Was the decision arbitrary and capricious or an abuse of discretion?*

A finding that the administrator acted arbitrarily or capriciously means that he or she acted without reason or on a whim. The judge begins with the presumption that the administrator acted lawfully, and examines the record to determine the justification for the administrative action advanced when the decision was announced. In most cases that means examining the opinion accompanying an agency order, the publication information accompanying the promulgation of a rule, or other type of agency policy announcement.[51] The judge is not interested in *post hoc* rationalizations of what the administrator might have considered when the decision was made, but rather in what he or she actually took into consideration.[52]

Determining whether an administrator abused his or her discretion is every bit as difficult as it sounds. The concept of administrative discretion is an exceedingly complex notion; Chapter 9 is devoted to considering it. For the present, an administrative decision may be considered an abuse of discretion if the administrator considered matters that are not appropriate in determining government action, such as the race or religion of the person before the agency, or if the administrator failed to take account of matters that are important to a decision,[53] as in *Overton Park,* where the court found that the Secretary of Transportation had not dealt with the environmental considerations that were required by statute.[54]

4. *Was there substantial evidence on the record as a whole to support the conclusion?*

Section 706(2)(E) of the APA provides that a court shall "hold unlawful and set aside agency action, findings and conclusions found to be . . . unsupported by substantial evidence *in a case subject to section 556 and 557 of this title or otherwise reviewed on the record of an agency hearing provided by statute."* (Emphasis added.) The point of this language is that judicial review of formal adjudications and formal rulemaking ought to be more formal and more careful than of other kinds of administrative actions. Presumably Congress required formal proceedings in specified situations because the issue was particularly important or because it was extremely difficult to resolve the type of dispute that was involved. More rigorous judicial review offers greater assurance of the integrity of the record, the adequacy of the record (whether there was a substantial amount of evidence to support the conclusion the administrator reached), and, finally, the proper application of the record (that the administrator considered the whole record and not just those parts of it that supported his or her predispositions).

Less formal administrative actions should receive a less formal review than the "substantial evidence" approach. These less formal administrative actions would satisfy the other requirements of §706, with particular attention to the so-called arbitrary and capricious standard noted earlier. As a practical matter, however, judges usually look to see whether there is substantial evidence in the record as a whole to support an administrative action. The reason that "substantial evidence" becomes a factor centers on the definition of "arbitrary and capricious." When a judge wishes to determine whether an administrative decision was "arbitrary, capricious, an abuse of discretion, or not otherwise in accordance with law" (§706), he or she looks to the record that supports the agency decision. If an arbitrary decision is one that is not based on reason or is a matter of whim, how is the judge to decide whether the record before the court fits that definition? When people say that a decision was without support in reason, they usually mean that there was no evidence to substantiate it. So viewed, one criterion for determining the validity of an administrative decision is whether there is evidence in the record that supports it. Clearly, a decision that relied only on that evidence in the record that supported the agency and not any opposing evidence would be arbitrary and capricious. The only check then is to see whether the administrator relied on substantial evidence in the record as a whole.

The meaning of the word "substantial" in administrative law is extremely vague, and determining whether there was substantial evidence requires judgment. The judge does not ask whether the evidence in the record proves the administrator's point beyond a reasonable doubt, or even whether there was a preponderance of the evidence in support of the decision he or she reached. Rather, the court wants to know whether there was enough evidence of the kind that reasonable people are accustomed to relying upon in serious matters[55] that the administrator reasonably could have reached the conclusion reached by the agency.

In sum, judges usually look to see whether there is evidence in the record as a whole to support the administrative action. If the case is a formal administrative action, they are aware that the review should be somewhat more probing than in other administrative matters. In any event, administrative records ought to contain some evidence to support the administrator's action.

5. Is there a constitutional violation?

Judges will entertain the argument that the statutes, regulations, or agency practices involved in a particular administrative action are unconstitutional. The claim that an administrator obeyed the requirements of the APA and the enabling act of his agency will, of course, not save an administrative action if there is a constitutional violation.[56]

JUDICIAL REVIEW AND TECHNICAL COMPLEXITY: WHERE IS THIS REASONABLE MAN EVERYONE KEEPS TALKING ABOUT?

Judicial review is perhaps most difficult where the agency administers policies governing complex scientific and technological activity. Administrative decisions in such areas as air and water pollution[57] and toxic substances control[58] involve difficult and often controversial scientific judgments about which even the recognized experts disagree. Of course, disputes over complex scientific and technological problems arise in cases other than administrative law, for example, in malpractice, personal injury, and infringement of patent suits. Chief Judge Carl McGowan recently described one case.

> The Clean Water Act of 1977 authorized the Environmental Protection Agency by informal rulemaking to issue regulations imposing effluent limitations for each industry discharging pollutants into the waters of the United States. The statutory standard prescribed for the guidance of EPA was that effluents throughout a five-year period from 1977-1983 should not exceed levels characteristic of plants using "the best practicable control technology currently available." . . . Sixteen different wood and paper companies individually brought petitions to review the regulations applicable to them. . . . The substantive claims made were essentially that in this industry manufacturing techniques vary widely from plant to plant in their scientific and engineering characteristics, and that EPA had been arbitrary and capricious in not providing a sufficient number of groupings to allow for these variations. To the extent that the court turned aside the claims of error made in respect of the hearing procedures followed and the Agency's interpretation of the underlying statute, it was left with the formidable task of acquiring an understanding of sixteen separate plant operations so that it could compare them with one another and with the many more noncomplaining plants and decide whether there had been irrationality in EPA's classifications. This presumably was to be done by the court's mastering the contents of the 140,000 pages of record replete with assertions by chemical engineering reports, assembled in the six-year period of notice and comment.
>
> This task was one to be approached by a court, wholly lacking in expert assistance of its own, with a modest view of its own capabilities in this area, and a firm grasp upon the standards of review properly to be observed by it.[59]

The court cannot ignore the basic requirements for judicial review and simply give an agency carte blanche to exceed the law, abuse its discretion, and act arbitrarily. Nor may it presume to judge the accuracy of administrators' scientific judgments. In this day and time, agency actions will be vigorously challenged, especially when administrative actions affect repeat players. Scientific data will be presented by all parties.[60]

The court is not generally asked to find that the agency is wrong on a scientific basis. Instead, the scientific arguments are made to show, as in the EPA example cited above, that the administrator acted arbitrarily by refusing to acknowledge competent scientific information or by making gross generalizations that are seen as irrational when viewed in light of the real-world situation as indicated by scientific evidence.

Judges are often painfully aware of their own weaknesses in deciding such matters.[61] In terms of workload, critical political rhetoric, and difficulty in drafting opinions, judges might be tempted to avoid such cases through technical devices or to rubber-stamp administrative decisions. To their credit, judges are aware of the importance of their role in the administrative justice system and understand the need for careful and thorough judicial review.[62] Finally, judges possess an expertise that is not inherently in conflict with the subject matter expertise of the agency:

> If the principal purpose of judicial review of agency action is thought to reside in assuring procedural fair play and reasoned decisionmaking, then we have an expertise to bring to bear that does not derogate from the expertise the agency members should have in their particular fields. The one is expertise that complements, rather than conflicts with the other.[63]

Review in Technical Cases: Present Situation and Future Prospects

Review in these complex cases begins like any other judicial review of administrative action. For many reasons, some of which were outlined in Chapters 4 and 5, agencies operating in technologically complex fields are required to make rules through the hybrid rulemaking process. The considerations judges often apply to ensure that such agency decisions were not arbitrary and capricious are summarized by Judge McGowan:

> We will be content . . . first, to insist upon an explanation of the facts and policy concerns relied on by the Agency in making its decision; second, to see if those facts have some basis in the record; and, finally, to decide whether those facts and those legislative considerations by themselves could lead a reasonable person to make the judgment that the Agency has made.[64]

The Supreme Court has indicated a desire to reduce the present scope of judicial review, particularly where scientific matters are concerned, but even the members of that court are not clear on whether or how far review should be reduced. The problems and prospects of judicial review can be best understood from a brief examination of two recent, and conflicting, Supreme Court decisions, *Vermont Yankee Nuclear Power Corporation v. Natural Resources Defense Council*[65] and *Industrial Union Department, AFL-CIO v. American Petroleum Institute.*[66]

Vermont Yankee and the NRC

The *Vermont Yankee* case arose on petitions for judicial review of two actions taken by the Nuclear Regulatory Commission. When the NRC began proceedings to license the Vermont Yankee Nuclear Power Plant, various groups, including the Natural Resources Defense Council, argued that the National Environmental Policy Act (NEPA) required that before a nuclear plant could be licensed, the NRC must consider fully the impact of the nuclear fuel cycle—including problems of transportation, processing, and storage of spent fuel—in the cost-benefit analysis.[67] The appeals board of the NRC required the licensing board to report on the impact of the transportation of fuel, but not on processing or storage.[68] The NRC then granted a license to the power facility.

The second NRC action grew out of the first. After the appeals board made its determination about the importance of the impact of the fuel cycle, the NRC, employing a hybrid rulemaking process, began a rulemaking proceeding to develop a policy statement on that subject. The NRC began with the informal notice and comment procedure and added an oral hearing at which interested parties could present evidence. The commission did not permit cross-examination of witnesses. In the end, the NRC concluded that the impact of the processing and storage of fuel was not of major significance, and such impact as there might be could be accommodated by adding a numerical factor from an impact chart into the cost/benefit analysis for any particular plant license application. These conclusions were apparently based on the testimony of Dr. Frank K. Pittman, director of the Atomic Energy Commission, Division of Waste Management and Transportation. Pittman testified in very general terms that the federal government had the responsibility for planning, constructing, and operating a nuclear fuel processing and storage facility, and that it was ready and able to do so. Pittman indicated that the government had plans for such a facility and studies to support its position that nuclear waste disposal would pose no difficulty.

> Dr. Pittman's description of the new plan—now also postponed indefinitely—to build a surface storage facility can only fairly be described as vague but glowing. . . .
>
> In less that two pages, he sets out a very general description of what the facility is supposed to do , [cite], accompanied by several schematic drawings. These show the facility will have a cooling system, a transfer area and storage basins, but do not attempt to describe how they will be built and operated, what materials will be used, where such a facility might be located, or what it might cost to build and operate. . . .
>
> No citations are given for these studies; in fact, there are no references to backup materials supporting any of Pittman's statement, or those portions of the Revised Environmental Survey drawn from it.[69]

The environmental groups objected that there was a great deal of evidence contradicting Pittman's testimony and that they should be permitted to cross-examine Pittman on those disputed points. They also argued that the NRC should require careful consideration of nuclear waste management in licensing, since a plant like Vermont Yankee would "produce approximately 160 pounds of plutonium wastes annually during its 40-year life span."[70] The commission rejected those arguments.

The Natural Resources Defense Council sought review of both NRC actions in the U.S. Circuit of Appeals for the District of Columbia Circuit. The Vermont Yankee Nuclear Power Corporation and the Baltimore Gas and Electric Company intervened on behalf of the NRC. Consolidated National Intervenors, Inc., a consortium of some eighty groups and individuals including the Sierra Club and the Union of Concerned Scientists, intervened on the side of the Natural Resources Defense Council. In addition, the state of New York filed an *amicus curiae* (friend of the court brief) urging reversal of the NRC actions, while Commonwealth Edison, Consolidated Edison of New York, Niagara Mohawk Power Corporation, Omaha

Public Power District Powers Authority, and Rochester Gas and Electric Corporation filed amicus briefs in support of the NRC.

Chief Judge Bazelon wrote for himself and Judge Edwards. Judge Tamm entered a concurring opinion. On the Vermont Yankee licensing decision based on the appeals board ruling, the court reversed the appeals board interpretation of the requirements of the National Environmental Policy Act. The NEPA requires detailed analyses of the environmental impact of such matters. The court noted that since a plant like Vermont Yankee would produce significant quantities of plutonium that would need to be safeguarded, by the agency's own admission, for some 250,000 years, as well as strontium 90 and cesium 137, which would be dangerous for from 600 to 1,000 years, licensing a plant clearly involved "irreversible and irretrievable commitments of resources."[71] The court remanded the Vermont Yankee licensing decision for further action in light of its ruling on the NRC rulemaking action.

The court then set aside the rulemaking proceeding and remanded it for further action. The basis for this ruling was that the agency's procedure did not demonstrate that there had been consideration of the arguments opposed to Pittman's testimony. Bazelon outlined the court's responsibility in such a review process.

> Absent extraordinary circumstances, it is not proper for a reviewing court to prescribe the procedural format which an agency must use to explore a given set of issues. Unless there are statutory directives to the contrary, an agency has discretion to select procedures which it deems best to compile a record illuminating the issues. Courts are no more expert at fashioning administrative procedures than they are in the substantive areas of responsibility which are left to agency discretion. What a reviewing court can do,
> however, is scrutinize the record as a whole to insure that genuine opportunities to participate in a meaningful way were provided, and that the agency has taken a good, hard look at the major question before it. . . .
>
> In order to determine whether an agency has lived up to these responsibilities, a reviewing court must examine the record in detail to determine that a real give and take was fostered on the key issues. This does not give a court a license to judge for itself how much weight should be given particular pieces of scientific or technical data, a task for which it is singularly ill-suited. It does require, however, that the court examine the record so that it may satisfy itself that the decision was based "on a consideration of the relevant factors." Where only one side of a controversial issue is developed in any detail, the agency may abuse its discretion by deciding the issues on an inadequate record.
>
> A reviewing court must assure itself not only that a diversity of informed opinion was heard but that it was genuinely considered.[72]

The court found that an examination of the record indicated that the NRC's procedures had been inadequate to ensure a thorough consideration of the issues. Specifically, the court found that in the absence of opportunities to challenge Dr. Pittman's testimony, the NRC acted arbitrarily.

> The Commission's action in cutting off consideration of waste disposal and reprocessing issues in licensing proceedings based on the cursory development of the facts which occurred in this proceeding was capricious and arbitrary. The portions of the rule pertaining to these matters are set aside and remanded.[73]

The Supreme Court in a unanimous opinion written by Justice Rehnquist (Justices Powell and Blackmun did not participate) reversed and remanded the ruling of the circuit court.[74] The opinion was lengthy, but conveyed one message: unless a statute required more, agency rulemaking procedures were up to the agency and procedural requirements were not to be increased by the courts. If a reviewing court finds the record insufficient to support a rule, it may vacate the rule and remand it, but it may not add procedures. Referring to the District of Columbia Circuit Court opinion as "Monday morning quarterbacking," the Court chastised the lower court for second-guessing the agency.

The decision in *Vermont Yankee* engendered a great deal of commentary and controversy.[75] The breadth and tenor of the *Vermont Yankee* opinion, coupled with apparent unanimity among the Supreme Court justices, suggested that reviewing courts would be called on to move toward the deference-to-agency-action end of the deference-versus-close-scrutiny continuum. However, the clarity and unanimity turned out to be more apparent than real. The review of the Occupational Safety and Health Administration's standard for worker exposure to benzene in 1980 found the Court badly divided and at the other end of the spectrum.

The Benzene Controversy

The Occupational Safety and Health Act of 1970 created the Occupational Safety and Health Administration in the Department of Labor. The act states:

> The Secretary, in promulgating standards dealing with toxic materials or harmful physical agents under this subsection, shall set the standard which most adequately assures, to the extent feasible, on the basis of the best available evidence, that no employee will suffer material impairment of health or functional capacity even if such employee has regular exposure to the hazard dealt with by such standard for the period of his working life. Development of standards under this subsection shall be based upon research, demonstration, experiments, and such other information as may be appropriate. In addition to the attainment of the highest degree of health and safety protection for the employee, other considerations shall be the latest available scientific data in the field, the feasibility of the standards, and experience gained under this and other health and safety laws.[76]

When the agency first began operation it was permitted by Congress to adopt national consensus standards (those generally agreed on) until it conducted OSHA's own investigations with an eye toward setting its own standards.[77] The agency began inquiries into toxic substances with primary research provided by OSHA's research support agency, the National Institute of Occupational Health and Safety (NIOSH). Of immediate interest was worker exposure to vinyl chloride, coke oven emissions, lead, asbestos, cotton dust in cotton mills, and benzene.

> Benzene is a familiar and important commodity. It is a colorless, aromatic liquid that evaporates rapidly under ordinary atmospheric conditions. Approximately 11 billion pounds of benzene were produced in the United States in 1976. Ninety-four percent of that total was produced by the petroleum and petrochemical industries and the remainder produced by the steel industry as a byproduct of coking operations. . . .

The entire population of the United States is exposed to small quantities of benzene ranging from a few parts per billion to 0.5 ppm [parts per million] in the ambient air. . . .

Benzene is a toxic substance. Although it could conceivably cause harm to a person who swallowed or touched it, the principal risk of harm comes from inhalation of benzene vapors. When these vapors are inhaled, the benzene diffuses through the lungs and is quickly absorbed into the blood. Exposure to high concentrations produces an almost immediate effect on the central nervous system. Inhalation of concentrations of 20,000 ppm can be fatal within minutes; exposure in the range of 250 to 550 ppm can cause vertigo, nausea, and other symptoms of mild poisoning. . . . Persistent exposures at levels above 25–40 ppm may lead to blood deficiencies and diseases of the blood-forming organs, including aplastic anemia, which is generally fatal.[78]

As early as 1948 benzene-related blood disorders caused Massachusetts to impose a 35-ppm level in work areas. By 1969 the American National Standards Institute recommended an average exposure over a normal workday to no more than 10 ppm. As NIOSH continued its investigation, it found that benzene had been linked to leukemia as early as 1920, and by 1976 a significant amount of data had accumulated showing a definite causal relationship between benzene and leukemia—even at relatively low levels of concentration, although NIOSH was not aware of just how low a level of exposure could lead to the cancer. NIOSH also found significant benzene impact on other nonmalignant blood disorders and chromosome damage, again even at relatively low levels of exposure. NIOSH urged OSHA to substantially reduce allowable worker exposure levels.

OSHA conducted the hybrid rulemaking process required by its statute, allowing extensive testimony. The record came to fifty volumes. The agency also contracted with a private accounting firm to determine the economic impact of its proposed 1 ppm standard. The statement of basis and purpose in the rule that was finally published was nearly two hundred pages in length, and included reasons why the arguments raised during the hearings against the agency standard were rejected.

In this case the Secretary of Labor found, on the basis of substantial evidence, that (1) exposure to benzene creates a risk of cancer, chromosomal damage, and a variety of nonmalignant but potentially fatal blood disorders, even at the level of 1 ppm; (2) no safe level of exposure has been shown; (3) benefits in the form of saved lives that would be derived from the permanent standard; (4) the number of lives that would be saved could turn out to be either substantial or relatively small; (5) under the present state of scientific knowledge, it is impossible to calculate even in a rough way the number of lives that would be saved, at least without making assumptions that would appear absurd to much of the medical community; and (6) the standard would not materially harm the financial condition of the covered industries.[79]

The American Petroleum Institute sought judicial review in the Fifth Circuit sitting in Louisiana. The Fifth Circuit struck the OSHA standard, primarily on the ground that the "to the extent feasible" language in the OSHA statute meant that a standard must be both technologically and economically feasible. The court interpreted economic feasibility to mean cost effective where that determination is reached through a cost-benefit analysis showing injury or death prevented per dollar of cost for implementation.[80]

The case went to the Supreme Court, but the cost-benefit analysis question wasn't reached. The Court was badly divided. The plurality opinion was written by Justice Stevens and was joined by Chief Justice Burger and Justice Stewart. Burger also wrote a separate concurring opinion. Powell joined in some parts of the plurality opinion but not others and entered his own concurring opinion. Justice Rehnquist concurred with the decision, but on entirely different grounds than the others. Justice Marshall wrote the dissent and was joined by Justices Brennan, White, and Blackmun. In short, there were five votes to affirm the lower court decision and set aside the OSHA benzene standard and four votes to uphold the standard, with the dissenters in greater agreement on the basis for their position.

The plurality never actually addressed the cost-benefit question because it found the OSHA action invalid on other grounds. The Court determined that the agency must find that existing exposure standards are dangerous, that a new standard is "reasonably necessary or appropriate," and that the new standard will significantly reduce the danger to workers. This threshold finding requirement was developed from a new interpretation of language in a different section of the OSHA act, which defined the term "standard." The Court's imposition of such a threshold finding step in developing a standard was very different from the rulings in *Overton Park* and *Vermont Yankee*, which had ruled that formal administrative findings are not necessary unless the agency enabling act specifically requires them. The plurality then engaged in a long and detailed analysis of the data concerning just how much exposure would lead to what amount of disease.

The Court also assumed that OSHA had based the rule on the carcinogenic effects of benzene and not on other hazards. OSHA's policy was that if a substance was clearly carcinogenic and safe levels had not been determined, it was to be assumed that no exposure level was safe and the standard should be set at the lowest feasible level. The plurality of the Court argued that the burden for proving that ambiguity at low levels of exposure was on the agency. But the agency argued that scientific evidence was not advanced enough to establish lower limits of safety and to make the agency prove minimum dosage levels would place the risk on the workers, contrary to the statute. The plurality disagreed.

The dissenting opinion was written by Justice Marshall for himself and others who had been part of the *Vermont Yankee* ruling. The dissent chastised the plurality for doing in the benzene situation exactly what it had told the lower court in *Vermont Yankee* not to do: second-guessing the administrator on technical policy issues and adding requirements in the decision process not established by statute. Recognizing that such scientifically complex rulings pose difficult problems of judicial review, Marshall observed:

> Such decisions were not intended to be unreviewable; they too must be scrutinized to ensure that the Secretary has acted reasonably and within the boundaries set by Congress. But a reviewing court must be mindful of the limited nature of its role. See *Vermont Yankee Nuclear Power Corp. v. NRDC.* . . .[81]

In short, today's decision represents a usurpation of decisionmaking authority that has been exercised by Congress and its authorized representatives. The plurality's construction has no support in the statute's language, structure or legislative history. The threshold finding that the plurality requires is the plurality's own invention.[82]

The dissenters concluded by reminding the others that while the guidelines for judicial review cannot be exact, review must be somewhat limited to avoid interference with properly exercised expert administrative judgment. Moreover, the review must be evenhanded. The decision here seemed to violate both principles.

> In the Occupational Safety and Health Act, Congress expressed confidence that the courts would carry out this important responsibility. But in this case the plurality has far exceeded its authority. . . . *Vermont Yankee Nuclear Power Corp. v. NRDC,* 435 U.S. 519, 558 . . . (1978).
>
> Because the approach taken by the plurality is so plainly irreconcilable with the Court's proper institutional role, I am certain that it will not stand the test of time. In all likelihood, today's decision will come to be regarded as an extreme reaction to a regulatory scheme that, as the Members of the plurality perceived it, imposed an unduly harsh burden on regulated industries. But as the Constitution "does not enact Mr. Herbert Spencer's Social Statics," *Lochner v. New York,* 198 U.S. 45, 75 . . . (1905) (Holmes, J., dissenting), so the responsibility to scrutinize federal administrative action does not authorize this Court to strike its own balance between the costs and benefits of occupational safety standards.[83]

The importance of these two cases is not merely that they represent two of the most important contemporary opinions on judicial review, but that they indicate why it is so difficult to attain the proper balance between appropriate judicial deference to agency expertise and the need for thorough review in complex cases. Just how far and in which direction the U.S. Supreme Court will move on this continuum is at present unclear.

SUMMARY

This chapter has examined judicial review as the third major element of the formal administrative process, noting especially the difficulties encountered by the judge. The judge who is called upon to review decisions of administrative agencies must avoid interference with proper administrative activities and yet ensure thorough review of agency action to prevent or terminate illegal or arbitrary administration. The task is carried out in complex cases that frequently involve many parties who submit intricate and lengthy volumes of argument and evidence. Review serves a number of functions in the administrative process. The nature of the cases and the purposes of review combine to produce a complex role for the judge. The black letter law rules that govern judicial review came primarily from statutes and common law. They govern which cases get into the courthouse for review and the kind of review they receive. Finally, judicial review, which in our time often involves difficult scientific and technological disputes, is a dynamic and continually developing process.

Chapters 5, 6, and 7 have focused on formal administrative law matters.

However, many of the tasks and problems of law and administration are not confined to the black letter law and decisions in particular court rulings. We turn to these problems of law and politics in administration in the remaining chapters.

NOTES

[1]*Citizens to Preserve Overton Park, Inc. v. Volpe*, 432 F. 2d 1307, 1309–10 (6th Cir. 1970).

[2]§4(f) of the Department of Transportation Act of 1966, as amended, 49 U.S.C §1653(f). Cited in *Citizens to Preserve Overton Park v. Volpe*, 401 U.S. 402, 405 n.3 (1971).

[3]See, e.g., *Nashville I-40 Steering Committee v. Ellington*, 387 F. 2d 179 (6th Cir. 1967) and *South Hill Neighborhood Ass'n Inc. et al. v. Romney et al.*, 421 F. 2d 455 (6th Cir. 1969), cited in *Citizens to Preserve Overton Park v. Volpe*, 309 F. Supp. 1189, 1191–92 (W.D. Tenn. 1970).

[4]*Citizens to Preserve Overton Park v. Volpe*, id., at 1191.

[5]Id., at 1194.

[6]"A threshold question—whether petitioners are entitled to any judicial review—is easily answered. Section 701 of the Administrative Procedure Act . . . provides that the action of 'each authority of the Government of the United States,' which includes the Department of Transportation, is subject to judicial review or where agency action is committed to agency discretion by law.' In this case, there is no indication that Congress ought to prohibit judicial review and there is most certainly no 'showing of clear and convincing evidence of a legislative intent' to restrict access to judicial review. *Abbott Laboratories v. Gardner*, 387 U.S. 136, 141 (1967).

"Similarly, the Secretary's decision does not fall within the exception for action 'committed by law to agency discretion.' This is a very narrow exception. Berger, 'Administrative Arbitrariness and Judicial Review,' 65 *Col. L. Rev.* 55 (1965). The legislative history of the Administrative Procedure Act indicates that it is applicable on those rare instances where 'statutes are drawn in such broad terms that in a given case there is no law to apply' S. Rep. no. 752, 79th Cong., 1st Sess., 26 (1945)." 401 U.S. at 410.

[7]Id., at 411.

[8]Id. The Court here refers to Rep. Holifield's comments on that point in the legislative history. 114 Cong. Rec. 19915.

[9]Id., at 412–13.

[10]Id., at 415–16.

[11]Id., at 419.

[12]Justices Black and Brennan would have gone even further. Justice Black, a man not considered an activist judge in most circles, wrote a separate opinion in which Justice Brennan joined:
"I agree with the Court that the judgment of the Court of

Appeals is wrong and that its action should be reversed. I do not agree that the whole matter should be remanded to the District Court. I think the case should be sent back to the Secretary of Transportation. It is apparent from the Court's opinion today that the Secretary of Transportation completely failed to comply with the duty imposed on him by Congress not to permit a federally financed public highway to run through a public park 'unless (1) there is no feasible and prudent alternative to the use of the land, and (2) such program includes all possible planning to minimize harm to such park. . . . I regret that I am compelled to conclude for myself that, except for some too late formulations, apparently coming from the Solicitor General's office, this record contains not one word to indicate that the Secretary raised even a finger to comply with the command of Congress." Id., at 422.

[13]*Citizens to Preserve Overton Park v. Volpe*, 335 F. Supp. 873, 874 (W.D. Tenn. 1972).

[14]Id., at 878.

[15]Id.

[16]*Citizens to Preserve Overton Park v. Brinegar*, 494 F. 2d, 1212 (6th Cir. 1974).

[17]The *Eldridge* case study illustrates the point. With an annual caseload in excess of one and a quarter million, the government considered the Social Security Administration to be involved in a litigation crisis when the number of cases taken for judicial review exceeded 5,000. See Appendix A.

[18]See, e.g., Clement E. Vose, *Caucasians Only: The Supreme Court, the NAACP, and the Restrictive Covenant Cases* (Berkeley: University of California Press, 1959).

[19]Professor Abram Chayes has written a very interesting and provocative article "The Role of the Judge in Public Law Litigation, 89 *Harvard L. Rev.* 1281 (1976). Chayes describes what he perceives as new characteristics of a new phenomenon, public law litigation, which he compares to the traditional model of private litigation that he feels has dominated the legal process since the late nineteenth century. There are important differences between public law and private law cases, some of which Chayes mentions. It is also true that a number of recent cases have presented difficult problems for the judges who decided the cases. However, public law litigation has been around for a very long time. There *are* new wrinkles, many of which are due to modern governmental context, but Chayes overstates his case.

[20]U.S. House of Representatives, Hearings Before the Subcommittee on Courts Civil Liberties, and the Administration of Justice of the Committee on the Judiciary, *State of the Judiciary and Access to Justice,* 95th Cong., 1st Sess. 135–36 (1977). Hereafter referred to as *Access to Justice.*

[21]U.S. Constitution, article III.

[22]Jurisdiction is particularly important because not all courts have the same characteristics. It is therefore a significant matter which tribunal has jurisdiction over a case. See, e.g., David P. Currie and Frank L. Goodman, "Judicial Review of Federal Administrative Action: Quest for the Optimum Forum," 75 *Columbia L. Rev.* 1 (1975). Jurisdiction is particularly important in determining where a case will be initially heard. This is known as primary jurisdiction. Primary jurisdiction is important because the record established in the initial decisionmaking process is the basis for all subsequent appeals. There can also be a qualitative difference in decisions, depending on the tribunal involved. See Burt Neuborne, "The Myth of Parity," 90 *Harvard L. Rev.* 1105 (1977).

[23]See also Henry Abraham, "The Sixteen Great Maxims," in *The Judicial Process* (New York: Oxford, 1980), pp. 373–400.

[25]*Baker v. Carr,* 369 U.S. 186 (1962).

[26]Sierra Club v. Morton, 405 U.S. 727 (1972). See also *Association of Data Processing Organizations v. Camp,* 397 U.S. 150 (1970).

[27]*Association of Data Processing Organizations v. Camp,* 397 U.S. at 152–54; *Barlow v. Collins,* 397 U.S. 159, 164–67 (1970); *Trafficante v. Metropolitan Life Ins. Co.,* 409 U.S. 205 (1972).

[28]*United States v. Richardson,* 418 U.S. 166 (1974). See also *Schlesinger v. Reservists Committee to Stop the War,* 418 U.S. 208 (1974).

[29]See, e.g., *Flast v. Cohen,* 392 U.S. 83 (1968). On the government records, see the Privacy Act of 1974, 5 U.S.C. §552 a(g)(1).

[30]*United States v. SCRAP,* 412 U.S. 669 (1973), and *NAACP v. Alabama,* 357 U.S. 449 (1958).

[31]There are sometimes exceptions where it would be difficult or impossible for the third party to defend his or her own interests. See *Singleton v. Wulff,* 428 U.S. 106 (1976), and *Barrows v. Jackson,* 346 U.S. 249 (1953).

[32]See generally *Warth v. Seldin,* 422 U.S. 490 (1975), and *Construction Ass'n of Sonora County v. Petaluma,* 522 F. 2d 897 (9th Cir. 1975), cert. denied, 424 U.S. 934 (1976).

[33]See, e.g., *Rescue Army v. Municipal Court,* 331 U.S. 549 (1947), and *Ashwander v. TVA,* 297 U.S. 288 (1936), Justice Brandeis concurring.

[34]Davis, supra note, 23, at p. 160.

[35]See, e.g., *Ortwein v. Schwab,* 410 U.S. 656 (1973).

[36]Burt Neuborne, "The Procedural Assault on the Warren Legacy: A Study in Repeal by Indirection," 5 *Hofstra L. Rev.* 545 (1977).

[37]Board of Governors of the Society of American Law Teachers, "Supreme Court Denial of Citizen Access to Federal Courts to Challenge Unconstitutional or Other Unlawful Actions: The Record of the Burger Court," in *Access to Justice,* supra note 20, at p. 696.

[38]*Simon v. Eastern Kentucky Welfare Rights Organization,* supra note 24; *Warth v. Seldin,* supra note 32, *Schlesinger v. Reservists,* supra note 28; *United States v. Richardson,* supra note 28; and *National Railroad Passenger Corp. v. National Ass'n of Railroad Passengers,* 414 U.S. 453 (1974). Of these developments, Justice Douglas wrote:

"Standing has become a barrier to access to the federal courts, just as the political question was in earlier decades. The mounting caseload of federal courts is well known. But cases such as this one reflect festering sores in our society; and the American dream teaches that if one reaches high enough and persists there is a forum where justice is dispensed. I would lower the technical barriers and let the court serve that ancient need." *Warth v. Seldin,* 422 U.S. at 519, Justice Douglas dissenting.

[39]*Eisen v. Carlisle & Jacquelin,* 417 U.S. 156 (1974), and *Zahn v. International Paper Co.,* 414 U.S. 291 (1973).

[40]*Alyeska Pipeline Serv. Co. v. Wilderness Society,* 421 U.S. 240 (1975).

[41]*Moore v. Sims,* 442 U.S. 415 (1979); *Trainor v. Hernandez* 431 U.S. 434 (1977); *Judice v. Vail,* 430 U.S. 1977); *Doran v. Salen Inn, Inc.,* 422 U.S. 922 (1975); *Hicks v. Miranda,* 422 U.S. 332 (1975); and *Huffman v. Pursue, Ltd.,* 420 U.S. 592 (1975).

[42]See, e.g., *Rizzo v. Goode,* 423 U.S. 362 (1976).

[43]See, e.g., the Civil Rights Attorneys' Fee Act, Public Law 94-559, 90 Stat. 2641, 42 U.S.C. §1988 (1976).

[44]Chapter 3 discusses the problem of the impact of Supreme Court opinions. See generally Stephen Wasby, *The Impact of the United States Supreme Court: Some Perspectives* (Homewood, Ill.: Dorsey, 1970).

[45]William J. Brennan, "State Constitutions and the Protection of Individual Rights," 90 *Harvard L. Rev.* 489 (1977), and Donald E. Wilkes, Jr., "The New Federalism in Criminal Procedure: State Court Evasion of the Burger Court," 62 *Kentucky L. J.* 421 (1973). Decisions concerning educational finance in California, *Serrano v. Priest,* 557 P. 2d 929 *(Calif. 1976); Connecticut, Horton v. Meskill,* 376 A 2d 359 (Conn. 1977); and New Jersey, *Robinson v. Cahill,* 303 A. 2d. 273 (NJ 1973) were clearly rejections by the state courts of the U.S. Supreme Court's ruling in *San Antonio Independent School Dist. v. Rodriguez,* 411 U.S. 1, (1973).

[46]Cited in Judge Frank M. Johnson, Jr., "The Role of the Judiciary with Respect to the Other Branches of Government." The John A. Sibley Lecture (University of Georgia School of Law, 1977), in *Access to Justice,* supra note 20 at pp. 750, 762. See also Judge A. Leon Higginbotham, Jr., "The Priority of Human Rights in Court Reform," 70 *Federal Rules Decisions* 134 (1976).

[47]See the testimony of Father William C. Cunningham, *Access to Justice,* supra note 20, at p. 167.

[48]On judicial deference to agency, see *International Brotherhood of Teamsters v. Daniel,* 439 U.S. 551, 556 n. 20 (1979); *Udall v. Tallman,* 380 U.S. 1, 4 (1965); and *Power Reactor Co. v. International Union of Electrical Workers,* 367 U.S.

376, 408 (1961). But the Court has the ultimate authority of statutory interpretation. *Int'l Brotherhood,* supra, at 566–67, and *Securities and Exchange Comm'n v. Sloan,* 436 U.S. 103, 117-19 (1978). See generally note 28, Chapter 5.

For a particularly interesting case in this area, see *East Oakland–Fruitvale Planning Council v. Rumsfeld,* 471 F. 2d 524 (9th Cir. 1972).

[49]*Morton v. Ruiz,* 415 U.S. 199, 235 (1974). See also Chapter 5, note 32.

[50]*Ashbacker v. Federal Communications Comm'n,* 326 U.S. 327 (1945).

[51]The discussion of *Overton Park* at the beginning of the chapter explains why this is important.

[52]*Burlington Truck Lines v. United States,* 371 U.S. 156, 168–69 (1962), and *Citizens to Preserve Overton Park v. Volpe,* supra note 2, at 419.

[53]"Arbitrary action may be colored by improper motivation; it may be action which has an impermissible basis as when Republicans or redheads are denied equal opportunity to do business with the government; or action which is unsupported by evidence, or turns on failure to consider relevant evidence, even in the presence of plenary discretion." Raoul Berger, "Administrative Arbitrariness and Judicial Review," 65 *Columbia L. Rev.* 55, 82–83 (1965).

[54]There is also a problem if it can be shown that there were related or conflicting statutes that should have been taken into account but were ignored by the administrators. See *Camp v. Pitts,* 411 U.S. 138 (1973), and *Investment Co. Inst. v. Camp,* 401 U.S. 617 (1971).

[55]See, e.g., *Richardson v. Perales* 402 U.S. 389, 402 (1971).

[56]See, e.g., *Goldberg v. Kelly,* 397 U.S. 24 (1970).

[57]See, e.g., *Alabama Power Co. v. Costle,* 636 F. 2d 323 (D.C. Cir. 1980); *Ethyl v. Environmental Protection Agency,* 541 F. 2d 1 (D.C. Cir. 1976), cert. denied, 426 U.S. 941 (1976); *International Harvester v. Ruckelshaus,* 478 F. 2d 615 (D.C. Cir. 1973); and *Environmental Defense Fund v. Ruckelshaus,* 439 F. 2d 584 (D.C. Cir. 1971).

[58]See, e.g., David Doniger, "Federal Regulation of Vinyl Chloride: A Short Course in the Law and Policy of Toxic Substances Control," 7 *Ecology L. Q.* 501 (1978).

[59]Earl McGowan, "Reflections on Rulemaking Review," 53 *Tulane L. Rev.* 681, 690–91 (1979). The case McGowan was describing was *Weyerhaeuser Co. v. Costle,* 590 F. 2d 1011 (D.C. Cir. 1978).

[60]Expertise has come to be extremely political. See, e.g.,

Guy Benveniste, *The Politics of Expertise,* 2d ed., (San Francisco: Boyd & Fraser, 1977), and Mark Green, *The Other Government* (New York: Norton, 1978).

[61]See, e.g., *National Resource Defense Council v. U.S. Nuclear Regulatory Comm'n,* 547 F. 2d 633, 643–44 (D.C. Cir. 1976).

[62]See McGowan, supra note 59.

[63]McGowan, supra note 59, at p. 686.

[64]Id., at p. 693. McGowan was citing language from *Weyerhaeuser,* supra note 59, at 1026–27.

[65]*Vermont Yankee Nuclear Power Corp. v. Natural Resources Defense Council,* 435 U.S. 519 (1978).

[66]*Industrial Union Dep't, AFL-CIO v. American Petroleum Inst.,* 448 U.S. 607 (1980)

[67]42 U.S.C. §4332(2)(C) (1976).

[68]*Natural Resources Defense Council v. U.S. Nuclear Regulatory Comm'n,* 547 F. 2d 633, 637 (D.C. Cir. 1976).

[69]Id., at 648-49.

[70]Id., at 638.

[71]Id., at 638–39.

[72]Id., at 644–46.

[73]Id., at 655. Judge Tamm concurred in the decision of the court but would simply have remanded the case to the agency on the ground that the record was inadequate to support its findings. He would avoid suggesting that the agency had to modify its procedures.

[74]Supra note 65.

[75]See Chapter 5, note 63.

[76]29 U.S.C. §655 (b)(5) (1976), cited in *Industrial Union Dep't,* supra note 66, at 612.

[77]29 U.S.C. §655(a) (1976).

[78]*Industrial Union Dep't,* supra note 66.

[79]Id. at 689, Justice Marshall dissenting.

[80]*American Petroleum Inst. v. Occupational Safety and Health Agency,* 581 F. 2d 493 (5th Cir. 1978).

[81]*Industrial Union Dep't,* supra note 66 at 706.

[82]Id., at 712–13.

[83]Id., at 723–24.

PART THREE

LAW, POLITICS, AND ADMINISTRATION

Chapter 8

Informal Process: "The Lifeblood of the Administrative Process"

A s early as 1941, the Attorney General's Committee on Administrative Procedure declared that informal action was "the lifeblood of the administrative process."[1] By the 1960s, Peter Woll had concluded that "requirements of public policy, expertise, and speed have rendered administrative adjudication today primarily informal in nature."[2] Indeed, it is very unusual, in terms of the percentage of total business done by administrative agencies, for the producers and consumers of administrative decisions to resolve problems of law and administration or develop policies in a formal way. The attempt is usually made to solve problems short of formal procedures. These informal methods of interaction range from a simple chat on the telephone to full-dress negotiations. This chapter assesses some of the reasons why informal processes are so important, the factors that condition informal administrative action, types of informal approaches to problem resolution, concepts and attitudes that characterize these proceedings, and the opportunities and problems these informal actions present compared to formal processes.

THE REAL-WORLD DECISIONMAKING ENVIRONMENT

Informal processes are employed by all types of agencies. In the case of single shot players dealing with social service or other agencies, the consumer of the decision may not fully understand that he or she is involved in an informal administrative proceeding. Americans are so attuned to a formal due-process approach to government action that they tend to ignore notices informing them that administrative action affecting them is in progress. Many believe that such notices are really *pro forma* and that, before any real action is taken, they will be personally contacted and accorded a formal means to present their views. It is difficult to convince them that such an attitude can be dangerous. Failure to acknowledge a letter from the Department of Motor Vehicles, for example, may bring a visit from an officer requesting surrender of one's drivers license. One who ignores a request for information from the VA risks losing educational or other benefits. Sadly, consumers often wait until it is too late to communicate with an agency. In some cases, the failure to respond to opportunities offered for discussion with an agency may permanently foreclose one's chance to contest agency action later.

Informal administrative process is also important to repeat players in dealing with regulatory agencies. The nuclear power plant licensing process, discussed in Chapter 7, is a useful example of this informal kind of activity.

Suppose Adam Smith, chief executive officer of the Consolidated Utility Company, decides in consultation with his staff to launch a development project for a nuclear power facility to be called Plant Omega. Smith is aware that the licensing process from construction to eventual operation of such a facility is a very long and complex one. His firm cannot wait until it has invested several years in such a project to prepare a licensing package for submission to the appropriate regulatory agencies. Nor is the company likely to purchase land and contract for materials and labor before beginning discussions with those administrators who are in positions to disapprove the project. From the planning stages through construction and application for licensing, a great deal of money will be expended at each stage of the plant development and that investment must be protected as much as possible.

Smith, being an astute businessman, will want to begin informal negotiations as early as possible. In this case the appropriate administrative authorities are the Nuclear Regulatory Commission and the State Utility Commission. There are a number of dimensions to the project that Smith will wish to assess. There is the economic dimension, of course, but there are also political dimensions. If, for example, members of the Utility Commission signal that they intend openly and adamantly to oppose the project, the company will understand that it faces an immediate local political battle. If, on the other hand, the company senses that it has allies in the commission, it is well to know that at the outset.

What Smith wishes to acquire is a strong sense of the decision environment within which his firm is operating. He attempts to learn the characteristics of that environment in informal discussions and negotiations with the relevant administrative decisionmakers as early as possible to avoid future problems. This is typical activity when the consumer of the decision is a repeat player, and especially where the decision concerns a big-ticket project.

From the perspective of the administrators, Mr. Washington of the NRC and Ms. Springfield of the State Utility Commission, it is equally important to make informal contact at the earliest opportunity. Plant Omega will be a major work project for the agencies as well as for the company. If the company proceeds with Omega, the administrators will develop a continuing relationship with the company over a period of years. The earlier the agencies become involved, the better administrators can plan to allocate their own resources.

Furthermore, the task of the administrators is not merely to process the papers submitted at various points in the process. Ms. Springfield's agency is charged with providing power that is needed by the community at the best possible cost consistent with a reasonable rate of return on investment for the company that builds and operates the power plants. Her responsibilities include fostering the development of power sources and ensuring that returns are sufficient to permit the power companies to compete for finances needed by the firms. At the same time, her agency is supposed to protect the purchasers of power from overpricing and poor service, problems that can be acute when businesses have a virtual monopoly in their service areas.

The relationship between the company and government is clearly not one-sided. The government wants power provided under the proper conditions. The company wants profits and continued financial strength. The initial informal negotiations during the development of the Omega facility will last two years or more. The total lead time for construction and licensing may last from seven to ten years. The process may be represented in this way:

$$T_1 \ldots T_2 \ldots T_3 \ldots T_4 \ldots \ldots \ldots T_{10}$$

The parties may begin informal negotiations on Omega at point T_1. At some point, T_2, the company and the government reach decisions committing themselves to push forward with the project. The actual formal licensing process for construction and later inspection and processing for the operating license occur years after the commitment point. Between T_1 and T_2, both Smith and his counterparts in government continue to assess the economic, technical, and political variables in the decisionmaking environment. The goal is to reduce uncertainty about the future of the project as much as possible before reaching the commitment point.

Once the commitment point is reached, government actors begin to factor the new project into their policy planning. They assume, however informally, that at a certain point in the future, T_{10}, Plant Omega will be operational, on line, and fully productive. The assumptions are made even though administrators know that problems might arise between T_2 and T_{10} that could delay access to power from the new facility. Nevertheless, the plant is now part of the decision environment of both the administrative and business personnel.

We now shift to the perspective of Robert Fisher, president of an environmental group opposed to the new nuclear power plant, which does not get involved until T_3 or T_4. Fisher's organization must convince the agencies involved to interpret the applicable statutes and regulations in such a way as to block the construction and licensing. Otherwise, the only real device available is delay through litigation. Even if Fisher's organization has a good argument, it will still be extremely difficult to convince agency personnel. So many human and fiscal resources have been invested by this stage that it becomes very difficult to stop the project. The administrators are no longer neutral actors. They have committed years of work to the project; Omega is part of their policy planning. Asking them to abandon the project now is asking them to admit that their efforts have been wasted. In effect, Washington and Springfield are being asked to tell their supervisors that the project is a white elephant. It is not necessarily bad faith that drives agency personnel forward (again assuming that the argument in opposition to the plant is valid), but sunk costs.

Similarly, it is hard to imagine Mr. Smith going to his board of directors and announcing that although the firm is five years and $25 million into the project, plans for Plant Omega ought to be discarded.

Informal procedures often develop slowly over a lengthy period. At some point, either before or after formal action is begun, the producers and consumers make important if unofficial commitments to a course of action. Both the informal relationship and the economic and political factors in the decision environment have important consequences for future decisionmaking.

FACTORS THAT CONDITION INFORMAL ADMINISTRATIVE PROCESSES

As the term "informal process" implies, the types of administrative actions that are informal in nature are very different from one another. It is possible, however, to single out recurring factors that shape and condition informal administration.

Sunk Costs

The first factor is the phenomenon of sunk costs. Once the point of commitment is reached by the parties involved in an informal administrative action, changes in policy or in direction are hard to make. Expended effort and fiscal resources provide an inertia that is all but irresistible. Writing of the problem of plant licensing, Justice William O. Douglas once warned:

> Plainly these are not findings that the "safety" standards have been met. They presuppose—contrary to the premise of the Act—that "safety" findings can be made *after construction is finished.* But when that point is reached, when millions have been invested, the momentum is on the side of the applicant, not on the side of the public. The momentum is not only generated by the desire to salvage an investment. No agency wants to be the architect of a "white elephant." (Emphasis in original.)[3]

If, at some point, an agency perceives its investment to be sufficiently large, it may become the advocate for the outside group or individual involved. Taken far enough, administrators may by virtue of perceived sunk costs find themselves coopted by the party before the agency.

Anticipated Costs

Another factor that influences the informal process is what might be termed "anticipated costs." That is, the costs of pursuing one's objectives through the formal administrative process may be sufficiently high that pressure is created to resolve problems informally. Attorneys often see their role as practicing preventive law or fostering alternatives to formal resolution of disputes. The costs of preparation and representation for trial or formal hearings escalate dramatically. In that spirit an attorney might attempt to convince a client who claims that an agency has wrongfully exacted several hundred dollars or more from him that he would be much better off settling for a negotiated compromise, and a loss of some of the funds, rather than spend more money for litigation and appeals and perhaps lose in the end anyway.[4]

Power Law

A third factor is the significance of what Mark Green has called "power law."[5] For many reasons, political scientists seem to have particular difficulty with the concept of power.[6] In general, power has negative connotations and taboos. Power is, presumably, something nice people do not deal with.

Green's study concentrated on the most prestigious Washington law firms, whose primary business is representing repeat players before different branches and

departments of government, but his thesis is more broadly applicable. He argues that
there are any number of individuals and organizations who use law as a tool to accomplish their ends, to achieve political power.[7] Such clients may say, as J. P. Morgan is
reputed to have declared, that they do not want a lawyer who tells them what they
cannot do. They want a lawyer who tells them how to do what they want to do.

Unless one goes about it in a corrupt or illegal manner, there is nothing
particularly sinister in this. If, for example, one who runs a business decides to pursue
a policy and commits resources in pursuit of policy goals, he or she may be unwilling
to face the loss, and perhaps the pressure, that comes from changing direction based
on a mere prediction that the firm may or may not win in court should a lawsuit
develop. One might more likely say something like: "I'm committed to this position.
I think I'm right and I'm prepared to use the tools at my disposal to defend my
policy."

Green's analysis suggests that power law matters because it affects: (1) the
development of statutes; (2) the shaping of cases that will produce important
precedents; (3) the adjudication of major public policy related disputes before
government agencies; and (4) the development of rules and other types of policy
statements issued by agencies. He argues that power law is practiced in both formal
and informal ways, and suggests that informal process is by far the preferred mode of
operation for these attorneys and their clients.

The practice of power law is based, according to Green, on what he terms the
"Ten Commandments of Washington Law." The following is a sketch of his
decalogue:

> I. *Reputation:* "The impression of power is power." Reputation can come
>   from previous government experience in a particular area, accumulated
>   legal, political and governmental experience, and political contacts.
> II. *Intelligence:* It is well to remember that many of those who practice power
>   law came to their position of prominence by virtue of superior intellectual
>   ability and well developed technical skill and not through some back door
>   to power.
> III. *Reconnaissance:* Since information is power, it is at the heart of power
>   law. The power lawyer's job is to be alert for developments that may
>   threaten his clients' interests and to work with the clients to avoid the
>   problems if it is possible to do so.
> IV. *Interlocking interests:* Lawyers who begin by representing a firm often
>   become part of the organization. This occurs as partial payment for
>   services. The interrelationships between law firms and client organization affects the performance of both sides.
> V. *Preferential access:* Being well enough known and connected to get
>   opportunities to make one's arguments is important. "Access without
>   brilliance is preferable to brilliance without access."
> VI. *Lobbying:* The techniques of lobbying may be far more important than
>   litigation ability from the standpoint of one's client.
> VII. *Law-writing:* Participation by an attorney in the drafting of legislation or
>   rules offers obvious advantages of molding policy in favorable terms and
>   less obvious advantages in recognition of prior knowledge in future
>   contests.

VIII. *Inundation:* By sheer dint of volume, legal papers may either exhaust an opponent or else delay the agency to the advantage of one's client.

IX. *Delay:* "For those who seek to avoid regulation, no decision is often a favorable decision." Delaying tactics are frequently used tools in power law.

X. *Corruption:* It is often difficult, when the stakes are high and the ethical problems obscured, to tell when one moves from legitimate advocacy to influence peddling or worse. Some attorneys make it a practice of working close to the line on purpose.[8]

Player Type

Perhaps more than in the formal process, it matters in the informal process whether the players are repeat players or single shot players. Repeat players have many more options than do single shot players. In many cases they are able to argue technical procedural legal points as well as or better than agency personnel, and they may have more financial and scientific resources at their disposal. Small businesspeople or individuals who have little expertise and are not financially able to acquire the services of first-rate administrative law attorneys may have few options in their interactions with the social service, regulatory, or second-generation regulatory agencies they encounter.

Felt Need for Individualized Justice

One of the factors that tends administrative actions toward informal process and away from rule-oriented formal administrative activity is a strongly felt need for individualized treatment by those before the agency. It is one of the great problems of public administration that Weberian theories of bureaucracy dictate rule-oriented behavior, standard operating procedures for getting work done, and a dispassionate approach to that work. It is a difficulty because those who come before an agency are likely to interpret those characteristics as rule-bound, rigid, and unfeeling bureaucratic behavior. Most of us have seen or felt this reaction to bureaucracy. An administrator explains to a client that a rule precludes granting the client's request. The client says, "But you don't understand! The rule doesn't apply in my case!" and walks away shaking his head and complaining, not about the rule but about the callous bureaucrat who applied the rule.

Jerome Frank, a member of the Securities and Exchange Commission and later a judge on the Second Circuit Court of Appeals, once wrote that discretionary decisionmaking by administrators is often prompted not by the administrator's desire for discretion and informality, but because those before agencies demand individualized consideration outside of normal procedures.[9]

The Power of the Raised Eyebrow

The perceptions of those dealing with an agency are important in another more coercive sense. The power of the raised eyebrow is the ability to cause an individual to act not by positive directive or by sanction but voluntarily, out of concern that an administrator might employ a sanction at some time in the future. Two examples are tax audits and broadcast licensing. Most people fear tax audits not because of what the Internal Revenue Service is going to do to them, but because of what the agency might *possibly* do. The threat of an audit may be enough to deter some taxpayers from cutting corners. A broadcaster might be concerned about FCC suggestions on adult programming or public service, not because the commission is likely to commence a formal discplinary proceeding against the station, but because lack of cooperation might be remembered by those at the commission when it comes time for station license renewal.

One of the most effective of the raised eyebrow agencies is the Securities and Exchange Commission. Even if one thought it likely that one's case would prevail in a formal administrative proceeding, it would be dangerous to ignore SEC suggestions concerning a new securities issue. A mere hint that one is under special scrutiny by the commission could destroy the marketability of the new issue.[10] The power of the raised eyebrow is important not because of what an agency can or will do, but because of what the party before the agency believes the agency could or would do.

The significance of this power varies depending on who is involved. Obviously, repeat players are not likely to be overawed by agency authority. They are likely to know exactly what an agency can and cannot do, and are not as likely as single shot players to be frightened by the mere possibility that an agency may institute a formal proceeding against them. In fact, the raised eyebrow can work in reverse. Administrators may be loath to take certain actions because they know that the repeat players affected might have sufficient legal, economic, and political resources to block or weaken the agency.

The Due Process and Efficiency Models

Finally, the pressure on agencies to process their workloads also has an effect. Herbert Packer made a study of the criminal justice system that is somewhat analogous to the administrative justice system. Packer suggested that there are models of how the system works, or ought to work, which he called the "due process" and "crime control" models.[11] The due process model is based on the proposition that the task of the criminal justice system is to investigate allegations of breaches of law and enforce the law. The party involved should be accorded all due process protections beginning with the presumption of innocence. The ultimate goal is to discover the truth and achieve justice. Packer suggests that most citizens, including participants in the criminal justice system, would agree with those ideals. On the other hand, Packer suggests that what an impartial observer of the actual operation of the system sees is less like the due process model than the crime control or efficiency model, which is based on the assumption that the task of the criminal justice system is to control crime. Crime is controlled by processing cases and achieving convictions. Given limited resources, accomplishing these goals requires efforts to improve the efficiency of case processing. In the criminal justice context, this means emphasizing informal processes such as plea bargaining.

Ideally, an administrative agency's goal is to implement and administer a policy or law. It has a formal process for doing so. In reality, agencies can be overloaded, regardless of what kind of agency is involved. The efficiency model may more accurately describe the operation of such an agency. The short-term goal may be to maximize efficient processing of the docket, and pressures to use informal processes for clearing cases become intense. The *Eldridge* case study in Appendix A is an example of such a situation.

THE NATURE OF INFORMAL PROCESSES

Informal processes are just that—informal. Therefore, one cannot establish a concise and specific taxonomy of informal processes in administrative law. One can describe a few of the more common types of informal mechanisms and the general attitudes that guide the use of these and other informal techniques. The informal devices may generally be classified as preformal, filtering, or opting-out procedures.

Preformal processes attempt to resolve problems early in the administrative process and avoid having to resort to the formal stages. The two most common approaches are informal negotiations and settlements and preclearance procedures. Almost all agencies use the first of these approaches to problem solving. Informal negotiated settlements have the obvious benefit of resolving problems congenially, which allows for continued good relationships between agency clients and administrators. Preclearance procedures take different forms in different agencies. Examples are Federal Trade Commission preclearance of proposed corporate mergers where antitrust laws could be a problem, and Securities and Exchange Commission deficiency letter procedures where the SEC reviews a prospectus for a security and notes deficiencies so that they may be corrected before formal registration and marketing of the securities issue. Another type of preclearance process is the issuance of advisory opinions, which were discussed briefly in earlier chapters. Advisory opinions are an agency's general views about how it expects to deal with certain situations that may arise. While agencies are not bound by such commentaries, it is in the interest of all concerned for the administrators to issue accurate advisory opinions and to follow them. Doing so may reduce the likelihood of formal procedures.

The second major type of informal action is what can be termed "filtering action." Filtering procedures serve two purposes: (1) they attempt to eliminate unnecessary formal procedures through a fairly structured negotiating process; and (2) where cases are going to move to formal action, efforts are made to simplify those procedures by reducing the number of issues in dispute and obtaining as much agreement as those involved are willing to provide. The predominant example of a filtering procedure is the prehearing conference. Prehearing conferences in administrative law are patterned after the pretrial conference model established in the Federal Rules of Civil Procedure[12] and authorized by the Administrative Procedure Act.[13] The ALJ can call a prehearing conference to ask the parties to limit the issues to be argued, the number of witnesses to be presented, and to stipulate to as many of the pertinent facts as possible. The conference is also one last chance to reach a settlement before the formal process gets under way. If no settlement can be obtained, at least the scope of the formal proceeding can be narrowed and the issues properly defined.

Finally, there are opting-out techniques, which are procedures that are often employed after a formal proceeding has begun aimed at resolving the difficulty short of completing the formal process. One of the most frequently used devices is the consent decree. Like most opting-out procedures, the consent decree is a negotiated or at least mutually agreed-on settlement. It is an agreement to cease a certain type of conduct that an agency asserts is illegal without admitting any guilt or liability. A consent decree may on occasion require an organization to conduct a recall of a product or change a particular practice, but it does not make the party automatically vulnerable to damage suits from private citizens. The agency gets the result it seeks, namely, a cessation of some unacceptable practices. The organization may be able to settle on terms that are less harsh than might have been imposed if the administrative process had run its course. Finally, the organization preserves all its legal options in the event that it faces future disputes. Consent decrees and other opting-out procedures could be employed at earlier stages of the process, but they are often seen as a last resort by those involved in an administrative dispute and frequently are not accepted until most other options have been exhausted.

Informal processes are by definition extremely flexible. In some respects it is better to think of these procedures in terms of the attitudes that characterize them rather than in terms of specific classes of procedure. Administrators often appear to be acting more in a supervision mode rather than in the more aggressive watchdog mold. They often settle for giving guidance to those before the agency rather than mandating specific types of conduct. Negotiation is preferred to adjudication. The informal approach works particularly well where both sides are more interested in conciliation than in confrontation.

ADVANTAGES AND DISADVANTAGES OF INFORMAL PROCESSES

As in any area of public policy, there are significant pluses and minuses associated with the use of informal administrative processes to resolve problems. The following is a brief summary of some of the most obvious costs and benefits. Chapter 9, on administrative discretion, and Chapter 10, on regulation, will deal in some detail with specific implications of the use of informal processes.

Advantages

The first obvious advantage to informal processes is speed. It is much easier and faster to resolve problems with a telephone call or a visit and a confirming letter than it is to proceed to formal methods. Given the number of problems on an average agency docket and the fact that formal processes can last for months and sometimes years, it is in the agency's best interest to do things the easy way. Depending on the type of player involved (consider, for example, the Social Security disability claimants' difficulties discussed in the *Eldridge* case study), delay can be a major concern.

A related advantage is low-cost resolution of problems. As soon as a case becomes a formal proceeding, costs escalate rapidly. Many single shot players are particularly hard-hit by legal fees and delayed benefit payments. The costs are also difficult for agencies and some repeat players to carry. Expense is a particular problem where there are lengthy administrative hearings that involve many parties and a large number of expert witnesses. Informal procedures are not without cost, but they are quite inexpensive relative to formal approaches to problem solving.

A third advantage is that informal processes take place in a more congenial atmosphere than might be present in a formal adversary-type proceeding. There are often more than two sides to an administrative disagreement or policy and exploration of the facets of a problem may be more relaxed and flexible in the informal setting.

A fourth advantage may be described in terms of game theory.[14] The use of informal processes allows those involved to more easily play a non-zero sum game. This conceptual framework assumes that interactions among political, economic, and social actors may be thought of as contests in which all the actors attempt to pursue their own best interests.[15] There are basically two kinds of games: zero sum games and non-zero sum games. In the first, there is one winner and one loser. The winnings of the winner equal the losses to the loser. In the non-zero sum game there is no absolute winner or loser. For example, in the National Football League championship, the champion is the winner of the Superbowl. In the world Grand Prix driving championship, one driver may win the money and prestige of a particular race, but another driver may accumulate points from several races to win the overall championship. Both drivers win something. The informal process, since it is not cast in rigid adversary terms, encourages non-zero sum games. In the real world, such games are easier to play and the results are often more acceptable to all concerned than the zero sum type.

Fifth, informal processes often make it possible to resolve problems without disrupting ongoing projects or life-styles. While negotiations are under way, it is often possible for those involved to continue in existing routines rather than face an immediate shutdown of an industrial plant or an immediate loss of income from benefits. The absence of the threat of traumatic disruption may allow for a less crisis-ridden and more reasoned approach to problems.

Finally, informal processes permit administrative discretion. Agencies can be more flexible in the informal environment than is possible once a formal procedure has been instituted. There is more room for judgment and individual consideration in the decision process.

Disadvantages

The use of informal administrative processes involves risks as well as opportunities. One danger is that the ability of an administrator to be particularly sensitive to an individual or group before the agency implies the ability to discriminate.[16] The possibility of falling victim to discrimination is somewhat higher in informal proceedings that in formal proceedings.

Second, and related to differences between the parties before the agencies, is the danger that the distinction between repeat players and single shot players can be extremely important in the informal process. If an administrator's concern about a repeat player's power is strong enough, the vigor with which the administrator pursues the wider public interest may be jeopardized.

Third, for reasons already established, the effects of sunk costs may subvert the objectivity of the decisionmaker and foster a combative attitude to latecomers to a particular policy discussion.

Fourth, related to the problem of sunk costs, is the fact that, particularly in informal processes, intra- or interorganizational politics may play a disproportionate role in the decision process. Bureaucratic politics and organization theory and behavior variables are almost always important in decisionmaking, but informal processes may permit these factors to play more of a role than they should.[17]

Fifth, access to the formal process may be deterred. Woll and others have observed that parties with matters pending before agencies may not really be able to move the dispute to a formal proceeding even if that option is technically available. Given the expense and the time required to pursue a formal remedy, there is sometimes no practical alternative to resolving a problem through the informal channel. When that happens the spirit of free negotiation mutually conducted may give way to a more coercive atmosphere without the protections afforded in the formal setting. The mere availability of access to the formal process may serve as an important check.

Sixth, the informal process provides no guarantee of openness. Closed or private proceedings may allow for more candid discussions, but they do not permit the check available in open proceedings where good records are kept and the forum is available to outsiders.

Seventh, informal processes provide no guidance or protection for the future for those who deal with an agency. The binding effect of advisory opinions and agency guidelines is questionable at best. Although it is in everyone's long-term best interest to establish consistent patterns of behavior and policy, it is not mandatory that an agency do so. Further, unlike formal proceedings, informal processes often do not result in any kind of formal written decision that can be referred to as precedent by others in the future. It is true that the binding effect of precedent in administrative law is more limited than in some other areas of jurisprudence, still, such opinions are available and can be studied with some likelihood that an agency will honor its precedents. Such options are not available from many informal decision processes.

Finally, the informal processes do permit more discretion to be exercised by administrators, which may have the salutory affect of allowing them more flexibility to deal with problems. But discretion also implies an opportunity for arbitrariness. It was, after all, in part in an effort to prevent or check arbitrariness that formal administrative procedures were initially instituted.

SUMMARY

Despite the preoccupation of the administrative law literature with the formal administrative process, much of the activity is informal rather than formal in nature. Many factors encourage the use of the informal process. A number of these factors, such as power law and sunk costs, also condition the operation of the informal processes.

In this chapter we noted that while it is not possible to categorize all the various forms of informal processes, they can generally be thought of in terms of preformal processes, which involve negotiation, filtering processes, which are used in connection with formal proceedings to simplify and shorten the process, and opting-out mechanisms for resolving disputes short of the full run of formal process.

There are several important advantages in using informal as against formal administrative process, but there are also a number of dangers or shortcomings that might attend their use. The role of administrative discretion, which is so important in informal processes, is both one of the major advantages and, because of the danger of arbitrariness, one of the great disadvantages. It is to this double-edged concept, administrative discretion, that we turn in Chapter 9.

NOTES

[1]U.S. Senate, Report of the Attorney General's Committee on Administrative Procedure, *Administrative Procedure in Government Agencies*, Sen. Doc. no. 8, 77th Cong., 1st Sess. (1941), p. 35.

[2]Peter Woll, *Administrative Law: The Informal Process* (Los Angeles: University of California Press, 1963), p. 3. For a short summary of Woll's findings, see "Informal Administrative Adjudication: Summary of Findings," 7 *UCLA L. Rev.* 436 (1960).

[3]*Power Reactor Development Co. v. International Union of Electrical, Radio and Machine Workers*, 367 U.S. 396, 417 (1961), Justice Douglas dissenting.

[4]See, e.g., Kenneth Culp Davis, *Discretionary Justice* (Baton Rouge: Louisiana State University Press, 1969), p. 158. See also *United Gas Pipeline Co. v. Ideal Cement Co.*, 369 U.S. 134, 136–37 (1962), Justice Douglas dissenting.

[5]Mark Green, *The Other Government: The Unseen Power of Washington Lawyers* (New York: Norton, 1978).

[6]One of the more interesting recent efforts to deal with the concept of power is described in James MacGregor Burns, *Leadership* (New York: Harper & Row, 1978), Part I.

[7]Burns's definition of power is a useful one for thinking about the nature and significance of power law. "On these assumptions, I view the power process as one in which power holders (P), possessing certain motives and goals, have the capacity to secure changes in the behavior of a respondent (R), human or animal, and in the environment, by utilizing resources in their power base, including factors of skill, relative to the targets of their power wielding and necessary to secure such changes. This view of power deals with three elements in the process: the motives and resources of power holders; the motives and resources of power recipients; and the relationship among all these." Id., at p. 13.

[8]Green, supra note 5, at pp. 12–16.

[9]Jerome Frank, *If Men Were Angels: Some Aspects of Government in a Democracy* (New York: Harper & Brothers, 1942), chap. 10.

[10]Precisely for this reason, SEC personnel are prohibited from discussing such matters. That does not mean word of an investigation will not get out. The risk that someone might learn of SEC concern is a rather powerful deterrent.

[11]Herbert L. Packer, "Two Models of the Criminal Justice Process," in George F. Cole, ed., *Criminal Justice: Law and Politics* (Belmont, Calif.: Duxbury Press, 1972), pp. 35–52.

[12]Rule 16, Federal Rules of Civil Procedure, 1 *Moore's Rule Pamphlet* 134 (1981).

[13]5 U.S.C. §554(c)(1).

[14]Robert Lineberry provides a very useful introductory discussion of this subject in his *American Public Policy: What Government Does and What Difference It Makes* (New York: Harper & Row, 1977), p. 30–36.

[15]Lineberry summarizes "The Prisoner's Dilemma" and "The Tragedy of the Commons," two stories that explain why it may often be difficult to know what is in one's best interest. Id.

[16]"The discretionary power to be lenient is an impossibility without a concomitant power not to be lenient, and injustice from the discretionary power not to be is especially frequent; the power to be lenient is the power to discriminate." Davis, supra note 4, at p. 170.

[17]See generally Graham Allison, *Essence of Decision* (Boston: Little, Brown, 1971); and Francis Rourke, *Bureaucracy, Politics and Public Policy* (Boston: Little, Brown, 1969).

Administrative Discretion: Uses, Abuses, Controversies, and Remedies

"DISCRETIONARY CLEMENCY"[1]

The United States Attorney for the District of Utah died in fall 1974. William J. Lockhart accepted an interim appointment to fill the vacancy. Lockhart assumed the office on November 22, a particularly difficult time. On September 16 President Ford had announced his clemency program for Vietnam draft evaders,[2] to be administered primarily by the United States Attorneys offices throughout the country. Amnesty was promised to those liable for prosecution for draft evasion on condition that they come forward and accept alternative service in public or charitable institutions for a period of up to two years.

Such a program would have been difficult to administer under the best of conditions, but administrative problems were exacerbated by the time limit for entry into the program imposed by the president. U.S. Attorneys were directed by the Department of Justice to prepare a list by January 13, 1975, of those cases that "retain[ed] prosecutive merit." Individuals whose cases "lack[ed] prosecutive merit" were to be cleared and told that they need not participate in the alternative service program to avoid future legal difficulties. The others were to be notified that they must report to U.S. Attorneys for consideration of alternative service or face possible prosecution.

As he began work on administering the clemency program in Utah, Lockhart established a set of basic assumptions about his responsibility. However he implemented the program, Lockhart felt constrained by "an obligation of reasoned decision" to be able first to explain logically and in writing his policy and findings.[3] Second, he observed that the administrator of the program has a "moral, legal, and constitutional obligation to make a reasonable effort to assure consistency in the exercise of prosecutorial discretion, and violates the requirements of equal protection if [h]e fails to make that reasonable effort."[4] Third, the administration of the program "should not have the effect of encouraging or causing prosecutions or other punitive action which would not have been initiated in the absence of clemency."[5]

After studying the program, Lockhart concluded that the vesting of unlimited discretion in U.S. Attorneys to deal with draft evaders more or less as each official saw fit led to arbitrary and inconsistent administration. He also found that the program was structured so that the individuals were open to more punishment than they might have been if the program had not been instituted.

The directive that required U.S. Attorneys to develop a list of individuals whose cases "retained prosecutive merit" did not define that language. Lockhart assumed that an assessment of prosecutive merit required that two judgments be made in each case. First, his office had to determine whether there was enough evidence and sufficiently strong circumstances in the file to assume that a prosecution, if instituted, would have some chance of success. Since U.S. Attorney staffs lacked sufficient manpower to investigate cases thoroughly, and becase draft evasion cases had had very low priority compared with other cases, many of the files had to be rejected for weak evidentiary and factual case development. Second, in Lockhart's view, the U.S. Attorney's office had to determine that the defendant could have a fair trial if a prosecution were actually undertaken. The age or weak preparation of case files suggested that a number of defendants might be unable to locate witnesses or that other speedy trial related rights might constitutionally bar prosecution.

Finally, Lockhart concluded that, when individuals whose cases were found to have prosecutive merit came in to negotiate alternative service, he and other U.S. Attorneys would have "an unreviewed power to impose a sentence, in the form of a period of two years' alternative service, without trial or other adequate processes for establishing the facts, and without any understandable or meaningful standards, either for determining the kind of violation or circumstances constituting 'prosecutive merit,' or for determining appropriate periods of alternative service."[6]

Several specific aspects of the program gave Lockhart concern that some alleged violators could be dealt with more harshly under the clemency program than they would otherwise have been. First, the requirement of a complete review of all case files would force some U.S. Attorney offices that had generally ignored the evader cases up to 1972–1973 to consider prosecutions. The case files might be selected as prosecutable or nonprosecutable simply because the cases that were poorly investigated offered little chance of successful prosecution, and not because one case was more or less deserving of prosecution than another. Unlike the usual situation in which a prosecutor could negotiate a case with a defendant, the clemency program permitted the U.S. Attorney to be prosecutor, jury, and sentencing judge without the check of a possible hearing before a judge at which the attorney would be made to explain his or her actions. After examining problems in his own and other districts, Lockhart determined that the structure and vagueness of the program might encourage prosecutors to avoid hard decisions in favor of a "split-the-difference" mentality in which alternative service would be required in questionable cases.

> Thus, ambiguity in program guidelines created a serious probability that alternative service would be imposed as a "lesser alternative" in many situations where exercise of prosecutorial discretion would have rendered prosecution unlikely.[7]

Lockhart examined the program, the problems, and his case files and concluded: "The final decision of the District of Utah, however, determined that none of the persons who had remained in the United States, and hence accessible for prosecution, would be required to render alternative service, thus exempting all Utah applicants from the Clemency Program."[8] Based on the lack of guidance in program administration and his assessment of the lack of justifiable decision criteria, Lockhart had decided that he could not recommend any cases as having prosecutive merit and requiring alternative service.

215

Administrative
Discretion:
Uses, Abuses,
Controversies,
and Remedies

Lockhart's difficulties and his ultimate assessment of the clemency program exemplify the problems and opportunities that are presented when administrators are granted considerable authority and a great deal of discretion in exercising that authority. In his attempts to administer the program, Lockhart quickly saw that the same discretion that permitted him to be sensitive to the individual problems and circumstances of one person seeking clemency also allowed him, if he chose, to be arbitrary or abusive toward another. Few administrators exhibit such self-awareness and concern for the double-edged nature of the discretion they exercise.

This chapter focuses on the nature, sources, uses, abuses, and perceptions of administrative discretion. Like "informal process," administrative discretion is a rather difficult concept to deal with. It takes any number of forms and may exist in varying levels or degrees.[9] There is almost no situation in which an administrator can be accurately described as having no discretion.[10] However, because we operate in a constitutional framework, no administrator has complete discretion either.

Ernst Freund defined administrative discretion as follows: "When we speak of administrative discretion, we mean that a determination may be reached, in part at least, on the basis of considerations not entirely susceptible of proof or disproof."[11] Indeed, there are any number of possible ways to define the term. For present purposes we shall define administrative discretion to mean the power of an administrator to make significant decisions that have the force of law, directly or indirectly, and that are not specifically mandated by the Constitution, statutes, or other sources of black letter law.

WHY IS ADMINISTRATIVE DISCRETION NECESSARY?

Administrative discretion is both necessary and, to some degree, desirable. It is necessary in part because, as scholars from Goodnow to Davis agree, it is not possible for a legislature to draft statutes clearly and specifically enough to dictate every action to be taken in the administration of a program at all points in the future.[12] Even if it were possible to draft extraordinarily specific legislation, it would be extremely difficult to get agreement in the legislature over all the minutiae in such a bill.[13] Jerome Frank once observed that those who argue for the elimination of all discretion by enactment of rigid statutes ignore the fundamental fact that administration is human behavior and human behavior is not analogous to the operation of machinery.

It is imperative that in a democracy it should never be forgotten that public office is, of necessity, held by mere men who have human frailties. . . . To pretend, then, that government, in any of its phases, is a machine; that it is not a human affair; that the language of statutes—if only they are adequately worded—plus appeals to the upper courts, will alone, do away with the effect of human weaknesses in government is to worship illusion. And it is a dangerous illusion. . . .

Yet curiously, it often happens that the very men who one day stress that truth [that public officers are human], the next day help to obscure it, by distorting the real truth contained in the phrase "a government of laws, and not of men." As a consequence, sometimes, hypnotized by those words, we picture as an existing reality—or at least as a completely achievable ideal—a government so contrived that it matters not at all what men, at any given moment, constitute government. Such an idea is a narcotic. It is bad medicine. It does not protect us from bad government. On the contrary, it invites bad government.[14]

In addition to the structural and behavioral reasons why discretion is necessary, there are functional arguments. A primary reason for the rise in administrative activity was the desire to improve the effectiveness and efficiency of administration through increased flexibility in management of administrative problems.[15] Therefore, it is important to remember that "flexibility, especially at early stages in an agency's development of its program, may facilitate the ultimate advancement of the legislative purpose, while standards and controls may tend to obscure . . . the purposes behind a statute."[16] Flexibility is needed both for management effectiveness and also to allow the law to evolve as agencies develop.[17] In fact, when the first Hoover Commission examined the problems of administering the government, one of its criticisms was not that government had excessive discretion, but that it was excessively rigid.

Many of the statutes and regulations that control the administrative practices and procedures of the Government are unduly detailed and rigid.

It is impossible to secure enough authority and discretion to seize opportunities for economic and effective operations.[18]

Finally, administrative discretion is necessary because the technical expertise that is the basis for a good deal of administrative activity is constantly changing. Agency structures and authorizations that are not flexible enough to permit the agency to keep pace are counterproductive.

On another level, discretion is desirable because it permits individualized consideration and treatment of those before an agency. As Freund puts it:

The plausible argument in favor of administrative discretion is that it individualizes the exercise of public power over private interests, permitting its adjustment to varying circumstances and avoiding an undesirable standardization of restraints, disqualifications, and particularity of requirements.[19]

The demand for individualized attention, discussed in Chapter 8, is never ending. Eliminating the discretion to make individual assessments could wreak havoc on those who must deal with agencies. Judge J. Skelly Wright, in a review of Davis's *Discretionary Justice*, summarized his own and Davis's views on this point.

This is not to say that he [Davis] argues for complete elimination of discretionary decisionmaking. He would not exchange Lewis Carroll's fantasy for Franz Kafka's nightmare. A tyranny of petty bureaucrats who

217

Administrative
Discretion:
Uses, Abuses,
Controversies,
and Remedies

lack power to change the rules even an iota in order to do justice is at least as bad as a tyranny of petty bureaucrats who make up the rules as they go along.[20]

Law and Administrative Discretion: In Search of the Optimum Combination

The fact that administrative discretion is necessary and relatively useful does not mean that the more discretion administrators have the better off we are. Lockhart's experience with the clemency program suggests a number of reasons why excessive discretion can be a problem. Recognizing the dangers, Davis observed: "Discretion is a tool when properly used; like an axe, it can be a weapon for mayhem or murder."[21] The language is a bit strong, but the point is well taken. There is no absolute positive or negative correlation between discretion and just and equitable decisions.

If one were to depict graphically the relationship between discretion and just decisionmaking, the ardent antibureaucratic position might be represented by straightline A in Figure 9-1. A more realistic presentation of the relationship is curved line B, which suggests that complete discretion and no discretion can both result in unfair, arbitrary, and inconsistent decisions. The curve indicates that there is some point at which adequate and appropriate discretion meets useful guidance by rules and standards to provide an optimum mix.

The relationship between discretion and flexibility to promote efficient administration can be similarly viewed. One of the major arguments for discretion is that it permits an agency to develop and apply its expertise in a flexible manner with a likelihood of more efficient administration than if the agency were required to operate in a rule-bound manner. Again, it is tempting to think in terms of a

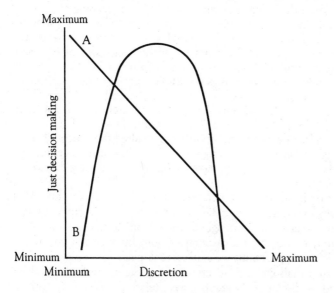

Figure 9-1 *The Relationship of Discretion to Just Decisions*

straight-line relationship; many administrators seem to think that the more discretion they have the more efficient they are likely to be. As a study conducted by Abraham Sofaer suggests, however, that assumption is wishful thinking.[22]

Sofaer's study of the United States Immigration and Naturalization Service (INS) was done for the Administrative Conference of the United States. The INS has one of the broadest grants of discretion in its decisionmaking processes of any agency in the federal government.[23] Sofaer examined cases involving so-called "change of status" requests in which resident aliens sought to have their status changed from temporary resident to permanent resident. The effect is the same as if the alien had obtained immigrant status from a U.S. embassy in the home country. Sofaer characterized the level of discretion in such proceedings as follows:

> Numerous discretionary decisions are made. The Examiner's initial determination to grant or deny an eligible alien's application on the basis of "discretion" is virtually ungoverned by standards. Several grounds for denying discretionary relief are identifiable; but adjudicators are given little guidance in applying them, and virtually no limits exist on their authority to decide any individual application one way or the other. The statutory prerequisites for eligibility incorporate many discretionary provisions that allow INS to waive ineligibility. In addition, aspects of the processes of administrative review and enforcement are highly discretionary.[24]

The results of the study did not support the argument that the more discretion granted, the better administration will be.

> First, the evidence seemed to confirm the hypothesis that relatively undefined grounds of decisions more frequently cause inconsistent results than well-defined grounds. We found that Examiners applied different standards in exercising discretion on the merits; that the Service's view of discretion has changed periodically; that extensive and successful political intervention on the merits strongly correlates with the presence of discretionary power; that official Service policy on the meaning of discretion permits inconsistent results; and that there are striking variations among INS districts in their rates of denial of section 245 cases that do not appear explainable in terms of the character of the districts involved. Many of the applications, initially denied, were granted on motions to reopen (by Examiners) or at deportation hearings (by SIO's [Special Inquiry Officers]). We found that, in cases where the facts had not changed upon "appeal," denials based on relatively undefined "discretionary" grounds were far more frequently reversed than denials based on the relatively well-defined "statutory" grounds. Moreover, this correlation resulted from inconsistent decision making, rather than from any other cause. Examiner reversals of discretionary decisions on the same record were overwhelmingly due to political intervention. . . .
> On the other hand, the evidence seemed to refute the hypothesis that discretion results in less costly, speedier administration. . . . The presence of discretionary power seemed throughout the administrative process, disproportionately to attract political intervention. Intervention on the merits of the denied applications we studied took place exclusively in connection with denials based on discretion. . . . Significantly, "appeals" of denials based on discretionary grounds were relatively more frequent than "appeals" of denials based on the more well-defined statutory grounds

219
Administrative
Discretion:
Uses, Abuses,
Controversies,
and Remedies

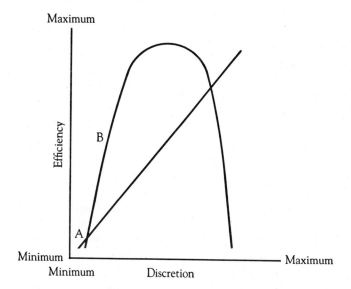

Figure 9-2 *The Relationship of Efficiency to Discretion*

Discretionary power to "reverse" decisions and to delay or suspend enforcement led to changed results in 55% of the random sample denials we examined; most of the other cases were either pending or involved aliens who departed the United States voluntarily.[25]

As was true of the discretion-to-justice relationship, the discretion-to-efficiency relationship is better represented by a curve rather than a straight line (see Figure 9-2). From his examination of the INS, which operates at the high-discretion end of the spectrum, Sofaer concluded: "Broad discretion in adjudication and enforcement at INS causes inconsistency, arbitrariness, and inefficiency."[26] The task of the administrator in any given situation is to operate as close to the optimum portion of the curve as possible.

Recognizing the ambiguity in the nature and purposes of discretionary administration, let us turn more specifically to the types and sources of discretion.

TYPES OF DISCRETIONARY DECISIONS

For analytical and practical purposes, it is possible to classify discretionary decisions into three general types: substantive, procedural, and complex.

A *substantive* discretionary determination is a decision in which the administrator by discretion determines a right, duty, or obligation, or promulgates a rule on particular questions of policy. Lockhart had the substantive discretion to determine whether any individual on whom he was holding a draft evader case file would be required to render alternative service and for what length of time up to two years.

A *procedural* discretionary decision is selection of a procedure to be used to gather facts or make policy decisions. Agency enabling acts and state or federal administrative procedures acts mandate a variety of processes, but administrators may nevertheless exercise considerable discretion on the means they use to deal with a problem. For example, an agency may elect to develop information by the use of consultants, through staff investigations, or in trial-type hearings.

Finally, a *complex* discretionary decision is both substantive and procedural. For example, an administrator may opt for an information-gathering technique that will bias the substantive decision, for example, when a regulatory agency seeks information and advice primarily from task forces made up predominantly of representatives of the regulated industry.[27] One of the most important and least understood complex discretionary decisions is the decision "not to decide or not to act at this time."[28] A serious problem in government is, on the one hand, to discourage administrators from inflicting harm through excessively zealous administration, and on the other, to get administrators to pursue their tasks aggressively. A decision not to act may mean that an agency will not adopt a fact-finding process to better understand a controversy and that the agency's current policy is to maintain the status quo. These are not neutral or trivial decisions.

Lockhart was making a complex discretionary decision when he established an informal set of criteria for determining whether to recommend any of his pending cases for alternative service. His assessment of the proper action to take was based upon an analysis of the operational weaknesses involved in implementing the clemency program and on consideration of the strengths and weaknesses of the case files. The decision rules he adopted and the procedure he used to establish them constituted a complex discretionary determination. In this situation, the result was that none of those who might have been confronted with alternative service or prosecution had to face those options.

SOURCES OF DISCRETIONARY AUTHORITY

The characteristics of discretionary decisionmaking and the limits on it are to some extent functions of the sources from which the authority to exercise discretion emanates. Some of the more common of these sources are: (1) broad legislative or executive delegations of authority to administrators; (2) expertise in a particular field; (3) experience in a specific area of activity; and (4) political support from groups and individuals both in and out of government.

Broad Delegations of Authority

For several reasons, some of which were noted earlier, legislatures frequently draft statutes which contain language that is vague or open to rather wide interpretation. Referred to by some commentators as "skeleton legislation,"[29] such legislative delegations of authority to administrative agencies provide the most basic source of discretion.

First, the legislature may endow an agency with plenary responsibilities in an area and plainly indicate that within that area its range of choice is entirely free. Second, the legislature may issue directives that are intended to control the agency's choice among alternatives but that, because of their generality, ambiguity, or vagueness, do not clearly determine choices in particular cases.[30]

221

Administrative
Discretion:
Uses, Abuses,
Controversies,
and Remedies

According to Freund:

> A statute confers discretion when it refers an official for the use of his powers to beliefs, expectations, or tendencies instead of facts, or to such terms as "adequate," "advisable," "appropriate," "beneficial," "competent," "convenient," "detrimental," "expedient," "equitable," "fair," "fit," "necessary," "practicable," "proper," "reasonable," "reputable," "safe," "sufficient," "wholesome," or their opposites.[31]

Judge Henry J. Friendly listed other commonly used statutory terms that, either accidentally or by design, confer discretion on administrators:

> There are numerous examples; just and reasonable rates, undue preference or prejudice, public convenience and necessity, discrimination in membership in a labor organization, bargaining in good faith, unfair methods of competition, are a sufficient sampling.[32]

There are indications that legislatures, and particularly the U.S. Congress, are attempting to draw statutory language more tightly to limit delegation of broad discretionary authority to executive agencies.[33] Even assuming that legislators understand the need for precision, significant factors remain that limit their ability to draft such legislation.[34] For example, state legislators rarely have the time and staff support necessary to develop detailed knowledge in special areas of administration.

The literature on administrative law seldom acknowledges the fact, but broad grants of authority from the chief executive are also important sources of discretion. The clemency program for draft evaders created by President Ford through an executive order, discussed earlier, is a prime example. Another important executive delegation was President Johnson's Philadelphia plan, also in an executive order. This order barred executive agencies from permitting the government to contract with firms that engaged in various forms of discriminatory employment practices.[35] A more recent example is President Reagan's executive order on regulatory activity, which vests considerable authority in the Office of Management and Budget to evaluate the cost-effectiveness and feasibility of regulations proposed by various executive agencies.[36]

Expertise and Discretion

One of the most important sources of administrative discretion is a *de facto* matter rather than a black letter law authority. It is the expertise or expertness (either term is employed in the literature of administrative law) that administrators possess in a particular field. Years before administrators were concerned with worker exposure to asbestos or disposal of nuclear and toxic chemical wastes, observers of the changing administrative environment noted: "The administration of general legislation by technical experts, skilled and trained in specialized fields, is 'the contemporary answer to the challenge to bridge the gap between popular government and scientific government'."[37] Scientific and technological knowledge confers a certain amount of authority on those who have it.[38] Agencies that have developed research staffs, have learned where to find technical information in the government and have learned how to use outside consultants have more flexibility and options in decisionmaking.[39]

Two federal agencies that have used their expert resources effectively in recent years are the Occupational Safety and Health Administration (OSHA) and the National Highway Traffic Safety Administration (NHTSA). OSHA was designed with a research arm, the National Institute of Occupational Safety and Health (NIOSH), and has used NIOSH research to advantage in such areas as standard setting for worker exposure to various toxic substances.[40] Until recently, NHTSA pursued vigorous in-house and contract research programs to raise automotive passenger safety standards.[41]

There is every reason to believe that expertise will continue to be an important source of discretionary authority. However, the administrative environment has become more complex in recent years. Particularly in the regulatory area, claims to expertise by administrative agencies will be challenged. In one case, environmental groups argued that administrative judgments about the danger of some pesticides were arbitrary because they ignored a significant body of scientific evidence.[42] In another now-famous case, automotive manufacturers challenged an Environmental Protection Agency determination that it was technologically feasible for the manufacturers to meet Clean Air Act standards even though a National Academy of Sciences report raised serious doubts about their capabilities.[43] Two points are clear, given recent administrative history: (1) agencies must develop a respectable level of expertness in their field to have any flexibility or effectiveness; and (2) beyond that threshold level, superior expertise by administrators in their field relative to other actors in the administrative process promises increased discretionary authority.

The Experience Factor

Discussion of administrative "expertise" masks the important difference in the quality of administration between expertness and experience. One may have a great deal of technical knowledge, yet no experience in the use of that knowledge. The experienced administrator, according to Gellhorn,[44] usually has a sense of the continuity of agency activity and is sensitive to the impact of agency decisions on those before the agency. Experience, like technical expertise, indirectly affords administrators discretion in judgment; it permits flexibility because it enables an administrator to understand what is workable as well as what may objectively be correct. Experience also enables an administrator to assess the political costs that may arise from a particular course of action.

Political Support from Groups and Individuals
Both In and Out of Government

Another *de facto* source of administrative discretion is the political support for its action that an agency can marshal from other levels and units within government, or from clientele groups outside the government.[45] When agencies take major actions, actions that affect more than just a small number of single shot players, they attract political support or opposition from groups and organizations that perceive themselves to be helped or injured. Examples of agency options altered by the vagaries of

223

Administrative
Discretion:
Uses, Abuses,
Controversies,
and Remedies

changing patterns of political support include the experiences of the Defense Department (DOD) and the Federal Trade Commission (FTC).

Support for DOD initiatives has, of course, fluctuated with changes in public opinion. Sentiment against the Vietnam war during the early 1970s translated into relatively low levels of support for DOD plans and projects. Since then, however, DOD has enjoyed a resurgence of support in public opinion and in the legislative arena. More specifically, the Defense Department has enjoyed some independence, quite apart from general public opinion, because of its ability to mobilize political support in important constituencies. Relationships between DOD and defense production and research and development industries is one source of such support. The closing of a major defense installation or the loss of jobs dependent on government contracts can mobilize constituent groups quickly.[46]

The Federal Trade Commission's ability to exercise options has varied considerably during the last decade. A. Lee Fritschler's well-known case study, *Smoking and Politics: Policymaking and the Federal Bureaucracy,*[47] shows how the FTC was able to build support in other units of government for its attempt to limit cigarette advertising. But Fritschler also noted the opposition engendered by the FTC antismoking effort. Since then, the FTC has found itself embroiled in major political controversies over its attempt to regulate advertising directed at small children and the merchandising activities of the funeral industry. In 1980, the opponents of the commission secured passage of the Federal Trade Commission Improvement Act of 1980, which specifically limited FTC action in some areas and reduced agency discretion by including a legislative veto option for Congress.[48]

CONFLICTING VALUES AND PERCEPTIONS ON ADMINISTRATIVE DISCRETION

Different actors in the administrative system operate from different sets of values, acquired during the professional development process. Administrators and judicial officials (both lawyers and judges) share many values, e.g., the importance of the democratic process and the principle of the rule of law, but their priorities are often quite different. And when officials with differing values or priorities approach basic problems (such as how to provide administrators sufficient discretion to accomplish the manifold purposes for which their agencies were created, and at the same time ensure against arbitrariness and abuse of discretion), the value conflicts can and do have important consequences. To understand how administrative discretion is used and how abuses are checked, one must be aware of the value conflicts between administratively oriented officials and those with legal orientations.

Administrative Imperatives: Expertise, Flexibility, and Efficiency

In tracing the history of public administration one soon comes across the scholarly debates over whether the field of public administration should be dominated by managerial rather than legalistic values. This extremely important and longstanding dispute had significant consequences for the training, thought, and practice of public administrators. When Frank Goodnow, often referred to as the father of modern public administration,[49] dealt with the problem of ensuring adequate discretion while protecting against abuses, he established a set of priorities. The first interest was governmental efficiency, then the preservation of individual rights and liberties, and, finally, the promotion of social welfare.[50] It is not surprising that one writing in the early years of the twentieth century focused on administrative expertise and efficiency as the goal of administrative activity. It was the age of the efficiency expert, when Taylorism was popular and the industrial managers of large enterprises were applauded for their skills. Nor is it surprising that lawyers and judicial scholars like Elihu Root and John Dickinson, writing during this same period, were so adamant in insisting that protection of individual rights was prior to efficiency and managerial values.[51] That tension was carried over to the newly developing academic and professional field of public administration. Leonard D. White, in his famous text *Introduction to the Study of Public Administration,* called for the public administration community to turn from the emphasis on legal aspects of the field to the managerial aspects. He asserted that "the study of administration should start from the base of management rather than the foundation of law."[52] His admonition was taken so seriously that in 1968 Dwight Waldo observed that it was his "opinion that we now suffer from lack of attention to constitutional-legal matters. Our early antilegal and antilawyer bias is understandable and forgiveable, but it is dangerously obsolete and self-defeating."[53]

At some point, one can observe the argument over priorities changing to a new kind of relationship between legal officers and administrators. Several factors suggest that administrators may consider, or be tempted to consider, judicial review and other legal aspects of administration as unfortunate and unwise constraints on administrative discretion. First, very few administration programs require the study of legal aspects of administration, and in fewer programs still are such courses taught by faculty whose primary area of research is law and administration. Second, an emphasis on management technique may lead an administrator to conclude that anything that constrains his or her flexibility to select management options is to be dealt with if necessary, to be avoided if possible. Sofaer's study of the Immigration and Naturalization Service, discussed earlier, provides an example.

Widespread concern over the amount of discretion exercised by the INS led, among other things, to efforts to guard against abuses. One of the least painful alternatives for the administrator is to make rules governing his or her own conduct. In 1971, the Administrative Conference of the United States (an advisory body charged with making studies and recommendations for improvements in the operation of the administrative justice system) recommended that the INS publish rules as to how it intended to exercise its discretion. The guidelines would, of course, be subject to change as the agency saw fit, but they would give those who must deal with the INS some idea how the agency would interact with them. The INS chose to respond to the Administrative Conference request by memorandum. Sofaer commented:

> The Service's official response to the Conference recommendation is hardly calculated to cause me to pause before accepting the need for mandatory rulemaking. Its comments, in total, consisted of these three sentences: "Exercise of discretion inherently requires flexibility in assessing diverse factual patterns. Decisions must necessarily be made on a case by case

basis utilizing criteria set forth in published precedents. Formulation of standards for the exercising of discretion is self-defeating since standards would impair flexibility.[54]

225
Administrative
Discretion:
Uses, Abuses,
Controversies,
and Remedies

The argument that greater discretion allows increased flexibility to take advantage of management opportunities, which will increase agency effectiveness and result in the most efficient performance of the people's business, is intuitively satisfying, but it does not come to grips with the legal and political elements of the modern administrative environment. This approach to administration lends itself to an impatient if not openly hostile view toward the relationship between courts and agencies.

Administrators with a strong antilegal and promanagement penchant may fail to bring agency counsel into decision processes until too late, and then only with the expectation that the lawyers will ward off perceived challenges to the agency. Some lawyers feel that there is an unwritten law of administration: attorneys should not be called in until the administrator is in so much difficulty that it is too late to do anything about the situation. If an administrator does adopt the posture that judicial interactions with one's agency are threatening or hostile and not justifiable in terms of management effectiveness, the instructions to agency attorneys may be to employ technical defenses against appeal or any other ethically acceptable devices to win for the agency. Kenneth Culp Davis has suggested that winning through discouraging full judicial review of agency actions is not necessarily supportive of the overall purpose of the agency.

> The needed escape, I think, has to be from the tendency of government lawyers, like any other lawyers, to use all available tricks to win for their client. That government lawyers use all legal ethical means to win their cases is, of course, only natural. But I think they can and should rise to a slightly higher degree of sophistication. Uncle Sam is not an ordinary client. Uncle Sam always wins when justice is done. This means that he may lose when judgment is entered for him, and he may win when judgment is entered against him. That this is so is not merely an idealist's dream but a hard-headed reality. It has *sometimes* been the basis on which government lawyers have exercised their important discretionary power. (Emphasis in original.)[55]

Finally, some administrators respond to the possibility of interaction with legal actors with anxiety as well as annoyance. Whether from lack of knowledge of judicial-administrative interactions or from horror stories (apocryphal or real) about judicial interference in agency activity, many administrators' efforts are hampered by the fear of becoming embroiled in a lawsuit. Taken far enough, such anxiety can lead to paralysis in which the administrator is afraid to depart in any way from proven standard operating procedures.

In sum, the perspectives that administrators have of judicial actors, institutions, and values affect how they perceive and use their discretion. If the legal actors and elements in the administrative environment are believed to be opponents of the managers, dysfunctional types of administrative behavior may result. Values and perceptions are, of course, also important to judicial actors.

Judicial Imperatives: Due Process, Equal Protection, and Substantial Justice

If the watchwords of public administration are expertise, flexibility, and efficiency, the terms that guide the judiciary in reviewing governmental actions are protection of the concept of due process of law, prevention of violations of equal protection of the laws, and general concern that government actions ought to be characterized by substantial justice or fundamental fairness. Two recurring themes in post–New Deal judicial opinions and articles by members of the judiciary are important to an understanding of administrative discretion. First, the judges sitting in various courts have found it difficult to define the role of the courts in reviewing administrative actions. Second, although judges recognize the need for judicial deference to administrative initiatives, they have been uncomfortable with the argument that administrative expertise, flexibility, and efficiency are always adequate to justify broad discretionary action.

Toward the end of the New Deal momentum grew in the judiciary to support administrative exercises of discretion. At the same time, however, there was a countertrend based on growing fear of administrative arbitrariness.[56] In the Supreme Court, these divergent themes emerge rather clearly, with the majority most often holding in support of administrative expertise and experience and the dissenters warning of "administrative authoritarianism."[57] For example, in *Securities and Exchange Commission v. Chenery*, a very important case defining the nature of judicial review of administrative action decided just at the time of the enactment of the APA, the Court stated:

> The scope of our review of an administrative order wherein a new principle is announced and applied is no different from what which pertains to ordinary administrative action. The wisdom of the principle adopted is none of our concern. . . . Our duty is at an end when it becomes evident that the Commission's action is based upon substantial evidence and is consistent with the authority granted by Congress. . . . The facts being undisputed, we are not free to disturb the Commission's judgment save where it has plainly abused its discretion in these matters. . . .
>
> The Commission's conclusion here rests squarely in that area where administrative judgments are entitled to the greatest amount of weight by the appellate courts. It is the product of administrative experience, appreciation of the complexities of the problem, realization of the statutory policies, and responsible treatment of the uncontested facts. It is the type of judgment which administrative agencies are best equipped to make and which justifies the use of the administrative process. . . . Whether we agree or disagree with the result reached, it is an allowable judgment which we cannot disturb.[58]

The basis for deference was the Court's belief in and acceptance of the need for flexibility for an agency to exercise its capacity in the public interest. But not everyone was convinced. Dissenting in *Chenery*, Justice Jackson wrote:

> I suggest that administrative experience is of weight in judicial review only to this point—it is a persuasive reason for deference to the Commission in the exercise of its discretionary powers under and within the law. It

cannot be invoked to support action outside the law. And what action is and what is not within the law must be determined by the courts, when authorized to review, no matter how much deference is due to the agencies' fact finding. Surely an administrative agency is not a law unto itself, but the Court does not really face up to the fact that this is the justification it is offering for sustaining the Commission action.[59]

By the time of the decision in *Universal Camera Corporation v. National Labor Relations Board*, the APA had come into its own.[60] The Court was busy applying the new statute and working out its own role in the administrative justice system.

Our power to review the correctness of application of the present standard ought seldom to be called into action. Whether on the record as a whole there is substantial evidence to support agency findings is a question which Congress has placed in the keeping of the Courts of Appeals. This Court will intervene only in what ought to be the rare instance when the standard appears to have been misapprehended or grossly misapplied.[61]

The Court was insisting that courts should not be in the business of judging the wisdom of agency decisions. They were to defer to the expertise of the administrator as long as the decision itself was within the legal power granted to the agency and as long as there was substantial evidence in the record as a whole to support the decision.

However, the more that deference to agency discretion was granted, the more fear grew that broad grants of power would inevitably lead to arbitrariness. Justice Douglas, who had himself spent a considerable time on the SEC, wrote:

Unless we make the requirements for administrative action strict and demanding *expertise,* the strength of modern government, can become a monster which rules with no practical limits on its discretion. Absolute discretion, like corruption, marks the beginning of the end of liberty. This case is perhaps insignificant in the annals. But the standard set for men of good will is even more useful to the venal.[62]

It was one thing for that debate to take place between the majority and minority members of the Supreme Court. It was quite another in the many courts below, where some judges maintained strict deference and others saw themselves as guardians against excess power in the hands of bureaucratic officials.[63] The latter group frequently reminded their judicial colleagues and administrators that,

absent any evidence to the contrary, Congress may rather be presumed to have intended that the courts shall fulfill their traditional role of defining and maintaining the proper bounds of administrative discretion and safeguarding the rights of the individual.[64]

For the contemporary administrator, the immediate impact may be conflicting interpretations of one's statutory authority or review of particular decisions by different judges sitting in different jurisdictions.[65]

The process of defining the judicial role continues as the administrative environment changes and new judges come to the bench. On the whole, there is a fair measure of judicial discretion in the review of administrative discretion. Like administrators, different judges may exercise their discretion in different ways.

Also like administrators, judges are socialized into their profession with a set of values that affects their actions. The fundamental priorities of due process, equal protection of the laws, and substantial justice necessarily often conflict with the administrative managerial emphasis on expertise, flexibility, and efficiency.

Judges *do* respect expertise in administration, but it is a cautious respect, which "does not eliminate the need for judicial review of agency actions, and inherent in that albeit limited power of review is the need for an agency to spell out its reasons."[66] This antipathy toward claims of expertise suggests general agreement with Justice Douglas's warning that expertise can become a monster that rules with no limits on its discretion,[67] and with Justice Jackson's fear of administrative authoritarianism justified by claims of expertise and experience.[68]

Judges are often skeptical of administrative action justified on the ground of administrative flexibility. "To permit flexibility under the APA does not, however, mean that agencies are granted carte blanche to proceed in any way they see fit. Flexibility is not synonymous with uncontrolled discretion."[69] Judges understand the advantages of flexibility, but prefer to have clear standards available where there is a good chance that someone may suffer a serious loss of property or liberty.[70]

If judges tend to be skeptical of expertise and claimed requirements for flexibility, many tend to be openly hostile to administrative efficiency and convenience when these are claimed to justify discretionary administrative action, unless the need for it is clearly demonstrated. "We must not play fast and loose with basic constitutional guarantees in the interest of administrative efficiency."[71]

This distrust stems in part from a fundamental tension built into the framework of government. The Supreme Court has often reminded administrators that

> The establishment of prompt efficacious procedures to achieve legitimate state ends is a proper state interest worthy of cognizance in constitutional adjudication. But the Constitution recognizes higher values than speed and efficiency. Indeed, one might fairly say of the Bill of Rights in general, and the Due Process Clause in particular, that they were designed to protect the fragile values of a vulnerable citizenry from the overbearing concern for efficiency and efficacy that may characterize praiseworthy government officials no less, and perhaps more, than mediocre ones.[72]

The Constitution was designed to ensure just but not efficient government, and judges often see their duty as ensuring against the natural tendency of officials to arrogate power to themselves, using the need for efficiency as justification.

Judges have also had long experience with repeated administrative rationalizations based on efficiency used to justify agency actions, many of which turned out to be arbitrary or actually violative of the constitutional or statutory rights of people before the agency. Administrative convenience and necessity were used in each case to support the administrator and urge judicial deference. In cases relying on irrebuttable presumptions, the Supreme Court observed: "The State's interest in administrative ease and certainty cannot, in and of itself, save the conclusive presumption from invalidity."[73] In cases challenging residency requirements for receipt of public services and benefits, the Court held: "The argument that the waiting period serves as an administratively efficient rule of thumb for determining residency will not withstand scrutiny."[74] The same arguments have been used by agencies to treat female employees and citizens differently from similarly situated males.[75]

229
Administrative
Discretion:
Uses, Abuses,
Controversies,
and Remedies

It must be emphasized that these differing values and perspectives are held to different degrees. Progress can and should be made in understanding and dealing with the inherent conflicts between those who exercise administrative discretion and those who must ensure against abuses of discretionary authority. Administrators who become more familiar with the law will be better able to anticipate judicial concerns and deal with them. They will also understand that judicial interaction with the agency, much more than an annoying interference, is inevitable and necessary to the successful operation of the administrative justice system. Judges have shown themselves to be increasingly sensitive to some aspects of agency acitivity. Still, progress can be made. Chapter 11 presents examples of how judicial awareness of administrative problems can be used in considering agency decisions in the areas of freedom of information and right to privacy.

REMEDIES FOR ABUSE OF DISCRETION

Administrative discretion is useful and necessary; it takes many forms and stems from several sources, and is a basic tool for solving problems. These factors make it likely that discretion will be abused intentionally or accidentally and make it difficult to fix remedies for those abuses. Although Chapter 10, on the law and politics of regulation, and Chapter 12 on law and the public employee, will discuss the more important remedies in more detail, it is useful to summarize here the most frequently used remedies for abuse of discretion.

Self-Help

The most obvious way for the administrator to protect against abuses is to take action to prevent it in the first place. Many scholars and study groups have long advocated that the best way for administrators to do this is to place all agency standards, policy positions, and procedures in rules promulgated so that they may be read and understood by all who must deal with the agency.[76] If an agency action is challenged and the administrator can show that the action was based on standards made known in published rules before the fact, the likelihood of judicial support and deference increases. A judge who feels that an administrator is making up the rules as he or she goes along is very likely to overturn an agency action. Agencies can change standards as the need arises, but the fact that standards are set and changed in an orderly, rational process is a sign of well-used authority.

A second mechanism for self-help is to develop a proper and complete record of each agency action. The record must be made while the agency action is in progress. Another trigger of judicial disfavor is the perception that a record was made up after the fact, as a *post hoc* rationalization of agency action.

Finally, administrators can assure adequate procedures to resolve administrative disputes, whether they are formal, e.g., administrative appeals processes, or informal, e.g., agency ombudsmen, to convince clients, the legislature, and the courts that the agency makes every effort to deal with such unfortunate instances of abuse of discretion as may arise.

Unfortunately, for many reasons, the self-help remedies have not been employed by enough administrators.[77] Hence, other approaches to the problem of abuse of discretion have been required.

Oversight by the Legislature and Supervision by the Executive

All agencies are accountable to a higher institutional authority for their actions. Executive branch agencies are responsible both to the chief executive (be it the president, the governor, or the mayor) and to the legislature. Independent commissions are accountable to the legislature even though they need not answer to the executive. Most agencies are required to report and justify their activities both to a subject area committee (a committee concerned with the substantive policy that an agency administers) and to an appropriations committee (a committee that is ostensibly concerned with ensuring that agency funds are properly expended, but in reality it often considers the substance of agency policy as well.)[78] For reasons that will be discussed in Chapter 10, executive supervision and legislative oversight have not proven to be effective as deterrents or as remedies to abuses of agency discretion. For one thing, neither the legislature (even a committee of the legislature) nor the chief executive has the time or the staff to pay attention to all the day-to-day activities of even one agency. For another, as Raoul Berger has noted, elections are not likely to be won or lost because a few people suffered from an abuse of administrative discretion.[79]

What the legislature can do is to take care in drafting or revising legislation for an agency to give as much discretion and guidance as possible in the statutes. Administrators can also be encouraged to promulgate rules and guidelines structuring and confining (as Davis put it) their own discretion.

The problem of executive supervision of agencies that are technically under his or her authority is complex. The *de facto* sources of authority discussed earlier, such as expertise and political support from agency clients, often frustrate executive attempts to control agencies. The executive's primary tools are the budget review process and judicious use of the appointment and dismissal powers. Beyond these mechanisms, executive supervision is more a matter of political acumen and management skill than of institutional checks and legal devices.

Judicial Remedies

Writers who have considered the problem of remedying abuses of administrative discretion since Goodnow's famous works on the subject have urged that the judiciary should not be the only means for dealing with the problem. The fact is, however, that the judiciary has been the most effective remedy for specific abuses by particular administrators. The courts use essentially four approaches to meet allegations of administrative arbitrariness: (1) standard judicial review; (2) judicial intervention in cases of maladministration through the use of injunctions; (3) judgments of money damages awarded to those injured by administrative actions; and (4) criminal convictions where prosecutions are brought for malfeasance or other delicts of law.

231

Administrative
Discretion:
Uses, Abuses,
Controversies,
and Remedies

Judicial review of the sort discussed in Chapter 7 may result in several kinds of actions. The judge may reverse or vacate an agency decision. More often, the judge will remand a decision for further proceedings before the agency. Such a disposition delays agency action; repeated remands may have the effect of nullifying a decision. The judge may refuse to enforce agency orders and subpoenas. Agencies like the National Labor Relations Board are virtually powerless without an enforcement order from a court.

In some situations, a mere judicial declaration that a policy or other action is illegal is not sufficient to solve the problem that gave rise to a lawsuit in the first place. Often the person bringing a suit is asking for a court to end maladministration. Administrators who fail to cease discriminatory actions in schools or housing, or who operate prisons or mental hospitals in what they know (or should know) are unlawful and inhumane conditions, may be told by a court to remedy the situation. For various reasons, generally political, administrators may not respond. In this event a court may use an injunction to force an administrator to do or remain from doing whatever is necessary to remedy the illegal administrative situation that exists.[80] Failure to obey such an order may result in a charge of contempt of court.

Cases in which judges are called on to issue such orders are often no-win situations. The judge is left with two unpalatable choices. He or she can require specific administrative actions from uncooperative or frightened administrators, and be accused of judicial usurpation and abuse of power, which interferes with the executive and legislative branches of government,[81] or, alternatively, the judge can tell someone who has proven that he or she is the victim of maladministration that although the law is on his or her side, nothing will be done to remedy the situation.

Illustrations of the latter choice have occurred frequently in prison and mental health institutions in recent years.[82] The public has repeatedly shown that it does not support significant expenditures to improve prisons or mental health facilities. Consequently many such facilities are overcrowded (often two or three times more people are housed in them than the institutions were designed for), understaffed, and underfunded. When patients, prisoners, or their families win suits showing that the conditions of confinement are illegal, the court often requests that the institution come up with voluntary plans for change. Unfortunately, the same political forces that prevented adequate support in the first place continue to block solutions, at which point the court is forced to take action. Astute politicians have learned that by forcing the courts to move by injunction to remedy such situations, the blame for increased taxes for improvements in state programs and institutions can be diverted to the judges. The use of such remedies is fraught with all manner of difficulties since, among other things, judges are not trained in the administration of schools, prisons, or mental health facilities. On the other hand, there are often few effective alternatives to ensure compliance with the law.

One alternative to injunctions is that a person injured by maladministration may be afforded an opportunity, under some limited circumstances, to sue for damages.[83] For reasons that will be discussed in Chapter 12, the opportunity to maintain such suits is very limited, and this is particularly true where one is disputing an action in an area involving administrative discretion. The utility of a money damages claim also assumes one can be made whole again by recompense in the form of money damages, which may or may not be true. The Supreme Court has indicated in recent years that it favors remedies for maladministration using money damage suits after the fact rather than injunctions that attempt to alter ongoing administrative patterns.[84] Just how far the Court will take that trend remains to be seen.

Finally, the judiciary may render judgment in criminal prosecutions for illegal activities by administrators. Such prosecutions do occur, but they are quite rare. For one thing, criminal laws affect only the most extreme of administrative abuses. Furthermore, political realities encourage superiors to fire questionable employees rather than keep them until criminal prosecutions can be mounted.

SUMMARY

In this chapter we have indicated a number of reasons why administrative discretion is both necessary and desirable. It stems from a variety of sources, which include broad delegations of authority from the legislature and the chief executive, as well as several *de facto* sources, including expertise, experience, and political support for one's agency. Problems of allowing constructive use of administrative discretion while limiting abuses are complicated by the fact that administrators and judicial officals come to the problem with different perspectives.

Despite good intentions, historical examples of abuses of administrative discretion are legion. Mechanisms have been developed to remedy such arbitrariness, including self-help, supervision by officials of the legislative and executive branches, and judicial remedies of several types.

Many times more decisions are made by administrators in social services administration than in regulation, but regulation has been the cause of the most vocal debates in administrative law and politics in recent years. The law and politics of regulation is considered in Chapter 10.

NOTES

[1] This case study is summarized and interpreted from William J. Lockhart, "Discretionary Clemency: Mercy at the Prosecutor's Option," 1976 *Utah L. Rev.* 55, 58 (1976). (Hereafter cited as Lockhart.)

[2] 10 *Weekly Compilation of Presidential Documents* 1150 (1974).

[3] Lockhart, supra note 1, at p. 58.

[4] Id., at p. 59.

[5] Id., at p. 60.

[6] Id., at p. 64.

[7] Id.

[8] Id., at p. 57.

[9] "Generalizations as to the allowable limits of administrative discretion is dangerous, for the field is peculiarly one where differences in degree become differences of substance. It is possible to say, on the one hand, that the responsibility for fashioning a policy, not only of great economic importance but also one that has divided the faiths and loyalties of classes of people, cannot appropriately be entrusted to the administrative; on the other, that the scope of administrative power should not be so narrowly defined as to take away from the administrative its capacity to achieve effectively the purposes of its creation." James M. Landis, *The Administrative Process* (New Haven, Conn.: Yale University Press, 1938), p. 55.

[10]Steve Wexler "Discretion: The Unacknowledged Side of Law," 25 *U. Toronto L. J.* 120, 122-23 (1972).

[11]Ernst Freund, *Administrative Powers over Persons and Property: A Comparative Survey* (Chicago: University of Chicago Press, 1928), p. 71.

[12]"There are many duties which the government is called upon to perform in a complex civilization which cannot be performed under a system of unconditional commands. No legislature has such insight or extended vision as to be able to regulate all the details in administrative law, or to put in the form of unconditional commands rules which in all cases completely and adequately express the will of the state. It must abandon the system of unconditional commands and resort to conditional commands which vest in the administrative officer large powers of discretionary character." Frank Goodnow, *The Principles of Administrative Law in the United States* (New York: Putnam, 1905), pp. 324-25.

[13]"In addition, there appear to be serious institutional constraints on Congress' ability to specify regulatory policy in meaningful detail. Legislative majorities typically represent coalitions of interests that must not only compromise among themselves but also with opponents. Individual politicians often find far more to be lost than gained in taking a readily identifiable stand on a controversial issue of social or economic policy." Richard B. Stewart, "The Reformation of American Administrative Law," 88 *Harvard L. Rev.* 1667, 1695 (1975). See also Landis, supra note 9, at pp. 51–55.

[14]Jerome Frank, *If Men Were Angels: Some Aspects of Government in a Democracy* (New York: Harper & Brothers, 1942), pp. 3–7. Landis once noted: "The prime key to the improvement of the administrative process is the selection of qualified personnel. Good men can make poor laws workable; poor men will wreak havoc with good laws." U.S. Senate, *Report on Regulatory Agencies to the President-Elect*, 86th Cong., 2d Sess. (1960), p. 66.

[15]"The *raison d'être* of the administrative process is the increasing need for more flexibility than is provided by either Congress or the courts. Modern regulation requires specialization, expertise, continuity of service, and flexibility for utilization of a variety of skills which would not be possible operating within a strict common-law framework." Peter Woll, *Administrative Law: The Informal Process* (Berkeley: University of California Press, 1963), p. 188. See also Dean Roscoe Pound, *Administrative Law: Its Growth, Procedure and Significance* (Pittsburgh, Pa.: University of Pittsburgh Press, 1942), p. 28.

[16]Abraham D. Sofaer, "Judicial Control of Informal Discretionary Adjudication and Enforcement," 72 *Columbia L. Rev.* 1293, 1296–97 (1972).

[17]"Advocates of discretionary decisionmaking can argue with some force that there is a value in flexible, empirical growth of the law and that the rules for resolving some problems are for one reason or another simply not susceptible of neat codification." J. Skelly Wright, "Beyond Discretionary Justice," 81 *Yale L. J.* 575, 593 (1972).

[18]*The Hoover Commission Report on the Organization of the Executive Branch of Government* (New York: McGraw-Hill, 1949), p. 6.

[19]Freund, supra note 11, at p. 97.

[20]Wright, supra note 17, at p. 576

[21]Kenneth Culp Davis, *Discretionary Justice: A Preliminary Inquiry* (Baton Route: Louisana State University Press, 1969), p. 25.

[22]Sofaer, supra note 16. The details of the study are presented in Abraham Sofaer, "The Change-of-Status Adjudication: A Case Study of the Informal Agency Process," 1 *Journal of Legal Studies* 349 (1972).

[23]Sofaer, supra note 16, at p. 1300.

[24]Id., at pp. 1300–1301.

[25]Id., at pp. 1301–2.

[26]Id., at p. 1374.

[27]This problem and the effort to deal with it through the enactment of the Federal Advisory Committee Act will be addressed in more detail in Chapter 11.

[28]Davis, supra note 21, at p. 4.

[29]Robert M. Cooper, "Administrative Justice and the Role of Discretion," 47 *Yale L. J.* 577, 582 (1938).

[30]Stewart, supra note 13, at p. 1676 n. 25.

[31]Freund, supra note 11, at p. 71.

[32]Henry J. Friendly, *The Federal Administrative Agencies: The Need for Better Definition of Standards* (Cambridge, Mass.: Harvard University Press, 1962), p. 8.

[33]Stephen R. Chitwood, "Legalizing Public Administration" (paper presented at the 1978 American Society for Public Administration Meeting.) The paper discusses the language of the Education for All Handicapped Children Act, Public Law 94-142, as a case in point.

[34]"The factors responsible for this lack of specificity are (1) the impossibility of specifying at the outset of new governmental ventures the precise policies to be followed; (2) lack of legislative resources to clarify directives; (3) lack of legislative incentives to clarify directives; (4) legislators' desire to avoid resolution of controversial policy issues; (5) the inherent variability of experience; (6) the limitations of language." Stewart, supra note 13, at p. 1677 n. 27.

[35]See, e.g., Thomas D. Morgan, "Achieving National Goals Through Federal Contracts: Giving Form to an Unconstrained Administrative Process," 1974 *Wisconsin L. Rev.* 301 (1974).

[36]Executive Order No. 12291, February 17, 1981, 46 Fed. Reg. 13193 (1981).

[37]Cooper, supra note 29, at p. 583. Cooper borrowed the language from John Dickinson, "Judicial Control of Official Discretion," 22 *American Political Science Rev.* 275, 277 (1928). Jerome Frank expressed a similar sentiment when he wrote: "It has been widely said that the first problem of today is to reconcile the Expert State and the Free State." Frank, supra note 14, at p. 18.

[38]This is true both of the use of expertise by organizations and the use of expertise by individuals within organizations. Michael Crozier's *The Bureaucratic Phenomenon* (Chicago: University of Chicago Press, 1964) provides a study of how lower level technicians in an industrial firm can use their technical expertise to their advantage. Managing so-called "knowledge workers" requires more sophisticated tech-

niques than earlier administrative environments precisely because employees understand that their expertise gives them power relative to others in an organization. See Frederick C. Mosher, "The Public Service in the Temporary Society," 31 *Public Admin. Rev.* 47 (1971). See also Peter Drucker, "Productivity and the Knowledge Worker," in *Business and Society in Change* (New York: American Telephone & Telegraph, 1975).

[39]Enough firms and organizations spend all or much of their time doing research for government agencies that they are often spoken of as the "third sector," as distinguished from the public and private sectors.

[40]See, e.g., *American Textile Manufacturers Inst. v. Donovan,* 69 L. Ed. 2d 185 (1981).

[41]An interesting case that shows the conflict over technical, political, and economic questions is *Pacific Legal Foundation v. Department of Transportation,* 593 F. 2d 1338 (D.C. Cir. 1979).

[42]*Environmental Defense Fund v. Ruckelshaus,* 439 F. 2d 584 (D.C. Cir. 1971).

[43]*International Harvester Co. v. Ruckelshaus,* 478 F. 2d 615 (D.C. Cir. 1973).

[44]See, e.g., Walter Gellhorn, *Federal Administrative Proceedings* (Baltimore: Johns Hopkins Press, 1941).

[45]Francis Rourke, *Bureaucracy, Politics, and Public Policy* (Boston: Little, Brown, 1969), and Philip Selznick, *TVA and the Grassroots* (New York: Harper & Row, 1949).

[46]W. Henry Lambright, *Governing Science and Technology* (New York: Oxford University Press, 1976).

[47]A. Lee Fritschler, *Smoking and Politics* 2d ed. (Englewood Cliffs, N.J.: Prentice-Hall, 1975).

[48]Federal Trade Commission Improvement Act of 1980, Public Law 96-252, 94 Stat. 374 (1980), 15 U.S.C. §§45, 46, 50, 57a, 57b-1 to 57b-4, 57c (1976).

[49]Oscar Kraines, *The World and Ideas of Ernst Freund: The Search for General Principles of Legislation and Administrative Law* (University: University of Alabama Press, 1974), pp. 10–11.

[50]Frank Goodnow, *Comparative Administrative Law* (New York: Putnam, 1893), pp. 138–40).

[51]See Elihu Root, "Public Service by the Bar," an address given April 30, 1916, and published in Robert Bacon and James Broun Scott, eds., *Addresses on Government and Citizenship* (Cambridge, Mass.: Harvard University Press, 1916), pp. 534–37, and John Dickinson, *Administrative Justice and the Supremacy of Law in the United States* (New York: Russell & Russell, 1927).

Scholars and practitioners of both law and administration had considerable difficulty dealing with the differences in the legal and managerial perspectives. Probably best known among this group is Woodrow Wilson, who leaned strongly to the managerial perspective in his famous 1887 article "The Study of Administration," later defined public administration as a subfield of public law. Arthur S. Link, "Woodrow Wilson and the Study of Administration" in Link, ed. *The Higher Realism of Woodrow Wilson and Other*

Essays (Nashville: Vanderbilt University Press, 1971), p. 42.

[52]Leonard D. White, *Introduction to the Study of Public Administration,* 4th ed. (New York: Macmillan, 1955), p. xvi.

[53]Dwight Waldo, 'Scope of the Theory of Public Administration," in James C. Charlesworth, ed., *Theory and Practice of Public Administration: Scope, Objectives, and Methods,* monograph no. 8, Annals of the American Academy of Political and Social Science (1968), pp. 14–15.

[54]Sofaer, supra note 16, at p. 1313.

[55]Davis, supra note 21, at p. 160.

[56]See, e.g., *Ohio Bell Telephone Co. v. Public Utilities Comm'n,* 301 U.S. 292 (1937), and *St. Joseph Stock Yards Co. v. United States,* 298 U.S. 38 (1936).

[57]*Securities and Exchange Comm'n v. Chenery,* 332 U.S. 194, 216 (1947), Justice Jackson dissenting.

[58]Id., at 207–9.

[59]Id., at 215, Justice Jackson dissenting.

[60]*Universal Camera Corp. v. National Labor Relations Board,* 340 U.S. 474 (1951).

[61]Id., at 490–91.

[62]*New York v. United States,* 342 U.S. 882, 884 (1951), Justice Douglas dissenting.

[63]See, e.g., *Klein v. Cohen,* 304 F. Supp. 275, 277 (D.C. Mass. 1969), and *Robertson v. Cameron,* 224 F. Supp. 60, 62 (D.C. D.C. 1063). See also *Jones v. Califano,* 576 F. 2d 12, 20 (2d Cir. 1978), and *Appalachian Power Co. v. EPA,* 477 F. 2d 495, 507 (4th Cir. 1973).

[64]*Capadora v. Celebreeze,* 356 F. 2d 1, 6 (2d Cir. 1966). See also *Aquavella v. Richardson,* 437 F. 2d 397, 403 (2d Cir. 1971); *Holmes v. New York City Housing Authority,* 398 F. 2d 262 (2d Cir. 1968); *Hornsby v. Allen,* 326 F. 2d 605 (5th Cir. 1964); *United States v. Atkins,* 323 F. 2d 733 (5th Cir. 1963); and *Shannon v. HUD,* 305 F. Supp. 205, 214 (E.D. Pa. 1969).

[65]It is a relatively common situation, at least for federal branch administrators, to find themselves facing conflicting interpretations of law. The cases over funding of abortions under Medicaid provide an example of this problem. See *Harris v. McRae,* 448 U.S. 297 (1980). Such conflicts may eventually be resolved by the Supreme Court, as was true of the Medicaid cases, but years can pass between the pronouncements of conflicting decisions and ultimate resolution of the conflict in the Supreme Court.

[66]*Citizens Ass'n of Georgetown v. Zoning Comm'n of Dist. of Columbia,* 477 F. 2d 402, 408 (D.C. Cir. 1973). See also *Airline Pilots Ass'n v. Civil Aeronautics Board,* 475 F. 2d 900, 906 (D.C. Cir. 1973); *Greater Boston Television Corp. v. Federal Communications Comm'n,* 444 F. 2d 841, 851 (D.C. Cir. 1971); *WAIT Radio v. Federal Communications Comm'n,* 418 F. 2d 1153, 1156 (D.C. Cir. 1969).

[67]Supra note 62.

[68]Supra note 57.

[69]*Mobil Oil Corp. v. Federal Power Comm'n,* 483 F. 2d 1238, 1254 (D.C. Cir. 1973).

[70]*American Iron and Steel Institute v. Environmental Protection Agency,* 526 F. 2d 1027, 1046 (3d Cir. 1975).

[71]*United States v. Fay,* 247 F. 2d 662, 669 (2d Cir. 1957).

[72]*Stanley v. Illinois*, 405 U.S. 645, 656 (1972).

[73]*Vlandis v. Kline*, 412 U.S. 441, 451 (1973). See also *Stanley v. Illinois*, supra note 72; *Cleveland Board of Education v. LaFleur*, 414 U.S. 632 (1974); *Bell v. Burson*, 402 U.S. 535 (1971).

[74]*Shapiro v. Thompson*, 394 U.S. 618, 636 (1969).

[75]*Frontiero v. Richardson*, 411 U.S. 677, 688 (1973). See also *Reed v. Reed*, 404 U.S. 71 (1971).

[76]U.S. House of Representatives, Task Force on Legal Services and Procedure, *Report on Legal Services and Procedure Prepared for the Commission on Organization of the Executive Branch of the Government*, House Doc. no. 128, 84th Cong., 1st Sess. (1955), p. 24. See also Davis, supra note 21.

[77]Wright, supra note 17, and Sofaer, supra note 16, both argue effectively that voluntary limitation of discretionary authority sounds good, but it does not generally happen.

[78]See, e.g., Lawrence C. Dodd and Richard L. Schott, *Congress and the Administrative State* (New York: Wiley, 1979).

[79]Raoul Berger, "Administrative Arbitrariness and Judicial Review," 65 *Columbia L. Rev.* 55, 81 (1965).

[80]See, e.g., *Columbus Board of Education v. Pennick*, 443 U.S. 449 (1979); *Milliken v. Bradley* (Milliken II), 433 U.S. 267 (1977); and *Swann v. Charlotte-Mechlenburg Board of Education*, 402 U.S. 1 (1971). These cases are concerned with school desegregation. In other areas of administration, see *Rhodes v. Chapman*, 69 L. Ed. 2d 59 (1981); *Hutto v. Finney*, 437 U.S. 678 (1978); *Halderman v. Pennhurst State School & Hospital*, 447 F. Supp. 495 (E.D. Pa. 1977); affirmed, 612 F. 2d 84 (1979), reversed on other grounds, 67 L. Ed. 2d 694 (1981); and *Wyatt v. Stickney*, 344 F. Supp. 387 (N.D. Ala. 1972).

[81]See, e.g., Donald L. Horowitz, *The Courts and Social Policy* (Washington, D.C.: The Brookings Institution, 1977).

[82]*Halderman* and *Wyatt*, supra note 80.

[83]See, e.g., *Owens v. City of Independence*, 445 U.S. 622 (1980), and *Maine v. Thiboutot*, 448 U.S. 1 (1980).

[84]See, e.g., *Rizzo v. Goode*, 423 U.S. 362 (1976).

Chapter 10

Politics and Regulatory Agencies:
Law and Politics in Administration

F ew words in modern English usage evoke such a strong and immediate reaction as does the word "regulation." The last two successful presidential candidates made the attack on the regulatory bureaucracy the cornerstone of their campaigns. However, although regulation is something Americans seemingly love to hate, they continue to clamor for more, different, or new types of regulation in response to problems that appear on the public agenda. In this chapter we consider the politics and administrative problems of regulation that affect many of the formal and informal administrative law processes discussed thus far. We examine first the paradoxical continued use of regulation as a policy instrument at the same time that antiregulatory sentiment is at a high point. Second, we consider the primary actors and institutions in the politics of regulatory agencies. Finally, we note efforts to "reform" the regulatory process in recent years.

THE WHY AND WHETHER OF REGULATION, OR "I HATE ALL OF BIG GOVERNMENT EXCEPT THE PART THAT BENEFITS ME"

The decade of the 1970s was marked by a reaction against extensive government regulation of various aspects of American life. Rhetoric was accompanied by action, for example, deregulation in airline operations,[1] rail service,[2] and trucking.[3] The arguments against different kinds of regulation range from a general dislike of having one's activities regulated, to calculations that regulation costs too much, to a more moderate but still strongly held view that regulation must be modified in response to demonstrated problems in administering it.

236   However, even as Americans expressed resentment at the polls by electing

237
Politics and
Regulatory
Agencies:
Law and
Politics in
Administration

candidates who promised deregulation, they were demanding that government—particularly the federal government—do something about the growing problem of toxic chemical and nuclear waste disposal. In 1971 the Council on Environmental Quality of the Nixon administration produced its report on the hazard to citizens and the environment from the inherent danger of misuse or lack of proper waste treatment of the over 1,000 new chemical compounds marketed each year.[4] In its investigations of toxic chemicals, Congress found brain damage was caused by exposure to Kepone, lead, mercury, and other heavy metals.[5] Products used to manufacture or refine items for commercial and retail markets, such as vinyl chloride, arsenic, asbestos, myrex, fluorocarbons, and polychlorinated biphenals (PCBs), were also found to be dangerous. In stating the need for the Toxic Substance Control Act,[6] the legislature noted that in 1975 as many Americans died of cancer as in all the battle deaths in Vietnam, Korea, and World War Two combined.[7] Congress also observed that the National Cancer Institute had found that 60 to 90 percent of those deaths could be attributed to environmental contaminants.[8]

These frightening reports began to attract public attention when studies found that significant medical problems were caused by low-level exposure to widely used substances such as asbestos and benzene.[9] Public opinion had seemingly become resistant to the barrage of reports that rats exposed to huge doses of some chemical contracted cancer. However, such news as the fact that a worker who has been exposed to asbestos and is a smoker has a likelihood of contracting cancer that is 92 times greater than average[10] had a great impact on public opinion.

In addition to the reports published in scientific journals and newspapers, specific incidents heightened anxiety and increased political pressure to deal with nuclear and toxic chemical wastes. The small upstate New York community of Pulaski, along with several neighboring towns, suffered an economic disaster when state fishery officials prohibited fishermen from keeping their catches because high levels of toxic chemicals in the waters had rendered the fish unsafe for human consumption.[11] Pulaski relied on the annual influx of sportsmen for its economic base. Then came the discovery of the Love Canal dump site.[12] Panic set in when the community realized that there were abnormally high incidences of cancer, especially among children who lived on or near the buried disposal site. The energy crisis of the early 1970s added to demands for wider use of nuclear-powered electrical generating facilities, but it was found that storing nuclear wastes in salt caves and other geological formations would not be safe.[13] Beyond that, it was learned that containers of nuclear wastes that had been dumped at sea in years past were leaking. The proverbial last straw was the realization, confirmed by private and governmental organizations, that illegally dumped chemicals and materials from unsafe dump sites were rapidly filtering into streams and underground aquifers from which communities draw drinking water. Hearings conducted in 1980 by a congressional subcommittee determined that there were some two hundred unprotected dump sites within one mile of the supply points for municipal water companies.[14] The subcommittee warned that the situation was actually worse, but inadequate or nonexistent monitoring facilities in various states and localities made it impossible to accurately assess the scope of the problem.

A number of groups demanded that the Environmental Protection Agency take action. Others urged the federal government not to act in haste, but to help state and local officials work out their own solutions with particular attention to local problems. Many state and local actors worried that federal government authorities would make their states dump sites for wastes generated elsewhere. One state attempted to prohibit transportation of nuclear wastes from other states to the dump site in that state.[15] On the other side, industrial officials were concerned that the federal administrators would overreact and impose detailed costly command and control regulations.

A compromise was reached under which state and local authorities would be permitted to develop waste disposal policies as long as they met minimum federal requirements.[16] Failure by state authorities to act would trigger federal administrative involvement. But, while state residents did not want action mandated by Washington, they were no more anxious to have disposal sites located in their communities by state officials. Some states began by establishing agencies to license private firms that wanted to establish and operate disposal facilities. The tension over disposal plant siting has been heightened by the fact that geological and population factors often severely limit the number of areas in a state where such facilities could be located. Conflict sometimes erupted between local officials and state authorities. In Georgia, for example, one firm sought a license from the state on property it was acquiring in rural Heard County. Local residents protested loudly; some even threatened violence.[17] Local officials countered the firm's plans by condemning the property involved for use as a county recreational facility. That tactic was under consideration by other Georgia communities when the state legislative session began. Though loath to be identified by their constituents as supporting state administrative authority over local sentiment, the legislators quickly realized that all or most communities would attempt to block the building of waste facilities in their areas. Under current law, state inaction would trigger federal intervention. The legislators gave a state authority power to deal with the situation, but it remains to be seen whether state officials can develop a set of rules and licensing processes that will survive the inevitable political and legal battle that will come with attempts to open waste treatment facilities

The Debate at the Macro-Level: Wiedenbaum versus Green

The inconsistency between regulatory rhetoric and action is in part attributable to the fact that the debate over the uses and abuses of regulation and the state of the regulatory establishment takes place at the macro-level. It is argued in general terms, with a few specific examples sprinkled in to prove one or another point. Decisions to employ regulatory tactics in particular problem areas, on the other hand, are often intensely pragmatic judgments.

The macro-level antiregulatory arguments have been so loudly and frequently repeated that one hardly needs to reiterate them.[18] Critics argue that regulation interferes with individual liberty and with the operation of the free market system. They also stress that the costs of regulatory administration are high, both in terms of the cost of the government institutions and officers needed to administer the regulatory programs and in terms of the costs of compliance with regulations to businesses, which are passed on to the consumer as increased costs for goods and services. The following comments by Nevada Senator Paul Laxalt and New Mexico Senator Harrison Schmitt are characteristic of antiregulatory rhetoric.

239

Politics and
Regulatory
Agencies:
Law and
Politics in
Administration

[Senator Laxalt:] Government regulation has become a popular subject. . . . Those who are regulated are almost unanimous in their criticism of regulation, how it affects their lives, and the amount of time and money they must spend complying, often with needless or conflicting regulations.[19]

[Senator Schmitt:] Mr. Chairman, . . . as you indicated in your opening statement, one does not have to spend more than a brief time with our constituents to find out what is troubling them. It is inflation and government regulation. . . .

Government is impersonal in the extreme. Service seems to be nonexistent. Through ever-increasing interference in our lives, regulation is eating the heart out of small- and medium-sized business and nonprofit institutions. Regulation is frustrating the initiative to be one's own boss, which is what made our country great. . . .

The growth of inflation and the growth of impersonal, frustrating Government closely parallels the growth of regulatory activity by the Federal Government. A study by Murray Weidenbaum of the Center for the Study of American Business found that the cost of administering the 41 agencies that are specifically regulatory in their activities increased from $2.2 billion in fiscal year 1974 to $4.8 billion in fiscal year 1979, a 115 percent increase. . . .

The Weidenbaum study concludes that Federal regulations alone will cost the private sector about $102.7 billion in 1979. . . . Whatever the figure is, it is big.

The Weidenbaum study . . . also states that federally mandated safety and environmental features have increased the price of the average automobile by $666 in 1978.[20]

Murray Weidenbaum, an economist formerly with the Nixon administration and at this writing a leading economic adviser in the Reagan administration, calculated the total economic impact of federal government regulations at more than $100 billion dollars. This assessment has been the centerpiece of antiregulatory rhetoric in Congress and in various interest group campaigns against regulation.

On a slightly different tack, the critics argue that the plethora of regulatory agencies has created major management problems in the federal government since the agencies are frequently multihead commissions whose policies are not coordinated by the chief executive.[21] Because they are independent of presidential control, critics contend that they are not held responsible to the electorate for their actions and are not responsive to the majority of the public.

Additionally, regulatory agencies have been charged with being staffed by overly zealous and impractical officials who are insensitive to the needs of the marketplace and who fail to place disagreements in their proper perspective. Administrators have been charged with "nitpicking" on trivial matters and bullying businessmen in what appears to be more an effort to win debating points than an attempt to accomplish the goals for which agencies were created. Indeed, the critics argue that the agencies have not accomplished their purposes.

Those who disagree with Weidenbaum, Friedman, and Laxalt et al. reply that the entire social and political order with its framework of laws is by definition a limitation on absolute freedom of action. It is natural that laws impose some limits on economic activity. The only time in our national history following industrialization that the marketplace was virtually free of regulation, it destroyed itself. Surely Adam Smith's *Wealth of Nations*[22] cannot be read to support deliberately false or deceptive trade practices or the rise of monopolies in important areas of the economy. Further, given the interrelatedness of the parts of the economy and complex interdependency of citizens in modern American society, government cannot avoid significant involvement in the economic life of the nation.

Admittedly, "federal regulation is often weak, wasteful, dilatory, and misguided. This conclusion, however, is the beginning of analysis, not its end. . . . Unfortunately, much of the debate over regulatory reform in our view is distorted by those who want not regulatory reform but regulatory abolition, not regulatory analysis but regulatory paralysis."[23] Mark Green of the Public Citizen's Congress Watch is one of the leading spokesmen for those opposed to widespread deregulation or restrictions on regulatory agency authority. Green et al. argue that while there may be a need to relax or restructure regulatory activity in some areas, for example, transportation route and rate determinations, this does not mean that government should abandon all active regulatory programs. In such areas as consumer, health, safety, and environmental regulation, government supplements the market by dealing with problems the market does not resolve.

In recent testimony before the Senate Government Affairs Committee, Green responded in detail to the deregulators. He asserted that "many regulated companies engaged in a massive propaganda campaign to smear federal consumer and environmental regulation."[24] Noting that the Business Roundtable study of the costs of regulation "cost about *200 times* the entire budget of the Public Citizen's Congress Watch," Green observed that the massive campaign in the media against regulation is extremely self-serving.[25] For example, one company "runs advertisements in national media with the Statue of Liberty hanging from a noose strung by Washington—the point, presumably, is that one of our basic liberties is the freedom to pollute. Indeed, [this company] understandably is unhappy with federal regulation: it paid the highest court-imposed fine ever for the destruction of wildlife, a fact omitted from its advertisements."[26]

Second, Green argued "corporate opponents of regulation have an incentive to exaggerate the costs of regulation—and they do."[27]

In the early 1970s, chemical manufacturers announced that a proposed OSHA standard on vinyl chloride, a proven carcinogen, could cost two million jobs and $65–$90 billion. "The Standard is simply beyond the compliance capability of the industry," said their trade association. OSHA implemented the standard and the industry complied, without job losses and at a cost one–two-hundreth of its original estimate. Recently, Secretary James Schlesinger wrote Secretary Ray Marshall to urge that he stop the proposed federal exposure standard for beryllium, another known carcinogen, because of its $150 million cost. DOE officials later conceded that their estimate derived from a "gross estimate based on rule of thumb" that was provided them by some beryllium manufacturers.[28]

Third, Green observed that every conceivable cost of regulation, real or imagined, is included in antiregulatory materials, but "the benefits of regulation are often ignored, immeasurable [and] substantial"[29] Some benefits arise because agencies have done what they were designed to do, while other benefits were positive externalities (unanticipated and unplanned dividends).

241
Politics and
Regulatory
Agencies:
Law and
Politics in
Administration

> An estimated 200,000 Americans are alive today who would be dead if the federal government wasn't regulating car and highway safety. By 1985 federal fuel economy standards will be saving 18 billion gallons of gasoline. . . . Between 1970 and 1976, air emissions of particulates declined by 41%. Also the two traditional measures of water pollution—biological oxygen demand and total suspended solids—fell by two-thirds due to the federal water pollution control program.[30]

Executives of major regulated industries admit that some regulatory programs do work:

> At a recent conference Fletcher Byrom, chairman of the Koppers Company, told a business audience that "you and I know that the market system would not give us environmental protection, worker safety and health. These are not economic things . . . they add value, not wealth; the only way to improve the quality of life is through intervention." Even Henry Ford, still vigorously opposing standards for passive restraint systems, told *Meet the Press* a year ago that "we wouldn't have the kind of safety built into automobiles that we had unless there had been a federal law."[31]

Green, citing a 1975 study by the MIT Center for Policy Alternatives, observed that firms forced by regulations to change products have developed products and processes that were better and more cost effective than the products that they earlier fought to save.[32] In addition, defenders of regulatory programs point out that new businesses with new jobs have been created as the result of such programs as water and air pollution control.

Green and his associates maintain that "many of the most cited studies of the costs of regulation are seriously flawed."[33] Because the calculations made by Weidenbaum and others have been so important in the debates over regulation, it is worthwhile to quote from two rather lengthy critiques of those estimates. First, the Subcommittee on Oversight and Investigations of the House Committee on Interstate and Foreign Commerce:

> Dr. Weidenbaum arrived at his figures in the following manner. First, he summed the available estimates of the cost of regulation by various regulatory agencies in 1976, and then he compared that figure to the budgets of those regulatory agencies. From these figures, he derived a multiplier of 20, i.e., the regulation cost to the private sector is 20 times that of the budget of the agency selected. In some cases where no estimates had been made of the cost of regulatory activity to the private sector, Dr. Weidenbaum carried those costs at zero, thus permitting him to argue that his numbers represent an underestimation of the true total cost to the private sector of regulatory initiatives.
>
> The major problem with using Dr. Weidenbaum's study to show that the cost of government regulation is excessive—as it has been used consistently—is that the study by itself, is meaningless. Even if its estimate is correct—or, for that matter, low—the study did not attempt to analyze

whether the benefits of those regulations exceed their dollar cost. Of course, if it were to be discovered that the benefits exceeded the cost, then most economists would agree that the effect of the regulations would be deflationary. . . .

The Subcommittee also believes that Dr. Weidenbaum's study misses the mark even in calculating the costs of regulation because it mixes apples and oranges. He includes old line cartel regulatory agencies such as the Interstate Commerce Commission with newer social regulatory agencies such as the Environmental Protection Agency. Students with such diverse viewpoints as James C. Miller III and Ralph Nader support the overhaul of the regulatory procedures and, indeed, of the basic laws involved in the cartel-type regulatory agencies. This widespread support helped result in the recently enacted laws deregulating airlines, trucking and railroads.

The regulatory reform debate does not center around these old-line cartel regulations. Nor does it focus on agencies whose sole function is to police the rules of the game, such as the Antitrust Division of the Justice Department or the Patent and Copyright Office. Nor does it focus on agencies whose primary purpose is to police certain activities which the public has long held to be anti-social and whose products the Congress has either banned or closely regulated, such as the Drug Enforcement Administration and the Bureau of Alcohol, Tobacco and Firearms in the Treasury Department. Yet, Dr. Weidenbaum includes these agencies in his estimate of the cost of regulation.

In addition, there is considerable debate as to the correctness of Dr. Weidenbaum's multiplier of 20. Of the $63 billion of costs Dr. Weidenbaum aggregated for 1976, some $25 billion involved an estimate of the cost imposed by the paperwork required by Federal agencies for such things as IRS forms, Census forms, and forms for government contracts, subsidies and loans, as well as for the social regulatory programs. This estimate was compiled by the Commission on Federal Paperwork. However, Green and Weitzman at the Subcommittee's hearings cited in rebuttal a later, November 17, 1978, General Accounting Office (GAO) report that estimated the paperwork burden for Federal programs which GAO and OMB monitor at $1 billion and the total cost of Federal paperwork at $5 billion.

Inasmuch as 40 percent of the $63 billion estimate of federal regulatory costs was attributable to this paperwork component in the Weidenbaum analysis, if its real cost is only one-fifth of Dr. Weidenbaum's assumption, then a drastic reduction in his multiplier to 20 would be in order. . . .

The Subcommittee made no attempt to revise Dr. Weidenbaum's estimates of the total cost of Federal regulation; however, we believe that several of his key assumptions are of questionable validity. If they are, indeed, incorrect, then his estimates would have to be revised downward drastically. Second, his figures are so broadbased as to be meaningless with respect to the central issue of the regulatory debate—the value of social regulation. Third, regardless of the inaccuracy of his figures, no judgments on the utility of Federal regulations can be made without having estimates for the benefits of these regulations.[34]

Green also rebuts Weidenbaum's figures:

243
Politics and
Regulatory
Agencies:
Law and
Politics in
Administration

• Most fundamentally, his emphasis on costs and neglect of benefits makes as much economic sense as denouncing Mobil for $32 billion in costs a year—and failing to say it also produces $34 billion in revenues. What is obviously meaningful is *net* costs, which Weidenbaum neither produces nor adequately acknowledges as he scores polemical points with his $100 billion scare number.

• In testimony and speeches he mostly attacks health/safety regulation, which comprises only about one-third of his aggregate total. The other two-thirds are the costs of classic cartel regulation—ICC, CAB—and federal paperwork. And most of the federal paperwork costs relates to IRS forms, not OSHA.

• His conclusion that federal environmental and safety standards add $666 to the price of a new car is based on a recalculation of BLS data that BLS officials have said is invalid. He wrongly assumes that the intial cost of a safety standard never goes down. But there is a learning curve for auto engineers, who over time can meet standards at lower cost. A NHTSA study in 1976 asked car companies how much lower their retail prices would be if there were no safety standards. The answer: an average of $80 per car.

• Recently, the Business Roundtable released its study, conducted by Arthur Anderson & Co., of the incremental costs of six federal programs (EPA, EEO, OSHA, DOE, ERISA, FTC) to 48 giant companies. The total pre-tax cost of $2.6 billion was reportedly described as the "tip of the iceberg" by Frank Cary, chairman of IBM and of the Roundtable's "Task Force on Regulation." But there is just no way that the Roundtable's conclusion of $2.6 billion in regulatory costs can be reconciled with Mr. Weidenbaum's $102.7 billion estimate. Since the 48 companies involved are the largest in the country and the six agencies among those most attacked by business, the Roundtable study is more the body of the iceberg than its tip.

• For example, the Roundtable estimates the incremental cost of OSHA regulations at *$184 million* a year to its subjects. Mr. Weidenbaum concludes that OSHA costs *$3.5 billion* a year. Yet as several studies have demonstrated, American business was spending nearly this amount *before* the creation of OSHA. Weidenbaum confuses ordinary business expenses for regulatory costs.

• A Library of Congress analysis also criticizes Weidenbaum because many of the studies he depends on are old and no longer applicable, because "there are unresolved problems of double counting and inaccurate addition," because his paperwork costs to corporations include filling out forms for federal contracts, subsidies and loans, and because his 1:20 multiplier—which is how he gets up to $100 plus billion—is largely conjectural. This September 1978 analysis concludes that his study has "enough questionable components to make the totals arrived at suspect and of doubtful validity."[35]

The debate between the macro-level critics and defenders of regulation will continue, with each side attempting to convince legislatures at all levels of government to take or refrain from taking some regulatory action.

Regulation as a Policy Option

The purpose here is not to tell the legislature what it should do in any given situation, but rather to examine situations in which a regulatory approach to problem solving has been chosen. Regulation is one of several possible types of policy that the legislature may elect to employ. Decisions about which approach should be pursued come from what is generally referred to as the public policy process.

The policy process is conceptualized in different ways by leading authors in the field,[36] but most ask a series of nearly identical questions for each stage of the process.[37] The following model is typical. Policymaking is made up of several stages of decisionmaking: problem identification; policy formulation; policy adoption; then implementation, evaluation, and, possibly, policy termination.

Once a problem arises, the process of identifying it begins. What is the problem? Should it be on the public agenda (those problems that require public rather than private attention)? What priority should this problem be assigned relative to other problems on the public agenda?

The next stage is policy formulation. What policy should government use to deal with this problem? What are the options available for resolving the problem? Frohock, relying heavily on Lowi's work, has developed a five-part typology describing the major types of policy options that the legislature might consider.[38]

The first category is *regulatory policy*. Regulatory programs place limits on various forms of activity. Regulatory bodies may, for example, limit access to business or the professions, as in the case of medical association or bar association controlled licensing of physicians and attorneys. They may set routes and rates, as for utility or taxi cab companies. Regulators may be charged with ensuring fair trade practices, or health, safety, or other aspects of business activity. Regulatory administrators may use a carrot-and-stick approach in dealing with regulated parties or develop innovative techniques of regulation,[39] but basically regulation is, to one degree or another, coercive.[40] The extent of coerciveness varies. One agency can threaten only bad publicity, while in another officials have substantial coercive power, "like a shotgun behind the door," but try to avoid using available sanctions. Some regulatory programs have authority to impose many sanctions, up to and including criminal prosecutions. Regulatory programs that rely heavily on the use of coercive authority are generally referred to as command-and-control type regulation.

A second category of policy option is *distributive policy*. "Distributive policies grant goods and services to specific segments of the population."[41] Such programs as Veterans benefits and Aid to Families with Dependent Children (AFDC) are intended to dispense assistance to those who qualify. The difficulty for the legislature, and later for administrators, is to properly define the eligible members of the target group and then to select the agencies and procedures by which to disburse the funds.

A third type of policy is *redistributive policy*, which is "aim[ed] at rearranging one or more of the basic schedules of social and economic rewards."[42] The most frequently cited example of a redistributive policy is the progressive income tax, which attempts to ease the burdens on the poorer members of the society by placing the major burden for support of social programs and governmental expenditures on the wealthier citizens.

A fourth type is what Frohock calls a *capitalization policy*. In some respects similar to distributive policies, capitalization policies provide subsidies, tax advantages, or other financial devices that aid in capital formation for plant or equipment modernization. The purpose is to provide incentives for the private sector to develop or expand industries in needed areas of the economy or to aid beleaguered businesses such as the family farm.

245

Politics and
Regulatory
Agencies:
Law and
Politics in
Administration

Finally, some responses to public problems come in the form of *ethical policies*,[43] of which the Ethics in Government Act[44] is an example. Although it has some regulatory aspects, the Ethics in Government Act encourages public servants to note and act on possible conflicts of interest, and attempts to promote public support for civil servants by publicizing their efforts to prevent unethical practices.

After the policymaking body has selected a type of policy and surveyed the specific options available within that policy area, it must consider which means will likely work best. What are the costs and benefits for each option as far as they can be analyzed?

The problems encountered in discussing costs and benefits of regulatory programs are central to policy formulation, adoption, and evaluation. The idea that there ought to be a relationship between costs and benefits is intuitively appealing, but, on reflection, turns out to be considerably more complex than is readily apparent.[45] For present purposes, two problems are particularly important: (1) economic versus political perspectives on regulatory policy, and (2) technical difficulties in computing costs and benefits.

James Q. Wilson has addressed the important differences between economic and political perspectives on regulatory policy. He observed that one need not give up all concern about making rational and effective public policies to understand that the attempt to apply hard economic analysis techniques to the public policy process will not explain behavior, and often will not lead to better policies.[46] He bases his conclusion on three differences in the economic and political perspectives on policy.

> First, politics concerns preferences that do not always have a common market measuring rod. In an economic market, we seek to maximize our "utility," a goal that substantively can be almost anything but in practice involves things that have, or can easily be given, money values. . . .
>
> In nonmarket relationships, such as in voluntary associations or in legislatures, we may also behave in a rationally self-interested manner—but we do so in a setting that does not usually permit monetary (or quantitative) values to be assigned to our competing preferences in any nonarbitrary way. . . .
>
> Second, political action requires assembling majority coalitions to make decisions that bind everyone whether or not he belongs to that coalition. When we make purchases in a market, we commit only ourselves, and we consume as much or as little of a given product as we wish. When we participate in making decisions in the political arena, we are implicitly committing others as well as ourselves, and we are "consuming" not only a known product (such as the candidate for whom we vote) but also a large number of unknown products (all the policies the winning candidate will help enact). . . .
>
> The third and most important difference between economics and politics is that whereas economics is based on the assumption that

preferences are given, politics must take into account the efforts made to change preferences.[47]

What problems ought to be on the public agenda, what priority to assign a particular problem, what policy options are available, who will benefit from alternative policy choices, and who will pay are political decisions shaped by a variety of forces and factors, only some of which are amenable to economic analysis. "Politics differs from economics in that it manages conflict by forming heterogenous coalitions out of persons with changeable and incommensurable preferences in order to make binding decisions for everyone."[48]

The major problem with failing to understand the important distinctions between these perspectives can be summed up by the statement: "Americans love numbers."[49] When offered what appears to be a scientific analysis of a problem and possible solutions it is tempting to let the numbers dominate the debate.[50] The Report of the Subcommittee on Oversight and Investigations gives an example of excessive reliance on cost-benefit economic-efficiency-oriented models of public policy analysis and decisionmaking:

> Let's examine . . . the variables which would have been involved if the government of Abraham Lincoln had been required to perform a cost-benefit analysis on a proposed Emancipation Proclamation.
>
> Some of the non-trivial variables on the cost side would have been the loss of equity (property value) to the slaveholders; the effect on economic production of a complete alteration of the system of production and distribution in the Southern States; the direct and indirect costs of introducing a wage system in those states; the impact on the war effort (increased Southern resistance); the extent and timing of a migration of unskilled Blacks into the North with resulting employment impacts and demands on private charities; and the additional costs of maintaining public order in the Southern military districts.
>
> Each of these costs would have had to have been estimated for a variety of industries and regions and then generalized into a single accounting system. Inasmuch as the impacts would not have occurred simultaneously, each one would have had to have been estimated for a given period of time.
>
> On the benefits side, some of the easier variables to estimate would have been essentially offsets to the cost, such as the potential long-run increase in productivity resulting from a switch to a wage system, the additional manpower available to the Northern Army, and the additional labor to be employed in post-war industrialization and to settle the West. The most difficult quantification problem would have been in assigning a dollar value to human dignity and freedom. Again, each one would have had to have been estimated for a given time to make the comparisons meaningful.
>
> Inasmuch as economic historians tell us that slavery was a profitable system, the cost benefit analysis, at least in the short run, probably would have deemed that Lincoln not free the slaves unless a substantial dollar value was assigned to human dignity and freedom.[51]

As President Roosevelt is reputed to have said to one of his policy analysts, the logic is fine, but the conclusion is absolutely wrong.[52]

247
Politics and
Regulatory
Agencies:
Law and
Politics in
Administration

The second concern in considering costs versus benefits is that there are a host of specific technical problems. The Subcommittee Report mentioned several. First, computations of costs of particular regulatory programs are often very weak.[53] The source of data for estimating costs is often the industry that is now, or is about to be, regulated. Such data have proven over the years to be fraught with problems of bias.[54] Second, it found that such analyses rarely take account of technological change (the learning curve) as a factor that reduces costs of programs over time.[55] Third, the subcommittee found that it is extremely difficult to deal with incremental costs, that is, to determine which costs are attributable to a particular government policy.[56] The subcommittee observed that techniques for calculating benefits are "primitive."[57] To calculate the benefits of a particular program, one must be able to anticipate the specific effects of a given policy decision.[58] This means forecasting accurately and at a level of specificity that in many instances exceeds our capacity for calculation. Another problem is "applying dollar values to items that lack a market price."[59] Nor are costs and benefits always distributed fairly, hence the costs and benefits of a given type of activity, and the policies created to deal with it, may not allow comparability in analysis.[60]

Finally, a major problem is the ethical complexity of the choice that is made. Although no one likes to place a dollar value on human life, the loss of a limb, or pain and suffering from an illness or injury, it is done all the time. Courts assign values in wrongful death suits and insurance companies assign costs and risks in actuarial judgments every day. But courts are acting after the fact, and insurance companies are merely making knowledgeable predictions about events over which they have little or no control. Policymakers have a choice, in which ethical considerations are involved.

After a policy is formulated, it must be adopted. Which organizations in government must approve the program? The determination of which congressional committees will consider a proposed policy can make all the difference to the success or failure of the policy. Advocates must determine where the money will come from to administer the program. Also extremely important are decisions on which organization will administer the program and who will provide oversight to ensure the proper administration of the policy. Few legislators wish to be accused of creating more bureaucracy by adding a new agency to administer a new policy, but there are drawbacks to assigning a new program to an existing agency. An old agency has an existing agenda of problems and responsibilities and a limited amount of resources to do its job. The new program, particularly if it is not adequately funded, may not receive the attention it would in a new agency whose existence revolves around administering the new program.

Once a policy is adopted, it must be implemented. The determinations as to the best strategies and tactics for executing the provisions of a new law are complex. The institutional mechanisms and processes to administer the program must be designed and constructed. Priorities for resource allocation must be developed. This can be particularly difficult if the legislation was poorly crafted, the agency must immediately resolve a crisis (as was the case with the Department of Energy), or if statutory time limits were placed on the development of rules or guidelines for the program.

Policy evaluation is, or should be, an ongoing process that determines how well the program in operation meets the objectives defined in the formulation and adoption stages. Evaluators must determine whether unexpected costs have arisen in administering the program, e.g., increased acid rain has come from encouraging the power industry to use more coal. The actual operating costs must be compared with the costs that were anticipated at the time of adoption.

Finally, and occasionally, the policy process comes to a stage known as policy termination. The problem is to determine how to bring an end to outdated or ineffective programs. Termination is difficult because of the loss of jobs to those involved in the program and because over the years agencies build strong relationships with client organizations. Interest groups may mobilize in support of the program.

Regulation is neither right or wrong, good or bad, in the abstract. Regulatory programs are policy choices selected from among available alternatives during the give and take of the policy process to deal with a public problem that found its way onto the public policy agenda. Public policies are political choices that may or may not be reconcilable with economic efficiency criteria. In some situations, regulatory programs may be appropriate, while other contexts might be better suited to alternative strategies. Ultimately, the choice is not based on economics or on the views of policy analysts, but is a political judgment.

Why Have Policymakers Opted for Regulation?

Monographs and articles are filled with explanations of why policymakers have chosen regulation in various policy contexts. The Ribicoff Committee's *Study on Federal Regulation* found a number of general recurring themes in regulatory programs.[61] What follows is a summary, based on the Ribicoff study, of the more frequently cited reasons.

1. *The need to regulate natural monopoly.*

Utility services such as natural gas, electricity, and, more recently, cable television are often monopolies within a particular service area. Theoretically, a purchaser has some choices in this area, but as a practical matter homeowners and apartment dwellers have little choice in where to buy their utilities. Regulation is used to substitute for the market forces which would not be present in a monopoly.

2. *Efforts to encourage proper use of natural resources.*

Though it is in everyone's long-run best interest to use natural resources wisely, near-term market pressures and incentives often cause abuse of those resources.[62] Regulatory programs often seek to curb such abuses.

3. *The need to ensure that participants in the marketplace take account of externalities or "spillover" effects of their actions.*

Frequently, actions have unanticipated consequences that market forces will not resolve. For example, the burning of fossil fuels in power facilities and industrial plants produces chemicals that are carried long distances on air currents. When these chemicals mix with atmospheric moisture and fall as precipitation, they become acid rain. A subcommittee of the House Committee on Interstate and Foreign Commerce found that 100 of 214 Adirondack (upstate New York) lakes are acidified to the point that fish and most organic life are unable to survive.[63] In a sample of 350 of its many lakes, Wisconsin officials found that 47 had been acidified; that most lakes tested had a level of acidity ten times higher than normal.[64] More than 75 percent of the sulfur pollution falling in New England comes from outside that region.[65] The people who burn the fuels have economic incentives to burn the cheapest fuel available, such as high sulfur coal, and to resist requests to install costly air pollution control equipment. They are not the people who feel the acid rain effects. On the other hand, those who have the acid rain and therefore the incentive to do something about the air pollution, are not in a position to take such action. Regulation is used to force producers and consumers to take account of the external effects of their actions.

249
Politics and
Regulatory
Agencies:
Law and
Politics in
Administration

4. *Problems of unavailability or inadequacy of information about health, safety or other concerns.*

A free market system assumes that one can choose among competing alternatives in the marketplace and that one can acquire information about those alternatives on which to base decisions. In a complex scientific world, it is often difficult or impossible for consumers to acquire information they need. Regulation can force sellers to provide labeling information on the contents or safety features of their products to enable the consumer to make rational market choices.

5. *Prevention of destructive competition.*

If price competition becomes active enough, it can have destructive consequences that may not be apparent until far enough into the future that consumers would not take the negative factors into consideration in their initial market choices.[66] Such competition can also destabilize the marketplace as it did during the depression of the '30s. Regulation seeks to moderate the negative effects.

6. *Protection of consumers from sharply rising prices and windfall profits.*

Dramatic shifts in market conditions such as gasoline, diesel, and fuel oil price increases during the 1970s had devastating impacts on the national economy in general. They also resulted in particularly harsh effects on those who live in cold climates or in areas with no public transportation systems, and on those living on fixed incomes. Price limits have been used on temporary or permanent bases in an attempt to mitigate the effects of such dramatic market forces.

7. *Dangers of price discrimination.*

Regulation historically has been used to curb attempts to control markets by using discriminatory pricing policies, for example, the battle in the late 1900s between the railroads and farmers, who asserted that the carriers were using price discrimination to force farmers to do business on railroad terms. Another example is the recent allegation that major oil companies have used discriminatory wholesale prices and supply policies to drive independent gasoline retailers out of business.

8. *Efforts to promote key industries.*

Regulation has been used to promote, protect, and guide (or drive, depending on one's ideological orientation) new or desired industries. The Civil Aeronautics Board was created to promote air transport using various kinds of regulation. Establishment of minimum rates by regulation insulates the industry from price competition and permits some of the costs of innovation and the development of management techniques to be passed through in pricing without penalties.

9. *Decisions to provide service to special groups through the use of cross-subsidies.*

Market forces may provide incentives for certain industries to limit service to particularly lucrative markets and abandon service to smaller communities. But national policy may favor continued service to ensure complete networks of services to all parts of the country. Regulation has been used with subsidies to permit, for example, air carriers to argue for higher air fares on all routes to subsidize continued service to smaller communities.

10. *Control of competing industries.*

It is sometimes felt to be in the national interest to have coherent national policies for particular areas. The legislature may charge an agency with responsibility to coordinate in that area so as to preserve the maximum number of options. Two examples are transportation and energy policy. The Interstate Commerce Commission was encouraged to set rates in such a way that railroads, trucking, and barge transport would all be available to future transportation planners. The Department of Energy has an obligation to assist in developing and maintaining a variety of energy options for the future.

11. *Preservation of established property rights.*

A television station license issued by the Federal Communications Commission makes the difference between a collection of electronics equipment and a prosperous business. Protecting this kind of asserted property right is a complex problem.

The history of regulatory policies shows that decisions to impose regulation are most often intensely pragmatic reactions to particular problems and not theoretical judgments about market deficiencies. Many times policies were adopted because individuals or firms had abused others by manipulations of the market system, or because certain problems were becoming increasingly unacceptable to the public. The Securities and Exchange Commission was created to administer a variety of regulatory programs because of massive repeated proven abuses of the securities markets by private individuals and business firms.[67] The Food and Drug Administration was created in response to wretched conditions in the food and drug industries that produced adulterated food and impure, unsafe and ineffective drugs.[68] The National Labor Relations Board came into existence, and was later strengthened, to ensure fair labor standards at a time when the nation was rocked by violent labor-management confrontations. Similarly, the new agencies created in the 1960s and '70s came about through pragmatic political judgments. Congress created the highway safety regulatory programs because 50,000 Americans were killed annually in traffic accidents and automobile manufacturers seemed unwilling to improve safety features.[69] The legislative history of the Consumer Product Safety Commission legislation indicates that this body was created because Congress determined that 20 million people were injured each year in product-related accidents; of this number 110,000 resulted in permanent disability and 30,000 died.[70] The legislative history of the Occupational Safety and Health Administration states that more workers were killed in job-related accidents in the four years prior to the act than had died in

Vietnam in the same period.[71] The Federal Elections Commission was created because the Watergate debacle had demonstrated gross abuses of campaign financing.[72] Similar findings can be found in most regulatory legislative histories.[73]

ORGANIZATIONAL ASPECTS OF REGULATORY ADMINISTRATION: LIFE IN A POLITICAL ENVIRONMENT

Whatever gave rise to a regulatory program, the policies are assigned to an agency, either an executive branch agency or an independent regulatory commission, for administration. Those who work in or deal with regulatory agencies should be alert to the opportunities and dangers that their organizations face in the political environment in which they operate.

Bernstein's Life Cycle of a Regulatory Commission

One of the most frequently cited critiques of regulatory agencies, and in particular of independent regulatory commissions, is Marver Bernstein's *Regulating Business by Independent Commission*.[74] Bernstein used a conceptual framework to describe the operation of regulatory commissions, which he called "The Life Cycle of a Regulatory Commission."[75] "Despite variations in time sequence and the particular circumstances surrounding the creation of each one, the national independent commissions have experienced roughly similar periods of growth, maturity, and decline."[76] Bernstein's work has itself been criticized because not all commissions have suffered the fate he described and because the pitfalls he ascribed to independent commissions may afflict other kinds of organizations. Nevertheless, Bernstein's model can illustrate both opportunities and problems that an administrator in a regulatory agency might see. His life cycle consists of four phases: "gestation," "youth," "maturity," and "old age."

The gestation of regulatory bodies begins, according to Bernstein, when a major problem appears. An example would be the OPEC embargo on the sale of oil. As the situation degenerates (e.g., when the gas lines formed), public distress increases. Interest groups emerge and demand that the legislature act to resolve the problem. For many reasons, says Bernstein, the legislature will enact a compromise bill that may very well be "out of date by the time it is enacted."

In its youth, the regulatory agency is at a disadvantage relative to regulated industry in terms of expertise and experience, but it does have crusading zeal.[77] Bernstein notes that new regulatory bodies have a relatively high level of political support in their first few years, which the administrators may or may not be able to exploit. They may take a relatively bold and expansive view of their opportunities and responsibilities in the initial months of the agency's life.

Once the regulated groups realize that the regulatory program will indeed be implemented, they will attempt to influence appointments to key positions in the agency.

> Most commissions have tried initially to achieve independence from regulated groups. They have embarked on the regulatory task with some exuberance and with a desire to clarify goals and mark out basic policies.

But the characteristics of youth have only a transitory existence and soon fade away. [78]

"In the period of maturity, regulation usually becomes more positive in its approach. Its functions are less those of a policeman and more like that of a manager of an industry." [79] At this point, the agency may be considered to be less an outside umpire of regulated activity and more like a facilitator. The Interstate Commerce Commission and the Civil Aeronautics Board are two examples of agencies that for years have been viewed in this light. In this period of operation, Bernstein holds, homeostasis takes over. Routine is comfortable and therefore important. Neither organizational life nor the policy it produces maintains vitality. The agency does not actively press issues that have not been forced on it. Existing rules, precedents, and court opinions tend to increase courtlike formality in agency proceedings.

> The close of the period of maturity is marked by the commission's surrender to the regulated. Politically isolated, lacking a firm basis of public support, lethargic in attitude and approach and bogged down by precedents and backlogs, unsupported in its demand for more staff and money, the commission finally becomes a captive of the regulated group. [80]

Finally, the agency slips into old age, the period Bernstein describes as "debility and decline." The agency is without sufficient power or initiative to take any significant action against those it is charged with regulating. [81] Many of the better people have left the agency and those who remain no longer have a strong sense of purpose. Both operations and the quality of management decisions decline.

Organizational Pressures, the Capture Thesis, and Political Styles

Those who disagree with Bernstein acknowledge that all agencies, including regulatory commissions, are vulnerable to the failings he described, but add that not all agencies, not even all commissions, actually succumb to them. James Q. Wilson points out that while some regulatory agencies may fall victim to the capture thesis, others do not. [82] In fact, in a number of instances agencies have made important policy decisions that adversely affect very powerful interests, contrary to Bernstein's captive agency theory. Wilson argues that regulatory agency behavior may be primarily conditioned by the style of political interactions that characterize an agency's political environment. Specifically, the political climate in which an agency operates is determined by the manner in which the costs and benefits of the policy administered by the agency are distributed. [83] But he warns that costs and benefits, in this context, refer to beliefs and values as well as to economic interests.

Wilson argues that where the public policy administered by an agency distributes benefits and costs widely across the population, what he calls "majoritarian politics" will prevail. (See Figure 10-1, which is a two-dimensional representation of Wilson's framework.) "Interest groups have little incentive to form around such issues because no small, definable segment of society (an industry, an occupation, a locality) can expect to capture a disproportionate share of the benefits or avoid a disproportionate share of the burdens." [84] Antitrust legislation is an example of a regulatory program born and operated in majoritarian politics.

253
Politics and
Regulatory
Agencies:
Law and
Politics in
Administration

Distribution of costs

		Wide	Narrow
Distribution of benefits	Wide	Majoritarian	Entrepreneurial
	Narrow	Client	Interest group

Figure 10-1 *Wilson's Framework: Political Styles and Regulatory Environments*
SOURCE: Derived from James Q. Wilson, *The Politics of Regulation* (New York: Basic Books, 1980).

Where the distribution of costs and benefits is narrow, Wilson says "interest group politics" predominate. In such situations, the general public may not become aroused, but the interest groups that stand to gain or lose from administration of the policy have a "strong incentive to organize and exercise political influence."[85] Wilson cites various labor-management relations regulations as situations in which interest groups compete but the conflict remains relatively narrow.

"Client politics" characterize situations in which costs are widely distributed and benefits narrowly concentrated.

> Some small, easily organized group will benefit and thus has a powerful incentive to organize and lobby; the costs of the benefit are distributed at a low per capita over a large number of people, and hence they have little incentive to organize in opposition—if, indeed, they even hear of the policy. . . . Absent . . . watchdog organizations, however, client politics produces regulatory legislation that most nearly approximates the producer-dominance [or capture] model.[86]

Finally, Wilson terms as "entrepreneurial politics" policy activity in areas in which costs are rather narrowly concentrated but benefits are widely distributed. Much of the health and safety regulatory activity of the past two decades involved entrepreneurial politics as a major factor in its origins and operation. Ralph Nader is one of the leading policy entrepreneurs of this period.[87]

Wilson's typology of political styles that affect the development and implementation of regulatory politics is descriptive of some aspects of regulatory activity. As a theoretical device it is vulnerable to several significant criticisms.[88] But Wilson's work does indicate that those who would understand regulatory politics solely from the premise that agencies behave as they do because they are captured by the regulated organizations vastly oversimplifies the situation. Over time, different agencies that administer regulatory programs face a variety of political styles from changing interest groups.

Internal Dynamics and Regulatory Organizations

In addition to an understanding of their political environment and the legislature's black letter law requirements, administrators must be sensitive to the internal dynamics of regulatory agencies.

As Graham Allison has argued, everyone wants to believe that his or her agency is a rational policymaker, but in fact, much agency decisionmaking can be better understood by examining patterns of interaction within an organization than by considering careful calculations about costs and benefits of all available policy options.[89] Subunits and departments within organizations shape routines and develop channels of communication. These organizational routines, communications links, and informal relationships among units have important effects on decisionmaking.

Second, the people who operate organizations are often not stable management teams. James Thompson observed that organizations are frequently directed by shifting coalitions of individuals.[90] The coalitions change as individuals within the organization perceive themselves to be affected by changing patterns of professional and personal rewards and risks. Those who expect regulatory agencies to operate consistently over an extended period of time may understand the importance of organizational routines, but may not be aware of changing patterns of influence among key agency personnel.

Individual bureaucratic politics also matter.[91] Personalities come and go, particularly in regulatory agencies, and each administrator comes to the agency with differing capabilities and skills for playing bureaucratic politics. Even experienced administrators vary in how well they can perform in a particular organization. Administrators also differ in terms of their skill in interacting with important elements in the political environment. This can have a significant effect on the overall ability of the organization to maximize its goals and to avoid or neutralize threats. Bureaucratic politics skills are particularly important internally in regulatory agencies, which employ experts from different scientific disciplines or professions, e.g., law or medicine. Effective working relations between technical experts and administrative generalists are often difficult to maintain.

Extensive consideration is often given to the size and structure of an agency. However, because regulatory agencies are created during different historical periods to deal with special problems in particular ways, they vary dramatically in both size and form. For example, the Ribicoff Committee asked:

> What is the optimal size of a regulatory Commission? As Professor Cushman has pointed out, "There is no ideal size. When Lincoln was asked how long a soldier's legs ought to be, he replied that they should be long enough to reach from his body to the ground; and so a commission ought to be big enough or small enough to perform efficiently the task assigned to it."[92]

A good deal has been written suggesting that regulatory agencies be standardized into single-administrator-headed executive branch agencies. Much of this commentary was prepared by people who worked for the chief executive and, not surprisingly, were interested in making regulatory agencies more manageable by and politically responsive to the President who is, after all, the chief executive officer of government.[93] This reorganization-standardization approach to regulatory agencies has not been widely accepted. The need for balanced commission membership, collegial decisionmaking, and varying degrees of independence from pressure from current political demands are still of concern to many legislators.[94] Many of the multiheaded commissions' statutes permit the president to designate the chair and vest in that person management authority for the basic administration of agency operations, as opposed to substantive policymaking, which remains with the entire commission.

This book has considered the laws and institutions that shape regulatory activities. It has also considered some of the problems and prospects faced by those who administer the agencies, the regulated parties, and the judges who review agency regulations or adjudications brought under regulations. We turn now to the other participants in the regulatory process: the President, the Congress, and the public.

THE PRESIDENT AND THE REGULATORY PROCESS

The President is an important figure in regulatory administration. However, the chief executive's opportunities and resources are more complex than most recognize. The key elements necessary to an understanding of the President's role are: an assessment of the actual power the chief executive possesses; a consideration of the appointments process; an awareness of White House budgetary authority; a view of the executive policy clearance process; and a critical assessment of presidential consultation, control, and coordination of regulatory policy.

Presidential Power: Real and Imagined

Presidents have several more or less formal sources of authority at their disposal to deal with regulatory agencies, including appointment and removal powers, budgetary authority, legislative clearance power, and coordination and control authority. However, the power of the chief executive over the regulatory bureaucracy may be more apparent than real. There are several reasons for this disparity.

First, there are limits to the President's formal powers. For example, legal doctrines prohibit the chief executive from firing members of independent regulatory commissions who perform adjudicatory functions unless good cause is shown. In addition, there are checks by other branches. For example, the President has the power to make appointments, but the appointments are subject to the Senate confirmation process.[95]

Second, the constitutional obligation to "take care that the Laws be faithfully executed"[96] requires the chief executive to respect properly enacted laws. Since most agencies operate on the basis of an enabling act and administer several additional statutes, and because each agency is different from the others, the President's authority is limited by a maze of statutes.

Finally, the sheer diversity and complexity of the agencies exceeds the capacity of any one individual for personal control or management. As Stephen Hess has said, the presidency is not one person, but is itself an organization.[97] Aware that technological expertise and interest group support have given agencies significant independence from presidential direction, presidents have built an impressive counterbureaucracy in the Executive Office of the President. The Executive Office consists of financial and technical advisers who help the President administer the executive branch. Hess points out that the managerial complexity of the administrative arm of government is exacerbated by political diversity in the agencies and in the regulated clientele. He observes that what a President can do is organize the White House as effectively as possible and staff it with the right personnel. The staffing problem is a continuing one because of high turnover and because some political executives are co-opted ("go native," in political parlance) by the agencies or their interest groups.[98]

Some presidents see presidential control as the need to directly challenge what they perceive to be contentious, unresponsive, and even unbridled agencies. President Nixon has been characterized as the clearest example of a President who saw his relationship to the regulatory bureaucracy as adversarial.[99] Two of the most common tactics used by presidents who wish to gain control of the bureaucracy have been reorganization and what might be referred to as counterstaffing. Presidents generally justify large-scale executive branch reorganizations on the ground of managerial efficiency. However, reorganizations do not save money and do not usually result in increased efficiency. Instead, reorganization is accomplished to move opponents out of key positions in the bureaucracy and to maneuver more amenable officials into important posts.[100] Reorganizations are often slow, low-key operations. Counterstaffing is a strategy in which key positions in an agency are filled by officials who are known to hold policy positions and practice management styles contrary to prevailing agency attitudes and practices. President Reagan has counterstaffed the high-level personnel in the Environmental Protection Agency, the Department of the Interior, the Department of Energy, the Occupational Safety and Health Administration, and other agencies. In counterstaffing, one assumes a conflict mode of interaction with the bureaucracy that will make dramatic changes in agency operation. While these tactics are available to presidents, historically the career administrators and interest groups tend to outlast the burst of energy expended by a new administration, whether it acts through reorganization or counterstaffing.[101]

Richard Neustadt has asserted that the real power of the presidency is the power to persuade.[102] One need not go quite that far to accept the proposition that the exercise of formal power is in itself insufficient to establish and maintain effective working relations with agencies.[103]

The Appointments Process

Glenn Robinson, a former FCC commissioner, observed that although presidents have the opportunity to place their mark on agency policy through their appointments, they rarely try to do so. In fact, presidents are often indifferent to the use of appointments except in the most general sense.[104] Judge Henry Friendly has argued that of the suggestions for reforming the regulatory system, one of the most important is the enhancement of the appointments process.[105] But few administrations have established systematic appointments procedures that include close personal consideration by the President of the qualifications of potential appointees beyond their political credentials. Following a very difficult period of service as chief counsel for a congressional committee investigating regulatory problems, Bernard Schwartz wrote, "Far too frequently those agencies are looked on only as political 'dumping-grounds.' Neither the President nor the Senate has really been interested in the men appointed to the commissions."[106]

257
Politics and
Regulatory
Agencies:
Law and
Politics in
Administration

Even assuming presidents had the time and knowledge to become active and effective in the area, a number of disincentives discourage them from personally selecting highly qualified regulators. Glenn Robinson writes that "neither the patronage value that the President attaches to individual appointments in particular nor the public importance he attaches to agency appointments in general outweighs the substantial political costs incurred by selecting an appointee who is too controversial."[107] The political costs for selecting individuals with established records in their fields (and hence with established friends and opponents) can be high. For example, the Carter administration was attacked when several individuals who had spent some years in environmental organizations were appointed to the Environmental Protection Agency.

Of course, Robinson's generalization does not hold if a President deliberately selects counterstaffing as a strategy for dealing with the bureaucracy. In that event, the President is accepting conflict and gambling that he will win. At least two tactics are available to implement counterstaffing. First, the President can select someone with a well-documented but not necessarily widely known record that is dramatically different from current agency policy and wager that, given traditional deference to presidential regulatory appointments, opposing groups inside or outside the agency will not be able to block the appointment or win the public relations contest in the media. President Reagan's selection of James Watt to head the Department of the Interior is a prime example. In the Watt appointment, the fact that the President's party was the Senate majority party helped.[108] Second, the President can select a highly visible candidate with a strongly held and advocated philosophical position, but without a well-known detailed record. An example is the Reagan appointment of former South Carolina Governor Edwards to the position of energy secretary. The costs in terms of adverse publicity of such conflict can be very high.

Another difficulty in making regulatory appointments is selecting a role model. Should the President look for an adjudicator who is familiar with quasi-judicial proceedings, a rulemaker who performs well as a policymaker in a complex environment, or a manager who can administer a complicated organization in a conflict-ridden and volatile political environment? In fact, most regulators must perform both adjudicatory and policymaking functions.[109] The Ash Council implied that the management qualities of potential appointees were particularly important, but the Ribicoff Committee argued effectively that, except for regulatory commission chairmen, the management aspects of most regulatory tasks are not particularly significant:

> Also inherent in the Council's conclusion is an important misconception of the appointment needs of the regulatory commissions. Again and again, the Council's report refers to the need for "talented executives" or "well-qualified men with executive ability" or "men of administrative excellence"—all of which suggests that the Council believed that the best regulators were people with demonstrated management ability. Indeed the report states, "it would be clearly easier to find one highly qualified executive than it is to find five, seven, or eleven for a single agency." The Ash Council misses the point on two counts.
>
> First, . . . there would be no better guarantee of chaos than a commission comprised of five, seven, or eleven administrators. The

concept of the office of commissioner does not call for a manager. Rather, commissioners operate as rule-makers and judges, individuals who are able to reach an informed justified decision.

The second oversight . . . was that [Ash Council] did not take into account the special and important role played by a vigorous commission chairman. It is in that office that an administrator is needed, and the present power of most chairmen is more than sufficient to assure an effective operation.[110]

Another major difficulty in the appointments process can be avoiding conflicts of interest. There are several facets to this problem. First, the President must avoid appointing people who will face opposition in confirmation proceedings or attract negative public opinion because they are so intimately tied to the industry they will regulate that they are, in general terms, in a conflict of interest. Second, the President is required to enforce conflict-of-interest rules among those who have been appointed to an agency.[111] Finally, he must be concerned that his appointments could be viewed as manifesting the revolving-door syndrome, that is, that those who serve come from the regulated industry and return to that industry when they leave office. William Cary tells one man's reaction to this problem:

When Newton Minow was being considered for a job at FCC, he was asked: "Just what makes you think you are qualified to be Chairman of the FCC?"

He answered: "Two things: first, I'm not looking for a job in the communications business, and second, I don't want to be reappointed."[112]

The Ribicoff Committee made the appointments process a major focus of its study of the federal regulatory process.[113] The committee found basis in fact for the thesis that the appointments process is, and has been for many years, unsystematic and not a priority consideration in most administrations. Drawing on interviews with those responsible for screening appointments over several administrations, the committee noted that appointments were often made by the BOGSAT method ("Bunch Of Guys Sitting Around a Table").[114] The following conclusions are drawn from the committee's list of major findings.

(1) The preeminent problem with the regulatory appointments process, as it has operated in the past, is that it has not consistently resulted in the election of people best equipped to handle regulatory responsibilities. For much of the past fifteen years, neither the White House nor the Senate has demonstrated a sustained commitment to high quality regulatory appointments.

(2) Highly competent men and women—in business and industry, in colleges, in the agency staff, and in state and federal government—are available to serve on a commission composed of multiple members. The reason why more qualified persons are not being appointed is not a problem of availability.

(3) The lack of balance is a matter of major concern for the independent regulatory commission. Generally, membership on the commissions is not well balanced, and we have not had broad representation of various backgrounds, talents, and outlook. Specifically:

(a) Women and members of so-called minority groups are woefully underrepresented in the regulatory commissions; out of a total of more than 150 appointments since 1961, only seven women and four blacks have been selected for the nine major commissions. Five of those agencies have never had a black commissioner, and three have never had a female member.

(b) The commissioners are predominantly composed of white males with legal backgrounds. Economists, engineers, political scientists, accountants and members of other professions are rarely selected.

(c) A comparatively large number of regulators come directly from the regulated industries, which is in sharp contrast to the rare selection of persons with clear identification with public interest group concerns.[115]

259
Politics and
Regulatory
Agencies:
Law and
Politics in
Administration

Although the committee found some exceptions, it concluded from its study of existing literature and from the experience of lawyers who practice before nine major regulatory bodies that the general quality of regulatory appointees has been unsatisfactory.[116] Not only are individual appointments questionable, but the entire leadership of particular agencies is badly unbalanced, with strong biases in favor of regulated industries.[117]

In sum, presidents have not taken advantage of their opportunities to appoint top-quality regulators. The politics of the appointments process are complex and presidents must exercise care in using the appointments mechanism as a tool to ensure effective regulatory administration.

Budgetary Authority

The most widely recognized means the President may use in dealing with regulators are the budget preparation process and White House negotiating strength in the congressional appropriations process.[118] However, although the budgetary power of the President is important, certain factors limit even this power.

First, most regulatory agencies are quite small compared to other agencies.

Most of the important influences at work upon a regulatory agency are the White House, on one hand, and Congress, on the other. . . . In fact, government regulatory agencies are stepchildren whose custody is contested by both Congress and the Executive but without very much affection from either one. Furthermore, as stepchildren they are often starvelings receiving only crumbs in the federal budget.[119]

Regulatory bodies are small in size, and in fiscal terms take up about 2 percent of the federal budget.[120] Many of the expenditures are mandated by statutes, so it can be rather difficult to get much leverage through the budget preparation process. Additionally, there is always a chance that an agency will be able to mobilize interest group support in the congressional appropriations process (what has been referred to as an "end run around the White House").

Nevertheless, the President can use the budget process either to help or hinder an agency, particularly if the agency wants to undertake a new project. The President's budget preparation power can be used in a variety of ways, including manipulations of the numbers and types of agency personnel.[121]

White House Policy Clearance

For some time White House clearance has been required for legislative initiatives generated by agencies. Many of the same factors that affect budget clearance are involved in policy clearance.

Recent developments may make the policy clearance process more important than it has been in the past. First, the Executive Office of the President has expanded to include a plethora of financial, political, and policy experts who can challenge the merits of policies that the agencies wish to send to the Hill. Second, executive orders by the Carter and Reagan administrations have mandated increasing oversight of regulatory analyses by the Office of Management and Budget (OMB), expanding White House powers of clearance.[122] Whether the OMB will be staffed at a level that will permit wide-ranging analysis of proposed regulations remains to be seen.

Presidential Consultation, Control, and Coordination of Regulatory Policy

The President is charged with responsibility for the executive branch of the federal government and is obligated by the Constitution's duty-to-take-care clause to ensure that agencies do execute the law. In carrying out these responsibilities, the President is expected to coordinate and direct executive branch operations and to generate and, later, to accept responsibility for executive branch policies. On the other hand, most agencies are created by statute (and their appropriations are drawn from the Treasury) to be operated according to their technical expertise, not to act as extensions of political parties. The APA and other statutes require that policy-making through rulemaking will not be upheld if it is arbitrary, capricious, or not in accord with statutory authority. Similarly, agency adjudications are quasi-judicial actions that determine important questions of legal status or obligation. They are also government actions that affect important individual interests. Partisan or political intervention in agency adjudications and some rulemaking processes, known as *ex parte* communication, is generally prohibited by the APA.[123] There can be, and frequently has been, conflict between the need for governmental accountability to the electorate through the President's office and some degree of neutral competence to be exercised by professional administrators in agencies free of political pressure from the White House.[124] The distinction between quasi-legislative and quasi-judicial activities by agencies is easily blurred.[125] Presidential efforts to control or coordinate policy in the former are permissible, but presidential intervention in the latter may not be. There are some means that presidents may clearly employ, but the debate over the extent of permissible presidential involvement in agency operations is unresolved.

As to acceptable avenues of influence, some statutes, e.g., the Civil Aeronautics Board legislation, authorize presidential intervention. Presidents are permitted to act on some CAB decisions because of the possible impact of air transport decisions on foreign policy. Certainly the President may submit information in rulemaking proceedings as long as that information is made part of the record. The President also has considerable authority through the Attorney General to determine litigation strategy, since agency litigation can be preempted in almost all cases by the Justice Department. Just how far beyond these types of intervention the President can go is a subject of continuing disagreement.

There have been any number of celebrated cases of impropriety in which the President or highly placed White House officials have intervened directly in agency proceedings.[126] But frequently the presidential role is considerably more complicated and less clear. For example, "when President Carter created a Regulatory Council in October [1978] to reconcile conflicting regulations and assess their economic impact, critics viewed it as an unwarranted Presidential intrusion into the regulatory process."[127] Actually, two such bodies were created by the Carter administration. The United States Regulatory Council, consisting of representatives of some thirty-six executive branch and independent regulatory agencies, brought regulators together with representatives from the Executive Office of the President to give broad consideration to regulatory programs and procedures.[128] The other group, the Regulatory Analysis Review Group (RARG), was created to perform regulatory analyses on particular regulations.[129] Proponents applauded the attempt to get coordinated regulatory action. Opponents argued that this was really policymaking behind closed doors and without normal protections against administrative arbitrariness. Pointing, for example, to the fact that RARG was to be "chaired by a member of the Council of Economic Advisers,"[130] critics argued that this kind of activity had no acceptable legal basis and in fact was contrary to several regulatory statutes.

Emmette Redford has been perhaps the leading advocate of active presidential involvement in regulatory decisionmaking.[131] Judge Friendly responded to Redford's proposal to "establish a 'focal point' in an 'executive center' to develop 'policy guides' which the Commission is then to carry out through 'day-to-day decisions.'" Friendly went on, "Quite simply, I find it hard to think of anything worse."[132]

> Surely, the administrative purists went too far in seeking to raise a wall between the agencies and the President. . . . Moreover, agency policies in certain areas might obstruct, whereas others might advance, the President's success in functions especially confided to him, such as national defense or the conduct of foreign affairs; it is by no means plain that all he may properly do in such matters is to appear before the agency as a litigant. Beyond all this the President has another very practical concern with the workings of the agencies—in all likelihood he will get the blame if things go too wrong.
>
> Having said all this, I still find difficulty in the proposal that the President should not merely see to it that the agencies function but should tell them how.[133]

William Cary found the debate both interesting and amusing—amusing because while he was Securities and Exchange Commission chairman he never saw the President officially.[134] Cary once called the White House to ask whether the President had any general ideas or comments on the commission that he would like to convey, and to ask why he had received no communication of any kind since his appointment. He was informed that if there had been any problems he would have heard from the White House. Cary concluded: "In general . . . it can be said that the White House is interested and involved in a regulatory agency only if there has been a scandal or widespread newspaper publicity about the industry it regulates."[135]

Cary found the presidential involvement issue interesting because he recognized the dilemmas of both the President and the regulators. Trying to place himself between Redford and Friendly, Cary suggested that the White House should not be able to force or control action in a commission, but should be able to communicate its views on policy matters before the commission.[136]

Some participants in the policy process have been willing to go beyond the scholarly debate on presidential involvement. Robert Rauch of the Environmental Defense Fund has been particularly active. Rauch presented President Carter and his leading advisers with a legal memorandum arguing that presidential intervention in Environmental Protection Agency rulemaking would be illegal, save for submission of written comments that would, like any other comment submitted to an agency, become a part of the record or participation in any open hearings the agency might hold.[137] Given the likelihood of increased White House interest in rulemaking, Rauch and others who share his view may be challenged to carry through with the legal threat to presidential intervention implied by the memorandum.

CONGRESS IN THE REGULATORY PROCESS

Congress, like the President, has in recent years been reexamining its relationship with the regulatory agencies. In part, the reevaluation is attributable to antiregulation political sentiment, which makes it politically profitable for members of Congress to be seen as leaders in the regulatory reform movement. One can also surmise that a number of representatives feel compelled to deal with the problems created by the political handoff of policy problems to agencies with broad grants of authority, little direction, and weak or ineffective oversight. Still others, having decided that the pendulum has swung too far in the direction of presidential dominance, seem to wish to reassert congressional power in the post-Watergate period.

Of particular importance to the legislative relationship between the legislature and regulatory agencies are oversight, the budgetary factor, and the varying quality of legislation.

Legislative Oversight

Several interesting studies have been made of legislative efforts to oversee the activities of regulatory agencies to ensure that they do what they were designed to do, and in the manner intended.[138] The present discussion draws heavily on the Ribicoff Committee report.[139] As Dodd and Schott have observed, oversight

> involves the attempts by Congress to view and control policy
> implementation by the agencies and officials of the executive branch. As
> an all-pervasive process, it can read Congress into every facet of
> administration; precisely for this reason, oversight is a slippery and
> ephemeral process that is difficult to identify, measure, or study in a precise
> manner.[140]

Oversight can indeed be a "slippery and ephemeral process." In part, the complexity arises from problems similar to those faced by the President. Legislators have an obligation to ensure the accountability of administrators but should not interfere for narrow partisan purposes with ongoing efforts by professional administrators. In providing the kinds of checks envisioned by the framers of the Constitution, they must respect the concept of the separation of powers.

263
Politics and
Regulatory
Agencies:
Law and
Politics in
Administration

Two examples highlight the difficulty of understanding the legislative role with respect to agencies. First, there is an ongoing conflict over whether the legislature should merely conduct oversight, or review, of past or existing practices of agencies or attempt to control present or future actions.[141] Members of Congress, not surprisingly, see themselves doing both.

> This report is grounded in the idea that oversight is not simply hindsight; oversight involves a wide range of congressional efforts to review and control policy implementation by the regulatory agencies. Thus, oversight includes study, review and investigations, but it also involves an active concern with the administration of policy during implementation. Congressional oversight thus includes both participation before agency action and review after the fact.[142]

If "control" simply means "active concern," there is no conflict. If control is taken to mean attempts to coerce agency action or inaction in a particular case, there may be legal difficulties.[143] Overly intrusive legislative actions may also have a detrimental impact apart from whatever legal questions might be involved.

> Legislative controls which are unduly detailed stifle initiative; make for inflexibility and inefficiency in the conduct of governmental programs; sometimes result in imposing the will of individual legislators, or small groups, in matters in which they do not speak for the entire legislature and which are best left to executive officials; and end in frustrating the basic will of the legislative body.[144]

A second example of the "slippery" nature of oversight is the concern with ensuring that an agency administers policy as Congress intended when it enacted the statute. The intent behind a statute is the consensus that existed at the precise moment the law was enacted. Members of Congress who discuss a statute after its passage are in no position to insist that their understanding of legislative intent is the correct interpretation. After all, no one legislator embodies the intentions of the entire Congress at any one time, much less across time. Members conducting oversight efforts can indicate what they thought the intent of the law originally was and what many members now think it should be, but the significance of such a claim is difficult to interpret. The Ribicoff Committee expressed the complexity of legislative intent.

> Unfortunately, it is not always easy to know what Congress' intent was with respect to a particular law. In many instances even supporters of a measure have quite different views of the purpose of that law. Sometimes the same statute will reflect conflicting goals, e.g., regulation and promotion. In those cases where congressional intent is unclear, oversight operates to indicate to the agencies what the current Congress thinks was the intent of the Congress that passed the law. The regulatory agencies are not legally bound by the interpretation.[145]

For present purposes, constituent casework by individual members of the legislature is not considered oversight.[146] When a legislator responds to a complaint from an individual or an organization in his or her home district, the expectation is not that the legislator will check to ensure that the bureaucracy is operating properly, but that the legislator will act as a personal political advocate. Complaints from constituents can and occasionally do lead to investigations and other forms of oversight, but there is no evidence to suggest that a concern for legislative oversight is what motivates legislators to hire caseworkers or to become involved in the process themselves. Indeed, a strong case could be made for the proposition that constituent casework is often detrimental to broader oversight efforts.

Several purposes are served by oversight. Senator Ribicoff developed one of the best summaries of those purposes in an article entitled "Congressional Oversight and Regulatory Reform."

> The primary purpose of oversight is to insure that agencies administer the laws enacted by Congress in accordance with congressional intent. Oversight also serves to promote a constant interchange with the regulatory agencies to see that the general concerns of the public are brought to the attention of the agencies and reflected in their policies. Oversight serves, too, to prevent dishonesty, waste, and abuse of the administrative process. Finally, and importantly, effective congressional oversight should prevent the agencies from making decisions that are properly left to the political process. In sum, legislative oversight of the regulatory agencies should insure the accountability of non-elected representatives of the people.[147]

Ribicoff omits one important purpose of oversight. Oversight should not merely be an adversarial interaction between the legislature and agencies to ensure that the latter perform properly. It should also be a cooperative effort to determine whether programs enacted by the legislature are effective in accomplishing their intended goals.[148]

Congressional oversight is conducted through the committee system, most often in subcommittees. To replace the earlier special investigating committee approach to oversight,[149] Congress mandated in the Legislative Reorganization Act of 1946 that standing committees are responsible for oversight of agencies.[150] Basically, there are three kinds of oversight, conducted by three types of committees.

> Within each House oversight of regulatory agencies is shared primarily by the appropriations, authorization and government operations committees. This tripartite structure was reaffirmed by the Legislative Reorganization Act of 1946. Under that Act appropriations committees had the responsibility for "fiscal" oversight, the spending of funds by Federal agencies. The authorizing committees were primarily responsible for "legislative" oversight of agencies within their jurisdiction. The authorizing committees were to determine whether a particular program was working and to propose remedies to problems they uncovered. The government operations committees were primarily responsible for "investigative oversight," a type of oversight which is often wider ranging than "fiscal" or "legislative" oversight.[151]

Authorization committees, also known as subject matter committees, create programs and, at least in theory, assess their effectiveness with an eye toward new or amended legislation. These committees consider the substantive authority on which legislation depends, and their bills authorize the Congress to appropriate funds for the program. Appropriations committees must meet to consider the budget requests for each fiscal year. Theoretically, they evaluate how agencies have guarded previously appropriated funds against fraud, abuse, and waste. In practice, many members of appropriations committees give substantive consideration to agency operations from a financial audit justification. For example, emphasis by regulators on a strong enforcement program that adversely affects a particular industry may lead an appropriations committee member to suggest that the program is an inappropriate use of agency resources. Government operations committees often carry out cross-agency investigations of administrative procedures. The *Study on Federal Regulation* is an example of such an investigation.

Oversight can be conducted both formally and informally. Legislative proposals for change in administrative operations or full-scale hearings to produce such evidence as is needed to make the legislative changes are, of course, formal processes. Informal methods include special hearings, preparation and publication of reports on the performance of an agency or policy,[152] references to agency performance in floor debates or speeches in Congress, and informal contacts by committee members or staff with an agency.[153]

> Our interviews with congressional staff members also show high levels of informal oversight activity. Communications between Members and the agencies are very frequent. In fact, the Commission–Committee study found, that staff communication with agency personnel was the most frequently used oversight technique. Some staff members claimed to be in daily contact with the agency they oversee.[154]

Informal techniques may be quite effective because informal studies or inquiries can easily become formal legislative action, with important consequences for administrators. The power of the raised eyebrow is a most effective tool for legislative oversight.[155]

The availability of resources that legislative committees can call on in support of oversight efforts is a continuing problem. Much of the oversight work is done by small subcommittees. The members of those committees often have particular interests in subjects in their own jurisdictions, but their schedules are crowded. They are often serving on several committees and subcommittees at the same time. Neither the legislators nor the members of their staffs have sufficient time to do in-depth analysis of agency activities. Drawing on a study by James P. McGrath of the Congressional Research Service, the Ribicoff Committee concluded that the 93rd and 94th Congresses held 1,077 hearings on major agencies. See Table 10-1. These hearings represent only a small part of the legislative workload. Committee staffs shoulder the primary burden of oversight detail work, but staffs are often too small to analyze the complex and very large agencies they are asked to study. Table 10-2 shows the number of available staff members and the budgets of the programs they must oversee.

To handle the workload and to add to the capacity for independent analysis, members of Congress have expanded their in-house staff capability in a fashion

265
Politics and
Regulatory
Agencies:
Law and
Politics in
Administration

Table 10-1 Number of Hearings of Major Regulatory
Agencies, 93rd and 94th Congresses

Agency	Hearings
Civil Aeronautics Board	55
Commodity Futures Trading Commission	5
Consumer Product Safety Commission	25
Environmental Protection Agency	208
Federal Energy Administration	120
Federal Maritime Commission	26
Federal Power Commission	90
Federal Reserve Board	77
Federal Trade Commission	144
Food and Drug Administration	80
Interstate Commerce Commission	70
National Highway Traffic Safety Administration	25
National Labor Relations Board	13
National Transportation Safety Board	33
Nuclear Regulatory Commission	21
Occupational Safety and Health Administration	20
Securities and Exchange Commission	65
Total	1,077

SOURCE: U.S. Senate, Committee on Governmental Affairs, *Study on Federal Regulation*, vol. 2 (1978), p. 81.

similar to the enhancement of the Executive Office of the President. Specifically, Congress has developed the Congressional Research Service, the Office of Technology Assessment, the Congressional Budget Office, and the General Accounting Office to assist the Congress as a whole, its committees, and its individual members. Table 10-3 summarizes the authority for and services provided by each of these legislative agencies.

Most observers agree that the legislature is doing more regulatory oversight now than it was before the 1970s.[156] Even so, Congress continues to receive low marks for the quality of its oversight efforts. The Ribicoff Committee concluded that "Congress oversees in an episodic, erratic manner."[157] Appropriation committees get higher marks than authorization committees, in that their efforts are more systematic and regular.[158] Of course, part of the reason is that the annual appropriations process automatically triggers periodic hearings. By contrast, unless regulatory agency statutes have reauthorization requirements, often referred to as "sunset" provisions, there is no regular requirement for other committees to conduct oversight proceedings. Because of the press of business, oversight tends to be haphazard and in response to some particular problem that has drawn public attention.

Oversight tends to be done on a crisis basis only. The crisis may be local, involving a constituent, or national in scope. The oversight effort is

267
Politics and
Regulatory
Agencies:
Law and
Politics in
Administration

Table 10-2 Appropriations Subcommittee Jurisdiction, Professional Staff, and FY 1977 Budget Request

Subcommittee	Regulatory Agencies	Combined Agency Request (thousands)	Total Request (thousands)	Subcommittee Professional Staff		Total Budget Request per Staff Member (millions)	
				House	Senate	House	Senate
Agriculture and related agencies	Commodity Futures Trading Commission, Food and Drug Administration.	$253,233	$12,575,892	3	3	$ 4,191,964	$ 4,191,964
HUD – independent agencies	Consumer Product Safety Commission, Environmental Protection Agency, Federal Home Loan Bank Board	808,087	45,306,198	3	3	15,102,066	15,102,066
Interior	Federal Energy Administration	193,157	5,786,054	2	4	2,893,027	1,446,514
Labor and Health, Education, and Welfare	Occupational Safety and Health Administration (Labor)	130,820	52,618,208	5	6	10,523,642	8,796,972
Public Works	Federal Power Commission, Nuclear Regulatory Commission	286,012	9,551,209	5	3	1,910,242	3,183,736
State, Justice, Commerce and Judiciary	Federal Communications Commission, Federal Maritime Commission, Federal Trade Commission, Securities and Exchange Commission	165,928	6,312,870	2	3	3,156,435	2,104,290
Transportation	Federal Aviation Administration (DOT), Civil Aeronautics Board, Interstate Commerce Commission, National Transportation Safety Board.	2,195,550	14,351,891	2	2	7,175,845	7,175,845

SOURCE: U.S. Senate, Committee on Governmental Affairs, *Study on Federal Regulation*, vol. 2 (1978), p. 25.

Table 10-3 Congressional Support Agencies

Agency	Statutory Authority	Services Provided
General Accounting Office	Budget and Accounting Act of 1921	Performs several functions mandated by law, including assisting Congress in its legislative and oversight activities; auditing the programs, activities, and financial operations of federal departments and agencies; helping to improve federal agency financial management systems. The Congressional Budget and Impoundment Control Act of 1974 authorized additional GAO oversight assistance to Congress. That act authorized GAO to establish an Office of Program Review and Evaluation (now a Division of Program Analysis). Its responsibilities are: (1) to review and evaluate the results of government programs or activities when ordered by Congress, a committee, or on the initiative of the Comptroller General; (2) to assist any committee in developing a statement of legislative objectives and goals, including methods of assessing and reporting actual program performance relative to its goals, and to assist such committees in analyzing and assessing program review or evaluation studies prepared by and for a federal agency; and (3) to develop and recommend to the Congress methods for review and evaluation of Government programs and activities carried on under existing law.
Congressional Research Service	Legislative Reorganization Act of 1946 and Legislative Reorganization Act of 1970	Provides such services as analyzing and evaluating legislative proposals, tracking major policy issues, submitting summaries of subjects for committee review and lists of program expiration dates at the beginning of each term, and offering greater consulting and advisory assistance. In addition, CRS assists Congress in performing oversight by providing more traditional services such as: assisting the hearing process by suggesting names for prospective witnesses, preparing questions, and analyzing testimony; preparing background studies, briefing papers, memoranda, and draft reports; loaning specialized personnel for temporary use during limited periods; compiling bibliographies, developing pro and con arguments on topics; analyzing, summarizing, and commenting on judicial decisions; providing copies of issue briefs, multilithed reports, on-demand bibliographies, and special studies on a variety of public questions and problems; securing copies of or abstracting books, magazine articles, newspaper items, scholarly journal writings, or other publications. Quick reference service for the retrieval of factual or statistical data.
Office of Technology Assessment	Technology Assessment Act of 1972	Provides unbiased information and technical expertise in the various applications of technology; secures, analyzes, and assesses data about the effects of technological developments; identifies existing or probable impacts

Table 10-3 Congressional Support Agencies (Continued)

Agency	Statutory Authority	Services Provided
		caused by new technology, ascertains cause-and-effect relationships; explores alternative technological methods for implementing programs, estimates and compares the impacts that alternative technological methods and programs might have; and reports findings of completed analyses and identifies areas for further research.
Congressional Budget Office	Congressional Budget and Impoundment Control Act of 1974	Although its primary mandate is to provide budget data to the budget committees of the Senate and House of Representatives, the Congressional Budget Office is also directed by law to furnish information on request to the committees on appropriations, ways and means, and finance to assist them in discharging duties within their jurisdiction.
		Provides on request, compiled information related to budget matters to other committees and members, and is authorized (to the extent practicable) to make available additional information related to budget matters that other committees or members may request.
		CBO personnel can be temporarily assigned to other congressional committees to assist them in matters related directly to budgetary activity.

source: Constructed from the descriptions of the offices in U.S. Senate, Committee on Governmental Affairs, *Study on Federal Regulation*, vol. 2 (1978), pp. 54–59.

usually initiated not in accordance with any preplanned set of priorities, but rather in response to a newspaper article, a complaint from a constituent or special interest group, or information from a disgruntled agency employee. "The regulatory agencies are generally left unsupervised until one of their policies or actions stirs up disapproval loud enough to reach congressional ears."

The ad hoc approach to oversight is illustrated by committee treatment of agency regulations. Very few committees or committee staff members systematically review the regulations issued by agencies under their jurisdiction. Issues of the Federal Register containing proposed agency rules are not regularly scrutinized. One committee staff member explained that he did not have time to review all of the regulations issued by "his" agency. Only when complaints were registered about a particular rule did he inquire about it. "You know how it is," he said, "The squeaky wheel gets the grease."[159]

In addition to the shortage of time, staff, information, and lack of regular procedures, legislative oversight suffers from a lack of generally agreed-on standards for agency performance. To determine whether an agency is performing properly, it is necessary to define what "properly" means. Proper agency performance might be defined as faithfully executing the provisions of law that the agency is charged with administering. However, poorly drafted or excessively broad statutes can make it difficult to know what an agency is supposed to do, let alone whether it is doing it well or badly. Another problem is that legislative oversight is conducted through a legislative committee structure that is badly fragmented.[160] The members of different committees often refuse to cooperate with each other.[161] Committee chairmen in particular are jealous of their prerogatives and their political "turf."

Finally, there are relatively few political incentives for representatives to shift their time and resources from other activities to concentrate on conducting oversight in any positive way. There may be political mileage in leading an attack on regulatory agencies in general, or on one agency in particular, but on the whole oversight is long, involved, and tedious. It rarely draws press coverage unless some particularly egregious agency error is uncovered. Few interest groups will make a special effort to aid a legislator's reelection bid in the home district because he or she found after a lengthy hearing that a particular agency was doing a good job. (Casework, on the other hand, has a rather direct, if occasionally small, payoff. The person for whom a congressman prodded the Social Security Administration to process a check will remember that service and tell others about it.) Constituents rarely know or care about oversight. Improving oversight requires a serious incentive to make it worth the legislator's while.

There can be a number of negative consequences of oversight. For one thing, it can be extremely burdensome to the agencies. Most agencies dedicate much time and effort each year to the preparation of testimony for hearings. But oversight hearings may more often be pursued for political notoriety or to score ideological debating points than to make careful analyses of agency performance. Hearings can also be used to punish or ridicule administrators in difficult positions who are attempting to do a good job. Finally, the concentration of the oversight function in small committees can allow a few individuals to wield tremendous power.

> Because only a few committees, and often only a few individuals, may
> oversee a regulatory agency, the goal of "representation of the public
> interest" may not always be achieved. . . . Individual staff members, too,
> can wield a great deal of influence with the agencies.[162]

That power can be easily abused.

The Budget Process

The budget process is also important because (1) it is a lever to force agency responsiveness to Congress and (2) it is the means by which government establishes priorities. As to the former, Congress can set levels and limits for funding certain regulatory programs, establish purposes for which funds can be spent, and include "limitations provisions" that specify activities for which agency funds may not be expended.[163] On the matter or priority setting, regulatory agencies can find themselves in a very difficult position between the president's budget recommendations and the budget actually produced by Congress. The Ribicoff Committee found that, historically, the Office of Management and Budget has reduced the budget requested by the agency and that Congress has given the agency somewhat more than OMB recommended.[164] Agency needs and expectations of funding may run afoul of executive branch budget-cutting pressures, meaning that administrators need congressional support. The fragile relationships with both the Hill and the White House can be difficult to maintain. The delicacy of the budgetary relationship can be extremely intimidating to a would-be watchdog.

271
Politics and
Regulatory
Agencies:
Law and
Politics in
Administration

The Problem of the Political Handoff

The pressures legislators face can tempt them to deal with policy problems by a political handoff. That is, it is easier to pass a law making an agency responsible for solving a problem than to resolve fundamental policy conflicts before assigning a statute to an agency for implementation. Broad grants of authority and discretion may permit an agency to be innovative, but if there is not regular, conscientious oversight, there are dangers for those who are regulated by the agency and for agency administrators. The danger of abuse of discretion is obvious. The danger for the administrator can be that a lack of regular interaction between Congress and the agency may lead to a campaign against the agency by a congressional newcomer or an incumbent who needs an issue around which to build a reelection campaign. In sum, there is great attractiveness to the idea that regulatory agencies should be the servants of Congress because the members of Congress are accountable to the electorate. But a host of political opportunities and incentives impinge on legislative performance apart from the substance or quality of regulatory programs. The framers of the Constitution were concerned that actions by the executive branch might automatically seem suspect to Americans, and those of the legislative branch might appear presumptively proper. It was for this reason that Madison warned in *Federalist Paper* No. 48,

> The legislative department is everywhere extending the sphere of its activity and drawing all power into its impetuous vortex. . . .
>
> In a representative republic where the executive magistracy is carefully limited, both in the extent and duration of its power; and where the legislative power is exercised by an assembly, which is inspired by a supposed influence over the people with an intrepid confidence in its own strength; which is sufficiently numerous to feel all the passions which actuate a multitude, yet not so numerous as to be incapable of pursuing the objects of its passions by means which reason prescribes; it is against the enterprising ambition of this department that the people ought to indulge all their jealousy and exhaust all their precautions.
>
> The legislative department derives a superiority in our governments from other circumstances. Its constitutional powers being at once more extensive, and less susceptible of precise limits, it can, with greater facility, mask, under complicated and indirect measures, the encroachments which it makes on coordinate departments.[165]

PUBLIC PARTICIPATION IN THE REGULATORY PROCESS

As this chapter has indicated, most aspects of law and regulatory administration are highly controversial. Surprisingly, in one area there seems to be relatively little disagreement. The need to both increase the amount and improve the quality of public participation in regulatory activities has been supported by a wide range of individuals and groups in the past decade or so. Although some differences of opinion on a few of the suggested remedies remain, there is even considerable consensus on the elements of the problem. In fact, one can practically overlay the outlines of the several articles and study reports on the subject.[166] Below we briefly summarize the reasons why expanded public participation is needed, noting the difficulties public interest groups face in participating, and discuss the points in the regulatory process where such interest groups or individuals intervene and how.

The Problem of Participation

Several factors merged in the '70s as it became clear that the level of public participation, as opposed to participation by the regulated organizations, was low and that there were substantial burdens discouraging increased public involvement. Groups that wanted to participate in particular regulatory proceedings pressed the claim that the law does and ought to require agencies to permit public participation.[167] They made essentially two arguments. First, rulemaking proceedings should be open to all who have a serious interest in the proposed rule and who have something to contribute to the deliberations on whether to promulgate the rule. Second, even where an agency is conducting a regulatory adjudication (or a licensing proceeding, which is a species of adjudication), there should be an opportunity for meaningful participation by those who can demonstrate a substantial interest (which is not necessarily the equivalent of legal standing) in the matter. The rationale for involvement in rulemaking is clear, but that for involvement in quasi-judicial actions is more troublesome. The argument is that there are at least three possible decisions that can be reached in, for example, a power plant licensing case: (1) a decision in the regulated firm's interest; (2) a decision that serves the agency's interest; and (3) a decision that serves the public interest. A decision can serve the interests of both the agency and the regulated industry, but may or may not be in the public interest. Public participation, even if it is not equal to that of the regulated group, may infuse outside ideas into what could be, and sometimes is, a too-congenial proceeding between an agency and its client organizations.

At the same time, some scholars and administrators, in evaluating what had happened during the '60s, began to look for ways to open the processes of government, both to improve those processes and to restore a greater sense of legitimacy to government. Civil rights, environmental, and consumer interest groups were also learning that they could be effective by using litigation or the threat of it as an interest group tactic.[168]

Finally, scholars and reformers in government had come to the conclusion that one need not look for sinister scenarios or accept power elite theories of decision-making to recognize that there was much truth in the assertion that regulatory agencies were often either dependent on or biased toward the groups and organizations they regulated.

> We do not need to subscribe to the theory of regulatory "capture" . . . to explain this tendency toward industry domination. Rather, the reason appears to be simply in the fact that regulatory agencies respond to the inputs they receive—in the same fashion as any other decisionmaking body. And, until the recent past, the source of almost all input to the agencies was the regulated industries. As the Landis report noted, ". . . it

273
Politics and
Regulatory
Agencies:
Law and
Politics in
Administration

is the daily machine-gun like impact on both agency and its staff of industry representation that makes for industry orientation on the part of many honest and capable agency members as well as agency staffs."[169]

Indeed, there have been some rather dramatic instances of real or potential conflicts of interest. For example, at the request of California Congressman John Moss the General Accounting Office did a study of the Federal Power Commission, which then regulated natural gas. When financial disclosure statements of 125 FPC executives were filed or brought up to date, GAO learned that "19 officials owned prohibited securities of the following companies: Exxon Corporation, Union Oil Company, Standard Oil of Indiana, Texaco Corporation, Pacific Power and Light Company, Tenneco Oil Company, Central Telephone and Utility Company, Cities Service, Commonwealth Edison, Northern Illinois Gas, Occidental Petroleum, Monsanto Company, Washington Gas Light Company, Atlantic Richfield Company, and Potomac Electric Power Company."[170] The appearance of industry mindedness in an agency charged with regulation of natural gas is not helped by such holdings.

But in general, potential conflict of interest is not so much the problem as the fact that outside input to regulatory bodies is unsystematic, while industry interaction with the agency is ongoing, well financed, and expertly prepared. Administrators want to believe that they can remain unaffected and stand as neutral arbiters of the public interest, but there are limits. Those limits are particularly tested when a regulatory body has both a regulatory and a promotional responsibility, as does the Federal Aviation Administration, the Federal Communications Commission, and bodies that regulate utilities. Such agencies must help the industry prosper and simultaneously act as its watchdog. Those who have studied this problem have encouraged Congress and the agencies to expand opportunities for participation, and to a degree this has been done.

Methods of Participation

Public interest groups participate in agency proceedings in several different forums and by a number of means. They may serve on task forces or advisory groups maintained by the agency. They may submit comments on notice-and-comment rulemaking processes. If a statute requires a hearing in connection with rulemaking (either a formal or a hybrid rulemaking proceeding), groups that can demonstrate a substantial interest may participate if the agency enabling act requires the opportunity to intervene or if agency rules permit it. Many agencies permit intervention in licensing or ratemaking proceedings, but this is often limited to nonrepetitive presentation of evidence and views. Adjudications are difficult to deal with because of the due process rights of the regulated party. Participation by third parties can create due process difficulties in terms of notice and in cross-examining those who give adverse evidence.[171] Whether, and in what manner, would-be private attorneys general will be permitted to participate in such proceedings depends on agency rules and judicial interpretations of statutory requirements.[172]

Public interest groups often participate in congressional oversight hearings, but what type of participation is permitted is up to the committee involved.

Finally, groups may seek to participate in regulatory proceedings before the courts. In certain situations, they may be able to obtain standing to bring an agency ruling up for judicial review. At other times, they may ask permission to intervene in proceedings brought by some other party.[173]

Roadblocks to Participation

Limitations on public participation may be defined as falling into several general categories: (1) lack of notice; (2) lack of organization; (3) lack of funds; (4) lack of expertise; and (5) procedural bars to participation.

It is extremely difficult for most citizens to get word of agency action, even if they are part of what is known as the informed public. Few know what the Federal Register is, much less how to read it. Few people read or understand legal notices in the newspaper. Often the newspapers do not even report that an important administrative hearing was conducted until after the fact.

Lack of organization is very important. Many people may be interested in a particular regulatory action, but they can have no effect unless they know of a group that will advance their cause or have the time and the skills to develop an organization from the ground up. In many cases, groups that wish to be effective must establish offices in the capital where they can develop channels of communication with agencies and congressional committees.

Participation in agency proceedings is extremely expensive.[174] Filing fees, copying costs, and transcript charges alone can be staggering.[175] Few groups can afford the expense if proceedings go on very long. After surveying the dockets of several major agencies and analyzing participation in those cases, the Ribicoff Committee concluded:

> In all of the preceding examples comparing public interest groups costs to industry costs is like comparing David and Goliath. Effective participation in a regulatory proceeding does indeed depend on the quality and extent of one's legal counsel. It also depends upon the quality and extent of expert testimony and technical submissions. It requires ample administrative and clerical resources, costs which are frequently taken for granted. Yet time after time, industry is able to spend 10, or 50, or 100 times as much money on participation as public interest groups. The persistence and ingenuity of the public interest groups in their efforts to participate effectively is laudable, but their lack of resources to insure adequate representation is lamentable.[176]

Effective participation in complex regulatory proceedings requires expertise. First, one must have a lawyer skilled in administrative law—preferably someone who knows the law, politics, and procedures of the agency involved. Technical experts and needed both to make one's case and to interpret the submissions of others in the proceedings. Such expertise is expensive and not easy to find. For one thing, it is often difficult to get experts to volunteer their services because they may want to be hired later by the firms against whom the public interest groups are proceeding. Government experts may not wish to serve because of possible conflict within their agencies, or between agencies if the expert is perceived to be making statements against the government's interests in a proceeding.

Finally, there are procedural roadblocks to participation both in agencies and in courts. Many regulatory agencies have not formulated clear rules on when and to what extent intervenors will be allowed to participate. It is frequently a matter of discretion with the administrative law judge conducting a proceeding to decide whether, and in what manner, a group will be heard. In the courts, there was for several years a strong movement to relax rules of standing and other procedural bars to review. But as Chapter 7 indicated, many of these doctrines have been reinterpreted since the early '70s and are again formidable barriers to many groups that would like to appeal administrative rulings.[177]

275

Politics and
Regulatory
Agencies:
Law and
Politics in
Administration

The difficulties of public participation in administrative proceedings are among regulatory law and administration problems for which reform efforts are under way. We turn now to a brief summary of some of the most widely discussed reform options.

EFFORTS AT REGULATORY REFORM

It is important to bear in mind the distinction between participants who debate at the macro-level whether and when to use regulation, and those who are primarily interested in improving the quality of regulation when the legislature has already decided on a regulatory approach to a particular policy problem. Both groups use the term "regulatory reform." This term is frequently used as political shorthand for regulatory reduction by some economists, business groups, and legislators. For example, in hearings on the proposed government-wide legislative veto, legislators did not discuss how the quality of regulations or the regulatory process would be improved by the veto. Instead, most of those testifying in favor of the bill concentrated on the need to eliminate regulations and supported the bill as a step in that direction.[178] Efforts to reduce regulation in general are also different, albeit by degrees, from attempts to deregulate in selected areas of the economy for specific reasons.

Reform initiatives may be grouped into six categories: (1) "innovative techniques" of regulation; (2) organizational reforms; (3) appointment improvements; (4) legislative oversight modifications; (5) rulemaking procedural modifications; and (6) public access and participation developments.

Innovative Techniques

A package of changes in regulatory administration known as "innovative techniques" was actively promoted by the Carter administration. This set of initiatives grew out of the Carter regulatory reform order, Executive Order No. 12044, promulgated in 1978. The order required executive branch heads to "approve significant regulations before they are published for comment in the Federal Register. At a minimum [they] . . . should determine that . . . alternative approaches have been considered and the least burdensome of the acceptable alternatives has been chosen."[179] In other words, where agencies have discretion in implementing regulatory statutes, they should seek to accomplish the purposes of the law without automatically selecting highly intrusive and burdensome command-and-control type regulations. Where possible, the administration urged that incentives be used. Working through the U.S. Regulatory Council,[180] the President pressed agencies to develop and report on the innovative techniques they had found appropriate to their agencies. Eight techniques were listed:

- Performance standards
- Tiering
- Marketable rights
- Economic incentives
- Compliance reform
- Enchanced competition
- Information disclosure
- Voluntary standards[181]

Table 10-4 is assembled from U.S. Regulatory Council documents on the innovative techniques program. It defines the techniques, provides an example of each one, and comments on anticipated benefits and possible problems associated with every option.

The political and legal controversies surrounding the use of innovative techniques remain to be settled. Political disputes may arise from any number of directions, but will most likely emerge as interest groups attempt to determine whether one or another technique will best serve their goals. Legal challenges are likely to come from those who suggest that there are statutory limits on just how far administrators may "innovate."

Organizational Reform

The argument that regulation can be improved by reorganizing the regulatory agencies is both intuitively and, for presidents, politically appealing. It is, of course, true that some agencies need reorganizing. The argument that there is one best way to organize a regulatory agency has, however, yet to be made convincingly. Analysts inside and outside the government have rejected the Ash Council proposal to make almost all regulatory bodies single-head executive branch agencies.[182]

Appointments Improvements

The Ribicoff Committee has suggested several reforms that would improve the quality of personnel in high-level regulatory posts. The committee's major finding is that no improvement in appointments will occur unless and until chief executives treat the appointments process with the attention it deserves. The process should be made systematic and, if possible, should be designed in such a manner that it could be used by future administrations.

To make substantive qualitative improvements, the committee argued that, political realities notwithstanding, the President should wherever possible make appointments with an eye toward achieving some balance in the appointees' backgrounds and general policy preferences.[183] Background checks on candidates should be thorough and, where necessary, conflict-of-interest laws ought to be clarified by statute or rulemaking to aid in this clearance process. Appointees should be required to commit themselves to serving the full term for which they are appointed or at least promise that they will give sufficiently early notice of intention to resign that the White House will have time to conduct a careful search for replacements.[184]

Table 10-4 Innovative Techniques of Regulation

Technique	Description	Examples	Benefits	Problems
Marketable rights	Distributing a limited number of rights to scarce resources that private parties can then buy, sell, or trade as market needs dictate. Can remove government from difficult, contentious, and lengthy decisions about who can best use the limited resources.	The Environmental Protection Agency has been studying a plan to allocate permits for the production or sale of CFC. [Chlorofluorocarbons are chemicals that eventually find their way to the upper atmosphere and damage the ozone.] These permits could be bought and sold among producers or users to bring about the highest economic efficiency. Since it is not environmentally important where or when CFC is emitted into the atmosphere, only one market would be necessary. One current idea for allocating valuable take-off and landing times at busy airports is to accept bids for slots at each hour of the day. These would be ranked from highest to lowest bid and the top 40 bids, for example, would qualify for the 40 slots available during a given hour. The lowest bid would become the price for all bidders. A carrier that bids successfully would then have to pair this slot with a compatible slot at another airport to move its plan between cities. If it cannot get both slots for a flight, then a carrier would have to trade.	Marketable rights might provide a way of offsetting externalities. Compliance costs are reduced. Administrative effort and expense is saved by easing of enforcement problems and the burdens of promulgating regulations. A market model less restrictive of individual choice is used.	The legality of government selling rights to permit users on a basis other than cost to the government has to be determined. There are problems of equivalence and equity. The value of permission to emit air pollutants in California is not the same as in Maine; air traffic slots at National Airport may be more valuable than slots at Dulles Airport. Timing is a problem because the detrimental effects of emissions may not be at a constant level throughout the year. The value of airports may vary according to the time of day. In an open market, the rights currently enjoyed by small businesses could be effectively eliminated, given the potential for larger businesses to monopolize trading in permits.

(continued)

SOURCE: Constructed from information in "Innovative Techniques in Theory and Practice," *Proceedings, U.S. Regulatory Council Conference,* July 22, 1980 (Washington, D.C.: United States Regulatory Council, 1980).

Table 10-4 Innovative Techniques of Regulation (Continued)

Technique	Description	Examples	Benefits	Problems
Economic incentives	Using fees or subsidies (rather than government enforced standards) to encourage private sector achievement of regulatory goals. Removes the government from having to eliminate or directly restrict the unwanted activity, but creates an incentive for the private sector to limit the activity itself.	Current Department of Interior regulations allow the use of economic incentives in lieu of a requirement for continuous operation. A lessee of federal coal lands can be given the option of paying advanced royalties, rather than continuing to produce, for a period of ten years. This allows the lessee greater flexibility to respond to the changing economic environment but still provides an incentive to resume operations. The National Credit Union Administration used an economic incentive to implement its Central Loan Fund (CLF). The CLF was set up as the equivalent of the Federal Reserve Bank for credit unions, but the NCUA found that credit unions were not interested in joining until the reserve requirements were redefined as a non-risk investment. This changed the credit union's economic equations, freeing other funds for more lucrative investments and made membership in CLF attractive.	Incentives may improve resource allocation. This approach provides incentives to innovate. Incentive techniques permit increased flexibility. Reduced enforcement burdens and litigation costs are faced by government.	The effectiveness of incentives are difficult to determine in advance. In some situations economic incentives cannot be made attractive enough. The Council reported that workers' compensation rates might be structured to reward firms with good records and penalize those with safety and health problems. But the report added: "However, it was noted that in one industry, companies have been forced to self-insure and even this has not changed their behavior."

Technique	Description	Examples	Benefits	Problems
Performance standards	Replacing regulations that specify the exact means of compliance (usually detailed design standards) with general targets that the regulated firms can decide how to meet. Performance standards reduce compliance costs and provide regulated firms more flexibility and discretion to discover new and more efficient compliance technologies.	The Environmental Protection Agency's "bubble" policy sets overall emission limits for particular pollutants for a plant or a region (consisting of many plants) and allows firms to implement any type of control that will achieve the overall standard. This policy allows a plant manager to use the most cost-effective strategy for meeting the pollution limits for his or her plant. EPA's former policy specified emission limits for each source of pollution and level of technology that must be used. It is estimated that the "bubble policy" will save between 15 and 20 percent of the total compliance costs for air pollution.	Performance standards allow regulated groups flexibility to use any means they deem appropriate to meet the required standards. They eliminate the need for detailed specification standards with the detailed rulemaking procedures required to promulgate them. Less detailed enforcement is possible. Performance standards encourage technical innovation.	It is possible to evade output monitoring without really improving performance unless performance monitoring measurement can be made exceedingly sensitive and complex. It is difficult or impossible to specify performance standards under some circumstances.

(continued)

Table 10-4 Innovative Techniques of Regulation (Continued)

Technique	Description	Examples	Benefits	Problems
Compliance reform	Replacing or supplementing strict governmental monitoring and enforcement with market-oriented mechanisms including third-party compliance, and supervised self-certification. Such measures can improve compliance incentives while curtailing costs to the taxpayer.	The Consumer Product Safety Commission allows producers to certify that their products meet appropriate standards. It also uses independent inspections and analyses (e.g., Underwriters Laboratories) to certify product quality and "consumer deputies" from trade associations and consumer organizations to ensure that products are in compliance.	Ends or reforms extensive governmental intrusion into the private sector. Reduces administrative costs such as the need for more inspectors. Seeks enforcement through cooperation and negotiation rather than formal adversarial proceedings. Reduces caseload because cases are based on sampling and checking rather than complete enforcement.	The flexibility to employ such techniques varies significantly from agency to agency, depending upon statutory mandate. Use of third-party inspection techniques requires availability of professionally competent, independent individuals within the regulated industry, or an adversary group like a union with qualified inspection personnel. Standards must be clear in themselves and clearly communicated. There must be adequate monitoring. The potential for abuse or avoidance of regulatory goals is high.
Enhanced competition	Removing barriers to market entry or limits on the services that may be provided by those already in the market. This free market approach can be an important source of cost savings and can improve the quality and diversity of products and services.	The primary examples of this technique are Civil Aeronautics Board efforts to ease restrictions on market entry and abandonment of service before and after the Airline Deregulation Act.	Relieves workload. Allows market mechanism to function. Permits more participants to enter a market. Reduces cross-subsidies and other inefficiencies.	Some industries remain essentially oligopolistic and market mechanisms do not work freely. Service to unprofitable markets would be lost. Competition in some industries and under some circumstances may be destructive. Limits opportunity for national policy planning in such areas as transportation.

Technique	Description	Examples	Benefits	Problems
Information disclosure	Providing users of a product or service with relevant information about the consequences of using it. Disclosure can replace centralized government decisions with informed freedom of choice among many users and can stimulate competition among suppliers for improved performance (e.g., low tar in cigarettes, lower life-cycle energy use).	Recent examples include requirements for energy efficiency ratings on appliances, nutrition and ingredient labeling for food, EPA mileage ratings for all new automobiles, and tar and nicotine labeling requirements for cigarettes.	As more information is made available to consumers, the effectiveness of the market mechanism increases, resulting in incentives for producers to make better and safer products. Even if producers do not feel a decrease in sales, they may see labeling as an incentive to improve the product and to use labeling as advertising. Labeling measures can help develop standardized measures as a comparative device for decisionmaking.	This technique is not useful where externalities are involved for which neither the producer nor the consumer pays directly. The Council provides an example of "a motorcycle noise standard which benefits third parties, not the purchaser." It is not useful where there are vulnerable consumers, such as children or elderly people, who are not sufficiently mobile or economically flexible to make use of market options. It is not useful where competition is weak or consumer choice is limited.

(continued)

Table 10-4 Innovative Techniques of Regulation (Continued)

Technique	Description	Examples	Benefits	Problems
Voluntary standards	Relying on regulatory standards developed by third parties or the regulated firms themselves. Cooperating firms may reach agreement faster than government procedures will allow, and private technical knowledge can be applied directly to the problem at the outset.	The Consumer Product Safety Commission encourages voluntary standards: television fire-safety problems and burn-safe furniture are specific examples. The Federal Communications Commission uses the Electronics Industry Association, the Land Mobile Communications Council, and the American Standards Institute for Electrical and Electronic Engineers to form joint technical committees to help develop many of its regulations.	Voluntary standards to not depend upon expensive and lengthy court litigation for enforcement. They cost little and can be developed quickly. They are one of the least intrusive ways of implementing policy.	Self-regulation is notoriously unsuccessful in dealing with many of the problems that brought on requirements for command and control regulation. The government has little or no effective control over compliance. Unless those involved perceive some benefit to compliance, they may well give only lip service to voluntary programs.

Technique	Description	Examples	Benefits	Problems
Tiering	Tailoring regulatory requirements, usually recordkeeping and reporting requirements, compliance responsibilities, and the meeting of eligibility requirements for government funding programs, to fit the size or nature of the regulated entity. This can reduce the disproportionate burden that falls on small businesses and other entities without forfeiting regulatory goals.	Under a program sponsored by the Office of Surface Mining, state surface mining regulatory authorities assist small operators in meeting regulatory requirements. Two reports, one hydrological and one geological must be submitted to a state before surface mining can begin. If an operator qualifies as a small operator, the state will pay for the expensive laboratory studies so that the operator can submit the reports and receive a mining permit. EPA has exempted approximately 695,000 generators of small amounts of hazardous wastes (less than one metric ton per month) from all reporting requirements for the hazardous waste program under the Resource Conservation and Recovery Act of 1976.	Reduces burdens of compliance on small businesses and organizations. May lead to more effective regulation because it is better tailored to the regulated organizations.	Defining tiers and comparing such definitions among various regulatory agencies and problems can be extremely difficult. The costs of administering tiered programs as compared with standardized programs can be quite high. While the negative impact of removing command and control regulations from one or a few small businesses may be minor, the cumulative impact, for example, in pollution-control can be very detrimental.

The committee also urged changes in the Senate confirmation process. It suggested creation of an Office of Regulatory Investigations to provide the legislature with an independent source of information on appointees.[185] Finally, it proposed standards to be employed in confirmation.

(1) That by reason of background, training, or experience, the nominee is affirmatively qualified for the office to which he or she is nominated.

(2) That, in considering a regulatory appointment, the Senate shall consider the character and nature of the office, and the needs of the agency to which the nominee has been named.

(3) That, in considering a regulatory appointment to a collegial body, the Senate shall consider the existing composition of that body and whether or not members of a single sector or group in society are too heavily represented.

(4) That the nominee is committed to enforcement of the regulatory framework as established by Congress in the statutes.

(5) That the nominee meet the statutory qualifications to hold the office to which he or she was nominated.[186]

Legislative Oversight Modifications

Over the past decade or so there have been efforts to alter the manner in which the legislature oversees regulatory activity. Again, the Ribicoff Committee recommendations are worthy of consideration. Basically, the proposals for oversight reform are of two types: general, broadly applicable suggestions and specific technique changes.

One of the most commonly suggested general improvements is for Congress to increase its staff. In fact, there is every indication that the legislature will continue to hire more staff members with a variety of technical skills. The recent development of an office of policy evaluation in the GAO is an example. There are several problems associated with proliferating staff offices and positions on the Hill, not the least of which is cost. The greatest hazard is that Congress will be unable to control its own bureaucracy. Turf fights between congressional staff agencies, such as the General Accounting Office and the Congressional Budget Office, have already broken out.[187]

Other frequently mentioned general changes include controlling casework (perhaps through some central clearinghouse in Congress),[188] educating members of Congress about the oversight techniques available to them (along with their potential uses and problems),[189] and enacting statutes that are more amenable to oversight.

The Ribicoff Committee proposed two techniques to make the oversight process more systematic, particularly with respect to oversight by authorization committees. It suggested that each committee should prepare an annual oversight plan indicating as specifically as possible what the committee anticipates doing and which agencies will be involved.[190] The plans would be compiled by the Congressional Research Service and distributed to members of the legislature, the various committees, and to the agencies to aid in their planning. In particular, the chairpersons of authorization and appropriations committees would be encouraged to

285
Politics and
Regulatory
Agencies:
Law and
Politics in
Administration

coordinate oversight hearings and share their findings. The major problem here, of course, would be breaking through jealously guarded prerogatives within the congressional committee structure. The Ribicoff Committee also supports the use of "sunset" provisions in legislation authorizing regulatory activity. These provisions state that unless an agency receives a new authorization within a given period, usually five or ten years, the sun will set (so to speak) on the agency and it will lose its authority. In theory, this will force periodic and presumably comprehensive reassessment of agency performance. In time, presumably "sunset" reviews would become systematized. A number of statutes now have sunset provisions and the process is well under way.[191] However, there is no guarantee that a sunset provision will trigger a careful, thoughtful, and systematic assessment of the performance of a regulatory agency. It may simply provide an opportunity to score political points and give a great deal of leverage to committee chairs. Then there is the problem of interest group imbalance. It is much easier to defeat legislation than it is to enact it. Some legislation came into being through a momentous effort to develop an interest group coalition around an issue, e.g., civil rights statutes. That kind of coalition generally breaks down after the law is enacted. The same is true of consumer-oriented legislation. Periodic reauthorization gives an advantage to smaller but better organized and financed interest groups over loose coalitions of public interest groups.

Two other suggested reforms would increase congressional access to information for use in the oversight process. The Ribicoff Committee suggests that regulatory statutes include a provision requiring agencies to provide information on request to the Congress and that funds be appropriated for that activity.[192] As it is presently, there are many problems in obtaining information from agencies and delays in processing congressional requests. This is a delicate problem because of the legal issues arising from the constitutional separation of powers and because it may further complicate already complex relationships between the White House and the Hill. However, how can Congress conduct proper oversight without information? A related recommendation by the Ribicoff Committee is for concurrent submission of budgets by agencies.[193] Some members of Congress have been concerned, particularly with respect to the independent regulatory commissions, that in deciding on appropriations they have seen only the recommendations in the president's budget prepared by the Office of Management and Budget. They would like to see the original agency requests.

One of the more controversial of recent legislative moves is the increasing use of the legislative veto of agency rulemaking[194] Indeed, the last several Congresses have considered imposing government-wide legislative veto rules through an amendment to the Administrative Procedure Act.[195] There are essentially two arguments in support of the veto. First, through the mechanism of a veto, Congress could respond quickly and specifically to a perceived administrative abuse of authority. Most of the veto provisions, either in the language of the law or in terms of their practical effect, focus congressional action is small subcommittees that can act to veto fairly quickly, if the need arises. Even where the veto is by one-house or a concurrent resolution, the recommendations of the subcommittee and the committee will very likely prevail. Second, the existence of a veto will presumably deter overly aggressive administrators who seek to promulgate unnecessary or excessively burdensome regulations. However, the veto is criticized on constitutional[196] and policy grounds.

The Ribicoff Committee analyzed the legislative veto and concluded:

Recommendation: Although the legislative veto may be appropriate in limited situations, the Congress should reject an across-the-board use of the legislative veto for regulatory agency rules. Congress should also refrain from routinely adding a legislative veto provision to regulatory agency statutes.[197]

The committee's assessment was that the veto "may: Increase delay in the regulatory process; Increase uncertainty in regulated industries and increase pressure on Congress; Diminish the usefulness of agency records: Encourage the agencies to decrease rulemaking and increase adjudication; [and] Have an adverse impact on entire regulatory programs."[198]

In a leading study on the implications of the legislative veto, Bruff and Gellhorn found that the veto is unlikely to make agencies more responsive to the public interest and may in fact make them more responsive to small well-organized interest groups or to a few members of Congress in pivotal subcommittee positions.[199] Congress could not possibly review all or even most regulations, so a veto process would involve selective review.[200] The rules that would be subjected to review would likely be those that well-financed interest groups would take on a political appeal from the agency rulemaking process to the congressional subcommittee. Agencies could be coerced into modifying their findings by a threatened veto.

It has also been noted that judicial review will be adversely affected since, if a court is eventually called on to review a regulation that went through the congressional process, it will be difficult for the court to determine legislative intent. Veto provisions often include statements that legislative clearance should not imply congressional approval for purposes of review, but that does not prevent the use of hearing records or other kinds of congressional record information in appealing cases. Just what courts will do with this problem remains to be seen.

Rulemaking Procedural Modifications

In recent years, Congress has imposed requirements for hybrid rulemaking procedures and has been considering several amendments to the APA. However, during the Carter and Reagan administrations much of the initiative for changes in rulemaking procedures has come from the White House. Carter's Executive Order No. 12044 imposed hybrid rulemaking requirements on virtually all executive branch agencies. It established a general requirement for regulatory impact analyses in cases of substantial rules (defined as those having an impact of more than $100 million on the economy). It required the development of a calendar of federal regulations in which agencies are required to publish, at the beginning of the fiscal year, the major rulemaking efforts they anticipate in the coming year along with sufficient descriptive material to enable interest groups or congressional committees to participate if they so desire. The order also required executive agencies to consider alternatives to regulation.

Shortly after he took office, President Reagan issued Executive Order No. 12291,[201] a revised version of Carter's No. 12044 with additional provisions that discourage rulemaking. Specifically, No. 12291 has several requirements for cost-

benefit analysis justification for new rules and permits the director of the Office of
Management and Budget to

> (5) identify duplicative, overlapping, and conflicting rules existing or
> proposed, and existing or proposed rules that are inconsistent with the
> policies underlying statutes governing agencies other than the issuing
> agency or with the purpose of this Order, and, in each such case, require
> appropriate interagency consultation to minimize or eliminate such
> duplication, overlap, or conflict;
> (6) Develop procedures for estimating the annual benefits and costs of
> agency regulations, on both an aggregate and economic or industrial sector
> basis, for purposes of compiling a regulatory budget.[202]

287
Politics and
Regulatory
Agencies:
Law and
Politics in
Administration

Additionally, the order authorizes the director of OMB, on his own motion or at
the request of the "President's Task Force on Regulatory Relief," to review the
required "Regulatory Impact Analysis" for a proposed rule and, if in the opinion of
the OMB it is warranted, delay publication of a proposed rule for comment or of a
final rule for implementation.[203] In sum, these two executive orders substantially
complicate the process of rulemaking for executive branch agencies, and in fact
they discourage rulemaking.

These presidential modifications must also be understood in connection with a
recent legislative change. The Regulatory Flexibility Act of 1980 imposes
essentially similar requirements on agencies as did Carter's No. 12044 when they
make rules that will have a significant economic effect on small entities. Small
entities under the act mean "small businesses," "small organizations (not for
profits)," and "small governmental jurisdictions." These regulatory flexibility
analyses must be submitted to the Small Business Administration for evaluation
and must be published in the Federal Register. The act specifically gives the chief
counsel for advocacy of the Small Business Administration the right to appear as
amicus curiae "in any action brought in a court of the United States to review a
rule."[204]

Presumably, some of the steps taken to modify administrative rulemaking will
create better records for future consideration as well as discourage unnecessary or
duplicative rulemaking. Also, agencies must take cognizance of the impact of their
proposed rules. Both orders enhance the president's opportunity to intervene in
agency rulemaking.

Unfortunately, these changes present many of the same problems as does the
legislative veto. Presidents who claim to be interested in streamlining the
governing process and reducing paperwork have created complex additional
procedures that will generate volumes of additional paperwork for each rule
developed. They offer a variety of mechanisms for political intervention in
rulemaking outside of the normal process. They foster many of the potential abuses
of cost-benefit calculation that have been discussed earlier in this book. They
discourage administrators from rulemaking at a time when most dispassionate
observers of the regulatory process call for the development of policy through
rulemaking rather than through adjudication. Finally, depending on how the chief
executive employs the techniques imposed on agencies and how they are
interpreted by the courts, these additional requirements for rulemaking could
spawn countless new and complex forms of litigation.

Public Participation

An annual calendar of proposed regulatory activity and hybrid rulemaking require-ments, imposed by the executive orders, do improve opportunities for public participation. Congress has also moved to make participation more available, although many difficulties remain. Specifically, the Freedom of Information Act, the Government in the Sunshine Act, and the Federal Advisory Committee Act all have the effect of opening up a variety of agency processes. These acts will be considered in Chapter 11. The legislature has also encouraged agencies to assist public interest participants through permitting access to information or, in some cases, by minimizing costs of participation. Agencies have moved to increase publication of notice of rulemaking or major adjudications in trade journals, by mailings to interest groups, and even by press releases and spot news announcements.

The three major problems of public participation continue to be the cost of intervention, the need for the widest possible notice of pending proceedings, and the need to clarify and develop the procedural rules governing public participation in proceedings both before the agency and possibly later before a court.

SUMMARY

In this chapter we have presented an overview of the problems and new directions in regulatory law and administration. We sought to distinguish between, on the one hand, careful, detailed consideration of particular problems of improving regulation as a policy technique chosen by the legislature to advance particular purposes, and, on the other, the macro-level debate over the inherent goodness or badness of regulation. Regulation is one of a number of policy options, it is selected most often not because it is particularly favored but because specific circumstances of problems seem more amenable to regulation than to other available solutions. The decisions as to which policy mechanism ought to be employed is a political decision, not an economic judgment.

Those interested in regulatory reform can learn a great deal about possible directions for change by examining the institutions and actors involved in the regulatory process. In particular, this chapter has considered: regulatory agencies as organizations; the role of the president in the regulatory process; the congressional task in regulatory activity; and the problems and prospects of public participation. For the President, the key aspects of regulatory administration appear to be improve-ments in the appointments process and the desire to improve control and coordina-tion within the executive branch. The Congress continues to try to improve its oversight of agency activity while recognizing the institutional constraints it faces in that effort. The problems of just what kinds and means of public participation will be useful and effective remain a major problem in regulatory administration.

Finally, we considered some of the efforts at regulatory reform that have emerged within the past decade or so, with particular attention to innovative techniques, appointment reforms, legislative oversight recommendations, and changes in the rulemaking process. Some of these changes are for the better. Others are more directed at regulatory reduction than regulatory reform.

The debate over regulatory politics and administration cuts across government and seems likely to be a focal point for discussion and action for the foreseeable future. Another such area of public law and public administration is the acquisition, use, and dissemination of information by government. Chapter 11 addresses itself to that subject.

289
Politics and
Regulatory
Agencies:
Law and
Politics in
Administration

NOTES

[1]Airline Deregulation Act of 1978, Public Law 95-504, 92 Stat. 1705, 49 U.S.C. §1301 et seq. (1976).

[2]Staggers Rail Act of 1980, Public Law 96-448, 94 Stat. 1895, 49 U.S.C §§10101a, 10501(a), 10505, 10701a, 10707a, 10709, 10712, 10713, 10729, 10730, 10731, 10741, 10751, 10752 (1976).

[3]Motor Carrier Act of 1980, Public Law 96-296, 94 Stat. 793, 49 U.S.C. §§10101(a), 10102(12), 10322, 10521, 10524, 10526, 10527, 10528, 10701, 10703(b), 10706, 10708, 10730, 10732, 10733, 10749, 10751, 10922, 10923(d), 10924, 10925, 10927, 10928, 10930(a), 11109, 11302(b), 11342, 11345, 11503a, 11701(c), 11902 (1976).

[4]Council on Environmental Quality, "Toxic Substances," in U.S. House of Representatives, Environment and Natural Resources Policy Division of the Library of Congress for the House Committee on Interstate and Foreign Commerce, *Legislative History of the Toxic Substances Control Act* (Committee Print, 1976). (Hereafter referred to as Toxic Substances Act History.)

[5]Id., at p. 4,

[6]Id., at pp. 3–6.

[7]Id., at p. 4.

[8]Id.

[9]The story of the growing awareness of low-level toxicity of such substances as benzene is summarized in *Industrial Union Department, AFL-CIO v. American Petroleum Inst.*, 448 U.S. 607, 615–27 (1980).

[10]History of Toxic Substances Control Act, supra note 4, at p. 4.

[11]Id., at p. 239. See also *New York Times*, April 1, 1978, p. 1.

[12]See, e.g., E. J. Dionne, Jr., "The Love Canal Legacy: Lawsuits and Bitterness," *New York Times*, September 7, 1981, p. 11.

[13]*Natural Resources Defense Council v. Nuclear Regulatory Comm'n*, 547 F. 2d 633, 648 (D.C. Cir. 1976).

[14]Irving Molotsky, "House Panel Lists Toxic Sites Threatening Water Supplies in U.S.," *New York Times*, September 28, 1980, p. 45.

[15]"State's Nuclear Waste Ban is Ruled Unconstitutional," *New York Times*, June 27, 1981, p. 6.

[16]See generally the Comprehensive Environmental Response, Compensation, and Liability Act of 1980, Public Law 96-510, 94 Stat. 2767, and associated EPA regulations. See particularly the act's legislative history in 1981 *U.S. Code Cong. and Admin. News* 6119–6240.

[17]See Charles Seabrook, "State Plan for Dumps Draws Fire," *Atlanta Constitution*, June 21, 1981, p. B-1; Fran Hesser, "Assembly May Act to Put State in Hazardous Waste Business," *Atlanta Constitution*, February 17, 1981, p. 1; and Fran Hesser and Sharon Bailey, "Attempt to Alter Hazardous Waste Bill Thwarted," *Atlanta Constitution*, March 6, 1981, p. 2-C.

[18]The shrillest critics have been such people as Friedrich von Hayek, *The Road to Serfdom* (Chicago: University of Chicago Press, 1944), and Murray Wiedenbaum, whose ideas appear in U.S. Senate, Hearings Before the Subcommittee on Administrative Practices and Procedure, *Administrative Procedure Reform Act of 1978*, 95th Cong., 2d Sess. (1978), pp. 425–28.

[19]In U.S. Senate, Hearings Before the Subcommittee on Administrative Practice and Procedure of the Committee on the Judiciary, *Administrative Procedure Act Amendments of 1978*, 95th Cong., 2d Sess. (1978), p. 1.

[20]Senator Schmitt, id., at pp. 2–4.

[21]See generally President's Advisory Council on Executive Organization (Ash Council), *A New Regulatory Framework: Report on Selected Independent Regulatory Agencies* (Washington, D.C.: Government Printing Office, 1971).

[22]Adam Smith, *An Inquiry into the Nature and Causes of the Wealth of Nations* (Chicago: University of Chicago Press, 1976).

On the self-destructive tendencies in the American marketplace, see Louis D. Brandeis, *Other People's Money* (New York: Harper & Row, 1967); John Kenneth Galbraith, *The Great Crash* (Boston: Houghton Mifflin, 1961); Ralph de Bedts, *The New Deal's SEC: The Formative Years* (New York: Columbia University Press, 1964); and William O. Douglas, *Democracy and Finance* (Port Washington, N.Y.: Kennikat Press, 1940).

[23]Statement of Mark Green and Nancy Diabble of Public Citizens Congress Watch before the Senate Governmental

Affairs Committee, "Regulatory Reform Act," May 1, 1979, mimeographed.

[24]Id., at p. 2.

[25]Id.

[26]Id., at p. 3.

[27]Id.

[28]Id.

[29]Id.

[30]Id., at p. 4.

[31]Id., at p. 5.

[32]Id.

[33]Id.

[34]U.S. House of Representatives, Report of the Subcommittee on Oversight and Investigation of the Committee on Interstate and Foreign Commerce, *Cost-Benefit Analysis: Wonder Tool or Mirage?*, 96th Cong., 2d Sess. (1980), pp. 9–10. (Hereafter cited as Subcommittee Report.)

[35]Green, supra note 23, at p. 6.

[36]See., e.g., Charles O. Jones, *An Introduction to the Study of Public Policy*, 2d ed., (North Scituate, Mass.: Duxbury Press, 1977), and Robert Lineberry, *American Public Policy* (New York: Harper & Row, 1977).

[37]See, e.g., James MacGregor Burns, J. W. Peltason, and Thomas E. Cronin, *Government by the People*, 10th ed. (Englewood Cliffs, N.J.: Prentice-Hall, 1978), p. 406.

[38]Fred M. Frohock, *Public Policy: Scope and Logic* (Englewood Cliffs, N.J.: Prentice-Hall, 1979), pp. 11–15.

[39]See, e.g., *Regulating with Common Sense: A Progress Report on Innovative Regulatory Techniques* (Washington, D.C.: U.S. Regulatory Council, 1980), and "Innovative Techniques in Theory and Practice," *Proceedings, U.S. Regulatory Council Conference* (Washington, D.C.: U.S. Regulatory Council, 1980).

[40]Theodore J. Lowi, "Four Systems of Policy, Politics and Choice," *Public Admin. Rev.* 298, 299–300 (1972).

[41]Frohock, supra note 38, at p. 13.

[42]Id.

[43]I should note in passing that I disagree with some of the classifications as applied by Frohock to specific policies. Id., at p. 14.

[44]On the Ethics of Government Act, see Chapter 12.

[45]Subcommittee Report, supra note 34, at p. 5.

[46]James Q. Wilson, "The Politics of Regulation," in Wilson, ed., *The Politics of Regulation* (New York: Basic Books, 1980), pp. 358–63.

[47]Id., at pp. 362–63.

[48]Id., at p. 363.

[49]Subcommittee Report, supra note 34, at p. 7.

[50]Also from the Subcommittee Report, p. 7: "While it is not nearly as easy to quantify the costs and benefits of a proposed regulation as it is to quantify baseball statistics, whenever some quantification is done—no matter how speculative or limited—the number tends to get into the public domain and the qualifications tend to get forgotten. When impor-

tant elements are not quantified or are quantified inadequately or unfairly, the quantification can have a pernicious effect. Dr. Lester Love commented upon this phenomenon in this testimony before the Subcommittee:

" 'There is a Gresham's law of decision making: quantified effects tend to dominate consideration, even if the unquantified effects are believed to be more important. Thus, quantification is likely to be pernicious if important aspects are left unquantified, if the quantification isn't evenhanded for benefits and costs, or if the quantification is inadequate.' "

[51]Id., at. p. 6.

[52]Luther Gulick, "The Twenty-fifth Anniversary of the American Society for Public Administration," 25 *Public Admin. Rev.* 1, 3 (1965).

[53]Subcommittee Report, supra note 34, at p. 10.

[54]Id., at p. 11.

[55]Id., at p. 16.

[56]Id.

[57]Id., at p. 17.

[58]Id.

[59]Id., at p. 20. Green has asked: "What is the value of avoiding pain and suffering to an auto crash victim, or the loss of consortium to the victim's spouse? Can a dollar figure be put on the benefit of a six-year-old not disfigured from flammable sleepwear? How do we calculate the environmental benefits of seeing across the Grand Canyon, of utilizing recreational areas, of avoiding property depreciation due to pollution? What is the dollar value of investor confidence in a sound securities market and of consumer confidence in safe food and drugs?" Green, supra note 23, at p. 4.

[60]Subcommittee Report, supra note 34, at p. 25.

[61]U.S. Senate, Committee on Governmental Affairs, *Study on Federal Regulation*, 95th Cong., 2d Sess. (1978), vol. 6, chap. 2.

[62]This problem is epitomized by the "tragedy of the commons." See Lineberry, supra note 36, at pp. 31–32.

[63]U.S. House of Representatives, Hearings Before the Subcommittee on Oversight and Investigations of the Committee on Interstate and Foreign Commerce, *Acid Rain*, 96th Cong., 2d Sess. (1980), p. 14.

[64]Id., at pp. 25–26.

[65]Id., at p. 2.

[66]Eddy, Potter, and Paige argue, based upon their analysis of evidence from trial records and other data, that the dramatic competition among aircraft manufacturers for orders for airbuses resulted in unsafe technical changes in design to save enough weight to allow one more seat in the aircraft. The design ultimately failed, resulting in the loss of a fully loaded airliner. Paul Eddy, Elaine Potter, and Bruce Page, *Destination Disaster* (New York: Ballantine, 1976).

Another recent example of destructive competition is the gasoline war, which has the most serious consequences for station owners operating on narrow profit margins. Such price battles result in the destruction of weaker competitors and in higher prices set by the survivors, as well as wasteful use of fuel in the near term.

[67]See note 22.

[68]The sad state of affairs that led to the creation of the Food and Drug Administration was presented in Upton Sinclair's

classic *The Jungle* (New York: Airmont, 1965). The enabling legislation has been reconsidered on at least three occasions since the 1930s, but each time a major incident involving food, drugs, or cosmetics caused legislators to strengthen the agency's authority.

[69]See the legislative histories of the National Traffic and Motor Vehicle Safety Act of 1966, Public Law 89-563, 80 Stat. 718, and the Highway Safety act of 1966, Public Law 564, 80 Stat. 731, in 1966 *U.S. Code Cong. and Admin. News* 2709, 2741 (1966).

[70]These are results of the study by the National Commission on Product Safety, cited in Kenneth Culp Davis, *Administrative Law: Cases–Text–Problems*, 6th ed. (St. Paul. Minn.: West, 1977), p. 9.

[71]U.S. Senate, Subcommittee on Labor of the Committee on Labor and Public Welfare, *Legislative History of the Occupational Safety and Health Act of 1970*, 92d Cong., 1st Sess. (1971), p. 142.

[72]See, e.g., Federal Election Commission, *Legislative History of Federal Election Campaign Act Amendments of 1974* (Washington, D.C.: Government Printing Office, 1977) and id, *Legislative History of Federal Election Campaign Act of 1976* (Washington, D.C.: Government Printing Office, 1977).

[73]See, e.g., U.S. Senate, Subcommittee on Labor of the Committee on Human Resources, *Legislative History of the Federal Mine Safety and Health Act of 1977*, 95th Cong., 2d Sess. (1978).

[74]Marver Bernstein, *Regulating Business by Independent Commission* (Princeton, N.J.: Princeton University Press, 1955).

[75]Id., chap. 3 (Bernstein was not alone in his life-cycle approach to regulatory agencies. See Galbraith, supra note 22, at p. 96.)

[76]Id., at p. 74.

[77]Id., at p. 79.

[78]Id., at p. 84.

[79]Id., at p. 87.

[80]Id., at p. 90.

[81]Id., at p. 92.

[82]Wilson, supra note 46.

[83]Id., at p. 366.

[84]Id., at p. 367.

[85]Id., at p. 368.

[86]Id., at p. 369.

[87]Id., at pp. 370-72.

[88]Wilson's essay does not explain many anamolous cases. Additionally, Wilson suggests that Bernstein's captive thesis does not come to grips with the fact that agencies *do* make decisions contrary to the regulated interests. He also argues that his own characterization of the politics that give rise to regulatory programs and guide their operations explains behavior better. Bernstein might answer that he did not say that agencies were not born in a variety of political environments. They did not come into existence as captives of the regulated interests; in fact, the captive process does not begin until a regulated interest recognizes that it has lost the battle to prevent regulation. Second, Bernstein might answer that agencies may decide against the wishes of regulated interest in their early years, but such decisions become more unusual over time. Finally, he might argue that it is an oversimplifica-

tion to assume that the "captive" thesis means that agencies will never act against the regulated group. A more sophisticated analysis might suggest that at least during what he describes as the years of maturity, the regulated party may have come to be in a superior debating position relative to outsiders who wish to affect agency policy.

[89]Graham T. Allison, *Essence of Decision* (Boston: Little, Brown, 1971), chap. 3.

[90]James D. Thompson, *Organizations in Action* (New York: McGraw-Hill, 1967), chaps. 9–10.

[91]See generally Francis Rourke, *Bureaucracy, Politics, and Public Policy* (Boston: Little, Brown, 1969), and W. Henry Lambright, *Governing Science and Technology* (New York: Oxford University Press, 1976).

[92]*Study on Federal Regulation*, supra note 61, vol. 1, p. 26.

[93]See, e.g., Ash Council, supra note 21.

[94]See, e.g., *Study on Federal Regulation*, supra note 61, vol. 1, p. 23, and Roger G. Noll, *Reforming Regulation: An Evaluation of the Ash Council Proposals* (Washington, D.C.: Brookings Institution, 1971).

[95]U.S. Constitution, Article II, §2, cl. 2.

[96]Id., article II, §3.

[97]Stephen Hess, *Organizing the Presidency* (Washington, D.C.: Brookings Institution, 1976).

[98]Surprisingly little has been written in public administration literature on high-level executive branch staffing. The leading work on top executives is Hugh Heclo, *A Government of Strangers* (Washington, D.C.: Brookings Institution, 1977).

[99]See, e.g., Richard Nathan, *The Plot That Failed* (New York: Wiley, 1975).

[100]Harold Seidman, *Politics, Position, and Power* 2d ed. (New York: Oxford University Press, 1976). See also Nathan, supra note 99.

[101]The changes in the Civil Service Service system that were instituted by creation of the Senior Executive Service during the Carter administration may weaken traditional bureaucratic defenses. See Bernard Rosen, "Uncertainty in the Senior Executive Service," 41 *Public Admin. Rev.* 203 (1981). This topic is considered further in Chapter 12.

[102]Richard Neustadt, *Presidential Power* (New York: Wiley, 1960).

[103]Burns has argued that power and leadership are not the same and that leadership is necessary for government to work well and effectively. James MacGregor Burns, *Leadership* (New York: Harper & Row, 1978), chap. 1.

[104]Glenn O. Robinson, "The Federal Communications Commission: An Essay on Regulatory Watchdogs," 64 *Virginia L. Rev.* 169, 183–85 (1978).

[105]Henry J. Friendly, *The Federal Administrative Agencies: The Need for Better Definition of Standards* (Cambridge, Mass.: Harvard University Press, 1962), pp. 142–43.

[106]Bernard Schwartz, *The Professor and the Commissions* (New York: Knopf, 1959), p. 203.

[107]Robinson, supra note 102, at p. 188.

[108]This tactic can be a high-risk venture. The dramatic Senate Foreign Relations Committee rejection of Ernest LeFever to head human rights policy in the State Department is an example. A similar example was the battle over Reagan's appointment of Dr. C. Everett Coop, a physician with, among other things, a widely known and ardently defended antiabortion record, as Surgeon General.

[109]Robinson, supra note 104, at p. 186.

[110]*Study on Federal Regulation*, supra note 61, vol. 1, p. 19.

[111]The Ethics in Government Act, discussed in Chapter 12, is an attempt to assist in this endeavor.

[112]William Cary, *Politics and the Regulatory Agencies* (New York: McGraw-Hill, 1967), p. 11.

[113]*Study on Federal Regulation*, supra note 61, vol. 1, *The Regulatory Appointments Process*.

[114]Id., at p. 6.

[115]Id., at p. xxxi.

[116]"The most recent study of appointments published in 1976 by the Senate Commerce Committee exhaustively reviewed the circumstances of appointment of more than fifty members of the Federal Trade Commission and the Federal Communications Commission over a twenty-five year period. The authors of that study concluded that "many selections can be explained in terms of powerful political connections and little else." Dissatisfaction with the quality of appointments is by no means limited to liberal reformers, as illustrated by the conclusions of an American Conservative Union study issued early in 1976: according to that report, President Ford "displays a predilection toward old-shoe mediocrity, rather than a desire to seek out excellence. . . . In terms of both quantity and quality, the appointments of the Ford Administration are a disaster for conservatives." In October 1976, the House Investigations and Oversight Subcommittee of the Commerce Committee noted with concern the importance of factors unrelated to quality in regulatory appointments. 'We found that the influence of partisanship or narrow economic interest in these appointments has not diminished. . . . We found little significant progess in improving the quality of nominees or the criteria and process of selection of candidates." Id., at p. 7.

[117]"A more major public concern in recent times is the balance of commission membership, and whether the varied interests within our society have been fairly represented on those collegial bodies. Few women or minority group members have been appointed to the commissions; for example the Securities and Exchange Commission has not had a black or female commissioner in its forty-year history. There is also a dearth of commissioners who, prior to appointment, had a clear association with consumer interests; that has been highlighted by the comparatively large number of regulators who were appointed directly from the ranks of the regulated industries. Indeed, the pro-industry imbalance on the Federal Power Commission in 1973 was a major reason for the rejection by the Senate of an FPC nominee—the first time in more than twenty years that the full Senate had rejected a regulatory appointment." Id., at p. 32.

[118]Cary, supra note 112, at p. 11.

[119]Id., at p. 4.

[120]"The expenditures of most regulatory activities are for salaries and expenses for operations. Budget requests for these activities have generally been reviewed by the appropriations committees, and with the exception of outlays from prior obligations, they are controllable. Total fiscal year 1977 budget authority requested in the President's January 1976 budget for fourteen major regulatory agencies was $4.4 billion." *Study on Federal Regulation*, supra note 61, vol. 2.

[121]Where an agency is in need of special varieties and levels of personnel such as scientists, lawyers or high level administrators, that presidential discretion can be extremely important.

[122]See, e.g., Executive Order No. 12044, 43 Fed. Reg. 12661 (1978) and Executive Order No. 12291, 46 Fed. Reg. 13193 (1981).

[123]5 U.S.C. §§554(d), 557 (d).

[124]See Hugh Heclo, "OMB and the Presidency: The Problem of Neutral Competence," 38 *Public Interest* 80 (1975), and Larry Berman, *The Office of Management and Budget and the Presidency* (Princeton N.J.: Princton University Press, 1979).

[125]See the discussion of the *Overton Park* case, Chapter 7.

[126]See, e.g., Schwartz, supra note 106, at pp. 218–28.

[127]Martin Tolchin, "Battle Intensifies Over Authority of President to Control Agencies," *New York Times*, January 17, 1979, p. 1.

[128]*Regulatory Reform Highlights: An Inventory of Initiatives, 1978–80* (Washington, D.C.: U.S. Regulatory Commission, 1980), p. 8.

[129]"To assist individual agencies in meeting the goals of Executive Order 12044, the President established the Regulatory Analysis Review Group (RARG) to review and comment upon selected regulatory analyses of proposed new rules. The group which is composed of representatives from executive branch economic and regulatory agencies and the Executive Office of the President, brings a perspective from outside the agency to newly proposed regulations. This group is chaired by a member of the Council of Economic Advisers." Id., p. 7.

[130]Id.

[131]See, e.g., Emmette Redford, "The President and the Regulatory Commissions," 44 *Texas L. Rev.* 288 (1965). Marver Bernstein, Robert Cushman, and the Ash Council have expressed similar views supporting an active presidential role. See, e.g., Bernstein, supra note 74, at p. 163; Robert Cushman, *The Independent Regulatory Commissions* (New York: Oxford University Press, 1941), p. 689; and Ash Council, supra note 21.

[132]Friendly, supra note 105, p. 153.

[133]Id., at pp. 148–49.

[134]Cary, supra note 112, at p. 7.

[135]Id., at p. 8.

[136]Id., at pp. 20–25. Actually, he was not far from Friendly's position in this regard. "I do not have much trouble with the President's informing the agency of his policy when the policy is a very general one, for which he desires the

cooperation not only of the particular agency but of all branches of government, although I am skeptical that this would accomplish anything approaching what its advocates expect. . . .

"On the other hand, I would see a number of difficulties in the President's enunciating a more specific merger policy for the agencies to follow." Friendly, supra note 132, at pp. 149–50.

[137]Memorandum from Robert Rauch to Environmental Protection Agency, President Jimmy Carter, Stuart Eisenstadt, Charles Schultze, William Nordhaus, Robert Strauss, and Douglas Costle, September 5, 1978.

[138]Lawrence C. Dodd and Richard L. Schott, *Congress and the Administrative State* (New York: Wiley, 1979); Morris Ogul, *Congress Oversees the Bureaucracy* (Pittsburgh: Pittsburgh University Press, 1976); and Joseph P. Harris, *Congressional Control of Administration* (Garden City, N.Y.: Doubleday, 1964).

[139]*Study on Federal Regulation*, supra note 61, vol. 2, *Congressional Oversight of Regulatory Agencies.* Another very useful study of legislative oversight is U.S. Senate, Congressional Research Service and General Accounting Office for the Subcommittee on Oversight Procedures of the Committee on Government Operations, *Congressional Oversight: Methods and Techniques*, 94th Cong., 2d Sess. (1976).

[140]Dodd and Schott, supra note 138, at p. 156; Harris, supra note 138, at p. 1. *Study on Federal Regulation*, supra note 61, vol. 2, p. 4.

[141]Harris, supra note 138, at p. 9.

[142]*Study on Federal Regulation*, supra note 61, vol. 2, p. 4.

[143]See, e.g., *Chadha v. Immigration and Naturalization Service*, 634 F. 2d 409 (9th Cir. 1981).

[144]Harris, supra note 138, at p. 2.

[145]*Study on Federal Regulation*, supra note 61, vol. 2, p. 4.

[146]On casework generally, see *Congressional Oversight*, supra note 139, chapter 13, "Casework and Projects: Oversight in the Members Office," pp. 67–70.

[147]Abraham Ribicoff, "Congressional Oversight and Regulatory Reform," 28 *Admin. L. Rev.* 415, 418 (1976).

[148]*Study on Federal Regulation*, supra, vol. 2, p. 4.

[149]Id., at pp. 16–17.

[150]"The 1946 Legislative Reorganization Act was the first statute requiring congressional committees to oversee federal agencies. Section 136 of the Act stated that:

"Each standing committee of the Senate and the House of Representatives shall exercise continuous watchfulness of the execution by the administrative agencies concerned of any laws, the subject matter of what is within the jurisdiction of such committees." Id. at p. 16.

[151]Id., at p. 15.

[152]Examples of each of these are provided in *Congressional Oversight*, supra note 139.

[153]*Study on Federal Regulation*, supra note 61, vol. 2, p. 51.

[154]Id., at p. 81.

[155]See Chapter 8.

[156]*Study on Federal Regulation*, supra note 61, vol. 2, pp. 80-81.

[157]Id., at p. 94.

[158]Id., at p. 66.

[159]Id., at pp. 66–67.

[160]Id., at p. 94.

[161]Id., at p. 156.

[162]Id., at p. 17.

[163]Id., at pp. 30–32.

[164]Id., at p. 123.

[165]Alexander Hamilton, James Madison, and John Jay, *The Federalist Papers* (New York: Mentor, 1961), pp. 309–10.

[166]This treatment draws heavily on the following studies, *Study on Federal Regulation*, supra, note 61, vol. 3, *Public Participation in Regulatory Agency Proceedings*; Ernest Gellhorn, "Public Participation in Administrative Proceedings," 71 *Reports of the Administrative Conference of the United States* 376 (1972), also published in 81 *Yale L. J.* 359 (1972); and Roger C. Cramton, "The Why, Where and How of Broadened Public Participation in the Administrative Process," 71 *Reports of the Administrative Conference of the United States* 422 (1972), also published in 60 *Georgetown L. J.* 525 (1972).

[167]The most frequently cited cases include *National Welfare Rights Organization v. Finch*, 429 F. 2d 725 (D.C. Cir. 1970); *Office of Communication of the United Church of Christ v. Federal Communications Comm'n*, 359 F. 2d 994 (D.C. Cir. 1966); and *Scenic Hudson Preservation Conference v. Federal Power Comm'n*, 354 F. 2d 608 (2d Cir. 1965).

[168]Probably the best treatment of the subject is Clement Vose, *Caucasians Only: The Supreme Court, The NAACP, and the Restrictive Covenant Cases* (Berkeley: University of California, 1959).

[169]*Study on Federal Regulation*, supra note 61, vol. 3, p. 2.

[170]Comptroller General of the United States, *Need for Improving the Regulation of the Natural Gas Industry and Management of Internal Operations* (Washington, D.C.: General Accounting Office B-180228, 1974), pp. 35–36.

[171]See Cramton, supra note 166, at pp. 428–32, and Gellhorn, supra note 166, at p. 388.

[172]See, e.g., *United Church of Christ v. FCC*, supra note 167.

[173]See the discussion of the *Overton Park* case in Chapter 7.

[174]See, e.g., *Study on Federal Regulation*, supra note 61, vol. 3, chap. 2, "Extent and Cost of Participation."

[175]Gellhorn, supra note 166, at pp. 406–7.

[176]*Study on Federal Regulation*, supra note 61, vol. 3, p. 22.

[177]Id., part II, "Procedural Barriers to Public Participation," and U.S. House of Representatives, Hearings Before the Subcommittee on Courts, Civil Liberties, and the Administration of Justice of the Committee on the Judiciary, *State of the Judiciary and Access to Justice*, 95th Cong., 1st Sess. (1977).

[178]See generally the testimony in support of H.R. 1776 in U.S. House of Representatives, Hearings before the Subcommittee on Rules of the House Rules Committee, *H.R. 1776, The Administrative Rule Making Reform Act, and Related Measures*, parts 1, 2, 3, 96th Cong., 1st Sess. (1979).

[179]Executive Order No. 12044, section 2(d)(3), 43 Fed. Reg. 12661 (1978).

[180]Member organizations included the Administrative Conference of the United States, Department of Agriculture, Department of Commerce, Department of Education, Department of Energy, Department of Health and Human Services, Department of Housing and Urban Development, Department of the Interior, Department of Justice, Department of Labor, Department of Transportation, Department of the Treasury, Environmental Protection Agency, Equal Employment Opportunity Commission, Federal Emergency Management Agency, General Services Administration, National Credit Union Association, Small Business Administration, United States International Trade Commission, Veterans Administration, Civil Aeronautics Board, Commodity Futures Trading Commission, Consumer Product Safety Commission, Federal Deposit Insurance Corporation, Federal Election Commission, Federal Energy Regulatory Commission, Federal Home Loan Bank, Federal Maritime Commission, Federal Mine Safety and Health Review Commission, Federal Reserve System, Federal Trade Commission, Interstate Commerce Commission, National Labor Relations Board, Nuclear Regulatory Commission, Occupational Safety and Health Review Commission, Postal Rate Commission, and Securities and Exchange Commission.

[181]*Regulating with Common Sense*, supra note 39, at p. 1.

[182]See note 94 supra.

[183]*Study on Federal Regulation*, supra note 61, vol. 1, p. xxii.

[184]Id., at p. xxvi.

[185]Id., at pp. xxiii–xxix.

[186]Id., at p. 179.

[187]For example, Comptroller General Elmer Staats stated: "However, we strongly recommend that the oversight role that the bill vests with the Congressional Budget Office should be assigned to the GAO." "Statement by Elmer B. Staats, Comptroller General of the United States before the United States Senate Committee on Government Affairs on The Reform of Federal Regulation Act of 1979 (S. 262), and the Regulation Reform Act of 1979 (S. 755)," GAO Release, May 23, 1979, p. 2

[188]*Study on Federal Regulation*, supra note 61, vol. 2, pp. 64–65.

[189]See *Congressional Oversight*, supra note 139.

[190]*Study on Federal Regulation*, supra note 61, vol. 2, pp. 95–98.

[191]See, e.g., Lawrence J. Dyckman, "GAO's First Sunset Review: Deciding Whether to Dismantle an Agency," 14 GAO Review 45 (1979).

[192]*Study on Federal Regulation*, supra note 61, vol. 2, pp. 99–105.

[193]Id., at p. 128.

[194]On the veto generally, see Chapter 5.

[195]See note 178 supra.

[196]See, e.g., Robert G. Dixon, "The Congressional Veto and Separation of Powers: The Executive on a Leash," 56 N. Carolina L. Rev. 423 (1978).

[197]*Study on Federal Regulation*, supra note 61, vol. 2, p. 122.

[198]Id., at p. 117.

[199]Ernest Gellhorn and Harold Bruff, "Congressional Control of Administrative Regulation: A Study of Legislative Vetoes," 90 Harvard L. Rev. 1369 (1977).

[200]See the CRS listing of the number of regulations that would be subject to review in one month, in note 178 supra, at p. 223.

[201]Executive Order No. 12291, 46 Fed. Reg. 13193 (1981).

[202]Id., section 6 (5)–(6).

[203]Id., section 3(3)–(f).

[204]5 U.S.C. §612(b).

Acquisition, Use, and Dissemination of Information: A System of Information Policy

As with regulatory law and administration, there is widespread concern about how governmental organizations acquire, use, and disseminate information about individuals, groups, and businesses. This pervasive law and policy issue affects all citizens and, in varying degrees, all administrative agencies.

Over the past decade, legal and political institutions at the national, state, and local levels have been feverishly attempting to come to grips with the information explosion, recognizing that it bodes both well and ill for consumers and producers of administrative decisions.[1] It bodes well if a decisionmaker is able to acquire and use relevant information to develop policies and resolve disputes. It is positive also for consumers of decisions who are now better able than in earlier times to acquire information about what government is doing to or for them. On the other hand, this knowledge, and the information-processing technology that goes along with it, may paralyze decisionmakers by the sheer volume of information that is available, rendering them ineffective.[2] They are also endangered by the declining ability of officials to maintain reasonable confidentiality within an agency.[3] From the consumer perspective, the specter of Orwell's "Big Brother" looms large as we move toward 1984.[4] The legislative histories of a number of bills document any number of abuses of personal privacy by a variety of public and private institutions.

In earlier chapters we noted the Freedom of Information Act (FOIA)[5] and the Right to Privacy Act[6] were designed to aid in the resolution of legal aspects of information problems. Indeed, a fair amount of what has been written on this subject follows a rather simple approach to agency information problems, based on those acts. These commentaries often begin with a recognition that we all "live in an information society."[7] They then suggest that what is needed is the development of a creative balance between the right to personal privacy and the government's need for social, political, economic, and scientific information. The common next step is to analyze particular information problems that arise in agencies by attempting to determine how the provisions of, and the many exceptions to, the FOIA and the Privacy Act apply to the dispute at hand. Often the cases and commentaries are focused very narrowly on the reports of the legislative histories of the information policy acts and the several government commission reports on the motivations that gave rise to the Freedom of Information and Right to Privacy acts.[8]

In this chapter we discuss problems of information policy in a broader sense. Specifically, we discuss why it is important for producers and consumers of administrative decisions to avoid casting problems of the acquisition, use, and dissemination of information too narrowly. We then consider the system of legal protections on acquisition, use, and dissemination of information. Finally, we suggest that the way to resolve legal controversies over information is through a broad conceptualization of information problems.

THE INFORMATION PARADOX

The conflict-laden relationship between the positive and negative implications of the increasing ability for those in government to acquire, use, and disseminate information is the "information paradox." Despite efforts to explain away the conflict, government policies which say that it is desirable to have minimum secrecy, on the one hand, and maximum privacy, on the other, are inherently in opposition.[9] Repeated claims that the attempt to deal with the paradox by enactment of complimentary privacy and FOIA statutes do not resolve the basic conflict.

It is not surprising or unusual that government is asked to deal with such conflicts as the information paradox. Ours is, after all, a system of government based on such tensions as the conflict between majority rule and minority rights. But there is a great danger for producers and consumers in adopting a narrow focus on the information paradox defined as a legal battleground between the federal FOIA and privacy acts. Let us consider a few of these difficulties.

Intergovernmental and Interorganizational
Information Sharing

Those who approach information conflicts with a narrow view of the information paradox often emphasize the federal government's role in information policy in an administrative environment characterized by increasingly complex intergovernmental relations. It is not enough to consider only how and when Washington uses information.

The analysis of problems related to the disclosure of genetic data by Leonard Riskin and Philip Reilly shows just how this intergovernmental complexity can affect information uses and abuses.[10] One can readily discern from their work that a number of major problems of information acquisition and dissemination have private as well as public, along with state and local governmental, dimensions, in addition to the more commonly recognized federal government aspects. Information moves among government units and between government and private sector organizations. Given the ambiguity in state statutes and tort law (tort law is the law governing civil disputes between private parties), the narrow federally oriented approach to information policy leaves out many of the more important aspects of the problem of information use and abuse. Consider the following examples.

Riskin and Reilly discuss several situations in which screening for specific genetic disease, such as phenylketonuria (PKU),[11] is required by law or by hospital policy. More than 2,000 diseases are recognized as genetically based and may, in the foreseeable future, be dealt with initially through screening processes.[12] Difficulties do not stem so much from the tests themselves, which by all accounts have saved a great deal of pain and suffering through early diagnosis and treatment of serious illnesses. (Newer methods, such as amniocentesis, offer even more sophisticated methods of gathering information.) Rather, the problem is how the data that are acquired through testing are employed.[13]

> It is the handling of personal information generated by these statutory programs that concerns us here. Although only a few genetic screening laws specifically require the storage of test results, data collection is often an integral part of such programs. In at least twenty-five states, health authorities must gather data in order to fulfill statutory commands to follow up persons with positive test results.[14]

The danger is that the information may "be improperly disclosed to third parties, possibly damaging the data subject's relationships with friends, relatives, employers, insurance companies, schools and law enforcement authorities."[15]

Aubrey Milunsky and Philip Reilly warned of the possible abuses:

> During major population screening efforts for carriers of genetic disease (such as sickle cell anemia), an appreciable number of unaffected screens will be detected who are carriers. In addition to the problems . . . [of] securing the privacy of such information, who ultimately will be responsible for holding the data and ensuring its availability to these children some years later? Resolution of such issues generates a certain urgency when the interests of insurance carriers and their possible duty to seek information about the genetic status of their clients are thrown into the equation. Conceivably, an individual could be penalized by having life insurance coverage denied because he was found to be a carrier in a compulsory screening test years before. Medical insurance companies, cognizant of the economic advantages of recent advances in the prevention of serious or fatal genetic diseases through prenatal studies, have already considered denying medical coverage to the defective offspring of patients who refused to have an amniocentesis and prenatal genetic studies. Are such actions, however, constitutionally acceptable? Traditionally, the physician, with the consent of his patient, has provided the insurance companies with all the information pertaining to the general health of the patient. Is there anything that should make his conduct change in the face of recently acquired knowledge of the genetic makeup of his patient?[16]

It is clear that there is intention to retain this data. Consider the optimism of Robert Guthrie:

> Given the further development and perfection of multiple screening tests, mass screening can become not merely a way of rapidly detecting PKU and other treatable genetic diseases but also a source of invaluable

information on biochemical differences in large populations. Given the fact that screening for PKU alone has proved itself not merely medically but also economically sound— . . . one can safely assume that specimens will continue to be collected by the hundred thousand and screened by one or another technique. And if that is the situation, it is surely common sense to seek screening procedures that, for the same outlay, will yield steadily increasing "fringe benefits" of data on both pathologic and benign innate metabolic differences.[17]

An incident in 1970 demonstrates the dangers of misuse of information for screening programs that seem at first benign. Four soldiers who died during a military exercise were reported to have the sickle cell anemia trait. The likelihood of having the sickle cell trait, but no disease, is very high among black people. After this incident some hypothesized that those with the trait might have difficulties under conditions of stress.

Although these hypotheses have never been proven, the concern raised by them caused temporary employment discrimination against persons with the sickle cell trait by the New York Fire Department and the Transit Authority of New York, the New York Telephone Company and several major airlines. The Secretary of the Army stated in 1972 that applicants for certain positions must be screened for the sickle cell trait and that carriers are ineligible. In addition, a number of life insurance companies, without any actuarial support, for a time charged extra-high premiums to, or dropped their coverage of, sickle cell carriers. It was only after a dramatic political attack by black physicians and business leaders that this genetic discrimination ceased.[18]

This kind of abuse of information cannot be resolved by using a narrow information paradox approach. Several units of government at the state and local level were involved. Their actions were responses to an incident that occurred in the armed forces as well as to speculation about that incident printed in a journal. The FOIA and the Privacy Act do not speak to that interaction at the state and local level. But in addition to the intergovernmental relations aspects, there were also private sector consequences from the public sector incident. The insurance companies reacted to state and local government decisions as well as professional speculation and sought genetic information on their clients.

It is also important to remain alert to the fact that many information policy problems concern inter- and intraorganizational information sharing. The effort to achieve a healthy workplace for American workers through research provides a case illustrating why the sharing of information by organizations can result in difficulties for both producers and consumers of administrative decisions. The Occupational Safety and Health Administration (OSHA) not only investigates for hazards that might result in accidents in the workplace, but is also charged with assisting research to study long term health hazards. As a part of its research and planning efforts, OSHA requires that employers collect and report medical data on employees.[19] There are some special problems connected with this data collection activity. For one thing, unlike doctors and hospitals, employers do not necessarily have a commonly accepted ethical or legal framework for deciding how to use or disseminate information. Beyond this problem, there are information-sharing difficulties. Data collected by OSHA go to the National Institute of Occupational Safety and Health

(NIOSH), which acts as a research arm for OSHA in providing the scientific expertise used in rulemaking procedures and in meeting other advisory requirements. But, although authorized, in 1976, by the same statute, NIOSH and OSHA report to different cabinet officers.[20] NIOSH is one of the National Institutes of Health within HEW (now Health and Human Services, HHS), and OSHA is part of the Department of Labor. These two cabinet agencies do not have identical information-reporting statutes. Among other requirements, HHS must comply with the provisions of the Health Services Research, Health Statistics, and Medical Libraries Act of 1974.

> This statute requires the Secretary of Health, Education, and Welfare to assist federal, state and local health agencies "in the design and implementation of a cooperative system for producing comparable uniform health information and statistics at the federal, state and local levels. . . ." The Secretary is required further to review HEW's statistical activities to assure that they are consistent with this cooperative system.[21]

NIOSH's collection, retention, and sharing requirements fit a mission-oriented or organizational perspective and are responsive to professional rationality in the medical community. To accomplish significant epidemiological studies, specific information must be collected from a large population over a long period of time. From the scientific perspective, the sharing advocated in the medical community is eminently logical, but the sharing of information among public and private organizations at the federal, state, and local levels creates dangers of misuse of information. The employee who stands to benefit in the long run from progress in occupational health may be injured in the near term by disclosure of information.

Again, danger stems from differing interests and requirements among organizations. A recent study shows how information collected for epidemiological research can find its way via information sharing into data banks used to set insurance premiums or to make personnel decisions.[22]

Several states have free information access laws with no privacy protections. An insurer or an employer can use such open government laws to obtain information from a state or local agency and then put that information in a national insurance data bank. An employer may use it, for example, to try to avoid future employee disability claims.

The popular federally oriented narrowly drawn information paradox approach completely ignores the intergovernmental and interorganizational dimensions of information problems, but they are important factors that must be considered. Consider the following summary of information-sharing dangers:

> The sharing of information among record-keeping organizations also transmits the stigma that goes with some kinds of information. One's own physician, for example, may heartily approve of taking a minor or temporary problem to a psychiatrist, but the potential consequences of disclosing the mere fact that one has had psychiatric treatment are too well known to need description. Equally serious for some individuals are the consequences of disclosing arrest records, military discharge codes, and previous adverse insurance decisions, and the simple fact that a number of credit grantors asked for credit reports on a particular individual during a short span of time can adversely affect an evaluation of his credit worthiness. Such problems stem in part from the tendency of organizations to accept at face value information they get about individuals from other organizations.[23]

Reputation and Privacy in Commercial Matters

Related to the FOIA–Privacy Act mindset is the idea that we have already established adequate controls over government use of information on individual financial activity. Two recent decisions of the Supreme Court suggest that we should not be sanguine about financial information or dissemination of information by government that may directly affect one in the marketplace.

In *United States v. Miller*, the Court held constitutional the obtaining of bank records by government officials through a subpoena issued to the bank instead of by a warrant, and without giving the individual involved either notice or an opportunity to object.[24] Banks, under the provisions of the inappropriately named Bank Secrecy Act of 1970,[25] are required to maintain and retain microfilm records of deposits, withdrawals, cancelled checks, deposited checks, and bank drafts, as well as account information on anyone with access to a bank account. Congress justified the statute as follows:

> The Congress finds that adequate records maintained by insured banks have a high degree of usefulness in criminal, tax, and regulatory investigations and proceedings. The Congress further finds that microfilm or other reproductions and other records made by banks of checks, as well as records kept by banks of the identity of persons maintaining or authorized to act with respect to accounts therein have been of particular value in this respect.[26]

Mr. Miller was arrested for producing liquor without a proper license and for violation of tax laws. It seems that the local fire department arrived at a warehouse fire only to find that the blaze came from a distillery that had exploded. The authorities found Miller, the burning still, and gallons of whiskey with no tax stamp.

Prior to indictment, the authorities wanted more evidence to connect Miller with sales of the liquor. Toward this end, they subpoenaed records from the C & S banks in which Miller maintained accounts. Following his conviction, Miller's attorney appealed, arguing that the records were held in confidence by the bank for the account holder. Removing the records without a warrant and without notice or an opportunity to object was, he asserted, an unreasonable search and seizure within the meaning of the Fourth Amendment.

The Supreme Court ruled against Miller. In so doing, it went far beyond merely upholding the particular government action involved.[27] It held that there is no expectation of privacy in financial records such as bank statements or cancelled checks.

> Even if we direct our attention to the original checks and deposit slips, rather than to the mircofilm copies actually viewed and obtained by means of the subpoena, we perceive no legitimate expectation of privacy in their contents.[28]

In the second case, *Paul v. Davis,*[29] Louisville police circulated bulletins to businesses in the area identifying serveral individuals as "active shoplifters." Mr. Davis sued on grounds that he was not a shoplifter and had never been convicted of shoplifting. He further asserted that this "designation would inhibit him from entering business establishments for fear of being suspected of shoplifting and possibly apprehended, and would seriously impair his future employment opportunities."[30] He sought damages[31] and an injunction to prevent the police from further distribution of such bulletins.

Justice Rehnquist, writing for a five-to-three majority, dismissed the claim for damages.[32] He went on to hold:

> While we have in a number of our prior cases pointed out the frequently drastic effect of the "stigma" which may result from defamation by the government in a variety of contexts, this line of cases does not establish the proposition that reputation alone, apart from some more tangible interests such as employment, is either "liberty" or "property" by itself sufficient to invoke the procedural protection of the Due Process Clause.[33]

The breadth and significance of the Rehnquist opinion was of concern to the dissenters on the Court. Taking the reasoning of the majority to its logical extreme, Justice Brennan wrote:

> The Court by mere fiat and with no analysis wholly excludes personal interest in reputation from the ambit of "life, liberty, or property" under the Fifth and Fourteenth Amendments, thus rendering due process concerns *never* applicable to the official stigmatization, however arbitrary, of an individual. The logical and disturbing corollary of this holding is that no due process infirmities would inhere in a statute constituting a commission to conduct *ex parte* trials of individuals, so long as the only official judgment pronounced was limited to the public condemnation and branding of a person as a Communist, a traitor, an "active murderer," a homosexual, or any other mark that "merely" carries social opprobrium.[34]

These two cases indicate that there is a great deal of uncertainty in policy and law where information is shared between public and private organizations or placed in what was once referred to as the stream of commerce. In a time when the lines between public and private sectors of the economy are blurred, that kind of ambiguity in information law is unacceptable. References to FOIA and Privacy Act provisions are not adequate to meet this challenge.

A SYSTEM OF INFORMATION ACQUISITION, USE, AND DISSEMINATION

Enough has been said to show that a narrow information paradox focus is inadequate for solving legal problems related to information. Previous attempts to come to grips with information issues have generally been ad hoc, unsystematic, and, in varying degrees, conflicting. A more useful approach is to assume that the legal framework, properly developed, should be a system for acquiring, using, and disseminating information. The application of that framework should be guided by a broad conception of information policy.

The System

In *The System of Freedom of Expression*, Thomas I. Emerson begins by rejecting an atomistic approach to the resolution of free speech issues. He writes:

A system of freedom of expression, operating in a modern democratic society, is a complex mechanism. At its core is a group of rights assured to individual members of the society. . . .

This interrelated set of rights, principles, practices, and institutions can be considered a system, at least in a rough way, because it has overall unity of purpose and operation. To view it in this manner facilitates the development of the rules for its governance, for such rules must be derived from the basic functions and dynamics of the system. Furthermore, they must accommodate the system of freedom of expression to the other features of our national life.[35]

Emerson continues for some seven hundred pages to define the elements of a system of free expression and to set the basis for the application of these elements to the body of law. His system considered only constitutional free expression. This chapter can do no more than outline a proposed system of acquisition, use, and dissemination of information.

An analogue of Emerson's system may be useful in examining and understanding information law. The various information laws can be considered a system, albeit a relatively primitive system at present. That system has a number of related elements.

At the heart of the system are the constitutional elements drawn from the language of the Constitution and the Supreme Court interpretations of that language. These elements include the provisions that ensure a representative and deliberative form of government with specifically protected rights of expression and political action.[36] One must also note the constitutional protection of privacy and the provisions barring unreasonable searches and seizures where unreasonable is defined as those conducted without a warrant.[37] That protection is afforded to private citizens and organizations,[38] both commercial[39] and political,[40] in administrative as well as in criminal contexts. There are limited special exceptions in which courts will permit warrantless surprise administrative inspections of certain types of businesses.[41] There is also constitutional recognition of a right to privacy,[42] which protects the family unit as well as the individual.[43]

From the constitutional base, we proceed to the statutes which, although they were separately drawn from a number of initial causes, must be understood together. They provide a further articulation of information law beyond the foundations established in constitutional development.

These statutes include protections for privacy interests of several types. They include the Privacy Act of 1974[44] and the various state privacy acts, generally found in state administrative procedure acts, that provide general protection for individual privacy. The essential principles of the Privacy Act of 1974 were set forth by the President's Commission on Privacy.

(1) There shall be no personal-data record-keeping system whose very existence is secret and there shall be a policy of openness about an organization's personal-data record-keeping policies, practices and systems. (The Openness Principle)

(2) An individual about whom information is maintained by a record-keeping organization in individually identifiable form shall have a right to see and copy that information. (The Individual Access Principle)

303

Acquisition, Use,
and Dissemination
of Information:
A System of
Information

(3) An individual about whom information is maintained by a record-keeping organization shall have a right to correct or amend the substance of that information. (The Individual Participation Principle)

(4) There shall be limits on the types of information an organization may collect about an individual, as well as certain requirements with respect to the manner in which it collects such information. (The Collection Limitation Principle)

(5) There shall be limits on the internal uses of information about an individual within a record-keeping organization. (The Use Limitation Principle)

(6) There shall be limits on the external disclosures of information about an individual a record-keeping organization may make. (The Disclosure Limitation Principle)

(7) A record-keeping organization shall bear an affirmative responsibility for establishing reasonable and proper information management policies and practices which assure its collection, maintenance, use, and dissemination of information about an individual is necessary and lawful and the information itself is current and accurate. (The Information Management Principle)

(8) A record-keeping organization shall be accountable for its personal-data record-keeping policies, practices, and systems. (The Accountability Principle)[45]

This general fair information practices statute is supplemented by more specific statutory requirements. The Family Educational Rights and Privacy Act of 1974[46] extends most of the privacy protections normally available to adults to schoolchildren and their parents, using the threat of deprivation of federal aid to education as the sanction to enforce compliance by state and local officials. Two other statutes, the Fair Credit Reporting Act[47] and the Right to Financial Privacy Act,[48] add very limited protections against abuses of information in the marketplace. The latter statute was added as Title XI of the Financial Institutions Regulatory and Interest Rate Control Act of 1978, in response to the Supreme Court holding in *United States v. Miller*. It was enacted as a much weaker version of the bill that was introduced and provides for notice and a limited opportunity to object to efforts to obtain one's financial records.[49]

Related to these laws are several statutes that protect the deliberative processes of government and ensure some degree of accountability. The best known is the Freedom of Information Act as amended in 1974.[50] Following enactment of the original version of the statute, the U.S. Attorney General summarized the policy goals of the FOIA as follows:

1. that disclosure be the general rule, not the exception;
2. that all individuals have equal rights of access;
3. that the burden should be on government to justify the withholding of a document, not on the person requesting it;
4. that individuals improperly denied access to a document should have a right to seek injunctive relief in the courts; and
5. that there should be a fundamental shift in the attitudes and policies regarding government information of those in positions of responsibility.[51]

The FOIA applies to government information Justice Brandeis's principle that "sunlight is the best disinfectant" in government operation, and also protects legitimate government secrecy in limited areas. Both the Privacy Act and the FOIA contain rather lengthy lists of exempted information practices, which can be quite confusing.

Another of the open government statutes is the Government in the Sunshine Act of 1976.[52] The Sunshine Act has the goal of opening meetings of collegial bodies "composed of two or more individual members, a majority of whom are appointed to such positions by the President with the advice and consent of the Senate, and any subdivision thereof authorized to act on behalf of the agency."[53] The statute requires published announcement of meetings, prior justification for closed meetings, complete transcripts of meetings held, whether open or closed, and an annual reporting of compliance.

The Federal Advisory Committee Act (FACA)[54] recognizes the importance of advisory committees in government decisionmaking. It is intended to foster fairness and openness in the operation of those groups that provide government with vital information in specialized areas. Henry Steck noted that the purposes of the act include the following:

> First, the Act is a committee management law designed to create an orderly set of standards and uniform procedures for regulating the establishment, operation, administration, and duration of advisory committees. . . . Second, the Act is a "sunshine law" requiring that "Congress and the public should be kept informed with respect to the number, purpose, membership, activities, and cost of advisory committees. . . ." Third, the Act is a fair balance law. It requires that the membership of advisory committees be "fairly balanced in terms of points of view represented and the functions to be performed."[55]

Two important problems remain with respect to this cluster of information and privacy statutes. First, most of these federal government information statutes require agencies to make rules indicating how each agency will implement the statutory provisions. For a variety of reasons, not all agencies have complied enthusiastically with those rulemaking requirements.[56] Second, there is a problem with the statutory elements of the system of information policy at the state and local levels. Although many states have adopted statutes similar to those governing federal agencies in the freedom of information area, they have been extremely inconsistent about developing state laws similar to the federal privacy, sunshine, and advisory committee legislation. In sum, while the federal statutes have a number of loopholes and problems, they make up enough pieces to provide an adequate statutory framework for information problem solving. The situation at the state level is not quite as bright.

Long before any of the present cluster of statutes and regulations were developed, there was concern for such problems as privacy in the common law. By all accounts, it was the seminal article by Samuel Warren and Louis Brandeis, published in 1890, "The Right to Privacy,"[57] which provided the focal point for discussion by jurists and commentators. It is difficult, after nearly a century of references to this article, to recall that theirs was a relatively limited concern for privacy against torts by those who would invade one's private life or threaten reputation or creative efforts. The privacy theme from that work has been broadly interpreted to support wider notions of a common law right to privacy. Even so, the controversy over the meaning and scope of privacy in tort law remains.[58] Despite the problems, it seems certain that we will continue to rely heavily on tort law protections to deal with private conflicts over the uses and abuses of information not dealt with by statutes. This will be particularly true until state laws are made more uniform.

This brief description of the system suggests there are in fact a number of significantly related elements extant that are closely interconnected. Viewing the system as a whole helps us to identify the gaps in the framework that must be filled by legislatures and courts. A complete articulation of the system and a survey of needs and rights is a more pressing matter than debating how to define the exemptions of the Privacy Act and the FOIA. Connections must be more clearly drawn among the constitutional elements, the statutory aspects, and the common law factors. In particular, the relationships of the federal laws to the state rules must be examined in detail.

The system has weaknesses. The Supreme Court continues to try to define the nature and scope of constitutional privacy in political, economic, and social problem areas. The federal statutes contain an intricate and lengthy list of exceptions that confuse those both in and out of government. The level of statutory development at the state and local level is extremely uneven. Similarly, the meaning of privacy in tort law continues to develop. Even so, this system of information framework offers a useful approach to understanding problems associated with information gathering, use, and dissemination. It will be particularly useful if those who must deal with information problems will employ the system framework with a broad conception of what the problems of information policy are. It is important to take account of both the legal and administrative problems raised and to avoid a narrow perspective.

ADMINISTRATIVE ELEMENTS OF INFORMATION DISPUTES

While one can employ the legal system of information acquisition, use, and dissemination as a framework for approaching information disputes, one must deal with such controversies with a realistic understanding of the problems in the administrative environment that affect such disputes. As Emerson put it, we "must accommodate the system . . . to other features of our national life."[59] Myopic approaches to information problems are unacceptable, whether they are taken by judges, administrators, those in the private sector, or consumers of administrative decisions. What follows is a discussion of some of the aspects of information problems with which decisionmakers ought to be familiar and that may be essential for effective resolution of legal disputes. We may consider these factors as facets of the environment in the legal system of information policy. They include terminology and human communications, as well as technical, linguistic, managerial, and organizational factors.

The Importance of Terminology

As in most areas of endeavor, one of the primary problems in information controversies is agreeing on the meaning of frequently used terms. Discussions of the "nature of information" become confusing because of varying views of concepts.[60] This is true even if one does not go into the philosophical debates in epistemology and related areas.[61] If this ambiguity can be dismissed with an agreement to disagree, the battles over standardization of terms can be fought at a leisurely pace in the pages of professional journals. In the meantime, many sound rather like Humpty Dumpty in Lewis Carroll's *Through the Looking Glass:* " 'When I use a word . . . it means just what I choose it to mean—neither more nor less.' "[62]

Unfortunately, those concerned with the law do not enjoy that luxury. A major duty of courts is, after all, to serve as government's arbiter of the meaning of words—the meaning of policies as expressed in statutes and regulations, of agreements as presented in commercial dispute resolutions, and of government authority as stated in the Constitution and enabling legislation.[63]

The Privacy Protection Study Commission, in its study of the implementation of the Privacy Act, encountered some practical examples of difficulties caused by unclear or conflicting definitions:

> Whereas the record definition refers to information about an individual that contains his name or identifier, the system-of-records definition refers to information about an individual that is retrieved by name, identifier, or specifying particular. The crucial difference between the two definitions is obvious, and the effect has been to exclude many records from the Act's requirements about individuals that are not accessed by name, identifier, or assigned particular. The Interior Department, for example, files its records on job candidates recommended by Congressmen under the Congressmans' names rather than the names of the applicants and the Maritime Administration (Department of Commerce) files information on directors of shipbuilding firms by shipyard and shipbuilding contract rather than by the directors' name.[64]

The deficiency in this definition is related in part to the failure to understand the relationship between the information concepts on which the information policy statutes are based and the technology that is used to deal with information maintained by government.

> A further and extraordinarily important flaw in the system-of-records definition is that it springs from a manual rather than a computer-based model of information processing. In a manual record-keeping system, records are apt to be stored and retrieved by reference to a unique identifier. This, however, is not necessary in a modern computer-based system that permits attribute searches. An attribute search, in contrast to the conventional "name search," or "index search," starts with a collection of data about many individuals and seeks to identify those particular individuals in the system who meet a set of prescribed conditions or who have a set of prescribed attributes or combination of attributes. For example, officials of the Veterans Administration (VA) testified in the Commission's hearings on medical records that the VA has produced lists of names for another agency by using psychiatric diagnosis, age, and several other personal attributes as the search keys.[65]

The definition of the term "agency" itself is troublesome. The information statutes generally permit a free flow of information within an agency (intraorganizational flow) so that the agency may effectively use the information to accomplish its goals.[66] But if "agency" is defined as a cabinet-level department, the records may flow with no protection at what most observers would refer to as an interorganizational level. This type of definition of agency is common.[67]

Apart from these statutory problems, a problem solver in this field quickly comes to realize that the most fundamental terms are disputed. Some analysts consider "knowledge" and "information" to be essentially the same.[68] Others are committed to distinguishing between the two.

> The knowledge that is needed is not to be confused with mere information. Knowledge is derived from information, and consequently the marshalling, collating, organizing, analyzing, focusing and testing information becomes, more than ever before, an essential element of public policy and administration.[69]

Still others prefer "intelligence" as a compromise term.[70]

The uses of terms in this chapter are predicated on the thesis that there are useful distinctions between basic terms. The information problems discussed here are based on the idea that a "datum" is a unit of fact or opinion, "information" is a coherent set of data, and "knowledge" is evaluated information.[71]

Human Communications Behavior

As judges and others in the legal community apply the elements of the legal system of information, they must be aware of the problems of human communications involved. There is a tendency in legal studies to refer to information problems as though the disputes centered on title to and use of a document, a computer tape, or some other physical entity. But most of the elements of the system were developed to deal with the substance of information and also the processes by which the information is obtained, used, and disseminated. These processes are human communications, with all the problems of selective perception, encoding, transmission, noise, reception, decoding, understanding, and feedback that are basic to communications behaviors. These factors must not be ignored.

Technology

Technology has been both the cause and effect of information difficulties.[72] As Jesse Shera and Donald Cleveland noted, the technological requirements and products of the space race fundamentally altered information collection, use, and dissemination.[73]

> If we have learned anything about this discipline in the last fifteen years, it is that information science is not be equated with machines and technology. But it is also true that without technology a significant proportion of information science activities would not exist.[74]

Those who identify information science with librarianship focus on the technical problems in acquisition, use, and dissemination as the core of their "science."[75] But neither the information statutes, nor judicial opinions related to them, recognize hardware, software, storage, retrieval, security, access, or interface considerations. In short, those who work with information and those who must reach legal conclusions about it tend to think of the subject matter in entirely different ways. As Shera and Cleveland observed, information technology isn't everything, but it is basic.

Linguistic Problems

Information is not only thought of in different ways, it is also discussed in what amount to different languages. When judges, who are generalists, are called on to resolve conflicts in which specialists are involved, they can easily be caught up in linguistic problems. One who reads administrative law materials soon realizes that several major languages are written and spoken in the field. See Table 11-1. In addition, one finds that there are several dialects extant within each of the languages. Some within the legal community have become acclimated to the linguistic difficulties, others have not.

Table 11-1   Common Languages and Dialects in Information Problem Analysis

Languages	Dialects
Legalese	State Federal Criminal Civil Administrative Constitutional
Medical	General practitioner Specialty medicine Pharmaceutical (PDR) HEW (HHS)
Social service	Intergovernmental relations State agency HEW (HHS) Food stamp Medicare/Medicaid Education
Regulatory	Old-line economic (ICC, SEC) Second-generation hybrid (OSHA, CPSC)
Engineering	Industrial management Mechanical Aeronautical Electronic ADP Nuclear Chemical Government contracting

Table 11-1 Common Language and Dialects in
Information Problem Analysis (Continued)

309
Acquisition, Use,
and Dissemination
of Information:
A System of
Information

Languages	Dialects
Scientific	Physical
	Biological
	Mathematical
	National Science Foundation
Political	Federal
	State
	Foreign policy
	Domestic policy
	Intergovernmental relations
	Education
	Criminal justice
	Health
	HUD
	Budget

In part at least, hybrid rulemaking, one of the most important and controverisal developments of the last decade in administrative law, can be understood as a reaction to this problem of language and specialized knowledge. Judges are responsible for reviewing the decisions of expert administrative agencies. As Chapter 7 explained, they are not to substitute their judgment for administrative expertise, yet they must ensure that administrators do not act arbitrarily or capriciously, do not exceed their statutory authority, comply with procedural limits on their activities, and do not abuse their discretion.[76] The court of appeals in the *Vermont Yankee* case discussed the problem of dealing with agency expertise.[77] Judge Bazelon, writing for the court, indicated that while courts would not and could not second-guess the substance of an agency decision, they do have the responsibility to ensure that the agency supply a record that is sufficiently clear and detailed so that other experts in the field, in government and out, can make their own analysis of the adequacy of the agency decision.[78] That decision was overturned by the Supreme Court,[79] but the problem of providing adequate review of highly technical records, frequently filled with specialized jargon, continues.

Managerial Considerations

Those who are in the business of managing information systems must be concerned with reassessment of organizational information needs, costs of information acquisition, use and dissemination, control of information and information technology, integration of information systems, whether manual or automated, and development of an increasingly sophisticated analytical capability. Above all, it is clear from an information manager's perspective that information is a resource.[80]

A major criticism of judges and lawyers who deal with information controversies is that they do not comprehend the management problems involved in the cases they decide.[81] Given the fact that information management practices and technologies, for example, the COURTRAN docket management system and on-line legal research systems, have only come into common use in the legal community very recently, it should not be surprising that many members of that community are not yet accustomed to thinking in information management terms.

In any event, there are significant management concerns that should be considered in information law cases. Agency compliance with judicial opinions in this area will be enhanced to the degree that judges recognize management problems and deal with them in their opinions.

Organizational Concerns

Along with the managerial factors, there are larger organization theory concerns related to information law. Although some organizational factors have been recognized in legislative histories of information laws, the statutes and court decisions appear to frame information questions primarily as though all that is at issue is an effort to deal with files on individuals. In fact, problems are often phrased as though information policy disputes are generally between *a* government bureaucrat and *a* private individual. But often the disputes over information are between organizations, not individuals.

As members of the legal community apply the elements of the legal system of information, they should be aware of the internal and external effects on organizations of the decisions they make. Additionally, they should be alert to the fact that information conflicts are conditioned by aspects of organization theory.

Harold Wilensky's *Organizational Intelligence: Knowledge and Policy in Government and Industry* is primarily concerned with the internal information policy.[82] Information within organizations is important to ordinary management problems, including planning, development, and personnel. Also important are intraorganizational liaisons, innovation, data used as a bargaining chip within the organization, and the use of specialized knowledge as a basis for jargon or in-group identification.

But organizations also carry built-in "information dysfunctions" or "intelligence failures."[83] When the possibility of these structural failures is added to the problem of secrecy within and among organizations, the nonrational aspects of organizational information practices become apparent.[84] In sum, organizations use information in some ways that are intentional and planned and in other ways that are accidental or matters of chance.

In terms of the external perspective on an organization's information concerns, there are two major considerations. First, organizations try to resist demands by outsiders for information that the organization maintains about its own operations. This kind of information includes "financial information about separate organizational, industrial, and geographical segments of business; the interrelationships of the segments; information on industrial and natural resources ownership and control; product information needed by consumers; information of new discoveries, and on how and why decisions are made to market or withhold new products and technologies; environmental impact information; and information on employment policies and working conditions."[85]

311

Acquisition, Use,
and Dissemination
of Information:
A System of
Information

Organizations have information that the society needs, but, according to Alan Westin, they also need privacy:

> The foregoing discussion of organizational behavior suggests that privacy is a necessary element for the protection of organizational autonomy, gathering of information and advice, preparation of positions, internal decision making, inter-organizational negotiations and timing of disclosure. Privacy is thus not a luxury for organizational life; it is a vital lubricant of the organizational system in free societies.[86]

The second consideration is the collection and control by organizations of information about individuals. Much of this information is obtained, held, and shared by private organizations that are not affected by FOIA versus Privacy Act factors. There are a number of specific premises about organizational information activity that should be recognized and understood by those who seek to develop policy in this area.

> First, while an organization makes and keeps records about individuals to facilitate relationships with them, it also makes and keeps records about individuals for other programs, such as documenting the record keeping organization's own actions and making possible for other organizations—government agencies for example—to monitor the actions of individuals.
>
> Second, there is an accelerating trend, most obvious in the credit and financial areas, toward the accumulation in records of more and more personal details about an individual.
>
> Third, more and more records about an individual are collected, maintained and disclosed by organizations with which the individual has no direct relationship but whose records help to shape his life.
>
> Fourth, most record-keeping organizations consult the records of other organizations to verify the information they obtain from an individual and thus pay as much or more attention to what other organizations report about him than they pay to what he reports about himself; and
>
> Fifth, neither law nor technology now gives an individual the tools he needs to protect his legitimate interest in the records organizations keep about him.[87]

No judge or lawyer will attempt to list and apply all the factors in the environment of the system of information law. What members of the legal and administrative communities can and should do is become more aware that disputes that center on information problems must be resolved with an understanding of and an appreciation for the context within which the controversies arise.

*

SUMMARY

This discussion of problems of information policy has suggested that the continuing focus on federal FOIA versus federal Privacy Act considerations is too narrow. That approach misses many important aspects of information policy, law, and politics. Specifically, it does not come to grips with interorganizational and intraorganizational information sharing. It was not designed to comprehend the intergovernmental component of information policy, which is of major importance. The intergovernmental dimension is crucial because it is at the local level that public sector and private sector information sharing most often occurs.

For these and other reasons, it is important for administrators, consumers of administrative decisions, and members of the legal community to take a more realistic approach to information problems. One way to do this is to consider information laws as a totality that comprise a legal system of information acquisition, use, and dissemination. The system is made up of constitutional, statutory, and common law elements, and reflects the interaction between the public and private sectors and among the various levels of government. The rules that make up the legal system, however, must be applied with a recognition of the administrative elements that affect information problems.

NOTES

[1]Harold L. Wilensky, *Organizational Intelligence: Knowledge and Policy in Government and Industry* (New York: Basic Books, 1967), p.8.

[2]Records developed in major administrative rulemaking proceedings are so extensive and complex that courts will frequently refuse to accept the entire record along with other documents when review of the administrative decision is sought. Instead, they receive a joint appendix that contains the important parts of the record which both sides in the case consider pertinent. Even the appendices can run to several volumes.

[3]Discussing the problem of maintaining organizational secrecy, Westin observed: "It is useful to recall that the Constitution itself was written in a closed meeting in Philadelphia; press and outsiders were excluded, and the participants sworn to secrecy. Historians are agreed that if the convention's work had been made public contemporaneously, it is unlikely that the compromise forged in private sessions could have been achieved, or even that their state governments would have allowed the delegates to write a new constitution." Alan F. Westin, *Privacy and Freedom* (New York: Atheneum, 1967), p. 46.

[4]The reference is to George Orwell's *1984* (New York: Signet Classics, 1971). One finds frequent reference in literature on information policy to Orwell, Aldous Huxley's *Brave New World* (New York: Harper & Row, 1946), and Franz Kafka's *The Trial* (New York: Penguin, 1953).

[5]5 U.S.C. §552 (1976).

[6]5 U.S.C. §552a (1976).

[7]Privacy Protection Study Commission, *Personal Privacy in an Information Society* (Washington, D.C.: Government Printing Office, 1977), p. 5.

[8]Two of the most commonly cited are U.S. Congress, Joint Committee Print of the Senate Committee on Government Operations and the Subcommittee on Government Information and Individual Rights of the House Committee on Government Operations, *Legislative History of the Privacy Act of 1974, Source Book on Privacy,* 94th Cong., 2d. Sess. (1976), hereafter cited as *Source Book on Privacy,* and U.S. Congress, Joint Committee Print of the Subcommittee on Government Information and Individual Rights and the Subcommittee on Administrative Practice and Procedure of the Senate Committee on the Judiciary, *Freedom of Information Act and Amendments of 1974, Source Book, Legislative History, Text, and Other Documents,* 94th Cong., 1st Sess. (1975), hereafter cited as the *Source Book on FOIA.*

[9]Much is made of the supposedly complementary nature of the two laws, but there is evidence that the sponsors of the two bills and the groups participating in the legislative battle over their passage were not so concerned with the fit of the legislation. Senator Edward Kennedy noted: "With the need to enact the Freedom of Information Act amendments over the veto of President Ford, and with the need to complete work on the Privacy Act in the closing days of the 93rd Congress, the two laws do not appear to mesh as easily as might have been desired. Two different committees in the Senate worked on the different bills; and while the Office of Management and Budget was pressing hard for enactment of privacy legislation, the Justice Department was pressing equally hard to defeat the Freedom of Information legislation." *Source Book on Privacy,* supra note 8, at p. 1173.

[10]Leonard L. Riskin and Philip P. Reilly, "Remedies for Improper Disclosure of Genetic Data," 8 *Rutgers Camden L. J.* 480 (1977).

[11]Other examples include sickle cell anemia, Tay-Sachs disease, and cystic fibrosis. See generally U.S. Senate, Committee on Labor and Public Welfare, Hearings before the Subcommittee on Health, *Amendments to Revise Programs for Sickle Cell Anemia and Other Genetic Disorders,* 94th Cong., 1st Sess. (1975); U.S. Senate, Committee on Labor and Public Welfare, Joint Hearings Before the Subcommittee on Health and the Special Committee on the National Science Foundation, *National Advisory Commission on Health, Science, and Society,* 92d Cong., 1st. Sess. (1975); and U.S. House of Representatives, Committee on Interstate and Foreign Commerce, Hearings Before the Subcommittee on Oversight and Investigations, *Getting Ready for National Health Insurance: Shortchanging Children,* 94th Cong., 1st Sess. (1975).

[12]Riskin and Reilly, supra note 10, at p. 480.

[13]If more testing is required through mandatory programs, serious questions may be raised concerning the acquisition of the information, as well as its use and dissemination, on the ground of constitutional privacy.

[14]"Storage of genetic data can also result from statutes that are not directly connected with genetic screening. North Carolina, for example, recently passed a statute granting a special income tax exemption to hemophiliacs. In order to avail themselves of this exemption, affected persons must certify their condition to a state health service agency and submit a supportive statement on their tax return. This process will inevitably result in a registry of exempt persons." Riskin and Reilly, supra not 10, at p. 483.

[15]Id., at p. 480.

[16]Aubrey Milunsky and Philip Reilly, "The New Genetics: Emerging Medicolegal Issues in the Prenatal Diagnosis of Hereditary Disorders," 1 *American J. of Law & Medicine* 71, 78 (1975).

[17]Robert Guthrie, "Mass Screening for Genetic Disease," *Hospital Practice* (June 1972), p. 100.

[18]Riskin and Reilly, supra note 10, at p. 489

[19]Comment, "OSHA Records and Privacy: Competing Interests in the Workplace," 27 *American U. L. Rev.* 953, 954 (1978), hereafter cited as "OSHA Records and Privacy."

[20]29 U.S.C. §651 (1976).

[21]"OSHA Records and Privacy," supra note 19, at p. 961.

[22]Id.

[23]*Personal Privacy,* supra note 7, at p. 10.

[24]*United States v. Miller,* 425 U.S. 435 (1976).

[25]12 U.S.C. §189b (1976).

[26]Id., §189b(a)(1).

[27]There were some relatively recent precedents on which the Court could have drawn for a narrower ruling in *Miller.* Specifically, it could have employed *Couch v. United States,* 409 U.S. 322 (1973), in which the need to protect financial records was recognized, but the Court upheld a government acquisition by subpoena of financial records, holding that an accountant has no authority to claim a privacy right for his client. But since the accountant had custody of the records, the client was also unable to assert a right to withhold them.

Justice Douglas's dissent in *Couch* applies with even greater force to the more recent *Miller* case. "The majority

contends, however, that petitioner cannot reasonably claim 'an expectation of privacy or confidentiality.' The reasons asserted for this position overlook the nature of the accountant . . . [who] bore certain fiduciary responsibilities to petitioner. One of those responsibilities was not to use the records given him for any purpose other than completing the returns. Under these circumstances, it can hardly be said that by giving the records to the accountant, the petitioner committed them to the public domain." 409 U.S. at 340.

[28]*United States v. Miller,* 425 U.S. at 443.

[29]*Paul v. Davis,* 424 U.S. 693 (1976).

[30]Id., at 697.

[31]Davis's claim for damages was brought under 42 U.S.C. §1983 (1976).

[32]*Paul v. Davis,* supra note 29, at 698–99.

[33]Id., at 701. Justice Rehnquist's attempt to differentiate the most direct precedent, *Wisconsin v. Constantineau,* 400 U.S. 433 (1971), was unconvincing. As Justice Brennan wrote for the dissenters: "*Jenkins* and *Constantineau,* and the decisions upon which they relied, are cogent authority that a person's interests in his good name and reputation falls within the broad term 'liberty'and clearly require that the government afford procedural protections before infringing that name and reputation by branding a person as a criminal." Id., at 731-32.

[34]Id., at 721.

[35]Thomas I. Emerson, *The System of Freedom of Expression* (New York: Random House, 1970), pp. 3–4.

[36]Emerson presents a thorough discussion of the First Amendment role. Other significant provisions are articles I and II and the Fourth, Fifth, Ninth, and Fourteenth amendments.

[37]See generally Mark A. Rothstein and Laura F. Rothstein, "Administrative Searches and Seizures: What happened to Camara and See?" 50 *Washington L. Rev.* 341 (1975); Frank P. Nargorney, "Administrative Law," *1973–74 Annual Survey of American Law* 441 (1974); and Jacob Landynski, *Search and Seizure and the Supreme Court: A Study in Constitutional Interpretation* (Baltimore: Johns Hopkins, 1966).

[38]*Camara v. Municipal Court,* 387 U.S. 523 (1967).

[39]*Marshall v. Barlows,* 436 U.S. 307 (1978), and See *v. Seattle,* 387 U.S. 541 (1967).

[40]See, e.g., *NAACP v. Alabama,* 357 U.S. 449 (1958).

[41]*Donovan v. Dewey,* 69 L. Ed. 2d 262 (1981); *United States v. Biswell,* 406 U.S. 311 (1972), and *Colonnade Catering Corp. v. United States,* 397 U.S. 73 (1970).

[42]*Griswold v. Connecticut,* 381 U.S. 479 (1965).

[43]See, e.g., *Moore v. East Cleveland,* 431 U.S. 494 (1977).

[44]5 U.S.C. §552a (1976). In addition to the *Source Book on Privacy,* supra note 8, those interested in this statute should examine U.S. Senate, Joint Hearings Before the Ad Hoc Subcommittee on Privacy and Information Systems of the Committee on Government Operations and the Subcommittee on Constitutional Rights of the Committee on the Judiciary, *Privacy: The Collection, Use, and Computerization of Personal Data,* 93d Cong., 2d Sess. (1974).

[45]Privacy Protection Study Commission, *The Privacy Act of 1974: An Assessment* (Washington, D.C.: Government Printing Office, 1977), chap. 2, pp. 76–77.

[46]Public Law 93-380, 88 Stat. 484, §513 (1974), 20 U.S.C. §1232g (1976).

[47]Public Law 91-508, 84 Stat. 1114, Title 6 (1970), 15 U.S.C. §1681 et seq. (1976).

[48]Public Law 95-630, 92 Stat. 3641 (1978), 12 U.S.C. §3401 et seq. (1976).

[49]"There have been a number of legislative responses to the Miller decision, including many bills which have been introduced over several Congresses to protect the privacy of financial records. Additionally, the House Suncommittee on Financial Institutions held hearings on the subject in late July of 1975.

"Last year Congressman Cavanaugh introduced H.R. 8133 which was based on many of the bills introduced in prior Congresses. This bill was introduced just before the release of the final report of the Privacy Protection Study Commission. Both the bill and the report were based on two key principles: one, that the customer be given prior notice of the Government's attempt to gain access to the bank records, and two, that the customer be given an opportunity to contest Government access in court." 1978 *U.S. Code Cong. and Admin. News* 9306 (1978).

[50]5 U.S.C. §552 (1976).

[51]Cited in Bernard Schwartz, *Administrative Law* (Boston: Little, Brown, 1976), p. 128.

[52]5 U.S.C. §552b (1976). On the Sunshine Act generally, see U.S. Congress, Joint Committee Print of the Senate Committee on Government Operations and the House Committee on Government Operations, *Government in the Sunshine Act, S. 5 (Pub. L. No. 94-409); Source Book, Legislative History, Texts, and Other Documents*, 94th Cong., 2d Sess. (1976).

[53]5 U.S.C. §552b(a)(1) (1976).

[54]See generally Jerry W. Markham, "The Federal Advisory Committee Act," 35 *U. Pittsburgh L. Rev.* 557 (1974).

[55]Henry J. Steck, "Private Influence on Environmental Policy: The Case of the National Industrial Pollution Control Council," 5 *Environmental Law* 241, 248–49 (1975).

[56]See, e.g., Harold C. Relyea, "Opening Government to Public Scrutiny: A Decade of Federal Efforts," 35 *Public Admin. Rev.* 3 (1975); Allen Schick, "The Short Sad History of Freedom of Information," 1 *Bureaucrat* 116 (1972); and Ralph Nader, "Freedom from Information: The Act and the Agencies," 5 *Harvard Civil Rights–Civil Liberties L. Rev.* 1 (1970).

[57]4 *Harvard L. Rev.* 193 (1890).

[58]See note 71.

[59]Emerson, supra note 35, at p. 4.

[60]Pranas Zunde and John Gehl, "Empirical Foundations of Information Science," in *Annual Review of Information Science and Technology*, vol. 14 (White Plains, N.Y.: American Society for Information Science, 1979), p. 68.

[61]Id.

[62]Quoted in Douglas E. Berninger and Burton W. Atkinson,"Interaction Between the Public and Private Sectors in National Information Policy," in *Annual Review*, supra note 60, vol. 13 (1978), p. 11.

[63]*United States v. Nixon*, 418 U.S. 683 (1974); *National Treasury Employees Union v. Nixon*, 492 F. 2d 587 (D.C. Cir. 1974); and *Jones v. United States*, 419 F. 2d 593 (8th Cir. 1969).

[64]*Privacy Act of 1974*, supra note 45, at pp. 5–6.

[65]Id., at pp. 6–7.

[66]5 U.S.C. §552a(b) (1976).

[67]*Privacy Act of 1974*, supra note 45, at p. 3.

[68]"By information and knowledge, I mean data that change us. This distinguishes information from data, which are merely raw facts that do not change us. By knowledge management, I mean public policy for the production, dissemination, accessibility and use of information as it applies to public policy formulation. In this sense, knowledge management constitutes what Yehezkel Dror calls 'metapolicy,' that is, policy for policymaking procedures." Nicholas L. Henry, "Knowledge Management: A New Concern for Public Administration," 34 *Public Admin. Rev.* 189 (1974). Compare Fritz Machlup, *The Production and Distribution of Knowledge in the United States* (Princeton, N.J.: Princeton University Press, 1962), chap. 2.

[69]Lynton K. Caldwell, "Managing the Transition to Post-Modern Society," 35 *Public Admin. Rev.* 570 (1975). See also Zunde and Gehl, supra note 60.

[70]"Intelligence denotes the information–questions, insights, hypotheses—relevant to policy. It includes both scientific knowledge and political or ideological information, scientific or not." Wilensky, supra note 1, at p. viii.

[71]Two other concepts in this area are badly in need of definition. The first—privacy—has received some attention. See, e.g., David M. O'Brien, "Privacy and the Right of Access: Purposes and Paradoxes of Information Control," 30 *Admin. L. Rev.* 45, 62–82 (1978); Tom Gerety, "Redefining Privacy," 12 *Harvard Civil Rights–Civil Liberties L. Rev.* 233 (1967); Westin, supra note 3; Hyman Gross, "The Concept of Privacy," *New York U. L. Rev.* 34 (1967); and William Prosser, "Privacy," 48 *California L. Rev.* 383 (1960). Nevertheless, we are a long way from agreement on a definition that links common law approaches. See O'Brien and Prosser on statutory concerns and constitutional factors.

The second concept in need of definition is the so-called "right to know." Until recently, the term was a vague notion related to freedom of speech. See O'Brien at pp. 56–57. Recently, however, the right to know has been recognized explicitly by the Supreme Court: "Freedom of speech presupposes a willing speaker. But where a speaker exists, as is the case here, the protection afforded is to the communication, to its source and to its recipients both." *Virginia Board of Pharmacy v. Virginia Consumers Council*, 425 U.S. 748, 756 (1976). The Court's opinion in this case was extremely broad. The right-to-receive-information argument was central to the Court's conclusion that the First Amendment protects commercial speech. "As to the particular consumer's interest in the free flow of information, that interest may be keen, if not keener by far, that his interest in the day's most urgent political debate." Id., at 763. The Court applied and expanded the "free flow" theory in *First Nat'l Bank v. Bellotti*, 435 U.S. 765 (1978). The Court relied primarily on "the role of the First Amendment in fostering individual self-expression but also on its role in affording the public access to discussion, debate and the dissemination of information and ideas." Id., at 783. In *Bellotti* the Court went so far as to conclude that "the First Amendment goes beyond protection of the press and the self-expression of individuals to prohibit government from limiting the stock of information from which members of the public may draw." Id.

[72]For a discussion of technology from a privacy perspective, see Westin, supra note 3, part 2.

[73]Jesse H. Shera and Donald B. Cleveland, "History and Foundations of Information Science," in *Annual Review*, supra note 60, vol. 12 (1977), p. 258.

In part, of course, the scientific and technological developments that brought industrialization and urbanization have fundamentally altered the potential for good or ill of information science. "The records of a hundred years ago tell little about the average American except when he died, perhaps when and where he was born, and if he owned land, how he got his title to it. Three quarters of the adult population worked for themselves on farms or in small towns. Attendance at the village schoolhouse was not compulsory and only a tiny fraction pursued formal education beyond it. No national military service was required, and few programs brought individuals into contact with the federal government. . . .

"Record keeping about individuals was correspondingly limited and local in nature. The most complete record was probably kept by churches, who recorded births, baptisms, marriages and deaths. Town officials and county courts kept records of similar activities. Merchants and bankers maintained financial accounts for their customers and when they extended credit, it was on the basis of personal knowledge of the borrower's circumstances. Few individuals had insurance of any kind, and a patient's medical records very likely existed only in the doctor's memory. Records about individuals never circulated beyond the place they were made." *Personal Privacy*, supra note 7, at pp. 3–4.

[74]Shera and Cleveland, supra note 73, at p. 259.

[75]See, e.g., J.M. Brittain, *Information and Its Uses* (Bath, United Kingdom: Bath University Press, 1970), chap. 1. See also Shera and Cleveland, supra note 73.

[76]5 U.S.C. §706 (1976).

[77]*Natural Resources Defense Council v. Nuclear Regulatory Comm'n*, 547 F. 2d 633 (D.C. Cir. 1976), reversed under the name *Vermont Yankee Nuclear Power Corp. v. Natural Resources Defense Council*, 435 U.S. 519 (1978).

[78]*NRDC v NRC*, id., at 644–46.

[79]*Vermont Yankee*, supra note 77, at 556–58.

[80]Wilensky, supra note 1, at p. 43. See Francis E. Rourke, "Introduction to Symposium: Administrative Secrecy: A Comparative Perspective," 35 *Public Admin. Rev.* 2 (1975).

[81]Of course, one must read the criticism with an understanding of the perspective of the critic. See generally Charles H. Koch, Jr., and Barry R. Rubin, "A Proposal for a Comprehensive Restructuring of the Public Information System," 1979 *Duke L. J.* 1 (1979). (The remedy that Koch and Rubin propose is worse than the problem.) See also Robert L. Salochin, "The Freedom of Information Act: A Government Perspective," 35 *Public Admin. Rev.* 10 (1975).

[82]Wilensky, supra note 1, at p. 8: "The resources an organization devotes to intelligence, the kinds of experts it uses, and the functions these experts serve are a product of several interrelated forces: the availability of intelligence, the relation of the organization to its external and internal environment, the degree of rationalization of the environment, and the organization's structural complexity."

[83]"Intelligence failures are rooted in structural problems that cannot be fully solved; they express universal dilemmas of organizational life that can, however, be resolved in various ways at varying costs." Id., at p. 42.

[84]Id., at p. 69.

[85]Mark V. Nadle, "Corporate Secrecy and Political Accountability," 35 *Public Admin. Rev.* 16 (1975). Much of the litigation under the Freedom of Information Act over the past several years has been "reverse" FOIA suits, in which a party attempts to prevent the government from releasing information about it in an FOIA response. See, e.g., David A. Drachsler, "The Freedom of Information Act and the Right of Non-Disclosure," 28 *Admin. L. Rev.* 1 (1976). The Supreme Court declared an end to reverse FOIA suits in *Chrysler Corp. v. Brown*, 441 U.S. 281 (1979). It remains to be seen whether these suits will reemerge in a different form.

[86]Westin, supra note 3, at p. 51.

[87]*Personal Privacy*, supra note 7, at p. 8.

Chapter 12

The Law and Public Employees

Chapters 8 through 11 have addressed problems of law, politics, and administration that have raised important and difficult issues for administrators, the public, and the courts. In this chapter we turn to another problem area: legal controversies that arise in connection with government employment. "One out of every six jobs in the country is a government job,"[1] so the rules that govern public employees affect the lives of a significant portion of the American work force and their families. Moreover, government, whether federal, state, or local, is a "special" employer.[2] Among other things, it represents all the people within its jurisdiction and is expected to be responsive and responsible to the citizenry.[3] Government is also special because it has only those powers granted to it by law, and even those powers are limited by the civil liberties of citizens and employees granted by the Constitution and statutes.

To understand how conflicts between employees and their government employer are managed, it is necessary to consider the setting within which such conflicts arise and the interests affected by their resolution, the constitutional protections afforded to public servants, and the statutory requirements that govern public employment.

THE SETTING AND THE INTERESTS

One of the great difficulties in legal and political discussions of public employees is that they are popularly assumed to be part of a more or less homogeneous group, a monolith unaffectionately known as "the bureaucracy." Actually, the public sector is exceedingly rich in talent and training and diverse in backgrounds and political perspectives. Unfortunately, so is the body of law that governs how these officials function and protects them from abuse.

316

Two recent examples of public employee disputes demonstrate the complexity of this area of administration.

Bessie Givhan was a junior high school teacher in the Western Line Consolidated School District, in Mississippi. She was terminated in 1971 and filed suit for reinstatement.[4] At that time the school district was under a desgregation order issued by the U.S. District Court for the Northern District of Mississippi.[5] Though the school district later advanced a number of alleged incidents that supported its decision to fire Givhan, the primary reason for her dismissal was altercations between the school principal and Ms. Givhan.

> In an effort to show that its decision was justified, respondent School District introduced evidence of, among other things, a series of private encounters between petitioner and the school principal in which petitioner allegedly made "petty and unreasonable demands" in a manner variously described by the principal as "insulting," "hostile," "loud," and "arrogant." . . . Finding that petitioner had made "demands" on but two occasions and that those demands "were neither 'petty' nor 'unreasonable,' insomuch as all the complaints in question involved employment policies and practices at [the] school which [petitioner] conceived to be racially discriminatory in purpose or effect," the District Court concluded that the primary reason for the school district's failure to renew [petitioner's] contract was her criticism of the policies and practices of the school district, especially the school to which she was assigned to teach.[6]

Givhan asserted that her termination was a reprisal by the principal for having the temerity to challenge his administrative practices, which she considered illegal and unjust. She claimed interference with her First Amendment right to freedom of speech. Givhan argued that the other charges levied against her after the dismissal were attempts to rationalize this unconstitutional reprisal.

The school board insisted that her constitutional rights had not been involved, arguing that she was fired because of "an antagonistic and hostile attitude to the administration."[7] The board insisted that Givhan's private encounters with the principal represented not free speech but insubordinate behavior that would cause disharmony in the school and disrupt administration of education. In any case, it asserted, Givhan had done a number of other things that would have justified her termination quite apart from the difficulties with the principal.[8]

The district court found a First Amendment violation and ordered reinstatement, but the Circuit Court of Appeals reversed. The Supreme Court vacated the lower court decision and sent the case back to the district court for a determination whether Givhan would or would not have been terminated "but for" the arguments with the principal, which it ruled were protected by the First Amendment.[9]

Another example of contemporary law and personnel conflict (more fully presented in an article by Mark Coven[10]) was the dismissal of a high-level New Hampshire executive.[11] Mr. Bennett was director of the New Hampshire Department of Resources and Economic Development. He was appointed by the governor and reported to the commissioner of the department. The governor and the commissioner promoted development of a pulp mill in the state, but Bennett disagreed and let his superiors know of his disapproval. They replied that while they would not force him to promote the project publicly, he should refrain from openly opposing the plan.[12] The plan was very controversial, everyone wanted economic progress, but many feared environmental damage from the proposed plant. The community that was the prospective site of the mill was planning a referendum that the company involved agreed would determine whether the mill would be constructed.[13] While all this was in progress, Mr. Bennett found himself in a difficult spot. Following a speech to a Chamber of Commerce group, he was asked a direct question about his opinion of the pulp mill proposal. He answered:

> I'll be short and sweet on that one. The official policy of the
> Administration because Governor Thomson unilaterally announced that
> the pulp mill will locate in the Connecticut River Valley, his official policy
> is that we are pro pulp mill. . . . I think that the idea of a pulp mill stinks.
> It contravenes everything that this state, everything that we are tying to
> do, that I've talked to you about, about quality it would be a catastrophe
> in my judgment. Don't quote me on that.[14]

Bennett was fired for insubordination, his dismissal was upheld by the state supreme court against claims that his termination violated his First and Fourteenth Amendment rights.

Both cases were complex disputes involving constitutional, statutory, and, to some degree, procedural dimensions. In both cases state or local government employees asserted federally protected rights. In one case the dispute was decided in a state agency and appealed to a state court; in the other the dispute was decided by a local administrative body and a suit challenging that decision was later brought in a federal district court.

More broadly, there are several general factors that complicate public personnel disputes. Since more than 80 percent of all public employees are state and local workers, contests involving them are frequently complex intergovernmental disputes implicating a variety of local, state, and federal legal questions.[15] Moreover, since a substantial portion of public employees are covered by some form of collective bargaining arrangement,[16] additional matters must be considered beyond the constitutional and statutory authorities. "Whereas previously to understand the personnel policies and procedures of a jurisdiction one had only to consult the civil service law and rules, now one must also study the contents of collective agreements entered into by the public employer with a union or unions."[17]

In addition, the tasks performed by government employees are manifold, complex, and often extremely important. They require quality people properly trained and experienced. Therefore, personnel difficulties must be dealt with in a manner that encourages professionalism and career development, not merely as a unilateral demand for obedience to the public employer. Finally, because of the lack of privacy in the society, a slow employment market, and the close connection (and, in some cases, overlap) between the public and private sectors, an adverse action taken by government against a government employee or job applicant can have a profound and lasting impact on the person's life and career. The stakes are often very high. It is against this backdrop that controversies involving public employees arise and must be resolved.

Producer and Consumer Perspectives

The differences between producer and consumer perspectives on problems of law and administration, discussed at several points in this book, are particularly important and difficult to deal with in personnel controversies. A public servant is a producer of administrative decisions for those outside government who must deal with the agency, for those at other levels of government who are affected by his or her decisions, for those in other agencies at the same level, and for subordinates within his or her agency whose careers are at stake. An employee is simultaneously a consumer as a citizen generally interested in the use of governmental authority and tax dollars, a client who makes demands on other agencies for services or law enforcement, an officer of an agency whose work is affected by decisions of other agencies and other levels of government, and an employee who is the consumer of decisions made by superiors and co-workers. The problems that arose in *Bennett* and *Givhan* can be properly understood only if one remains aware of these varying perspectives and their implications. Furthermore, there are occasions—for example, "whistleblowing"—in which apparent conflicts in the public servant's role can complicate his or her position.

Types of Employees

Because there are so many different kinds of jobs and titles in public service, it is difficult to generalize about employee rights and responsibilities. One can work from a simple typology as a basis for discussion. Most public servants can be described as general civil service employees, political officers, or special employees. Indeed, the case law often draws these distinctions.

General civil service employees are employed and managed in accordance with the merit principle.

> The merit concept [holds] that appointments, promotions, and other personnel actions should be made on the basis of relative ability. For appointments and promotions, this has usually meant the administration of competitive examinations, scores on which have been believed to distinguish between the candidates according to capacity to perform satisfactorily on the job. For other personnel actions such as salary increases, reduction-in-force, and dismissals, the assumption has also been that the employee's "merit" could be determined and he or she should be treated accordingly.[18]

Above all, the merit principle requires skill and professionalism to be preferred over political connections. In fact, general civil servants are those who possess the skills and experience to do the day-to-day work of most agencies.

Political officials are those who can be considered policymaking or confidential employees. Ranging from cabinet-level appointees to press aides, policymaking officials are those for whom partisan affiliation or political loyalty is an appropriate employment consideration.[19] The chief executive is elected to govern on the basis of law and a political platform. Political officers are the appointed officials who help the elected officer implement that policy agenda; they are employed and managed by elected or highly placed appointees. Just which public positions are or ought to be political as opposed to general civil service posts is a matter of continuing conflict.[20]

Special employees are public servants holding particularly sensitive posts that serve special government requirements. More will be said about special employees later, but for the moment administrative law judges and officials who deal in national security affairs are examples. These employees may or may not be covered by general civil service requirements, but there are generally additional rules that apply to their specific tasks. The two most common types of special rules are provisions guaranteeing independence from certain kinds of interference and special guidelines to ensure accountability in addition to normal performance evaluations.

The category into which one's position is placed can be extremely important in establishing the type and amount of legal protections that are available against adverse actions by the government.

Modes of Adverse Action

There are three basic ways in which the government as an employer can legally affect or limit one's exercise of perceived rights or liberties. First, it can regulate certain activities by employees. For example, government may regulate the time, place, and manner of such recognized rights as union participation or peaceful picketing.[21] Citizens have the right to use peaceful picketing as a form of protected political expression, but they may not block access to public buildings or otherwise interfere with the normal functioning of government.[22]

Second, government may punish employees who violate agency rules or statutes. Standard adverse personnel actions include reduction in pay grade, reductions in responsibility, suspension, and, if the case warrants, termination of employment.[23] If such an adverse action is taken or an employee brings a grievance, dispute resolution procedures are triggered. Normally, at the federal level, a general civil service employee is entitled to proceed either through the dispute resolution procedure specified in the collective bargaining agreement or through the agency standard procedure, with the possibility of a review by the Merit System Protection Board in some instances.[24] If a constitutional question is raised, there may be recourse to litigation in court in the event of adverse action.[25]

Finally, government may act by prohibition. Government units may bar the exercise of claimed employee rights, e.g., statutes and regulations that prohibit partisan political campaigning. Another common prohibition on public employees is the general ban on public employee strikes. The 1981 firing of air traffic controllers who struck against the FAA is a dramatic case in point.

A Multiplicity of Interests

Recognizing that cases of adverse action by government against employees often present strong arguments for both the protection of the worker and the needs of the employer, courts often use a balancing test to resolve difficult cases.[26] The balance is usually struck by weighing the interests of the employee as a worker and as a citizen against "the interest of the State as an employer in the efficiency of the public services it performs through its employees."[27] In fact, however, disputes between public servants and government units raise a multiplicity of interests.[28]

Employees, of course, do have an important personal interest in job security and advancement. They also often have a professional interest in effective and even-handed performance of their duties. The career civil service is based on the notion that it is possible to develop a cadre of government employees who are professionals in the business of operating government and who have something approaching "neutral competence."[29] Neutral competence can be roughly defined as nonpartisan professionalism in administration of government programs and services. Additionally, for many public servants public administration is a second profession.[30] That is, many of those in administrative posts entered government as lawyers, doctors, and engineers, and they brought their professional standards with them. It is a fact of life that public servants are on occasion forced to deal with conflicts between their personal and professional interests. Finally, government workers are also part owners of the institutions in which they are employed and have a citizenship interest in how those institutions perform.

Employers (supervisors) also have important interests. Like any manager, a government supervisor has a managerial interest in effective, efficient, and harmonious organizational operations. On the other side, a government supervisor has a responsiveness interest in maintaining an organization that is responsive to public needs. As a public organization, an agency may have to respond to acute needs for which there is no alternative but service by that agency. Employee demands that interfere with this responsiveness jeopardize the agency and run counter to the interests of its clients. The supervisor also has an accountability (or responsibility) interest in implementing public policy choices made by the political process, which may engender conflict with subordinates who think the new policies incorrect. Finally, supervisors are also employees and share the employee interests.

The public also has interests in employee performance. First, there is a service interest in the effective, efficient, and fundamentally fair operation of government agencies and employees. Second, the public has a fiduciary interest or expectation of public office in all forms as authority held in trust for the benefit of the public. Third, the citizenry has a deliberative interest in being informed on public problems and administrative difficulties, in order to make political decisions through the democratic process. This interest may clash with the asserted interests of government supervisors.

> More importantly, the question whether a school system requires additional funds is a matter of legitimate public concern on which the judgment of the school administration, including the School Board, cannot, in a society that leaves such questions to popular vote, be taken as conclusive. On such a question free and open debate is vital to informed decision-making by the electorate. Teachers are, as a class, the members of a community most likely to have informed and definite opinions as to how funds allotted to the operation of the schools should be spent. Accordingly, it is essential that they be able to speak out freely on such questions without fear of retaliatory dismissal.[31]

The *Bennett* case presents this problem in rather clear terms. The governor had employer's interests in blocking adverse commentary on the pulp mill project, Bennett had a variety of employee's interests in making his views known, and the public, in particular the community that was to vote in the referendum, had interests in hearing an informed public servant speak on a subject within the jurisdiction of his office.[32]

In sum, because the legal environment of public employment is so complex and because the problems encountered by public servants implicate such a wide range of essential interests, they give rise to a considerable amount of litigation. In much of that litigation employees assert their constitutional rights, and it is to a summary of major developments in the constitutional law of public employment that we turn next.

CONSTITUTIONAL ISSUES IN PUBLIC SERVICE

Among the most commonly presented constitutional issues in public employee controversies are the rights to expression and association (First Amendment), to due process of law (Fifth and Fourteenth amendments), to equal protection of the law (Fifth and Fourteenth amendments), and to privacy (Fourth, Ninth, and Fourteenth amendments). Since Chapter 6 dealt with due process in some detail, those matters will not be repeated here.

The Doctrine of Unconstitutional Conditions

The cornerstone of constitutional protection for public employees is the doctrine of unconstitutional conditions, a rule of law created by the Supreme Court in a number of cases from the 1950s on. This doctrine holds that although there may be no constitutional right to hold a public job or receive a government benefit, government may not condition a job or a benefit on an agreement to forfeit constitutional rights.[33]

> For at least a quarter-century, this Court has made clear that even though a person has no "right" to a valuable governmental benefit and even though the government may deny him the benefit for any number of reasons, there are some reasons upon which the government may not rely. It may not deny a benefit to a person on a basis that infringes his constitutionally protected interests—especially, his interest in freedom of speech. . . .
>
> We have applied this general principle to denials of tax exemptions, *Speiser v. Randall* [357 U.S. 513], unemployment benefits, *Sherbert v. Verner*, 374 U.S. 398 . . . , and welfare payments, *Shapiro v. Thompson*, 394 U.S. 618 . . . ; *Graham v. Richardson*, 403 U.S. 365. . . . But, most often, we have applied the principle to denials of public employment. *United Public Workers v. Mitchell*, 330 U.S. 75, . . . ; *Wieman v. Updegraff*, 344 U.S. 183 . . . ; *Shelton v. Tucker*, 364 U.S. 479, . . . ; *Torcaso v. Watkins*, 367 U.S. 488, . . . ; *Cafeteria Workers v. McElroy*, 367 U.S. 886, . . . ; *Cramp v. Board of Public Instruction*, 368 U.S. 278, . . . ; *Baggett v. Bullitt*, 377 U.S. 360, . . . ; *Elfbrandt v. Russell*, 384 U.S. 11, . . . ; *Keyishian v. Board of Regents*, 385 U.S. 589, . . . ; *Whitehill v. Elkins*, 389 U.S. 54, . . . ; *United States v. Roble*, 389 U.S. 258, . . . ; *Pickering v. Board of Education*. . . . We have applied the principle regardless of the public employee's contractual or other claim to a job.[34]

Public employees may challenge actions by their superiors that interfere with their fundamental constitutional rights. Government actions that infringe on these rights must cease unless the government can demonstrate a compelling state interest, an interest so vital that it justifies the interference with the employee's freedom.

First Amendment Freedoms: Speech and Association

Government has engaged in a variety of activities that have been held to violate employees' First Amendment freedoms. The Court has struck down any number of loyalty oaths for employees as a condition of employment.[35] Most of the oaths required an employee to swear that he or she was not at the time and had not been a member of or associated with any organization that was considered subversive. In most cases, the oaths were struck because they were extremely vague.[36] As Chapter 6 indicated, many groups were placed on lists of subversive organizations that clearly were not subversive. (The NAACP was a prime example.) Not only was it difficult to know whether one had at some point been even loosely associated with a group that might turn up on someone's list, but the words used in the oaths were often subject to differing interpretations. In one case, the Court struck down a state civil service law under which a teacher who assigned readings from Marx or Engels could find that he or she had violated state loyalty oath requirements forbidding seditious conduct.[37] The reason that some government requirements are declared void for vagueness is that one who cannot understand what speech is permitted or which organizations are acceptable is likely to engage in self-censorship for fear of inadvertently committing some breach of law. Such uncertainty has a "chilling effect" on the exercise of fundamental rights. The Court has *not* ruled out oaths in which employees are asked to promise to properly perform the duties of their office and to enforce the law. Indeed, the Constitution contains some oath requirements.[38] Where oaths are prospective rather than retrospective and do not force surrender of beliefs or associations, they have been upheld.[39]

A number of government restrictions on employment have been struck down because they violate the First Amendment right to freedom of association and the right to privacy in those associations. The Supreme Court first announced that freedom of association was protected by the First Amendment in 1958.[40] The Court has held that there are very few instances in which it is the government's business to know which organizations one belongs to. Such information would be relevant to a Democrat President who does not want a Republican press representative or to Stragetic Air Command staff officers who do not want to assign to a missile command center a Communist officer who declared his intentions to overthrow the government, but these considerations certainly do not apply to general civil servants. Given the fact that guilt by association was so widely used in recent U.S. history to deprive people of jobs, the Court has required that only *knowing* membership, that is, membership in which one knew of the unlawful aims of an organization and actively pursued those aims, could be relevant to public employment in all but the most unusual circumstances.[41] A major problem with government requirements that employees disclose *all* of their organizational affiliations is what is termed "overbreadth." The Supreme Court has ruled that even if the government has a compelling enough reason to justify interference with fundamental freedoms, like the right to association, its method of accomplishing its goals should be narrowly tailored to that task and should not be overly broad.[42] Again, the concern is that broad requirements for disclosure may intimidate citizens from exercising their basic freedoms.

In a general sense, the Court has held that public employees may not be fired merely for exercising their right to freedom of expression.[43] That is true whether one is a tenured employee or not.[44] However, the Court's rulings suggest that there may be some limits on political[45] and special employees.[46] And, although the Court has repeatedly held that employees may not be terminated merely for making statements that criticize the current administration in matters of public concern,[47] that is not the end of the matter. The Court has recognized the problem of balancing employee rights against employer concerns in maintaining effective and efficient operation of public organizations.[48] Where the employer is able to show that the comments made by the employee were knowingly false or resulted in severe damage to the effective operation of the agency, the employee may yet be in trouble.[49] Fortunately, from the employee's standpoint, the Supreme Court has not found any such claims justified in the cases it has heard on the matter. On the other hand, in several cases employers claimed that an employee was dismissed for other reasons, not because he or she exercised protected First Amendment freedoms.[50] Two of the most common charges are conduct unbecoming an officer and insubordination. Against this, the employee must prove that he or she was fired because of the exercise of the free speech right. Earlier U.S. Supreme Court opinions suggested that if the exercise of freedom of speech was a significant factor in one's dismissal, reinstatement was required.[51] But two recent cases have made it more difficult for the employee to prevail. In *Mt. Healthy Board of Education v. Doyle*, the Court held:

> Initially, in this case, the burden was properly placed upon respondent to show that his conduct was constitutionally protected, and that this conduct was a "substantial factor"—or, to put it in other words, that it was a "motivating factor" in the board's decision not to rehire him. Respondent having carried that burden, however, the District Court should have gone on to determine whether the Board had shown by a preponderence of the evidence that it would have reached the same decision as to respondent's reemployment even in the absence of the protected conduct.[52]

In *Givhan*, the Court wrote: "And while the District Court found that petitioner's 'criticism' was the 'primary' reason for the School District's failure to rehire her, it did not find that she would have been rehired *but for* her criticism."[53] (Emphasis in original.)

A related question that surfaces from time to time is whether anyone, including a public employee, has a right *not* to speak. Originally, this question emerged in response to the abuse of public servants before congressional and state legislative investigating committees during the McCarthy era.[54] In general, the U.S. Supreme Court decisions held that there is no First Amendment right not to speak as a corollary to the freedom of speech that would allow one to refuse to answer appropriate questions from a properly constituted legislative investigating committee.[55] In a 1977 case, however, the Court held that: "The right to speak and the right to refrain from speaking are complementary concepts for the broader concept of 'individual freedom of mind.' "[56] Whether that right will be accorded to public employees remains to be seen. The Court has held that public employees can be required to answer questions about their public duties on pain of dismissal.[57] If the questioning might lead to criminal charges against the employee, he or she may not be compelled to testify or face dismissal unless the employee is granted immunity from prosecution for what he or she might say.[58]

Finally, a continuing First Amendment problem concerns political activity by employees and the imposition of political pressures on employees by their superiors. Many public employees have long argued that the federal government's Hatch Act and the state legislation referred to as "little Hatch Acts," which prohibit active participation in partisan politics, interferes with their rights to freedom of expression and association. The Supreme Court has upheld the federal act and some state acts on the ground that such interference as there is is justified by the compelling government interest in keeping the civil service free of corruption and the effects of machine politics.[59]

In recent years, partisan decisions by officials that affect the careers of civil servants have provided a number of interesting cases. In *Abood v. Detroit*,[60] the Court ruled that employees in unionized government jobs could not be forced to pay those portions of union service fees that were to be used to advance political causes. The Court had decided a year earlier, in *Buckley v. Valeo*,[61] that the expenditure of funds to support a political candidate or issue was a form of free speech protected by the First Amendment. In *Abood* the Court ruled that public employees could not be forced to participate in that expression by means of fees deducted from their salary by their employer and given to the union for purposes not directly related to collective bargaining, contract administration, and grievance adjustment. Potentially more important are several decisions that have directly challenged the entire notion of political patronage hiring and termination of employees. Writing for the plurality in *Elrod v. Burns*,[62] which challenged the Cook County, Illinois, machine of the late Mayor Richard Daley, Justice Brennan observed that cases alleging interference with protected fundamental rights, in this instance Republican employees who were fired by a Democratic county administration, involved three determinations. First, the Court had to decide whether there was a substantial infringement of the employees' protected freedom. In this case there was no question but that the employees were being terminated because of their political association. Second, some infringements of liberties may be justified if the government can demonstrate a sufficiently compelling reason. Justice Brennan acknowledged that party affiliation might be appropriate for some jobs in some circumstances. Third, the court had to decide whether, given that the government action did serve compelling interests, patronage practices as used were overbroad and not sufficiently tailored to achievement of the goals without excessive interference with protected rights. Justice Brennan concluded that the patronage system failed on the third ground. In *Elrod*, a process server and other low-level employees were being fired solely because they belonged to the wrong party. While the criterion of party affiliation may be appropriate and necessary for some high-level policymaking positions, it was not justified as a blanket practice. Justice Stewart wrote the concurring opinion, which along with the three justices in the plurality made up a majority of the court, but he and his colleague, Justice Blackmun, only went so far as to say that a "nonpolicymaking, nonconfidential government employee" could not be discharged solely because of party affiliation.[63] In 1980, however, the Court held:

> In sum, the ultimate inquiry is not whether the label "policymaker" or "confidential" fits a particular position; rather, the question is whether the

hiring authority can demonstrate that party affiliation is an appropriate requirement for the effective performance of the public office involved.[64]

Equal Protection: The Problem of Discrimination

In recent times First Amendment claims and Fifth and Fourteenth Amendment discrimination suits have accounted for the largest share of noncriminal constitutional adjudication. Elimination of the historical discrimination against women and minority groups has been a difficult challenge. In particular, the attempt to deal with discrimination in public employment based on race, sex, and alienage has been most complex. But before reaching cases that outline these particular problems, it is necessary to outline the premises and assumptions on which courts depend in handling claims of unconstitutional discrimination.

Almost all laws and regulations classify people, things, or actions. Laws are directed at particular groups of people, such as residents of a community, business persons, doctors, minors, or pension recipients. But not all laws that classify or treat different groups of people differently can be said to involve unconstitutional, or invidious, discrimination in violation of the equal protection clause of the Fourteenth Amendment. (Where the federal government is involved, charges of discrimination are brought under the Fifth Amendment.[65]) The problem for courts is to determine what kinds of unequal treatment are unlawful. That problem is complicated by the fact that some laws that appear to be fair and nondiscriminatory as written are administered in a discriminatory manner.[66] The Supreme Court has developed a general framework for dealing with such cases.

In most instances, the courts will assume that government officials act lawfully.[67] Therefore, one who asserts that government officials have discriminated in law (that is, in the manner in which a law is written) or under color of law (the manner in which law or policy is administered) carries the burden of proving that those officials have acted unlawfully. All the government need do is demonstrate that its actions are rationally related to a legitimate government interest. For example, suppose a group of fifteen-year-olds challenge a state law requiring mandatory school attendance until the age of sixteen. True, the law classifies and treats people differently based on age, but the state will merely claim that mandatory attendance until approximately sixteen years of age is rationally related to the legitimate state purpose of ensuring a minimum level of education for all its citizens. The law would stand.

The Supreme Court has found over the years that certain criteria used to treat people differently are inherently suspicious because they have historically been used to discriminate unconstitutionally. They are referred to as "suspect classifications," the best example being government action that treats people differently on the basis of race.[68] Where the person charging discrimination shows that the government treats citizens differently on the basis of a suspect classification or discriminates in providing opportunities to exercise fundamental rights (e.g., when the right to due process, in a criminal case, the right to marry, or the right to travel are made to depend on one's ability to pay), the Court becomes more vigilant and imposes strict judicial scrutiny. At the point where the Court is convinced that government is treating people differently on the basis of a suspect classification or with respect to their fundamental rights, the burden of proof shifts to the government to justify the discrimination. The government must do more than merely show that its actions are rationally related to some legitimate state purpose. It must demonstrate a compelling interest, sufficiently grave to overcome the harm done to those who were discriminated against.[69] The Court has ruled that suspect classifications are those that involve a "discrete and insular minority," which has suffered a history of discrimination, has been "relegated to such a position of powerlessness as to command extraordinary protection from the majoritarian political process,"[70] and may possess the characteristic that distinguishes them from others as an accident of birth.[71] Race, illegitimacy, and alienage have all been treated as suspect classifications at one time or another.[72] Obviously, it is and should be extremely difficult to justify discrimination and stand the test of strict judicial scrutiny.

Unfortunately, there is another element to the problem. The equal protection clause prohibits discrmination in law or under color of law(de jure), but it does not prohibit accidental or existing discrimination (de facto). This is important because those who practiced discrimination long ago became sophisticated enough to avoid using words or writing policies that actually stated the intention to discriminate. For that reason, the courts have generally looked to the effect of the government action to decide whether there was de jure discrimination, rather than attempting to determine what was in the minds of the officials when they acted or wrote a law.[73] If the action complained of had the effect of treating, for example, blacks differently from others, strict scrutiny would be triggered and the government would be required to justify the differential treatment. In *Washington v. Davis*, a 1976 case, the Supreme Court held that it is necessary to demonstrate both discriminatory effect and discriminatory intent to trigger strict judicial scrutiny.[74] Those who felt they were being subjected to discrimination had to prove that the discrimination was intentional. In 1977, the Court gave examples of guidelines to prove intent, including an examination of the impact or effect of the government action, the "historical background of the decision," the "specific sequence of events leading up to the challenged decision," a determination whether there had been "departures from the normal procedural sequence," and the "legislative or administrative history" of the action, including records, minutes, or hearing transcripts.[75]

In 1979, a woman brought a suit against the personnel administrator of Massachusetts, arguing that the state's veterans preference law was unconstitutional discrimination on the basis of sex.[76] She argued that, until relatively recently, U.S. military guidelines limited the number of women who could serve in the military to roughly 2 percent of the members of the armed services, hence limiting the number of women who could qualify for veterans preference. The challengers proved that, at the time the law was extended during the Vietnam years, the legislature had been told that its program, which provided a lifetime absolute preference over all nonveterans, was making it all but impossible for most women to break out of the lowest-paid clerical positions into more responsible government jobs. The women produced figures to show that the number of women who were able to get beyond the minimal civil service levels was indeed very low and that a variety of men had been hired over women who had higher scores on civil service examinations. They argued that some form of preference to help returning veterans or to encourage others to serve might be justified, but that the life-long absolute preference enacted in the face of an awareness of its impact on women was unconstitutional. The Supreme Court disagreed, holding that the program was not intentional gender-based discrimination.

Discriminatory purpose, however, implies more than intent as volition or intent as awareness of consequences. It implies that the decisionmaker, in this case a state legislature, selected or reaffirmed a particular course of action at least in part "because of," not merely "in spite of," its adverse effects upon an identifiable group.[77]

In sum, recent developments in equal protection indicate some difficulty for those who wish to pursue constitutional claims under the equal protection clause. On the other hand, they also suggest a slightly less adversarial relationship between government officials or units and the courts with respect to equal protection claims brought under the Constitution.

In recent years most of the litigation brought in federal courts alleging racial discrimination in government employment has been launched under Title VII of the Civil Rights Act of 1964, as amended in 1972.[78] That legislation and the Civil Service Reform Act of 1978[79] (CSRA) have made most legislation barring discrimination in employment practices applicable to the government as an employer, or else provided a government equivalent. The existence of this statutory alternative plus efforts by government managers to eliminate discrimination in employment, together with the rulings of the Supreme Court making it more difficult to prosecute constitution-based claims of discrimination, have resulted in a change in litigation patterns.

There has, however, been a variety of litigation brought by white males alleging that affirmative action programs, implemented to bring more minority employees into government service and to eliminate the effects of past discrimination, are illegal. Specifically, challengers to affirmative action programs governing hiring and promotions assert that these programs are reverse racial discrimination which violates the equal protection provisions of the Constitution, as well as Title VII and Title VI of the Civil Rights Act of 1964 (which prohibits discrimination in any government program financed by federal funds).

Three such cases have been decided by the United States Supreme Court, all three badly dividing the Court. Ordinarily, any government action that deliberately provides an advantage or disadvantage to a citizen on the basis of race is unconstitutional. However, where a case of discrimination is proven in a court according to the rules discussed earlier, the question is what should the court provide as a remedy to the person who was discriminated against? In most cases, the victim would not be made whole again by an award of money damages. In such situations, the court may impose a race-conscious equitable remedy, ordering the government to hire the person who had been discriminated against and to remedy the effects of its past discriminatory actions. A race conscious remedy ordered in a proven case of discrimination is lawful and the scope of a judge's authority in writing such a remedial order is broad, but only where a case of discrimination has actually been proven.[80] It has been argued that racial discrimination has been pervasive in American society for generations and that individuals in the job market and attempting to obtain professional educations have been disadvantaged by that discrimination, both directly and indirectly.[81] Is it lawful for employers to seek minority applicants more aggressively than their white male counterparts to meet this broader conception of the need to remedy past discrimination, whether or not it has been proven in court? In *Regents v. Bakke,* the Court concluded that race might be considered as one factor in the admissions process for applicants to the University of California Medical School at Davis, absent a proven case of past discrimination, but the school was not justified in establishing a special minority admissions program that set aside a specific number of spaces in the class for minority students.[82] In *United Steelworkers v. Weber,*[83] a white employee of Kaiser Aluminum charged that an affirmative action agreement voluntarily entered into between the firm and the union calling for a given percentage of minority workers to be accepted into a job training program was illegal reverse discrimination under Title VII. Title VII contained a provision that barred the government from forcing an affirmative action program on an employer who had not been proven guilty of discrimination, but in *Weber* the question was whether it banned voluntary plans. Justice Brennan wrote for a badly divided Court, arguing that it did not. Justice Blackmun wrote an interesting concurring opinion suggesting that the real problem is to provide a way for an employer to make serious attempts to make up for questionable past practices without having first to lose a law suit proving discrimination, with the costs and possible money damages that might come out of such litigation.[84] The points that saved this affirmative action plan apparently were that it was voluntarily agreed on, rather than government imposed, and was for a set time period, namely, the duration of that contract. The third case, *Fullilove v. Klutznick,*[85] challenged the minority business enterprise section of the Public Works Employment Act of 1977, which required those who administer grant funds under the statute to set aside 10 percent of the funds for contracts with minority business enterprises. Again, a divided Court upheld the program, this time on the ground that Congress had designed this program as a limited and time-bound response to a well-documented history of discrimination in small business contracting.

Some employers, both public and private, operate programs that mandate specific hiring and promotion requirements as remedies for specific proven cases of past discrimination.[86] Others, including the federal government, operate under a system that has no mandatory quotas but that requires diligent efforts to seek out and encourage qualified minority candidates to enter government service.[87] Finally, there are a variety of special situations in which the courts have upheld some limited voluntary programs that set percentage requirements for hiring, job training, and promotion. Most government employees and employers operate under the second of these modes of affirmative action.

Given that we are a nation of immigrants, it is embarrassing for Americans to be reminded of the discrimination against aliens in our history, particularly since World War I. A declining economy and a more competitive job market, along with a major increase in the number of refugees, immigrants and permanent resident aliens have increased tensions. A host of suits have been brought by aliens who permanently reside in this country, some with the expectation of becoming citizens, paying taxes, and being subject to all other laws (including compulsory military service if required), who would like to work for government at all levels in jobs ranging from clerk typist, to teacher, police officer, or engineer. The Supreme Court has generally treated laws that bar professionals from practicing,[88] prevent persons from receiving benefits from public programs,[89] or preclude resident aliens from public employment as illegal discrimination.[90] The Court grants considerably more deference to the federal government in these matters because of the relationship between immigration and naturalizatin policy and foreign policy,[91] but blatant and unjustified discrimination in hiring is not permitted.[92] In 1978 and 1979, the Supreme Court handed down rulings permitting state governments considerably more latitude in restricting certain kinds of jobs to citizens only. The Court held that where the nature of a government job is such that it is of particular importance and involves a considerable amount of discretion, a state may be able to justify a limitation.[93] Specifically, the Court upheld a New York restriction on the certification of teachers[94] and a state restriction that citizens only be hired as state troopers.[95] Given the present political environment, it is likely that there will be continued litigation over public employment for aliens for the foreseeable future.

Suits charging sex discrimination under the equal protection clause have also been plentiful in the past decade. The Court has held that government programs may not automatically assume dependency of women on men (and not the reverse) in terms of job-related benefits or survivors' benefits under Social Security.[96] A number of cases in which women were provided with a benefit because of previous sex-related discrimination in the society as a whole have been upheld.[97] For example, a male military officer who was a victim of the military's "up-or-out" program, which requires that officers be promoted within certain time constraints or be separated from the service, sued because of less stringent retention requirements for female officers. The government acknowledged that it was treating women differently from men, but argued that this action was justified because female officers were barred from combat-type line assignments, which often help officers in promotion consider-ations. Because of this limitation on their career opportunities, the government argued that women should be accorded slightly more favorable terms for retention. The Court agreed.[98]

Judges have had a difficult time determining whether or not gender-based classifications are inherently suspect and require strict judicial scrutiny.[99] As a kind of judicial compromise, the Supreme Court has determined that government actions that intentionally discriminate on the basis of gender will be judged according to a standard somewhere between strict scrutiny and the mere rational basis test. "Classifications by gender must serve important governmental objectives and must be substantially related to achievement of those objectives."[100] Given the Massa-chusetts veterans preference case and the recent male-only draft registration case,[101] it is difficult to tell just what direction sex discrimination suits brought under the Constitution will take.

The Constitutional Conflict over Privacy and Life-style

A continuing area of controversy among government employers and public servants is the degree to which government employees must adjust their life-styles and off-duty conduct to conform to the public image of the government. Colorful characters may enliven cocktail parties, but they also often attract public attention in a manner that many government supervisors would rather avoid. From the employer's point of view, they may also injure public confidence in the professionalism or integrity of the public service. From the employees' perspective, as long as their conduct does not endanger others or affect their actual performance on the job, their lives should be their own. Some challenges by employees to rules of public employment are based on the constitutionally protected right to privacy. Of course, there is no specifically articulated right to privacy in the Constitution, but, as was true of the right to association, the Supreme Court has determined that this right is implied by other provisions of the Bill of Rights.[102] In one case, local school boards required pregnant teachers to take maternity leave five months before their projected delivery date. The Court ruled that this restriction unduly interfered with the woman's protected rights concerning family life and the decision to bear children.[103] Similar arguments have been made by government employees who object to restrictions on their sexual conduct or lifestyle. Some lower federal courts have supported the employees,[104] but the Supreme Court has carefully avoided several cases that raised questions about prohibitions against homosexuality or firings of public employees who underwent sex change operations. Challenges have also been brought by public servants who asserted that restrictions on dress or personal appearance interfered with their freedom of expression. However, the Supreme Court ruled that regulations limiting the style and length of, for example, a police officer's hair are not unconstitutional violations of the employee's liberty.[105] A related life-style consideration that has prompted constitutional litigation is the frequently imposed requirement that one live within the government jurisdiction in which one is employed. Police officers, firemen, and teachers have brought suits challenging such rules. In *McCarthy v. Philadelphia Civil Service Commission,* the Supreme Court held that a requirement that city employees reside in the city did not violate the employee's right to travel or his liberty under the Constitution.[106]

STATUTORY PROTECTIONS FOR PUBLIC EMPLOYEES

In addition to the evolving body of constitutional law protecting the rights of public employees, there are several statutory developments that public employers and employees should be aware of, if not familiar with. These are statutes that govern employee political activity, discriminatory activity, and the general operation of the civil service system.

The Practical Side of Hatch Act Limitations

The Hatch Act and its state-level counterparts limiting partisan political activity by public employees have been upheld in constitutional challenges. But this is the beginning of the difficulty, not the end. The Supreme Court concluded that the rules issued under the statute are sufficiently clear that an ordinary person should be able to understand them, but the evidence is that most public employees do not know what is and is not permitted under the act.[107] The Office of Personnel Management has published a pamphlet listing activities that are open and those prohibited to public employees, as follows:[108]

What Employees May Do	What Employees May Not Do
• You have the right to register and vote as you choose in any election. . . .	The general prohibitions on Federal employees are that they may not use their official authority or

• You have the right to express your opinions as an individual, privately and publicly, on all political subjects and candidates as long as you don't take an active part in partisan political management or partisan political campaigns.

• You may wear a political badge or button or display a sticker on your private automobile, subject to work-related limitations.

• You may make a voluntary campaign contribution to a political party or organization.

• You may accept appointment to public office, provided service in the office will not conflict or interfere with the efficient discharge of your Federal duties.

• You may participate in a non-partisan election either as a candidate or in support of . . . a candidate, and you may, if elected, serve in the office if such service will not conflict or interfere with your Federal duties.

• You may serve as an election clerk or judge, or in a similar position, to perform non-partisan duties as prescribed by state or local law.

• You may be politically active in connection with an issue not specifically identified with a political party, such as a constitutional amendment, referendum, approval of a municipal ordinance, or similar issue.

• You may participate in the non-partisan activities of a civic, community, social, labor, professional, or similar organization.

• You may be a member of a political party or other political organization and attend meetings

influence to interfere with or affect the result of an election, and that they may not take an active part in partisan political management or in partisan political campaigns.

• You may not be a candidate for nomination or election to a national or state office.

• You may not become a partisan candidate for nomination or election to public office.

• You may not campaign for or against a political party or candidate in a partisan election for public office or political party office.

• You may not serve as an officer of a political party, a member of a national, state or local committee of a political party, an officer or member of a committee of a partisan political club, or be a candidate for any of these positions.

• You may not solicit, receive, collect, handle, disburse, or account for assessments, contributions, or other funds for a partisan political purpose or in connection with a partisan election. Federal criminal statutes impose restrictions concerning contributions in connection with the election for Federal office. Specifically, you may not solicit political contributions from other Federal employees and no person may solicit or receive political contributions in buildings where Federal employees work. Also, one of these criminal statutes restricts your ability to make political contributions to Federal employees.
. . .

• You may not sell tickets for or otherwise actively promote such activities as political dinners.

• You may not take an active part in managing the political campaign of and vote on issues, but you may not take an active part in managing the organization.

• You may attend a political convention, rally, fund-raising function, or other political gathering, but you may not take an active part in conducting or managing such gatherings.

• You may sign petitions, including nominating petitions, but may not initiate them or canvass for signatures in partisan elections.

• You may petition Congress or any Member of Congress, such as by writing to your Representatives and Senators to say how you think they should vote on a particular issue.

a candidate, in a partisan election for public office or political party office.

• You may not work at the polls on behalf of a partisan candidate or political party by acting as a checker, challenger, or watcher, or in a similar partisan position.

• You may not distribute campaign material.

• You may not serve as a delegate, alternate, or proxy to a political party convention.

• You may not address a convention, rally, caucus, or similar gathering of a political party in support of or in opposition to a candidate for public office or political party office, or on a partisan political question.

• You may not endorse or oppose a candidate in a partisan election through a political advertisement, broadcast, campaign literature, or similar material.

• You may not use your automobile to drive voters to the polls on behalf of a political party or candidate in a partisan election.

These restrictions in themselves are rather confusing, but there are two further complicating factors. First, the federal Hatch Act applies to state employees whose work is primarily or substantially funded by federal funds. Second, many states with little Hatch Acts do not provide descriptive guides of permissible activities.

Statutory Antidiscrimination Programs

The statutes enacted by the federal government to eliminate discrimination fall into three general categories: (1) broad attacks on discriminatory practices in employment; (2) specific attempts to deal with sex discrimination; and (3) attempts to deal with special problems of discrimination.

For several years the primary mechanism for dealing with discrimination in employment was the Civil Rights Act of 1964.[109] The act prohibits discrimination on the basis of race, sex, religion, and national origin, and established the Equal Employment Opportunity Commission (EEOC) as an enforcement agency. But that act was passed during a period of severe conflict over federal enforcement of fair employment practices, and the bill that was eventually enacted contained many compromises and changes from the one that was originally introduced. For one thing, the EEOC had extremely limited enforcement powers, serving primarily as a clearing house for complaints by employees. The 1964 act was amended and substantially strengthened by the Equal Employment Opportunity Act of 1972.[110] Among other things, the amendments extended the coverage of the Title VII antidiscrimination provisions to most federal, state, and local employees. Second, EEOC was given substantial enforcement authority, including the power to prosecute cases in court.

An important aspect of the amendments to the Civil Rights Act is that they were designed with a concern for the need to deal with sex discrimination. The original bill was primarily designed to deal with racial discrimination in employment and places of public accommodation. The women's movement was still quite weak when the 1964 act was passed, but by the early '70s more women were politically active and more were employed. The EEOC has since attempted to deal with such matters as sexual harassment of employees through issuance of guidelines and dispute resolution procedures.[111] Other important statutory developments on sex discrimination include the Equal Pay Act[112] and the pregnancy discrimination amendments to the Civil Rights Act.[113] The Equal Pay Act was intended to eliminate widespread pay disparities between males and females doing the same kind of work. The pregnancy discrimination amendments were designed as a response to a Supreme Court ruling that employers need not consider pregnancy-related problems as medical disabilities in insurance plans or other benefit programs.[114] Efforts are now under way in the EEOC and in courts to integrate the several protections against gender-based discrimination into a coherent body of law.

Two special problems of discrimination have also engendered protective statutes. The Age Discrimination in Employment Act of 1967[115] was enacted to deal with major problems faced by workers between the age of forty and sixty-five as a flood of young workers entered the work force. The statute simply states that employers should not discriminate in hiring, promotions, or other personnel decisions on the basis of age unless there is some *bona fide* job-related reason for doing so. Many governmental units were not covered by this act, and, following a decision in which the Supreme Court held that there was no constitutional ground for claiming protection against age-based discrimination,[116] Congress amended the ADEA to make it applicable to most government employees.[117] The second problem was discrimination against handicapped citizens. To deal with this problem, Congress enacted the Rehabilitation Act of 1973.[118]

Finally, a major part of the effort to update civil service legislation that brought about the Civil Service Reform Act of 1978 was the attempt to unite and clarify the antidiscrimination legislation. The CSRA states:

> (b) Any employee who has authority to take, direct others to take, recommend, or approve any personnel action, shall not, with respect to such authority—
>> (1) discriminate for or against any employee or applicant for employment—
>>> (A) on the basis of race, color, religion, sex, or national origin, as prohibited under section 717 of the Civil Rights Act of 1964 (42 U.S.C. 2000e-16);

(B) on the basis of age, as prohibited under sections 12 and 15 of the Age Discrimination in Employment Act of 1967 (29 U.S.C. 631, 633a);

(C) on the basis of sex, as prohibited under section 6(d) of the Fair Labor Standards Act of 1938 (29 U.S.C. 206 (d));

(D) on the basis of handicapping condition, as prohibited under section 501 of the Rehabilitation Act of 1973 (29 U.S.C. 791); or

(E) on the basis of marital status or political affiliation, as prohibited under any law, rule, or regulation.[119]

The Civil Service Reform Act

The Civil Service Reform Act is a long and complex statute that fundamentally restructured the civil service. In general terms, it divided the former Civil Service Commission into two basic parts, according to their functions. The Office of Personnel Management is charged with general administration of the civil service system, particularly including efforts to improve governmental personnel management techniques and performance evaluations. The Merit System Protection Board (MSPB) was created as an independent organization designed to resolve civil disputes of several kinds. Where the dispute involves allegations of discrimination, the CSRA contains provisions under which the EEOC can be called on to review the board's rulings. A reconciliation process is available should the two agencies disagree.

Although there are a number of constitutional law protections for employees, statutes to govern public personnel matters, and a new organizational structure for the management at least of the federal civil service, two major problems remain. First, there are gaps or ambiguities in the law on the problems encountered by special employees and the supervisors who manage those employees. Second, the black letter law and public policy pronouncements may offer several options for public servants who encounter problems in employment, but the informal interactions within the bureaucracy can make it difficult for the civil servant to use the formal protections. Indeed, the pressures can force public servants into moral dilemmas.

Special Employees in the Public Service

Several kinds of public service jobs are sufficiently special as to require exceptions to some of the standard rules that govern general civil service personnel. However, many special employees are not primarily political employees in a patronage sense, and consequently they cannot be deprived of all the usual protections afforded to civil servants. In fact, some positions require added independence and security. Regulatory decisionmakers are one such group. Chapter 10 noted the conflict between the need of regulatory officials to maintain independence and the President's attempts to coordinate regulatory policy. The courts have held that executives may not fire regulatory commissioners who make quasi-judicial decisions without good cause.

For similar reasons, the Administrative Procedure Act established administrative law judges as officers protected by civil service procedures and rules, but it gave them additional protections. Specifically, ALJs may not be assigned to tasks other than normal ALJ duties. The APA insulates their pay and promotion decisions from attempts at retribution by agency employers. However, providing such extraordinary protections to ALJs means that few mechanisms are available by which to evaluate ALJ performance or to provide the ALJs with incentives to improve their productivity. A number of studies have been done to find ways to preserve needed protections for ALJs and at the same time allow agencies to

- identify unsatisfactory Administrative Law Judges and take personnel action,
- make effective use of Administrative Law Judges to assure maximum productivity,
- plan adequately for Administrative Law Judge requirements to meet workload,
- provide the Civil Service Commission (OPM) with information to determine the adequacy of its Administrative Law Judges certifying practices,
- develop Administrative Law Judges to their maximum potential through training or diversity of experience, and
- establish appropriate management feedback mechanisms to determine the effectiveness of an Administrative Law Judge personnel management system.[120]

Another group of special employees for which the conflict between civil service protections and accountability remains a problem is the Senior Executive Service. However, in the case of the SES, the employees are somewhat more vulnerable than they were before the establishment of this category, rather than more protected. Indeed, the Senior Executive Service was created by the Civil Service Reform Act precisely to develop a body of senior executives who could be rewarded for outstanding performance through such devices as merit pay, could be used more flexibly in varying jobs as the need presented itself, and could be removed from important positions if they failed to perform effectively without the necessity of satisfying standard civil service adverse personnel action procedures. But, as Bernard Rosen pointed out in a recent article, the removal of standard protections can make it difficult for senior career executives to perform one of their important traditional roles, that is, to aid new administrations or inexperienced political appointees to understand all aspects of their various problems and opportunities without fear of reprisal for failing to be sufficiently responsive to political agendas.

> The mythology about political executives having to overcome resistant career executives originates largely in the tensions of an administration's first year and are subsequently publicized in the "war stories" of a few departed officials. There is no persuasive evidence, however, that the alleged resistance goes beyond the responsible action of making sure that the political decision makers see all aspects of an issue before they decide.[121]

Given the frequent turnover in political executives and the complexity of agencies and their problems, there is a danger that high-level civil servants with valuable experience and knowledge may not be available to advise new administrations or may be unwilling to risk "speaking truth to power."

Another group that might, with qualifications, be referred to as special employees are not direct government employees, but are employed by firms that depend to a large extent on government contracts. Contracting is much more than an agreement to acquire goods and services for government at the best price possible, consistent with a fair rate of return for the business. It is also a policy tool that can be used as a lever to accomplish a variety of purposes.[123] In a general sense, government contractors are required to conform to a host of approved personnel practices, such as affirmative action, as a condition of receiving their contracts. Their progress in meeting those personnel requirements is monitored by the Office of Federal Contract Compliance (OFCCP) and the Equal Opportunity Commission, among other government agencies. In a very real sense, the conditions of employment for those employed by government contractors are heavily influenced by federal personnel policies. On the other hand, they do not enjoy civil service protections.[124] Just what directions the law and politics of the contract process will take in the near term is unclear, and so is the environment of the contract worker and his or her supervisor.

Employees of the federal courts and of the Congress are also special employees. Congress, as a matter or prerogative and in some instances out of respect for the judiciary as a coequal and independent third branch of government, has exempted itself and the federal courts from certain requirements, including the strictures of the APA and some civil rights legislation. As the size of the judicial and congressional bureaucracies has grown, however, there has been increasing concern by some employees that they should be afforded standard civil service benefits and protections even if the rules governing their pay and retirement remain separate.[125] On the other hand, many employers and employees might like some standardization in personnel practices, but few relish the prospect of losing the flexibility they now enjoy.

Finally, a significant group of special employees can be classified under the rubric of military or national security personnel. There are two problems for these employees. First, courts traditionally grant a considerable amount of deference to the military and the President in matters of national security or military administration. Second, many of the statutes designed to protect civil servants and private citizens contain exemptions for national security affairs. Because of the reluctance of the courts to interfere in such matters, military and security workers have been subjected to serious abuses in the name of national security. Some of the worst abuses have come in the application process. For example, a congressional investigation found that:

> Applicants for federal jobs in some agencies, and employees in certain cases, have been subjected to programs requiring them to answer forms of psychological tests which contained questions such as these:
>
> I am very troubled by constipation.
> My sex life is satisfactory.
> At times I feel like swearing.
> I have never been in trouble because of my sex behavior.
> I do not always tell the truth.
> I have no difficulty in starting or holding my bowel movements.

I am very strongly attracted by members of my own sex.

I like poetry.

I go to church almost every week.

I believe in the second coming of Christ.

I believe in a life hereafter.

My mother was a good woman.

I believe my sins are unpardonable.

I have used alcohol excessively.

I loved my Mother.

I believe there is a God.

Many of my dreams are about sex matters.

At periods my mind seems to work more slowly than usual.

I am considered a liberal "dreamer" of new ways rather than a practical follower of well-tried ways. (a) true, (b) uncertain, (c) false.

When telling a person a deliberate lie, I have to look away, being ashamed to look him in the eye. (a) true, (b) uncertain, (c) false.[126]

In addition to such intrusive and biased psychological testing, there are well-documented abuses of polygraph or "lie detector" testing.[127] A third area of frequently reported abuses for military and security affairs workers is wiretapping of telephones of current and past employees.[128]

Fortunately, there have been efforts to remedy these abuses in recent years. If properly administered, the Privacy Act and the Civil Service Reform Act in particular could be used and were intended to provide protections for such employees along with other citizens. Employees may be able to sue employers who violate their constitutional and statutory rights to privacy.[129] On the other hand, supervisors must be able to safeguard legitimate national security information and maintain military discipline. This is another area in which competing interests make policy development difficult.

WHISTLEBLOWING AND OTHER ETHICAL PROBLEMS

Most civilian public servants do not fit into the political or special employee categories and enjoy a wide range of protections in their relationships with their employers. But, as this book has stressed, one who would understand law and administration must understand both the law and the environment in which it operates. The reality is that although the black letter law may provide a number of options and protections for employees who are mistreated or who perceive their agencies to be badly administered, informal mechanisms may discourage recourse to those legal options. The problem of the availability of legal actions versus the problems encountered in employing them has been highlighted in the debate over whistleblowing. Obviously, legislators and citizens would like public servants who encounter examples of fraud, abuse, waste, mismanagement, or maladministration to come forward so that the problem can be dealt with and the public interest served.

On the other hand, supervisors can hardly accomplish their tasks if subordinates ignore standard channels of authority whenever they disagree with a management decision. For the employee who finds such a problem, a difficult conflict among his or her job security and advancement, professionalism, and citizenship interests may arise. Long after one blows the whistle, colleagues and supervisors will be in a position to affect one's career in more or less subtle ways. Even though formal protections exist to protect those who blow the whistle against reprisals, the decision to go public is still a difficult one to make.

These and other ethically based decisions have been of particular concern to policymakers in the aftermath of Watergate. Ethics for administrators is again considered an important topic. Two general initiatives have been undertaken in recent years to revitalize ethical considerations in administration. First, the Civil Service Reform Act and the Ethics in Government Act both provide mechanisms to encourage ethical conduct. The Ethics in Government Act requires disclosures of possible conflicts of interests and discourages the movement of administrators from agencies into attractive positions with the firms they formerly regulated. It also encourages concern for ethical standards among those in government. The CSRA provides specific protections for whistleblowers through the Office of the Special Counsel of the Merit System Protection Board. The special counsel may initiate proceedings both informally with the agency and formally through the MSPB to block adverse personnel actions against employees who come forward with evidence of fraud, abuse, waste, or maladministration. Unfortunately, early oversight hearings are not encouraging. In hearings conducted in spring 1980, ten witnesses from a variety of agencies who had blown the whistle testified on the insidious reprisals taken against them and the costs and delays associated with attempts to protect themselves.[130] When asked whether they would encourage others to blow the whistle, relying on the MSPB protections, none replied in the affirmative. Since that time, however, the Office of Special Counsel has been expanded and given more independence. Whether that will enable the authorities to implement the whistleblower protections more effectively remains to be seen.

The second, and perhaps more important, initiative has been taken by some scholars, led by John Rohr,[131] who are reexamining the basic values that underlie public service in general and the responsibilities of public servants in the American government in particular. Preparation for ethical difficulties in the education of public servants or in their professional development may be far more important than the availability of black letter law protections after the fact.

IN SEARCH OF RESPONSIBLE BUREAUCRACY

In part at least, many of the tensions among public employees, their supervisors, and the public may be recast and seen as an effort to determine how administrators can be made and kept responsible.[132] Two of the leading writers on administrative responsibility, Carl Friedrich and Herman Finer, emphasized the importance of two major facets of this responsibility: (1) internal mechanisms to ensure responsibility, and (2) external devices to check abuses and discourage irresponsible bureaucratic behavior.[133] Internal checks are self-imposed limits on conduct, obtained through the educational process and through appropriate socialization as a professional public servant. External checks are formal organizational, political or legal constraints on one's behavior. Finer emphasized the need for objective external methods to ensure accountability, and Friedrich argued that because of the manner in which the bureaucracy operates, responsibility can only be guaranteed by eliciting responsible behavior from administrators as an internal control and not by simply trying to enforce it.[134] This and earlier chapters have argued that internal (informal and often personal) norms and external political, managerial, and legal checks are both necessary.

This chapter has emphasized three internal mechanisms for ensuring responsible behavior: (1) professionalism, (2) a recognized need to represent unpopular or unrepresented views on a policy problem, and (3) ethical considerations. For a public servant, professionalism means a commitment to technical proficiency in one's area of specialization, as assessed by other professionals, and also a recognition that public servants do govern and have an obligation to do so in the public interest and in a statesmanlike manner.[135] Of course, the higher one moves in the bureaucracy the more obvious is the need for statesmanship, but from the consumer's perspective the sensitivity and evenhandedness that characterize statesmanlike behavior are important qualities for the street-level bureaucrat. The task of representing all facets of a problem in administrative decision processes may be difficult to accomplish, but it serves the important goal of presenting those who are not adequately heard in the political process and helps counter the tendency toward myopia that can afflict decisionmakers bogged down in a policy problem. Stephen Bailey has suggested that some of these problems can be dealt with only if administrators operate from strong ethical commitments. In particular, he notes that the "essential moral qualities of the ethical public servant are: (1) optimism, (2) courage, and (3) fairness tempered by charity."[136]

As to external mechanisms for ensuring responsible administrative behavior, Chapter 10 considered in some detail efforts by the executive and the legislature to impose political accountability on the bureaucracy. This chapter has emphasized the need for agency managers to ensure responsible behavior by subordinates, through adverse personnel actions if necessary, in order to maintain the effectiveness of the organization. Some limitations on civil servants are external, not internal, but have their effect informally rather than formally. For example, the treatment of whistle-blowers by colleagues within an organization can be extremely chilling. There are, of course, a number of judicially administered external checks: judicial review; judicial intervention in maladministration through injunctions and similar devices; criminal prosecutions; and judgments of money damages awarded to those injured by administrative abuses. The constitutional, statutory, and procedural legal checks complement the other external and internal mechanisms to make up a framework for responsible bureaucracy.

Chapters 7 and 9 dealt with the legal checks on bureaucracy. Because lawsuits for money damages brought against units of government and individual public employees have become popular in recent years, they are worthy of brief discussion here. Judges have historically varied in their opinions on what kinds of suits could be brought against what types of public officers or government units, and whether some immunities should be available to protect officials from frivolous actions or suits brought primarily to harass them.[137]

In general, with respect to suits brought in federal courts, the federal government,[138] state governments,[139] judges,[140] legislators,[141] prosecuting attorneys in the criminal and administrative systems,[142] and regulatory adjudicators,[143] are immune from suits for money damages. State and local government *officials*[144] and others acting under color of government authority[145] *are* subject to suit under the provisions of the Civil Rights Act of 1871, which states:

> Every person who, under color of any statute, ordinance, regulation, custom, or usage, of any State or Territory, subjects, or causes to be subjected, any citizen of the United States or other person within the jurisdiction thereof to the deprivation of any rights, privileges, or immunities secured by the Constitution and laws, shall be liable to the party injured in an action at law, suit in equity, or other proper proceeding for redress.[146]

Local government units are considered "persons" within the meaning of the act and may be sued for actions taken pursuant to their policies.[147] They do not enjoy any immunity against such suits in federal court.[148] As opposed to units, state and local officials sued in federal court do enjoy a "qualified good faith immunity." The Supreme Court has held that public officials should be protected from suits for mere mistakes in judgment. Such an official is immune unless "he knew or reasonably should have known that the action he took within the sphere of his official responsibility would violate the constitutional rights of the [person] affected, or if he took the action with the malicious intention to cause a deprivation of constitutional rights or other injury to the [person]."[149] Officials cannot be required to guess whether or not a right is protected. In a 1974 case, the Supreme Court held that officials would not be held liable unless "the constitutional right allegedly infringed by them was clearly established at the time of the challenged conduct."[150] The same rules apply if a suit was brought with respect to a right based in a statute rather than in the Constitution.[151]

The Civil Rights Act of 1871 speaks to actions taken by state or local officials, but the Supreme Court has held that the same rules apply to federal officials.[152]

Each state has its own laws on what types of suits may be brought by citizens or employees against state or local officials in state courts. In all but ten states, claims to absolute common law immunities against suit have been waived either by state court opinions or by state legislative enactments.[153] Similarly, the degree to which governmental organizations will represent their employees in suits of this nature and the extent to which the government will indemnify officials against damage awards returned against them varies from jurisdiction to jurisdiction. Indeed, just what government units are going to do about the increasing number of suits and how they will protect their employees is a fast-changing area of law and administration. In the final analysis, suits for money damages make up only one element in the array of techniques needed to ensure administrative accountability.

SUMMARY

This chapter has presented problems and developments that have emerged in the area of public law and public administration that is concerned with the relationship between public employees and their supervisors. The problems may vary considerably, depending on whether one speaks of general civil service employees, political executives, or special employees. Many disputes center on adverse actions of several types taken against employees by their supervisors. It is true that there simply may be a conflict between the needs and rights of the individual as against the concerns of the organization, but many conflicts involve a multiplicity of interests that are associated with the goals of the employees, their employers, and the general public for whose benefit the public organizations exist.

Aware of some of these conflicting interests, the courts have worked to ensure that public employees do receive protection for their constitutional rights under the Bill of Rights and the Fourteenth Amendment. Legislatures have gone further, developing a set of statutory protections for public employees. Given the modern administrative context within which these rights are exercised, a variety of problems are still in need of resolution so that employees may feel both protected and responsible. In particular, this chapter addressed the problems of special employees and the ethical difficulties that may be presented by the clash of interests in public employment.

Finally, the maintenance of administrative responsibility, a topic that has run through most of this book, was briefly touched on in light of recent developments in the area of lawsuits against public employees and their organizations. Like the issues of informal process, administrative discretion, regulation, and information policy, problems of the law and public employees are not merely legal but are also political and administrative; they require broad analysis and resist narrow conceptualizations.

NOTES

[1] Robert D. Lee, Jr., *Public Personnel Systems* (Baltimore: University Park Press, 1979), p. 4.

[2] Id., at pp. 1–4.

[3] See generally Frederick Mosher, Jr., *Democracy and the Public Service* (New York: Oxford University Press, 1968); Thomas I. Emerson, *The System of Freedom of Expression* (New York: Vintage Books, 1970), chap. 15; and Paul Appleby, *Big Democracy* (New York: Knopf, 1949).

[4] The case eventually went to the U.S. Supreme Court as *Givhan v. Western Line Consolidated School Dist.*, 439 U.S. 410 (1979).

[5] Givhan brought her action against the school district as an intervenor in the pending desegregation case. Id., at 411–12.

[6] Id., at 412–13.

[7] Id., at 412 n. 1.

[8] On the other allegations, the court of appeals found:

"Appellants also sought to establish these other bases for the decision not to rehire: (1) that Givhan 'downgraded' the papers of white students; (2) that she was one of a number of teachers who walked out of a meeting about desegregation in the fall of 1969 and attempted to disrupt it by blowing automobile horns outside the gymnasium; (3) that the school district had received a threat by Givhan and other teachers not to return to work when schools reopened on a unitary basis in February, 1970; and (4) that Givhan had protected a student during a weapons shakedown at Riverside, in March, 1970, by concealing a student's knife until completion of a search. The evidence on the first three of these points was inconclusive and the district judge did not clearly err in rejecting or ignoring it. Givhan admitted the fourth incident, but the district judge properly rejected that as a justification for her not being rehired, as there was no evidence that [the principal] relied on it in making his decision [cites]." Id., at 412 n. 2.

⁹Id., at 417.

¹⁰Mark Coven, "The First Amendment Rights of Policy-making Public Employees," 12 *Harvard Civil Rights–Civil Liberties Law Rev.* 559 (1977).

¹¹The case was *Bennett v. Thompson*, 116 N.H. 453, 363 A. 2d 187 (N.H. 1976), appeal dismissed, 429 U.S. 1082 (1977).

¹²Coven, supra note 10, at pp. 560–61.

¹³Id., at p. 562.

¹⁴*Bennett v. Thomson*, quoted in Coven, supra note 10, at p. 561.

¹⁵See Lee, supra note 1, at p. 5.

¹⁶Felix A. Nigro and Lloyd G. Nigro, *The New Public Personnel Administration*, 2d ed. (Itasca, Ill.: Peacock, 1981), p. 12.

¹⁷Id., at p. 13.

¹⁸Id., at p. 2.

¹⁹*Branti v. Finkel*, 445 U.S. 507, 518 (1980).

²⁰No clear line can be drawn between policymaking and nonpolicymaking positions. While nonpolicymaking individuals usually have limited responsibility, that is not to say that one with a number of responsibilities may have only limited objectives. An employee with responsibilities that are not well defined or are of broad scope more likely functions in a policymaking position. In determining whether an employee occupies a policymaking position, consideration should also be given to whether the employee acts as an adviser or formulates plans for the implementation of broad goals. Thus, the political loyalty 'justification is a matter of proof, or at least argument, directed at particular kinds of jobs.' " *Elrod v. Burns*, 427 U.S. 347, 367–68 (1976).

"Under some circumstances, a position may be appropriately considered political even though it is neither confidential nor policymaking in character. As one obvious example, if a State's election laws require that precincts be supervised by two election judges of different parties, a Republican judge could be legitimately discharged solely for changing his party registration. That conclusion would not depend on any finding that the job involved participation in policy decisions or access to confidential information. Rather, it would simply rest on the fact that party membership was essential to the discharge of the employee's governmental responsibilities.

"It is equally clear that party affiliation is not necessarily relevant to every policymaking or confidential position. The coach of a state university's football team formulates policy, but no one could seriously claim that Republicans make better coaches than Democrats, or vice versa, no matter which party is in control of the state government. On the other hand, it is equally clear that the Governor of a State may appropriately believe that the official duties of various assistants who help write speeches, explain his views to the press, or communicate with the legislature cannot be performed effectively unless those persons share his political beliefs and party commitments." *Branti v. Finkel*, supra note 19, at 518.

²¹See, e.g., *United States v. O'Brien*, 391 U.S. 367 (1968), and *Grayned v. Rockford*, 408 U.S. 104 (1972). But see

Carey v. Brown, 447 U.S. 455 (1980), and *Chicago Police Dep't v. Mosely*, 408 U.S. 92 (1972).

²²*Adderley v. Florida*, 385 U.S. 39 (1966).

²³See, e.g., Nigro and Nigro, supra note 16, Chap. 14 "Justice for the Worker Grievances and Appeals."

²⁴U.S. Office of Personnel Management, *Manager's Handbook* (Washington, D.C.: Government Printing Office, 1981), pp. 197–204.

²⁵See, e.g., *Perry v. Sindermann*, 408 U.S. 593 (1972), and *Pickering v. Board of Education*, 391 U.S. 563 (1968).

²⁶*Pickering*, Id., at 568.

²⁷*Mt. Healthy Board of Education v. Doyle*, 429 U.S. 274, 284 (1977).

²⁸Coven, supra note 10, at p. 559. Coven's discussion of the public's deliberative interest is particulary interesting.

²⁹See, e.g., Hugh Heclo, "OMB and the Presidency: The Problem of Neutral Competence," 38 *Public Interest* 80 (1975), and Larry Berman, *The Office of Management and Budget and the Presidency, 1921–1979* (Princeton, N.J.: Princeton University Press, 1978).

³⁰Frederick C. Mosher, ed., *American Public Administration: Past, Present, Future* (University: University of Alabama Press, 1975), p. 7.

³¹*Pickering*, supra note 25, at 571–72.

³²Coven, supra note 10, at pp. 573–75.

³³*Keyishian v. Board of Regents*, 385 U.S. 589 (1967).

³⁴*Perry*, supra note 25, at 577.

³⁵With the exception of three cases decided in 1951 and 1952 (*Adler v. Board of Education*, 342 U.S. 485 [1952]; *Garner v. Board of Public Works* 341 U.S. 716 [1951]; *Gerende v. Board of Supervisors*, 341 U.S. 56 [1951]) and nullified by later decisions, the Court has struck down virtually every retrospective loyalty oath or association disclosure statement to come before it. See, e.g., *Wieman v. Updegraff*, 344 U.S. 183 (1952); *Speiser v. Randall*, 357 U.S. 513 (1958); *Shelton v. Tucker*, 364 U.S. 479 (1960); *Cramp v. Board of Public Instruction*, 368 U.S. 278 (1961); *Baggett v. Bullitt*, 377 U.S. 360 (1964); *Elfbrandt v. Russell*, 384 U.S. 11 (1966); and *Keyishian v. Board of Regents*, supra note 33. See also *Baird v. State Bar*, 401 U.S. 1 (1971); *In re Stolar*, 401 U.S. 23 (1971); and *Law Student Civil Rights Research Council v. Wadmond*, 401 U.S. 154 (1971).

³⁶An excellent example of how vague and sweeping the language of such oaths has been is the Oklahoma oath at issue in *Wieman v. Updegraff*, supra note 35, at 184 n. 1.

³⁷Supra note 33.

³⁸See, e.g., U.S. Constitution, Article II, §1, cl. 8, and Article VI, §3.

³⁹*Cole v. Richardson*, 405 U.S. 676 (1972).

⁴⁰*NAACP v. Alabama*, 357 U.S. 449 (1958). See also *Bates v. Little Rock*, 361 U.S. 516 (1960).

⁴¹*Yates v. United States*, 354 U.S. 298 (1957); *Scales v. United States*, 367 U.S. 203 (1961); *Noto v. United States*, 367 U.S. 290 (1961); *Aptheker v. Secretary of State*, 378

U.S. 500 (1964); *Keyishian v. Board of Regents*, supra note 35; *United States v. Robel*, 389 U.S. 258 (1967); and *Communist Party of Indiana v. Whitcomb*, 414 U.S. 441 (1974).

⁴²*Buckley v. Valeo*, 424 U.S. 1, 25 (1976); *Kusper v. Pontikes*, 414 U.S. 51, 57 (1973); and *Shelton v. Tucker*, 364 U.S. 479 (1960).

⁴³*Pickering*, supra note 25, at 568.

⁴⁴*Perry*, supra note 25, at 596.

⁴⁵See generally *Elrod v. Burns*, supra note 20 and *Branti v. Finkel*, supra note 19.

⁴⁶See *Snepp v. United States*, 444 U.S. 507 (1980); and *United States v. Marchetti*, 466 F. 2d 1309 (4th Cir. 1972), cert. denied, 409 U.S. 1063 (1972).

⁴⁷*Pickering*, supra note 25, at 570.

⁴⁸Id., at 568.

⁴⁹Id., at 569–70. See also *Givhan v. Western Line Consolidated School Dist.*, supra note 4, at 414–15 (1979).

⁵⁰That was the case in *Givhan*, supra note 4, and *Mt. Healthy Board of Education v. Doyle*, supra note 27.

⁵¹That is precisely the manner in which the district courts in *Mt. Healthy* and *Givhan* had interpreted *Pickering* and *Perry v. Sindermann*.

⁵²Supra note 27, at 287.

⁵³Supra note 4, at 417.

⁵⁴See, e.g., *Watkins v. United States*, 354 U.S. 178 (1957); *Siweezy v. New Hampshire*, 354 U.S. 234 (1957); *NAACP v. Alabama*, supra note 40; *Uphaus v. Wyman*, 360 U.S. 72 (1959); and *Barenblatt v. United States*, 360 U.S. 109 (1959).

⁵⁵*Barenblatt*, id., and *Gibson v. Florida Legislative Investigating Comm.*, 372 U.S. 539 (1963).

⁵⁶*Wooley v. Maynard*, 430 U.S. 705 (1977).

⁵⁷*Gardner v. Broderick*, 392 U.S. 273 (1968).

⁵⁸*Lefkowitz v. Cunningham*, 431 U.S. 801 (1977); *Lefkowtiz v. Turley*, 414 U.S. 70 (1973); and *Garrity v. New Jersey*, 385 U.S. 493 (1967).

⁵⁹*National Ass'n of Letter Carriers v. Civil Service Comm'n*, 413 U.S. 548 (1973); *Broadrick v. Oklahoma*, 413 U.S. 601 (1973); and *United Public Workers v. Mitchell*, 330 U.S. 75 (1947).

⁶⁰*Abood v. Detroit*, 431 U.S. 209 (1977).

⁶¹*Buckley*, supra note 42.

⁶²Supra note 45.

⁶³*Elrod*, supra note 20, at 374–75.

⁶⁴*Branti*, supra note 19, at 518.

⁶⁵See, e.g., *Weinberger v. Weisenfeld*, 420 U.S. 636 (1975); *Frontiero v. Richardson*, 411 U.S. 677 (1973); and *Bolling v. Sharpe*, 347 U.S. 497 (1954).

⁶⁶The classic example is *Yick Wo v. Hopkins*, 118 U.S. 356 (1886).

⁶⁷This two-tier framework for equal protection analysis is found in *San Antonio Independent School Dist. v. Rodriguez*, 411 U.S. 1 (1973).

⁶⁸See, e.g., *Loving v. Virginia*, 388 U.S. 1 (1967), and *Strauder v. West Virginia*, 100 U.S. 303 (1880).

⁶⁹One of the few examples in which the Court has upheld a clear race-based classification was the Japanese exclusion order case, *Korematsu v. United States*, 323 U.S. 214 (1944).

⁷⁰*San Antonio*, supra note 67, at 28.

⁷¹*Frontiero v. Richardson*, 411 U.S. 677, 686 (1973).

⁷²On alienage, see *Nyquist v. Mauclet*, 432 U.S. 1 (1977), and *Graham v. Richardson*, 403 U.S. 365 (1971). On illegitimacy see *Levy v. Louisiana*, 391 U.S. 68 (1968); *Glova v. American Guarantee & Liability Ins. Co.*, 391 U.S. 73 (1968). More recently, however, the Court has backed away from treating all classifications based on legitimacy (*Mathews v. Lucas*, 427 U.S. 495 [1976], and *Lalli v. Lalli*, 439 U.S. 259 [1978]) or alienage (*Folie v. Connelie*, 435 U.S. 291 [1978], and *Amback v. Norwick*, 441 U.S. 68 [1979]) as inherently suspect.

⁷³Justice Black was particularly concerned that courts should focus on the effect of government action and not on guesses about intent of government officials. He wrote:

"It is difficult or impossible for any court to determine the 'sole' or 'dominant' motivation behind the choices of a group of legislators. Furthermore, there is an element of futility in a judicial attempt to invalidate a law because of the bad motives of its supporters. If the law is struck down for this reason, rather than because of its facial content or effect, it would presumably be valid as soon as the legislature or relevant governing body repassed it for different reasons.

"It is true that there is language in some of our cases interpreting the Fourteenth and Fifteenth Amendments which may suggest that the motive or purpose behind a law is relevant to its constitutionality. [cites] But the focus in those cases was on the actual effect of the enactments, not upon the motivation which led the states to behave as they did." *Palmer v. Thompson*, 403 U.S. 217, 225 (1971). See *Wright v. Council of the City of Emporia*, 407 U.S. 451, 461–62 (1972), and *Norwood v. Harrison*, 413 U.S. 455, 466 (1973).

⁷⁴*Washington v. Davis*, 426 U.S. 229 (1976).

⁷⁵*Village of Arlington Heights v. Metropolitan Housing Development Corp.*, 429 U.S. 252, 267–68 (1977).

⁷⁶*Personnel Administrator v. Feeney*, 442 U.S. 256 (1979).

⁷⁷Id., at 279.

⁷⁸42 U.S.C. §2000e et seq. (1976).

⁷⁹Civil Service Reform Act of 1978, Public Law 95-454, 92 Stat. 1111 (1978).

⁸⁰*Swann v. Charlotte-Mechlenburg Board of Education*, 402 U.S. 1 (1971).

⁸¹See *Regents v. Bakke*, 438 U.S. 265, 395–96 (1978), Justice Marshall in a separate opinion.

⁸²Id.

⁸³*United Steelworkers v. Weber*, 443 U.S. 193 (1979).

⁸⁴Id., at 209–211, Justice Blackmun concurring.

⁸⁵*Fullilove v. Klutznick*, 448 U.S. 448 (1980).

⁸⁶During the October 1980 term the Court avoided a complicated case involving state correctional employees brought under affirmative action rules by remanding it to the state

courts. *Minnick v. California Dep't of Corrections*, 68 L. Ed. 2d 706 (1981).

[87]See *Manager's Handbook*, supra note 24, chap. 12.

[88]*In re Griffiths*, 413 U.S. 717 (1973), and *Examining Board v. Flores de Otero*, 426 U.S. 572 (1976).

[89]*Graham v. Richardson*, 403 U.S. 365 (1971), and *Nyquist v. Mauclet*, supra note 72.

[90]*Sugarman v. Dougall*, 413 U.S. 634 (1973), and *Hampton v. Mow Sun Wong*, 426 U.S. 88 (1976).

[91]See, e.g., *Mathews v. Diaz*, 426 U.S. 67 (1976).

[92]*Hampton*, supra note 90.

[93]*Amback v. Norwick*, 441 U.S. 68, 75–80 (1979).

[94]Id.

[95]*Foley v. Connelie*, 435 U.S. 291 (1978).

[96]See, e.g., *Frontiero v. Richardson*, supra note 71; *Weinberger v. Weisenfeld*, 420 U.S. 636 (1975); and *Califano v. Goldfarb*, 430 U.S. 199 (1977).

[97]See, e.g., *Kahn v. Shevin*, 416 U.S. 357 (1974), and *Califano v. Webster*, 430 U.S. 313 (1977).

[98]*Schlesinger v. Ballard*, 419 U.S. 498 (1975).

[99]Compare *Frontiero*, supra note 71, and *Schlesinger*, supra note 98.

[100]*Craig v. Brown*, 429 U.S. 190 (1976).

[101]*Rostker v. Goldberg*, 69 L. Ed 2d 478 (1981).

[102]*Griswold v. Connecticut*, 381 U.S. 479 (1965).

[103]*Cleveland Board of Education v. La Fleur*, 414 U.S. 632 (1974).

[104]See, e.g., Nigro and Nigro, supra note 16, at pp. 418–20.

[105]*Kelley v. Johnson*, 425 U.S. 238 (1976).

[106]*McCarthy v. Philadelphia Civil Service Comm'n*, 424 U.S. 645 (1976).

[107]Lee, supra note 1, at 219.

[108]Office of Personnel Management, "Fed Facts: Political Activity of Federal Employees" (Washington, D.C.: Government Printing Office, 1980), pp. 3–6.

[109]Public Law 88-352, 78 Stat. 241 (1964), 42 U.S.C. §2000e (1976).

[110]Public Law 92-261, 86 Stat. 103 (1972), 42 U.S.C. §2000e (1976).

[111]See 45 Fed. Reg. 74676, November 10, 1980, and 45 Fed. Reg. 25024, April 11, 1980.

[112]Public Law 88-38, 77 Stat. 56 (1963), 29 U.S.C. §§203 and 206(d).

[113]Public Law 95-555, 92 Stat. 2076 (1978), 42 U.S.C. §2000e (1976).

[114]*General Electric Co. v. Gilbert*, 429 U.S. 125 (1976). But see *Nashville Gas Co. v. Satty*, 434 U.S. 136 (1977).

[115]Public Law 90-202, 81 Stat. 602 (1967), 29 U.S.C. §621 et seq. (1976).

[116]*Massachusetts v. Murgia*, 427 U.S. 307 (1976).

[117]Public Law 95-256, 92 Stat. 189 (1978), 5 U.S.C. §§3322, 8335, 8339; 29 U.S.C. §§623, 624, 626, 631, 633a, 634 (1978).

[118]Public Law 93-112, 87 Stat. 355 (1973), 29 U.S.C §701 et seq. (1976).

[119]Public Law 95-454, 92 Stat. 1111 (1978), 5 U.S.C. §2302(b) (1976).

[120]*Administrative Law Process: Better Management Is Needed* (Washington, D.C.: General Accounting Office, 1978), p. iv. In May 1979, the GAO issues another report, *Management Improvements in the Administrative Law Process: Much Remains to Be Done*, in which it concluded that very little had been done by agencies to improve the problems noted in the earlier report and called for an effort to achieve the same goals advanced earlier. Id., at pp. 1–2. See also U.S. House of Representatives, Hearings Before the Committee on Post Office and Civil Service, *Selection and Oversight of Administrative Law Judges*, 96th Cong., 2d Sess., 1980, and Hearings Before the Subcommittee on Investigations of the Committee on Post Office and Civil Service, *Administrative Law Judge Program of the Federal Trade Commission*, 96th Cong., 2d Sess. (1980).

[121]Bernard Rosen, "Uncertainty in the Senior Executive Service," 41 *Public Admin. Rev.* 203, 204 (1981).

[122]Aaron Wildavsky, *Speaking Truth to Power* (Boston: Little, Brown, 1979), p. 12.

[123]I have dealt with the relationship of such law and administration concerns in government contracting in a preliminary way in Phillip J. Cooper, "Government Contracts in Public Administration: The Role and Environment of the Contracting Office," 40 *Public Admin. Rev.* 459 (1980).

[124]See, e.g., *Becker v. Philco Corp.*, 389 U.S. 979 (1967), Justice Douglas dissenting from denial of cert.

[125]See, e.g., *Davis v. Passman*, 442 U.S. 228 (1979).

[126]U.S. House of Representatives, *Legislative History of the Privacy Act of 1974: Source Book on Privacy*, 94th Cong., 2d Sess. (1976), pp. 165–66.

[127]Id., at pp. 558–59.

[128]See, e.g., *Halperin v. Kissinger*, 606 F. 2d 1192 (D.C. Cir. 1979), affirmed by an equally divided court, 69 L. Ed. 2d 367 (1981).

[129]Id. See also *Owen v. City of Independence*, 445 U.S. 622 (1980), and *Monell v. Department of Social Services*, 436 U.S. 658 (1978).

[130]U.S. House of Representatives, Hearings Before the Subcommittee on the Civil Service of the Committee on Post Office and Civil Service, *Civil Service Reform Oversight, 1980 —Whistleblower*, 96th Cong., 2d Sess. (1980), pp. 79–149.

[131]John Rohr, *Ethics for Bureaucrats* (New York: Marcel Dekker, 1978).

[132]There is a considerable body of literature on administrative responsibility, including: Herman Finer, "Better Government Personnel: America's Next Frontier," 51 *Political Science Quarterly*, 569 (1936); Carl Friedrich, "Public Policy and the Nature of Administrative Responsibility" in C. J Friedrich and T. S. Mason, eds., *Public Policy* (Cambridge, Mass.: Harvard University Press, 1940); Herman Finer, "Administrative Responsibility in Democratic Government," 1 *Public Admin. Rev.* 335 (1941); David Levitan, "The Responsibility of Administrative Officials in a Democratic Society," 61 *Political Science Quarterly* 562 (1946);

Paul Appleby, *Big Democracy* (New York: Knopf, 1949); Charles Hyneman, *Bureaucracy in a Democracy* (New York: Harper & Brothers, 1950); Norton Long, "Bureaucracy and Constitutionalism," 46 *American Political Science Rev.* 808 (1952); idem, "Public Policy and Administration: The Goals of Rationality and Responsibility," 14 *Public Admin. Rev.*, 22 (1954); Emmette Redford, *Ideal and Practice in Public Administration* (University: University of Alabama Press, 1958); Herbert Storing, "The Crucial Link: Public Administration, Responsibility and the Public Interest," 24 *Public Admin. Rev.*, 39 (1964); and Roscoe Martin, ed., *Public Administration and Democracy: Essays in Honor of Paul Appleby* (Syracuse, N.Y.: Syracuse University Press, 1965).

[133]See works by Friedrich and Finer, supra note 132.

[134]Friedrich, "Public Policy and the Nature of Administrative Responsibility," supra note 132, at p. 19.

[135]See Herbert Storing, "American Statesmanship: Old and New," in R. Goldwin, ed., *Bureaucrats, Policy Analysts, Statesmen: Who Leads?* (Washington, D.C.: American Enterprise Institute, 1980), p. 88.

[136]Stephen Bailey, "Ethics and the Public Service," in Martin, ed., *Public Administration and Democracy*, supra note 132, at pp. 285–86.

[137]Some who have written on the subject of immunities against suits for money damages argue that until the last few years the law of sovereign and official immunities was well established and the case law was consistent. But that has not been the case in the United States historically. For example, compare *Chisholm v. Georgia*, 2 Dallas 419 (1793); *Little v. Barreme*, 2 Cranch 170 (1804); *United States v. Judge Peters*, 5 Cranch 115 (1805); *Wise v. Withers*, 3 Cranch 331 (1806); *Osborne v. President and Directors and Company of the Bank of the United States*, 9 Wheaton 738 (1824); *City of Providence v. Clapp*, 17 Howard 161 (1855); *Weightman v. Corporation of Washington*, 1 Black 39 (1862); *Levy Court of Washington County v. Woodward*, 2 Wallace 501 (1864); *Board of Supervisors of Mercer County v. Cowles*, 7 Wallace 118 (1869); *The Siren*, 7 Wallace 152 (1869); *The Davis*, 77 U.S. 875 (1870); *Davis v. Gray*, 83 U.S. 203 (1873); *Bates v. Clark*, 95 U.S. 204 (1877); *Ex Parte Virginia*, 100 U.S. 339 (1880); *United States*, 106 U.S. 196 (1882); *Poindexter v. Greenhow*, 114 U.S. 270 (1885); and *Lincoln County v. Luning*, 133 U.S. 529 (1896); with *Kendall v. United States*, 3 Howard 87 (1845); *Wilkes v. Dinsman*, 7 Howard 89 (1849); *Hill v. United States*, 9 Howard 385 (1850); *Bradley v. Fisher*, 80 U.S. 335 (1872); *Louisiana v. Jumel*, 107 U.S. 711 (1882); *Cunningham v. Macon and Brunswick R.R. Co.*, 109 U.S. 446 (1883); *Hagood v. Southern*, 117 U.S. 52 (1886); *Ex Parte Ayers*, 123 U.S. 443 (1887); *Hans v. Louisiana*, 134 U.S. 1 (1890); *Belknap v. Schild*, 161 U.S. 10 (1896) and *Spalding v. Vilas*, 161 U.S. 483 (1896).

[137]The federal government is exempt from suit under the doctrine of sovereign immunity; one may, however, sue for money damages under the Federal Tort Claims Act, 28 U.S.C. §§1291, 1346, 1402, 1504, 2110, 2401, 2411, 2412, 2671–80, or other statutes that specifically authorize such suits. Unfortunately—or fortunately, depending upon one's perspective—the Federal Tort Claims Act exempts a great deal of federal government action from suits.

[139]States are immune under the Eleventh Amendment of the U.S. Constitution from suits for money damages, but are subject to suits for injunctive relief. See *Edelman v. Jordan*, 415 U.S. 651 (1974).

[140]*Bradley v. Fisher*, 80 U.S. 335 (1872); *Pierson v. Ray*, 386 U.S. 547 (1967); and *Stump v. Sparkmun*, 435 U.S. 349 (1978).

[141]*Tenney v. Brandhove*, 341 U.S. 367 (1951), and *Lake Country Estates v. Tahoe Regional Planning Agency*, 440 U.S. 391 (1879).

[142]*Imbler v. Pachtman*, 424 U.S. 409 (1976), and *Butz v. Economou*, 438 U.S. 478 (1978).

[143]*Butz v. Economou*, id.

[144]*Scheuer v. Rhodes*, 416 U.S. 232 (1974); *Wood v. Strickland*, 420 U.S. 308 (1975); and *Procunier v. Navarette*, 434 U.S. 555 (1978).

[145]There are some situations under which private citizens may be considered to act unlawfully while acting "under color of" state law. See *Adickes v. S & H Kress & Co.*, 398 U.S. 144 (1970).

[146]42 U.S.C. §1983 (1976).

[147]*Monell*, supra note 129.

[148]*Owen*, supra note 129.

[149]*Wood*, supra note 144, at 321–22.

[150]*Procunier*, supra note 144, at 562.

[151]*Maine v. Thiboutot*, 448 U.S. 1 (1980).

[152]*Bivens v. Six Unknown Named Agents of Federal Bureau of Narcotics*, 403 U.S. 388 (1971), and *Butz v. Economou*, supra note 143.

[153]See generally *Muskopf v. Corning Hospital District*, 11 Cal. Reptr. 89, 359 P. 2d 457 (Cal. 1961); *Hicks v. State*, 88 N.M. 588, 544 P. 2d 1153 (N.M. 1976); and *Spanel v. Mounds View School Dist.*, No. 621, 118 N.W. 2d 795 (N.M. 1962). See generally *The New World of Municipal Liability: Current City Trends and Legislative Actions in the Fifty States* (Washington, D.C.: National League of Cities, 1978); Charles Rhyne, William Rhyne, and Stephen Elmendorf, *Tort Liability of Municipal Officers*, (Washington, D.C.: National Institute of Municipal Law Officers, 1976); John P. Lichty, *Redress Against Sovereignty: A Study of the Increasing Liabilities of Municipalities in Tort* (Grand Forks, N.D.: Bureau of Government Affairs, 1972); and William Olson, "Governmental Immunity from Tort Liability: Two Decades of Decline: 1959–1979," 31 *Baylor L. Rev.* 485 (1979).

Chapter 13

Law and Administration: Perspectives and Directions

I n this book we have examined the ways in which those who govern try to resolve complex problems under conditions of change and, sometimes, stress. In particular, we have analyzed the interactions between administrators and those who make demands on or request services from administrative agencies. To understand these interactions requires that administrative law, which is the shorthand way of referring to public law and public administration, be broadly defined and approached. Administrative law is more than a collection of legal procedures. Indeed, foregoing chapters have indicated the need to understand not only what is formally known as administrative law, but also its political, historical, and philosphical underpinnings. Only then can one push beyond, to the problems of politics, law, and administration that make up the living context within which administrative law contests are conducted and resolved.

This concluding chapter offers a brief sketch of the highlights considered, suggests guidelines for dealing with present-day administrative law problems, and offers some ideas about what problems will and should occupy the attention of scholars and practitioners of public law and public administration in the immediate future.

THE ELEMENTS RECONSIDERED

The actors, institutions, and processes that deal with problems of public law and public administration make up a loosely defined entity known as the administrative justice system. Individuals, institutions, and groups with varying economic, political, and legal resources make demands on that system. Although the goal and value of equal justice under law is of great importance, in reality there is a

347

considerable difference in how the administrative justice responds to demands, depending on whether one is a single shot player or a repeat player.

Whatever their characteristics or sources, demands are handled by many different institutions and processes. One who would understand or follow the flow of those demands through the system should evaluate the phenomena observed from both the perspectives of those who produce the decisions and those who may be seen as consumers of those decisons. Possible constitutional, statutory, procedural, and factual elements in each problem should also be considered.

In general, of course, legal problems are resolved in accordance with the black letter law. The formal legal guidelines may be found, with practice, by using some fairly simple sources and techniques. But the law in action is a product of the law in books plus a variety of other factors, including: the jurisprudence of the legal decisionmaker; the analytical tools and rules used by judges and those who perform judge-like duties to resolve cases; the institutional and political constraints on legal decisionmaking; and the difficult and complex interactions among legal decision-makers, who find it hard to work together in collegial bodies or to reconcile their decisions with those of other adjudicators.

One cannot understand administrative law as it exists today without under-standing the course and elements of its development. Administrative law is not new, just more complex than it was in earlier times. Its history can be roughly divided into a few periods. The most recent period has been characterized by a plethora of efforts to resolve problems in the administrative justice system that have surfaced on the public policy agenda during the 1970s and early '80s. Specific changes are in the process of being implemented and at the same time the environment of administrative law itself is changing.

Rulemaking is one of the key elements of the formal administrative law process. Several types of agency rules are created by means of specialized processes. The hybrid process is a primary mechanism advanced by courts, the legislature, and the executive to improve the quality of rulemaking and, in particular, to make it a more open and effective process. Other recently developed devices in rulemaking, including regulatory analyses and the legislative veto, are still experimental.

Adjudications are the second major element of formal administrative law. These are decisions by agencies that determine important legal rights, status, or obligations of citizens and organizations. Efforts are under way to find alternatives to full trial-type administrative hearings to settle disputes. The search is for simpler alternatives that will be acceptable both to courts and to those who deal with the agencies, permitting less expensive administrative proceedings and reducing delay. Unfortunately, many of those who come before the agencies want a reduction in formal proceedings but want to retain all their own formal legal options at the same time.

Judicial review is the third element of formal administrative law. The difficulties involved in reviewing administrative decisions are best understood by placing one's self in the position of the judge. The judge must resolve complex cases with complex political and legal aspects. The primary difficulty is to hold the middle ground between judicial interference in the administrative process and excessive deference to administrators that fails to provide the necessary check on administrative abuses.

The fact is that most administrative law matters are resolved through alternatives to formal proceedings. These informal techniques of problem solving provide a range of benefits over their formal alternatives, but they also have disadvantages, particularly for those less experienced and less able to wage contests with the government than others.

Fundamental to all administrative law questions are the problems and opportunities posed by administrative discretion. Drawn from a variety of sources, the administrator's discretion to be sensitive to one person or organization carries the danger of arbitrary treatment of another. Mechanisms for maintaining discretion within bounds continue to develop, with the judiciary carrying the major burden.

Few topics are more difficult to deal with in the current political environment than the law and politics of regulatory administration. Yet when macro-level political arguments are set aside, it is possible to deal with regulation as one of a number of policy instruments. Presidential, congressional, and public interest group involvement in the problems of regulatory administration has resulted in many changes in the conduct of regulation; these changes have only recently been implemented and will be tested.

Information policy exemplifies why modern administrative law problems must be understood as combining management, legal, and political considerations. The laws and management problems associated with information policy may usefully be considered as a system of information acquisition, use, and dissemination. It is, in fact, a developing subsystem of administrative justice. The goal is to maintain an open deliberative form of government that has all the information it needs to properly perform its manifold functions and at the same time preserve individual privacy in a society in which privacy is becoming increasingly scarce.

The laws and administrative practices covering public employees affect a substantial percentage of the population. These laws and procedures seek to resolve the varying interests of public employees, their supervisors, and the public. They determine what kind of people enter and remain in government service and their incentives to act in the public's interest rather than their own.

LIVING WITH LAW AND ADMINISTRATION

Although it is certainly true that the administrative justice system is complex and the problems it must resolve are vexing, administrative law is not mysterious and need not be approached with a sense of futility. In this book we have not attempted to prescribe answers to the many administrative law problems that confront producers and consumers of administrative law decisions, but we can offer a few simple common sense suggestions for those on both sides of administrative law problems.

Consumers of Administrative Decisions

1. Get the name of a good lawyer, in case the need for one should arise. Like finding a good physician, it's better to find a lawyer in advance than when one is in the legal analogue of the emergency room. It is particularly helpful to find a lawyer who is experienced in administrative law matters.

2. Try to understand the producer perspective on the problem at hand. If possible it is useful to learn and understand the administrator's limitations.
3. Before reaching for a telephone or a typewriter, attempt to the degree possible to understand the problem in terms of its constitutional (if applicable), statutory, procedural, and factual dimensions.
4. Decide carefully whether, when, and how to escalate interaction from informal discussions to a formal adversarial relationship.
5. Have access to a depository library or other research center where basic research tools, including the U.S. Code, the Code of Federal Regulations, the *Federal Register*, the *U.S. Government Manual*, and their state or local counterparts, are available.
6. If in a field requiring frequent interaction with a particular agency, use the rounding-out processes described in Chapter 2 to stay generally current on new developments.
7. Affiliate with appropriate interest groups for effective action on agency rulemaking or major litigation. Caution: Be aware of Hatch Act limitations in any activities that are partisan in nature. If in doubt, ask a lawyer for help.

Producers of Administrative Decisions (Including Supervisors)

1. Do a basic legal research analysis:
   a. Examine the content and legislative history of the statutes or executive orders that created the agency and that outline agency responsiblities.
   b. Do a general survey of agency regulations paying particular attention to the operational guidelines that are relevant to one's responsibilities and that codify the agency's response to public employee statutory or constitutional rights.
   c. Establish a pattern, based on the rounding-out processes described in Chapter 2, of publications to be monitored on a regular basis.
   d. Develop a collection of useful pamphlets and guidebooks from such agencies as the Office of Personnel Management, Merit System Protection Board, the Office of Federal Contract Compliance, the Equal Employment Opportunity Commission, and their state and local counterparts where applicable.
   e. Read carefully any collective bargaining agreement that applies to one's position.
2. Get to know the agency staff counsel or, if the chief staff counsel is new or inaccessible, an experienced hand in the counsel's office.
3. Maintain thorough records of all significant actions from rulemaking to employee discipline.
4. Employ informal administrative processes if possible.
5. Assume that litigation is likely at some point and be prepared for it.
6. Be aware of the consumer perspective in problem resolution.

PROBLEMS, ISSUES, AND PROSPECTS

In conclusion, it is worthwhile to note some important breaking developments in the field, to suggest items for the law and administration research agenda, and to comment briefly on the place of law and administration in public administration curricula.

Constitutional issues in public administration have re-emerged in a variety of new forms in recent years. As was observed in Chapter 6, the concept of administrative due process underwent a substantial shift during the late 1970s, away from its direction in the late Warren Court period. This is also true of judicial opinions on allegations of various forms of discrimination brought under the equal protection clause. In addition to the highly visible constitutional rights and liberties questions, however, a number of questions have been raised recently concerning the basic constitutional power to regulate in certain activities. The line of decisions establishing commercial free speech and protecting the expenditure of money to advance political causes as a related form of First Amendment expression raises interesting questions about the authority of federal and state governments to regulate in these areas.[1] Additionally, the Supreme Court's opinion in overturning the extensions of the wage and hour provisions of the Fair Labor Standards Act has had two immediate impacts.[2] First, it has called into question some federal legislation that affects state and local government employees. Second, it has prompted a number of groups to begin to challenge the power of Congress under the commerce clause to regulate, even though in most areas such questions had long since been considered closed.[3]

Other developments noted in Chapter 7 on judicial review but not widely considered in recent years are changes in the rules that govern access to litigation in federal courts. Particularly worthy of discussion are the changes in the rules of standing, abstention, comity, and those that govern the operation of class action suits. It will be interesting to see whether and to what extent the lower federal courts respond to the leadership of the Burger Court.

Related to some of the changing patterns of litigation and administrative politics are important developments in state administrative law. Some interest groups have already shifted their litigation strategy from the federal courts to the state courts. Challenges to property tax based school financing arrangements, for example, moved from the federal forum to state courts, with differing results. Another factor that may make the states the focal point for important developments are recent attempts to enact statutes that permit either state or federal administration, for example, in such matters as strip mining and waste disposal. And to the degree that law and administration activity increases at the state level, it will be interesting to discover whether the states will prove to be laboratories for innovation or not.

Much of the administrative law of the post-New Deal era has concerned allegations that some agencies have overreached their delegated powers. OSHA, for example, has been charged with being overly aggressive. But the use of counterstaffing and other tactics by the Reagan administration to cut back dramatically on the federal administrative establishment raises a slightly different problem. It has been observed over the years that the major problem is not how to prevent administrators from being overly aggressive, but how to get them to take any action at all. If reduced administrative pressure becomes an official policy rather than a mere incident of inertia, there is a potential for a storm of suits that attempt to force administrative action.

In addition to these recent developments, researchers in law and administration might consider a number of items for their research agendas in the near term. Certain actors in the administrative justice system, for one reason or another, have only recently begun to attract much attention. They are administrative law judges, agency attorneys, and agency legislative liaison officers. ALJs have been the subject of a number of articles that have appeared sporadically over the past four decades, but they have not attracted nearly as much attention as they deserve.

Another area of inquiry that needs further attention is the legislative role in administrative justice, although the rise in importance of the legislative veto has given some impetus for work in this field in the last several years. As the framers of the Constitution noted, the executive and judiciary bear watching, but there is just as much reason to take an interest in the activities of the legislative branch.

One who reads in the history of administrative law notes that the early writings were mostly comparative studies, yet there is very little comparative administrative law literature of recent vintage—with the exception of material on ombudsmen and the Schwartz and Wade British-American comparative project, that is now ten years old.[4] It may be that comparative state and cross-national studies of law and administration will provide the best fields in which to search for innovative techniques and ideas.

The relationship between law and policy process remains a fertile area for investigation. Of particular promise are studies of the role that the law and the courts play in policy implementation. A second fruitful field is likely to be the development of techniques to manage law and policy conflict in crisis situations, such as the Three Mile Island nuclear power plant leak, the Chicago DC-10 plane crash, and Love Canal. We have not yet developed effective mechanisms for dealing with complex legal and technical problems under conditions of stress.

Finally, this book has demonstrated in some detail that law, administration, and politics are intimately intertwined. Law is an essential element in public administration, but it is only one element. This inescapable fact is often overlooked in education for public service. We cannot return to the days when all administration was considered law and management was a separate field. On the contrary, the field of public administration is sufficiently mature that it can include in its curricula the variety of subject matter that is needed to educate public administrators and those who will deal with them. Only if we bring about such a blending of public law and public administration can we achieve a well-administered government that is truly a government under law.

NOTES

[1]See *Buckley v. Valeo*, 424 U.S. 1 (1976); *Virginia State Board of Pharmacy v. Virginia Consumer Council*, 425 U.S. 748 (1976); and *First National Bank v. Bellotti*, 435 U.S. 765 (1978).

[2]*National League of Cities v. Usery*, 426 U.S. 833 (1976).

[3]See, e.g., *Hodel v. Virginia Surface Mining and Reclamation Association*, 69 L. Ed. 2d 1 (1981).

[4]Bernard Schwartz and H.W.R. Wade, *Legal Control of Government in Britain and the United States* (Oxford, United Kingdom: Clarendon Press, 1972).

APPENDIXES

Mathews v. Eldridge:
The Anatomy of an Administrative Law Case

NOTE

This case study is an independent piece to be used with several portions of this book. The reader should be aware that some changes have been made in the administrative and political operations of the program that is the focal point of this study. For example, HEW is now the Department of Health and Human Services (HHS). There have also been changes in the Social Security statute and regulations. Many of the same problems, however, continue to exist. But this case study is not intended as a commentary on the Social Security Administration. It is a study of a major administrative law case in the modern administrative environment and, as such, it reveals some of the many difficulties of operating the administrative justice system.

INTRODUCTION

The Social Security Administration, headquartered in Baltimore, handles more legal disputes in a year than all of the federal courts in the United States combined. Its cases are substantial, with the average Social Security disability claim running approximately $25,000. These decisions are complex determinations made through an intergovernmental decisionmaking system that involves federal officials and state departments of vocational rehabilitation. Most citizens are much more likely to find themselves in this type of legal controversy—a benefit claim dispute—than they are to face criminal prosecution, or even to defend against or maintain a substantial civil suit in local courts. The stakes can be very high. One might begin the struggle with a home, furniture, and a fair standard of existence and end it a decade later with no home, little furniture, and substantial debts.

This article investigates one such case, *Mathews v. Eldridge*.[1] This is a useful case to study, for it is in some ways typical. It demonstrates how a contest over benefits arises and is conducted. At the same time, it is a particularly important and unique case which, unlike the thousands of other contested benefit cases raised each year, found its way to the United States Supreme Court and resulted in the resolution of an extremely important controversy in a farreaching decision from the Court. In *Eldridge*, the Court held that there is no constitutional right to an oral hearing prior to the termination of Social Security disability benefits. Since that opinion was delivered in 1976, the Supreme Court has applied the *Eldridge* ruling to a wide range of administrative law controversies. Just how the case got to the Court and the significance of its result are the subjects of this study.* In particular, this investigation will present commentary on the perspective of George Eldridge, the claimant. Eldridge, and all those who make such claims, was the ultimate consumer of the administrative decision and the legal judgment produced by the administrative justice system. That consumer perspective is an important one for other consumers of administrative decisions and for the producers of those determinations.

From an analytic perspective,** the study of this case reveals a number of interesting factors that may inform the study of administrative law. These phenomena include: (1) the significance of the interaction of the several levels and units of government involved; (2) the special problems that arise in social service claims as opposed to the more publicized and more frequently analyzed regulatory cases; (3) the essential meaning and complexity of the concept of due process of law in theory and in practice; (4) the presence of what appears to be a conflict between the essential values of the administrative process and the judicial process; (5) the basic distinctions between administrative and judicial proceedings; (6) the relationship of precedent to policy; (7) the significance of judicial politics with the change from the Warren to Burger Court; and (8) the relationship of law to the policy process.

GEORGE ELDRIDGE ENTERS THE SYSTEM

George Eldridge lives in Norton, Virginia, a small coal mining city of approximately 5,500 citizens in the southwestern corner of the state. His disagreement with the Social Security Administration and the Virginia Department of Vocational Rehabilitation began in 1967 and continued off and on until March of 1978. Before it was over, "George Eldridge had his home foreclosed. He and his six children were sleeping in one bed because all of their furniture had been repossessed." How did this happen?

Mr. Eldridge: The Person and the Predicament

Eldridge was born in Lee County, Virginia. He was removed from school in the fifth grade by a bout with pneumonia. While he was recovering from this illness, the family moved to the mountain community of Norton in 1936, in connection with the father's transfer. He was employed by the L & N Railroad, the same company that would later employ George.

When he was able to do so, George took a job doing section labor for the L & N. Section labor involved laying new track, cross ties, making repairs, and installing and maintaining rail lines and switches at mine entrances and near the coal tipples where trucks loaded the coal through chutes into waiting rail cars. It was hard work and, as he now adds with some pride, the tasks were performed by hand as opposed to the more recently developed mechanical means.

The biggest snow we had come in March of '41 or '42. It measured 46 inches here at the bus station. I walked from Endover, that's up in the hollow from

---

*This study has, from an instructional perspective at least, a clear debt to Anthony Lewis's *Gideon's Trumpet* (New York: Random House, 1964) and Alan F. Westin's *The Anatomy of a Constitutional Law Case* (New York: Macmillan, 1958).

**The substantive analysis of social security disability issues employs Haviland and Glomb's "The Disability Insurance Benefits Program and Low Income Claimants in Appalachia," 73 *W. Virginia L. Rev.* 109 (1971), as a conceptual base.

Appalachia tool house, two miles and a half in that snow to sweep switches so the trainmen could get to the switches to throw them and pick up their loads.

And I walked back—there was no way to ride. When I got back home, it was so cold, I pulled off my pants and stood them up against the wall.[2]

357

Mathews v.
Eldridge: The
Anatomy of an
Administrative
Law Case

Eldridge worked for the L & N for almost three years before he was drafted into the army. Upon his discharge, he went back to work on the railroad as an employee of the Interstate Railroad before it was acquired by the Southern Railroad Company.

After about nine years with that rail line, Eldridge switched jobs. He became a soft drink distributor for Royal Crown Cola, and it was during his work for RC that Eldridge became totally disabled. He had been diagnosed as having spinal arthritis in the '40s, but, since he lacked educational prerequisites, Eldridge saw no alternative to the strenuous delivery job. His health degenerated, but, by this time he had a house and a large family to consider. Finally, after eight years at the delivery job, his working days came to an end.

I was working in the town of Coeburn. I got down from the truck and then I couldn't raise my legs to get up on the running board of the truck to get back into the truck. They had to come and get me. . . .

I laid thirty-one days in the hospital unable to move my legs.[3]

Some time after he became disabled, Eldridge began to suffer from diabetes. He found himself learning to deal with a multiplicity of medications for the arthritis and diabetes, including insulin injections and a new diet.

Gaining Entrance to the Program: The First Round

In 1967 Eldridge applied at the local Social Security office in Norton for complete disability benefits under the Social Security Act. His application for benefits was initially rejected and that decision was upheld in an administrative review routinely conducted by the Social Security headquarters office in Baltimore. His case was reconsidered at his request by the state agency. A decision against him was rendered in late 1967. Eldridge requested and received a hearing before a hearing examiner (these examiners have since been designated as administrative law judges[4]), in spring 1968. One June 2, the hearing examiner announced his decision in Eldridge's favor. Shortly thereafter Eldridge was placed on the disability program and informed, though he does not remember ever having been notified, that his condition would be periodically reevaluated to determine his continued eligibility for benefits.

In June 1969 he was contacted and asked to submit information showing that he was still disabled.[5] He filled out the forms, which included comments about treatment that he had been receiving from physicians along with the names and addresses of the doctors. He was not physically examined by government doctors.

In February 1970 Eldridge was notified that the state agency had concluded that his disability had ended as of January and that his benefits would be terminated the next month. To understand what happened to Eldridge from this point on, it is necessary to investigate briefly the procedures involved in the termination of benefits.[6]

Disability Benefit Terminations

Under the regulations issued by the Department of Health, Education, and Welfare, which has overall responsibility for the Social Security Administration (SSA), and the legislation that provides for the disability program, there are several stages of review to which one has recourse when a decision is made by the state vocational rehabilitation agency to terminate benefits.[7] The rehabilitation agencies act for the Social Security Administration in the initial stage of decisionmaking. They monitor recipients of benefits on a regular basis to ensure their continued disability. They do not usually actually examine the recipients. Instead, a staff doctor and a case worker evaluate the papers sent in by people like Eldridge. They request medical reports from the recipient's physician and have access to vocational specialists and psychiatrists for advice. It is a process of paper review.

If the state agency staff workers conclude that the recipient is no longer eligible because he or she is physically able to be employed at some substantial gainful employment existing in the national economy, whether there would be a specific position for the claimant or not, they notify the individual and indicate in general terms why they believe the disability no longer exists. The recipient is told that he or she has ten days to submit additional reports or other pertinent evidence and that it might be possible to obtain an extension of the time limit if it is necessary to obtain further evidence of continued eligibility. Claimants are told that termination normally occurs two months from the date that the person was determined to be no longer eligible.

If no additional evidence is submitted to the state agency, the entire record is sent to the Baltimore office of the SSA for review and final determination. The headquarters may not reverse an unfavorable decision to the claimant, but it may return a determination by the state agency in favor of the benefit recipient.[8] If the SSA headquarters does determine that the benefits are to be terminated, the recipient is told of that decision and of the termination date. The claimant is also advised that it is possible to have the case reconsidered by the state agency. If reconsideration is requested, a different team of reviewers should be chosen in the state agency to review the file again. If they agree with the earlier determination, the recipient may request further proceedings. Benefits do not continue through the reconsideration process or later administrative review. Benefits cease as of the date indicated by the SSA headquarters. If the claimant wins at some point in the process, back benefits are paid.

The next stage in the process of review is an oral hearing conducted before an administrative law judge at which the claimant may appear with an attorney, although most do not,[9] or someone else to speak on his or her behalf. Representation is permitted, but it is neither required nor provided by the government. Further, the amount of compensation that an attorney may receive for representing a client in such a hearing is limited by law.[10] The standard fee in such a case, assuming that there is no special problem in computation or payment, is 25 percent of the back benefit payments recovered. The purpose of the hearing is to determine whether the individual meets the requirements of the program.

In the event that the claimant is dissatisfied with the decision of the administrative law judge, an appeal may be taken to the Appeals Council of the Social Security Administration. This is a paper appeal.

If the claimant is still unhappy, the case may be taken to a federal district court for judicial review of the administrative record.[11] Here, of course, testimony is taken before a federal district judge, although the review is limited to examination of the record to determine whether there was substantial evidence on which the agency could have reached its final determination. Finally, if one alleges a federal legal question, it might be possible to appeal the decision of the district court, but such cases are rare.

MR. ELDRIDGE AND THE APPEALS PROCESS

The Second Round: 1969–1971

As things stood in February 1970, Eldridge had lost his 1969 review. He and his family faced an immediate loss of the disability benefits. It was a frightening prospect for a man with six children, a home to pay for, and a wife who was dying of cancer.

But the terse letter informing him of the termination decision evoked anger and frustration as well as fear. Eldridge could not understand how the officials could determine that he was no longer disabled without having seen him or performing any sort of medical tests. As he saw it, nothing had changed in the eighteen months since he had won his dispute before the administrative law judge.

Perhaps most upsetting to Eldridge was the manner in which the decision was made. Eldridge argued that he was not asking for charity. He had paid premiums into the program while he was able to work. He had proven in his hearing in 1968 that he was completely disabled within the meaning of the applicable statute and regulations. Now, without an opportunity to be heard, the benefits would end.

But of course there was an opportunity to fight the decision after the payments were stopped. Eldridge had fought the 1968 eligibility decision by himself, but this time he felt that he needed help despite the cost. His concern and his anger prompted Eldridge to respond to the notice from SSA in two ways.

First, he began his administrative appeals process by requesting that the agency reconsider his case. On April 11 and again on April 23 he contacted the local office requesting a prompt decision. But Eldridge knew that he was unlikely to get through the reconsideration process and on to a hearing without a lengthy delay. He'd been through it before. It would probably be months before his benefits were restored. In fact, the mean time from termination to eventual reinstatement for successful claimants was then just over eighteen months.

An Attempt to Challenge SSA

In addition to his administrative efforts, Eldridge's anger at what he felt was an unfair and arbitrary process of decisionmaking prompted him to challenge the Social Security Administration on constitutional grounds in court. On April 27, 1970, Mr. McAfee of Cline, McAfee, Adkins & Gillenwater, a Norton law firm, filed suit for Eldridge in the United States District Court for the Western District of Virginia. The legal issue that the court was to decide can be easily stated, but a decision either way would have profound implications both for those receiving benefits—the consumers of administrative decisions—and for the administrators of the program—the producers of administrative judgments.

Eldridge's attorney argued that it was a violation of due process of law protected by the Fifth Amendment of the Constitution of the United States for the Secretary of Health, Education, and Welfare, responsible for SSA, to terminate a disability recipient's benefits without first providing the person with an oral hearing. Such a hearing would permit a claimant to appear in person, to present evidence in his behalf, to question witnesses and to respond to adverse evidence which had been placed in his disability file. The hearing, it was argued, should be held before an administrative law judge who has independence from those who administer the program. In short, Eldridge wanted the same kind of hearing that he would be entitled to *later* in the process to be provided *before* his benefit checks were stopped.

In June, the district court ordered the government to resume the benefit payments pending the outcome of the litigation. In that same month, Eldridge's wife died. His total income until that point had consisted of a VA payment of $136 per month. Eldridge remembered with bitter feelings the fact that discontinuance of benefits prevented him from providing his wife with the few things that she had requested.

While the constitutional case was pending before the court, the administrative appeal continued. The reconsideration decision was unfavorable. Eldridge's attorney immediately filed requesting a hearing, which did not occur until March 17, 1971. The administrative law judge, a different examiner than the one Eldridge had faced in 1968, concluded that he was still completely disabled and ordered that payments be resumed with back payments to be paid for the several months during which the benefits had been interrupted. Had it not been for the intervention of the court, Eldridge would have faced a financial nightmare. As it was, he had to pay medical bills for himself and his family as well as attorney fees.

When the administrative appeal was resolved in Eldridge's favor, the district court dismissed the constitutional suit as moot. That is, Eldridge no longer had an actual live case or controversy with the government. To be sure, he disagreed with the government's policy, but the law requires more than general disagreement. It demands that an individual have standing to sue. He must be substantially injured or stand in imminent danger of being injured by the party he is suing.[12] Further, the dispute must be a continuing disagreement or the suit will be dismissed for mootness.[13]

ONCE MORE INTO THE BREACH

Round Three: One More Time

It was not long, though, before Eldridge was again engaged in a controversy with the Social Security Administration. A year after his second victory in a hearing, Eldridge received another set of forms from the state agency. He frowned as he read the same form letter that had started his last year-long battle.

> When your disability payments began, you were notified by the Social Security Administration that your condition might improve and your claim was scheduled for review. The Social Security Administration has requested us . . . to develop current evidence as to whether your condition still prevents you from working.[14]

Once again Eldridge filled out the forms. He indicated that his situation had not changed. He answered the questions about the kinds of medical treatment he was receiving and when he had last seen his physician. With the hope that things would go better this time, he mailed the package.

In May 1972, Eldridge received another letter from the Social Security Administration:

> Although you indicated in the report you recently completed for us that you do not feel your condition has improved so that you are able to return to work, the other information and evidence in your case shows that you are able to work and have been since May 1972. You were initially found to be disabled due to chronic anxiety and back strain. In addition you have been found to have diabetes. Medical evidence shows no significant motion limitations of your back which would impose severe functional restrictions. Diabetes is under control and no complications have been noted, secondary to this. Although you remain somewhat anxious, there is no indications [sic] of your continued emotional problems of sufficient severity to preclude all work for which you are qualified.
>
> Therefore, disability benefits being paid on your Social Security number may be stopped unless additional evidence is submitted which shows that you are still unable to work because of your impairment.[15]

Now Eldridge was really furious. Twice he had proven his case in person. Stacks of medical reports had been submitted. He had yet to be examined by a physician who worked for the government.[16] For the third time he prepared to fight the state agency. He wrote back to the agency.

> In regards to your letter of May 1972 asking for more evidence to prove my disability, I think you should already have enough evidence in my files to prove the disability already. Besides if I was able to work I would have worked because if I was able to work I could make more money than social security paid me. Another thing, if you will check my reports a little closer I think that you will find that I have arthritis of the spine rather than a strained back as you stated in your letter. The people at the disability section in Richmond have never made a yes decision in my case. I have always had to have a hearing in order to get the decision made properly. Even at the last hearing that was held in my case I had to employ an attorney, and the examiner made his decision wholly in my favor and stated in his decision for me for my checks to continue without interruption. So

go ahead and make your own decision in the case. I know I'm not able to work, if I ever get able to work I will, I will get by some way without the social security even though I've paid into it while I was able to work.[17]

It was false bravado. Eldridge knew full well that he couldn't do without the benefits. He just couldn't understand why he was being treated in what he perceived to be an inhumane fashion. Even more than seven years after he wrote that letter, his blue eyes flashed with indignation when he discussed the episode.

The state agency entered a determination against him and forwarded the findings to Baltimore for final decision. The Social Security Administration wrote Eldridge again on June 12 comfirming the earlier judgment of the state agency and informing him that his benefits would end in July. He could, of course, file for reconsideration any time within six months after termination.

He was already exhausted. The cost of the proceedings and the breaks in payments over the several years of dealing with SSA meant that by the time this round of adjudication ended, Eldridge would lose his home, a mobile home, his automobile, and his furniture.

The Journey to the Supreme Court Begins

Eldridge again followed the dual strategy. He turned to the courts, represented this time by a different attorney, Mr. Donald Earls, then with Cline, McAfee et al., later with Earls, Wolfe and Farmer, also of Norton, Virginia. He filed suit in the district court in Abingdon, Virginia in August 1972. The issue was the same due process claim that Eldridge's attorney had raised a year earlier in that same court, but this time the judge did not order continuation of payments pending the outcome of the litigation.

The case was not a review of an administrative decision as such. Under other circumstances, Eldridge might have battled his way through reconsideration, hearing, and Appeals Council stages to get to the district court. This process is known as exhaustion of administrative remedies. The so-called exhaustion doctrine is intended to reduce court review of individual administrative decisions. If he had pursued this route, his case would have been reviewed by a district court judge. The judge in such a case would have examined the decision of the agency to terminate benefits in light of what is known as the "substantial evidence rule."[18] He or she would have examined the record to determine whether on the record as a whole there was substantial evidence to support the decision of the agency.[19]

But Eldridge was *not* seeking judicial review of a substantive agency decision. Speaking for Eldridge, Earls argued that they were willing to concede that the agency had examined the benefit termination in the manner prescribed by statute and regulations. The complaint was that the regulations and other guidelines, insofar as they provided no pretermination hearing, were themselves unconstitutional. That sort of case was brought as a civil suit naming the then Secretary of Health, Education, and Welfare, Caspar Weinberger.

His case came on for argument before Judge Turk, a judge whose docket frequently contained Social Security disability cases. On April 9, 1973, the judge announced his ruling for Eldridge. Before analyzing his opinion, it is necessary to understand the background of the constitutional problem that Eldridge had raised.

WHY DID GEORGE ELDRIDGE INSIST ON A CONSTITUTIONAL REMEDY?

Eldridge sued because he was convinced that he had been treated in a manner that was patently unfair. In more formal terms than he would use, he felt that the several decisions made in his case by unseen and unnamed administrators who, on three separate occasions, had withdrawn his benefits, had been made arbitrarily and capriciously. In fact, his argument was even more basic. His attorney, Mr. Earls, asserted that the procedure employed by the Department of Health, Education, and Welfare violated the longstanding principle that administrators should not be able to seriously injure a citizen's liberty or property interests without giving an opportunity for a hearing.

The Fear of Administrative Arbitrariness

Ever since administrative agencies have been in use, there has been fear of abuse of authority by administrators.[20] Years before administrative law was recognized as a major branch of American law, the Supreme Court noted that there exist dangers of possible arbitrary administration of an otherwise useful law.

> When we consider the nature and theory of our institutions of government, the principles upon which they are supposed to rest, and review the history of their development, we are constrained to conclude that they do not mean to leave room for the play and action of purely personal and arbitrary power. Sovereignty itself is, of course, not subject to law, for it is the author and source of law, but in our system, while sovereign powers are delegated to the agencies of government, sovereignty itself remains with the people, by whom and for whom all government exists and acts. And the law is the definition and limitation of power. . . . For the very idea that one man may be compelled to hold his life, or the means of living, or any material right essential to the enjoyment of life, at the mere will of another seems to be intolerable in any country where freedom prevails, as being the essence of slavery itself.[21]

As this country entered the twentieth century and faced the social, economic, and political changes that were on the horizon, serious questions were asked about the manner in which administrative agencies would be dealt with, particularly where they were charged with making decisions in individual cases.[22] In such situations, the agencies were acting like courts.[23] The generally accepted solution was to require the agencies to provide some basic elements of due process of law.[24] Fair procedure and the possibility of review by a court of law would serve as a sufficient check, or so it was thought.[25]

Due process includes, at least, notice to those to be affected by the agency, an opportunity to be heard, decision by an impartial decisionmaker, and the availability of review of the initial decision.[26] In the *Eldridge* case, this discussion of procedural due process raises at least three questions. (1) What kind of problems are presented by the increases in social service benefit cases? (2) What is the significance of the so-called right-privilege dichotomy, which is mentioned in discussions of benefit claims adjudications? (3) At what point in a dispute between the government and a citizen is a hearing required?

The major regulatory commissions like the Interstate Commerce Commission deal primarily with businesses rather than individual citizens. With increased social service demands brought on by the growth of urban areas, the Great Depression, World War II, and the postwar need for education and other services has come an increase in disputes involving individual claimants for disability, retirement, welfare, medical aid, educational support, and veterans' benefits. These individuals are relatively less able than organizations to wage legal battles with government. In particular, they suffer immediately and personally from delays in the administrative law processes. They frequently do not understand the complex legal issues at stake, are not represented by attorneys, and are unable to understand all the "red tape" that stands between them and what they perceive to be benefits they are entitled to receive. An additional complication is the fact that several of these programs are administered by federal, state, and, in some cases, local officials.

The benefit cases also focus attention on what was earlier known as the right-privilege dichotomy, which doctrine held that due process requires hearings and other procedural protections where an individual faces an injury to a liberty or property right, but not where a mere privilege is at stake. Such benefit programs as Aid to Families with Dependent Children were considered matters of privilege, hence not protected by due process.[27] The Supreme Court rejected this view and, in *Sherbert v. Verner* held:

Nor may the South Carolina court's construction of the statute be saved from constitutional infirmity on the ground that employment compensation benefits are not appellant's "right" but merely a "privilege." . . . For example, the Court recognized with respect to Federal social security benefits that the interest of a covered employee under the Act is of sufficient substance to fall within the protection from arbitrary governmental action afforded by the Due Process Clause.[28]

363
*Mathews v.
Eldridge:* The
Anatomy of an
Administrative
Law Case

Students of due process such as Judge J. Skelly Wright observed that social benefit programs are essential parts of modern life, and cannot be relegated to the status of mere privilege.[29]

Finally, assuming that some process is due in a particular case, at what point in the interaction between the government and the claimant is the hearing required? Before this question can be answered, one must understand a number of cases that were to be at the heart of George Eldridge's case.

Development of Administrative Due Process:
Goldberg v. Kelly and Related Cases

The Court had ruled that before a final tax assessment decision, citizens must be afforded an opportunity for a hearing that is more than a mere chance to complain. "A hearing in its very essence demands that he who is entitled to it shall have a right to support his allegations by argument however brief, and, if need be, by proof, however informal."[30] After all, "the fundamental requisite of due process is the opportunity to be heard."[31]

Of course, not every administrative action requires a hearing, but:

> In administrative proceedings of a quasi-judicial character, the liberty and property of the citizen shall be protected by the rudimentary requirements of fair play. These demand a fair and open hearing.[32]

And "whether any procedural protections are due depends upon the extent to which an individual will be condemned to suffer grievous loss."[33] The court has found such "grievous loss" where an organization's name was placed on the Attorney General's list of subversive organizations without a hearing,[34] where dismissal from government employment will bring public approbation and cause a mark on the character of the individual,[35] where an individual faced forfeiture of unemployment benefits for refusal to work on Saturdays for religious reasons,[36] and where garnishment of wages is undertaken without due process,[37] all require some form of due process hearing protection.

In 1970 came the landmark case of *Goldberg v. Kelly*,[38] in which the court concluded that the due process clause required that recipients of Aid to Families with Dependent Children (AFDC) be afforded an evidentiary hearing, though not a full trial in the traditional sense, prior to termination of their benefits. New York and other states had employed a procedure by which the claimants could object to termination, but would not actually receive a "fair hearing" before a state hearing officer until after termination. If the claimant succeeded at that hearing, back benefits would be paid.

Justice Brennan wrote for the seven-to-two majority in *Goldberg*. Justices Black and Burger dissented. Justice Brennan wrote:

> Appellant does not contend that procedural due process is not applicable to the termination of welfare benefits. Such benefits are a matter of statutory entitlement for persons qualified to receive them.[39]

Brennan then made reference to a significant footnote.

> It may be realistic today to regard welfare entitlements as more like "property" than a "gratuity." Much of the existing wealth in this country takes the form of rights that do not fall within traditional common-law concepts of property. It has

been aptly noted that "[s]ociety today is built around entitlement. The automobile dealer has his franchise, the doctor and lawyer their professional licenses, the worker his union membership, contract, and pension rights, the executive his contract and stock options: all are devices to aid security and independence. Many of the most important of these entitlements flow from government: subsidies to farmers and businessmen, routes for airlines and channels for television stations; long term contracts for defense, space, and education; social security pensions for individuals. Such sources of security, whether private or public, are no longer regarded as luxuries or gratuities; to the recipients they are essentials, fully deserved, and in no sense a form of charity. It is only the poor whose entitlements, although recognized by public policy, have not been effectively enforced." Reich, "Individual Rights and Social Welfare: The Emerging Legal Issues," 74 *Yale L.J.* 1245, 1255 (1965). See also Reich, "The New Property," 73 *Yale L.J.* 733 (1964).[40]

The majority opinion continued as follows:

Their [benefit payments] termination involves state action that adjudicates important rights. The constitutional challenge cannot be answered by an argument that public assistance benefits are "a privilege and not a right." *Shapiro v. Thompson*, 394 U.S. 618.[41]

Brennan observed that qualified recipients were in no position to fight a posttermination proceeding.

Since he lacks independent resources, his situation becomes immediately desperate. His need to concentrate upon finding the means for daily subsistence, in turn, adversely affects his ability to seek redress from the welfare bureaucracy.[42]

The government argued that administrative due process is a flexible concept that should not be read to require the increased administrative burden and financial costs involved, which outweighed, in its view, possible injury to claimants. Brennan rejected that notion.

Thus, the interest of the eligible recipient in uninterrupted receipt of public assistance, coupled with the State's interest that his payments not be erroneously terminated, clearly outweighs the State's competing concern to prevent any increase in its fiscal and administrative burdens.[43]

Brennan's due process calculation was not a simple balance. He discussed the role of the constitutional principle at stake as well as the societal interest in fair administration of public policy.

The majority opinion, however, did not read the concept of "welfare" or social benefit narrowly. Neither did it limit the requirement of pretermination hearing to AFDC. A companion case to *Goldberg*, *Wheeler v. Montgomery*,[44] indicated that the Court did not intend to have its opinion read so narrowly. The case involved a challenge to old-age benefits procedures, which required some notice and related procedures prior to termination. The Court struck the decision as violative of due process under *Goldberg* since "the procedure does not, however, afford the recipient an evidentiary hearing at which he may appear and offer oral evidence and confront and cross-examine witnesses against him."[45]

Following the *Goldberg* decision, the right to a hearing before adverse action was recognized in parole revocation (*Morrissey v. Brewer*[46]), in probation revocation (*Gagnon v. Scarpelli*[47]), in prison disciplinary procedures (*Wolff v. McDonnel*[48]), in suspension of drivers' licenses (*Bell v. Burson*[49]), in opportunity to demonstrate *bona fides* as a state resident for tuition purposes (*Vlandis v. Kline*[50]), in suspension from secondary school for more than ten days (*Goss v. Lopez*[51]), in various forms of attachment of goods or bank accounts (*Fuentes v. Shevin*[52]), and in removal without hearing from public housing projects (*Caulder v. Durham*[53]).

Richardson v. Wright: One Direct Challenge Avoided

365

*Mathews v.
Eldridge:* The
Anatomy of an
Administrative
Law Case

Of course, by the time of the *Goldberg* ruling, Eldridge was well into the second round of his contest with the Social Security Administration. A number of other disability recipients who were in predicaments similar to Eldridge's launched litigation aimed at obtaining a clear application by the Supreme Court of *Goldberg* to the disability program.[54]

The Court noted probable jurisdiction in *Richardson v. Wright.*[55] But while that case was pending, HEW issued new regulations for termination that were only slightly different from the existing procedures. The justices vacated the lower court judgment and remanded the case for consideration in light of the new rules. It was clearly an attempt by HEW to avoid a ruling, and it worked.[56] Justice Brennan, author of the *Goldberg* decision, filed a dissent for himself and Justice Marshall in the *Richardson* case which asserted that the same maneuver had been attempted unsuccessfully in *Goldberg.* In his view, *Goldberg* was clearly applicable and the delay in declaring that fact would only cause hardship for wrongfully terminated claimants.

THE DISTRICT COURT ACTS

Judge Turk and the Due Process Cases

It was against this developing body of law on administrative due process that Judge Turk of the District Court for the Western District of Virginia dealt with the case of *Eldridge v. Weinberger.*[57] In addition to an obvious facility with the due process cases, Judge Turk's opinion in *Eldridge* indicated a familiarity with the stages and problems of disability decisionmaking.

Given the location in which Judge Turk sits and his reference to Haviland and Glomb's study, "The Disability Insurance Program and Low Income Claimants in Appalachia,"[58] it is also clear that Judge Turk understood the particular problems faced by people like Eldridge in proving their disability.[59] The comments of administrative law judges and experienced attorneys indicate that the special difficulties in shouldering the requisite burden of proof are what make the availability of hearings a significant issue.[60]

Haviland and Glomb, who had studied a series of cases drawn from a sample over time of their practice in disability claims in Appalachia, argued as follows:

The hypothesis of this articles is that the Disability Insurance Benefits program is not geared to the pattern of cases described herein and, accordingly, will not work well for a predictably significant group of claimants throughout the nation who suffer from chronic diseases or injuries of a non-traumatic nature. Rather, the program is geared to the more middle-class claimant who has worked on a regular basis all of his life until some traumatic event robbed him of his ability to work. This person would usually have little difficulty with the medical evidence requirement in establishing that he is suffering from a physical or mental impairment—this could be documented by the trauma itself and his subsequent medical treatment for that trauma.

Since the onset of his disability can be pin-pointed, he will have very little difficulty with the current insurance requirement. The pre-existing skills and residual capacity for retraining of our hypothetical middle-class worker make him more suited for rehabilitation for jobs which actually exist in the "national economy." For the middle class worker, the "national employability tests" may be a realistic standard of employment, but for the type of person described in this study, it is not a realistic test, since his age, existing skills, and lack of trainability severely limit the likelihood of his rehabilitation.

The hypothesis, that the persons studied herein do not fit the programmed image of the Disability Insurance Benefit program, should alert the advocate to the fact that in presenting the cases of claimants who fit into the factual pattern discussed they will be "swimming against the current" of the programmed image.[61]

Some explanation is needed to indicate why there might be difficulty in proving disability.

"The idea of the disability benefit program is simple. If a worker or one of his surviving dependents, who normally would not qualify for social security benefits until achieving retirement age, becomes disabled, he may begin to receive his retirement benefits at once and need not wait until retirement age is reached."[62] But it may not be as simple as it sounds. An experienced administrative law judge explains.

> The most common misconceptions of entitlement for disability benefits are the following: the claimant paid into the Social Security fund for many years, and he is, therefore, entitled to his money; the claimant has been found disabled by some other unit of government, i.e., the Veterans' Administration or state compensation board and he is, therefore, automatically entitled to benefits; and the claimant has an attending physician's medical report that confirms the disability. Of course, the opinions of attending physicians cannot be ignored, but such conclusions are valid only if they are supported by objective medical findings and if the physician follows the specific definition of disability in the Social Security Act. Usually, when doctors identify a patient as "disabled," they mean that the patient is unable to perform his regular job.[63]

The first problem for the claimant is to prove that he is eligible to receive benefits in terms of timing. That is, he must show that he was insured at the time that the disability began. Specifically, he must show that he had been insured for twenty quarters out of the forty quarters prior to the beginning of his injury, roughly five out of the previous ten years. If the injury was a traumatic accident such as an on-the-job incident, the beginning of the disability is easy to determine and prove. If, on the other hand, one is dealing with something like chronic serious arthritis or progressive lung disorders, it may be nearly impossible to pinpoint precisely the onset of the disease. Assuming that one can make such a showing, the next problem is to show eligibility at that time. In a number of cases cited by Haviland and Glomb, proving insured status is difficult because unskilled or semiskilled workers often worked in marginal operations that did not maintain adequate records.

The second problem is proving total disability. The Social Security Disability program is an all-or-nothing arrangement that covers only total disability as demonstrated by medical evidence. That requirement contains two different adjudicatory problems. (1) What is meant by total disability? (2) What type and level of proof is needed?

> The regulations defining the methods of proving disability under section 223 (d) (1) provide two basic methods of proof. The first method provides for proof of disability by medical evidence showing the existence of certain specified pathologies which is apparently presumed to be disabling without any actual showing that the pathology has any relationship to the claimed inability to work. The second method provides that the claimant must prove that a physical condition, regardless of the severity of the condition as contrasted to section 1502 (a), in fact prevents him from functioning in jobs theoretically available to him in the national economy. The claimants burden of producing the medical evidence required by either method of proof of disability is usually met by the submission of written reports signed by licensed physician reflecting an examination and a course of treatment.[64]

The specific pathologies are frequently dealt with in terms of a list of disabling conditions provided in the regulations. The burden of proof for showing such disability and for demonstrating its continued existence, should the claimant be placed on the program, rests with the claimant. Additionally, in cases where chronic disorders in skeletal conditions or cardiovascular systems are complicated by age and long exposure to chemicals and the like, the evidence needed may be exceedingly hard to gather. Simple laboratory tests may not detect or properly portray the actual condition of the claimant. Beyond that, a number of the tests are not absolutely reliable because they may be improperly administered or because they test for specific disorders rather than the synergistic effects of more than one medical malady.[65]

Finally, assuming that one can develop a complete set of medical evidence and the necessary data proving the eligibility of the claimant at the time of the onset of the disabling injury or disease, the problem of the national employability standard must be dealt with.

> Proof of disability under the functional method of 1502 (b) requires proof not only that the claimant's impairment precludes him from engaging in his "previous employment" or any equivalent employment, but also that he cannot, "considering his age, educational, and work experience, engage in any other kind of substantial gainful work which exists in the national economy, regardless of whether such work exists in the immediate area in which he lives, or whether a specific job vacancy exists for him or whether he would be hired if he applied for work.[66]

In short, the determination of eligibility and disability is a complex fact-finding process involving data on medical diagnoses and treatment, vocational possibilities, and legal interpretation. The evidence submitted in the form of medical reports does not necessarily speak for itself. In fact, studies of the hearing process have found that a major aspect of the hearing examiner's task is to complete the often inadequate record that gets through the initial and reconsideration stages to the hearing stage.[67] Most claimants, particularly those who are poorly educated and lack independent financial means, do not have attorneys to aid them in preparing and asserting their claims.[68] Finally, there are complex problems of proof in cases where, like the one in which Eldridge was a claimant, the person seeking benefits is an older, unskilled, poorly educated person who suffers from nontraumatic interacting diseases rather than a traumatic injury.

The Decision and the Court of Appeals Affirmance

On April 9, 1973, Judge Turk announced his decision in favor of Eldridge, holding specifically that *Goldberg v. Kelly* and other related cases clearly mandated that the government provide a pretermination hearing for those receiving disability benefits under Title II of the Social Security Act, just as the Supreme Court had required pretermination hearings for those receiving benefits under Title I, old age survivors benefits (*Wheeler v. Montgomery*), and under Title IV, Aid to Families with Dependent Children (*Goldberg v. Kelly*).[69]

The government argued that recipients of Title II benefits are to be distinguished from those involved in programs under the other titles. In particular, those receiving benefits under AFDC are by definition destitute, while benefit claimants under the disability program are not made eligible for the program by proof of poverty. Beyond that, the federal government attorneys argued, the nature of the evidence and the kind of questions dealt with in a disability case are unlike those at issue in a welfare termination hearing. In the latter case, there might be hearsay and possibly even rumors involved, which require complex fact-finding processes to sort out and verify. Disability claims, on the other hand, are decided on the basis of scientific evidence submitted by doctors and vocational experts. The evidence in the disability cases is, in legal terms, more accurate and probative than some of the material presented in welfare cases. Finally, the government attorneys contended that a decision in favor of Eldridge would result in an intolerable financial and administrative burden on the federal government because of the funds required to provide the increased number of hearings and the likely increases and continued benefit costs for ineligible recipients who would continue to receive benefits while their cases dragged through the hearing process. Certainly, they said, such a burden is not justified to provide a relatively minor increase in the accuracy of the fact-finding process beyond the existing procedural protections available to claimants. After all, those who lost payments, but later succeeded with their claims in a hearing would be entitled to receive back benefits.

Judge Turk rejected each of these contentions. From a doctrinal viewpoint, he found that the cases in the area of administrative due process clearly required a hearing before termination.[70] As for government claims about administrative overload, he observed that the Supreme Court had specifically rejected the increased costs and administrative burdens argument in both *Goldberg* and *Wheeler*. Moreover, he observed that the experience under *Goldberg* requirements had not produced any evidence of the anticipated administrative and financial overburden.

Judge Turk began by noting that it seemed strange to assert that it is constitutionally necessary to provide hearings in cases of Titles I and IV of a statute while rejecting the same requirement from Title II of that law. He recited the holding of *Goldberg* and its companion case, *Wheeler v. Montgomery*. He also noted that a case regarding the application of the prehearing requirement to disability claimants had been taken to the Supreme Court, in *Wright v. Richardson*.[71] While the *Wright* case was en route to the Court, the Social Security Administration added a requirement to its termination regulations that required the agency to notify the claimant of the reasons for termination and permit the claimant to submit within ten days additional written information relating to his claim. The Court remanded the case for reconsideration in light of the new regulations. Justices Brennan, Douglas, and Marshall would have decided the case at that time and in favor of the application of *Goldberg* evidentiary hearing rule.[72]

Following these more or less introductory remarks, Judge Turk moved to the core of his opinion. He began by recognizing the fact that procedural due process is a somewhat flexible concept.

> In deciding whether the requirements of due process have been satisfied in this case, it is important first to recognize that due process safeguards vary with the rights sought to be protected. In *Cafeteria Workers v. McElroy*, 367 U.S. 886, 895, . . . the Supreme Court stated:
>
> > "The very nature of due process negates any concept of inflexible procedures universally applicable to every imaginable situation . . . what procedures due process may require under any given set of circumstances must begin with a determination of the precise nature of the government function involved as well as of the private interest that has been affected by government action."
>
> The court in *Goldberg* presented the issue in a similar manner as follows:
>
> > "The extent to which procedural due process must be afforded to the recipient is influenced by the extent to which he may be 'condemned to suffer grievous loss.' *Joint Anti-Fascist Refugee Committee v. McGrath*, 341 U.S. 123, 168, . . . (1951) (Frankfurter, J., concurring), and depends upon whether the recipient's interest in avoiding that loss outweighs the governmental interest in summary adjudication. 397 U.S. 254 at 262–263, . . . (1970)."[73]

The government's attempt to draw a distinction between the "grievous loss" to be suffered by the welfare recipient and the problems faced by the disability claimant "is not persuasive for purposes of due process."[74]

> Although disability beneficiaries are not by definition dependent on benefit payments for their livelihood, they are by definition unable to engage in substantial gainful activity, and to cut off payments erroneously may create a loss as "grievous" as that which concerned the Supreme Court in the cases of welfare and old age beneficiaries.[75]

But, argued Judge Turk, this decision does not hinge alone on the narrow issue of the similarity of welfare recipients and disability claimants. The due process question is more basic than that and the answer to it requires an examination of these more fundamental concerns.

Turk's consideration then turned to a demonstration of the fact that the Supreme Court had clearly applied a prior hearing requirement to diverse cases of government decisions respecting individuals in which the loss would quite plainly be "less grievous" than that suffered by George Eldridge and others like him. He focused on *Sniadach v. Family Finance Corporation*,[76] *Bell v. Burson*,[77] and *Fuentes v. Shevin*.[78] These cases were decided both before and after the *Goldberg v. Kelly* decision. In *Sniadach*, the Supreme Court had struck down as violative of due process a Wisconsin wage garnishment statute that permitted creditors to "freeze ½ of the wages due an employee without notice or a prior hearing."[79] In *Fuentes*, the Court voided Florida and Pennsylvania repossession laws that did not provide prior due process safeguards. Finally, the Court in *Bell v. Burson* struck down a Georgia law which contained an irrebuttable presumption. While the Reverend Bell was having Sunday dinner with parishioners of his circuit ministry, his parked car was struck by a young girl who rode her bicycle into the car. The law, based on insurance requirements, would have resulted in the revocation of Bell's license or posting of a bond, neither of which the minister could afford. The statute held that since he was uninsured he was presumed to have been at fault. He argued, and the Supreme Court concurred, that to deprive him of his license without a prior hearing to prove that he could not possibly be found liable was a violation of due process.

Turk concluded that these cases rejected the government's insistence on a narrow meaning of procedural due process.

> In *Fuentes* it was argued that *Sniadach* and *Goldberg* should be narrowly read as limited to cases involving absolute necessities. In rejecting a narrow reading of those cases the court states
>
> > "Both decisions were in the mainstream of past cases, having little or nothing to do with the absolute 'necessities' of life but establishing that due process requires an opportunity for a hearing before a deprivation of property takes effect. . . . While *Sniadach* and *Goldberg* emphasized the special importance of wages and welfare benefits, they did not convert that emphasis into a new and more limited constitutional doctrine.
> >
> > "Nor did they carve out a rule of 'necessity' for the sort of nonfinal deprivations of property that they involved.' 407 U.S. at 88."
>
> The court in *Fuentes* also made reference to the case of *Bell v. Burson*, . . . in which the court had held that there must be an opportunity for a hearing on the issue of fault before the license of an uninsured motorist could be suspended. The court in *Fuentes* noted that the driver's license involved in *Bell* did not rise to the level of a "necessity" as in the cases of wages or welfare benefits but was nevertheless an important interest entitled to the protection of procedural due process. From the above cases it is thus apparent that *Goldberg* is not distinguishable from the case at bar in terms of the criterion for benefits.[80]

Having disposed of the need for a hearing argument, Turk turned to the two remaining government contentions on the nature of evidence in disability claims and the burden on government resources.

The government contention that the evidence involved in disability cases is easily understood and well suited to a clear interpretation is, according to Turk, incorrect. First, the facts of the *Eldridge* case refute such a simplistic assumption. On several occasions Eldridge's paper record had been reviewed and reconsidered with a decision against his claim. Yet on each occasion when his case was heard before a hearing examiner, the decision was in his favor.

Second, disability evidentiary problems fall within the *Goldberg v. Kelly* ruling.

> It is true that the court in *Goldberg* stated that "[p]articularly where credibility and veracity are at issue, as they must be in many termination proceedings, written submissions are a wholly unsatisfactory basis for decision." . . . But the court also characterized the pretermination hearing as important "where recipients

have challenged proposed terminations as resting on incorrect or misleading factual premises or on the misapplication of rules or policies to the facts of particular cases." . . . There is no doubt that medical evidence may be conflicting, *Richardson v. Perales*, 402 U.S. 389 . . . (1971), and the Secretary must exercise judgment in resolving the conflicting medical evidence, 20 C.F.R. §404.1526. Thus there will be a resolution of factual issues in disability cases, and the exercise of subjective judgment to resolve conflicting evidence of a factual nature makes the value of a hearing self-evident. But in addition, it is noteworthy that determinations of total disability are not exclusively a function of medical evidence. The four elements of proof required for the establishment of a disability claim were set forth in *Underwood v. Ribicoff*, 298 F.2d. 850, 851 (4th Cir. 1962) as follows:

> (1) the objective medical facts, . . .
> (2) the diagnosis . . . of . . . treating and examining physicians on subsidiary questions of fact,
> (3) the subjective evidence of pain and disability testified to by Claimant, and corroborated by his wife and . . . neighbors, [and]
> (4) claimant's educational background, work history, and present age.

There is no requirement that a disability under the Social Security Act be proven by "objective" medical evidence. *Flake v. Gardner*, 399 F.2d. 532, 540 (9th Cir. 1968); *Whitt v. Gardner*, 389 F.2d. 906, 909 (6th Cir. 1968). The testimony of the claimant or witnesses in his behalf may be crucial in establishing a disability. See *Page v. Celebreeze*, 311 F.2d. 757 (5th Cir. 1963).[81]

Finally, even if the evidence were more clear, the right to due process protections prior to deprivation of liberty or property interests is not dependent on the fact that the claimant is likely to win the case.

In response to the contention that defendants could repossess goods without first affording plaintiffs a hearing in the case of a default in payments on a conditional sales contract, the court [in *Fuentes*] stated:

"The right to be heard does not depend on an advance showing that one will surely prevail at the hearing. To one who protests against the taking of his property without due process of law, it is no answer to say that in his particular case due process of law would have led to the same result because he had no adequate defense upon the merits." *Coe v. Armour Fertilizer Works*. . . . It is enough to invoke the procedural safeguards of the Fourteenth Amendment that a significant property interest is at stake. . . .

The Court also stated:

"The issues decisive of the ultimate right of continued possession, of course, may be quite simple. The simplicity of the issues might be relevant to the formality or scheduling of a prior hearing." See, *Lindset v. Normet*, . . . But it certainly cannot undercut the right to a prior hearing of some kind.[82]

The arguments concerning the catastrophic impact of a pretermination hearing requirement were presented, said Turk, in almost exactly the same terms in *Goldberg*, in which the Supreme Court responded that the right to due process was not to be forfeited to possible increases in administrative inconvenience. Beyond that, Justice Brennan, writing for the *Goldberg* court, indicated that the rearranging of existing agency procedures could result in a substantial savings.[83]

The government advanced the same argument in *Richardson v. Wright*. Brennan wrote for the dissenters in *Richardson*, arguing that the figures advanced by HEW were inflated and misleading. Judge Turk summarized Brennan's critique.

He there noted that the Secretary had assumed that all beneficiaries will demand a prior hearing. The Secretary's own figures show that of the 39,078 cases in which determinations of cessation of disability were rendered in 1972 only 2,801 post-termination hearings were held. It is certainly likely that even a smaller percentage of disability beneficiaries would demand pre-termination hearings due to the fact that the new regulations provide for notice and an opportunity to respond in writing before termination.

Justice Brennan also noted that the Secretary assumes that all of those demanding hearings will lose, and that the Secretary will be unable to recover any of the benefits paid to the beneficiaries pending the hearing. Both of these assumptions are unwarranted. Not only do a substantial number of persons demanding a hearing prevail, but the Secretary is directed to require a refund from the beneficiary or decrease future benefits in the case of an overpayment. 20 C.F.R. §§404.501–404.502. The Secretary also assumes that a pre-termination hearing would entail a two-month delay in the termination of disability benefits. But under current procedures benefits are paid for two months after a disability ceases, and it is hard to believe that it would take an additional two months (four months after an initial determination that disability had ceased) to have a hearing.[84]

Turk concluded by indicating that procedural due process does not exist to minimize costs and maximize administrative efficiency.

What the Supreme Court said in a related area is worth repeating here in light of the Secretary's argument.

"A prior hearing always imposes some costs in time, effort, and expense, and it is often more efficient to dispense with the opportunity for such a hearing. But these rather ordinary costs cannot outweigh the constitutional right." See *Bell v. Burson*, supra 402 U.S. at 540–541 . . . ; *Goldberg v. Kelly*, supra 397 U.S. at 261. . . . Procedural due process is not intended to promote efficiency or accommodate all possible interests; it is intended to protect the particular interests of the person whose possessions are about to be taken. "The establishment of prompt efficacious procedures to achieve legitimate state ends is a proper state interest worthy of cognizance in constitutional adjudication. But the Constitution recognizes higher values than speed and efficiency. Indeed, one might fairly say of the Bill of Rights in general, and the Due Process Clause in particular, that they were designed to protect the fragile values of a vulnerable citizenry from the overbearing concern for efficiency and efficacy that may characterize praiseworthy government officials no less, and perhaps more, than mediocre ones." *Stanley v. Illinois*, 405 U.S. 645, 656 . . . *Fuentes v. Shevin*, . . .

In *Bell v. Burson*, . . . the court rejected the argument that the additional cost of an expanded hearing was sufficient to forego a hearing as to fault prior to the revocation of a drivers license. The court there stated:

"[I]t is fundamental that except in emergency situations (and this is not one) due process requires that when a State seeks to terminate an interest such as that here involved, it must afford 'notice and opportunity for hearing appropriate to the nature of the case' before the termination becomes effective. . . ."

In *Fuentes*, supra . . . , the court stated:

"There are extraordinary situations that justify postponing notice and opportunity for a hearing. . . . These situations, however, must be truly unusual. Only in a few limited situations has this Court allowed outright seizure without opportunity for a prior hearing."[85]

The government promptly appealed Judge Turk's decision to the United States Circuit Court of Appeals for the Fourth Circuit. The case came on for hearing nearly a year after the district court ruling in February 1974. The appeals court affirmed that ruling in a per curiam opinion (an unsigned opinion for the court) on April 1, 1974. The terse opinion merely held that the affirmance was predicated on the opinion as presented by Judge Turk. Again the government appealed, this time to the United States Supreme Court.

POLICY CRISIS: LAW AND THE POLICY PROCESS

Shocking the System

Judge Turk's decision in the *Eldridge* case was a shock to the Social Security policy system. It was not the only such challenge to the existing pattern of administration, but it was a significant one. It was all the more important because it came at a time when the Social Security Administration was facing a number of serious problems, many of which were related to the disability program.

The *Eldridge* case was a shock because it meant that the policy system that operated the disability program would be forced from its routine, if problematic, day-to-day administrative mode into a more active phase of the policy process. The Social Security Administration had begun life with responsibility only for the Old Age and Survivor's Insurance program. That responsibility was significantly expanded with the creation of the Disability Program as part of Title II of the Social Security Act.[86]

A problem had been recognized as early as the 1940s. Clearly, there were a number of people who, to use the bureaucratic parlance, fell between the cracks in existing social insurance policies. Some couldn't qualify for retirement benefits because of age. Others could not be retrained because they were completely disabled. These people weren't covered by private plans, because many of them were unskilled or semiskilled workers whose previous work experiences had not included major benefit packages. Finally, they weren't covered by unemployment compensation programs of other types.

A policy was formulated. With a recognition by the government that disability insurance programs are the most difficult of all such plans to administer, and with an understanding of the ideological and emotional concerns over the status of this program as welfare or as social insurance, the plan was drafted.[87] The policy intentionally set up a complex intergovernmental mechanism for administering the program through the use of state vocational rehabilitation agencies. The purpose, of course, was to identify those who were in a position to benefit from rehabilitation and to get them into the system for treatment. Additionally, since the program was designed to be a total disability program as opposed to an unemployment compensation plan, the state agencies would provide expert vocational counselors to evaluate claimants with regard to the entire spectrum of possible employment, rather than from a concern for whether the claimant was able to return to his or her previous area of employment.

Congress adopted the policy as part of Title II of the Social Security Act. Amendments were added in 1967 to maintain the program as a total disability program rather than permitting it to lean toward an unemployment compensation activity.[88]

The plan was implemented and has been extremely active, processing more than 1.2 million claims in 1974 alone. The Bureau of Disability Insurance and the Bureau of Hearings and Appeals grew. The SSA developed a reputation for self-examination and evaluation.[89] It contracted for several major evaluation projects conducted by independent researchers.[90]

Still, the agency had settled into a more or less routine mode of operation until the 1970s. Then things began to deteriorate. The black lung and SSI programs were implemented without additional staff. Delays increased, congressional concern over problems of administration grew, hearing demands increased, and the reversal rate at the hearing stage exceeded 50 percent.[91] Not only were these problems serious, they promised to worsen. The number of cases appealed from the agency to the federal district courts increased significantly. What is perhaps more significant is the fact that the government was losing a major portion of the cases taken to the federal courts. It faced not only losses through individual claims, but also significant challenges to the entire administrative mechanism used to manage the disability system. It became clear that the Social Security Administration would have to take a hard look at its program with a view toward implementation of the many suggestions and, in some cases, mandates given with regard to the disability program. Insider and critic alike could agree on at least two things: (1) the program was serving a vital need for many people; and (2) there were major weaknesses in the program that were inherent in programs of this type, regardless of the effectiveness of the administrative efforts focused on the program.

There is a temptation to look at cases like Mr. Eldridge's with great sympathy for the claimant and a predictable indignation about the individual hardship inflicted by what appears to be an uncaring bureaucracy. Unfortunately, such reaction is myopic since it ignores the many pressures that affect an agency, especially a social service agency that has a tremendous responsibility in times of economic difficulty in the national economy. Let us examine briefly a few of the more significant shocks to the administrative system of the Social Security disability program during the time that Eldridge's case was winding its way to a decision in the Supreme Court. In particular, the agency was concerned by an increased procedural caseload, a high reversal rate at the hearing stage, increasing appeals of agency decisions to federal courts, along with a corresponding increase in agency losses in those judicial challenges, a recognition of weaknesses in the existing Social Security disability program appeals process, and the growing awareness of the impact of intergovernmental relations on the administration of the program.

Growing Caseload

The problem that administrators saw was the growing caseload coming from state agencies for hearing. As the caseload grew, so did the length of time necessary to process cases.

> The reasons for this increase in median processing time are not difficult to identify: 52,000 hearing requests were received in 1971; 155,000 hearing requests were received in 1975. And while the work load increased 300 percent, personnel (presiding officers and supporting staff) increased by only 200 percent. Unless dramatic increases in efficiency were achieved, increases in processing times and backlogs were certain to develop.
>
> Constant consideration has been given to increasing the productivity of each presiding officer. As a consequence, average case dispositions per year were up from 227 per exerpienced ALJ (administrative law judge) in 1975 to 302 per ALJ in 1976. With hearing requests holding relatively constant, the backlog of pending cases plummeted from 111,000 to 90,000 in 1976 alone.[92]

An examination of case flow in one year in the mid-1970s illustrates the magnitude of the problem. In calendar 1974 1,250,400 initial claims for disability were made and processed in the state agencies of which 60 percent were disallowed. Of that 60 percent, 29 percent, or 215,000 cases, were dealt with on reconsideration in the state agencies with 69 percent disallowed. Of that 69 percent, 35 percent were taken to hearing stage. Administrative law judges, at the federal level, delivered 51,900 decisions of which approximately 51 percent were disallowed. About half of those cases disapproved at hearing stage were taken for an administrative appeal to the Social Security Appeals Council. Of these 13,300 decisions, 86 percent were against the claimant. Finally, roughly 2,500 of the denials by the Appeals Council were taken to judicial review in federal district courts where some 28 percent were allowed.[93]

One of the significant aspects of this caseload is the length of time needed by a claimant to get through the various levels of administrative process to a hearing and eventually to a final award decision by the Bureau of Disability of the SSA. Figure A-1 shows the time 214 cases took, from date of application for benefits to award, from a study done by the staff of the Social

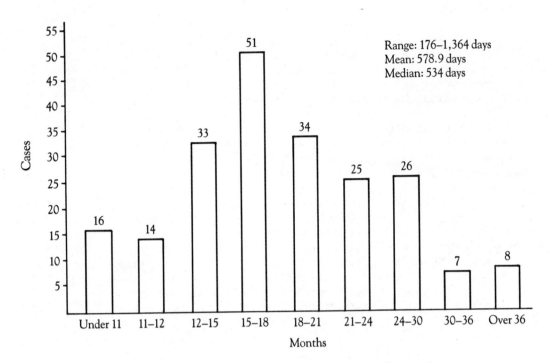

Figure A-1 *214 Cases: Time from the Date an Application Was Filed to the Date of Award Notice*[96]

Security Subcommittee of the House Ways and Means Committee, published just a month before Eldridge's case went to oral argument before the Supreme Court.

These time figures must be understood in light of the case load figures. Table A-1 presents the hearing demand on the agency.

Table A-1 Requests for Hearing: Receipts, Processed, and Pending[95]

Fiscal Year	Receipts	Processed	Pending
1970	42,573	38,480	13,747
1971	52,427	45,301	20,873
1972	103,691	61,030	63,534
1973	72,202	68,356[a]	36,780
1974	121,504	80,783[b]	77,233
1975	154,945	121,009	111,169

[a]Excludes 30,000 black lung cases transferred back to BDI.
[b]Excludes 268 black lung cases transferred back to BDI.

Reversals at Hearing

Not only were there more hearings, but the rate of decisions in those hearings, contrary to the initial findings of the state agencies, increased rather dramatically. In 1960, the rate of reversals at hearings was approximately 30 percent. This figure increased to roughly 39 percent by 1966. By 1974, however, the rate was approximately 50 percent reversal.

A number of reasons were advanced to explain the high rate of reversal. For example, it was suggested that only those with borderline cases took cases to appeal, meaning that it is not unlikely that borderline cases would have an approximately equal chance for success on appeal.[96] However, that doesn't account for the dramatic increase in the rate of reversal. Critics suggested that there were other reasons, one of which was that many meritorious claims could only be satisfactorily resolved by a face-to-face meeting between government officials and the claimant.[97]

Increasing Losses

In addition to having more proceedings that resulted in reversals in administrative hearings, the Social Security Administration noticed a significant increase in the number of cases being taken to federal district courts on appeal. Table A-2 gives an indication of the magnitude of

Table A-2   End-of-year Growth in Pending Cases[98]

Calendar Year	Total Social Security Cases	Disability Cases
1960	337	
1968	1,751	1,307
1969	2,370	1,748
1970	2,769	2,001
1971	3,148	2,251
1972	3,775	2,676
1973	4,033	3,018
1974 (June 17)	5,092[a]	4,187
1974	6,191[a]	4,301
1975 (August 31)	9,226[a]	4,723

[a]Including black lung cases. On June 17, 1974, 384 black lung cases were pending; 1,200 were pending on January 1, 1975; and 3,338 were pending on August 31, 1975.

the problem. The extent of the caseload in the federal courts can be understood in some measure by reference to the fact that, for example, in August 1975 the office of legal counsel prepared 502 briefs for Social Security and black lung cases.[99] Roughly 75 to 80 percent of the total Social Security caseload is made up of disability cases.[100]

Another problem was that the court activity was unevenly distributed across the nation, suggesting some difficulty with the manner in which the program was administered in certain locations.[101]

More claimants seem to apply for benefits and to appeal denials with more frequency in certain parts of the country than in others. For instance of the 2,595 pending social security cases at the end of fiscal 1973, 887 (34 percent) [arose in]

Puerto Rico	252
South Carolina	182
West Virginia–Southern	111
Kentucky–Eastern	297
Kentucky–Western	42

The jurisdictions noted account for considerably less than 10 percent of the disabled workers receiving benefits, even though they have an extremely high incidence of disability compared to the national average.

In terms of court workload by circuit the same disparity existed. The fourth and fifth circuits have had 47 percent of all the disability court cases. The fourth, fifth, and sixth circuits taken together have had 69 percent of the cases and they will be even harder hit when the black lung cases mature. On the other hand, New York and California which have roughly 20 percent of the disability caseload have had only 6 percent of the court cases. . . .

Obviously, the impact of the social security disability caseload on various courts in the country is uneven and, undoubtedly, will be of crisis proportions in certain judicial districts in the next few years. For instance, in the second and tenth circuits social security cases constituted only 1 percent of civil caseloads; but in the fourth circuit they made up 5 percent. In the District Court for Eastern Kentucky they were 22 percent of the civil caseload.[102]

This growing caseload in the courts, of course, is burdensome to the administration in that it requires time and personnel costs. But more has been at issue than numbers. There had been a growing qualitative difference in the manner in which the district courts addressed the cases coming to them from the Social Security Administration. As judges became more dissatisfied with agency decisionmaking in individual cases, their decisionmaking tended to range somewhat further than in former years. The reversal rate at the district court level reached nearly 30 percent during the time when Eldridge's case was winding its way through the federal courts. The courts were also dealing losses on substantial constitutional issues to the administration. The *Eldridge* case was one such loss.[103]

Criticism in the Literature

Literature generated during the early '70s added insight to the problems already apparent to those in Social Security policy. Four generalizations emerged in articles and books during these years. First, most commentators in and out of government agreed that some form of oral hearing, whether or not a full evidentiary hearing, at which the claimant could appear and obtain full explanation of the agency ruling in his case, is needed.[104] Second, with the exception of one or two major authors, most writers agreed at least implicitly that the *Goldberg v. Kelly* pretermination fair hearing requirements would apply to disability claimants.[105] Third, they were nearly unanimous in concluding that the preparation of the record at the initial determination and reconsideration stages was in many cases inadequate.[106] Finally, they were virtually unanimous in concluding that the ones victimized by the weaknesses in the process and most severely affected by the existing decision structure of the disability program were the claimants, who were in no position to bear such burdens.[107]

Experiments were conducted to determine whether some form of early conference would improve the quality of decisionmaking. The results of the program were promising. Table A-3 indicates some of the results.

Investigators and those in the agencies acknowledged that such a program would, if applied to all disability appeals, result in a higher rate of allowances of claims. On the other hand, it would probably mean a reduction in the number of hearing requests and ultimate reversals. In monetary terms, most observers felt that the program would still result in slightly higher costs. On the other hand, delays might be reduced. Moreover, there was a general recognition that the claimants were much more satisfied if they were afforded a fair hearing even if it was not a formal trial-type proceeding. Unless they obtain a hearing, claimants do not see the evidence that the agency has on hand when it makes its initial determination nor do they get more than a terse general statement in the agency termination letter explaining why they are no longer considered disabled.[109] Month after month they wait, with no more indication of their fate than an occasional form letter from either the state agency or the Baltimore office indicating the status of the claim as each milestone in the appeals process occurs.

Table A-3   Results of SSA Hearing Experiment

377

*Mathews v.
Eldridge:* The
Anatomy of an
Administrative
Law Case

	Interview cases		Noninterview cases	
	Number	Percent	Number	Percent
Denials changed to allowances	132	19.6	8	1.3
Denials upheld	539	—	576	—
Total number of denials	671	—	584	—
Requested hearing	214	39.7	241	41.8
Decision changed at hearing	46	22.2	73	37.2
Decision changed: total cases, reconsideration and hearing	178	26.0	81	14.0

SOURCE: Staff Report, "Background Material on Social Security Hearings and Appeals."[108]

There seemed to be little doubt in the minds of those writing on the subject that the *Goldberg* fair hearing requirement would be imposed on the Social Security disability program. That small amount of doubt rested on the likely impact of the changes in personnel on the Supreme Court rather than on the appropriate doctrinal evaluation.[110] There was, on the other hand, some question as to just how formal such a fair hearing must be. Just what kind of process was due was the central theme of a seminal article authored in 1975 by Judge Henry J. Friendly.[111] Judge Friendly was interested in the confusion surrounding the nature and extent of procedural due process required in administrative proceedings. Among other conclusions, Judge Friendly was concerned that the due process requirements had been extended too far and had cast administrative proceedings in an adversary model, which was not appropriate in some situations. The question before those considering changes in the Social Security process was whether such a change would pass constitutional muster. Most observers agreed that the Court's decision in the *Eldridge* case would be the key to those inquiries.[112]

At least among those who had studied the hearings process, there was a great deal of agreement that one of the reasons for the high rate of reversal of early decisions and for delays at the hearing stage was that the records sent up to the administrative law judge from the state agencies were woefully inadequate.[113] Consider the following story recounted by Representative B. F. Sisk of California.

Another of my constituents, Miss F., had her disability claim twice denied before her doctors' reports were even obtained and reviewed. Her case appears to be a prime example of the many cases that are being denied without adequate review and then appealed. The backlog of cases awaiting hearings, according to many hearing judges with whom I've been in contact and as evidenced in the many complaints I receive from claimants, could be alleviated if claims were properly developed and reviewed at the initial and reconsideration stages of processing.

Miss F., who is going blind from uncontrollable diabetes and who suffers from other diabetes complications, applied for disability benefits in November of 1974 at which time she signed permission slips for Social Security officials to contact her physicians to obtain information about her condition. Her claim was denied in April of this year (1975) and she immediately requested reconsideration of the claim. She talked with her doctors and they advised her that they had not been contacted by the Social Security Administration at the time she received the first denial. Miss F.'s claim was denied again after reconsideration in May. Interestingly, at the time she was notified of the second denial, one of her doctors had just submitted his report two days before she received the denial notice and the other doctor had not yet submitted his report. In May she requested a hearing on the claim and she has not yet been notified [as of October] of the hearing date.

In this case, it appears to me, if Social Security personnel were not going to contact the physicians as indicated to the claimant when she signed the consent forms at the Social Security office, then she should have been instructed to submit the medical reports herself. At any rate, the obvious problem here is that this claim was never properly developed prior to the issuance of the initial and reconsideration decisions.[114]

This weakness in record preparation is a recurring theme that is especially highlighted in the writing of administrative law judges,[115] who know that the record will have to be properly supplemented or it will surely be overturned on judicial review for lack of substantial evidence to support the administrative determination.

Finally, observers of the Social Security system were very much concerned that, given the existing procedures, the claimants were forced to bear the costs of the weaknesses and inequities of the system since benefits were withheld or terminated pending the outcome of an excessively lengthy administrative process. "Understandably, the Social Security Administration, like all government agencies, has been under heavy pressure to cut costs. Unfortunately, this has happened at the expense of their program beneficiaries."[116] Representative Claude Pepper of Florida put it this way:

In *Goldberg* the Court recognized that: "Termination of aid pending resolution of a controversy over eligibility may deprive an eligible recipient of the very means to live while he waits. Since he lacks independent resources, his situation becomes immediately desperate." These same considerations that the *Goldberg* Court deemed so important in requiring the Government to continue making uninterrupted payments until an evidentiary hearing has been held, are equally compelling in the case of disability applicants and should require that the Government provide an appeals process designed to resolve the claims of the applicants with reasonable promptness.[117]

After describing a particularly maddening case involving one of his constituents, Representative John Heinz III of Pennsylvania said: "Personally, I think that the Social Security Administration has treated Mr. S and his parents with the consideration that one would expect of George Orwell's big brother in his novel *1984*, and the rationality of the investigator in Kafka's *The Trial*. This case would truly make for theater of the absurd."[118] One case recounted by Congressman Sisk presented the problem in stark terms.

One of my constituents, Mr. H., a man terminally ill with cancer, filed his claim for disability benefits in December of 1973, and after having his claim denied at the initial and reconsideration levels, he requested a hearing on July 15, 1974. The claim was not scheduled for a hearing until February 21, 1975, 7 months later, and by that time my constituent was hospitalized for the last time.

The hearing decision reversed the two earlier denials, approving a period of disability for this man back to October of 1973. Unfortunately, however, the claimant died before benefit payments were made to him, and his poor widow suffered further frustration after the benefits which were due her late husband were erroneously issued to her in his name; and a delay of 4 months occurred before the proper payments were issued to the widow. The family had no other financial resources on which to depend during this time.[119]

The Intergovernmental Process

379

*Mathews v.
Eldridge:* The
Anatomy of an
Administrative
Law Case

Given the description of the process for determining disability claims, it should be clear that the fact that both state and federal agencies are continuously interacting both in the administration of the Social Security Disability program and in decisions in specific claims is of major importance. Initially, Congress sought to involve state agencies in such a way that vocational rehabilitation organizations with existing connections with the medical community and an understanding of local needs would be the most effective mechanism for ensuring success of the program.[120] While the *Eldridge* case was en route to the court, that concept was facing substantial criticism from two different perspectives.

On the one hand, experienced state and federal administrators as well as members of Congress were greatly concerned about the inconsistency among various state agencies. An example of the disparity is found in the staff report done in 1975 for the Subcommittee on Social Security of the House Ways and Means Committee.

> The percent of reversals by the State agencies on reconsideration over the years have been relatively stable—between 30 and 40 percent. The variation in rates between State agencies—like that on initial determinations—was quite substantial in calendar 1974, varying from a low of 19.5 percent in Kentucky to 45.9 percent in New Jersey with a national average of 30.5[121]

Marie Clark, supervisor of Disability Determination Services of Cheyenne, Wyoming, described the plight of the claimant in the following graphic terms.

> I think the claims become involved in an incredible administrative ping-pong game when they are filed. They are kicked back and forth between State and Federal Offices until the claimants don't know where to go for help in pursuing their claims.[122]

Second, the intergovernmental significance of the process relates to the problems of administering a highly decentralized system without clear standards.[123] The original idea was to provide a basic insurance manual to the states and to supplement that document with letters until revisions of the basic manual could be prepared and distributed. Additionally, a series of precedents were to be developed that would focus on court decisions and rulings of the Appeals Council. Problems emerged because the precedents that were prepared had to be "sanitized" to ensure privacy for the claimants.[124] That meant that the cases were generalized beyond usefulness as precedents, and the idea soon faded.[125] During hearings in 1975, Congressmen Pickle of Texas and Steiger of Wisconsin questioned a panel of state directors of Disability Determination Services:

> Mr. Pickle: Let me ask you, are the directives which come from the social security offices, regional or national, are they clear and concise, or is there confusion on the kind of Federal instruction that you get?

> Mr. Brown: The most recent one is a very good example of a very confused one. I have not been through it. Some of the staff have, and it is most difficult to decipher.
>   Interestingly enough, we got it the same day that our regional offices in Atlanta did. They had no more advance notice than we did, and the next day we had to implement it.

> Mr. Gaughan: Needless to say, some of us have not implemented it yet.

> Mr. Pickle: Have you understood it yet?

> Mr. Gaughan: No, sir.

Mr. Pickle: Is this average or normal?

Mrs. Clark: Over the years, the instructions from BDI have been very good until the advent of the SSI program. When we got SSI instructions, there was confusion in the whole system due to a number of reasons, and this was reflected in the instructions.

Mr. Pickle: I am primarily talking about the advent of the SSI.

Mrs. Clark: All right. I think that lately we have noticed a strong effort by BDI to upgrade the DISM, to clarify instructions and to bring order, clarity and ease of reference into the manual.

Mr. Steiger: Hold on a minute, Jake! You talk about confusion. What is the "DISM"?

Mrs. Clark: It is the Disability State Insurance Manual.

Mr. Steiger: All right. There also is a BDI, which I assume is the Bureau of Disability Insurance, and there is DIL. What is the DIL?

Mr. Sorenson: Disability Insurance Letter.

Mr. Gaughan: They put it out in letter form until they get the printing completed.

Mr. Steiger: I appreciate that clarification. That is DIL?

Mr. Pickle: I thought that was a pickle. [Laughter]

Mr. Steiger: Did I ever open myself up for that one![126]

The testimony of these and other state officials showed concern over the problems of information flow between their offices and the federal government. Particularly troublesome was the problem of inadequate lead time to implement new policy decisions emanating from the Bureau of Disability Insurance in Baltimore, which has overall federal responsibility for the program. The state officers also pointed out that while much of the discussion of the disability program has centered on the hearing process, approximately 96 percent of disability decisions are made in the state agencies by people who make less money than their federal counterparts and who have inadequate support staffs and training programs.[127]

In summer 1975, the Subcommittee on Social Security of the Ways and Means Committee published its "Staff Survey of State Disability Agencies Under Social Security and SSI Programs."[128] This document provided responses by all the state disability agencies to questions posed by the committee staff relating to the intergovernmental problems involved in the administration of the disability program and the Supplemental Security Income program. The responses reveal general dissatisfaction with communication, coordination, and training activities by the federal offices.[129] Many states called for outright federalization of the programs.[130] Half of the state agencies indicated that the reasons advanced by the Ways and Means Committee in 1954 for dividing the program administration among state and federal agencies no longer existed or were not being realized under the existing organization. Most of the states did, however, have positive comments about the work of the regional Social Security offices.

ELDRIDGE ON THE CONGRESSIONAL AGENDA

The Committee Staff Reports

In April 1974 the Circuit Court of Appeals affirmed Eldridge's victory in the district court; the case would not be heard before the United States Supreme Court until October 1975. In the interim, Congress focused its attention on problems in the Social Security disability program. The forthcoming decision in the *Eldridge* case figured prominently in all its deliberations. The congressional activity took place mainly in the Social Security Subcommittee of the House **381**

*Mathews v.
Eldridge:* The
Anatomy of an
Administrative
Law Case
Ways and Means Committee. Two factors were particularly noteworthy in connection with
the committee's work. First, the subcommittee had a very thorough staff that provided clear
and succinct background data on the particularly significant aspects of this policy problem.
Second, Social Security problems hit home for each member of Congress because a large part
of the case work done by members' staffs is related to chasing down claims for frightened or
unhappy constituents.[131] The subcommittee, in turn, felt the pressure from colleagues from
both houses of Congress and from both sides of the aisle to do something about the problems of
administering the disability program.

Those involved were nearly unanimous in support of the role performed by the Social
Security Disability Program and, in general, by the administrators involved in the program.
Their concern was with improving the system in terms of both equity and cost effectiveness.
The fact that these concepts are in some senses contradictory was a significant factor in the
discussions.

The first signal of forthcoming congressional activity came with the publication in 1974
of the "Committee Report on the Disability Insurance Program," which has become known in
the literature of the field as the "Staff Report." That report highlighted a number of significant
problems in the program, and was reinforced when more than seventy members of Congress
addressed letters to the Subcommittee on Social Security requesting that some action be taken
to deal with the "appeals crisis" in Social Security in particular and with the delays in Social
Security disability proceedings in general.

Social Security Subcommittee Hearings
on the Appeals Crisis

In 1975, plans were made to conduct hearings in the fall before the subcommittee to deal with
the problem of delays and other subjects. Meanwhile, at the Social Security Administration,
Commissioner Caldwell was working to make what improvements he could.[132] He reported his
efforts to the subcommittee staff in July of that year, just as the staff was preparing its important
report, "Background Materials on Social Security Hearings and Appeals." This document
summarized the hearings process, the problems noted earlier in the discussion of the policy·
area, impending significant decisions like the *Eldridge* case, which promised to seriously
challenge the administration of the program, and a summary of data on problems of time delay
and variance in decisionmaking among administrative law judges and state agencies. The
report was prepared for the hearings scheduled in September and October.

Also published in summer 1975 was the "Staff Survey of State Disability Agencies Under
Social Security and SSI Programs." This report highlighted the intergovernmental problems
in the programs.[133]

Hearings were conducted by the subcommittee on September 19, 26, and October 3 and
20, 1975. Those called included several prominent scholars of Social Security law, the head of
administrative law judge activities for the Civil Service Commission, a panel of state
administrators, and a number of members of Congress who recited case after case of damage
they attributed to the delays and inaccurate decisions that they felt harmed their constituents.
The *Eldridge* case popped up in each of these panels and the statements submitted to support the
testimony.

On Friday, October 3, just three days before the case was to be heard in the Supreme
Court, John Rhinelander, former general counsel of HEW, appeared before the subcommittee
along with Donald Gonya, deputy assistant general counsel for the Social Security Division,
and Frank Dell Aqua, head of the Litigation Branch. Rhinelander led the testimony in which
the *Eldridge* case was a focal point. He felt that the case was significant enough to submit into
the hearing record all 140 pages of the briefs filed for the government and Eldridge.

The proceedings of the hearings were published in December while the *Eldridge* case was pending before the Court. The subcommittee also published another important document during December, "Recent Studies Relevant to the Disability Hearings and Appeals Crisis." This report contained the so-called Boyd Report of the Social Security Task Force on the Disability Claims Process, Edwin Yourman's "Report on a Study of Social Security Benefit Hearings, Appeals and Judicial Review," and Professor Victor Rosenblum's study, "The Administrative Law Judge in the Administrative Process: Interrelationships of Case Law with Statutory and Pragmatic Factors in Determining ALJ Roles."[134]

It was within this complex political and administrative context that the *Eldridge* case came to the Supreme Court of the United States.

BEFORE THE BURGER COURT

Preparations for the Judicial Confrontation

Of the thousands of cases brought to the Supreme Court every year, only a few will receive a full oral argument and result in a full signed opinion. Most of the cases that merit such treatment are almost by definition major questions of law and public policy. As such, the policy impact of a decision in this type of case is a matter of concern to the justices. On the other hand, the Court does operate under decision rules that are set by norms of constitutional interpretation, statutory interpretation, and *stare decisis* or common law principles. The *Eldridge* case was presented from two quite different perspectives. The government argued the case primarily—almost exclusively—as a public policy problem set in cost-benefit terms. Counsel for Eldridge argued the case as a constitutional claim based on a specific line of precedents, particularly *Goldberg v. Kelly* and associated rulings.

Mr. Eldridge was very surprised to learn that his case was being appealed by the government to the Supreme Court.

Question: What did you think when you heard that the government was going to appeal your case to the Supreme Court of the United States?

Answer: Well, I thought that by them carrying it that far, that they was really out to try to beat me, because that was the first case that I'd ever heard of them taking to the Supreme Court.

Question: How did you find out about that? Did Mr. Earls call you and tell you "Mr. Eldridge, we're going to have to go to the Supreme Court?" What did you think then?

Answer: Well, I thought that if they was going to spend money to carry it that far, that they were just out to finish it off. That's what I thought.

Question: Did you ever understand why they were taking your case to the Supreme Court?

Answer: No, I didn't understand it. I knowed I couldn't work.

Question: And you've never understood why the government, the Solicitor General, and the Supreme Court were tied up with your case?

Answer: No, I don't guess I ever will.[135]

Despite the fact that Mr. Earls explained the case to him, Eldridge just couldn't understand why this was happening.

Question: All of this time, you felt that they were out to get you for winning—is that it?

Answer: Well, from the way they done me, I never knowed of them doing anybody else that way.

Question: You mean you think because you won somebody got angry at you because you beat them? They just didn't care?

Answer: No, I've always thought that there was somebody in there that was handling my claim that really didn't understand the whole situation, or didn't care or something![136]

When the Supreme Court granted the writ of certiorari, Mr. Earls acquired some unanticipated assistance from attorneys for two different legal aid societies. David Webster from Atlanta Legal Aid Society and an attorney from California Rural Legal Assistance contacted Earls and volunteered their services to do research and help in preparing for the oral argument to come.

The Briefs

Earls and his colleagues were rather surprised by the tack taken by the government in their brief. In fact, he believed that the attorneys for the government had "missed the case."

The brief for the government was fifty-six pages in length with an appendix of sixty-seven pages. Only about five pages of this document were given to the constitutional doctrine of due process.

The statement of facts in the government's brief was somewhat deceptive, for it gave the impression that Eldridge had not really been reasonable and patient in his dealings with the government.

> Respondent, a resident of Virginia, applied for disability benefits under the Social Security Act, which were awarded by the Secretary, acting through the Social Security Administration, effective in June 1968. Respondent was informed that his claim would be reexamined due to the possibility of his medical recovery, and that his benefits would be terminated if the review demonstrated that he was no longer disabled.
> The Virginia state agency scheduled respondent's case for review in 1972 and in March 1972 sent him a questionnaire. The letter requested respondent to complete and return the questionnaire within ten days, and also informed him that if he required assistance or had any questions he could visit or telephone any Social Security office. . . .
> The state agency asked respondent to furnish within ten days any further evidence relating to the reasons it gave or to request further time to obtain such evidence. In response he disputed one characterization of his claim made in the state agency's statement of reasons and stated that the agency already had "enough evidence" in the file upon which to base a decision.
> Upon the basis of this information, the state agency determined that respondent had ceased to be disabled in May of 1972 and forwarded that determination to the Social Security Administration. . . . Social Security notified respondent in writing of this determination and of his right to request reconsideration within six months.
> Respondent did not seek reconsideration. Rather, on August 3, 1972, he filed this complaint in this case.[137]

Conveniently relegated to footnotes were the comments about the battle for the initial benefit decision before the hearing examiner in 1968 and the battle through the process that had lasted from February 1970 through the spring of 1971, less than a year before the immediate decision that led to this suit.

There were essentially four parts to the government's brief. First, it argued that the existing procedures were fair, but Eldridge was just not patient enough to avail himself of the alternatives available.[138] Second, the government asserted that the interests of the government in "avoiding unneeded administrative burdens and costs" outweighed the "worker's interest in continued receipt of disability insurance benefits assessed in light of the reliability of the existing procedures."[139] Third, a point related to the second line of argument, it was suggested that because the statute did not require proof of indigency, disability recipients were not as needy as welfare recipients.[140] Fourth, and this was the core of the argument, the government argued that a pretermination hearing requirement would pose unacceptable administrative and economic burdens on the agency. In short, the government could not afford to provide pretermination hearings.

The government did not get to the discussion of the constitutional point until page 35 of the brief. Several cases were cited for the proposition that procedural due process is a flexible concept. All but one of the cases, it should be noted, had actually resulted in decisions for the aggrieved party demanding a hearing before the adverse action to which they objected.

The only major Social Security disability case cited by the government was *Richardson v. Perales*,[141] used to support the proposition that the medical reports were good evidence of disability and provided sufficient certainty to protect the claimant. *Richardson*, of course, had only been concerned with whether such reports, absent the presence in the hearing room of their authors, could be admitted in a hearing at all since they were clearly of a hearsay character. Again, that case concerned admissibility in a hearing of reports; the Court was not talking about a situation in which the report was considered outside the hearing context and that, after all, was all that Eldridge wanted. On two other occasions he had succeeded against the reports in hearings while the paper review of the record prior to the hearing stage had worked against his claim. It was also what was at the heart of the decision in *Underwood v. Ribicoff*, cited by the district court in *Eldridge* and accepted by the court of appeals.[142] *Underwood* rejected the proposition that there was nothing more involved in a disability determination than an examination of medical reports of physicians.[143] That case was not mentioned at all by the government.

The government brief quickly moved away from the constitutional issue and back to the cost argument. Using figures that the Solicitor General admitted during the oral argument were "a little misleading," the government argued that to require pretermination hearings would result in as many as 11,000 additional hearings at a total cost, given possible wrongful benefit payments, of some 25 million dollars. What it failed to say was that even at that outside estimate the total cost would have been less than one-tenth of one percent of the cost of the entire program on an annual basis.

> Moreover, some beneficiaries who now accept an adverse initial determination would be likely to request a pretermination hearing if the effect would be to prolong the payment of benefits.[144]

The appendix was given over to a continuation of the statistical analysis and copies of the forms and letters used in the termination process.

In sum, except for the comment that the statute did not require that the claimant be destitute by definition, it was the same argument that the government had advanced in *Goldberg v. Kelly* and again in *Richardson v. Wright*.

The brief for respondents was terse by comparison, totaling a mere eleven pages. Eldridge's counsel felt that since it was essentially the same argument that had been rejected in the earlier case and not materially affected by the barrage of statistics, the Court would cut through the bulk and reject the differentiation from *Goldberg* on the merits attempted by the government.[145]

The brief for Eldridge made a brief supplementary comment on the statement of facts presented by the government. The argument was in three parts. First, George Eldridge had been through the administrative process completely twice and was now into his third foray. On each of the earlier occasions he had lost in the paper reviews and had prevailed in the hearing because of the complexity of judging disability under the *Underwood v. Ribicoff* standard. The second round has stretched some eighteen months between the decision that disability had ceased and the judgment by a hearing examiner awarding the benefits. Second, Earls argued that the welfare option was not a viable one because:

Qualification for welfare benefits may require more stringent standards than qualifications for Social Security disability benefits; (2) A welfare recipient may submit his property to a lien for the amount of assistance received; (and) (3) Welfare benefits do not commence spontaneously but rather start after a sometimes lengthy investigation.[146]

Finally, he argued,

> George Eldridge is as much entitled to an opportunity for an evidentiary hearing concerning his termination of disability benefits as: (1) A welfare recipient concerning his welfare check, *Goldberg f. Kelly, supra*; (2) A wage earner concerning his paycheck, *Sniadach v. Family Finance Corp.*, 395 U.S. 337 (1969); (3) A parolee concerning his freedom, *Morrisey v. Brewer*, 408 U.S. 471 (1972); (4) A prison inmate concerning his good time credits, *Wolf v. McDonnell, supra*; (5) A consumer concerning his old stove, *Fuentes v. Shevin*, 407 U.S. 67 (1972); (6) An uninsured motorist concerning his license, *Bell v. Burson*, 402 U.S. 535 (1971); (7) An elderly person concerning his Medicare benefits, *Martinez v. Richardson*, 472 F.2d. 421 (10 Cir. 1973); (8) A student concerning his suspension from school, *Goss. v. Lopez*, 43 L.W. 4181 (1975).[147]

In each of these cases some prior hearing was required.

Strategy and Tactics

Given the existing string of precedents, the support in journals, and the narrow four-to-three decision conflict on the same legal question in *Richardson v. Wright*, what prompted the government to risk what many observers felt would be a major loss in a significant case? There were at least two reasons that an analyst of this case might highlight.

One force compelling the government to fight was fear. Reversal rates were climbing, losses in district courts were increasing, and pressure, both economic and political, seemed to be mounting on all sides. In short, the government fought because there seemed to be no alternative.

But there was a more positive reason to take on the challenge. Since *Goldberg* and *Richardson*, the composition of the Court had changed. By the mid-'70s, the Court had clearly established an identity as the Burger Court. Of the original Warren Court only Justices Brennan, Marshall, and Douglas remained.

Given Justice Douglas's uphill battle to recover from a stroke suffered a year before, it seemed unlikely that he would be able to participate fully in the consideration and decision in *Eldridge*. As it happened, while he was able to be on the bench at the time of the oral argument, Douglas was seriously weakened by his illness and was forced to resign while *Eldridge* was pending.

Chief Justice Burger and Justice Blackmun voted to dismiss in *Richardson v. Wright* along with Justice Stewart and White. Since then, Justices Powell and Rehnquist had joined the Court. There was little doubt that the latter two members would join the Chief Justice and Justice Blackmun on this kind of case.

One of the major themes of the Burger Court had been the Chief Justice's concern for reducing the use of judicial mechanisms for problem resolution.[148] In his speeches he urged the courts to resist the temptation to engage in activities beyond the traditional bounds of courts.[149] He urged reduction in federal court jurisdiction, streamlined administration, and deference to state courts.[150] Fear of increased dockets and judicialization of government were central themes in his comments and opinions.[151]

Finally, by fall 1975 there were signals in at least two major decisions rendered by the Court that its members were about to reverse the direction of doctrinal development in the area of procedural due process in administrative proceedings. In a 1974 decision, *Arnett v. Kennedy*,[152] the Court faced a request by a nonprobationary federal civil servant that he be given a hearing prior to the termination of his employment under *Goldberg, Fuentes*,[153] *Sniadach*,[154] *Bell*,[155] and *Board of Regents v. Roth*.[156] The civil servant had made allegations of corrupt practices in the ill-fated Office of Economic Opportunity. Under existing statutes and regulations, he was given written notice of the reasons for his dismissal and could appear before the person who fired him, in this case the person he had accused of malfeasance. to object to his discharge. After termination, he could ask for an administrative appeal, which would eventually (the average was more than eleven months) result in a later hearing. If he succeeded at that hearing, he could be reinstated with back pay.

Justice Rehnquist wrote the plurality opinion, which was joined by Chief Justice Burger and Justice Stewart. Rehnquist dismissed the precedents advanced, holding that all that was required was that the employee get a chance at some point to clear his name.[157] Rehnquist chose the one major case in the past two decades that gave him the takeoff point he needed. *Cafeteria Workers v. McElroy*.[158] Because this case figured prominently in *Eldridge*, it deserves comment here.

Cafeteria Workers was a 1961 case in which a pretermination hearing was denied to Rachael Brawner. Mrs. Brawner had been employed at a cafeteria on a naval installation. When she arrived for work one morning, she was denied access to the facility for alleged security reasons that were never revealed. She was employed by the concessionaire who operated the cafeteria, but lost her job because she was not permitted access to her place of employment. She demanded a hearing to learn on what grounds she had been marked as a security risk. The Court held:

> What procedural due process may require under any given set of circumstances must begin with a determination of the precise nature of the government function involved as well as the public interest that has been affected by government action.[159]

That decision was written by Justice Stewart. It stood as an exception, an exception justified by the particular defense and national security environment in that case.[160]

Justices Powell and Blackmun concurred in the *Arnett v. Kennedy*, but not on the grounds of *McElroy*. In fact, Justice Powell observed that the plurality opinion was "incompatible with the principles laid down in *Roth* and *Sindermann*" and "misconceives the origin of the right to procedural due process. That right is conferred not by legislative grace but by constitutional guarantee."[161] Nevertheless, Powell and Blackmun concurred on grounds that just when the hearing must be afforded

> depends on a balancing process in which the Government's interest in expeditious removal of an unsatisfactory employee is weighed against the interest of the affected employee. . . .
> [Since the employee] would be reinstated and awarded back pay if he prevails on the merits [any] actual injury would consist of a temporary interruption of his income during the interim. [That] could constitute a serious loss in many cases. But the possible deprivation is considerably less severe than that involved in *Goldberg*.[162]

The dissent, written by Justice Marshall and joined by Justices Douglas and Brennan, was a powerful statement.

> During the period of delay, the employee is off the government payroll. His ability to secure other employment to tide himself over may be significantly hindered by the outstanding charges against him. Even aside from the stigma that attends a dismissal for cause, few employers will be willing to hire and train a new employee knowing that he will return to a former Government position as soon as an appeal is successful. And in many states, including Illinois, where appellee resides, a worker discharged for cause is not even eligible for employment compensation.

Many workers, particularly those at the bottom of the pay scale, will suffer severe and painful economic dislocations from even a temporary loss of wages. Few public employees earn more than enough to pay their expenses from month to month. . . . Like many of us, they may be required to meet substantial fixed costs on a regular basis and lack substantial savings to meet those expenses while not receiving a salary. The loss of income for even a few weeks may well impair their ability to provide the essentials of life to buy food, meet mortgage or rent payments, or procure medical services. . . . The plight of the discharged employee may not be far different from that of the welfare recipient in Goldberg who, "pending resolution of a controversy . . . may [be] deprived . . . of the very means by which he waits." Appellee, although earning an annual salary of $16,000 before his dismissal, far above the mean salary for federal employees, was nonetheless driven to the brink of financial ruin while he waited. He had to borrow money to support his family, his debts went unpaid, his family lost the protection of his health insurance and, finally, he was forced to apply for public assistance. In this context justice delayed may well be justice denied.

To argue that dismissal from tenured Government employment is not a serious enough deprivation to require a prior hearing because the discharged employee may draw on the welfare system in the interim is to exhibit a gross insensitivity to the plight of these employees. First, it assumes that the discharged employee will be eligible for welfare. Often welfare applicants must be all but stripped of their worldly goods before being admitted to the welfare rolls, hence it is likely that the employee will suffer considerable hardship before becoming eligible. . . . He may have to give up his home or cherished personal possessions in order to become eligible. The argument also assumes all but instant eligibility which is, sadly, far from likely even when all the employee's other sources of support have been depleted. [163]

The government received another favorable sign in June 1975 when the Court decided *Weinberger v. Salfi*. [164] The facts were these. Mrs. Salfi married Londo Salfi in May 1972. Approximately a month later, he was hospitalized following a heart attack. He died the following November. She promptly applied for survivors' benefits under the Social Security Act for herself and children's benefits for her daughter by a previous marriage. The Social Security Administration disapproved her claim on the ground that the statute presumes that those married less than nine months prior to the death of the insured wage earner were married for the purpose of taking advantage of Social Security benefits.

Mrs. Salfi sued claiming that such an irrebuttable presumption was a violation of the due process clause in the same sense as the presumption that a father of a child born out of wedlock was an unfit parent, held unconstitutional by the Court in 1972 in *Stanley v. Illinois*, or the assumption of nonresidence for tuition purposes, struck down in 1974 in *Vlandis v. Kline*. What Mrs. Salfi wanted was a hearing to show that since her husband was in good health at the time of their wedding with no history of serious illness, let alone coronary disease, she could not possibly have married him to take advantage of survivors' benefits.

In the opinion written for the Court by Justice Rehnquist, equal protection arguments raised in earlier cases such as *Dandridge v. Williams*, [165] *Fleming v. Nestor*, [166] and *Richardson v. Belcher*[167] were used to say that Congress could make such classifications. It is true that these cases claimed a violation of the due process clause of the Fifth Amendment, but this is a deceptive generalization. Each of these cases claimed discriminatory action in violation of the concept of equal protection. But since there is no equal protection clause in the Fifth Amendment, the Court has frequently said that that amendment includes within its due process clause equal protection guarantees against discrimination by the federal government paralleling those of the Fourteenth Amendment regarding state government actions. [168] In sum, the cases cited by those disagreeing with the government in *Dandridge* etc. objected to unequal treatment and to denial of a hearing. In the irrebuttable presumption cases, all of which had gone against the government in the last decade, it was indeed a claim for a hearing that was at issue.

What was at the heart of Rehnquist's concern did not appear until relatively late in the opinion.

> Large numbers of people are eligible for these programs and are potentially subject to inquiry as to the validity of their relationship to wage earners. . . . Not only does the prophylactic approach thus obviate the necessity for large numbers of individualized determinations, but it also protects large numbers of claimants who satisfy the rule from the uncertainties and delays of administrative inquiry into the circumstances of their marriage. Nor is it at all clear that individual determinations could effectively filter out sham arrangements, since neither marital intent, life expectancy, nor knowledge of terminal illness has been shown by appellees to be reliably determinable.[169]

The Rehnquist opinion also sought to resurrect the right-privilege dichotomy that had been buried years before.[170] He observed:

> We hold that these cases [*Stanley* and *Vlandis*] are not controlling on the issue before us now. Unlike the claims involved in *Stanley* and *LaFleur*, a noncontractual claim to receive funds from the public treasury enjoys no constitutionally protected status.[171]

Justice Brennan rebutted the argument on the merits. Brennan demonstrated that *Stanley*, *LaFleur*, *Vlandis*, and the other irrebuttable presumption cases were exactly on point and could not be differentiated. On the nature of the presumption in *Salfi*, Brennan wrote:

> We have been presented with no evidence at all that the problem of collusive marriages is one which exists at all. Indeed, the very fact that Congress has continually moved back the amount of time required to avoid the rebuttable presumption . . . suggests that it found, for each time period set, that it was depriving people of benefits without alleviating any real problem of collusion. There is no reason to believe that the nine-month period is any more likely to discard any high proportion of collusive marriages than the five-year, three-year, or one-year periods employed earlier.
>
> The Court says: "The Administrative difficulties of individual eligibility determinations are without doubt matters which Congress may consider when determining whether to rely on rules which sweep more broadly than the evils with which they seek to deal." . . . But, as we said in *Stanley v. Illinois, supra*:
>
> "The Constitution recognizes higher values than speed and efficiency."[172]

The changes in Court personnel and the two decisions considered augered well for the government. The signals were not lost on Solicitor General Bork, who was to present the oral argument in the Supreme Court. He would couch much of the language of his argument in *Arnett* and *Salfi* terms and references to judicial administration, efficiency, and increasing caseloads.[173]

Still, no one seemed ready to predict victory for the government in the *Eldridge* case. In fact, implicit in most of the reports and testimony issued in the year before the case was heard was an expectation that the precedents were strong and more likely than not to result in a loss for HEW, particularly in light of the documented injustices to claimants in their battles with the SSA.

There had also been doubts at the time of *Richardson v. Wright* and the government diverted the litigation. The amended regulations obtained a remand for further consideration from the Court. A similar ploy had been attempted by New York in *Goldberg* without success.

In *Eldridge*, a last ditch effort was made to stave off the Supreme Court decision by interposing a jurisdictional question. The decision in *Salfi* had been rendered in late June, but it was not until two days before the oral argument in the Court, October 4, 1975, that Mr. Earls was served with typescript of a supplemental brief by the government. In that brief, the government argued that there was no jurisdiction for the district court to have heard *Eldridge* since the decision was not final. That is, George Eldridge had not taken the case all the way through the administrative process. It was very nearly the same argument that the government had made and lost in *Salfi*. After all, this case did not present a matter of judicial review of an agency decision in a particular case. It was a constitutional claim against the constitutionality of agency regulations. Further, the government had brought the case on appeal and had never before raised any question of the jurisdiction of the federal courts to hear the case. Why now?

There were at least two possibilities, either of which might benefit the government. First, one may ask whether the government hoped that the Court might take the out afforded and once again avoid dealing directly with the constitutional question. Such a jurisdictional decision would blunt the effect of the decision of the lower courts in *Eldridge*. It would also give the government an opportunity to select a case for Supreme Court review that would have facts that were not clearly adverse to the government's case. Second, this tactic, if indeed it was a tactic, permitted attorneys for the government to get *Salfi* into the *Eldridge* litigation even though the legal question involved was not the same. *Salfi* was a very recent decision in which the Court had treated a Social Security claim in a manner quite unlike other recent due process claims for hearing.

Preparation for *Eldridge*'s presentation was quite different from that of the Solicitor General. For Mr. Earls it was "quite a weekend." This would be Earls's first appearance before the Supreme Court of the United States.

Mr. Earls is a native of Norton, Virginia. Educated at the University of Virginia and the Washington and Lee School of Law, he had clerked in a federal district court after law school. He returned to Norton where he married and began practice with a local firm. He had been in practice just long enough to qualify for admission to the Supreme Court bar when the *Eldridge* case arose.

Earls and his colleagues met at Earls's hotel room and worked through the weekend before the argument. Earls hadn't been particularly moved by the fact that Mr. Bork was personally handling the *Eldridge* case and would present the argument. He did take note when his colleagues informed him that Bork did not usually play such a personal role unless the case was a matter of top priority.[174]

Counsel for Eldridge wanted to approach the case in straightforward constitutional due process terms. The oral argument would be in two parts. First, there would be an analysis of the relationship of *Eldridge* to *Goldberg v. Kelly* and associated cases. Second, the facts of the *Eldridge* case would be recounted to illustrate in graphic terms what happens to people who face delays and the physical and monetary costs associated with terminations without hearings. Such an analysis, Earls felt, would clearly demonstrate the correctness of Judge Turk's opinion in the district court. It would also refute the government's contention that harm from a lack of pretermination proceedings is unlikely and, in any case, would probably not impose severe hardship like that of the welfare recipient in *Goldberg*.

It was crucial, from Earls's point of view, that the Court understand Judge Turk's opinion. Turk had clearly delineated the confusing pattern of facts in the *Eldridge* case as the claim and appeals moved through the complex procedures involved in disability determination. Turk had carefully, through consideration of both precedent and policy problems, placed that adjudicatory process as it affected Eldridge into the stream of constitutional doctrine on procedural due process. That melding of substance and process was, for Earls, the crux of the case. The argument before the Court would not, however, work out as planned. It was instead characterized by procedural confusion and conceptual complexity.

The Oral Argument: A Survey and Analysis

The oral argument presented by Mr. Bork continued with the fiction that this case began in 1972. Bork began as follows:

> Here the secretary of HEW terminated the respondent's disability payments in 1972 on the basis of medical reports and the respondent was given a summary of that evidence; (and) given an opportunity to submit additional evidence in a written rebuttal. There were post-termination procedures available to him, including a full evidentiary hearing which I shall describe in a moment, but he brought this suit instead of availing himself of those procedures, claiming a constitutional right to pre-termination oral hearing.[175]

Again, Bork later said: "He was entitled to administrative reconsideration, to an evidentiary hearing and so forth. He availed himself of none of this, but brought suit before the Secretary had made a final decision after a hearing."[176] No mention is made of the fact that Eldridge had gone through the entire process two and one-half times before the case ever got to the courts. The government's effort clearly was to cast the case in terms of judicial review rather than as a constitutional challenge.

As he turned to the merits, Bork used *McElroy* as a takeoff point and then took up the "balance" argument that has become popular to an extreme.

> We are, in effect, dealing with a cost benefit judgment; and so viewed the question becomes really how many? The decision of this case will have a heavy impact upon the decision of how many decisional processes of government must be conformed to a judicial model rather than to an administrative model. I think that is important and clearly there has to be a stopping point somewhere to the imposition of judicial models upon governmental decision-making because it is very expensive; and in some circumstances, which I would contend this is one, adds little or nothing to the alternative procedures provided.

Bork sharpened the point a short time later:

> It would be nice to say, I suppose, that the system must be perfect. Nobody must ever be terminated no matter how temporarily, but indeed I don't think any legal process, any chemical process or any industrial process ever can afford to remove the last bit of impurities in that process. It gets extraordinarily expensive. Indeed, it begins to defeat the ends of the process. *I can put an approximate dollar value on both sides of this due process equation.* (Emphasis added.)

He then equated what would be paid out in eventually denied claims and the costs of the program with the interest at 8 percent on claims withheld from rightful claimants for a year on the claim. The total figure that he computed for increased government costs of an adverse decision in the case was $25,000,000, which is less than one-tenth of one percent of the program expenditures per year.[177] Bork neglected to inform the Court that, unlike the case of welfare recipients, the Secretary can recover from wrongful payments and there is no such thing as being judgment proof in such a proceeding because the common practice is to wait until the claimant applies for any other Social Security benefits, including old age benefits, and then subtract a base 25 percent per month until the wrongful payment is recouped. His cost-benefit calculus also neglected the fact that the standard attorney fee for a disability benefit case is 25 percent of the back payments.

The government used figures not given by SSA in any of the hearings nor found by the studies conducted by independent researchers or by the staff of the Social Security subcommittee of the House Ways and Means Committee during their continuing efforts to deal with the problems of the program. Beyond that, as the briefs showed, welfare is not available to many disability claimants.

Speaking for Eldridge, Earls asked where the figure was that accounted for the loss of

Eldridge's house during the last delay, the nights his children went hungry, and the pain suffered because he couldn't give his dying wife food she requested? Earls contended that Bork's argument was an abstraction based on little or no case law, an apocryphal cost-benefit analysis, and a studied ignorance of the full record and lower court ruling in the case.

391

Mathews v.
Eldridge: The
Anatomy of an
Administrative
Law Case

The success of the government's diversionary tactic was immediately apparent as Earls began his oral argument. Earls managed to get out just two sentences before the questions started. Justice Rehnquist, author of the *Salfi* opinion, immediately attempted to cast the case as one involving only judicial review. In addition, he accepted the fact pattern as presented by the government and asked a stream of questions about finality and the assertion that Eldridge didn't take advantage of procedures available to him. Finally, he was joined by Justice White. They asked:

What is your case or controversy? Have they terminated you or not?

Mr. Earls: The Secretary did terminate Mr. Edlridge's benefits. The district court reinstated his benefits until such time as he was afforded an evidentiary hearing.

Justice White: The government challenged the district court order. The Secretary terminated you, right? The district court reinstated you, right?

Mr. Earls: That's correct.

Justice White: Now the government is challenging the district court order reinstating those benefits?

Mr. Earls: Challenging the district court order and the Fourth Circuit Court of Appeals order upholding the district court.

Justice White: You never exhausted your administrative remedies.

Mr. Earls: Your honor, what we're . . .

Justice White: Well, did you? You did not exhaust them. And you might have won.

Mr. Earls: That is the government's argument, Mr. Justice White. Our contention is this, that by benefits being terminated prior to being afforded an evidentiary hearing, we were denied due process. We went twice, Mr. Eldridge, factually speaking, went twice through an administrative hearing.

That was one of the few lengthy passages that Earls managed until the end of his argument. From this point on it appeared that either the government had successfully cast the case as one in which Eldridge just gave up too soon or they had not fully read and understood Judge Turk's decision. Earls and his colleagues saw at once what was happening. So did Justice Brennan.

Brennan attempted to lead Earls step by step out of the procedural quagmire, but by then it was too late. Time was passing rapidly and there was to be another tangential line of discussion before Earls could get back to the constitutional argument that he had planned to make.

As soon as Justice Brennan had assisted Earls in straightening out the fact pattern of the case, Justices White and Rehnquist began asking questions about the procedural adequacy of the evidentiary hearing, such as whether Earls was satisfied with the subpoena and cross-examination provisions of the regulations. Earls tried to indicate that all he wanted was to move the existing hearing up to pretermination and not to change or expand the provisions of the hearing itself.[178]

He did respond briefly to the cold medical record argument made by Bork. The idea was to suggest that the medical records were enough. That view had been rejected in Judge Turk's opinion, but Bork had carefully avoided any reference to that decision. Earls saw an opportunity and interjected:

Your honor, in the case of *Underwood v Ribicoff*, the Fourth Circuit held that the main element in determining benefits is not only the objective cold medical record as the Secretary says. They said that subjective evidence such as the claimant's appearance before an administrative law judge, and the testimony of the claimant, his wife and neighbors as to his ability to work and in many of these cases, and George Eldridge is a good example, you can look at him and tell he is disabled.

Earls was trying to indicate the significance of the fact that he had three times been denied benefits during paper reviews but had won twice at hearings.

Earls tried to return to his argument that the hypothetical advanced by the government that a claimant would not suffer because of the benefits was wrong. At least it was certainly wrong with respect to Eldridge.

The Secretary's figures point out that 90 percent of the total [Social Security] benefit population earn nothing, so I would say that as opposed to *Goldberg v. Kelly* and need, they are indistinguishable. I feel in the George Eldridge case, where Mr. Eldridge was required to sleep in one bed with five children, lost his home that he had worked all his life for, as a laborer on the railroad and then as a soda distributor, driving a truck and carrying cases of soda: there cetainly he lost everything which could not be recouped. . . . This is what happened in the George Eldridge case, and this is what happens in many of the cases.[179]

As Earls and his colleagues walked the length of the great marble hall from the courtroom and down the front staircase into the afternoon, everyone knew what had happened. The alignment on the Court seemed clear. The government had framed the case as it had wished and successfully diverted the argument from a constitutional matter to a narrow procedural discussion.

"A DOLLAR VALUE ON BOTH SIDES OF THIS DUE PROCESS EQUATION": THE GOVERNMENT'S BALANCING FORMULA SUCCEEDS

The government succeeded beyond its most optimistic expectations. The opinion of the Court was to be little more than an amalgamation of the government's brief, its argument, and the Court's language from *Arnett v. Kennedy* and *Salfi*. Perhaps more significant was the fact that the government had managed to get a clear mandate for a straight balance between administrative efficiency and due process requirements, something that was unprecedented except for *Cafeteria Workers v. McElroy*, which was a special case involving defense and security claims.

Justice Powell's Balancing Test

The alignment of the Court was predictable. Powell wrote for Burger, White, Blackmun, and Rehnquist. Brennan wrote for himself and Justice Marshall. By this time, February 1976, Justice Douglas had retired and had been replaced by Justice John Paul Stevens who, of course, did not take part in *Eldridge*.

Justice Powell accepted the facts as stated by the government.[180] The only facts noted were that Eldridge was placed on benefits in 1968 and when, in 1972, he was declared ineligible he ignored his administrative alternatives and ran directly to the district court.[181] Not so much as a footnote indicates that he had been through the entire process two and a half times. Nor was there any indication of the fact that he had lost in paper proceedings and had won on each opportunity for a hearing. Neither was there any reference to the loss of his house, his car, or his furniture. The name Smith could have been substituted for Eldridge without changing a thing. The government had presented the case as an abstract policy issue and that is how the Court treated it. Justice Powell disposed of Judge Turk's complex decision in one paragraph.[182] The government did not win its jurisdiction argument on *Salfi*, but then, from a tactical point of view, winning on the issue was quite insignificant.

On the merit's, Powell developed a balancing test by reading *Goldberg* as though it had set forth a simple balance test.

More precisely, our prior decisions indicate that identification of the specific dictates of due process generally requires consideration of three distinct factors; first, the private interest that will be affected by the official action; second, the risk of an erroneous deprivation of such interest through the procedures used, and the probable value, if any, of additional or substitute procedural safeguards; and finally, the government's interest, including the function involved and the fiscal and administrative burdens that the additional or substitute procedural requirement would entail.

But when Justice Brennan, who wrote the *Goldberg* opinion, discussed the fact that due process must not be inflexible, he clearly did not imply that a straight balance test was at issue. To the degree that he was concerned with examining the burdens on government, he was adamant in rejecting simple dollar calculations and on including what appear to be intangibles.

Moreover, important governmental interests are promoted by affording recipients a pre-termination evidentiary hearing. From its foundation the Nation's basic commitment has been to foster the dignity and well-being of all persons within its borders. We have come to recognize that forces not within the control of the poor contribute to their poverty. This perception, against the background of our traditions, has significantly influenced the development of the contemporary public assistance system. Welfare, by meeting the basic demands of subsistence, can help bring within the reach of the poor the same opportunities that are available to others to participate meaningfully in the life of the community. At the same time, welfare guards against the societal malaise that may flow from a widespread sense of injustified frustration and insecurity. Public assistance, then, is not mere charity, but a "means to promote the general Welfare, and to secure the Blessings of Liberty to ourselves and our Posterity." The same governmental interests that counsel the provision to those eligible to receive it; pretermination evidentiary hearings are indispensable to that end.

Appellant does not challenge the force of these considerations but argues that they are outweighed by countervailing governmental interests in conserving fiscal and administrative resources. These interests, the argument goes, justify the delay of any evidentiary hearing until after discontinuance of grants. Summary adjudication protects the public fisc by stopping payments promptly upon discovery of reason to believe that a recipient is no longer eligible. Since most terminations are accepted without challenge, summary adjudication also conserves both the fisc and administrative time and energy by reducing the number of evidentiary hearings held. We agree with the District Court, however, that these governmental interests are not overriding in the welfare context. The requirement of a prior hearing doubtless involves some greater expense, and the benefits paid to ineligible recipients pending decision at the hearing probably cannot be recouped [unlike Social Security], since these recipients are likely to be judgment-proof. But the State is not without weapons to minimize these costs.

Justice Powell applied his balance test to Social Security disability benefits. Following the lead of the government's argument, Justice Powell reasoned from the premise that the statute does not require a demonstration of financial need to the conclusion that disability claimants are not needy, though he referred to no supporting data. He concluded:

In view of the torpidity of this administrative review process, . . . and the typically modest resources of the family unit of the physically disabled worker, the hardship imposed on the erroneously terminated disability recipient may be significant. Still, the disabled worker's need is likely to less than that of a welfare recipient. In addition to the possibility of access to private resources, other forms of government assistance will become available where the termination of disability benefits places a worker or his family at or below the subsistence level.[183]

The only evidence in this case on the matter is to the contrary.

Powell then turned to the question of the quality of adjudication. Again, he adopted the government's theoretical position that it is probably relatively easy to prove disability from medical reports, hence hearings are not especially necessary. That doesn't address the fact that hearings result in reversal in more than 50 percent of the cases brought on appeal, or that Eldridge had won twice in hearings but had lost three times in paper reviews. Nor does it come to grips with the problems noted in the congressional hearings of claimants whose claims were rejected even before medical records were obtained.

Powell's acceptance of the government theory is all the more surprising in light of the fact that two law review articles were cited in the record, one in the brief in the Supreme Court and the other by Judge Turk in his opinion, which demonstrate conclusively why medical reports alone, as a cold paper record, so frequently result in incorrect or unjust decisions.[184] In particular, Turk referred to the Haviland and Glomb study, which focused on Appalachia and demonstrated empirically just why people like Eldridge have a particularly difficult time winning a paper review but do much better in hearings. Also ignored was the controlling law on proof of disability, *Underwood vc. Ribicoff*, cited both in Supreme Court and in the lower court briefs.

Finally, Powell arrived at the crux of his argument, the question of cost and administrative burden.

In striking the appropriate due process balance the final factor to be assessed is the public interest. This includes the administrative burden and other societal costs that would be associated with requiring, as a matter of constitutional right, an evidentiary hearing upon demand in all cases prior to the termination of disability benefits. The most visible burden would be the incremental cost resulting from the increased number of hearings and the expense of providing benefits to ineligible recipients pending decision. No one can predict the extent of the increase, but the fact that full benefits would continue until after such hearings would assure the exhaustion in most cases of this attractive option. Nor would the theoretical right of the Secretary to recover undeserved benefits result, as a practical matter, in any substantial offset to the added outlay of public funds. The parties submit widely varying estimates of the probable additional financial cost. We only need say that experience with the constitutionalizing of government procedures suggests that the ultimate additional cost in terms of money and administrative burden would not be insubstantial.[185]

However, as mentioned earlier, the ability of the Secretary to recover is very real, since the government need not sue for back payments. The agency is authorized to withhold overpayment from future benefits and does so at the rate of approximately 25 percent per month until the bill is paid. After his initial discussion on costs versus benefits, Justice Powell drops, almost in passing, his comment about constitutionalizing government. His comment presumes that everyone knows and agrees that "constitutionalizing of government procedures" is bad. Students of constitutional law would respond that this government's actions are legitimate because they are "constitutionalized."

Justice Powell then continued with his assessment of costs.

Financial cost alone is not a controlling weight in determining whether due process requires a particular procedural safeguard prior to some administrative decisions. But the Government's interest, and hence that of the public, in conserving scarce fiscal and administrative resources, is a factor that must be weighed. At some point the benefit of an additional safeguard to the individual affected by the administrative action and to society in terms of increased assurance that the action is just, may be outweighed by the cost. . . .

But more is implicated in cases of this type than ad hoc weighing of fiscal and administrative burdens against the interests of a particular category of claimants. The ultimate balance involves a determination as to when, under our constitutional system, judicial-type procedures must be imposed upon administrative action to assure fairness. . . . In assessing what process is due in this case, substantial weight must be given to the good-faith judgments of the individuals charged by Congress with the administration of the social welfare system that the procedures they have provided assure fair consideration of the entitlement claims of individuals.[186]

395
*Mathews v.
Eldridge:* The
Anatomy of an
Administrative
Law Case

The majority opinion, for obvious reasons, does not in any way refer to the proposition advanced by the lower court or to the precedents called forth in the previous *Eldridge* decision that the Bill of Rights was added to the Constitution precisely because the citizenry and a number of the framers of that document were not prepared to yield to the "good-faith judgments"[187] of any government officials.

Dissenters Fear Debased Constitutional Currency

Justice Brennan's brief dissent expresses the utter disdain that, as the author of the decision in *Goldberg v. Kelly,* he felt in examining this opinion. He was joined by Justice Marshall. There is no doubt that they would have been joined by Justice Douglas had he remained with the Court. Brennan's dissent had two parts. First, he responded to the merits of the *Eldridge* case itself and manner in which the Court dealt with it.

> I would add that the Court's consideration that a discontinuance of disability benefits may cause the recipient to suffer only a limited deprivation is no argument. It is speculative. Moreover, the very legislative determination of need in fact, presumes a need by the recipient which is not this Court's to denigrate. Indeed, in the present case, it is indicated that because disability benefits were terminated there was a foreclosure upon the Eldridge home and the family's furniture was repossessed, forcing Eldridge, his wife and children to sleep in one bed. . . . Finally, it is no argument that a worker who has been placed in the untenable position of having been denied disability benefits, may still seek other forms of public assistance.[188]

(Brennan's comment was inaccurate with regard to Eldridge's wife, who had died of cancer shortly before he lost the house.) Second, Brennan referred to his dissenting opinion in *Richardson v. Wright* for comments on the precedents and discussion of specific policy matters relevant to Social Security disability claims in general. Dissenting in *Richardson,* Brennan had argued as follows:

> The Secretary does not contend that disability beneficiaries differ from welfare and old-age recipients with respect to their entitlements to benefits or the drastic consequences that may behall them if their benefits are erroneously discontinued.[189]

Of course, the government changed its position on whether the disability claimant faced the same degree of harm when it presented its arguments in *Eldridge.* Brennan continued:

> The only distinctions urged are that the evidence ordinarily adduced to support suspension and termination of disability benefits differs markedly from that relied upon to cut off welfare benefits and that an undue monetary and administrative burden would result if prior hearings were required. Neither distinction withstands analysis. . . . Hence, the Secretary concludes, while procedural due process requires a pretermination evidentiary hearing for welfare and old age recipients, for disability beneficiaries a written presentation will suffice.
> The Secretary seriously misconstrues the holding in *Goldberg.* The Court there said that "the pretermination hearing has one function only: to produce an initial determination of the validity of the welfare department's grounds for discontinuance of payments in order to protect a recipient against an erroneous termination of his benefits." . . . The Secretary does not deny that due process

safeguards fulfill the same function in disability cases. In *Goldberg*, the Court held that welfare recipients were entitled to hearings because decisions to discontinue benefits were challenged "as resting on incorrect or misleading factual premises or on misapplication of rules or policies to the facts of particular cases." Id., at 268 the Court expressly put aside consideration of situations "where there are no factual issues in dispute or where the application of the rule of law is not intertwined with factual issues." However reliable the evidence upon which a disability determination is normally based, and however rarely it involves questions of credibility and veracity, it is plain that, as with welfare and old-age determinations, the determination that an individual is or is not "disabled" will frequently depend upon the resolution of factual issues and the application of legal rules to the facts found. It is precisely for that reason that a hearing must be held.[190]

Brennan was particularly upset by the attempt to narrow the language of *Goldberg* to make issues of credibility and veracity the touchstone of pretermination hearings.

[The Secretary] first quotes the statement that "particularly where credibility and veracity are at issue, as they must be in many termination proceedings, written submissions are a wholly unsatisfactory basis for decisions." . . . Apart from the obvious fact that that was not an absolute statement intended to limit hearings solely to those instances, it was but one of three reasons given to demonstrate that written submissions are insufficient. The Court also said that written submissions "are an unrealistic option for most recipients, who lack the educational attainment necessary to write effectively and who cannot obtain professional assistance" and that they "do not afford the flexibility of oral presentations; they do not permit the recipient to mold his argument to the issues the decision maker appears to regard as important." Significantly, the Secretary does not deny that those reasons are as fully applicable to disability beneficiaries as to welfare recipients.[191]

Brennan then turned to a recitation of the specific regulations involved in disability termination and a consideration of how each fits in the hearing debate.

Brennan did not accept the cost argument. He concluded the *Richardson* dissent on that note.

I do not deny that prior hearings will entail some additional administrative burdens and expense. Administrative fairness usually does. Despite the Secretary's protestations to the contrary, I believe that in the disability, as in the welfare, area "much of the drain on fiscal and administrative resources can be reduced by developing procedures for prompt pretermination hearings and by skillful use of personnel and facilities." . . . The Court's conclusion on this point in *Goldberg* is fully applicable here:

". . . Thus the interest of the eligible recipient in uninterrupted receipt of public assistance, coupled with the State's interest that his payments not be erroneously terminated, clearly outweighs the State's competing concern to prevent any increase in its fiscal and administrative burdens."[192]

THE COURT HAD SPOKEN

George Eldridge Responds

The decision of the Court in the *Eldridge* case was significant for several reasons. For administrators, the opinion signalled a major shift in how much process is due and just what agencies will be expected to provide. To legal scholars, the decision set forth the new controlling law on the test for procedural due process,[193] which would be broadly applied to processes as diverse as commitment of juveniles to mental health facilities and removal of drivers' licenses. Some of the concerns about this doctrinal development will be recounted shortly. But Eldridge and his counsel had not thought of the case in policy terms. For them, the question was what was to happen to Eldridge and his family.

Earls called Eldridge as soon as the decision was announced to give him the news. Eldridge couldn't understand how it had happened, but his more immediate concern was how to deal with his impending loss of disability benefits—again. After all, the Supreme Court decision overturning Judge Turk and the Fourth Circuit meant that the *Eldridge* case was back to where it had been in July 1973. His benefits had been terminated.

Eldridge requested reconsideration by the Virginia office. He didn't receive a response until October 1977, approximately eighteen months after the Supreme Court decision. Earls promptly requested another hearing for Eldridge. In March 1978, two full years after the decision against him in the Supreme Court and ten years after his initial victory in his first hearing, Eldridge was found by an administrative law judge, the third such judge, to be eligible for benefits. It is reported that when the record arrived for consideration by the administrative law judge, it was delivered in two cartons. [194]

Eldridge still doesn't understand what happened. He does feel strongly that the off-and-on status with continuing controversy has harmed him irreparably. He is tired of asking the local Social Security official to call the local power company to ask them not to turn off the electricity while administrative decisions come and go.

> I think somebody is responsible for the things I've lost. They're responsible for making my health worse. They're responsible for the hardships that they've caused me and my children.
>
> I don't want to lay up no big treasures in this world. But if I get disabled to work and they've got a program to take care of me, then I want it. I don't want to beat around no bush about it after paying into it when I was able to work.
>
> All I want out of life is something to eat, wear and a place to stay. Well, hell, they won't let you have a place to stay. [195]

It is insecurity as to his dwelling that particularly upsets George Eldridge.

> When it boils down to where, after a man working hard all of his life that he's able to work, they won't let him have a home to live in by stopping his money and causing his little kids to go to the table and find nothing on it, well . . . [196]

Eldridge's unending problem was that he would take money from his back payments to attempt to start anew, but would soon find himself pressed again. Back payments less fees never were quite what they were expected to be. That is how he lost his home, his mobile home, and other items.

> I've lost a lot of money. In fact, the money what they've given me, two thirds of it has been lost trying to have a home. Just trying to have a home. [197]

For George Eldridge this case continues since his claim can be reevaluated in the future. Given his past experiences, that is not a comforting prospect.

Scholarly Criticisms of the Simplistic Balancing Test

Several law reviews noted the delivery of the *Eldridge* decision[198] although the full significance of the balancing test set forth in Justice Powell's opinion has only recently come to light. [199] In an early critique of the decision, Jerry Mashaw[200] concluded:

> The *Eldridge* approach is unsatisfactory both as employed in that case and as a general formulation of due process review of administrative procedures. The failing of *Eldridge* is its focus on technique rather than questions of value. That focus, it is argued, generates an inquiry that is incomplete because unresponsive to the full range of concerns embodied in the due process clause. [201]

The decision was not justified by precedent. It was not an example of judicial self-restraint, but was instead judicial activism in a conservative political and economic direction. The opinion in *Eldridge,* particularly when it is considered in light of the rationale of *Weinberger v. Salfi*[202] and *Arnett v. Kennedy,*[203] moves due process doctrine backward toward a reemergence of the right-privilege dichotomy, which most commentators had thought died more than a decade earlier.[204]

It is no argument to maintain that some kind of hearing at some point is due process of law. Where citizens suffer significant injury at the hands of government officials, such as was endured by George Eldridge, and repeated studies indicate that his is not an unusual set of circumstances, justice delayed is in a very real and tangible way justice denied.

SUMMARY

An examination of Eldridge's journey through the Social Security disability process is a lesson in the anatomy of an administrative law case. It demonstrates the complexity of due process of law in theory and practice. His case illustrates the interaction of state and federal agencies in social service claims as well as the relationship between those agencies and the federal courts.

Cases like *Eldridge* do not arise and are not resolved in a policy vacuum. The process of policymaking is ongoing. In the case of social service programs, there are constant tensions between administrative problems and judicial values. These programs continually present the dilemma of administering a massive program efficiently while simultaneously demonstrating a concern for individual problems and peculiar circumstances.

The manner in which the Supreme Court dealt with the case is illustrative of the significance of judicial policymaking. It demonstrates the significance of personnel changes on the Court. When the judicial process is considered from the vantagepoint of the administrator with an eye toward a particular policy area, one can see the relationship of law to the process of policy implementation. The decision in *Eldridge* highlights the relationship, whether properly or improperly evaluated, between policy and precedent in Supreme Court decisionmaking.

One of the goals of this piece has been to view a complex administrative problem from a number of relevant perspectives, emphasizing the view of the claimant, who is the ultimate consumer of the decisions that issue from the administrative justice system. It is important that the claimant's feelings and concerns be understood. One is reminded of Justice Douglas's comments in dissent in another Social Security disability case.

> This case is minuscule in relation to the staggering problems of the Nation. But when a grave injustice is wreaked on an individual by the presently powerful federal and state bureaucracy, it is a matter of concern to everyone, for these days the average man can say "There but for the grace of God go I."[205]

NOTES

[1]*Mathews v. Eldridge,* 424 U.S. 319 (1976).

[2]Interview with Mr. George Eldridge by the author in Norton, Virginia, August 27, 1979.

[3]Id.

[4]5 C.F.R. §930.203a (1980).

[5]A copy of the form letter is shown in Brief for Petitioner, *Mathews v. Eldridge,* p. 32a.

[6]See.generally Fred Davis and James Reynolds, "Profile of a Social Security Disability," 42 *Missouri L. Rev.* 541 (1977). There continue to be changes in regulations but most of the procedures remain roughly like those that existed during the ten-year period covered by this study.

[7]U.S. House of Representatives Subcommittee on Social Security of the Committee on Ways and Means, *Background Materials on Social Security Hearings and Appeals,* 94th Cong., 1st Sess. (1975), p. 2.

[8]Davis and Reynolds, supra note 6, at p. 548.

9Jerome Smith, "Social Security Appeals in Disability Cases," 28 *Admin. L. Rev.* 13, 14 (1976). See also Jerry L. Mashaw et al., *Social Security Hearings and Appeals: A Study of the Social Security Administrative Hearing System* (Lexington, Mass.: Heath, 1978), pp. 66–69.

10Davis and Reynolds, supra note 6, at p. 543.

11See generally Mashaw et al., supra note 9, chap. 5.

12*Simon v. Eastern Kentucky Welfare Rights Organization,* 426 U.S. 26 (1976). See also *Warth v. Seldin,* 422 U.S. 490 (1975).

13*DeFunis v. Odegaard,* 416 U.S. 312 (1974).

14Brief for Petitioner, supra note 5, p. 32A.

15Id., at 7 n. 5.

16He was seen at one point in this process, but not physically examined, by a consulting psychiatrist.

17Reproduced in Jerry L. Mashaw, "The Supreme Court's Due Process Calculus for Administrative Adjudication in *Mathews v. Eldridge*: Three Factors in Search of a Theory of Value," 44 *U. Chicago L. Rev.* 28, 35 (1976).

18The substantial evidence rule, though it is a fairly complex rule in particular cases, is based on the relatively simple notion that since the administrator is considered to be expert, there should be no major burden of proof in administrative cases. Instead, the administrator must have relied on some evidence and not have merely acted arbitrarily.

19See, e.g., *Richardson v. Perales,* 402 U.S. 389 (1971).

20See *Rooke's Case,* 5 Co. Rep. 996, 77 Eng. Rep. 209 (1599).

21*Yick Wo v. Hopkins,* 118 U.S. 356, 359–60 (1886).

22See generally John Dickinson, *Administrative Justice and the Supremacy of Law in the United States* (New York: Russell & Russell, 1927).

23Id., at pp. 35–36.

24Walter Gellhorn, *Federal Administrative Proceedings* (Baltimore: Johns Hopkins Press, 1941) and James M. Landis, *The Administrative Process* (New Haven, Conn.: Yale University Press, 1938).

25U.S. Senate, Report of the Attorney General's Committee on Administrative Procedure, *Administrative Procedure in Government Agencies,* Sen. Doc. no. 8, 77th Cong., 1st Sess. (1941).

26Albert H. Meyerhoff and Jeffrey A. Mishkin, "Application of *Goldberg v. Kelly* Hearing Requirements to Termination of Social Security Benefits," 26 *Stanford L. Rev.* 549, 549–50 (1974).

27See, e.g., William W. Van Alstyne, "The Demise of the Right-Privilege Distinction in Constitutional Law," 81 *Harvard L. Rev.* 1439 (1968).

28*Sherbert v. Verner,* 374 U.S. 398, 404–5 (1963).

29J. Skelly Wright, "Poverty, Minorities, and Respect for Law," 1970 *Duke L. J.* 425 (1970). See also Charles Reich, "The New Property," 78 *Yale L. J.* 733 (1964).

30*Londoner v. Denver,* 210 U.S. 373 (1908).

31*Grannis v. Ordean,* 234 U.S. 385, 394 (1913); *Dent v. West Virginia,* 129 U.S. 114, 124–25 (1889); and *Armstrong v. Manzo,* 380 U.S. 545, 552 (1965).

32*Morgan v. United States,* 304 U.S. 1, 14–15 (1938).

33*Joint Anti-Fascist Refugee Committee v. McGrath,* 341 U.S. 123, 168 (1951).

34*McGrath,* id. *Greene v. McElroy,* 360 U.S. 474 (1959).

35*Wieman v. Updegraff,* 344 U.S. 183 (1952).

36*Sherbert v. Verner,* supra note 28.

37*Sniadach v. Family Finance Corp.,* 395 U.S. 337 (1969).

38*Goldberg v. Kelly,* 397 U.S. 254 (1970).

39Id., at 261–62.

40Id., at 262 n. 8.

41Id., at 262.

42Id., at 264.

43Id., at 266.

44*Wheeler v. Montgomery,* 397 U.S. 280 (1970).

45Id., at 281–82.

46*Morrissey v. Brewer,* 408 U.S. 471 (1972).

47*Gagnon v. Scarpelli,* 411 U.S. 778 (1973).

48*Wolff v. McDonnel,* 418 U.S. 539 (1974).

49*Bell v. Burson,* 402 U.S. 535 (1971).

50*Vlandis v. Kline,* 412 U.S. 441 (1973).

51*Goss v. Lopez,* 419 U.S. 565 (1975).

52*Fuentes v. Shevin,* 407 U.S. 67 (1972). See also *Mitchell v. W.T. Grant,* 416 U.S. 600 (1974) and *North Georgia Finishing v. Di-Chem,* 419 U.S. 601 (1975).

53*Caulder v. Durham,* 433 F. 2d 998 (4th Cir., 1970), certiorari denied 401 U.S. 1003 (1971). See also *Escalera v. New York City Housing Authority,* 425 F. 2d 853 (2d Cir. 1970), certiorari denied 400 U.S. 853 (1970).

54See, e.g., *Messer v. Finch,* 314 F. Supp. 511 (E.D. Ky 1970), and *Wright v. Finch,* 321 F. Supp. 383 (D. D.C. 1971).

55*Richardson v. Wright,* 405 U.S. 208 (1972).

56Id., at 212.

57*Eldridge v. Weinberger,* 361 F. Supp. 520 (W.D. Va. 1973).

58James M. Haviland and Michael B. Glomb, "The Disability Insurance Benefits Program and Low Income Claimants in Appalachia," 73 *West Virginia L. Rev.* 109 (1971).

59Until relatively recently there were few judges hearing Social Security disability cases in the mining areas of Virginia.

60See Gerald Hayes, "Profile of a Social Security Disability and the Administrative Law Judge," 1975 *Air Force L. Rev.* 73 (1975). See also Smith, supra note 9, and Davis and Reynolds, supra note 6.

61Haviland and Glomb, supra note 58, at pp. 113–14.

62Davis and Reynolds, supra note 6, at p. 542.

63Hayes, supra note 60, at p. 75.

64Haviland and Glomb, supra note 58, at pp. 115–16.

65Id., at pp. 126–27.

66Id., at p. 128.

67Mashaw et al., supra note 9, at pp. 50–51.

[69]*Eldridge v. Weinberger*, supra note 57.

[70]Id., at 525–26.

[71]*Wright v. Richardson*, 405 U.S. 208 (1972).

[72]Id., at 209–27.

[73]*Eldridge v. Weinberger*, supra note 57.

[74]Id.

[75]Id.

[76]*Sniadach v. Family Finance Corp.*, supra note 37.

[77]*Bell v. Burson*, 402 U.S. 535 (1971).

[78]*Fuentes v. Shevin*, 407 U.S. 67 (1972).

[79]*Eldridge v. Weinberger*, supra note 57, at 524.

[80]Id.

[81]Id., at 524–24.

[82]Id., at 525.

[83]Id., at 525–26.

[84]Id., at 526.

[85]Id., at 527.

[86]See generally Robert G. Dixon, *Social Security Disability and Mass Justice: A Problem in Welfare Adjudication* (New York: Praeger, 1973).

[87]This debate over the insurance or social welfare base for the disability program will remain a significant dispute for the foreseeable future.

[88]See generally Dixon, supra note 86.

[89]Such investigations as U.S. House of Representatives, Hearings Before the Subcommittee on Social Security of the Committee on Ways and Means, *Delays in Social Security Appeals*, 94th Cong., 1st Sess. (1975) contain a great deal of criticism, but they also acknowledge SSA efforts to improve performance.

[90]See, e.g., Mashaw et al., supra note 9. See also "Report of the Disability Claims Process Task Force"; Edwin Yourman, "Report on a Study of Social Security Benefit Hearings"; and Victor G. Rosenblum, "The Administrative Law Judge in the Administrative Process," all in U.S., House of Representatives, Subcommittee on Social Security of the House Ways and Means Committee, *Recent Studies Relevant to the Disability Hearings and Appeals Crisis*, 94th Cong., 1st Sess. (1975).

[91]For a presentation of reversal rates, see *Background Materials*, supra note 7, at p. 25.

[92]Mashaw et al., supra note 9, at pp. 1–2.

[93]*Background Materials*, supra note 7, at p. 28.

[94]Id., at p. 21.

[95]Id., at p. 23.

[96]Mashaw et al., supra note 9, at p. 24.

[97]See generally Haviland and Glomb, supra note 58.

[98]*Background Materials*, supra note 7, at p. 13.

[99]Id.

[100]Id.

[101]Id.

[102]Id.

[103]See the statement of John B. Rhinelander, in *Delays in Social Security Appeals*, supra note 89, at p. 267 et seq.

[104]See generally *Delays in Social Security Appeals*, supra note 89.

[105]See, e.g., Meyerhoff and Mishkin, supra note 26.

[106]Mashaw et al., supra note 9, at pp. 46–64.

[107]Id., at p. 30.

[108]*Background Materials*, supra note 7, at p. 10.

[109]Transcript of oral argument in *Mathews v. Eldridge*, p. 10.

[110]Meyerhoff and Mishkin, supra note 26.

[111]Henry J. Friendly, "Some Kind of a Hearing," 123 *U. Pennsylvania L. Rev.* 267 (1965).

[112]See the testimony of John Rhinelander, in *Delays in Social Security Appeals*, supra note 89.

[113]Mashaw et al., supra note 9, at pp. 49–64.

[114]*Delays in Social Security Appeals*, supra note 89, at p. 231.

[115]See, e.g., Smith, supra note 9.

[116]Testimony of Representative John A. Siberling, in *Delays in Social Security Appeals*, supra note 89, at p. 247.

[117]Id., at p. 236.

[118]Id., at p. 242.

[119]Id., at p. 231.

[120]U.S. House of Representatives, Subcommittee on Social Security of the Committee on Ways and Means, *Staff Survey of State Disability Agencies Under Social Security and SSI Programs*, 94th Cong., 1st Sess (1975), pp. 1–3.

[121]*Background Materials*, supra note 7, at p. 12.

[122]*Delays in Social Security Appeals*, supra note 89, at p. 445.

[123]See generally Dixon, supra note 86. See also Dixon's testimony in *Delays in Social Security Appeals*, supra note 89, at pp. 111–20.

[124]Dixon, *Delays in Social Security Appeals*, supra note 89, at p. 154.

[125]Yourman, id., at pp. 148–49.

[126]*Delays in Social Security Appeals*, supra note 89, at p. 471.

[127]Id., at pp. 442, 469–70.

[128]See *Staff Survey*, supra note 120.

[129]Id., at pp. 8–10.

[130]Id., at p. 4. See also the comments of Marie A. Clark, in *Delays in Social Security Appeals*, supra note 89, at p. 445.

[131]Id., at pp. 227–66.

[132]See Caldwell's testimony, id., at pp. 35–45.

[133]"Twenty-four State agencies believe that the reasons given by the Committee on Ways and Means in 1954 for having State agencies under the vocational rehabilitation agency make disability determinations are no longer valid." *Staff Survey*, supra, note 120, at p. 2.

[134]U.S. House of Representatives, Subcommittee on Social Security of the Committee on Ways and Means, *Recent Studies Relevant to the Disability Hearings and Appeals Crisis*, 94th Cong., 1st Sess. (1975).

[135]Eldridge interview, supra note 2.

[136]Id.

[137]Brief for Petitioner, *Mathews v. Eldridge*, pp. 5–6 nn. 1–2.

[138]Id., at p. 11.

[139]Id.

[140]Id., at p. 12.

[141]*Richardson v. Perales*, 402 U.S. 389 (1971).

[142]*Eldridge v. Weinberger*, supra note 57, at 524–25.

[143]*Underwood v. Ribicoff*, 298 F.2d 850 (4th Cir. 1962).

[144]Brief for Petitioner, supra note 5, at p. 51.

[145]Interview with Donald Earls, August 27, 1979.

[146]Brief for Respondent, *Mathews v. Eldridge*, at pp. 9–10.

[147]Id., at p. 11.

[148]Warren E. Burger, "The State of the Federal Judiciary," in Walter F. Murphy and C. Herman Pritchett, *Courts, Judges, and Politics* (New York: Random House, 1974). See also Warren E. Burger, "1976 Annual Report of the State of the Judiciary," in *National Conference on the Causes of Popular Dissatisfaction with the Administration of Justice* (St. Paul, Minn.: Judicial Conference of the United States, 1976).

[149]Id. See also Warren E. Burger, "Annual Report on the State of the Judiciary,' 1979.

[150]Tom Goldstein, "Burger Asks Judges to Help Preserve Role of State Courts," *New York Times*, March 20, 1970, p. B12.

[151]See, e.g., *Santobello v. New York*, 404 U.S. 257 (1971), and *Stone v. Powell*, 428 U.S. 465 (1976), Chief Justice Burger concurring.

[152]*Arnett v. Kennedy*, 416 U.S. 134 (1974).

[153]*Fuentes v. Shevin*, supra note 52.

[154]*Sniadach v. Family Finance Corp.*, supra note 37.

[155]*Bell v. Burson*, supra note 49.

[156]*Board of Regents v. Roth*, 408 U.S. 564 (1972).

[157]*Arnett v. Kennedy*, supra note 152, at 157.

[158]*Cafeteria Workers v. McElroy*, 367 U.S. 886 (1961).

[159]Id., at 895–96.

[160]Compare *United States v. Robel*, 389 U.S. 258 (1967).

[161]*Arnett v. Kennedy*, supra note 152, Justice Powell concurring.

[162]Id., at 166–69.

[163]Id., at 219–221.

[164]*Weinberger v. Salfi*, 422 U.S. 749 (1975).

[165]*Dandridge v. Williams*, 397 U.S. 471 (1970).

[166]*Flemming v. Nestor*, 363 U.S. 603 (1960).

[167]*Richardson v. Belcher*, 404 U.S. 78 (1971).

[168]See, e.g., *Frontiero v. Richardson*, 411 U.S. 677 (1973), and *Weinberger v. Wiesenfeld*, 420 U.S. 636 (1975).

[169]*Weinberger v. Salfi*, supra note 164, at 781–82.

[170]Van Alstyne, supra note 27.

[171]*Weinburger v. Salfi*, supra note 164, at 771–72.

[172]Id., at 803–4, Justice Brennan dissenting.

[173]Transcript of oral argument in *Mathews v. Eldridge*, pp. 3–4.

[174]Interview with Donald Earls.

[175]Transcript of oral argument, in *Mathews v. Eldridge*, p. 1.

[176]Id., at 3.

[177]Brief for Petitioner, supra note 5, at p. 66A.

[178]Transcript of oral argument, in *Mathews v. Eldridge*, p. 24.

[179]Id., at pp. 24–26.

[180]*Mathews v. Eldridge*, supra note 1, at 323–26.

[181]Id.

[182]Id., at 325–26.

[183]Id., at 342.

[184]Haviland and Glomb, supra note 58; and Meyerhoff and Mishkin, supra note 26.

[186]Id., at 348–49.

[187]See generally Robert A. Rutland, *The Birth of the Bill of Rights, 1776–1791* (Chapel Hill: University of North Carolina Press, 1955).

[188]*Mathews v. Eldridge*, supra note 1, Justice Brennan dissenting.

[189]*Richardson v. Wright*, supra note 55, at 215.

[190]Id., at 215–17.

[191]Id., at 218.

[192]Id., at 227.

[193]See, e.g., *Parham v. J.R.*, 442 U.S. 584, 599–600 (1979), and *Mackey v. Montrym*, 443 U.S. 1, 10–11 (1979).

[194]Interview with Donald Earls.

[195]Interview with George Eldridge.

[196]Id.

[197]Id.

[198]Jerry L. Mashaw, "The Supreme Court's Due Process Calculus for Administrative Adjudication in *Mathews v. Eldridge*: Three Factors in Search of a Theory of Value," 44 *U. Chicago L. Rev.* 28 (1976).

[199]See note 193, supra.

[200]Recently Mashaw served as project director on the social security process conducted under the auspices of the National Center for Administrative Justice. See note 11, supra.

[201]See, e.g., Mashaw, supra note 198, p. 30.

[202]*Weinberger f. Salfi*, supra note 164.

[203]*Arnett v. Kennedy*, supra note 152.

[204]Van Alstyne, supra note 27.

[205]*Richardson v. Perales*, supra note 19, at 413, Justice Douglas dissenting.

Appendix B-1

1. The Administrative Procedure Act (5 U.S.C. §551 et seq.)

§551. Definitions

For the purpose of this subchapter—

(1) "agency" means each authority of the government of the United States, whether or not it is within or subject to review by another agency, but does not include—

(A) the Congress;

(B) the courts of the United States;

(C) the governments of the territories or possessions of the United States;

(D) the government of the District of Columbia;

or except as to the requirements of section 552 of this title—

(E) agencies composed of representatives of the parties or of representatives of organizations of the parties to the disputes determined by them;

(F) courts martial and military commissions;

(G) military authority exercised in the field in time of war or in occupied territory; or

(H) functions conferred by sections 1738, 1739, 1743, and 1744 of title 12; chapter 2 of title 41; or sections 1622, 1884, 1892–1902, and former section 1641(b)(2), of title 50, appendix;

(2) "person" includes an individual, partnership, corporation, association, or public or private organization other than an agency;

(3) "party" includes a person or agency named or admitted as a party, or property seeking and entitled as of right to be admitted as a party, in an agency proceeding, and a person or agency admitted by an agency as a party for limited purposes;

(4) "rule" means the whole or a part of an agency statement of general or particular applicability and future effect designed to implement, interpret, or prescribe law or policy or describing the organization, procedure, or practice requirements of an

agency and includes the approval or prescription for the future of rates, wages, corporate or financial structures or reorganization thereof, prices, facilities, appliances, services, or allowances therefor or of valuations, costs, or accounting, or practices bearing on any of the foregoing;

(5) "rule making" means agency process for formulating, amending, or repealing a rule;

(6) "order" means the whole or a part of a final disposition, whether affirmative, negative, injunctive, or declaratory in form, of an agency in a matter other than rule making but including licensing;

(7) "adjudication" means agency process for the formulation of an order;

(8) "license" includes the whole or a part of an agency permit, certificate, approval, registration, charter, membership, statutory exemption or other form of permission;

(9) "licensing" includes agency process respecting the grant, renewal, denial, revocation, suspension, annulment, withdrawal, limitation, amendment, modification, or conditioning of a license;

(10) "sanction" includes the whole or a part of an agency—

(A) prohibition, requirement, limitation, or other condition affecting the freedom of a person;

(B) withholding of relief;

(C) imposition of penalty or fine;

(D) destruction, taking, seizure, or withholding of property;

(E) assessment of damages, reimbursement, restitution, compensation, costs, charges, or fees;

(F) requirement, revocation, or suspension of a license; or

(G) taking other compulsory or restrictive action;

(11) "relief" includes the whole or a part of an agency—

(A) grant of money, assistance, license, authority, exemption, exception, privilege, or remedy;

(B) recognition of a claim, right, immunity, privilege, exemption, or exception; or

(C) taking of other action on the application or petition of, and beneficial to, a person;

(12) "agency proceeding" means an agency process as defined by paragraphs (5), (7), and (9) of this section;

(13) "agency action" includes the whole or a part of an agency rule, order, license, sanction, relief, or the equivalent or denial thereof, or failure to act; and

(14) "ex parte communication" means an oral or written communication not on the public record with respect to which reasonable prior notice to all parties is not given, but it shall not include requests for status reports on any matter or proceeding covered by this subchapter.

§552. Public information; agency rules, opinion, orders, records, and proceedings

(a) Each agency shall make available to the public information as follows:

(1) Each agency shall separately state and currently publish in the Federal Register for the guidance of the public—

(A) descriptions of its central and field organization and the established places at which, the employees (and in the case of a uniformed service, the members) from whom, and the methods whereby, the public may obtain information, make submittals or requests, or obtain decisions;

(B) statements of the general course and method by which its functions are channeled and determined, including the nature and requirements of all formal and informal procedures available;

(C) rules of procedure, descriptions of forms available or the places at which forms may be obtained, and instructions as to the scope and contents of all papers, reports, or examinations;

(D) substantive rules of general applicability adopted as authorized by law, and statements of general policy or interpretations of general applicability formulated and adopted by the agency; and

(E) each amendment, revision, or repeal of the foregoing.

Except to the extent that a person has actual and timely notice of the terms thereof, a person may not in any manner be required to resort to, or be adversely affected by, a matter required to be published in the Federal Register and not so published. For the purpose of this paragraph, matter reasonably available to the class of persons affected thereby is deemed published in the Federal Register when incorporated by reference therein with the approval of the Director of the Federal Register.

(2) Each agency, in accordance with published rules, shall make available for public inspection and copying—

(A) final opinions, including concurring and dissenting opinions, as well as orders, made in the adjudication of cases;

(B) those statements of policy and interpretations which have been adopted by the agency and are not published in the Federal Register; and

(C) administrative staff manuals and instructions to staff that affect a member of the public;

unless the materials are promptly published and copies offered for sale. To the extent required to prevent a clearly unwarranted invasion of personal privacy, an agency may delete identifying details when it makes available or publishes an opinion, statement of policy, interpretation, or staff manual or instruction, However, in each case the justification for the deletion shall be explained fully in writing. Each agency shall also maintain and make available for public inspection and copying current indexes providing identifying information for the public as to any matter issued, adopted, or promulgated after July 4, 1967, and required by this paragraph to be made available or published. Each agency shall promptly publish, quarterly or more frequently, and distribute (by sale or otherwise) copies of each index or supplements thereto unless it determines by order published in the Federal Register that the publication would be unnecessary and impracticable, in which case the agency shall nonetheless provide copies of such index on request at a cost not to exceed the direct cost of duplication. A final order, opinion, statement of policy, interpretation, or staff manual or instruction that affects a member of the public may be relied on, used, or cited as precedent by an agency against a party other than an agency only if—

(i) it has been indexed and either made available or published as provided by this paragraph; or

(ii) the party has actual and timely notice of the terms thereof.

(3) Except with respect to the records made available under paragraphs (1) and (2) of this subsection, each agency, upon any request for records which (A) reasonably describes such records and (B) is made in accordance with published rules stating the time, place, fees (if any), and procedures to be followed, shall make the records promptly available to any person.

(4) (A) In order to carry out the provisions of this section, each agency shall promulgate regulations, pursuant to notice and receipt of public comment, specifying a uniform schedule of fees applicable to all constituent units of such agency. Such fees shall be limited to reasonable standard charges for document search and duplication and provide for recovery of only the direct costs of such search and duplication. Documents shall be furnished without charge or at a reduced charge where the agency determines that waiver or reduction of the fee is in the public interest because furnishing the information can be considered as primarily benefiting the general public.

(B) On complaint, the district court of the United States in the district in which the complainant resides, or has his principal place of business, or in which the agency records are situated, or in the District of Columbia, has jurisdiction to enjoin the agency from withholding agency records and to order the production of any agency records improperly withheld from the complainant. In such a case the court shall determine the matter de novo, and may examine the contents of such agency records in camera to determine whether such records or any part thereof shall be withheld under any of the exemptions set forth in subsection (b) of this section, and the burden is on the agency to sustain its action.

(C) Notwithstanding any other provision of law, the defendant shall serve an answer or otherwise plead to any complaint made under this subsection within thirty days after service upon the defendant of the pleading in which such complaint is made, unless the court otherwise directs for good cause shown.

(D) Except as to cases the court considers of greater importance, proceedings before the district court, as authorized by this subsection, and appeals therefrom, take precedence on the docket over all cases and shall be assigned for hearing and trial or for argument at the earliest practicable date and expedited in every way.

(E) The court may assess against the United States reasonable attorney fees and other litigation costs reasonably incurred in any case under this section in which the complainant has substantially prevailed.

(F) Whenever the court orders the production of any agency records improperly withheld from the complainant and assesses against the United States reasonable attorney fees and other litigation costs, and the court additionally issues a written finding that the circumstances surrounding the withholding raise questions whether agency personnel acting arbitrarily or capriciously with respect to the withholding, the Special Counsel shall promptly initiate a proceeding to determine whether disciplinary action is warranted against the officer or employee who was primarily responsible for the withholding. The Special Counsel, after investigation and consideration of the evidence submitted, shall submit its findings and recommendations to the administrative authority of the agency concerned and shall send copies of the findings and recommendations to the officer or employee or his representative. The administrative authority shall take the corrective action that the Commission recommends.

(G) In the event of noncompliance with the order of the court, the district court may punish for contempt the responsible employee, and in the case of a uniformed service, the responsible member.

(5) Each agency having more than one member shall maintain and make available for public inspection a record of the final votes of each member in every agency proceeding.

(6) (A) Each agency, upon any request for records made under paragraph (1), (2), or (3) of this subsection, shall—

   (i) determine within ten days (excepting Saturdays, Sundays, and legal public holidays) after the receipt of any such request and shall immediately notify the person making such request of such determination and the reasons therefor, and of the right of such person to appeal to the head of the agency any adverse determination; and

   (ii) make a determination with respect to any appeal within twenty days (excepting Saturdays, Sundays, and legal public holidays) after the receipt of such appeal. If on appeal the denial of the request for records is in whole or in part upheld, the agency shall notify the person making such request of the provisions for judicial review of that determination under paragraph (4) of this subsection.

(B) In unusual circumstances as specified in this subparagraph, the time limits prescribed in either clause (i) or clause (ii) of subparagraph (A) may be extended by written notice to the person making such request setting forth the reasons for such extension and the date on which a determination is expected to be dispatched. No such notice shall specify a date that would result in an extension for more than ten working days. As used in this subparagraph, "unusual circumstances" means, but only to the extent reasonably necessary to the proper processing of the particular request—

   (i) the need to search for and collect the requested records from field facilities or other establishments that are separate from the office processing the request;

   (ii) the need to search for, collect, and appropriately examine a voluminous amount of separate and distinct records which are demanded in a single request; or

   (iii) the need for consultation, which shall be conducted with all practicable speed, with another agency having a substantial interest in the determination of the request or among two or more components of the agency having substantial subject-matter interest therein.

(C) Any person making a request to any agency for records under paragraph (1), (2), or (3) of this subsection shall be deemed to have exhausted his administrative remedies with respect to such request if the agency fails to comply with the applicable time limit provisions of this paragraph. If the Government can show exceptional circumstances exist and that the agency is exercising due diligence in responding to the request, the court may retain jurisdiction and allow the agency additional time to complete its review of the records. Upon any determination by an agency to comply with a request for records, the records shall be made promptly available to such person making such request. Any notification of denial of any request for records under this subsection shall set forth the names and titles or positions of each person responsible for the denial of such request.

(b) This section does not apply to matters that are—

   (1) (A) specifically authorized under criteria established by an Executive order to be kept secret in the interest of national defense or foreign policy and (B) are in fact properly classified pursuant to such Executive order;

   (2) related solely to the internal personnel rules and practices of an agency;

(3) specifically exempted from disclosure by statute (other than section 552b of this title), provided that such statute (A) requires that the matters be withheld from the public in such a manner as to leave no discretion on the issue, or (B) establishes particular criteria for withholding or refers to particular types of matters to be withheld;

(4) trade secrets and commercial or financial information obtained from a person and privileged or confidential;

(5) inter-agency or intra-agency memorandums or letters which would not be available by law to a party other than an agency in litigation with an agency;

(6) personnel and medical files and similar files the disclosure of which would constitute a clearly unwarranted invasion of personal privacy;

(7) investigatory records compiled for law enforcement purposes, but only to the extent that the production of such records would (A) interfere with enforcement proceedings, (B) deprive a person of a right to a fair trial or an impartial adjudication, (C) constitute an unwarranted invasion of personal privacy, (D) disclose the identity of a confidential source and, in the case of a record compiled by a criminal law enforcement authority in the course of a criminal investigation, or by an agency conducting a lawful national security intelligence investigation, confidential information furnished only by the confidential source, (E) disclose investigative techniques and procedures, or (F) endanger the life or physical safety of law enforcement personnel;

(8) contained in or related to examination, operating, or condition reports prepared by, on behalf of, or for the use of an agency responsible for the regulation or supervision of financial institutions; or

(9) geological and geophysical information and data, including maps, concerning wells.

Any reasonably segregable portion of a record shall be provided to any person requesting such record after deletion of the portions which are exempt under this subsection.

(c) This section does not authorize withholding of information or limit the availability of records to the public, except as specifically stated in this section. This section is not authority to withhold information from Congress.

(d) On or before March 1 of each calendar year, each agency shall submit a report covering the preceding calendar year to the Speaker of the House of Representatives and President of the Senate for referral to the appropriate committees of the Congress. The report shall include—

(1) the number of determinations made by such agency not to comply with requests for records made to such agency under subsection (a) and the reasons for each such determination;

(2) the number of appeals made by persons under subsection (a) (6), the result of such appeals, and the reason for the action upon each appeal that results in a denial of information;

(3) the names and titles or positions of each person responsible for the denial of records requested under this section, and the number of instances of participation for each;

(4) the results of each proceeding conducted pursuant to subsection (a) (4) (F), including a report of the disciplinary action taken against the officer or employee who was primarily responsible for improperly withholding records or an explanation of why disciplinary action was not taken;

(5) a copy of every rule made by such agency regarding this section;

(6) a copy of the fee schedule and the total amount of fees collected by the agency for making records available under this section; and

(7) such other information as indicates efforts to administer fully this section.

The Attorney General shall submit an annual report on or before March 1 of each calendar year which shall include for the prior calendar year a listing of the number of cases arising under this section, the exemption involved in each case, the disposition of such case, and the cost, fees, and penalties assessed under subsections (a) (4) (E), (F), and (G). Such report shall also include a description of the efforts undertaken by the Department of Justice to encourage agency compliance with this section.

(e) For purposes of this section, the term "agency" as defined in section 551(1) of this title includes any executive department, military department, Government corporation, Government controlled corporation, or other establishment in the executive branch of the Government (including the Executive Office of the President), or any independent regulatory agency.

§552a. Records maintained on individuals

(a) Definitions.—For purposes of this section—

(1) the term "agency" means agency as defined in section 552(e) of this title;

(2) the term "individual" means a citizen of the United States or an alien lawfully admitted for permanent residence;

(3) the term "maintain" includes maintain, collect, use, or disseminate;

(4) the term "record" means any item, collection, or grouping of information about an individual that is maintained by an agency, including, but not limited to, his education, financial transactions, medical history, and criminal or employment history and that contains his name, or the identifying number, symbol, or other identifying particular assigned to the individual, such as a finger or voice print or a photograph;

(5) the term "system of records" means a group of any records under the control of any agency from which information is retrieved by the name of the individual or by some identifying number, symbol, or other identifying particular assigned to the individual;

(6) the term "statistical record" means a record in a system of records maintained for statistical research or reporting purposes only and not used in whole or in part in making any determination about an identifiable individual, except as provided by section 8 of title 13; and

(7) the term "routine use" means, with respect to the disclosure of a record, the use of such record for a purpose which is compatible with the purpose for which it was collected.

(b) Conditions of disclosure.—No agency shall disclose any record which is contained in a system of records by any means of communication to any person, or to another agency, except pursuant to a written request by, or with the prior written consent of, the individual to whom the record pertains, unless disclosure of the record would be—

(1) to those officers and employees of the agency which maintains the record who have a need for the record in the performance of their duties;

(2) required under section 552 of this title;

(3) for a routine use as defined in subsection (a) (7) of this section and described under subsection (e) (4) (D) of this section;

(4) to the Bureau of the Census for purposes of planning or carrying out a census or survey or related activity pursuant to the provisions of title 13;

(5) to a recipient who has provided the agency with advance adequate written assurance that the record will be used solely as a statistical research or reporting record, and the record is to be transferred in a form that is not individually identifiable;

(6) to the National Archives of the United States as a record which has sufficient historical or other value to warrant its continued preservation by the United States Government, or for evaluation by the Administrator of General Services or his designee to determine whether the record has such value;

(7) to another agency or to an instrumentality of any governmental jurisdiction within or under the control of the United States for a civil or criminal law enforcement activity if the activity is authorized by law, and if the head of the agency or instrumentality has made a written request to the agency which maintains the record specifying the particular portion desired and the law enforcement activity for which the record is sought;

(8) to a person pursuant to a showing of compelling circumstances affecting the health or safety of an individual if upon such disclosure notification is transmitted to the last known address of such individual;

(9) to either House of Congress, or, to the extent of matter within its jurisdiction, any committee or subcommittee thereof, any joint committee of Congress of subcommittee of any such joint committee;

(10) to the Comptroller General, or any of his authorized representatives in the course of the performance of the duties of the General Accounting Office; or

(11) pursuant to the order of a court of competent jurisdiction.

(c) Accounting of Certain Disclosures.—Each agency, with respect to each system of records under its control, shall—

(1) except for disclosures made under subsections (b) (1) or (b) (2) of this section, keep an accurate accounting of—

(A) the date, nature, and purpose of each disclosure of a record to any person or to another agency made under subsection (b) of this section; and

(B) the name and address of the person or agency to whom the disclosure is made;

(2) retain the accounting made under paragraph (1) of this subsection for at least five years or the life of the record, whichever is longer, after the disclosure for which the accounting is made;

(3) except for disclosures made under subsection (b) (7) of this section, make the accounting made under paragraph (1) of this subsection available to the individual named in the record at his request; and

(4) inform any person or other agency about any correction or notation of dispute made by the agency in accordance with subsection (d) of this section of any record that has been disclosed to the person or agency if an accounting of the disclosure was made.

(d) Access to records.—Each agency that maintains a system of records shall—

(1) upon request by an individual to gain access to his record or to any information pertaining to him which is contained in the system, permit him and upon his request, a person of his own choosing to accompany him, to review the record and have a copy made of all or any portion thereof in a form comprehensible to him, except that the agency may require the individual to furnish a written statement authorizing discussion of that individual's record in the accompanying person's presence;

(2) permit the individual to request amendment of a record pertaining to him and—

(A) not later than 10 days (excluding Saturdays, Sundays, and legal public holidays) after the date or receipt of such request, acknowledge in writing such receipt; and

(B) promptly, either—

(i) make any correction of any portion thereof which the individual believes is not accurate, relevant, timely, or complete; or

(ii) inform the individual of its refusal to amend the record in accordance with his request, the reason for the refusal, the procedures established by the agency for the individual to request a review of that refusal by the head of the agency or an officer designated by the head of the agency, and the name and business address of that official;

(3) permit the individual who disagrees with the refusal of the agency to amend his record to request a review of such refusal, and not later than 30 days (excluding Saturdays, Sundays, and legal public holidays) from the date on which the individual requests such review, complete such review and make a final determination unless, for good cause shown, the head of the agency extends such 30-day period; and if, after his review, the reviewing official also refuses to amend the record in accordance with the request, permit the individual to file with the agency a concise statement setting forth the reasons for his disagreement with the refusal of the agency, and notify the individual of the provisions for judicial review of the reviewing official's determination under subsection (g) (1) (A) of this section;

(4) in any disclosure, containing information about which the individual has filed a statement of disagreement, occurring after the filing of the statement under paragraph (3) of this subsection, clearly note any portion of the record which is disputed and provide copies of the statement and, if the agency deems it appropriate, copies of a concise statement of the reasons of the agency for not making the amendments requested, to persons or other agencies to whom the disputed record has been disclosed; and

(5) nothing in this section shall allow an individual access to any information compiled in reasonable anticipation of a civil action or proceeding.

(e) Agency requirements.—Each agency that maintains a system of records shall—

(1) maintain in its records only such information about an individual as is relevant and necessary to accomplish a purpose of the agency required to be accomplished by statute or by executive order of the President;

(2) collect information to the greatest extent practicable directly from the subject individual when the information may result in adverse determinations about an individual's rights, benefits, and privileges under Federal programs;

(3) inform each individual whom it asks to supply information, on the form which it uses to collect the information or on a separate form that can be retained by the individual—

(A) the authority (whether granted by statute, or by executive order of the President) which authorizes the solicitation of the information and whether disclosure of such information is mandatory or voluntary;

(B) the principal purpose or purposes for which the information is intended to be used;

(C) the routine uses which may be made of the information, as published pursuant to paragraph (4) (D) of this subsection; and

(D) the effects on him, if any, of not providing all or any part of the requested information;

(4) subject to the provisions of paragraph (11) of this subsection, publish in the Federal Register at least annually a notice of the existence and character of the system of records, which notice shall include—

(A) the name and location of the system;

(B) the categories of individuals on whom records are maintained in the system;

(C) the categories of records maintained in the system;

(D) each routine use of the records contained in the system, including the categories of users and the purpose of such use;

(E) the policies and practices of the agency regarding storage, retrievability, access controls, retention, and disposal of the records;

(F) the title and business address of the agency official who is responsible for the system of records;

(G) the agency procedures whereby an individual can be notified at his request if the system of records contains a record pertaining to him;

(H) the agency procedures whereby an individual can be notified at his request how he can gain access to any record pertaining to him contained in the system of records, and how he can contest its content; and

(I) the categories of sources of records in the system;

(5) maintain all records which are used by the agency in making any determination about any individual with such accuracy, relevance, timeliness, and completeness as is reasonably necessary to assure fairness to the individual in the determination;

(6) prior to disseminating any record about an individual to any person other than an agency, unless the dissemination is made pursuant to subsection (b) (2) of this section, make reasonable efforts to assure that such records are accurate, complete, timely, and relevant for agency purposes;

(7) maintain no record describing how any individual exercises rights guaranteed by the First Amendment unless expressly authorized by statute or by the individual about whom the record is maintained or unless pertinent to and within the scope of an authorized law enforcement activity;

(8) make reasonable efforts to serve notice on an individual when any record on such individual is made available to any person under compulsory legal process when such process becomes a matter of public record;

(9) establish rules of conduct for persons involved in the design, development, operation, or maintenance of any system of records, or in maintaining any record, and instruct each such person with respect to such rules and the requirements of this section, including any other rules and procedures adopted pursuant to this section and the penalties for noncompliance;

(10) establish appropriate administrative, technical, and physical safeguards to insure the security and confidentiality of records and to protect against any anticipated

threats or hazards to their security or integrity which could result in substantial harm, embarrassment, inconvenience, or unfairness to any individual on whom information is maintained; and

(11) at least 30 days prior to publication of information under paragraph (4) (D) of this subsection, publish in the Federal Register notice of any new use or intended use of the information in the system, and provide an opportunity for interested persons to submit written data, views, or arguments to the agency.

(f) Agency rules.—In order to carry out the provisions of this section, each agency that maintains a system of records shall promulgate rules, in accordance with the requirements (including general notice) of section 553 of this title, which shall—

(1) establish procedures whereby an individual can be notified in response to his request if any system of records named by the individual contains a record pertaining to him;

(2) define reasonable times, places, and requirements for identifying an individual who requests his record or information pertaining to him before the agency shall make the record of information available to the individual;

(3) establish procedures for the disclosure to an individual upon his request of his record or information pertaining to him, including special procedure, if deemed necessary, for the disclosure to an individual of medical records, including psychological records, pertaining to him;

(4) establish procedures for reviewing a request from an individual concerning the amendment of any record or information pertaining to the individual, for making a determination on the request, for an appeal within the agency of an initial adverse agency determination, and for whatever additional means may be necessary for each individual to be able to exercise fully his rights under this section; and

(5) establish fees to be charged, if any, to any individual for making copies of his record, excluding the cost of any search for and review of the record.

The Office of the Federal Register shall annually compile and publish the rules promulgated under this subsection and agency notices published under subsection (e) (4) of this section in a form available to the public at low cost.

(g) (1) Civil remedies.—Whenever any agency

(A) makes a determination under subsection (d) (3) of this section not to amend an individual's record in accordance with his request, or fails to make such review in conformity with that subsection;

(B) refuses to comply with an individual request under subsection (d) (1) of this section;

(C) fails to maintain any record concerning any individual with such accuracy, relevance, timeliness, and completeness as is necessary to assure fairness in any determination relating to the qualifications, character, rights, or opportunities of, or benefits to the individual that may be made on the basis of such record, and consequently a determination is made which is adverse to the individual; or

(D) fails to comply with any other provision of this section, or any rule promulgated thereunder, in such a way as to have an adverse effect on an individual,

the individual may bring a civil action against the agency, and the district courts of the United States shall have jurisdiction in the matters under the provisions of this subsection.

(2) (A) In any suit brought under the provisions of subsection (g) (1) (A) of this section, the court may order the agency to amend the individual's record in

accordance with his request or in such other way as the court may direct. In such a case the court shall determine the matter *de novo*.

(B) The court may assess against the United States reasonable attorney fees and other litigation costs reasonably incurred in any case under this paragraph in which the complainant has substantially prevailed.

(3) (A) In any suit brought under the provisions of subsection (g) (1) (B) of this section, the court may enjoin the agency from withholding the records and order the production to the complainant of any agency records improperly withheld from him. In such a case the court shall determine the matter *de novo*, and may examine the contents of any agency records in camera to determine whether the records or any portion thereof may be withheld under any of the exemptions set forth in subsection (k) of this section, and the burden is on the agency to sustain its action.

(B) The court may assess against the United States reasonable attorney fees and other litigation costs reasonably incurred in any case under this paragraph in which the complainant has substantially prevailed.

(4) In any suit brought under the provisions of subsection (g) (1) (C) or (D) of this section in which the court determines that the agency acted in a manner which was intentional or willful, the United States shall be liable to the individual in an amount equal to the sum of—

(A) actual damages sustained by the individual as a result of the refusal or failure, but in no case shall a person entitled to recovery receive less than the sum of $1,000; and

(B) the costs of the action together with reasonable attorney fees as determined by the court.

(5) An action to enforce any liability created under this section may be brought in the district court of the United States in the district in which the complainant resides, or has his principal place of business, or in which the agency records are situated, or in the District of Columbia, without regard to the amount in controversy, within two years from the date on which the cause of action arises, except that where an agency has materially and willfully misrepresented any information required under this section to be disclosed to an individual and the information so misrepresented is material to establishment of the liability of the agency to the individual under this section, the action may be brought at any time within two years after discovery by the individual of the misrepresentation. Nothing in this section shall be construed to authorize any civil action by reason of any injury sustained as the result of a disclosure of a record prior to September 27, 1975.

(h) Rights of legal guardians.—For the purposes of this section, the parent of any minor, or the legal guardian of any individual who has been declared to be incompetent due to physical or mental incapacity or age by a court of competent jurisdiction, may act on behalf of the individual.

(i) (1) Criminal penalties.—Any officer or employee of an agency, who by virtue of his employment or official position, has possession of, or access to, agency records which contain individually identifiable information the disclosure of which is prohibited by this section or by rules or regulations established thereunder, and who knowing that disclosure of the specific material is so prohibited, willfully discloses the material in any manner to any person or agency not entitled to receive it, shall be guilty of a misdemeanor and fined not more than $5,000.

(2) Any officer or employee of any agency who willfully maintains a system of records without meeting the notice requirements of subsection (e) (4) of this section shall be guilty of a misdemeanor and fined not more than $5,000.

(3) Any person who knowingly and willfully requests or obtains any record concerning an individual from an agency under false pretenses shall be guilty of a misdemeanor and fined not more than $5,000.

(j) General exemptions.—The head of any agency may promulgate rules, in accordance with the requirements (including general notice) of sections 553(b) (1), (2), and (3), (c), and (e) of this titled, to exempt any system of records within the agency from any part of this section except subsections (b), (c), (1) and (2), (e) (4) (A) through (F), (e) (6), (7), (9), (10), and (11), and (i) if the system of records is—

(1) maintained by the Central Intelligence Agency; or

(2) maintained by an agency or component thereof which performs as its principal function any activity pertaining to the enforcement of criminal laws, including police efforts to prevent, control, or reduce crime or to apprehend criminals, and the activities of prosecutors, courts, correctional, probation, pardon, or parole authorities, and which consists of (A) information compiled for the purpose of identifying individual criminal offenders and alleged offenders and consisting only of identifying data and notations of arrests, the nature and disposition of criminal charges, sentencing, confinement, release, and parole and probation status (B) information compiled for the purpose of a criminal investigation, including reports of informants and investigators, and associated with an identifiable individual; or (C) reports identifiable to an individual compiled at any stage of the process of enforcement of the criminal laws from arrest or indictment through release from suprevision.

At the time rules are adopted under this subsection, the agency shall include in the statement required under section 553 (c) of this title, the reasons why the system of records is to be exempted from a provision of this section.

(k) Specific exemptions.—The head of any agency may promulgate rules, in accordance with the requirements (including general notice) of sections 553(b), (1), (2), and (3), (c), and (e) of this title, to exempt any system of records within the agency from subsections (c), (3), (d), (e), (1), (e) (4), (G), (H), and (I) and (f) of this section if the system of records is—

(1) subject to the provisions of section 552(b) (1) of this title;

(2) investigatory material compiled for law enforcement purposes, other than material within the scope of subsection (j) (2) of this section: *Provided, however,* that if any individual is denied any right, privilege, or benefit that he would otherwise be entitled by Federal law, or for which he would otherwise be eligible, as a result of the maintenance of such material, such material shall be provided to such individual, except to the extent that the disclosure of such material would reveal the identity of a source who furnished information to the Government under an express promise that the identity of the source would be held in confidence, or prior to the effective date of this section, under an implied promise that the identity of the source would be held in confidence;

(3) maintained in connection with providing protective services to the President of the United States or other individuals pursuant to section 3056 of title 18;

(4) required by statute to be maintained and used solely as statistical records;

(5) investigatory material compiled solely for the purpose of determining suitability, eligibility, or qualifications for Federal civilian employment, military service, Federal contracts, or access to classified information, but only to the extent that the disclosure of such material would reveal the identity of a source who furnished information to the Government under an express promise that the identity of the source would be held in confidence, or, prior to the effective date of this section,

under an implied promise that the identity of the source would be held in confidence;

(6) testing or examination material used solely to determine individual qualifications for appointment or promotion in the Federal service the disclosure of which would compromise the objectivity or fairness of the testing or examination process; or

(7) evaluation material used to determine potential for promotion in the armed services, but only to the extent that the disclosure of such material would reveal the identity of a source who furnished information to the Government under an express promise that the identity of the source would be held in confidence, or, prior to the effective date of this section, under an implied promise that the identity of the source would be held in confidence.

At the time rules are adopted under this subsection, the agency shall include in the statement required under section 553(c) of this title, the reasons why the system of records is to be exempted from a provision of this section.

(l) (1) Archival records.—Each agency record which is accepted by the Administrator of General Services for storage, processing, and servicing in accordance with section 3103 of title 44 shall, for the purposes of this section, be considered to be maintained by the agency which deposited the record and shall be subject to the provisions of this section. The Administrator of General Services shall not disclose the record except to the agency which maintains the record, or under rules established by that agency which are not inconsistent with the provisions of this section.

(2) Each agency record pertaining to an identifiable individual which was transferred to the National Archives of the United States as a record which has sufficient historical or other value to warrant its continued preservation by the United States Government, prior to the effective date of this section, shall, for the purposes of this section, be considered to be maintained by the National Archives and shall not be subject to the provisions of this section, except that a statement generally describing such records (modeled after the requirements relating to records subject to subsections (e) (4) (A) through (G) of this section) shall be published in the Federal Register.

(3) Each agency record pertaining to an identifiable individual which is transferred to the National Archives of the United States is a record which has sufficient historical or other value to warrant its continued preservation by the United States Government, on or after the effective date of this section, shall, for the purposes of this section, be considered to be maintained by the National Archives and shall be exempt from the requirements of this section except subsections (e) (4) (A) through (G) and (e) (9) of this section.

(m) Government contractors.—When an agency provides by a contract for the operation by or on behalf of the agency of a system of records to accomplish an agency function, the agency shall, consistent with its authority, cause the requirements of this section to be applied to such system. For purposes of subsection (i) of this section any such contractor and any employee of such contract, if such contract is agreed to on or after the effective date of this section, shall be considered to be an employee of an agency.

(n) Mailing lists.—An individual's name and address may not be sold or rented by an agency unless such action is specifically authorized by law. This provision shall not be construed to require the withholding of names and addresses otherwise permitted to be made public.

(o) Report on new systems.—Each agency shall provide adequate advance notice to Congress and the Office of Management and Budget of any proposal to establish or alter any system of records in order to permit an evaluation of the probable or potential effect of such proposal on the privacy and other personal or property rights of individuals or the disclosure of information relating to such individuals, and its effect on the preservation of the constitutional principles of federalism and separation of powers.

(p) Annual report.—The President shall submit to the Speaker of the House and the President of the Senate, by June 30 of each calendar year, a consolidated report, separately listing for each Federal agency the number of records contained in any system of records which were exempted from the application of this section under the provisions of subsections (j) and (k) of this section during the preceding calendar year, and the reasons for the exemptions, and such other information as indicates efforts to administer fully this section.

(q) Effect of other laws.—No agency shall rely on any exemption contained in section 552 of this title to withhold from an individual any record which is otherwise accessible to such individual under the provisions of this section.

§552b. Open Meetings

(a) For purposes of this section—

(1) the term "agency" means any agency, as defined in section 552(e) of this title, headed by a collegial body composed of two or more individual members, a majority of whom are appointed to such position by the President with the advice and consent of the Senate, and any subdivision thereof authorized to act on behalf of the agency;

(2) the term "meeting" means the deliberations of at least the number of individual agency members required to take action on behalf of the agency where such deliberations determine or result in the joint conduct or disposition of official agency business, but does not include deliberations required or permitted by subsection (d) or (e); and

(3) the term "member" means an individual who belongs to a collegial body heading an agency.

(b) Members shall not jointly conduct or dispose of agency business other than in accordance with this section. Except as provided in subsection (c), every portion of every meeting of an agency shall be open to public observation.

(c) Except in a case where the agency finds that the public interest requires otherwise, the second sentence of subsection (b) shall not apply to any portion of an agency meeting, and the requirements of subsections (d) and (e) shall not apply to any information pertaining to such meeting otherwise required by this section to be disclosed to the public, where the agency properly determines that such portion or portions of its meeting or the disclosure of such information is likely to—

(1) disclose matters that are (A) specifically authorized under criteria estalished by an Executive order to be kept secret in the interests of national defense or foreign policy and (B) in fact properly classified pursuant to such Executive order;

(2) relate solely to the internal personnel rules and practices of an agency;

(3) disclose matters specifically exempted from disclosure by statute (other than section 552 of this title), provided that such statute (A) requires that the matters be withheld from the public in such a manner as to leave no discretion on the issue, or (B) establishes particular criteria for withholding or refers to particular types of matters to be withheld;

(4) disclose trade secrets and commercial or financial information obtained from a person and privileged or confidential;

(5) involve accusing any person of a crime, or formally censuring any person;

(6) disclose information of a personal nature where disclosure would constitute a clearly unwarranted invasion of personal privacy;

(7) disclose investigatory records compiled for law enforcement purposes, or information which if written would be contained in such records, but only to the extent that the production of such records or information would (A) interfere with enforcement proceedings, (B) deprive a person of a right to a fair trial or an impartial adjudication, (C) constitute an unwarranted invasion of personal privacy, (D) disclose the identity of a confidential source and, in the case of a record compiled by a criminal law enforcement authority in the course of a criminal investigation, or by an agency conducting a lawful national security intelligence investigation, confidential information furnished only by the confidential source, (E) dislcose investigative techniques and procedures, or (F) endanger the life or physical safety of law enforcement personnel;

(8) disclose information contained in or related to examination, operating, or condition reports prepared by, on behalf of, or for the use of an agency responsible for the regulation or supervision of financial institutions;

(9) disclose information the premature disclosure of which would—

   (A) in the case of an agency which regulates currencies, securities, commodities, or financial institutions, be likely to (i) lead to significant financial speculation in currencies, securities, or commodities, or (ii) significantly endanger the stability of any financial institution; or

   (B) in the case of any agency, be likely to significantly frustrate implementation of a proposed agency action,

   except that subparagraph (B) shall not apply in any instance where the agency has already disclosed to the public the content or nature of its proposed action, or where the agency is required by law to make such disclosure on its own initiative prior to taking final agency action on such proposal; or

(10) specifically concern the agency's issuance of a subpoena, or the agency's participation in a civil action or proceeding, an action in a foreign court or international tribunal or an arbitration, or the initiation, conduct, or disposition by the agency of a particular case of formal agency adjudication pursuant to the procedures in section 554 of this title or otherwise involving a determination on the record after opportunity for a hearing.

(d) (1) Action under subsection (c) shall be taken only when a majority of the entire membership of the agency (as defined in subsection (a) (1)) votes to take such action. A separate vote of the agency members shall be taken with respect to each agency meeting a portion or portions of which are proposed to be closed to the public pursuant to subsection (c), or with respect to any information which is proposed to be withheld under subsection (c). A single vote may be taken with respect to a series of meetings, a portion or portions of which are proposed to be closed to the public, or with respect to any information concerning such series of meetings, so long as each meeting in such series involves the same particular matters and is scheduled to be held no more than thirty days after the initial meeting in such series. The vote of each agency member participating in such vote shall be recorded and no proxies shall be allowed.

(2) Whenever any person whose interests may be directly affected by a portion of a

meeting requests that the agency close such portion to the public for any of the reasons referred to in paragraph (5), (6), or (7) of subsection (c), the agency, upon request of any one of its members, shall vote by recorded vote whether to close such meeting.

(3) Within one day of any vote taken pursuant to paragraph (1) or (2), the agency shall make publicly available a written copy of such vote reflecting the vote of each member on the question. If a portion of a meeting is to be closed to the public, the agency shall, within one day of the vote taken pursuant to paragraph (1) or (2) of this subsection, make publicly available a full written explanation of its action closing the portion together with a list of all persons expected to attend the meeting and their affiliation.

(4) Any agency, a majority of whose meetings may properly be closed to the public pursuant to paragraph (4), (8), (9) (A), or (10) of subsection (c), or any combination thereof, may provide by regulation for the closing of such meetings or portions thereof in the event that a majority of the members of the agency votes by recorded vote at the beginning of such meeting, or portion thereof, to close the exempt portion or portions of the meeting, and a copy of such vote, reflecting the vote of each member on the question, is made available to the public. The provisions of paragraphs (1), (2), and (3) of this subsection and subsection (e) shall not apply to any portion of a meeting to which such regulations apply: *Provided,* That the agency shall, except to the extent that such information is exempt from disclosure under the provisions of subsection (c), provide the public with public announcement of the time, place, and subject matter of the meeting and of each portion thereof at the earliest practicable time.

(e) (1) In the case of each meeting, the agency shall make public announcement, at least one week before the meeting, of the time, place, and subject matter of the meeting, whether it is to be open or closed to the public, and the name and phone number of the official designated by the agency to respond to requests for information about the meeting. Such announcement shall be made unless a majority of the members of the agency determines by a recorded vote that agency business requires that such meeting be called at an earlier date, in which case the agency shall make public announcement of the time, place, and subject matter of such meeting, and whether open or closed to the public, at the earliest practicable time.

(2) The time or place of a meeting may be changed following the public announcement required by paragraph (1) only if the agency publicly announces such change at the earliest practicable time. The subject matter of a meeting, or the determination of the agency to open or close a meeting, or portion of a meeting, to the public, may be changed following the public announcement required by this subsection only if (A) a majority of the entire membership of the agency determines by a recorded vote that agency business so requires and that no earlier announcement of the change was possible, and (B) the agency publicly announces such change and the vote of each member upon such change at the earliest practicable time.

(3) Immediately following each public announcement required by this subsection, notice of the time, place, and subject matter of a meeting, whether the meeting is open or closed, any change in one of the preceding, and the name and phone number of the official designated by the agency to respond to requests for information about the meeting, shall also be submitted for publication in the Federal Register.

(f) (1) For every meeting closed pursuant to paragraphs (1) through (10) of subsection (c), the General Counsel or chief legal officer of the agency shall publicly certify that, in his or her opinion, the meeting may be closed to the public and shall state each relevant exemptive provision. A copy of such certification, together with a statement from the presiding officer of the meeting setting forth the time and place of the meeting, and the persons present, shall be retained by the agency. The agency shall maintain a complete transcript or electronic recording adequate to record fully the proceedings of each meeting, or portion of a meeting, closed to the public, except that in the case of a meeting, or portion of a meeting, closed to the public pursuant to paragraph (8), (9) (A), or (10) of subsection (c), the agency shall maintain either such a transcript or recording, or a set of minutes. Such minutes shall fully and clearly describe all matters discussed and shall provide a full and accurate summary of any actions taken, and the reasons therefor, including a description of each of the views expressed on any item and the record of any rollcall vote (reflecting the vote of each member on the question). All documents considered in connection with any action shall be identified in such minutes.

(2) The agency shall make promptly available to the public, in a place easily accessible to the public, the transcript, electronic recording, or minutes (as required by paragraph (1)) of the discussion of any item on the agenda, or of any item of the testimony of any witness received at the meeting, except for such item or items of such discussion or testimony as the agency determines to contain information which may be withheld under subsection (c). Copies of such transcript, or minutes, or a transcription of such recording disclosing the identity of each speaker, shall be furnished to any person at the actual cost of duplication or transcription. The agency shall maintain a complete verbatim copy of the transcript, a complete copy of the minutes, or a complete electronic recording of each meeting, or portion of a meeting, closed to the public, for a period of at least two years after such meeting, or until one year after the conclusion of any agency proceeding with respect to which the meeting or portion was held, whichever occurs later.

(g) Each agency subject to the requirements of this section shall, within 180 days after the date of enactment of this section, following consultation with the Office of the Chairman of the Administrative Conference of the United States and published notice in the Federal Register of at least thirty days and opportunity for written comment by any person, promulgate regulations to implement the requirements of subsections (b) through (f) of this section. Any person may bring a proceeding in the United States District Court for the District of Columbia to require an agency to promulgate such regulations if such agency has not promulgated such regulations within the time period specified herein. Subject to any limitations of time provided by law, any person may bring a proceeding in the United States Court of Appeals for the District of Columbia to set aside agency regulations issued pursuant to this subsection that are not in accord with the requirements of subsections (b) through (f) of this section and to require the promulgation of regulations that are in accord with such subsections.

(h) (1) The district courts of the United States shall have jurisdiction to enforce the requirements of subsections (b) through (f) of this section by declaratory judgment, injunctive relief, or other relief as may be appropriate. Such actions may be brought by any person against an agency prior to, or within sixty days after, the meeting out of which the violation of this section arises, except that if public announcement of such meeting is not initially provided by the agency in accordance with the requirements of this section, such action may be instituted pursuant to this section at any time prior to sixty days after any public announcement of such meeting. Such actions may be brought in the district court of the United States for the district in which the agency meeting is held or in which the agency in question has its headquarters, or in the District Court for the District of Columbia. In such actions a defendant shall serve his answer within thirty days after the service of the complaint. The burden is on the defendant to sustain his action. In deciding such cases the court may examine in camera any portion of the transcript, electronic recording, or minutes of a meeting closed to the public, and may take such additional evidence as it deems necessary. The court, having due regard for orderly administration and the public interest, as well as the interests of the parties, may grant such equitable relief as it deems appropriate, including granting an injunction against future violations of this section or ordering the agency to make available to the public such portion of the transcript, recording, or minutes of a meeting as is not authorized to be withheld under subsection (c) of this section.

(2) Any Federal court otherwise authorized by law to review agency action may, at the application of any person properly participating in the proceeding pursuant to other applicable law, inquire into violations by the agency of the requirements of this section and afford such relief as it deems appropriate. Nothing in this section authorizes any Federal court having jurisdiction solely on the basis of paragraph (1) to set aside, enjoin, or invalidate any agency action (other than an action to close a meeting or to withhold information under this section) taken or discussed at any agency meeting out of which the violation of this section arose.

(i) The court may assess against any party reasonable attorney fees and other litigation costs reasonably incurred by any other party who substantially prevails in any action brought in accordance with the provisions of subsection (g) or (h) of this section, except that costs may be assessed against the plaintiff only where the court finds that the suit was initiated by the plaintiff primarily for frivolous or dilatory purposes. In the cases of assessment of costs against an agency, the costs may be assessed by the court against the United States.

(j) Each agency subject to the requirements of this section shall annually report to Congress regarding its compliance with such requirements, including a tabulation of the total number of agency meetings open to the public, the total number of meetings closed to the public, the reasons for closing such meetings, and a description of any litigation brought against the agency under this section, including any costs assessed against the agency in such litigation (whether or not paid by the agency).

(k) Nothing herein expands or limits the present rights of any person under section 552 of this title, except that the exemptions set forth in subsection (c) of this section shall govern in the case of any request made pursuant to section 552 to copy or inspect the transcripts, recordings, or minutes described in subsection (f) of this section. The requirements of chapter 33 of title 44, United States Code, shall not apply to the transcriptions, recordings, and minutes described in subsection (f) of this section.

(l) This section does not constitute authority to withhold any information from Congress, and does not authorize the closing of any agency meeting or portion thereof required by any other provision of law to be open.

(m) Nothing in this section authorizes any agency to withhold from any individual any record, including transcripts, recordings, or minutes required by this section, which is otherwise accessible to such individual under section 552a of this title.

§553. Rule Making

(a) This section applices, according to the provisions thereof, except the extent that there is involved—

(1) a military or foreign affairs function of the United States; or

(2) a matter relating to agency management or personnel or to public property, loans, grants, benefits, or contracts.

(b) General notice of proposed rule making shall be published in the Federal Register, unless persons subject thereto are named and either personally served or otherwise have actual notice thereof in accordance with law. The notice shall include—

(1) a statement of the time, place, and nature of public rule making proceedings;

(2) reference to the legal authority under which the rule is proposed; and

(3) either the terms or substance of the proposed rule or a description of the subjects and issues involved.

Except when notice or hearing is required by statute, this subsection does not apply—

(A) to interpretative rules, general statements of policy, or rules of agency organization, procedure, or practice; or

(B) when the agency for good cause finds (and incorporates the finding and a brief statement of reasons therefor in the rules issued) that notice and public procedure thereon are impracticable, unnecessary, or contrary to the public interest.

(c) After notice required by this section, the agency shall give interested persons an opportunity to participate in the rule making through submission of written data, views, or arguments with or without opportunity for oral presentation. After consideration of the relevant matter presented, the agency shall incorporate in the rules adopted a concise general statement of their basis and purpose. When rules are required by statute to be made on the record after opportunity for an agency hearing, sections 556 and 557 of this title apply instead of this subsection.

(d) The required publication or service of a substantive rule shall be made not less than 30 days before its effective date, except—

(1) a substantive rule which grants or recognizes an exemption or relieves a restriction;

(2) interpretative rules and statements of policy; or

(3) as otherwise provided by the agency for good cause found and published with the rule.

(e) Each agency shall give an interested person the right to petition for the issuance, amendment, or repeal of a rule.

§554. Adjudications

(a) This section applies, according to the provisions thereof, in every case of adjudication required by statute to be determined on the record after opportunity for an agency hearing, except to the extent that there is involved—

(1) a matter subject to a subsequent trial of the law and the facts de novo in a court;

(2) the selection of tenure of an employee, except an administrative law judge appointed under section 3105 of this title;

(3) proceedings in which decisions rest solely on inspections, tests, or elections;

(4) the conduct of military or foreign affairs functions;

(5) cases in which an agency is acting as an agent for a court; or

(6) the certification of worker representatives.

(b) Persons entitled to notice of an agency hearing shall be timely informed of—

(1) the time, place, and nature of the hearing;

(2) the legal authority and jurisdiction under which the hearing is to be held; and

(3) the matters of fact and law asserted.

When private persons are the moving parties, other parties to the proceeding shall give prompt notice of issues controverted in fact or law; and in other instances agencies may by rule require responsive pleading. In fixing the time and place for hearings, due regard shall be had for the convenience and necessity of the parties or their representatives.

(c) The agency shall give all interested parties opportunity for—

(1) the submission and consideration of facts, arguments, offers of settlement, or proposals of adjustment when time, the nature of the proceeding, and the public interest permit; and

(2) to the extent that the parties are unable so to determine a controversy by consent, hearing and decision on notice and in accordance with sections 556 and 557 of this title.

(d) The employee who presides at the reception of evidence pursuant to section 556 of this title shall make the recommended decision or initial decision required by section 557 of this title, unless he becomes unavailable to the agency. Except to the extent required for the disposition of ex parte matters as authorized by law, such an employee may not—

(1) consult a person or party on a fact in issue, unless on notice and opportunity for all parties to participate; or

(2) be responsible to or subject to the supervision or direction of an employee or agent engaged in the performance of investigative or prosecuting functions for an agency.

An employee or agent engaged in the performance of investigative or prosecuting functions for an agency in a case may not, in that or a factually related case, participate or advise in the decision, recommended decision, or agency review pursuant to section 557 of this title, except as witness or counsel in public proceedings. This subsection does not apply—

(A) in determining applications for initial licenses;

(B) to proceedings involving the validity or application of rates, facilities, or practices of public utilities or carriers; or

(C) to the agency or a member or members of the body comprising the agency.

(e) The agency, with like effect as in the case of other orders, and in its sound discretion, may issue a declaratory order to terminate a controversy or remove uncertainty.

§555. Ancillary matters

(a) This section applies, according to the provisions thereof, except as otherwise provided by this subchapter.

(b) A person compelled to appear in person before an agency or representative thereof is entitled to be accompanied, represented, and advised by counsel or, if permitted by the agency, by other qualified representative. A party is entitled to appear in person or by or with counsel or other duly qualified representative in an agency proceeding. So far as the orderly conduct of public business permits, an interested person may appear before an agency or its responsible employees for the presentation, adjustment, or determination of an issue, request, or controversy in a proceeding, whether interlocutory, summary, or otherwise, or in connection with an agency function. With due regard for the convenience and necessity of the parties or their representatives and within a reasonable time, each agency shall proceed to conclude a matter presented to it. This subsection does not grant or deny a person who is not a lawyer the right to appear for or represent others before an agency or in an agency proceeding.

(c) Process, requirement of a report, inspection, or other investigative act or demand may not be issued, made, or enforced except as authorized by law. A person compelled to submit data or evidence is entitled to retain or, on payment of lawfully prescribed costs, procure a copy or transcript thereof, except that in a nonpublic investigatory proceeding the witness may for good cause be limited to inspection of the official transcript of his testimony.

(d) Agency subpoenas authorized by law shall be issued to a party on request and, when required by rules of procedure, on a statement or showing of general relevance and reasonable scope of the evidence sought. On contest, the court shall sustain the subpoena or similar process or demand to the extent that it is found to be accordance with law. In a proceeding for enforcement, the court shall issue an order requiring the appearance of the witness or the production of the evidence or data within a reasonable time under penalty of punishment for contempt in cases on contumacious failure to comply.

(e) Prompt notice shall be given of the denial in whole or in part of a written application, petition, or other request of an interested person made in connection with any agency proceeding. Except in affirming a prior denial or when the denial is self-explanatory, the notice shall be accompanied by a brief statement of the grounds for denial.

§556. Hearings; presiding employees; powers and duties; burden of proof; evidence; record as basis of decision

(a) This section applies, according to the provisions thereof, to hearings required by section 553 or 554 of this title to be conducted in accordance with this section.

(b) There shall preside at the taking of evidence—

(1) the agency;

(2) one or more members of the body which comprises the agency; or

(3) one or more administrative law judges appointed under section 3105 of this title.

This subchapter does not supersede the conduct of specified classes of proceedings, in whole or in part, by or before boards or other employees specially provided for by or designated under statute. The functions of presiding employees and of employees participating in decisions in accordance with section 557 of this title shall be conducted in an impartial manner. A presiding or participating employee may at any time disqualify himself. On the filing in good faith of a timely and sufficient affidavit of personal bias or other disqualification of a presiding or participating employee, the agency shall determine the matters as a part of the record and decision in the case.

(c) Subject to published rules of the agency and within its powers, employees presiding at hearings may—

(1) administer oaths and affirmations;

(2) issue subpoenas authorized by law;

(3) rule on offers of proof and receive relevant evidence;

(4) take depositions or have depositions taken when the ends of justice would be served;

(5) regulate the course of the hearing;

(6) hold conferences for the settlement or simplification of the issues by consent of the parties;

(7) dispose of procedural requests or similar matters;

(8) make or recommend decisions in accordance with section 557 of this title; and

(9) take other action authorized by agency rule consistent with this subchapter.

(d) Except as otherwise provided by statute, the proponent of a rule or order has the burden of proof. Any oral or documentary evidence may be received, but the agency as a matter of policy shall provide for the exclusion of irrelevant, immaterial, or unduly repetitious evidence. A sanction may not be imposed or rule or order issued except on consideration of the whole record or those parts thereof cited by a party and supported by and in accordance with the reliable, probative, and substantial evidence. The agency may, to the extent consistent with the interests of justice and the policy of the underlying statutes administered by the agency, consider a violation of section 557(d) of this title sufficient grounds for a decision adverse to a party who has knowingly committed such violation or knowingly caused such violation to occur. A party is entitled to present his case or defense by oral or documentary evidence, to submit rebuttal evidence, and to conduct such cross-examination as may be required for a full and true disclosure of the facts. In rule making or determining claims for money or benefits or applications for initial licenses an agency may, when a party will not be prejudiced thereby, adopt procedures for the submission of all or part of the evidence in written form.

(e) The transcript of testimony and exhibits, together with all papers and requests filed in the proceeding, constitutes the exclusive record for decision in accordance with section 557 of this title and, on payment of lawfully prescribed costs, shall be made available to the parties. When an agency decision rests on official notice of a material fact not appearing in the evidence in the record, a party is entitled, on timely request, to an opportunity to show the contrary.

§557. Initial decision; conclusiveness; review by agency; submissions by parties; contents of decisions; record

(a) This section applies, according to the provisions thereof, when a hearing is required to be conducted in accordance with section 556 of this title.

(b) When the agency did not preside at the reception of the evidence, the presiding employee or, in cases not subject to section 554(d) of this title, an employee qualified to preside at hearings pursuant to section 556 of this title, shall initially decide the case unless the agency requires, either in specific cases or by general rule, the entire record to be certified to it for decision. When the presiding employee makes an initial decision, that decision then becomes the decision of the agency without further proceedings unless there is an appeal to, or review on motion of, the agency within time provided by rule. On appeal from or review of the initial decision, the agency has all the powers which it would have in making the initial decision except as it may limit the issues on notice or by rule. When the agency makes the decision without having presided at the reception of the evidence, the presiding employee or an employee qualified to preside at hearings pursuant to section 556 of this title shall first recommend a decision, except that in rule making or determining application for initial licenses—

(1) instead thereof the agency may issue a tentative decision or one of its responsible employees may recommend a decision; or

(2) this procedure may be omitted in a case in which the agency finds on the record that due and timely execution of its functions imperatively and unavoidably so requires.

(c) Before a recommended, initial, or tentative decision, or a decision on agency review of the decision of subordinate employees, the parties are entitled to a reasonable opportunity to submit for the consideration of the employees participating in the decisions—

(1) proposed findings and conclusions; or

(2) exceptions to the decisions or recommended decisions of subordinate employees or to tentative agency decisions; and

(3) supporting reasons for the exceptions or proposed findings or conclusions.

The record shall show the ruling on each finding, conclusion, or exception presented. All decisions, including initial, recommended, and tentative decisions, are a part of the record and shall include a statement of—

(A) findings and conclusions, and the reasons or basis therefor, on all the material issues of fact, law, or discretion presented on the record; and

(B) the appropriate rule, order, sanction, relief, or denial thereof.

(d) (1) In any agency proceeding which is subject to subsection (a) of this section, except to the extent required for the disposition of *ex parte* matters as authorized by law—

(A) no interested person outside the agency shall make or knowingly cause to be made to any member of the body comprising the agency, administrative law judge, or other employee who is or may reasonably be expected to be involved in the decisional process of the proceeding, an *ex parte* communication relevant to the merits of the proceeding;

(B) no member of the body comprising the agency, administrative law judge, or other employee who is or may reasonably be expected to be involved in the decisional process of the proceeding, shall make or knowingly cause to be made to any interested person outside the agency an *ex parte* communication relevant to the merits of the proceeding;

(C) a member of the body comprising the agency, administrative law judge, or other employee who is or may reasonably be expected to be involved in the decisional process of such proceeding who receives, or who makes or knowingly causes to be made, a communication prohibited by this subsection shall place on the public record of the proceeding;

(i) all such written communications;

(ii) memoranda stating the substance of all such oral communications; and

(iii) all written responses, and memoranda stating the substance of all oral responses, to the materials described in clauses (i) and (ii) of this subparagraph;

(D) upon receipt of a communication knowingly made or knowingly caused to be made by a party in violation of this subsection, the agency, administrative law judge, or other employee presiding at the hearing may, to the extent consistent with the interests of justice and the policy of the underlying statutes, require the party to show cause why his claim or interest in the proceeding should not be dismissed, denied, disregarded, or otherwise adversely affected on account of such violation; and

(E) the prohibitions of this subsection shall apply beginning at such time as the agency may designate, but in no case shall they begin to apply later than the time at which a proceeding is noticed for hearing unless the person responsible for the communication has knowledge that it will be noticed, in which case the prohibitions shall apply beginning at the time of this acquisition of such knowledge.

(2) This subsection does not constitute authority to withhold information from Congress.

§558. Imposition of sanctions; determination of applications for licenses; suspension, revocation, and expiration of licenses

(a) This section applies, according to the provisions thereof, to the exercise of a power or authority.

(b) A sanction may not be imposed or a substantive rule or order issued except within jurisdiction delegated to the agency and as authorized by law.

(c) When application is made for a license required by law, the agency, with due regard for the rights and privileges of all the interested parties or adversely affected persons and within a reasonable time, shall set and complete proceedings required by law and shall make its decision. Except in cases of willfulness or those in which public health, interest, or safety requires otherwise, the withdrawal, suspension, revocation, or annulment of a license is lawful only if, before the institution of agency proceedings therefor, the licensee has been given—

(1) notice by the agency in writing of the facts or conduct which may warrant the action; and

(2) opportunity to demonstrate or achieve compliance with all lawful requirements.

When the licensee has made timely and sufficient application for a renewal or a new license in accordance with agency rules, a license with reference to an activity of a continuing nature does not expire until the application has been finally determined by the agency.

§559. Effect on other laws; effect of subsequent statutes.

This subchapter, chapter 7, and sections 1305, 3105, 3344, 4301 (2)(E), 5362, and 7521 of this title, and the provisions of section 5335(a)(B) of this title that relate to administrative law judges, do not limit or repeal additional requirements imposed by statute or otherwise recognized by law. Except as otherwise required by law, requirements or privileges relating to evidence or procedure apply equally to agencies and persons. Each agency is granted the authority necessary to comply with the requirements of this subchapter through the issuance of rules or otherwise. Subsequent statutes may not be held to supersede or modify this subchapter, chapter 7, sections 1305, 3105, 3344, 4301(2)(E), 5372, or 7521, or the provisions of section 5335(a)(B) of this title that relate to administrative law judges, except to the extent that it does so expressly.

§601. Analysis of Regulatory Functions—Definitions.

For purposes of this chapter—

(1) the term "agency" means an agency as defined in section 551(1) of this title;

(2) the term "rule" means any rule for which the agency publishes a general notice of proposed rulemaking pursuant to section 553(b) of this title, or any other law, including any rule of general applicability governing Federal grants to State and local governments for which the agency provides an opportunity for notice and public comment, except that the term "rule" does not include a rule of particular applicability relating to rates, wages, corporate or financial structures or reorganizations thereof, prices, facilities, appliances, services, or allowances therefor or to valuations, costs or accounting, or practices relating to such rates, wages, structures, prices, appliances, services, or allowances;

(3) the term "small business" has the same meaning as the term "small business concern" under section 3 of the Small Business Act, unless an agency, after

consultation with the Office of Advocacy of the Small Business Administration and after opportunity for public comment establishes one or more definitions of such term which are appropriate to the activities of the agency and publishes such definition(s) in the Federal Register;

(4) the term "small organization" means any not-for-profit enterprise which is independently owned and operated and is not dominant in its field, unless an agency establishes, after opportunity for public comment, one or more definitions of such term which are appropriate to the activities of the agency and publishes such definition(s) in the Federal Register;

(5) the term "small government jurisdiction" means governments of cities, counties, towns, townships, villages, school districts or special districts, with a population of less than fifty thousand, unless an agency establishes, after opportunity for public comment, one or more definitions of such term which are appropriate to the activities of the agency and which are based on such factors as location in rural or sparsely populated areas or limited revenues due to the population of such jurisdiction, and publishes such definition(s); in the Federal Register; and

(6) the term "small entity" shall have the same meaning as the terms "small business," "small organization" and "small governmental jurisdiction" defined in paragraphs (3), (4) and (5) of this section.

§602. Regulatory agenda.

(a) During the months of October and April of each year, each agency shall publish in the Federal Register a regulatory flexibility agenda which shall contain—

(1) a brief description of the subject area of any rule which the agency expects to propose or promulgate which is likely to have a significant economic impact on a substantial number of small entities;

(2) a summary of the nature of any such rule under consideration for each subject area listed in the agenda pursuant to paragraph (1), the objectives and legal basis for the issuance of the rule, and an approximate schedule for completing action on any rule for which the agency has issued a general notice of proposed rulemaking, and

(3) the name and telephone number of an agency official knowledgeable concerning the items listed in paragraph (1).

(b) Each regulatory flexibility agenda will be transmitted to the Chief Counsel for Advocacy of the Small Business Administration for comment, if any.

(c) Each agency shall endeavor to provide notice of each regulatory flexibility agenda to small entities or their representatives through direct notification or publication of the agenda in publications likely to be obtained by such small entities and shall invite comments upon each subject area on the agenda.

(d) Nothing in this section precludes an agency from considering or acting on any matter not included in a regulatory flexibility agenda, or requires an agency to consider or act on any matter listed in such agenda.

§603. Initial regulatory flexibility analysis.

(a) Whenever an agency is required by section 553 of this title, or any other law, to publish general notice of proposed rulemaking for any proposed rule, the agency shall prepare and make available for public comment an initial regulatory flexibility analysis. Such analysis shall describe the impact of the proposed rule on small entities. The initial regulatory flexibility analysis or a summary shall be published in the Federal Register at the time of the publication of general notice of proposed rulemaking for the rule. The agency shall transmit a copy of the initial regulatory flexibility analysis to the Chief Counsel for Advocacy of the Small Business Administration.

(b) Each initial regulatory flexibility analysis required under this section shall contain—

(1) a description of the reasons why action by the agency is being considered;

(2) a succinct statement of the objectives of, and legal basis for, the proposed rule;

(3) a description of and, where feasible, an estimate of the number of small entities to which the proposed rule will apply;

(4) a description of the projected reporting, recordkeeping and other compliance requirements of the proposed rule, including an estimate of the classes of small entities which will be subject to the requirement and the type of professional skills necessary for preparation of the report or record;

(5) an identification, to the extent practicable, of all relevant Federal rules which may duplicate, overlap or conflict with the proposed rule.

(c) Each initial regulatory flexibility analysis shall also contain a description of any significant alternatives to the proposed rule which accomplish the stated objectives of applicable statutes and which minimize any significant economic impact of the proposed rule on small entities. Consistent with the stated objectives of applicable statutes, the analysis shall discuss significant alternatives such as—

(1) the establishment of differing compliance or reporting requirements or timetables that take into account the resources available to small entities;

(2) the clarification, consolidation, or simplification of compliance and reporting requirements under the rule for such small entities;

(3) the use of performance rather than design standards; and

(4) an exemption from coverage of the rule, or any part thereof, for such small entities.

§604. Final regulatory flexibility analysis.

(a) When an agency promulgates a final rule under section 553 of this title, after being required by that section or any other law to publish a general notice of proposed rulemaking, the agency shall prepare a final regulatory flexibility analysis. Each final regulatory flexibility analysis shall contain—

(1) a succinct statement of the need for, and the objectives of, the rule;

(2) a summary of the issues raised by the public comments in response to the initial regulatory flexibility analysis, a summary of the assessment of the agency of such issues, and a statement of any changes made in the proposed rule as a result of such comments; and

(3) a description of each of the significant alternatives to the rule consistent with the stated objectives of applicable statutes and designed to minimize any significant economic impact of the rule on small entities which was considered by the agency, and a statement of the reasons why each one of such alternatives was rejected.

(b) The agency shall make copies of the final regulatory flexibility analysis available to members of the public and shall publish in the Federal Register at the time of publication of the final rule under section 553 of this title a statement describing how the public may obtain such copies.

§605. Avoidance of duplicative or unnecessary analyses.

(a) Any Federal agency may perform the analyses required by sections 602, 603, and 604 of this title in conjunction with or as part of any other agenda or analysis required by any other law if such other analysis satisfies the provisions of such sections.

(b) Sections 603 and 604 of this title shall not apply to any proposed or final rule if the head of the agency certifies that the rule will not, if promulgated, have a significant economic impact on a substantial number of small entities. If the head of the agency makes a certification under the preceding sentence, the agency shall publish such certification in the Federal Register, at the time of publication of general notice of proposed rulemaking for the rule or at the time of publication of the final rule, along with a succinct statement explaining the reasons for such certification, and provide such certification and statement to the Chief Counsel for Advocacy of the Small Business Administration.

(c) In order to avoid duplicative action, an agency may consider a series of closely related rules as one rule for the purpose of sections 602, 603, 604 and 610 of this title.

§606. Effect on other law.

The requirements of sections 603 and 604 of this title do not alter in any manner standards otherwise applicable by law to agency action.

§607. Preparation of analyses.

In complying with the provisions of sections 603 and 604 of this title, an agency may provide either a quantifiable or numerical description of the effects of a proposed rule or alternatives to the proposed rule, or more general descriptive statements if quantification is not practicable or reliable.

§608. Procedure for waiver or delay of completion.

(a) An agency head may waive or delay the completion of some or all of the requirements of section 603 of this title by publishing in the Federal Register, not later than the date of publication of the final rule, a written finding, with reasons therefor, that the final rule is being promulgated in response to an emergency that makes compliance or timely compliance with the provisions of section 603 of this title impracticable.

(b) Except as provided in section 605(b), an agency head may not waive the requirements of section 604 of this title. An agency head may delay the completion of the requirements of section 604 of this title for a period of not more than one hundred and eighty days after the date of publication in the Federal Register of a final rule by publishing in the Federal Register, not later than such date of publication, a written finding, with reasons therefor, that the final rule is being promulgated in response to an emergency that makes timely compliance with the provisions of section 604 of this title impracticable. If the agency has not prepared a final regulatory flexibility analysis pursuant to section 604 of this title within one hundred and eighty days from the date of publication of the final rule, such rule shall lapse and have no effect. Such a rule shall not be repromulgated until a final regulatory flexibility analysis has been completed by the agency.

§609. Procedures for gathering comments.

When any rule is promulgated which will have a significant economic impact on a substantial number of small entities, the head of the agency promulgating the rule of the official of the agency with statutory responsibility for the promulgation of the rule shall assure that small entities have been given an opportunity to participate in the rulemaking for the rule through techniques such as—

    (1) the inclusion in an advanced notice of proposed rulemaking, if issued, of a statement that the proposed rule may have a significant economic effect on a substantial number of small entities;

    (2) the publication of general notice of proposed rulemaking in publications likely to be obtained by small entities;

    (3) the direct notification of interested small entities;

    (4) the conduct of open conferences or public hearings concerning the rule for small entities; and

    (5) the adoption or modification of agency procedural rules to reduce the cost or complexity of participation in the rulemakings by small entities.

§610. Periodic review of rules.

  (a) Within one hundred and eighty days after the effective date of this chapter, each agency shall publish in the Federal Register a plan for the periodic review of the rules issued by the agency which have or will have a significant economic impact upon a substantial number of small entities. Such plan may be amended by the agency at any time by publishing a revision in the Federal Register. The purpose of the review shall be to determine whether such rules should be continued without change, should be amended or rescinded, consistent with the stated objectives of applicable statutes, to minimize any significant economic impact of the rules upon a substantial number of such small entities. The plan shall provide for the review of all such agency rules existing on the effective date of this chapter within ten years of that date for the review of such rules adopted after the effective date of this chapter within ten years of the publication of such rules as the final rule. If the head of the agency determines that completion of the review of existing rules is not feasible by the established date, he shall so certify in a statement published in the Federal Register and may extend the completion date by one year at a time for a total of not more than five years.

  (b) In reviewing rules to minimize any significant economic impact of the rule on a substantial number of small entities in a manner consistent with the stated objectives of applicable statutes, the agency shall consider the following factors—

    (1) the continued need for the rule;

    (2) the nature of complaints or comments received concerning the rule from the public;

    (3) the complexity of the rule;

    (4) the extent to which the rule overlaps, duplicates or conflicts with other Federal rules, and, to the extent feasible, with State and local governmental rules; and

    (5) the length of time since the rule has been evaluated or the degree to which technology, economic conditions, or other factors have changed in the area affected by the rule.

  (c) Each year, each agency shall publish in the Federal Register a list of the rules which have a substantial economic impact on a substantial number of small entities, which are to be reviewed pursuant to this section during the succeeding twelve months. The list shall include a brief description of each rule and the need for and legal basis of such rule and shall invite public comment upon the rule.

§611. Judicial review.

(a) Except as otherwise provided in subsection (b), any determination by an agency concerning the applicability of any of the provisions of this chapter to any section of the agency shall not be subject to judicial review.

(b) Any regulatory flexibility analysis prepared under sections 603 and 604 of this title and the compliance or noncompliance of the agency with the provisions of this chapter shall not be subject to judicial review. When an action for judicial review of a rule is instituted, any regulatory flexibility analysis for such rule shall constitute part of the while record of agency action in connection with the review.

(c) Nothing in this section bars judicial review of any other impact statement or similar analysis required by any other law if judicial review of such statement or analysis is otherwise provided by law.

§612. Reports and intervention rights.

(a) The Chief Counsel for Advocacy of the Small Business Administration shall monitor agency compliance with this chapter and shall report at least annually thereon to the President and to the Committees on the Judiciary of the Senate and House of Representatives, the Select Committee on Small Business of the Senate, and the Committee on Small Business of the House of Representatives.

(b) The Chief Counsel for Advocacy of the Small Business Administration is authorized to appear as amicus curiae in any action brought in a court of the United States to review a rule. In any such action, the Chief Counsel is authorized to present his views with respect to the effect of the rule on small entities.

(c) A court of the United States shall grant the application of the Chief Counsel for Advocacy of the Small Business Administration to appear in such action for the purposes described in subsection (b).

§701. Application; definitions

(a) This chapter applies, according to the provisions thereof, except to the extent that—
    (1) statutes preclude judicial review; or
    (2) agency action is committed to agency discretion by law.
(b) For the purpose of this chapter—
    (1) "agency" means each authority of the Government of the United States, whether or not it is within or subject to review by another agency, but does not include—
        (A) the Congress;
        (B) the courts of the United States;
        (C) the governments of the territories or possessions of the United States;
        (D) the government of the District of Columbia;
        (E) agencies composed of representatives of the parties or of representatives of organizations of the parties to the disputes determined by them;

(F) courts martial and military commissions;

(G) military authority exercised in the field in time of war or in occupied territory; or

(H) functions conferred by sections 1738, 1739, 1743, and 1744 of title 12; chapter 2 of title 41; or sections 1622, 1884, 1891–1902, and former section 1641 (b) (2), of title 50, appendix; and

(2) "person," "rule," "order," "license," "sanction," "relief," and "agency action" have the meanings given them by section 551 of this title.

§702. Right of review

A person suffering legal wrong because of agency action, or adversely affected or aggrieved by agency action within the meaning of a relevant statute, is entitled to judicial review thereof. An action in a court of the United States seeking relief other than money damages and stating a claim that an agency or an officer or employee thereof acted or failed to act in an official capacity or under color of legal authority shall not be dismissed nor relief therein be denied on the ground that it is against the United States or that the United States is an indispensable party. The United States may be named as a defendant in any such action, and a judgment or decree may be entered against the United States: *Provided,* That any mandatory or injunctive decree shall specify the Federal officer or officers (by name or by title), and their successors in office, personally responsible for compliance. Nothing herein (1) affects other limitations on judicial review or the power or duty of the court to dismiss any action or deny relief on any other appropriate legal or equitable ground; or (2) confers authority to grant relief if any other statute that grants consent to suit expressly or impliedly forbids the relief which is sought.

§703. Form and venue of proceeding

The form of proceeding for judicial review is the special statutory review proceeding relevant to the subject matter in a court specified by statute or, in the absence or inadequacy thereof, any applicable form of legal action, including actions for declaratory judgments or writs of prohibitory or mandatory injunction or habeas corpus, in a court of competent jurisdiction. If no special stautory review proceeding is applicable, the action for judicial review may be brought against the United States, the agency by its official title, or the appropriate officer. Except to the extent that prior, adequate, and exclusive opportunity for judicial review is provided by law, agency action is subject to judicial review in civil or criminal proceedings for judicial enforcement.

§704. Actions reviewable

Agency action made reviewable by statute and final agency action for which there is no other adequate remedy in a court are subject to judicial review. A preliminary, procedural, or intermediate agency action or ruling not directly reviewable is subject to review on the review of the final agency action. Except as otherwise expressly required by statute, agency action otherwise final is final for the purposes of this section whether or not there has been presented or determined an application for a declaratory order, for any form of reconsideration, or, unless the agency otherwise requires by rule and provides that the action meanwhile is inoperative, for an appeal to superior agency authority.

§705. Relief pending review

When an agency finds that justice so requires, it may postpone the effective date of action taken by it, pending judicial review. On such conditions as may be required and to the extent necessary to prevent irreparable injury, the reviewing court, including the court to which a case may be taken on appeal from or on application for certiorari or other writ to a reviewing court, may issue all necessary and appropriate process to postpone the effective date of an agency action or to preserve status or rights pending conclusion of the review proceedings.

§706. Scope of review

To the extent necessary to decision and when presented, the reviewing court shall decide all relevant questions of law, interpret constitutional and statutory provisions, and determine the meaning or applicability of the terms of an agency action. The reviewing court shall—

(1) compel agency action unlawfully withheld or unreasonably delayed; and

(2) hold unlawful and set aside agency action, findings, and conclusions found to be—

(A) arbitrary, capricious, an abuse of discretion, or otherwise not in accordance with law;

(B) contrary to constitutional right, power, privilege, or immunity;

(C) in excess of statutory jurisdiction, authority, or limitations, or short of statutory right;

(D) without observance of procedure required by law;

(E) unsupported by substantial evidence in a case subject to sections 556 and 557 of this title or otherwise reviewed on the record of an agency hearing provided by statute; or

(F) unwarranted by the facts to the extent that the facts are subject to trial *do novo* by the reviewing court.

In making the foregoing determinations, the court shall review the whole record of those parts of it cited by a party, and due account shall be taken of the rule of prejudicial error.

§1305. Administrative law judges

For the purposes of sections 3105, 3344, 4301(2)(D), and 5372 of this title and the provisions of section 5335(a)(B) of this title that relate to administrative law judges, the Office of Personnel Management may, and for the purpose of section 7521 of this title the Merit System Protection Board may investigate, require reports by agencies, issue reports, including an annual report to Congress, prescribe regulations, appoint advisory committees as necessary, recommend legislation, subpoena witnesses and records, and pay witness fees as established for the courts of the United States.

§3105. Appointment of administrative law judges

Each agency shall appoint as many administrative law judges as are necessary for proceedings required to be conducted in accordance with sections 556 and 557 of this title. Administrative law judges shall be assigned to cases in rotation so far as practicable, and may not perform duties inconsistent with their duties and responsibilities as administrative law judges.

§3344. Details, administrative law judges

An agency as defined by section 551 of this title which occasionally or temporarily is insufficiently staffed with administrative law judges appointed under section 3105 of this title may use administrative law judges selected by the Office of Personnel Management from and with the consent of other agencies.

§5362. Administrative law judges

Administrative law judges appointed under section 3105 of this title are entitled to pay prescribed by the Office of Personnel Management independently of agency recommendations or ratings and in accordance with subchapter III of this chapter and chapter 51 of this title.

§7521. Actions against administrative law judges

(a) An action may be taken against an administrative law judge appointed under section 3105 of this title by the agency in which the administrative law judge is employed only for good cause established and determined by the Merit System Protection Board on the record after opportunity for hearing before the Board.

(b) The actions covered by this section are—
   (1) a removal;
   (2) a suspension;
   (3) a reduction in grade;
   (4) a reduction in pay; and
   (5) a furlough of 30 days or less;
   but do not include—
      (A) a suspension or removal under section 7532 of this title;
      (B) a reduction-in-force action under section 3502 of this title; or
      (C) any action initiated under section 1206 of this title.

2. Executive Order 12291
46 *Federal Register* 13193 (1981)

By the authority vested in me as President by the Constitution and laws of the United States of America, and in order to reduce the burdens of existing and future regulations, increase agency accountability for regulatory actions, provide for presidential oversight of the regulatory process, minimize duplication and conflict of regulations and insure well-reasoned regulations, it is hereby ordered as follows:

Section 1. *Definitions.* For the purposes of this Order:

(a) "Regulation" or "rule" means an agency statement of general applicability and future effect designed to implement, interpret, or prescribe law or policy or describing the procedure or practice requirements of an agency, but does not include:

    (1) Administrative actions governed by the provisions of Sections 556 and 557 of Title 5 of the United States Code;

    (2) Regulations issued with respect to a military or foreign affairs function of the United States; or

    (3) Regulations related to agency organization, management, or personnel.

(b) "Major rule" means any regulation that is likely to result in:

    (1) An annual effect on the economy of $100 million or more;

    (2) A major increase in costs or prices for consumers, individual industries, Federal, State, or local government agencies, or geographic regions; or

    (3) Significant adverse effects on competition, employment, investment, productivity, innovation, or on the ability of United States-based enterprises to compete with foreign-based enterprises in domestic or export markets.

(c) "Director" means the Director of the Office of Management and Budget.

(d) "Agency" means any authority of the United States that is an "agency" under 44 U.S.C. 3502(1), excluding those agencies specified in 44 U.S.C. 3502(10).

(e) "Task Force" means the Presidential Task Force on Regulatory Relief.

435

Sec. 2. *General Requirements.* In promulgating new regulations, reviewing existing regulations, and developing legislative proposals concerning regulations, all agencies, to the extent permitted by law, shall adhere to the following requirements:

(a) Administrative decisions shall be based on adequate information concerning the need for and consequences of proposed government action;

(b) Regulatory action shall not be undertaken unless the potential benefits to society for the regulation outweigh the potential costs to society;

(c) Regulatory objectives shall be chosen to maximize the net benefits to society;

(d) Among alternative approaches to any given regulatory objective, the alternative involving the least net cost to society shall be chosen; and

(e) Agencies shall set regulatory priorities with the aim of maximizing the aggregate net benefits to society, taking into account the condition of the particular industries affected by regulations, the condition of the national economy, and other regulatory actions contemplated for the future.

Sec. 3. *Regulatory Impact Analysis and Review.*

(a) In order to implement Section 2 of this Order, each agency shall, in connection with every major rule, prepare, and to the extent permitted by law consider, a Regulatory Impact Analysis. Such Analyses may be combined with any Regulatory Flexibility Analyses performed under 5 U.S.C. 603 and 604.

(b) Each agency shall initially determine whether a rule it intends to propose or to issue is a major rule, *provided that,* the Director, subject to the direction of the Task Force, shall have authority, in accordance with Sections 1(b) and 2 of this Order to prescribe criteria for making such determinations, to order a rule to be treated as a major rule, and to require any set of related rules to be considered together as a major rule.

(c) Except as provided in Section 8 of this Order, agencies shall prepare Regulatory Impact Analyses of major rules and transmit them, along with all notices of proposed rulemaking and all final rules, to the Director as follows:

(1) If no notice of proposed rulemaking is to be published for a proposed major rule that is not an emergency rule, the agency shall prepare only a final Regulatory Impact Analysis, which shall be transmitted along with the proposed rule, to the Director at least 60 days prior to the publication of the major rule as a final rule;

(2) With respect to all other major rules, the agency shall prepare a preliminary Regulatory Impact Analysis, which shall be transmitted, along with a notice of proposed rulemaking, to the Director at least 60 days prior to the publication of a notice of proposed rulemaking, and a final Regulatory Impact Analysis, which shall be transmitted along with the final rule at least 30 days prior to the publication of the major rule as a final rule;

(3) For all rules other than major rules, agencies shall submit to the Director, at least 10 days prior to publication, every notice of proposed rulemaking and final rule.

(d) To permit each proposed major rule to be analyzed in light of the requirements stated in Section 2 of this Order, each preliminary and final Regulatory Impact Analysis shall contain the following information:

(1) A description of the potential benefits of the rule, including any beneficial effects that cannot be quantified in monetary terms, and the identification of those likely to receive the benefits;

(2) A description of the potential costs of the rule, including any adverse effects that cannot be quantified in monetary terms, and the identification of those likely to bear the costs;

(3) A determination of the potential net benefits of the rule, including an evaluation of effects that cannot be quantified in monetary terms;

(4) A description of alternative approaches that could substantially achieve the same regulatory goal at lower cost, together with an analysis of this potential benefit and costs and a brief explanation of the legal reasons why such alternatives, if proposed, could not be adopted; and

(5) Unless covered by the description required under paragraph (4) of this subsection, an explanation of any legal reasons why the rule cannot be based on the requirements set forth in Section 2 of this Order.

(e) (1) The Director, subject to the direction of the Task Force, which shall resolve any issues raised under this Order or ensure that they are presented to the President, is authorized to review any preliminary or final Regulatory Impact Analysis, notice of proposed rulemaking, or final rule based on the requirements of this Order.

(2) The Director shall be deemed to have concluded review unless the Director advises an agency to the contrary under subsection (f) of this Section:

(A) Within 60 days of a submission under subsection (c)(1) or a submission of a preliminary Regulatory Impact Analysis or notice of proposed rulemaking under subsection (c)(2);

(B) Within 30 days of the submission of a final Regulatory Impact Analysis and a final rule under subsection (c)(2); and

(C) Within 10 days of the submission of a notice of proposed rulemaking or final rule under subsection (c)(3).

(f) (1) Upon the request of the Director, an agency shall consult with the Director concerning the review of a preliminary Regulatory Impact Analysis or notice of proposed rulemaking under this Order, and shall, subject to Section 8(a)(2) of this Order, refrain from publishing its preliminary Regulatory Impact Analysis or notice of proposed rulemaking until such review is concluded.

(2) Upon receiving notice that the Director intends to submit views with respect to any final Regulatory Impact Analysis or final rule, the agency shall, subject to Section 8(a)(2) of this Order, refrain from publishing its final Regulatory Impact Analysis or final rule until the agency has responded to the Director's views, and incorporated those views and the agency's response in the rulemaking file.

(3) Nothing in this subsection shall be construed as displacing the agencies' responsibilities delegated by law.

(g) For every rule for which an agency publishes a notice of proposed rulemaking, the agency shall include in its notice:

(1) A brief statement setting forth the agency's initial determination whether the proposed rule is a major rule, together with the reasons underlying that determination; and

(2) For each proposed major rule, a brief summary of the agency's preliminary Regulatory Impact Analysis.

(h) Agencies shall make their preliminary and final Regulatory Impact Analyses available to the public.

(i) Agencies shall initiate reviews of currently effective rules in accordance with the purposes of this Order, and perform Regulatory Impact Analyses of currently effective major rules. The Director, subject to the direction of the Task Force, may designate currently effective rules for review in accordance with this Order, and establish schedules for reviews and Analyses under this Order.

Sec. 4. *Regulatory Review.* Before approving any final major rule, each agency shall:

(a) Make a determination that the regulation is clearly within the authority delegated by law and consistent with congressional intent, and include in the Federal Register at the time of promulgation a memorandum of law supporting that determination.

(b) Make a determination that the factual conclusions upon which the rule is based have substantial support in the agency record, viewed as a whole, with full attention to public comments in general and the comments of persons directly affected by the rule in particular.

Sec. 5. *Regulatory Agendas.*

(a) Each agency shall publish in October and April of each year, an agenda of proposed regulations that the agency has issued or expects to issue, and currently effective rules that are under agency review pursuant to this Order. These agendas may be incorporated with the agendas published under 5 U.S.C. 602, and must contain at the minimum:

   (1) A summary of the nature of each major rule being considered, the objectives and legal basis for the issuance of the rule, and an approximate schedule for completing action on any major rule for which the agency has issued a notice of proposed rulemaking;

   (2) The name and telephone number of a knowledgeable agency official for each item on the agenda; and

   (3) A list of existing regulations to be reviewed under the terms of this Order, and a brief discussion of each such regulation.

(b) The Director, subject to the direction of the Task Force, may, to the extent permitted by law:

   (1) Require agencies to provide additional information in an agenda; and

   (2) Require publication of the agenda in any form.

Sec. 6. *The Task Force and Office of Management and Budget.*

(a) To the extent permitted by law, the Director shall have authority, subject to the direction of the Task Force, to:

   (1) Designate any proposed or existing rule as a major rule in accordance with Section 1(b) of this Order;

   (2) Prepare and promulgate uniform standards for the identification of major rules and the development of Regulatory Impact Analyses;

   (3) Require an agency to obtain and evaluate, in connection with a regulation, any additional relevant data from any appropriate source;

   (4) Waive the requirements of Sections 3, 4, or 7 of this Order with respect to any proposed or existing major rule;

   (5) Identify duplicative, overlapping and conflicting rules, existing or proposed, and existing or proposed rules that are inconsistent with the policies underlying statutes governing agencies other than the issuing agency or with the purposes of this Order, and, in each such case, require appropriate interagency consultation to minimize or eliminate such duplication, overlap, or conflict;

   (6) Develop procedures for estimating the annual benefits and costs of agency regulations, on both an aggregate and economic or industrial sector basis, for purposes of compiling a regulatory budget;

   (7) In consultation with interested agencies, prepare for consideration by the President recommendations for changes in the agencies' statutes; and

(8) Monitor agency compliance with the requirements of this Order and advise the President with respect to such compliance.

(b) The Director, subject to the direction of the Task Force, is authorized to establish procedures for the performance of all functions vested in the Director by this Order. The Director shall take appropriate steps to coordinate the implementation of the analysis, transmittal, review, and clearance provisions of this Order with the authorities and requirements provided for or imposed upon the Director and agencies under the Regulatory Flexibility Act, 5 U.S.C. 601 *et seq.*, and the Paperwork Reduction Plan Act of 1980, 44 U.S.C. 3501 *et seq.*

Sec. 7. *Pending Regulations.*

(a) To the extent necessary to permit reconsideration in accordance with this Order, agencies shall, except as provided in Section 8 of this Order, suspend or postpone the effective dates of all major rules that they have promulgated in final form as of the date of this Order, but that have not yet become effective, excluding:

(1) Major rules that cannot legally be postponed or suspended;

(2) Major rules that, for good cause, ought to become effective as final rules without reconsideration. Agencies shall prepare, in accordance with Section 3 of this Order, a final Regulatory Impact Analysis for each major rule that they suspend or postpone.

(b) Agencies shall report to the Director no later than 15 days prior to the effective date of any rule that the agency has promulgated in final form as of the date of this Order, and that has not yet become effective, and that will not be reconsidered under subsection (a) of this Section;

(1) That the rule is excepted from reconsideration under subsection (a), including a brief statement of the legal or other reasons for that determination; or

(2) That the rule is not a major rule.

(c) The Director, subject to the direction of the Task Force, is authorized, to the extent permitted by law, to:

(1) Require reconsideration, in accordance with this Order, of any major rule that an agency has issued in final form as of the date of this Order and that has not become effective; and

(2) Designate a rule that an agency has issued in final form as of the date of this Order and that has not yet become effective as a major rule in accordance with Section 1(b) of this Order.

(d) Agencies may, in accordance with the Administrative Procedure Act and other applicable statutes, permit major rules that they have issued in final form as of the date of this Order, and that have not yet become effective, to take effect as interim rules while they are being reconsidered in accordance with this Order, *provided that,* agencies shall report to the Director, no later than 15 days before any such rule is proposed to take effect as an interim rule, that the rule should appropriately take effect as an interim rule while the rule is under reconsideration.

(e) Except as provided in Section 8 of this Order, agencies shall, to the extent permitted by law, refrain from promulgating as a final rule any proposed major rule that has been published or issued as of the date of this Order until a final Regulatory Impact Analysis, in accordance with Section 3 of this Order, has been prepared for the proposed major rule.

(f) Agencies shall report to the Director, no later than 30 days prior to promulgating as a final rule any proposed rule that the agency has published or issued as of the date of this Order and that has not been considered under the terms of this Order:

(1) That the rule cannot legally be considered in accordance with this Order, together with a brief explanation of the legal reasons barring such consideration; or

(2) That the rule is not a major rule, in which case the agency shall submit to the Director a copy of the proposed rule.

(g) The Director, subject to the direction of the Task Force, is authorized, to the extent permitted by law, to:

(1) Require consideration, in accordance with this Order, of any proposed major rule that the agency has published or issued as of the date of this Order; and

(2) Designate a proposed rule that an agency has published or issued as of the date of this Order, as a major rule in accordance with Section 1(b) of this Order.

(h) The Director shall be deemed to have determined that an agency's report to the Director under subsections (b), (d), or (f) of this Section is consistent with the purposes of this Order, unless the Director advises the agency to the contrary:

(1) Within 15 days of its report, in the case of any report under subsections (b) or (d); or

(2) Within 30 days of its report, in the case of any report under subsection (f).

(i) This Section does not supersede the President's Memorandum of January 29, 1981, entitled "Postponement of Pending Regulations", which shall remain in effect until March 30, 1981.

(j) In complying with this Section, agencies shall comply with all applicable provisions of the Administrative Procedure Act, and with any other procedural requirements made applicable to the agencies by other statutes.

Sec. 8. *Exemptions.*

(a) The procedures prescribed by this Order shall not apply to:

(1) Any regulation that responds to an emergency situation, *provided that*, any such regulation shall be reported to the Director as soon as is practicable, the agency shall publish in the Federal Register a statement of the reasons why it is impracticable for the agency to follow the procedures of this Order with respect to such a rule, and the agency shall prepare and transmit as soon as is practicable a Regulatory Impact Analysis of any such major rule; and

(2) Any regulation for which consideration or reconsideration under the terms of this Order would conflict with deadlines imposed by statute or by judicial order, *provided that*, any such regulation shall be reported to the Director together with a brief explanation of the conflict, the agency shall publish in the Federal Register a statement of the reasons why it is impracticable for the agency to follow the procedures of this Order with respect to such a rule, and the agency, in consultation with the Director, shall adhere to the requirements of this Order to the extent permitted by statutory or judicial deadlines.

(b) The Director, subject to the direction of the Task Force, may, in accordance with the purposes of this Order, exempt any class or category of regulations from any or all requirements of this Order.

Sec. 9. *Judicial Review.* This Order is intended only to improve the internal management of the Federal government, and is not intended to create any right or benefit, substantive or procedural, enforceable at law by a party against the United States, its agencies, its officers or any person. The determinations made by agencies under Section 4 of this Order, and any Regulatory Impact Analyses for any rule, shall be made part of the whole record of agency action in connection with the rule.

Sec. 10. *Revocations.* Executive Orders No. 12044, as amended, and No. 12174 are revoked.

Selected Readings on Law and Administration

ABA, Administrative Law Section, Symposium: "The Administrative Conference of the United States," 26 *Admin. L. Rev.* 259 (1974).

ABA, National Institute, Symposium: "Federal Agencies and the Public Interest." 26 *Admin. L. Rev.* 207 (1974).

American University Law Review. "First Annual Administrative Law Issue: Informal Administrative Practices." 26 *American U. L. Rev.* 795 (1975).

Baker, Warner. "Policy by Rule or Ad Hoc Approach—Which Should It Be?" 22 *Law and Contemp. Problems* 658 (1957).

Baram, Michael S., "Cost-Benefit Analysis: An Inadequate Basis for Health, Safety, and Environmental Regulatory Decisionmaking." 8 *Ecology L. Q.* 473 (1980).

Bazelon, David L. "The Impact of the Courts on Public Administration." 52 *Indian L. J.* 101 (1976).

———. "Risk and Responsibility." 65 *ABA Journal* 1066 (1979).

Becker, Theodore and Malcolm Feeley. *The Impact of Supreme Court Decisions.* 2d ed. New York: Oxford University Press, 1973.

Benjamin, Robert. *Administrative Adjudication in the State of New York.* Albany: New York State, 1942.

Berger, Raoul. "Administrative Arbitrariness and Judicial Review." 64 *Columbia L. Rev.* 55 (1965).

———. "Administrative Arbitrariness— A Rejoinder to Professor Davis." 114 *U. Pennsylvania L. Rev.* 816 (1966).

———. "Administrative Arbitrariness—A Reply to Professor Davis' 'Final Word.' " 114 *U. Pennsylvania L. Rev.* 783 (1966).

———. "Administrative Arbitrariness—Sequel." 51 *Minnesota L. Rev.* 601 (1967).

———. *Government by the Judiciary.* Cambridge, Mass.: Harvard University Press, 1977.

———. "Synthesis." 78 *Yale L. J.* 965 (1969).

Berle, Adolf A., Jr. *The Three Faces of Power.* New York: Harcourt, Brace & World, 1959.

————, and Gardiner Means. *The Modern Corporation and Private Property.* New York: Macmillan, 1932.

Berman, Harold, and William Greiner. *The Nature and Functions of Law.* Mineola, N.Y.: Foundation Press, 1972.

Berstein, Marver H. *Regulating Business by Independent Commission.* Princeton, N.J.: Princeton University Press, 1955.

————, ed. *The Government as Regulator.* Annals, vol. 400. American Academy of Political and Social Science, 1972.

Bock, Edwin, ed. *Government Regulation of Business.* Englewood Cliffs, N.J.: Prentice-Hall, 1965.

Brandeis, Louis D. *Other People's Money.* New York: Harper & Row, 1967.

Cardozo, Benjamin N. *The Nature of the Judicial Process.* New Haven, Conn.: Yale University Press, 1921.

Carrow, Milton M. *The Background of Administrative Law.* Newark, N.J.: Associated Lawyers, 1948.

Cary, William L. *Politics and the Regulatory Agencies.* New York: McGraw-Hill, 1967.

Case, C., and D. Schoenbrod. "Electricity or the Environment: A Study of Public Regulation Without Public Control," 61 *California L. Rev.* 961 (1973)

Chayes, Abraham. "The Role of the Judge in Public Law Litigation," 89 *Harvard L. Rev.* 1281 (1976).

Christensen, Craig W., and Roger G. Middlekauf. *Federal Administrative Law: Practice and Procedure.* New York: Practicing Law Institute, 1977.

Comment: "Recombinant DNA: A Case Study in Regulation of Scientific Research," 8 *Ecology L. Q.* 55 (1979).

Cooper, Frank E. *Administrative Agencies and the Courts.* Ann Arbor: University of Michigan Press, 1951.

————. *The Lawyer and Administrative Agencies.* Englewood Cliffs, N.J.: Prentice-Hall, 1957.

————. *State Administrative Law.* New York: Bobbs-Merrill, 1965.

Cooper, Robert M. "Administrative Justice and the Role of Discretion." 47 *Yale L. J.* 577 (1938).

Davis, Kenneth Culp. "Administrative Arbitrariness—A Final Word." 114 *U. Pennsylvania L. Rev.* 874 (1966).

————. "Administrative Arbitrariness Is Not Always Reviewable." 51 *Minnesota L. Rev.* 643 (1967).

————. "Administrative Arbitrariness—Postscript." 114 *U. Pennsylvania L. Rev.* 823 (1966).

————. *Administrative Law: Cases—Texts—Problems.* 6th ed. St. Paul, Minn.: West, 1976.

————. *Administrative Law for the Seventies.* Rochester: Lawyers Cooperative, 1977. (Now published by K.C. Davis Publishing, University of San Diego).

————. "Administrative Law Surprises in the Ruiz Case." 75 *Columbia L. Rev.* 823 (1975).

————. *Administrative Law Treatise.* St. Paul, Minn.: West, 1958 (Supplements have been added).

————. "A New Approach to Delegation." 36 *U. Chicago L. Rev.* 713 (1969).

————. *Discretionary Justice: A Preliminary Inquiry.* Baton Rouge: Louisiana State University, 1969.

Davison, J. Forrester, and Nathan Grundstein. *Administrative Law: Cases and Problems.* Indianpolis, Ind.: Bobbs-Merrill, 1952.

Dickinson, John. *Administrative Justice and the Supremacy of Law in the United States.* New York: Russell & Russell, 1927.

Dixon, Robert G., "Independent Commissions and Political Responsibility," 27 *Admin. L. Rev.* 1 (1975).

———. "The Congressional Veto and Separation of Powers: The Executive on a Leash." 56 *North Carolina L. Rev.* 423 (1978).

Duke University Law Review. *Annual Administrative Law Issue.*

Esteicher, Samuel. "Pragmatic Justice: The Contributions of Judge Harold Leventhal to Administrative Law." 80 *Columbia L. Rev.* 894 (1980).

Fellmeth, Robert. *The Interstate Commerce Commission.* New York: Grossman, 1970.

Forkosch, Morris D. *A Treatise on Administrative Law.* Indianapolis, Ind.: Bobbs-Merrill, 1956.

Frank, Jerome. *If Men Were Angels: Some Aspects of Government in a Democracy.* New York: Harper & Brothers, 1942.

Frankfurter, Felix. "The Task of Administrative Law," 75 *U. Pennsylvania L. Rev.* 614 (1927).

Friendly, Henry J. *The Federal Administrative Agencies.* Cambridge, Mass.: Harvard University Press, 1962.

———. "Some Kind of a Hearing." 123 *U. Pennsylvania L. Rev.* 1267 (1965).

Freund, Ernst. *Administrative Powers Over Persons and Property.* Chicago: University of Chicago Press, 1928.

———. *Standards of American Legislation: An Estimate of Restrictive and Constructive Factors.* Chicago: University of Chicago Press, 1917.

Fritschler, A. Lee. *Smoking and Politics.* Englewood Cliffs, N.J.: Prentice-Hall, 1975.

Gellhorn, Ernest. *Administrative Law and Process in a Nutshell.* St. Paul, Minn.: West, 1972.

———. "Public Participation in Administrative Proceedings," 81 *Yale L. J.* 359 (1972).

———, and Harold Bruff. "Congressional Control of Administrative Regulation: A Study of Legislative Vetoes," 90 *Harvard L. Rev.* 1369 (1977).

———, and Glenn O. Robinson. "Perspectives on Administrative Law." 75 *Columbia L. Rev.* 771 (1975).

Gellhorn, Walter. *Federal Administrative Proceedings.* Baltimore: Johns Hopkins Press, 1941.

———. *Ombudsman and Others: Citizens Protectors in Nine Countries.* Cambridge, Mass.: Harvard University Press, 1967.

———. *When Americans Complain: Government Grievance Procedures.* Cambridge, Mass.: Harvard University Press, 1966.

———. "Deregulation: Delight or Delusion?" 24 *St. Louis U. L. J.* 469 (1980).

———, and Clark Byse. *Administrative Law: Cases and Comments.* Mineola, N.Y.: Foundation Press, 1974.

———, and Paul Verkuil. *Administrative Law Problems.* Mineola, N.Y.: Foundation Press, 1978.

Gifford, Daniel J. "Administrative Rulemaking and Judicial Review: Some Conceptual Models." 65 *Minnesota L. Rev.* 63 (1980).

Goldberg, Arthur J. "A Defense of the Bureaucracy in Corporate Regulation and Some Personal Suggestions for Corporate Reform." 48 *George Washington L. Rev.* 514 (1980).

Goodnow, Frank. *The Principles of the Administrative Law of the United States.* New York: Putnam, 1905.

Gray, John Chipman. *The Nature and Sources of Law.* New York: Macmillan, 1927.

Hart, James. *An Introduction to Administrative Law: With Selected Cases.* New York: Appleton-Century-Crofts, 1950.

Harvard Law Review. "*Vermont Yankee Nuclear Power Corp. v. Natural Resources Defense Council, Inc.*: Three Perspectives," 91 *Harvard L. Rev.* 1805 (1978).

Hector, Louis. "Government by Anonymity: Who Writes Our Regulatory Opinions?" 45 *ABA Journal* 1260 (1959).

Jaffe, Louis L. *Judicial Control of Administrative Action.* Boston: Little, Brown, 1965.

———. "Book Review of Discretionary Justice by Davis." 14 *Villanova L. Rev.* 773 (1969).

———. "The Illusion of the Ideal Administration." 86 *Harvard L. Rev.* 1183 (1937).

———, and Nathaniel L. Nathanson. *Administrative Law: Cases and Comment.* Boston: Little, Brown, 1968.

Johnson, Nicholas, and John Distel. "A Day in the Life: The Federal Communications Commissions." 82 *Yale L. J.* 1575 (1973).

Kaiser, Frederick M. "Congressional Action to Overturn Agency Rules: Alternatives to the Legislative Veto." *Admin. L. Rev.* 667 (1980).

Kohlmeier, Louis M. *The Regulators: Watchdog Agencies and the Public Interest.* New York: Harper & Row, 1969.

Krislov, Samuel, and Lloyd Musolf. *The Politics of Regulation.* Boston: Houghton Mifflin, 1964.

Landis, James M. *The Administrative Process.* New Haven, Conn.: Yale University Press, 1938.

Leventhal, Harold. "Public Contracts and Administrative Law." 52 *ABA Journal* 85 (1966).

Levi, Edward H. *An Introduction to Legal Reasoning.* Chicago: University of Chicago Press, 1949.

Levy, Lewis, and Martin. *Social Welfare and the Individual: Cases and Materials.* Mineola, N.Y.: Foundation Press, 1971.

Lockhart, William J. "Discretionary Clemency: Mercy at the Prosecutor's Option. 1976 *Utah L. Rev.* 55 (1976).

———. "Irrational, But Arbitrary: Should Reviewing Courts Draw So Fine a Line?" 1979 *Utah L. Rev.* 649 (1979).

Loevinger, Lee. "The Administrative Agency as a Paradigm of Government: A Survey of the Administrative Process." 40 *Indiana L. J.* 287 (1965).

Lorch, Robert S. *Democratic Process and Administrative Law.* Detroit: Wayne State University Press, 1969.

Lowi, Theodore. *The End of Liberalism.* New York: Norton, 1969.

McCarran, P. "Three Years of the Federal Administrative Procedure Act—A Study in Legislation." 38 *Georgetown L. J.* 574 (1950).

MacDonald, James. *Environmental Litigation.* Madison: University of Wisconsin, 1972.

McFarland, Carl. *Judicial Control of the Federal Trade Commission and the Interstate Commerce Commission, 1920–1933.* Cambridge, Mass.: Harvard University Press, 1933.

———. "Landis' Report: The Voice of One Crying in the Wilderness." 47 *Virginia L. Rev.* 373 (1961).

———, and Arthur T. Vanderbilt. *Cases and Materials on Administrative Law.* New York: Matthew Binder, 1947.

Macy, John W., Jr., "The APA and the Hearing Examiner." 27 *Federal B. J.* 4 (1967).

Mans, Thomas. "Selecting the 'Hidden Judiciary:' How the Merit Process Works in Choosing Administrative Law Judges." 63 *Judicature* 60 (1979).

Mason, Malcolm S. "Current Trends in Federal Grant Law—Fiscal Year 1976," 35 *Federal B. J.* 163 (1976).

Markham, Jerry W. "Sunshine on the Administrative Process: Wherein Lies the Shade." 28 *Admin. L. Rev.* 463 (1976).

Medicine, David. "The Noise Control Act: Legislative and Administrative Problems of Implementation." 9 *Environmental L.* 311 (1979).

Michigan Law Review. *Project: Government Information and the Rights of Citizens.* 73 *Michigan L. Rev.* Part II 971 (1975).

Miller, Arthur S. *The Supreme Court and American Capitalism.* New York: Free Press, 1968.

Morgan, Thomas D. "Achieving National Goals Through Federal Contracts." 1974 *Wisconsin L. Rev.* 301 (1974).

Murphy, Walter F. *Elements of Judicial Strategy.* Chicago: University of Chicago Press, 1964.

Musolf, Lloyd D. *Federal Examiners: The Conflict of Law and Administration.* Cambridge, Mass.: Harvard University Press, 1955.

Nader, Ralph, Peter Petkas, and Kate Blackwell. *Whistle Blowing.* New York: Grossman, 1972.

Nathanson, Nathaniel N. "Probing the Mind of the Administrator." 75 *Columbia L. Rev.* 721 (1975).

Noll, Roger G. *Reforming Regulation.* Washington, D.C.: Brookings Institution, 1971.

Nonet, Phillippe. *Administrative Justice: Advocacy and Change in a Government Agency.* New York: Russell Sage Foundation, 1969.

Note: "Delegation and Regulatory Reform: Letting the President Change the Rules." 89 *Yale L. J.* 561 (1980).

Ogden, Gregory L. "Analysis of Three Current Trends in Administrative Law: Reducing Administrative Delay, Expanding Public Participation, and Increasing Agency Accountability." 7 *Pepperdine L. Rev.* 553 (1980).

Parker, Reginald. "The Administrative Procedure Act: A Study in Overestimation." 60 *Yale L. J.* 581 (1951).

Peltason, Jack W. *Federal Courts in the Political Process.* Garden City, N.Y.: Doubleday, 1955.

Pfeiffer, P. "Hearing Cases Before Several Agencies—Odyssey of an Administrative Law Judge." 27 *Admin. L. Rev.* 217 (1975).

Pierce, Richard J., Jr. "The Choice Between Adjudicating and Rulemaking for Formulating and Implementing Energy Policy." 31 *Hastings L. J.* (1979).

Pound, Roscoe. *Administrative Law, Its Growth, Procedure and Significance.* Pittsburgh, Pa.: University of Pittsburgh Press, 1942.

———. "The Rule of Law and the Modern Social Welfare State." 7 *Vanderbilt L. Rev.* 1 (1953).

President's Advisory Council on Executive Organization. *A New Regulatory Framework.* (Ash Council Report.) Washington, D.C.: Government Printing Office, 1971.

Pritchett, C. Herman. "Public Law and Judicial Behavior." 30 *Journal of Politics* 480 (1968).

"Proceedings of the National Conference on Federal Regulation: Roads to Reform," 32 *Admin. L. Rev.* 123 (1980).

Redford, Emmette. "The President and the Regulatory Commission." 44 *Texas Rev.* 288 (1966).

Reich, Charles. "The New Property." 73 *Yale L. J.* 733 (1964)

Rumble, Wilfred E., Jr. *American Legal Realism.* Ithaca, N.Y.: Cornell University Press, 1968.

Schmidhauser, John. *The Supreme Court as Final Arbiter in Federal State Relations.* Chapel Hill: University of North Carolina Press, 1958.

Schwartz, Bernard. *Administrative Law.* Boston: Little, Brown, 1976.

———. "Administrative Law: The Third Century." 29 *Admin L. Rev.* 291 (1977).

———. "Of Administrators and Philosophers—Kings: The 'Republic,' the 'Laws,' and Delegations of Power." 72 *Northwestern U. L. Rev.* 443 (1978).

———. "Administrative Law and the Burger Court." 8 *Hofstra L. Rev.* 325 (1980).

———, and H. W. R. Wade. *Legal Control of Government.* Oxford: Clarendon Press, 1972.

Schubert, Glendon. *Judicial Policy-Making.* Glenwood, Ill.: Scott, Foresman, 1965.

Segal, Bernard. "The Administrative Law Judge: Thirty Years of Progress and the Road Ahead." 62 *ABA Journal* 1424 (1976).

Sewell, W. R. Derrick, and Susan D. Phillips. "Models for the Evaluation of Public Participation Programmes." 19 *Natural Resources J.* 337 (1979).

Shapiro, Martin. *The Supreme Court and Administrative Agencies.* New York: Free Press, 1968.

———. "Stability and Change in Judicial Decision-Making: Incrementalism or *Stare Decisis*." 2 *Law in Transition Q.* 134 (1965).

Sharfman, Isaiah. *The Interstate Commerce Commission.* New York: Commonwealth Fund, 1937.

Sharon, Amiel T. "The Measure of an Administrative Law Judge." 19 *Judges J.* 20 (1980).

Sheldon, Charles H. *The American Judicial Process: Models and Approaches.* New York: Dodd, Mead, 1974.

Sirico, Louis J., Jr. "Agencies in Conflict: Overlapping Agencies and The Legitimacy of the Administrative Process." 33 *Vanderbilt L. Rev.* 101 (1980).

Sofaer, Abraham. "Judicial Control of Informal Discretionary Adjudication and Enforcement." 72 *Columbia L. Rev.* 1293 (1972).

Stason, E. Blythe, and Frank Cooper. *The Law of Administrative Tribunals.* Chicago: Callaghan, 1957.

Stewart, Milton D. "The New Regulatory Flexibility Act." 67 *ABA Journal* 66 (1981).

Stewart, Richard B. "The Reformation of American Administrative Law." 88 *Harvard L. Rev.* 1667 (1957).

Symposium: "Administrative Litigation." 5 *Litigation* 7 (1979).

Symposium: "Current Trends in Common Carrier Deregulation." 47 *ABA Antitrust L. J.* 1267 (1979).

Symposium: "Empirical Research in Administrative Law." 31 *Admin. L. Rev.* 443 (1979) and 32 *Admin. L. Rev.* 1 (1980).

Symposium: "Regulation and Innovation." 43 *Law and Contemp. Problems* 148 (1979).

Tucker, Edwin W. *Text–Cases–Problems on Administrative Law, Regulation of Enterprise and Civil Liberties.* St. Paul, Minn.: West, 1975.

Turkeheimer, B. W. "Veto by Neglect: The Federal Advisory Committee Act." 25 *American U.L. Rev.* 53 (1975).

U.S. Congress, House of Representatives, Task Force on Legal Services and Procedure. *Report on Legal Services and Procedure Prepared for the Commission on the Executive Branch of Government.* House doc. no. 128, 84th Cong., 1st Sess., 1955.

U.S. Congress, Senate. James M. Landis. *Report on Regulatory Agencies to the President-Elect.* 86th Cong., 2nd Sess., 1960.

U.S. Congress, Senate. Report of the Attorney General's Committee on Administrative Procedure. *Administrative Procedure in Government Agencies.* Sen. doc. no. 8, 77th Cong., 1st Sess., 1941.

Verkuil, Paul R. "Judicial Review of Informal Rulemaking." 60 *Virginia L. Rev.* 185 (1974).

———. "Jawboning Administrative Agencies: *Ex Parte* Contacts by the White House." 80 *Columbia L. Rev.* 943 (1980).

Vom Bauer, F. Trowbridge. "Fifty Years of Government Contract Law." 29 *Federal B. J.* 305 (1970).

Warren, George L., ed. *The Federal Administrative Procedure Act and the Administrative Agencies: Proceedings of an Institute Conducted by the New York University School of Law, February 1–8, 1947.* New York: N.Y.U. School of Law, 1947.

Wasby, Stephen L. *The Impact of the United States Supreme Court: Some Perspectives.* Homewood, Ill.: Dorsey Press, 1970.

White, Byron R., "Supreme Court Review of Agency Decisions," 26 *Admin. L. Rev.* 107 (1974).

Williams, Stephen. "Hybrid Rulemaking Under the Administrative Procedure Act: A Legal and Empirical Analysis." *U. Chicago L. Rev.* 401 (1975).

Woll, Peter. *Administrative Law: The Informal Process.* Berkeley and Los Angeles: University of California Press, 1963.

———. "Administrative Law in the Seventies." 32 *Public Admin. Rev.* 557 (1972).

Wright, J. Skelly. "Beyond Discretionary Justice." 81 *Yale L. J.* 575 (1972).

———. "The Courts and the Rule Making Process." 59 *Cornell L. Rev.* 375 (1974).

Zwerdling, R. "Reflections and Functions of the Federal Hearing Examiners." 25 *Admin. L. Rev.* 9 (1973).

Appendix D

Selected Sources on Law and Administration in the States*

STATES IN GENERAL

Merrill, Maurice H. "Calling Attention to a Proposal for Advance in State Administrative Procedure." 170 *Oklahoma B. J.* 1751 (1946).

Jeffrey, B.S. "Reforms in Administrative Procedures of State Agencies." 22 *Kansas Judicial Council Bulletin* 12 (1948).

Symposium: "State Administrative Procedure." 33 *Iowa L. Rev.* 193 (1948).

Heady, Ferrel. "State Administrative Procedure Laws: An Appraisal." 12 *Public Admin. Rev.* 10 (1972).

Note: "State Administrative Procedure—Scope of Judicial Review." 4 *Case Western Reserve L. Rev.* 45 (1952).

Harris, W.R. "Administrative Practice and Procedure: Comparative State Legislation." 6 *Oklahoma L. Rev.* 29 (1953).

Note: "Model State Administrative Procedure Act." 7 *Rutgers L. Rev.* 459 (1953).

Schenker, E. "Another Look at State Regulatory Agencies." 62 *Public Utilities Fortnightly* 1008 (1958).

Cooper, Frank E. "Turning the Spotlight on State Administrative Procedure." 49 *ABA Journal* 29 (1963).

Symposium. "The State Administrative Procedure Act." 16 *Admin. L. Rev.* 50 (1963).

Davis, Frederick. "Recent Noteworthy Administrative Law Developments in Selected Areas." 17 *Admin. L. Rev.* 1972 (1964).

Hill, Herbert. "Twenty Years of State Fair Employment Practice Commissions: A Critical Analysis with Recommendations." 17 *Buffalo L. Rev.* 22 (1964).

Note: "Administrative Procedure Legislation Among the States." 49 *Cornell L. Q.* 34 (1964).

*Presented by state, and chronologically within each state.

449

Selected
Sources
on Law and
Administration
in the States

Note: "Gubernational Executive Orders as Devices for Administrative Direction and Control." 50 *Iowa L. Rev.* 78 (1964).

Bomar, James L., Jr. "Due Process and Red Tape." 17 *Admin. L. Rev.* 206 (1965).

Cohen, Morris L. "Publication on State Administrative Reform in Slow Motion." 14 *Buffalo L. Rev.* 410 (1965).

Cooper, Frank E. *State Administrative Law.* Indianapolis, Ind.: Bobbs-Merrill, 1965.

Cohen, Morris. "Publication of State Administrative Regulations—Reform in Slow Motion." 14 *Buffalo L. Rev.* 410 (1965).

Merrill, Maurice H. "Revised Model State Administrative Procedure Act." 26 *Alabama Lawyer* 375 (1965).

Note: "Administrative Inspections and the Fourth Amendment—A Rationale." 65 *Columbia L. Rev.* (1965).

Note: "State Statute to Create the Office of Ombudsman." 2 *Harvard J. of Legislation* 213 (1965).

Note: "State Municipal Administrative Procedure Act." 3 *Harvard J. of Legislation* 323 (1966).

Gellhorn, Walter. "Ombudsman's Relevance to American Municipal Affairs." 54 *ABA Journal* 134 (1968).

Note: "Discovery in State Administrative Adjudication." 56 *California L. Rev.* 56 (1968).

Gould, David. "Developments in the Law—State Administrative Law." 22 *Admin. L. Rev.* 59 (1969).

Merrill, Maurice H. "Local Administrative Agencies." 22 *Vanderbilt L. Rev.* 775 (1969).

Ashman, Allan. "Representation for the Poor in State Rulemaking." 24 *Vanderbilt L. Rev.* (1970).

Bronstein, David A. "State Regulation of Powerplant Siting." 3 *Environmental Law* 273 (1973).

Force, Robert. "Administrative Adjudication of Traffic Violations Confronts the Doctrine of Separation of Powers." 49 *Tulane L. Rev.* 84 (1974).

Klein, Fannie J. *Federal and State Court Systems—A Guide.* Cambridge, Mass.: Ballinger, 1977.

Levine, Ted M. "Lawyer's Guide to State Development Agencies." 59 *ABA Journal* 998 (1973).

Note: "Due Process Limitations on Occupational Licensing." 59 *Virginia L. Rev.* 1097 (1973).

Note: "Administrative Search Warrants." 58 *Minnesota L. Rev.* 607 (1974).

Note: "Procedural Due Process and the Separation of Functions in State Occupational Licensing Agencies." 1974 *Wisconsin L. Rev.* 833 (1974).

Note: "Statutory Framework for State Economic Development Programs." 11 *Harvard J. of Legislation* 703 (1974).

Davis, Frederick. "*Withrow v. Larkin* and the Separation of Functions Concept in State Administrative Proceedings." 27 *Admin. L. Rev.* 407 (1975).

Hoffman, P. Browning, and Robert C. Dunn. "Beyond Rouse and Wyatt: An Administrative-law Model for Expanding and Implementing the Mental Patients' Right to Treatment." 61 *Virginia L. Rev.* 297 (1975).

Hornby, D. Brock. "Delegating Authority to the Community of Scholars." 1975 *Duke L. J.* 279 (1975).

Lewin, L. S.; A.R. Sommers, and H.M. Sommers. "State Health Cost Regulation: Structure and Administration." 6 *U. Toledo L. Rev.* 647 (1975).

Nichols, H. Louis. "Powers and Duties of the Zoning Board of Adjustment." 1975 *Planning, Zoning and Eminent Dom. Ist.* 121 (1975).

Note: "Administrative Discharge Procedures for Involuntary Civilly-committed Mental Patients: An Alternative." 50 *Indiana L. J.* 865 (1975).

Note: "Due Process Standards for Quasi-Judicial Proceedings of Municipal and County Agencies." 54 *North Carolina L. Rev.* 83 (1975).

Note: "Powers of Administrative Agencies Regulating the Healing Arts—Do They Include the Power to Require a Physical or Psychiatric Examination?" 52 *Denver L. J.* 939 (1975).

Note: "Enforcement of State Deceptive Trade Practice Statutes." 42 *Tennessee L. Rev.* 689 (1975).

Gifford, Daniel J. "Declaratory Judgments Under the Model State Administrative Procedure Acts." 13 *Houston L. Rev.* 825 (1976).

O'Grady, James P., Jr. "Grievance Mediation Activities by State Agencies." 31 *Arbitration J.* 125 (1976).

Note: "Combination of Investigatory and Adjudicatory Functions in an Administrative Body Does Not Violate Due Process." 35 *Maryland L. Rev.* 704 (1976).

Note: "Emerging State Programs to Protect the Environment: 'Little NEPA's' and Beyond." 5 *Environmental Affairs* 567 (1976).

Note: "Office of Public Counsel: Institutionalizing Public Interest Representation in State Government," 64 *Georgetown L. J.* 895 (1976).

Note: "Standing to Sue Under the Model Land Development Code." 9 *U. Michigan J. L. Ref.* 147 (1976).

Best, Arthur, and Bernard Brown. "Government Facilitation of Consumerism: A Proposal for Consumer Action Groups." 50 *Temple L. Q.* 253 (1977).

Davis, Frederick. "Judicialization of Administrative Law: The Trial Type Hearing and the Changing Status of the Hearing Officer." 1977 *Duke L. J.* 389 (1977).

Levinson, L. Harold. "Elements of the Administrative Process: Formal, Semi-Formal, and Free-Form Models." 26 *American U. L. Rev.* 872 (1977).

Peterson, Craig A., and Claire McCarthy. "Farmland Preservation by Purchase of Development Rights: The Long Island Experiment." 27 *De Paul L. Rev.* 447 (1977).

Schramm, Carl J. "Role of Hospital Cost-Regulating Agencies in Collective Bargaining." 28 *Labor L. J.* 519 (1977).

Note: "Economic Impact Disclosure Act." 10 *U. Michigan J. L. Ref.* 566 (1977).

Note: "Impartial Decision Maker: Authority of School Board to Dismiss Striking Teachers." 1977 *Wisconsin L. Rev.* 521 (1977).

Note: "Zero-Base Sunset Review." 14 *Harvard J. of Legislation* 505 (1977).

Symposium. "State Administrative Law." 13 *Willamette L. J.* 393 (1977).

Roddis, Richard S.L. "Limited Omnipotence: The Bases and Limitations of the Powers of Insurance Regulators." 13 *Forum* 386 (1978).

Salsich, Peter W., Jr. "Housing Finance Agencies: Instruments of State Housing Policy or Confused Hybrids?" 21 *St. Louis U. L. J.* 595 (1978).

Frank, Stephen. "Oversight of Administrative Agencies by State Supreme Courts: Some Macro Findings." 32 *Admin. L. Rev.* 477 (1980).

Noam, Eli M. "The Interaction of Federal Deregulation and State Regulation," 9 *Hofstra L. Rev.* 195 (1980).

Currie, David P., "State Pollution Statutes," 48 *U. Chicago L. Rev.* 27 (1981).

ALABAMA

McGill, J.D., Jr. "Alabama Administrative Regulatory Agencies—Development and Powers." 4 *Alabama Lawyer* 75 (1943).

Burton, W.H. "Administrative Procedure Before Certain Agencies of the States." 17 *Alabama Lawyer* 125 (1956).

Note: "Procedural Regulations of the New Alabama Water Improvement Commission." 34 *Alabama Lawyer* 72 (1973).

451
Selected
Sources
on Law and
Administration
in the States

ARIZONA

Davis, Ray J. "Administrative Procedure Act for Arizona." 2 *Arizona L. Rev.* 12 (1960).

Comment: "Judicial Review of Administrative Action in Arizona." 1975 *Arizona State L. J.* 739 (1975).

Comment: "Arizona's Agricultural Inspection: Search for a Suspect Species, or a Species of Suspect Search." 197 *Arizona State L. J.* 143 (1976).

ARKANSAS

Parker, Reginald. "Administrative Law in Arkansas." 4 *Arkansas L. Rev.* 107 (1950).

Arnold, Richard S. "An Ombudsman for Arkansas." 21 *Arkansas L. Rev.* 327 (1967).

Wilson, Zachary D. "Taxpayer Status to Challenge Administrative Actions Under the Arkansas Administrative Procedure Act." 25 *Arkansas L. Rev.* 160 (1971).

Wilson, Zachary D., and Charles N. Carnes. "Judicial Review of Administrative Agencies in Arkansas." 25 *Arkansas L. Rev.* 297 (1972).

CALIFORNIA

Kreps, R. N. "California Administrative Procedure Reform." 20 California S. B. J. (1945).

Elliot, Sheldon D. "California Administrative Law and Procedure." 21 So. *California L. Rev.* 21 (1947).

Kreps, R. N. "The California Administrative Procedure Act." 22 *California S. B. J.* (1947).

Symposium: "California Administrative Law." 44 *California L. Rev.* 190 (1956).

Boas, Maxwell S. "Insights and Guideposts: Administrative Law." 39 *California S. B. J.* 894 (1964).

Molinari, John B. "California Administrative Process: A Synthesis Updated." 10 *Santa Clara L. Rev.* 274 (1970).

Traub, Leon B. "California's Ombudsmen for Licensees—The Office of Administrative Procedure." 45 *Los Angeles Bar Bulletin* 190 (1970).

Henke, Dan F. *California Legal Research Handbook, State and Federal.* Walnut Creek, Calif.: Tex-Cal-Tex, 1971.

Grunschlag, Don. M. "Lawyer/Non-Lawyer Decisions in the Adjudication of Public Contract Claims: A Study of Administrative Process." 12 *Santa Clara L. Rev.* 36 (1972).

Overman, D. "Freedom of Information—Writ of Mandamus Granted Requiring Pesticide Applicators' Reports Open to Public Inspection." 20 *U. Kansas L. Rev.* 525 (1972).

Symposium: "Legal Problems of Administrative Practice," 5 *U. California Davis L. Rev.* 1 (1972).

Layman, Patrick J. "Quasi-Judicial Administrative Hearings: Is a Dual System of Discovery Necessary?" 7 *U. San Francisco L. Rev.* 306 (1973).

Berry, Steven C. "Scope of Judicial Review—An Administrative Grant of Variance Must Be Accompanied by Administrative Findings Regardless of Whether or Not Legal Legislation Makes Such Findings Mandates." 52 *J. Urban L.* 409 (1974).

Dudman, Jan M. "Defense of Entrapment in Administrative Proceedings." 1 *Pepperdine L. Rev.* 316 (1974).

Livingston, Gene. "Organizations and Administrative Practice—A Balance to the Corporate State." 26 *Hastings L. J.* 89 (1974).

Christie, Mary Lu. "*Strumsky v. San Diego County Employees Retirement Association*: Determining the Scope of Judicial Review of Administrative Decisions in California." 26 *Hastings L. J.* 1465 (1975).

Marsh, Lindell L. "Innovative Programs and Proposals for the Reconciliation of Private and Public Interests in the California Coastal Zone." 10 *Natural Resources Lawyer* 257 (1977).

Coan, George R. "Operational Aspects of a Central Hearing Examiners Pool: California's Experiences." 3 *Florida State U. L. Rev.* 86 (1975).

Collins, Ronald K. "Sufficiency of Uncorroborated Hearsay in Administrative Proceedings: The California Race." 8 *Loyala of Los Angeles L. Rev.* (LA) 632 (1975).

Patterson, Timothy R. "Passenger Vehicle Air Pollution Control in California: Enforcement, Progress and Problems." 15 *Santa Clara L. Rev.* 695 (1975).

Tobriner, Michael. "California Fair Employment Practices Commission—The Frustration of Potential." 10 *U. San Francisco L. Rev.* 37 (1975).

Collins, Ronald K. "Hearsay and the Administrative Process: A Review and Reconsideration of the State of the Law of Certain Evidentiary Proceedings Applicable in California Administrative Proceedings," 8 *Southwestern U. L. Rev.* 577 (1976).

Douglas, Peter M., and Joseph E. Petrillo. "California's Coast: The Struggle Today—A Plan for Tomorrow." 4 *Florida State U. L. Rev.* 177 (1976).

Henke, Joseph T. "Judicial Review of Local Governmental Administrative Decisions in California." 10 *U. San Francisco L. Rev.* 361 (1976).

Miller, Robert A. "Clarifying Muddy Waters: Justice Sullivan and the Appropriate Scope of Judicial Inquiry." 10 *U. San Francisco L. Rev.* 733 (1976).

Myers, Susan Ann. "California Occupational Safety and Health Act of 1973." 9 *Loyala U. L. Rev.* (LA) 905 (1976).

Van Alstyne, Debra Manning. "Environmental Decision Making Under CEQA: A Quest for Uniformity." 24 *UCLA L. Rev.* 838 (1977).

Abrams, Norman. "Administrative Law Judge Systems: The California View." 29 *Admin. L. Rev.* 487 (1977).

Asperger, James R. "California's Energy Commission: Illusions of a One-Stop Power Plant Siting Agency." 24 *UCLA L. Rev.* 1313 (1977).

Dauer, Paul F. "State Public Contract Disputes: A Prospectus for Comprehensive Reform." 8 *Pacific L. J.* 533 (1977).

Finkelberg, Louis. "Effectiveness of Environmental Impact Reports as an Implementation of the California Environmental Quality Act." 6 *San Fernando Valley L. Rev.* 127 (1978).

Crawford, Thomas. "Bay Area Air Quality Management District: Air Pollution Control at the Local Level." 19 *Santa Clara L. Rev.* 617 (1979).

COLORADO

Symposium: "Administrative Law and Practice in Colorado." 29 *Dicta* 431 (1952).

Goldberg, Mitchell, R., and Jack N. Hyatt. "Investigative Procedures of the Colorado Civic Rights Commission. 40 *U. Colorado L. Rev.* 97 (1967).

Henry, Hubert D. "Colorado Administrative Procedure Act: Exclusions Demanding Reform." 44 *Denver L. J.* 42 (1967).

Mall, Loren L. "Colorado's Ombudsman Office." 45 *Denver L. J.* 93 (1968).

Note: "Colorado Civil Rights Commission—Judicial Denial of Effective Investigatory Powers." 43 *Colorado L. Rev.* 345 (1972).

Laitos, Jan G. "Limits of the Law: Functional Failures of the Air Pollution Variance Board." 44 *U. Colorado L. Rev.* 513 (1973).

Clowdus, William M. "The Colorado Administrative Procedure Act—Colo. rev. stat. Ann. 3–16–6: Application a Matter of Construction." 51 *Denver L. J.* 275 (1974).

Ertle, Susan E. "Standing of State Political Subdivisions to Challenge State Agency Rulings Under the Colorado Administrative Procedure Act." 53 *Denver L. J.* 437 (1976).

Walker, Timothy B., Murray Blumenthal, and John R. Reese. "Empirical Examination of Citizen Representation in Contested Matters Before State Administrative Agencies: The Colorado Experience." 29 *Admin. L. Rev.* 321 (1977).

CONNECTICUT

Sands, Hubert. "Administrative Law: The Ombudsman Concept—Possibility of Adaptation to Connecticut." 42 *Connecticut B. J.* 277 (1968).

Trubek, Louise. "Will the Connecticut Administrative Procedure Act Frustrate Environmental Protection?" 46 *Connecticut B. J.* 438 (1972).

Zirkel, Perry A. "Guidelines for Teacher–Board Negotiations in Connecticut." 50 *Connecticut B. J.* 127 (1976).

Sacks, Howard R. "Promises, Performance, and Principles: An Empirical Study of Parole Decision Making in Connecticut." 9 *Connecticut L. Rev.* 347 (1977).

Feigen, Arnold B. "The Uniform Administrative Procedure Act—An Overview." 54 *Connecticut B. J.* 537 (1981).

FLORIDA

Comment: "Judicial Review of Administrative Action in Florida." 2 *Miami L. Q.* 181 (1947).

Klein, J. Velma. "Florida's Administrative Agencies." 195 *Insurance L. J.* 403 (1953).

Parsons, Malcolm B. "Substantial Evidence Rule in Florida Administrative Law." 6 *U. Florida L. Rev.* 481 (1953).

Fuquay, Robert F. "Rule Making and Adjudication in Florida Administrative Law." 9 *U. Florida L. Rev.* 260 (1956).

French, Harriett L. *Research in Florida Law,* 2d (Dobbs Ferry, N.Y.: Oceana, 1965).

Evans, Mark A. "Procedural Due Process: Florida's Uniform Administrative Procedure Act." 21 *U. Miami L. Rev.* 145 (1966).

Barnes, Ruth Mayes, "Government in the Sunshine: Promise or Placebo?" 23 *U. Florida L. Rev.* 361 (1971).

Mancusi-Ungaro, Ursula. "Rulemaking and Adjudication Under the Florida Administrative Procedure Act." 27 *U. Florida L. Rev.* 755 (1973).

Alford, Walter A. "Administrative Procedure Act," 48 *Florida B. J.* 683 (1974).

453
Selected
Sources
on Law and
Administration
in the States

Comment: "Reports of State Agencies Constitute Competent Substantial Evidence to Support Denial of Dredge and Fill Permit Application Even Though Reporting Agency Has No Jurisdiction Over Proposed Project." 2 *Florida State U. L. Rev.* 816 (1974).

Levinson, L. Harold. "The Florida Administrative Procedure Act: 1974 Revision and 1975 Amendments." 29 *U. Miami L. Rev.* 617 (1975).

Oertel, Kenneth G. "Hearings Under the New Administrative Procedure Act." 49 *Florida B. J.* 356 (1975).

Symposium: "The New Florida Administrative Procedure Act: Selected Presentations from the Attorney General's Conference." 3 *Florida State U. L. Rev.* 64 (1975).

Whisenand, James D. "Model Rules of Florida Administrative Practice—Chaos or Uniformity." 49 *Florida B. J.* 361 (1975).

Cleveland, C. Anthony. "Can the Joint Administrative Procedures Committee Adequately Solve Administrative Conflict." 4 *Florida State U. L. Rev.* 350 (1976).

Symposium: "Regulating the Environment: A Look at the Florida Environmental Reorganization Act." 50 *Florida B. J.* 263 (1976).

Pelham, Thomas G. "Regulating Developments of Regional Impact: Florida and the Model Code." 29 *U. Florida L. Rev.* 789 (1977).

Waas, George L. "The Administrative Appeal." 51 *Florida B. J.* 276 (1977).

Rice, Bob. "Sunshine Law." 6 *Florida State U. L. Rev.* 199 (1978).

Karl, Frederick B., and Paul A. Lehrman. "Trends in Administrative Law." 54 *Florida B. J.* 24 (1980).

GEORGIA

Sellers, A. "Administrative Law in Georgia." 1939 *Georgia B. A. J.* 219 (1939).

Field, D. Meade. "The Georgia Uniform Administrative Procedure Act." 1 *Georgia S. B. J.* 269 (1965).

Note: "Administrative Muddle in Georgia." 32 *Mercer L. Rev.* 359 (1980).

HAWAII

Ikeda, Walter H. "Ombudsman in Hawaii: The Basic Premises." 7 *Hawaii B. J.* 17 (1970).

Holmes, Thomas M. "The *Reinecker* Case: A Study in Administrative Injustice." 12 *Hawaii B. J.* 3 (1976).

Lowry, G. Kem, Jr. "Evaluating State Land Use Control: Perspective and Hawaii Case Study." 18 *Urban L. Annual* 85 (1980).

IDAHO

Haman, Gary M., and Robert Tunncliff. "Idaho Administrative Agencies and the New Idaho Administrative Procedure Act." 3 *Idaho L. Rev.* 61 (1966).

ILLINOIS

Comment: "The Illinois Administrative Review Act." 42 *Illinois L. Rev.* 636 (1947).

Dodd, Walter F. "Illinois Administrative Procedure Today—An Appraisal." 1949 *U. Illinois L. F.* 181 (1949).

Symposium: "Illinois Administrative Procedure." 1949 *U. Illinois L. F.* 181 (1949).

Davies, Bernita J., and Francis J. Rooney. *Research in Illinois Law.* Dobbs Ferry, N.Y.: Oceana, 1954.

Symposium: "Practice Before Illinois Administrative Tribunal." 40 *Illinois B. J.* 670 (1954).

Bauer, William J. "Present County Government System—Best of All Possible Worlds?" 17 *De Paul L. Rev.* 524 (1965).

Freehling, Paul E. "Administrative Procedure Legislation in Illinois." 57 *Illinois B. J.* 364 (1969).

Hunt, John W. "Administrative Procedure: An Additional Plea." 57 *Illinois B. J.* 644 (1969).

Polelle, Michael J. "Illinois Environmental Protection Act: Constitutional Twilight Zone of Criminal and Civil Law." 61 *Illinois B. J.* 584 (1973).

Tarrel, Robert L. "Illinois Commerce Commission." 22 *De Paul L. Rev.* 779 (1973).

Note: "Administrative Law—Illinois Supreme Court Upholds Discriminatory Administrative Fines." 1974 *U. Illinois L. F.* 695 (1974).

Bullwinkel, George E. "Environmental Law: The Uneasy Accommodation Between State and Federal Agencies." 25 *De Paul L. Rev.* 423 (1976).

Note: "Illinois Administrative Procedure Act." 1976 *U. Illinois L. F.* 803 (1976).

Gleason, John F. "Practice and Procedure Before the Motor Carrier Division of the Illinois Commerce Commission." 66 *Illinois B. J.* 92 (1977).

Cohn, Rubin G. "Administrative Procedural Reform in Illinois." 17 *Admin. L. Rev.* 91 (1964).

Stephens, Robert C. "Illinois Environmental Protection Act and the Power of an Administrative Agency to Impose a Fine." 50 *Chicago-Kent L. Rev.* 466 (1973).

Currie, David P. "Enforcement Under the Illinois Pollution Law." 70 *Northwestern U. L. Rev.* 389 (1975).

———. "Rulemaking Under the Illinois Pollution Law." 42 *U. Chicago L. Rev.* 457 (1975).

Gray, Kenneth. "Administrative Law in Illinois: Recent Trends and Developments." 8 *Loyola L. J.* (Chicago) 511 (1977).

Hovland, Daniel L. "Suspension or Revocation of a Driver's License Without Prior Hearing Deemed Constitutionally Adequate." 54 *North Dakota L. Rev.* 274 (1977).

Comment: "Legislative Review of Administrative Action: Is the Cure Worse Than the Illness?" 1978 *So. Illinois U. L. J.* 579 (1978).

Jost, Dean Timothy. "Exhaustion of Administrative Remedies in Illinois: The State of the Law at the Close of an Active Decade." 11 *Loyola U. L. J.* (Chicago) (1979).

INDIANA

Fuchs, Ralph F. "Judicial Control of Administrative Agencies in Indiana." 28 *Indiana L. J.* 1 (1952–53).

Note: "Judicial Review of Administrative Agency Actions in Indiana." 37 *Indiana L. J.* 259 (1962).

Skaare, Janet. "Administrative Reform in Indiana," 19 *Admin. Law Rev.* 472 (1967).

Kunz, Christina L. "Indiana Environmental Protection Agencies: A Survey and Critique." 10 *Indiana L. Rev.* 955 (1977).

IOWA

Comment: "Beer-Permit Revocations in Iowa: The Need for a More Rational Approach," 57 *Iowa L. Rev.* 1409 (1972).

455

Selected
Sources
on Law and
Administration
in the States

Note: "Safeguards, Standards, and Necessity: Permissible Parameters for Legislative Delegation in Iowa." 58 *Iowa L. Rev.* 974 (1973).

Bonfield, Arthur E. "The Iowa Administrative Procedure Act: Background, Construction, Applicability, Public Access to Agency Law, the Rulemaking Process," 60 *Iowa L. Rev.* 731 (1975).

Comment: "A Proposal for Increased Administrative Discretion in the Formulation of Iowa's Surface Mining Reclamation Requirements." 62 *Iowa L. Rev.* 522 (1976).

Symposium: "Contemporary Studies Project: General Assistance in Iowa." 61 *Iowa L. Rev.* 1155 (1976).

Uthus, Don C., and Diane McIntire. "Public Utility Rate Regulation and the Iowa Administrative Procedure Act—Extending Maximum Procedural Protection to Public Utilities at Public Expense." 26 *Drake L. Review* 483 (1976–77).

Bonfield, Arthur E. "The Definition of Formal Agency Adjudication Under the Iowa Administrative Procedure Act." 63 *Iowa L. Rev.* 285 (1977).

Note: "Due Process Refocused: Implications for Public Employment in Iowa." 62 *Iowa L. Rev.* 1489 (1977).

Note: "A Procedural Framework for Implementing Non-Point Source Water Pollution Control in Iowa." 63 *Iowa L. Rev.* 184 (1977).

Note: "State Housing Financing Agencies: The Iowa Blueprint." 62 *Iowa L. Rev.* 1524 (1977).

KANSAS

Smith, James B. "An Administrative Procedure Code for Kansas." 1 *U. Kansas L. Rev.* 51 (1952).

Note: "Kansas Administrative Procedure." 28 *J. B. A. Kansas* 322 (1960).

Granger, Kenton. "Judicial Review of Administrative Decisions in Kansas: A Legislative Enigma." 33 *J. B. A. Kansas* 291 (1964).

Hinkle, Winton M. "Kansas Administrative Regulations: A Tentative Step." 7 *Washburn L. J.* 61 (1967).

Davis, John E. "Corporation Commission Practice." 37 *J. B. A. Kansas* 87 (1968).

Adam, Fred B. "Practice and Procedure Before the State Corporation Commission." 41 *J. B. A. Kansas* 199 (1972).

Hostetler, David L. "Constitutional Law–Administrative Agencies–Subpoena Power–Prevalence Right to Privacy." 9 *Akron L. Rev.* 360 (1975).

Buckley, Mert. "Administrative Law: *De Novo* Review of Administrative Action—What Are the Limits?" 15 *Washburn L. J.* 475 (1976).

Brookens, John R., and James N. Clymer. "Scope of Review of Administrative Agency Actions in Kansas." 17 *Washburn L. J.* 312 (1978).

Gregg, Larry E. "Motor Carrier Case Before the State Corporation Commission." 48 *J. Kansas B. A.* 107 (1979).

Ainsworth, Merilyn V. and Sidney Shapiro. "Rethinking Kansas Administrative Procedure." 28 *Kansas L. Rev.* 419 (1980).

KENTUCKY

Cullen, Robert K. "Practice Before Kentucky Administrative Agencies." 11 *Kentucky S. B. J.* 222 (1947).

Daniel, Marilyn S., Douglas W. Becker, Carla J. Allen, et al. "Energy v. Environment: Who Wins in the Race for Coal in Kentucky." 64 *Kentucky L. J.* 641 (1975–57).

Pancake, Jon E. "Precomplaint Investigations Under the Kentucky Consumer Protection Act: Validity and Scope of Civil Investigative Demand." 65 *Kentucky L. J.* 168 (1976–77).

Ziegler, Edward H., Jr. "Legitimizing the Administrative State: The Judicial Development of the Nondesegregation Doctrine in Kentucky." 4 *N. Kentucky L. Rev.* 87 (1977).

Note: "Kentucky Open Records Act: A Preliminary Analysis." 7 *Kentucky L. Rev.* 7 (1980).

457

Selected
Sources
on Law and
Administration
in the States

LOUISIANA

Dakin, Melvin G. "Revised Model State Administrative Procedure Act—Critique and Commentary." 25 *Louisiana L. Rev.* 799 (1965).

Parker, John T. "Land-Use Control in Louisiana: Administrative Law and Urban Growth." 39 *Tulane L. Rev.* 558 (1965).

Alltmant, Jack M. "Judicial Review of Administrative Abuse of Discretion." 43 *Tulane L. Rev.* 854 (1969).

Wallace, Kate. *Louisiana Legal Research Manual.* Baton Rouge, La.: Institute for Continuing Legal Education, 1972

Karre, Karen M. "Louisiana's 'New' Administrative Procedure Act." 35 *Louisiana L. Rev.* 629 (1975).

Payne, Roy S. "Due Process for Drivers Under the Louisiana Revocation Statutes." 36 *Louisiana L. Rev.* 852 (1976).

MAINE

Sawyer, Richard G. "The Quest for Justice in Maine Administrative Procedure: The Administrative Code in Application and Theory." 18 *Maine L. Rev.* 218 (1966).

Benjamin, Thomas B., and Nancy G. Blair. "Implementation of Education Laws Relating to Exceptional Children in the Maine Experience." 11 *Clearinghouse Rev.* 449 (1977).

MARYLAND

Sybert, C. Ferdinand. "Maryland Administrative Procedure—the Law and the Lawyer." 61 *Maryland S. B. A.* 175 (1956).

Cohen, Leonard E., "Some Aspects of Maryland Administrative Law." 24 *Maryland L. Rev.* 1 (1964).

Define, William T. "Administrative Inspections and the Right of Privacy: The Frank Compromise." 11 *Villanova L. Rev.* 357 (1966).

Seinhardt, Michael D. "Procedural Guideline for Implementing the Right to Free Public Education for Handicapped Children." 4 *U. Baltimore L. Rev.* 136 (1974).

Tomlinson, Edward A. "Constitutional Limits on the Decisional Powers of Courts and Administrative Agencies in Maryland." 35 *Maryland L. Rev.* 414 (1976).

Bulman, Leonard Z. "Recent Changes in the Law Affecting Educational Hearing Procedures for Handicapped Children." 7 *U. Baltimore L. Rev.* 41 (1977).

MASSACHUSETTS

Segal, Robert M. "Administrative Procedure in Massachusetts: Rule Making and Judicial Review." 33 *Boston U. L. Rev.* 1 (1953).

Sacks, Albert M. "Proposed Administrative Procedure Act for Massachusetts." 5 *Harvard L. School Bull.* 5 (1954).

Segal, Robert M. "New Administrative Procedure Act of Massachusetts," 39 *Massachusetts L. Q.* 31 (1954).

Curran, William J., and Albert M. Sacks. "The Massachusetts Administrative Procedure Act." 37 *Boston U. L. Rev.* 70 (1957).

Coyne, Coleman G., Jr. "Confusion of Exhaustion of Administrative Remedies and Primary Jurisdiction Doctrines." 7 *Suffolk U. L. Rev.* 124 (1972).

Delaney, John. "An Administrative Court for Massachusetts?" 58 *Massachusetts L. Q.* 373 (1974).

Glantz, Leonard H. "Certificate of Need: The Massachusetts Experience." 1 *Am. J. Law and Medicine* 13 (1975).

MICHIGAN

Hoyt, Ralph M. "Michigan Administrative Procedure: Should Michigan Adopt an Administrative Procedure Code?" 29 *Michigan S. B. J.* 33 (1950).

Cooper, Frank E. "The Administrative Law of Michigan." 36 *ABA Journal* 527 (1951).

Needham, Roger A. "Michigan Administrative Code of 1954." 39 *Michigan S. B. J.* (1951).

Eley, Lynn W. "Michigan's Professional and Occupational Licensing Boards: Organization and Powers." 1 *U. Detroit L. J.* 347 (1964).

Reese, Robert. "How to Get a Hearing Practice Before City Boards and Commissions." 32 *Detroit Lawyer* 193 (1964).

Cramton, Roger. "Doctrine of Exhaustion of Administrative Remedies in Michigan." 44 *Michigan S. B. J.* 10 (1965).

Steiber, J., and B.W. Wolkinson. "Fact-finding Viewed by Fact-Finders: the Michigan Experience," 28 *Labor L. J.* 89 (1971).

Note: "Assimilating Human Activity into the Shoreland Environment: The Michigan Shoreland Protection and Management Act of 1970." 62 *Iowa L. Rev.* 149 (1976).

Eizelman, Michael J. "*Roger's Beauty School v. Michigan State Board of Cosmetology* (Mich) 244 NW2d 201: License Revocation and Procedural Due Process." 1977 *Detroit Coll. L. Rev.* 167 (1977).

MINNESOTA

Note: "Minnesota Pollution Control Agency—A Study in State Administrative Law." 56 *Minnesota L. Rev.* 997 (1972).

Riesenfeld, Stefan A., John A. Bauman, and Richard C. Maxwell. "Judicial Control of Administrative Action by Means of the Extraordinary Remedies in Minnesota." 33 *Minnesota L. Rev.* 569 (1949).

Cardin, Michael, and Lawrence B. Brillant. "Search for Effective State Decision Making About Toxic Substances: Michigan's Toxic Substance Control Commission Act." 25 *Wayne L. Rev.* 1217 (1979).

MISSISSIPPI

Franks, Ross L., and Thomas C. Collier. "Administrative Practice and Procedure Before the Mississippi Banking Board," 45 *Mississippi L. J.* 915 (1974).

MISSOURI

Shewmaker, R. D. "Missouri Administrative Law—SB 196: An Important First Step." 2 *J. Missouri B.* 159 (1946).

Symposium: "Administrative Agencies in Missouri." 19 *U. Kansas City L. Rev.* 233 (1951).

Comment: "Federal and Missouri Administrative Procedure Acts—A Comparison." 17 *Missouri L. Rev.* 286 (1952).

Spradley, R.C., and J.A. Daugherty. "Present Look at Administrative Law Practice in Missouri." 27 *Missouri B. J.* 257 (1971).

Special Project: "Fair Treatment for the Licensed Professional: The Missouri Administrative Hearing Commission." 37 *Missouri L. Rev.* 410 (1972).

Davis, Frederick. "Missouri Public Service Commission." 42 *UMKC L. Rev.* 279 (1974).

Note: "Administrative Law—Standing or Political Subdivisions to Secure Judicial Review of Non-Contested Cases in Minnesota." 40 *Missouri L. Rev.* 653 (1975).

Barwick, William M. "Public Advocacy Before the Missouri Public Service Commission." 6 *UMKC L. Rev.* 181 (1977).

Davis, Frederick. "Missouri Administrative Procedure Act and the Cities." 35 *Missouri B. J.* 433 (1979).

Note: "Disclosure of Protected Records Under the Missouri Sunshine Law." 45 *Missouri L. Rev.* 154 (1980).

MONTANA

Note; "Filing and Publication of Administrative Rules and Regulations in Montana." 19 *Montana L. Rev.* 43 (1957).

Sullivan, R.E. "Case for an Administrative Procedure Act." 21 *Montana L. Rev.* 168 (1960).

NEBRASKA

Brumley, Steven D. "Administrative Justice and Conclusory Findings." 46 *Nebraska L. Rev.* 712 (1967).

Peters, Geoffrey, Larry Teply, James Wunsch, and Joel Zimmerman, "Administrative Civil Commitments: the Ins and Outs of the Nebraska System." 9 *Creighton L. Rev.* 266 (1975).

Willborn, Steven L. "Time for Change: A Critical Analysis of the Nebraska Administrative Procedure Act." 60 *Nebraska L. Rev.*, (1981).

NEW HAMPSHIRE

D'Ambruoso, Dom C. "New Hampshire Public Utilities Commission: Functions and Jurisdiction." 15 *New Hampshire B. J.* 177 (1974).

Stusse, Michael B. "Wetlands Legislation in New Hampshire." 18 *New Hampshire B. J.* 265 (1977).

NEW JERSEY

Thomas, N.C. "New Jersey Administrative Law: The Nature and Scope of Judicial Review." 8 *Villanova L. Rev.* 120 (1952).

459
Selected
Sources
on Law and
Administration
in the States

Symposium: "Comparative Study of Administrative Procedure in New Jersey and the Model State Administrative Procedure Act." 7 *Rutgers L. Rev.* 465 (1953).

Davis, Kenneth C. "New Jersey's Unique Conception of 'Fair Play' in the Administrative Process." 10 *Rutgers L. Rev.* 660 (1957).

Frakt, Arthur N. "Administrative Enforcement of Equal Opportunity Legislation in New Jersey." 21 *Rutgers L. Rev.* 442 (1967).

Graham, James L. "Civil Liberties Problems in Welfare Administration," 43 *NYU L. Rev.* 836 (1968).

Penn, Arthur. "Public Interest Law Joins the Government: Advocate from Within." 12 *Trial* 20 (1976).

Note: "Department of Public Advocate—Public Interest Representation and Administrative Oversight." 30 *Rutgers L. Rev.* 386 (1977).

Roberts, Paula. "Child Care in New Jersey: An Experiment in Community Control." 10 *Clearinghouse Rev.* 861 (1977).

NEW MEXICO

Vaught, J. S. "Administrative Procedure in New Mexico and Court Decisions with Reference Thereto." 194 *New Mexico S. B.* 46 (1942).

Utton, Albert E. "Constitutional Limitations on the Exercise of Judicial Functions by Administrative Agencies." 7 *Natural Resources J.* 599 (1967).

Glidden, T. W., and Albert E. Utton. "Administrative Procedure Act for New Mexico." 8 *Natural Resources J.* 114 (1968).

Note: "Inherent Power of Administrative Agency to Reconsider Final Decisions." 8 *Natural Resources J.* 341 (1968).

Utton, Albert E. "How to Stand Still Without Really Trying: A Critique of the New Mexico Administrative Procedures Act." 10 *Natural Resources J.* 840 (1970).

Note: "Public Service Commission: A Legal Analysis of an Administrative System." 3 *New Mexico L. Rev.* 81 (1973).

Canepa, Joseph F., and Larry M. Reecer. "Age Discrimination in Employment: A Comparison of the Federal and State Laws and Remedies in New Mexico." 7 *New Mexico L. Rev.* 51 (1976–1977).

Note: "Delegation of Legislative Authority on the State Level: Environmental Protection in New Mexico." 17 *Natural Resources J.* 521 (1978).

NEW YORK

Fraser, Henry S. "The Benjamin Report on Administrative Adjudication in New York." 28 *Cornell L. Q.* 23 (1942).

Schwartz, Bernard. "A New York Administrative Procedure Act." 24 *NYU L. Q. Rev.* 55 (1949).

Note: "New York Administrative Procedure for the Dismissal of Teaching Personnel." 16 *Buffalo L. Rev.* 815 (1967).

Castrataro, George J. "Housing Code Enforcement: A Century of Failure in New York City." 14 *New York L. Rev.* 60 (1968).

Hollands, John H. "Ombudsman in Buffalo." 26 *Legal Aid Brief Case* 224 (1968).

Note: "Administrative Law: A Tenant May Not Be Deprived of Continued Tenancy in Public Housing Without First Being Afforded the Minimum Procedural Safeguards Guaranteed by Due Process." 37 *Brooklyn L. Rev.* 184 (1970).

Tibbles, Lance. "Ombudsmen for Local Government? The Buffalo Experiment." 2 *Urban Lawyer* 364 (1970).

Bossert, Walter A., Jr. "Improving Administrative Procedures in the State of New York." 26 *Record* 684 (1971).

"Survey of New York Administrative Law, 1971–1972." 37 *Albany L. Rev.* 726 (1973).

Marino, Ralph J. "New York Freedom of Information Law." 43 *Fordham L. Rev.* 83 (1974).

Note: "Deceptive Practices in the Marketplace: Consumer Protection by New York Government Agencies." 3 *Fordham Urban L. J.* 491 (1975).

Note: "Utility Rates, Consumers, and the New York State Public Service Commission." 37 *Albany L. Rev.* 707 (1975).

Gold, Peter A. "Establishing a Methadone Maintenance Treatment Program: Prior History Procedures and Problems." 21 *New York L. F.* 40 (1976).

Griffith, Emlyn I. "Public Comes First in Professional Discipline," 48 *New York S. B. J.* 100 (1976).

Osborn, John E. "New York's Urban Development Corporation, a Study of the Unchecked Power of a 'Public Authority.' " 43 *Brooklyn L. Rev.* 237

Note: "Administrative Rights of Handicapped Children to Educational Opportunities: Recent Developments in New York Law." 14 *Columbia J. of Law and Social Problems* 491 (1979).

Osterman, Elaine Pevar. "Discipline of Public Employees: The New York State Experience." 34 *Arbitration J.* 25 (1979).

Walsh, Albert A. "Housing Code Enforcement in New York City—Another Look at an Administrative Tribunal." 17 *Urban L. Annual* 51 (1979).

NORTH CAROLINA

Note: "Judicial Review and Separation of Powers." 45 *North Carolina L. Rev.* 467 (1967).

Hanft, Frank W. "Some Aspects of Evidence in Adjudications by Administrative Agencies in North Carolina." 49 *North Carolina L. Rev.* 635 (1971).

Bell, Richard G. "Administrative Law: The Proposed North Carolina Statutes for Registration and Publication of State Administrative Regulations." 8 *Wake Forest L. Rev.* 309 (1972).

Kavass, Igor I., and Bruce A. Christensen. *Guide to North Carolina Legal Research.* Buffalo, N.Y.: William Shein, 1973.

Daye, Charles E. "North Carolina's New Administrative Procedure Act: An Interpretive Analysis." 53 *North Carolina L. Rev.* 833 (1975).

Note: "Administrative Law—Proceeding Under the North Carolina Occupational Safety and Health Act." 53 *North Carolina L. Rev.* 1005 (1975).

Note: "Unauthorized Delegation of Legislative Authority to Administrative Agencies Under Article I, Section 6 and Article II, Section 1 of the North Carolina Constitution." 11 *Wake Forest L. Rev.* 269 (1975).

Note: "Problem of Procedural Delay in Contested Case Hearings Under the North Carolina Administrative Procedures Act." 7 *North Carolina Central L. J.* 347 (1976).

Butler, Patricia A. "Assuring the Quality of Care and Life in Nursing Homes: The Dilemma of Enforcement." 57 *North Carolina L. Rev.* 1317 (1979).

Wing, Kenneth. "Health Care Regulation: Dilemma of a Partially Developed Public Policy." 57 *North Carolina L. Rev.* 1165 (1979).

461
Selected
Sources
on Law and
Administration
in the States

NORTH DAKOTA

Leahy, J.E. "Judicial Review of Administrative Decisions in North Dakota." 24 *North Dakota Bar Briefs* 211 (1948).

Note: "Right to Notice and Hearing—North Dakota Administrative Agencies Uniform Practice Act." 27 *North Dakota L. Rev.* 218 (1951).

Note: "Judicial Review of an Agency's Determination of Fact in North Dakota." 40 *North Dakota L. Rev.* 292 (1964).

Note: "Energy Facility in North Dakota." 52 *North Dakota L. Rev.* 703 (1976).

OHIO

Symposium: "Administrative Law in Ohio," 13 *Ohio State L. J.* 427 (1952).

Note: "Scope of Review Under Recent Amendments to the Ohio Administrative Procedure Act," 23 *U. Cincinnati L. Rev.* 307 (1954).

Note: "Comparative Analysis of the Federal and Ohio Administrative Procedure Acts." 24 *U. Cincinnati L. Rev.* 365 (1955).

Fulda, Carl H. "Proposed Administrative Court for Ohio." 22 *Ohio State L. J.* 734 (1961).

Note: "Appeals under the Ohio Workmen's Compensation Act," 17 *Western Res. L. Rev.* 282 (1965).

Bingham, Theodore C. "Ombudsmen: The Dayton Model." 41 *U. Cincinnati L. Rev.* 807 (1972).

Note: "Judicial Review of Administrative Decisions in Ohio." 34 *Ohio State L. J.* 853 (1973).

Symposium: "Judicial Review of State and Local Administrative Agencies." 22 *Cleveland State L. Rev.* 229 (1973).

Note: "Ohio Division of Securities Rulemaking, the Administrative Procedure Act and the Ohio Securities Bulletin." 36 *Ohio State L. J.* 662 (1975).

Smith, B.H. "Development of Environmental Law Through the Administrative Process." 4 *Capital U. L. Rev.* 203 (1975).

Note: "Availability of Mandamus as a Vehicle for Administrative Review." 9 *Akron L. Rev.* 713 (1976).

Symposium: "State Government Symposium." 37 *Ohio State L. J.* 469 (1976).

Gotherman, J.E. "Ohio Privacy Act." 7 *Capital U. L. Rev.* 177 (1977).

Note: "*State ex rel. Osborn v. Jackson:* Roadmap for Administrative and Judicial Review in the Ohio Civil Service System." 6 *Capital U. L. Rev.* 429 (1977).

Tseng, Henry P. "Recent Developments in Ohio Administrative Law: Regulating the Regulators?" 4 *Ohio Northern U. L. Rev.* 317 (1977).

OKLAHOMA

Merrill, Maurice H. "Administrative Law of Oklahoma." 4 *Oklahoma L. Rev.* 286 (1951).

Note: "Administrative Law: Delegation of Legislative Power to Administrative Agencies in Oklahoma." 25 *Oklahoma L. Rev.* 553 (1972).

Note: "Administrative Law: Dismissal of Tenured Faculty in Oklahoma Colleges and Universities." 29 *Oklahoma L. Rev.* 370 (1976).

Fleming, Horace W., Jr. "Oklahoma Literature Commission: A Case Study in Administrative Regulation of Obscenity." 29 *Oklahoma L. Rev.* 882 (1976).

OREGON

463

Selected
Sources
on Law and
Administration
in the States

Hazard, Geoffrey C., Jr. "Oregon Administrative Procedure Act: Status and Prospects." 39 *Oregon L. Rev.* 97 (1960).

Note: "Oregon Administrative Procedure Act." 1 *Willamette L. J.* 233 (1960).

"Symposium on Oregon Administrative Law." 1 *Willamette L. J.* 145 (1960).

Quesseth, Cecil H. "Water Pollution Control Laws of Oregon—Problems on Enforcement." *Willamette L. J.* 284 (1965).

Note: "Judicial Review Under the Oregon APA: The Present Act and S.B. 300 Compared." 49 *Oregon L. Rev.* 394 (1970).

Note: "Validity of Agency Action Under the Oregon APA: The Acid Test." 51 *Oregon L. Rev.* 626 (1972).

Wyden, R. "Public Regulation of Private Supplements: Medicare and Medicaid in Oregon." 9 *Connecticut L. Rev.* 450 (1977).

Larsen, Alan S. "Legislative Delegation and Oversight: A Promising Approach From Oregon." 14 *Willamette L. J.* 1 (1977).

Frohnmayer, David B. "Oregon Administrative Procedure Act: An Essay on State Administrative Rulemaking Procedure Reform." 58 *Oregon L. Rev.* 411 (1980).

PENNSYLVANIA

Byse, Clark. "Administrative Procedure Reform in Pennsylvania." 97 *U. Pennsylvania L. Rev.* 22 (1948).

Forman, Howard J. "Administrative Law in Pennsylvania: Its Present Status and Recommendations for Improvement." 55 *Dickinson L. Rev.* 129 (1951).

Hanna, W. Clark. "Lights and Shadows in State Administrative Procedure Under Pennsylvania Administrative Agency Law." 24 *Temple L. Q.* 261 (1951).

Symposium: "Administrative Practice and Procedure in Pennsylvania." 36 *Temple L. Q.* 385 (1963).

Note: "Judicial Process Study of the Review of Licensing Decisions of the Pennsylvania Liquor Control Board." 113 *U. Pennsylvania L. Rev.* 1043 (1965).

Surrency, Erwin C. *Research in Pennsylvania Law.* 2d ed. Dobbs Ferry, N.Y.: Oceana, 1965.

Frank, Bernard. "Proposals for Pennsylvania Ombudsman." 39 *Pennsylvania B.A.Q.* 84 (1967).

Note: "Release Procedure Under the Pennsylvania Mental Health and Mental Retardation Act of 1966." 5 *Duquesne L. Rev.* 446 (1967).

Griswold, Robert H. "Problem of Public Confidence." 43 *Pennsylvania B.A.Q.* 253 (1972).

Zeiter, William E. "New General Rules of Administrative Practice and Procedure and the Commonwealth Documents Law," 44 *Pennsylvania B.A.Q.* 109 (1972).

———. "Pennsylvania General Rules of Practice and Procedure—A Surprising By-product of a State Register System." 24 *Admin. L. Rev.* 275 (1972).

Survey: "The Pennsylvania Human Relations Commission." 77 *Dickinson L. Rev.* 522 (1973).

Note: "Pennsylvania Human Relations Commission's Pattern and Practice Complaint Failed to Meet Statutory Particularity Requirement, Thus Precluding Use of Commission's Full Investigatory Powers." 21 *Villanova L. Rev.* 103 (1974).

Note: "Pennsylvania Local Agency Law." 15 *Duquesne L. Rev.* 133 (1976).

Note: "Municipal Corporations—Zoning Applicability of Municipal Zoning Laws to State Agencies." 15 *Duquesne L. Rev.* 721 (1977).

Symposium: "Administrative Process in Pennsylvania—Current Issues." 15 *Duquesne L. Rev.* 573 (1977).

Note: "Judicial Review of Administrative Action in Pennsylvania: An Updated Look at Reviewability and Standing." 16 *Duquesne L. Rev.* 20 (1977–78).

Johnson, Charles A. "Judicial Decisions and Organization Change: Some Theoretical and Empirical Notes on State Court Decisions and State Administrative Agencies." 14 *Law & Society Rev.* 27 (1979).

SOUTH CAROLINA

Mills, Robin K., and Jon S. Schultz. *South Carolina Legal Research Method.* Buffalo, N.Y.: William S. Hein, 1976.

SOUTH DAKOTA

Note: "South Dakota's Administrative Procedure Act and the Bank Charter Application—Is It a 'Contested Case'?" 17 *South Dakota L. Rev.* 394 (1972).

TENNESSEE

Boone, George Street. "Tennessee Law of Administrative Procedure." 1 *Vanderbilt L. Rev.* 339 (1948).

Note: "Delegation of Power to Administrative Agencies in Tennessee." 27 *Tennessee L. Rev.* 569 (1966).

Gifford, Daniel J. "Report on Administrative Law to the Tennessee Law Revision Commission." 20 *Vanderbilt L. Rev.* 777 (1967).

Cantrell, Ben H. "Review of Administrative Decisions by Writ of Certorari in Tennessee." 4 *Memphis State U. L. Rev.* 19 (1973).

Norton, Mike. "Tennessee Department of Revenue and the Uniform Administrative Procedures Act." 6 *Memphis State U. L. Rev.* 303 (1976).

Symposium: "Tennessee Uniform Administrative Procedures Act," 6 *Memphis State U. L. Rev.* 258 (1976).

Porteous, David C. "College and University Disciplinary Proceedings Under the Tennessee Uniform Administrative Procedure Act: Undue Process." 7 *Memphis State U. L. Rev.* 345 (1977).

Note: "Unemployment Compensation—Waiver and Recoupment of Overpayments." 7 *Memphis State U. L. Rev.* 683 (1977).

TEXAS

Harris, Whitney R. "Administrative Law of Texas." 29 *Texas L. Rev.* 213 (1950).

Note: "Symposium: An Administrative Procedure Act for Texas," 5 *Southwestern L. J.* 125 (1951).

"A Survey of Texas Administrative Law." 33 *Texas L. Rev.* 635 (1955).

Note: "Proposed Texas Administrative Procedure Act." 33 *Texas L. Rev.* 499 (1955).

Note: "Judicial Review of Administrative Agency Action—A Need for Texas Reform." 40 *Texas L. Rev.* 992 (1962).

Note: "Dismissals for Public School Employees in Texas—Suggestions for a More Effective Administrative Process." 44 *Texas L. Rev.* 1309 (1966).

Note: "Administrative Government in Texas." 47 *Texas L. Rev.* 805 (1969).

465

Selected
Sources
on Law and
Administration
in the States

Reavley, Thomas M. "Substantial Evidence and Insubstantial Review in Texas." 23 *Southwestern L. J.* 239 (1969).

Note: "Texas Open Meetings Act has Potentially Broad Coverage But Suffers From Inadequate Enforcement Provisions." 49 *Texas L. Rev.* 764 (1971).

Phillips, John C. "Evolution of the Administrative Process Under the 'New' Texas Savings and Loan Act." 6 *St. Mary's L. J.* 333 (1974).

Boner, Marian. *A Reference Guide to Texas Law and Legal History: Sources and Documentation.* Austin: University of Texas Press, 1975.

Means, Robert C., and Barry Chasnoff. "State Regulation of American Transportation: The Texas Aeronautics Commission." 53 *Texas L. Rev.* 653 (1975).

Hamilton, Robert W., and J.J. Jewett III. "Administrative Procedure and Texas Register Act: Contested Cases and Judicial Review." 54 *Texas L. Rev.* 285 (1976).

Note: "Beyond the Substantial Evidence Rule: *Lewis v. Metropolitan Savings and Loan Association.*" 31 *Southwestern L. J.* 927 (1977).

Note: "Public Utility Commission: Appellate Procedure and Judicial Review." 28 *Baylor L. Rev.* 1001 (1976).

Ventura, Joe. "Energy Policy Development in Texas." 29 *Baylor L. Rev.* 821 (1977).

UTAH

Kimball, Spencer L., and W. Eugene Hansen. "Utah Insurance Commissioner: A Study of Administrative Regulation in Action." 6 *Utah L. Rev.* 1 (1958).

Note: "Utah Practice in Publishing Administrative Rules and an Index to Agency Publications." *Utah L. Rev.* 222 (1960).

Aaron, Richard I. "Utah Ombudsman: The American Proposals." 1967 *Utah L. Rev.* 32 (1967).

VIRGINIA

Symposium: "The Virginia Stock Corporation Commission," 14 *William and Mary L. Rev.* 523 (1973).

WASHINGTON

"Symposium on Washington Administrative Law." 33 *Washington L. Rev.* 1 (1958).

Rodgers, William H., Jr. "When Seattle Citizens Complain." 2 *Urban Lawyer* 386 (1970).

Note: "Combination of Functions: May an Administrative Tribunal Be Both Prosecutor and Judge?" 46 *Washington L. Rev.* 411 (1971).

Note: "Licensing by Municipal Bodies: A Judicial Function." 53 *Washington L. Rev.* 597 (1973).

Note: "*Seattle v. Pullman*, 514 P 2d 1059." 13 *J. Family L.* 651 (1973–74).

McClintock, Michael C., and Steven A. Crumb. "Washington's New Public Records Disclosure Act: Freedom of Information in Municipal Labor Law." 11 *Gonzaga L. Rev.* 13 (1975).

Note: "Judicial Review of Compliance with the State Environmental Policy Act of 1971: Recent Developments." 10 *Gonzaga L. Rev.* 803 (1975).

Note: "Shorelines Management: Judicial Review of Shorelines Hearings Board Decisions." 51 *Washington L. Rev.* 405 (1976).

WEST VIRGINIA

Note: "Civil Rights–Administration Enforcement–Damages as an Appropriate Remedy." 75 *W. Virginia L. Rev.* 253 (1973).

WISCONSIN

Hoyt, Ralph M. "Wisconsin Administrative Procedure Act." 1944 *Wisconsin L. Rev.* 214 (1944).

Halsted, Orrin L., and Earl Sachse. "Study of Administrative Rulemaking in Wisconsin." 1954 *Wisconsin L. Rev.* 368 (1954).

Knudson, William. *Wisconsin Legal Research Guide.* 2d ed. Madison: University of Wisconsin, 1972.

Note: "Scope of Judicial Review of Administrative Agency Decisions in Wisconsin." 1973 *Wisconsin L. Rev.* 554 (1973).

Bunn, George, and Jeff Gallagher. "Legislative Committee Review of Administrative Rules in Wisconsin." 1977 *Wisconsin L. Rev.* 935 (1977).

Note: "Agency Decisionmaking Under the Wisconsin Environmental Policy Act." 1977 *Wisconsin L. Rev.* 11 (1977).

Klizke, Ramon A. "Administrative Decisions Eligible for Judicial Review in Wisconsin." 61 *Marquette L. Rev.* 405 (1978).

WYOMING

Note: "Scope of Judicial Review of An Administrative Agency in Wyoming." 9 *Wyoming L. J.* 65 (1954).

Symposium: "Administrative Law in Wyoming." 16 *Wyoming L. J.* 191 (1962).

Note: "Wyoming Administrative Procedure Act." 1 *Land & Water L. Rev.* 497 (1966).

DISTRICT OF COLUMBIA

Note: "D.C. Administrative Procedure Act Becomes Effective on October 21, 1969." 12 *Canadian Bar J.* 38 (1968).

Frana, Louis J. "Current Problems Concerning the District of Columbia Administrative Procedure Act." 23 *Admin. Law Rev.* 3 (1970).

Griffin, Robert C. "Synopsis of the D.C. Administrative Procedure Act: As Applied to the City Council and a Selected Agency." 16 *Howard L. J.* 67 (1970).

Note: "Administrative Procedure in the District of Columbia—The APA and Beyond." 20 *American U. L. Rev.* 457 (1970–1971).

Griffin, Joseph P. "District of Columbia Administrative Procedure Act: Its History, Provisions, and Interpretation." 61 *Georgetown L. J.* 575 (1973).

Index

Jurisprudence, 37, 42; schools of, 43–48